PEREGRINE B

Y11

AUBREY'S BRIEF LIVES

EDITED BY

OLIVER LAWSON DICK

AUBREY'S BRIEF LIVES

EDITED FROM THE ORIGINAL MANUSCRIPTS

AND WITH AN INTRODUCTION BY

OLIVER LAWSON DICK

Penguin Books

IN ASSOCIATION WITH

Secker & Warburg

Penguin Books Ltd, Harmondsworth, Middlesex
AUSTRALIA: Penguin Books Pty Ltd, 762 Whitehorse Road
Mitcham, Victoria

—

First published by Secker and Warburg 1949
Reprinted, without bibliography, glossary of persons, and
references, by Secker and Warburg 1958
Published in Peregrine Books 1962

—

—

Made and printed in Great Britain
by Western Printing Services Ltd, Bristol
Set in Monotype Garamond

TO

Sir Stephen Tallents

Acknowledgements

MY thanks are due first to Bodley's Librarian, the Corporation of the City of London, the Wiltshire Archaeological and Natural History Society, the Council of the Royal Society, and the Keeper of the Manuscripts at the British Museum, for permission to reproduce portions of the manuscripts in their archives.

I am also indebted to Bertrand Russell and Messrs George Allen and Unwin Ltd for permission to base my biographical notes on Descartes, Erasmus, Thomas Hobbes, and Sir Thomas More on material contained in *A History of Western Philosophy*: to Dr G. M. Trevelyan, OM and Longmans Green & Co. Ltd, for their permission to quote from *English Social History*: to J. M. Dent and Sons Ltd, for permission to base some of my biographical notes on the Everyman edition of their *Dictionary of English Literature*: and to the Oxford University Press for allowing me to quote from *The Concise Oxford Dictionary of English Literature* and *The Dictionary of National Biography*.

I have received invaluable assistance from Mr Eric Bligh in all parts of the book, but especially in regard to the Bibliography: and Mr Hugh Lloyd-Jones has helped me throughout with the Latin quotations. I have also received help and information from Mr John Bowle: Mr James Watson-Gandy: Mr Laurence Tanner, Keeper of the Muniments at Westminster Abbey: Mr Charles Stuart: Mr Arthur Bryant: Mrs Jacqueline Hope-Nicholson: the Librarian of the House of Commons: the Librarian of the Royal Society: the Director of the Wellcome Historical Medical Museum: the Librarian of the County of Surrey: the late James Ross, City Librarian of Bristol: Mr H. D. Simmons: Dr John F. Fulton of Yale University: Sir Edmund Craster: Major the Hon. Rupert Craven: and the late Bernard Shaw.

Contents

CONTENTS

CONTENTS

Foreword

THE original material used in this edition has been taken from fifty volumes in the Bodleian Library at Oxford and from sixteen volumes in the libraries of the Wiltshire Archaeological and Natural History Society, The Royal Society, the Corporation of London, and the British Museum. The passages from the original manuscripts that have been included in this edition have been selected on the following plan:

1. Any life that has nothing of intrinsic value to offer has been discarded. The four hundred and twenty-six lives which Aubrey wrote vary considerably in length (one consists of two words, another of twenty-three thousand) and many of them are of no interest whatsoever, consisting either of extracts from books or of mere lists of dates and facts. All that Aubrey has to say of John Holywood, for instance, is *Dr Pell is positive that his name was Holybushe.*

2. In the one hundred and thirty-four lives that have been selected, many sentences have been rejected. For Aubrey starts one life as follows: *James Harrington, Esq; the son of . . . Harrington of . . . in the Countie of . . . , by . . . , daughter of Sir . . . Samuel, was borne at . . . (Sir . . . Samuel's house in Northamptonshire) anno . . .* All sentences like this, which display nothing more than Aubrey's ignorance of a date or a place or the title of a book, have been omitted.

3. The majority of the remaining lives have been incorporated into the biography of John Aubrey; 26,989 words of Aubrey's text appear in this edition that were not given by Andrew Clark in his 1898 transcription of the Bodleian manuscript.

4. The imperfections of Aubrey's copy have been amended in the way that he intended they should be. A choice has been made between the alternative words he jotted down, and the several versions of his favourite stories, which he repeated sometimes as many as seven times, have been collated and a single version produced. As an instance, the two-page life of William and Philip Herbert was assembled from eleven different manuscripts; and this whole edition has been built up, like a jigsaw, until the disconnected pieces have at last resolved themselves into a complete picture.

5. All notes, quotation marks, and other distractions to continuous reading have been excluded from the text, and each life has been prefaced with a paragraph, written by the editor, outlining those facts about the subject which Aubrey has ignored.

6. Wherever a Latin quotation in the text is not self-explanatory, its translation has been given in square brackets. The word 'pounds' has also been substituted throughout for the Latin 'libri'.

7. Aubrey's many mistakes have been left uncorrected, except in the case of two gross misquotations of famous poems. On the few occasions when Aubrey has not only left a gap to be filled in later, but has also given the reference from which the fact can be obtained, that fact has been supplied. For instance, in the

life of Sir William Petty Aubrey says: *Anno Domini . . . happened that memorable accident and experiment of the reviving Nan Green, which is to be ascribed and attributed to Dr William Petty, as the first discoverer of life in her, and author of saving her. Vide and insert the material passages in the Tryal, and anatomicall experiment of Nan Green at Oxon: vide the narrative.* In the face of such clear instructions, I have felt justified in including seven lines describing the incident from Anthony Wood's 'Journal'. Nowhere else has such an insertion been made, but on a few occasions the word 'some' has been introduced to make good the omission of a figure; and in one place a word which Aubrey uses elsewhere, *denigrating*, has been inserted in the life of William Camden to complete a sentence.

8. Aubrey's original spelling has been retained throughout, except that merely artificial tricks of writing (y^t for that, wch for which, m for mm) have been neglected. Aubrey's use of capital letters has also been followed. Wherever possible, his original punctuation has been given, and italics have been used, when necessary, to clarify the meaning.

9. In 'The Life and Times of John Aubrey', however, italics have been used merely to distinguish those passages which occur in Aubrey's own handwriting in the manuscripts.

10. Aubrey's use of sign language has been abandoned, and wherever possible this form of shorthand has been translated into words.

11. Lastly, there comes the vexed question of obscenity. In the seventeenth century sex had not yet been singled out as the sin par excellence, it was merely one among many failings, and Aubrey no more thought of concealing it than he dreamed of avoiding the mention of gluttony or drunkenness. After judging his work, therefore, by its general tendency and not by particular details, it has been decided not to bowdlerize it in the slightest degree, but to print it as it was written, without emphasis and without concealment.

The Life and Times of John Aubrey

NOT long after John Aubrey's death, a wise man warned us against treating books like members of the nobility: that is, against learning their titles and bragging afterwards of acquaintance with them. Yet this has been peculiarly Aubrey's fate; for his reputation is founded almost entirely upon hearsay and the piecemeal quotation of his work by other writers.

The reason for the extraordinary neglect of this man of genius is not hard to find, and the fault, it must be admitted, is entirely his own. For Aubrey's love of life was so intense, his curiosity so promiscuous and so insatiable, that he proved quite incapable of completing any work he undertook. Each one was started in a most businesslike and practical fashion, but before long the original plan was always buried beneath the flood of digressions and notes, of horoscopes, letters, and stories, which his restless mind seemed powerless to control.

Having decided to write a life, Aubrey selected a page in one of his notebooks and jotted down as quickly as possible everything that he could remember about the character concerned: his friends, his appearance, his actions, his books, and his sayings. Any facts or dates that did not occur to him on the spur of the moment were left blank, and as Aubrey was so extremely sociable that he was usually suffering from a hangover when he came to put pen to paper, the number of these omissions was often very large. In the first flush of composition, too, his mind raced so far beyond his pen that he frequently resorted to a sort of involved shorthand and made use of signs instead of words.

He then read over what he had just written, and put in any stories that he thought were even vaguely relevant, wrote alternatives to words and phrases, inserted queries, numbered words, sentences, and paragraphs for transposition, and disarranged everything.

Any facts that occurred to him later were jotted down quite at random, in the margin if there was still room, otherwise on another page or in the middle of another life, often in a different volume, sometimes even in a letter to a friend. And there the text was left, for he rarely made a fair copy of anything that he had written, because, as he confessed, he *wanted patience to go thorough Knotty Studies.*

Even the optimistic author despaired at last of ever reducing his life's work to a manageable shape. *Considering therefore that if I should not finish and publish what I had begun*, he wrote, *My Papers might either perish, or be sold in an Auction, and some body else* (*as is not uncommon*) *put his name to my Paines:*

and not knowing any one that would undertake this Design whilst I live, I have tumultuarily stitcht up what I have many yeares since collected: I hope, hereafter it may be an Incitement to some Ingeniose and publick-spirited young Man, to polish and compleat, what I have delivered rough hewen: For I have not leisure to heighten my Stile. Accepting this clear mandate and electing myself the *Ingeniose and publick-spirited young Man*, I have taken Aubrey at his word, and, using his manuscripts as if they were my own notes, I have constructed the following book: with the important reservation that I have nowhere departed from the original text, although I have ruthlessly rearranged it.

Of this behaviour Aubrey would have thoroughly approved, for he purposely left his manuscripts in note form. *I know here be several Tautologies,* he wrote to Anthony Wood, when he sent him what the latter rightly called 'the foul draught of Mr Hobbs life', *but I putt them downe thus here, that upon reviewe I should judge where such or such a thing would most aptly stand,* and his considered opinion was that *First Draughts ought to be as rude as those of Paynters, for he that in his first essay will be curious in refining will certainly be unhappy in inventing.*

The present book, in the editor's opinion, approximates as nearly as possible to Aubrey's original intention. During the preparation of this edition, moreover, so much new information about Aubrey himself has come to light, that it is now possible to give a full account of his life. For when he came to write his own biography, Aubrey was overcome by a modesty which is quite inexplicable when one considers the care with which he preserved even the smallest trivialities about other people. But the three pages on which he did finally jot down a few bare facts about himself were accompanied none the less by the instruction, *To be interposed as a sheet of wast paper only in the binding of a booke.*

He was borne, he says, (*longaevous, healthy kindred*) *at Easton Pierse, a Hamlet in the Parish of Kington Saint Michael, in the Hundred of Malmesbury in the Countie of Wilts, his mother's* (*daughter and heir of Mr Isaac Lyte*) *inheritance, March the 12* (*St Gregorie's day*) *A.D. 1625, about Sun-riseing, being very weake and like to dye that he was Christned before morning prayer.*

His father, Richard Aubrey, was of the Aubreys of Herefordshire, a family which had built up a considerable estate on the foundations laid by William Aubrey, *Doctor of Lawes*, a man of some importance at the Court of Queen Elizabeth, *who loved him and was wont to call him 'her little Doctor'. He was one of the Delegates for the tryall of Mary, Queen of Scots*, according to John Aubrey, *and was a great Stickler for the saving of her life, which kindnesse was remembred by King James att his comeing-in to England, who asked after him, and probably would have made him Lord Keeper, but he dyed a little before that good opportunity happened. His Majestie sent for his sonnes, and knighted the two eldest, and invited them to Court, which they modestly and perhaps prudently declined. They preferred a Country life.* And in the country the family stayed, slowly enlarging its estates by good management and strategic marriages, until within a generation the Aubreys had so firmly established their place amongst the richer gentry of England that Aubrey's father was three times fined 'for not taking the Order of Knighthood at the Coronation of King Charles I'. But one less agreeable legacy descended from this worthy to his children: *He engrossed all the witt of the family*, said his great-grandson sadly, *so that none descended from him can pretend to any.*

John Aubrey was born during one of the Golden Ages of history, when *there had been a long serene Calme of Peace, and Men minded nothing but peace and Luxury.* The English Renaissance was at its height, and despite the squalor and the dirt and the barbarity that surrounded the material side of life (and which the modern world, mistaking comfort for civilization, is too apt to overemphasize) the art of living reached its peak in England during the early years of Charles I's reign. When Erasmus had described, a century before, the things upon which the various nations prided themselves, the Scots their nobility and logical sense, the French their breeding, he said of the English that they 'particularly challenge to themselves Beauty, Music and Feasting'. And upon these specifically human virtues the nation still prided itself. For it was an aristocratic age, which had no admiration for the Little Man, and its inhabitants were not ashamed to admit that there were many excellencies which were not universally attainable. And loneliness, the plague of modern civilization (with all its attendant discontents), had still not subdued the medieval gregariousness of the English people.

But though a true aristocracy existed, it was soundly based on worth, and the social classes, though clearly marked and unquestioningly accepted, were very fluid. Aubrey, besides noting with approval both John Gadbury's saying that *the Heavens are the best Heraulds* and Ben Jonson's remark *the most worthy men have been rokked in mean Cradles*, added on his own account *Poets and Bravos have Punkes to their Mothers.* For the rewards for ability were unlimited, no matter how humble one's circumstances might have been: *The father of Richard Neile, ArchBishop of Yorke, was a Tallow-Chandler in Westminster:* and the newly ennobled were so little ashamed of their mean origins that Aubrey falls severely upon Lord Burghley for his absurd pride. *The true name is Sitsilt*, he says, *and is an ancient Monmouthshire family but now come to be about the degree of yeomanry. 'Tis strange that they should be so vaine as to leave off an old British name for a Romancy one, which I beleeve Mr Verstegen did putt into their heads, telling his Lordship, in his Booke, that they were derived from the ancient Roman Cecilii.*

The reasons for this sudden blossoming of the spirit were largely religious. The power of the Church had only recently been broken, and had not yet been replaced by the tyranny of the State, and the consequent feeling of freedom and infinite opportunity made it a blessed time to live. For the destruction of the Church of Rome brought with it a release from the burden of sin which had weighed down the English spirit in the past, and life became, for a few short generations, not a thing to be put up with, but a gift to be enjoyed with zest. Even more important, the Puritans were still only a religious sect, and their prejudices, so soon to become the accepted opinions of the middle classes, were still looked upon as fanatic delusions; nor had they yet infected the whole nation with their pernicious idea of the seriousness of work, which has ever since distorted the idea of recreation into mere idleness or games. In the Stuart Century the great mass of the nation still followed Aristotle's rule that 'the first principle of all action is leisure', and leisure to the seventeenth-century man was not relaxation, but another form of activity. For the simultaneous discovery of the New Learning and the New World had so fired the imagination that there had emerged a whole society of full-grown men and women, to whom Milton could justly say: 'Lords and Commons of England – Consider what nation it is whereof ye are: a nation not slow and dull, but of quick, ingenious and piercing spirit; acute to invent, subtile and sinewy to discourse, not beneath the reach of any point that human capacity can soar to.' And it was into this world that John Aubrey was born.

I think I have heard my mother say I had an Ague shortly after I was borne, says Aubrey, taking up his own life again. *1629: about 3 or 4 years old, I had a grievous Ague: I can remember it. I gott not strength till I was 11 or 12 yeares old; but had sicknesse of vomiting (the Belly-ake: paine in the side) for 12 houres every fortnight for several yeares, then about monethly, then quarterly, and at last once in halfe a yeare. About 12 it ceased. This Sicknesse nipt my strength in the bud.*

1633: 8 yeares old, I had an Issue (naturall) in the coronall suture of my head, which continued running till 21. 1634: October: I had a violent Fever that was like to have carried me off. 'Twas the most dangerous sicknesse that ever I had. About 1639 (or 1640) I had the Measills, but that was nothing: I was hardly Sick.

This catalogue of illnesses marks perhaps the sharpest difference between Aubrey's time and our own. For death was everywhere, and the dozen or so children born to every marriage kept it firmly before each man's eyes: it being as unusual then for a child to live, as it is now for one to die. *Ten children in one Grave! a dreadful Sight!* lament the tombs,

Could Beauty, Youth, or Innocence
Their frail Possessors save
From Death, sweet Babe, a sure Defence

Thou'd'st had, and not been hurryed hence
Into the silent Grave.

But mortal Creatures, borne to dye,
To Nature must submit:
When that commands, all must comply,
No Parts can sheild from Destiny,
We then the Stage must quitt.

To a generation which was ever conscious that man was, as Marcus Aurelius had said, 'a pigmy soul carrying a dead body to its grave', there seemed to be some strange comfort in the fact that all nature shared the same doom:

Like to the Damask Rose you see,
Or like the Blossome on the Tree,
Or like the dainty Flower of May,
Or like the Morning of the Day,
Or like the Sun, or like the Shade,
Or like the Gourd which Jonas had,
Even so is Man, whose Thread is spun,
Drawn out, and cutt, and so is done.
The Rose withers, the Blossom blasteth,
The Flower fades, the Morning hasteth,
The Sun setts, the Shadow flies,
The Gourd consumes, and Man he dies.

Out of this constant grief there arose at last the very glorification of death. 'What a noble animal is man, splendid in ashes, pompous in the grave', intones Sir Thomas Browne; and Sir Walter Raleigh exults: 'It is therefore Death alone that can suddenly make man to know himself. He holds a glass before the eyes of the most beautiful and makes them see therein their deformity and rottenness and acknowledge it.' This praise of death even made men gloat over the corruption that was only too evident in the shallow graves and gibbeted felons of the time. *It is still accounted undecent for Widows to marry within a yeare (I thinke)*, John Aubrey says, *because in that time the husbands body may be presumed to be rotten*. And in what other century could a man have written of his own child:

Christopher Michell's Sonn lyeth here, Richard Michell was his Name,
His Father's Love was so to him, he caus'd to write the same:
He was but 4 Yeares 5 Moneths old, and then was buryed here,
And of his Body the Wormes did find a Dish of dainty chere.

But it was not only in childhood that death threatened. The law, not yet having learnt to distinguish between crime and sin, punished both with the utmost savagery, for in the absence of a police force or any method of detection, the few wrongdoers who were caught had to suffer a painful and public death as a sufficient discouragement to others. 'The Court doth award that you be drawn upon a hurdle to the place of execution and there shall be hanged by the neck, and, being alive, shall be cut down and your entrails to be taken out of your body, and, you living, the same to be burnt before your eyes, and your head to be cutt off, your body divided into four quarters, and head and quarters to be disposed of at the pleasure of the King's Majesty: and the Lord have mercy on your soul!' The most educated and sensitive men were onlookers at these dreadful spectacles: even the kindly Aubrey reports, *I did see Mr Chr. Love beheaded on Tower-hill in a delicate cleare day*, although he seems to have had some doubts about the ceremony, for he added, *about half an hour after his Head was struck off, the Clouds gathered blacker and blacker, and all that night and till next noon such terrible Claps of Thunder lightning and Tempest as if the Machine of the World had been dissolving.* Aubrey never deceived himself, however, as to the real reason for his interest in these exhibitions. *Ah! 'tis the best lechery to see 'em suffer Correction*, observes one of the characters in his play. *Your London Aldermen take great Lechery to see the poor wretches whipt at the Court at Bridewell. Were it not for the Law there were no living*, he decided. *Some would take delight in killing of men.*

The absence of any sure method of redressing private wrongs, the law being so cumbersome and so corrupt, led to the continuation of the personal feud in the unlighted and unpatrolled streets. *Capt. Yarrington dyed at London about March last*, Aubrey noted. *The cause of his death was a Beating and throwne into a Tub of Water.* Furthermore, the sword was still a part of everyday dress, and this made men, when they were in drink, *verie apt to doe bloudy Mischiefes.* However, we soon become indifferent to the lethal weapons of our own times, and there is no reason to think that the danger of stabbing worried the men of the seventeenth century any more than the prospect of a motoring accident troubles us. In fact, the attitude was remarkably similar. *Edmund Wyld, Esq. had the misfortune to kill a man in London, upon a great provocation, about A.D. 1644*, Aubrey reports, and he himself, despite all his benevolence, was three times in *Danger of Expiration* in this way. *Memorandum*, he jotted down, *St John's night, 1673, in danger of being run through with a sword at Mr Burges' chamber in the Middle Temple. Quaere the yeare that I lay at Mris. Neve's*, he continued, *for that time I was in great danger of being killed by a drunkard in the street opposite Grayes-Inn gate – a gentleman whom I never sawe before, but (Deo Gratias) one of his companions hindred his thrust.* On the third occasion, though, there was no doubt as to the identity of the culprit. *Danger of being killed by William, Earl of Pembroke, then Lord Herbert, at the Election of Sir William Salkeld for New Sarum*, Aubrey reported bluntly, and ever afterwards his writing took on a peculiarly spiteful tone at any mention of the Herberts. But sometimes even this violence had good results: *After Dr Lamb was killed in the streets by the Apprentices of London*, Aubrey mentions, *the City was fined 10,000 pounds which payd for the Building of the Banquetting house.*

Far more worrying than this occasional violence were the continual outbreaks of the plague in the early years of the century, when the Black Death of the Middle Ages flared into a dying fury before destroying itself finally in the Great Plague of 1665. At the time, there was no reason to suppose that this disaster was the last visit of the scourge that had lain upon the country for so long, and as late as 1680 we find Aubrey making this ominous note: *Mr Fabian Philips sayes the winter 1625 before the Plague was such a mild winter as this: quod N.B.*

As the medieval plague finally consumed itself with its own violence: *At Petersham the Plague made so great a Destruction, that there survived only five of the Inhabitants:* its place was taken by a new pestilence, syphilis, which had been brought back from the New World by Columbus's crew to rage with dreadful fury in the fresh soil of Europe. For the first outbreak of the disease was so violent, its progress was so rapid, and the symptoms so revolting, that even the lepers refused to live beside its victims.

Small-pox, too, raged throughout the land with a dreadful regularity. *The Small-Pox is usually in all great Towns*, says Aubrey complacently, *but it is observed at Taunton in Somersetshire, and at Sherburne in Dorsetshire, that at the one of them every Seventh Year, and at the other every Ninth Year comes a Small-Pox, which the Physitians cannot master.*

Nor was it from disease alone that death threatened, for Aubrey mentions that George Villiers's mother, *the Countesse of Bucks, died of a dropsi and Phisick.* For the medical profession, with neither knowledge nor traditions, was groping its way so unsurely from quackery towards enlightenment that many people must have come, like Robert Boyle, to 'apprehend more from the physician than the disease'.

The majority of even the most eminent practitioners were still amateurs, like *Fish, MD, or so called*, who *practised Physick and Astrologie, and had a good practise in both, in Convent Garden London*, and each jealously guarded the secrets of his cures from his rivals, so that no advance in the science was possible. And perhaps they were wise to conceal their methods after all, for William Harvey sadly confessed to Aubrey that *after his Booke of the Circulation of the Blood came-out, he fell mightily in his Practize, and 'twas beleeved by the vulgar that he was crack-brained.*

In each generation, therefore, the doctors started from scratch again, and, pursuing their own strange remedies, dealt death indiscriminately until they stumbled by chance on a treatment that did less harm than good, and then they concealed the secret until they were able to take it with them to the grave, unless they had previously managed to sell it for a good profit, like that 'kinswoman of Sir A. King's, which', Robert Hooke noted in his Diary, 'had a certain cure for a Leprosy or Scaled head. Shee had £100 per annum of St Bartholomews hospitall to which she promised to Leave the Receipt.'

Very few men were so scientific as Dr Jacquinto, Physician to Queen Anne, James I's consort, *who went into the Marshes of Essex, where they putt their sheep to cure them of the Rott, where he lived sometime purposely, to goe after the sheep, and observe what plants they did eat: and of those Herbes he made his Medicine for the Consumption, which did great Cures.* The great majority still depended largely on magic for their treatments, and dreams and prayers were considered far more valuable than any research. Dr Napier, for instance, who *was no Doctor, but a divine (rector Lindfordiensis) and practised Physick, when a Patient, or Quaerent came to him, presently went to his Closet to Pray: It appears by his Papers*, says Aubrey, *that he did converse with the Angel Raphael, who told him if the Patient were curable or incurable*; and the popularity of this treatment is proved by the fact that *his Knees were horny with frequent Praying.*

That visionary prescriptions were not always to be relied on, however, is shown by a gentlewoman of Aubrey's acquaintance, *who had a beloved Daughter, who had been a long time Ill, and received no benefit from her Physitians. She dream'd that a Friend of hers deceased, told her, that if she gave her Daughter a Drench of Yewgh pounded, she would recover. She gave her the Drench and it killed her, whereupon she grew almost distracted. Her Chamber Maid to Complement her, and to mitigate her Grief, said surely that could not Kill her; she would adventure to take the same her self; she did so and died also. This was about the Year 1670 or 1671*, Aubrey concludes, *I knew the Family*. Sometimes, though, this indiscriminate dosing did bear unexpected fruit for medical science: *A woman (I thinke in Italy) endeavoured to poyson her Husband (who was a Dropsicall Man) by boyling a Toade in his Potage; which cured him; and this was the occasion of finding out the Medicine.* Not altogether unexpectedly, all the same, for the therapeutic value of frogs had long been known, and Aubrey himself has noted down a proven remedy *To cure the Thrush. Take a living Frog*, he says, *and hold it in a Cloth, that it does not go down into the Childs Mouth; and putt the Head into the Childs Mouth till it is dead; and then take another Frog.* It was little wonder, after treatments like this, if the patients reacted strangely too, like *Oliver Cromwell, when he was so dangerously ill in Scotland of a kind of calenture or high Fever, that he pistolled one or two of his Commanders that came to visit him in his delirious rage.*

To Cure the Tooth-Ach, Aubrey jots down elsewhere, *Take a new Nail, and make the Gum bleed with it, and then drive it into an Oak. This did Cure William Neal, Sir William Neal's Son, a very stout Gentleman, when he was almost Mad with the Pain, and had a mind to have Pistoll'd himself.* For in the dreadful days before the discovery of anaesthetics or analgesics, even the simplest treatment was to be feared. *The Duke of Southampton (who was a most lovely Youth) had two fore-teeth, that grew out very unhandsome*, wrote Aubrey about Charles II's son by Barbara Villiers. *His Cruel Mother caused Him to be bound fast in a Chaire, and had them draw'n-out; which has caused the want of his understanding.* To show that such a disastrous result was not unique, Aubrey mentions another case of which he had personal knowledge. *At Broad-Chalke is a Cottage-Family, that the Generation hath two Thumbes. A poore Womans Daughter in Westminster, being born so, the Mother gott a Carpenter to amputate one of them with his Chizel and Mallet. The Girl was then about seven yeares Old: and was a lovely Child. Immediately after the Thumbe was struck-off: the fright and Convulsion was so extreme; that she lost her understanding, even her Speech: she lived till seventeen in that Sad condition.* And more serious operations were so rarely successful that Aubrey recorded with especial interest that *a Mariner (1688) of Bristowe having the Stone in his Kidney did adventure the cutting of it: The Surgeon took it out: and the Man recovered. Mr Cole of Bristowe sent this account to the Royal Societie: I think he sent the stone too.*

One can see, therefore, why Aubrey congratulated himself so strongly on having outwitted death so many times during his childhood, for in this he was more fortunate than his brothers and sisters, none of whom survived infancy, until William was born, in 1643, when John was already an undergraduate at Oxford.

When a Boy, Aubrey was *bred at Eston, an Eremeticall Solitude*, which he much resented. *'Twas a great disadvantage to me in my childhood*, he said later, *to be bred up in a kind of Parke, far from Neighbours and no Child to converse withall: so that I did not speake till late. My father had one to teach me in the house, and I was pent-up in a Roome by my selfe melancholy.* But because of this loneliness, the main lines of his character were laid down very early. *He was very curious*, he says of himself, *his greatest delight to be continually with the artificers that came there (e.g. Joyners, carpenters, coupers, masons) and understood their trades.* So soon appeared that indiscriminate curiosity about other people's business which was to plague him throughout his life, and already it was combined with a corresponding inability to concentrate upon his own work. *About Priorie St Maries, and in the Minchin-meadowes there*, he says, *but especially at Brown's-hill which is opposite to the house where, in an unfortunate hour, I drew my first breath, there is infinite variety of plants; and it would have tempted me to be a botanist had I had leisure, which is a jewell I could never master of.*

This solitary childhood forced Aubrey to rely for companionship on the country people who lived round about, and here he imbibed the second mainstay of his character – superstition. *When I was a child (and so before the Civill Warres)*, he says, *the fashion was for old women and mayds to tell fabulous stories nightimes, of Sprights and walking of Ghosts, &c. This was derived down from mother to daughter, from the Monkish Ballance which upheld Holy Church, for the Divines say, Deny Spirits, you are an Atheist. When the warres came, and with them Liberty of Conscience and Liberty of inquisition, the phantoms vanished. Now children feare no such things, having heard not of them; and are not checked with such feares.* But Aubrey, in his isolation, was surrounded by these tales. *Our Country-people would talke much of Faeries*, he said. *They swept-up the Harthe cleane at night: and did sett their shoes by the fire, and many times should find a threepence in one of them.* In this belief the rustics were not alone, for later in life Aubrey reported that *Mris. Markey (a daughter of Serjeant Hoskyns the Poet) told me, that her mother did use that Custome and had as much money as made her a little Silver-cup of thirtie shillings value. Elias Ashmole sayes: there was in his time, a Piper in Lichfield that did know what Houses were Faiery-ground: and that the Piper had oftentimes seen them.* All Aubrey's early education, in fact, seemed purposely designed to encourage his gullibility, for he points out that *in the old ignorant times, before woomen were Readers, the history was handed down from Mother to daughter: and W. Malmesburiensis pickt up his history from the time of Ven. Bede to his time out of Old Songs: for there was no writer in England from Bede to him. So my Nurse had the History from the Conquest down to Carl I. in Ballad.* And it was upon this unsure foundation that Aubrey's historical knowledge was based, for his later education, still in those days entirely classical, did nothing to counteract the superstitions of his childhood.

A further element of his character, *a strong and early impulse to Antiquitie*, was also present long before he went to school. *I was inclin'd by my Genius, from my Childhood to the Love of Antiquities*, he reports, *and my Fate dropt me in a Country most suitable for such Enquiries.* His taste for historical gossip appeared early too, for he mentions that, *when a Boy*, he *did ever love to converse with old men, as Living Histories*, and it was particularly to his mother's parents, Isaac and Israel Lyte, that he turned for information. *I was alwayes enquiring of my grandfather of the Old time, the Rood-loft, etc., ceremonies of the Priory, etc.*, he says, and in one of these conversations his grandfather told him a story that sums up the whole difference between the seventeenth century and the twentieth: *My Grand Father Lyte told me that at one Lord Majors shew there was the Representation of the Creation of the World, and writt underneath AND ALL FOR MAN.*

Besides this love of history, Aubrey had developed a practical side. *At 8*, he tells us, *I was a kind of Engineer; and I fell then to drawing, beginning first with plaine outlines, e.g. in draughts of curtaines. Then at 9 (crossed herein by my father and schoolmaster) to colours, having no body to instruct me: copied pictures in the parlour in a table booke.*

When he was eight years old, Aubrey *entred into his Grammar at the Latin schoole at Yatton Keynel, in the Church: where the Curate Mr Hart taught the eldest Boyes, Virgil, Ovid, Cicero etc.*, and where the eldest boys taught the new pupils a lesson in morality. *I was 8 yeares old before I knew what theft was*, he says with understandable bitterness, *scilicet, I had a fine Box top which was stolen from me*. His grandfather Lyte had also studied here as a child, for Aubrey had heard him say that *when he went to Schoole in this Church, in the S. Windowe of the chancell, were severall escutcheons, which a herald that passed by tooke note of: which window*, the future antiquary was quick to note, *is now dammed up with stones, and now no memorie left of them*. The loss of their stained glass made the authorities no more careful of the relics of the past that still survived, however, for Aubrey says, *the fashion then was to save the Ferules of their Bookes with a false cover of Parchment, sc. old Manuscript, which I was too young to understand; but I was pleased with the Elegancy of the Writing, and the coloured initiall letters. I remember the Rector here (Mr Wm. Stump, great grand Son of Stump the Cloathier of Malmesbury) had severall Manuscripts of the Abbey. He was a proper Man and a good Fellow, and when He brewed a barrell of Speciall Ale, his use was to stop the bung-hole (under the clay) with a Sheet of Manuscript; he sayd nothing did it so well; which me thought did grieve me then to see*. So early did Aubrey come to regret that wanton destruction of antiquities which was to trouble him till he died.

In the next year, 1634, Aubrey was transferred to a school in the neighbouring parish, which he described as *a mile's fine walke*, although he was careful to point out later to Anthony Wood, *I had then a fine little horse and commonly rode (but this is impertinent) i.e. I was not a vulgar boy and carried not a Satchell at my back. Sed hoc inter nos.* At this new school, *where was the like use of covering of Bookes*, Aubrey *was entred in* his *Latin Grammar by Mr R. Latimer, Rector of Leigh de-la-mere, who had an easie way of teaching: and every time we askt leave to goe forth, we had a Latin word from him which at our return we were to tell him again – which in a little while amounted to a good number of Words. 'Twas my unhappiness in halfe a yeare to loose this good Enformer by his death*, Aubrey added, for he was old and *wore a Dudgeon, with a knife, and bodkin, as also my old grandfather Lyte and Alderman Whitson of Bristowe, which I suppose was the common fashion in their young dayes*. But before he died,

Robert Latimer was responsible for a meeting which was to influence his young pupil's whole life. *This summer*, Aubrey says, *I remember 'twas in Venison season (July or August) Mr Thomas Hobbes came into his Native Country to visitt his Friends, and amongst others he came to see his old schoolmaster, Mr Robert Latimer, at Leigh de-la-mer, where I was then at Schoole in the church. Here was the first place and time that ever I had the honour to see this worthy, learned man, who was then pleased to take notice of me, and the next day visited my relations. His conversation about those times was much about Ben Jonson, Mr Ayton, etc. He was then a proper man, briske, and in very good habit: his hayre quite black, and with moist curles. He stayed at Malmsbury and in the neighbourhood a weeke or better. 'Twas the last time that ever he was in Wiltshire.* This friendship, so pleasantly begun between the fifty-five-year-old philosopher and a *little youth* of eight, was to last for nearly forty years and was only to be broken then by death.

After Robert Latimer's death, Aubrey complains that he was *under severall ignorant rest-in-house teachers*, and for this he lays the blame upon his father, *who was not educated to learning, but to Hawking*. However, in 1638, he was *transplanted to Blandford Schoole in Dorset, to William Sutton BD, who was ill-natured*, and although Aubrey refers proudly to the fact that *Blandford was the most eminent Schoole for the education of Gentlemen in the West of England*, his solitary upbringing left him at a sad disadvantage with the other boys. *I was like a Bird that was gott-out of his cage amongst the free Citizens of the aire*, he complained. *'Twas the first time I knew the world, and the wickedness of Boies. The boies mockt me, and abused me, that were stronger then my selfe; so I was faine to make friendship as a strong line to protections.* Amongst his tormentors seem to have been Walter and Tom Raleigh, the great Sir Walter's grand-nephews, for although Aubrey admits that they had *excellent tuneable voices, and playd their parts well on the violl*, he summed them up as *ingeniose, but all proud and quarrelsome.*

Here, he says, *I recovered my health, and gott my Latin and Greeke best of any of my contemporaries. Our Usher, Thomas Stephens, a very good and ingeniose person, by whom I reap't much information, had (by chance) a Cowper's Dictionary, which I had never seen before. I was then in Terence. Perceiving his method, I read all in the booke where Terence was, and then Cicero – which was the way by which I gott my Latin. 'Twas a wonderfull helpe to my phansie, my reading of Ovid's Metamorphy in English by Sandys, which made me understand the Latin the better. Also, I mett accidentally a booke of my Mothers, Lord Bacon's Essaies, which first opened my Understanding as to Moralls (for Tullie's Offices was too crabbed for my young yeares) and the excellence of the Style, or Hints and transitions. It* seems from this that Aubrey was still a rather serious child, and he confirms that *he cared not for play, but on play-dayes he gave himselfe to Drawing and*

Painting, or to visiting *the shop and furnaces of Old Harding, the only Country-glasse-painter that ever I knew.*

His curiosity about other people's business continued unabated, and this appetite was whetted by the periodic holidays that he spent with Alderman Whitson of Bristol, who besides being his godfather and step-grandfather, was also the owner of the *Mayflower. I was wont* (*I remember*) *much to lament with my selfe that I lived not in a City, e.g. Bristoll, where I might have accesse to watchmakers, locksmiths, etc.*, he said, for it seems that he *did not very much care for Grammar: apprehension enough*, he explains, *but memorie not tenacious. So that then a promising morne enough of an inventive and philosophicall head. My witt was alwaies working, but not adroict for verse*, he added, a fact which might perhaps be traced to the extraordinary licence allowed to schoolboys in those days, for he mentions that *at Curry-Yeovill in Somerset-shire, where there is a How schole in the Church, they have annually a Barrel of good Ale brought into the church; and that night they have the priviledge to breake open their Masters Cellar-dore.* The summing up of his schooldays concludes: *Mild of spirit; mightily susceptible of Fascination. My Idea very cleer; Phansie like a Mirrour, pure chrystal water which the least wind does disorder and unsmooth. Never riotous or prodigall; but* (*as Sir E. Leech said*) *Sloath and carelessnesse are equivalent to all other vices.*

On the second of May 1642, at the age of sixteen, Aubrey was entered as a gentleman-commoner at Trinity College, Oxford; and here at last he was to find his proper element, despite the harshness of the discipline, which he was quick to note. *At Oxford* (*and I doe believe the like at Cambridge*) *the Rod was frequently used by the Tutors and Deanes on his pupills, till Bachelaurs of Arts; even gentlemen-Commoners*, he reported. *One Doctor I knew right well* (*Dr Hannibal Potter, Trin. Coll. Oxon*) *that whipt his scholar with his Sword by his side when he came to take his leave of him to goe to the Innes of Court.* For though the undergraduates were younger in those days (the second Duke of Buckingham was a Master of Arts by the time he was fourteen) they were expected to be more serious, and organized games played no part in their education. Castiglione's instruction 'to joyne learnying with cumlie exercise' was still obeyed, and our modern games were not looked on as 'cumlie': football, in fact, 'is to be put in perpetual silence', being 'nothing but beastly fury and extreme violence'. The 'Courtly exercises and Gentlemanlike pastimes' which 'young men should use and delight in' were listed as follows by Queen Elizabeth's tutor, Roger Ascham: 'to ride comely: to run fair at tilt or ring: to play at all weapons: to shoot fair in bow, or surely in gun: to vault lustily: to run: to leap: to wrestle: to swim: to dance comely: to sing, and play of instruments cunningly: to hawk: to hunt: to play at tennis'; these were the pastimes for 'a Courtly Gentleman to use'. None of them, you will notice, fostered the team spirit, but what was lost in co-operative virtues was more than made up for in individuality: for the men of the past were above all individuals, even to the point of eccentricity, and from this variety sprang the great strength of the nation.

In Aubrey's day the false distinction had not yet been drawn between work, regarded as drudgery, and play, regarded as a good time; and educated men naturally sought their recreation in the study, rather than on the golf-course. For in the seventeenth century learning was part of the joy of life, just as much as drinking or love-making, and it was just as often overdone. John Evelyn, writing on the death of his five-year-old son, said: 'So insatiable were his Desires of Knowledge, that upon a Time hearing one discourse of Terence and Plautus, and being told (upon his Enquiry concerning these Authors) that the Books were too difficult for him, he wept for very Grief, and would hardly be pacified'; and Aubrey mentions that *Lord Ellesmere was so hard a Student, that in three or 4 yeares time he was not out of the House: Edward Brerewood*, too, *went not out of the College gates in a good while, nor (I thinke) out of his Chamber, but was in his slip-shoes, and wore out his Gowne and cloathes on the bord and benches of his chamber, but profited in knowledge exceedingly*. Even when they reached years of discretion, the men of the Renaissance seemed unable to moderate their studies. *Laurence Rooke was a temperate man and of a strong constitution*, says Aubrey, *but tooke his sicknesse of which he dyed by setting up often for Astronomicall Observations*, while *Michaell Dary, Mathematician and a Gunner of the Tower (by profession a Tobacco-cutter) an admirable Algebrician*, came to grief rather like Francis Bacon, for *with writing in the frostie weather his fingers rotted and gangraened*.

Lookt through Logique and some Ethiques, says Aubrey of his own studies, for he had now graduated from the Classics to the Humanities; and then comes a most pregnant note: *1642, Religio Medici printed, which first opened my understanding*. For at this time learning suddenly took a great leap forward, upon the unexpected recognition that *the British language is as copious in expressing congruous Termes of Art as the Greeke: or any language whatsoever*. English had, indeed, reached complete fluency a century before, but it had continued to develop so fast that, even for the Stuarts, the language of the Elizabethans had become antiquated: *Henry, the last Earle of Cumberland, was*, according to Aubrey, *an ingeniose Gentleman for those times and writt a Poeme in English upon the Psalmes, and very well, but the language being now something out of fashion, like Sir Philip Sidney's, they will not print it*. But when James I authorized a new translation of the Bible in 1604, he unwittingly caused the English language to crystallize at its very peak, and gave to it a permanence that it had never enjoyed before; and as soon as the constant change in the tongue slowed down to a manageable rate, learned works came more and more to be written in English, instead of Latin. The result was that for the first time the new printing presses began to affect the whole nation: not wholly for good, as Aubrey shows, for already the first blow had been struck at the imaginative faculty, which was finally to be smothered under the flood of precise newspaper information in our own time. *Before Printing, Old-wives Tales were ingeniose*, he says regretfully, *and since Printing came in fashion, till a little before the Civill-warres, the ordinary sort of People were not taught to reade. Now-a-dayes Bookes are common, and most of the poor people understand letters; and the many good Bookes, and variety of Turnes of Affaires, have putt all the old Fables out of doors: and the divine art of Printing and Gunpowder have frighted away Robin-goodfellow and the Fayries.*

Another abandonment of the Classics was to have even more far-reaching results. *All old accounts are in numerall letters*, Aubrey says. *Even to my remembrance, when I was a youth, Gentlemen's Bayliffs in the Country used no other, e.g. i. ii. iii. iiii. v. vi. vii. viii. ix. x. xi. etc: and to this day in the accounts of the Exchecquer. And the Shopkeepers in my Grandfathers times used to reckon with Counters: which is the best and surest way: and is still used by the French.* But now, at last, these Roman numerals were abandoned and the bonds that had confined science for two thousand years were broken. For without mathematics there could be no theory, and the Greeks and Romans had been limited to practical matters, simply because their numerals, though sufficient for counting, were useless for calculating. But while Europe was covered by the Dark Ages, the Arabs had made what is probably the greatest single discovery in the history of thought, the invention of a symbol for nought, and the adoption of the Arabic numerals at the time of the Renaissance opened up a whole new world of thought, which the men of the seventeenth century explored with voluptuous delight.

For *the Mathematicks* was the most popular of all studies during the Stuart Century, and *it was Edmund Gunter who, with his Booke of the Quadrant, Sector and Crosse-staffe did open men's understandings and made young men in love with that Studie. Before, the Mathematicall Sciences were lock't up in the Greeke and Latin tongues and there lay untoucht, kept safe in some libraries. After Mr Gunter published his Booke, these Sciences sprang up amain, more and more to that height it is at now* (1690).

Soldiers, sailors, courtiers, clerics, all devoted themselves to this intoxicating study, and many a young man was, like Henry Gellibrand, *good for little a great while, till at last it happened accidentally, that he heard a Geometrie Lecture. He was so taken with it, that immediately he fell to studying it, and quickly made great progresse in it. The fine Diall over Trinity Colledge Library is of his owne doeing*. This *dialling*, however, was so comparatively easy, and other tricks so impressive and so common, that Thomas Hobbes felt obliged to issue a warning: 'Not every one that brings from beyond seas a new Gin, or other jaunty devise, is therefore a Philosopher,' he said, 'for if you reckon that way, not only Apothecaries and Gardiners, but many other sorts of Workmen will put-in for, and get the Prize.' Unabashed, however, some of Aubrey's friends persisted in their unorthodox ways, like Seth Ward, Bishop of Salisbury, who *when he was President of Trinity College, Oxon, did draw his Geometricall Schemes with black, red, yellow, green and blew Inke to avoid the perplexity of A, B, C, etc.*, and William Oughtred, who achieved undying fame with his invention of the multiplication sign, which, he said, *came into my head, as if infused by a Divine Genius*. And the controversies that raged over *Arithmeticall Problemes* reached such a pitch of emotion (particularly when Hobbes thought that he had squared the circle and Dr Wallis knew that he had not) that poor Aubrey was driven to the conclusion: *sure their Mercuries are in □ or opposition. Ludolph van Keulen*, who had been *first, by Profession, a Fencing-Master; but becomeing deafe, betooke himselfe to the studie of the Mathematiques wherin he became famous and wrote a learned booke in 4to of the Proportion of the Diameter of a Circle to the Peripherie*, carried the obsession even further, for *on his Monument (according to his last Will) is engraved the Proportion abovesayd.*

The excitement caused by this serious study is not so surprising when one recalls that Professor Trevelyan has said, 'every reader had in some sort to be a student, for apart from poetry and the stage, there was hardly any literature that was not serious. . . . Not newspapers and novels but ballads and songs were hawked about by Autolycus and his comrades to satisfy the common appetite in the city street and on the village green.' For the host of adult infants for whom our magazines and films now cater had not yet appeared, and the Bible held undisputed sway over the minds of men. 'If there had been newspapers, magazines and novels', Professor Trevelyan continues, 'to compete with the Bible in manor-house, farm and cottage, there would have been no Puritan revolution.'

The result of this monopolizing of men's minds by the Scriptures was not long in coming; the battle of ideas mounted in violence until *the first brush occurred between the Earl of Northampton and Lord Brooke, near Banbury, which was the latter end of July, or the beginning of August, 1642. But now Bellona thundered, and as a cleare skie is sometimes suddenly overstretched with a dismall Cloud and thunder, so was this Serene Peace by the Civill Warres through the Factions of those times.*

The outbreak of the Great Rebellion was the more depressing because of the long peace that had preceded it. As far back as living memory could reach, since the fires of Smithfield had died out on Queen Mary's death eighty-four years before, the country of England had been at quiet within itself, and for the first time in history a man could have lived out his whole life in peace. England had been involved in wars, it is true, but none had touched her shores, and the fighting on the Continent had really increased the tranquillity of this country, by drawing off the more bellicose of her sons into the service of some foreign prince. But now the wars which had plagued England ever since the Romans left broke out again, and the mercenary ruffians who made up the continental armies of those days were to transfer their attentions to this prosperous land. No wonder William Oughtred cried out that he was 'daunted and broken with these disastrous times'. For the people of England had been so long unused to violence that the results of the conflict were unusually severe; *The Lady Jordan being at Cirencester, when it was besieged (Anno aetatis 75°) was so terrified with the Shooting, that her understanding was so spoyled, that She became a tiny-child, that they made Babies for her to play withall.*

Though the causes of the war were largely intellectual (and Aubrey mentions in the life of Thomas May that *Mr Decretz was present at the debate at their parting before Sir Richard Fanshawe went to the King, where both Camps were most rigorously banded*) the rebellion gave an excuse for private grudges and family quarrels to flare up into unexampled savagery. Henry Martin sat as one of Charles's judges, because of an insult delivered by the King many years before, and even Sir John Danvers, *a great friend of the King's partie and a Patron to distressed and cashiered Cavaliers*, abandoned his principles to spite his family. *To revenge himselfe of his sister, the Lady Gargrave*, explains Aubrey, *and to ingratiate himselfe more with the Protector to null his brother, Earl of Danby's, Will, he contrary to his owne naturall inclination, did sitt in the High Court of Justice at the King's Triall.*

In these circumstances the savagery of man, about which our ancestors shared none of our perfectionist illusions, had full play. *On this Oake*, says Aubrey in his *Naturall Historie of Wiltshire*, *Sir Francis Dodington hung up thirteen after quarter. He made a Sonn hang his Father or e contra.* And this bestiality was to continue for half a decade, until *the King was beaten out of the field.*

The result of *the first brush* on Aubrey was immediate. *In August following*, he reports, *my father sent for me home, for feare.* But it was not only Aubrey's life that was interrupted: the very continuity of English culture was broken. *When I was a little Boy (before the Civill Warres)* Aubrey was to repeat over and over again in talking of the vanished customs and beliefs of the so-recent past, for a whole way of life disappeared in the convulsion; a way of life which Aubrey has crystallized in a single sentence: *When I was a Boy every Gentleman almost kept a Harper in his house: and some of them could versifie.* But now the harpers were no more, for it was the life of the rich which suffered annihilation first; a life which could be traced back as far as history would reach. *After the comeing in of the Goths, the Roman Games and Cirques, were turned into Tilts and Turnaments. Tilting breath'd its last when King Charles Ist left London. The Tilt-yard was where the Guard-house is now, opposite to White-hall. In those dayes all Gentlemen of a thousand pounds per annum kept a Horse or Horses for a Man at Arms.*

It was not only the rich who were to suffer, though, and as soon as the whole people was involved, the customs and beliefs of the past collapsed before the storm. *When I was a Boy (before the Civill-warres)*, Aubrey says again, *I heard 'em tell that in the old time, they used to put a Penny in the dead persons mouth to give to St Peter: and I thinke that they did doe so in Wales and in the North Country;* and in Yorkshire, too, *in the Countrey churches, at Christmas in the Holy-daies after Prayers, they will dance in the Church, and as they doe dance, they cry (or sing) Yole, Yole, Yole.* For, as Aubrey explains, *in the Infancy of the Christian Religion it was expedient to plough (as they say) with the heifer of the Gentiles, i.e. to insinuate with them and to let them continue and use their old Ethnick Festivals which they new named with Christian names, e.g. Floralia, they turnd to the Feast of St Philip and Jacob, etc, the Saturnalia into Christmas. Had they donne otherwise, they could not have gain'd so many Proselytes or established their Doctrine so well, and in so short a time. The Gentiles would not perfectly relinquish all their Idols; so, they were persuaded to turne the Image of Jupiter with his thunderbolt to Christ crucifixus, and Venus and Cupid into the Madonna and her Babe, which Mr Th. Hobbes sayth was prudently donne.* But now these links with Imperial Rome, which had survived first the coming of the Catholic Church and then the Reformation, were finally destroyed; and many native myths perished at the same time. *It was a Custome for some people that were more curious then ordinary to sitt all night in their church porch of their Parish on Midsomer-eve; and they should see the apparitions of those that should die in the parish that yeare come and knock at the dore.* As these regional customs vanished under the stress of war, uniformity began to spread across the land, until at last even the shepherds of Aubrey's native Wiltshire were affected: *Their Habit (I believe) is that of the Roman or Arcadian Shepherds too*, he says, *sc. a long white Cloake with a very deep cape, which comes downe half way their backs, made of the locks of the Sheep; their Armature was a Sheep Crooke, a Sling, a Scrip, their Tar-box, a Pipe (or Flute) and their Dog. But since 1671 they are grown so luxurious as to neglect their ancient warme, and usefull fashion, and goe à la mode.* Every one of these changes was resented by Aubrey as a personal blow, until he was sadly led to conclude that *the Civill Warres comeing on have putt out all these Rites, or customs quite out of fashion. Warres doe not only extinguish Religion and Lawes: but Superstition; and no Suffimen is a greater fugator of Phantosmes, than Gun-powder.*

By far the worst result of the Rebellion for an antiquary like Aubrey was the acquisition of power by the Puritans, those Philistines whom he despised so much and who, in their turn, despised his kind. Speaking of Robert Sanderson, Lord Bishop of Lincoln, he says scornfully that *the very Parliamentarians reverenced him for his Learning and his vertue: so that he alwayes kept his living.* The accidental destruction of antiquities had been bad enough in the past, for the wanton use of the monastical manuscripts, which he had witnessed as a child, still preyed upon his mind. *In my grandFather's dayes, the Manuscripts flew about like Butter-flies,* he repeated sadly. *All Musick bookes, Account-bookes, Copie bookes, etc, were covered with old Manuscripts, as wee cover them now with blew Paper, or Marbled Paper. And the Glovers at Malmesbury made great Havock of them, and Gloves were wrapt up no doubt in many good pieces of Antiquity. Before the late Warres a World of rare Manuscripts perished here about; for within half a dozen miles of Easton-Piers were the Abbey of Malmesbury, where it may be presumed the Library was as well furnished with choice Copies, as most Libraries of England: Broadstock-Priory, Stenley-Abbey, Farleigh-Abbey, Bath-Abbey and Cyrencester-Abbey. One may also perceive by the Binding of old Bookes how the old Manuscripts went to wrack in those dayes. About 1647, I went to see Parson Stump out of curiosity to see his Manuscripts, whereof I had seen some in my Child-hood; but by that time they were lost and disperst; His sonns were gunners and souldiers, and scoured their gunnes with them.* But at least this destruction had been due to ignorance, and not to policy. The Puritans, on the other hand, knew what they were doing and destroyed on purpose and on principle. *My old cosen Parson Whitney told me that in the Visitation of Oxford in Edward VI's time they burned Mathematical bookes for Conjuring bookes, and, if the Greeke Professor had not accidentally come along, the Greeke Testament had been thrown into the fire for a Conjuring booke too.* This had happened during the only reign in which the Puritans had so far held power, but since then any form of unnecessary destruction had been discouraged: *Neer Dunnington Castle was an Oake, under which Sir Jeofry Chaucer was wont to sit, called Chaucer's oake, which was cutt downe, tempore Caroli I^{mi},* Aubrey says, *and so it was, that . . . was called into the Starre chamber and was fined for it. Judge Richardson harangued against him long, and like an orator, had topiques from the Druides, etc.*

It was against idolatry, however, that the fury of the Puritans was chiefly turned and, long before the Civil War, untoward incidents had begun to occur again. *In St Edmunds Church at Salisbury were curious painted Glasse-windowes (especially in the Chancell) where there was one Window (I think the East window) of such exquisite worke, that Gundamour the Spanish Ambassadeur did offer some hundreds of Pounds for it, if it might have been bought. In one of the Windowes was the Picture of God the Father, like an Old Man (as the fashion then was) which much offended Mr Shervill, the Recorder, who out of Zeale came, and brake some of these Windowes about 1631; and clambering upon one of the Pews (to be able to reach high enough) fell downe and brake his Legg; but that did not excuse him for being question'd in the Starre-chamber for it, and had a great Fine layd upon which I thinke did undoe him.* But soon the Star Chamber was abolished, and the Puritans, having achieved power, set about their iconoclasm with such a will that Aubrey noted sadly: *But what Mr Shervill left undonne, the Soldiers since have gonne through with, that there is not a piece of glass-painting left.* And as the war continued, the merchants of London put the whole thing on a proper business footing, for Aubrey mentions that *at Croydon in Surrey in the Rebellion, one Bleese was hir'd, for half a Crown per Day, to break the painted Glass-Windows, which were formerly fine.*

When the glass was finished, the zealots turned their attention to the altars and the statues, the vestments, painted tombs and organs, until Aubrey could write of Corston: *In the Church nothing to be found, the modern zeale has been a reforming here, as hereabout.* For at nearby Slaughterford, he had noted: *Here is a prettie small Church, the most miserably handled that ever I saw, the very barres are taken out of the windowes by the fanatique rage of the late times; here have been two good South windowes, and the doores are gone and the paving, and it serves for any use, viz. Weavers. The Font has gone to make a trough.*

Having gutted the churches, the Parliamentarians then turned their attention to the buildings themselves. Churches *were pulled-downe to the ground, that the Enemie might not shelter themselves against the Garrison;* castles, like Dunnington, which had been *Sir Geoffrey Chaucer's, a noble seate and strong castle, which was held by the King,* were *dismanteled; tuneable Bells were converted into Ordinance;* and many houses were burnt. The destruction in fact was so widespread that it led Aubrey, though he was only eighteen, to make his first practical antiquarian move: *I gott Mr Hesketh, Mr Dobson's man, a Priest, to drawe the Ruines of Osney, 2 or 3 wayes before 'twas pulled down,* he says. *Now the very foundation is digged up.* And thirty years later, one of these drawings, the only record of the Abbey, was to be reproduced in Dugdale's 'Monasticon', with the following inscription: 'The Noble Ruines of this Fabrick were drawn from a love to Antiquity, while yet a Youth at Oxford, and (which was not a little lucky) but a short time before they were entirely destroyed in the Civil War, secured now and as it were revived, are dedicated to Posterity, by John Aubrey of Easton Piers in the County of Wilts, Esq.'

In February 1643, Aubrey says, *with much adoe I gott my father to lett me to beloved Oxon againe, then a Garrison pro Rege,* and a very different place from the University which he had left a few short months before. For the Court had come to Oxford in the preceding November, taking the colleges for its lodgings and driving the older dons, like Dr Kettell of Aubrey's own college, into a premature grave.

Like Aubrey, most of the scholars had left Oxford on the outbreak of the war. The few who had remained were, according to one don, 'debauched by bearing Armes, and doing the Duties belonging to Soldiers, as Watching, Warding, and sitting in Tipling-Houses for whole Nights together'. So the atmosphere of the city cannot have been conducive to work, especially for someone so easily distracted as Aubrey. First, there was the King to be seen: *When I was a Freshman at Oxford*, Aubrey says, *I was wont to go to Christ Church to see King Charles I at Supper: Where I once heard him say, that as he was Hawking in Scotland, he rode into a Quarry, and found the Covey of Partridge falling upon the Hawk: and I do remember this expression further, viz. and I will swear upon the Book 'tis true. When I came to my Chamber, I told this Story to my Tutor: said he, That Covey was London.* And then there was the Court itself, which in those days was particularly fascinating for a young scholar. For at Court, as Professor Trevelyan has pointed out, 'the gentlemen of England learnt not only the intrigues of love and politics, but music and poetry, and a taste for scholarship and the arts, seeds which they took back to their rural homes to plant there'. For 'the mediaeval distinction between the learned clerk and the barbarous fighting baron was coming to an end, blending in the ideal of the all-accomplished "gentleman"'. In this ideal, the Stuart sovereigns led the way, although at their real 'business as King' they were to prove either woefully incompetent or grossly corrupt. James I, indeed, was so much of a scholar that he was moved to say on his first visit to the Bodleian Library at Oxford: 'If I were not a King, I would be a University man; and if it were so that I must be a prisoner, if I might have my wish, I would desire to have no other prison than that Library, and to be chained together with so many good Authors and dead Masters.' Charles, his son, *that great Antiquary*, was also the finest connoisseur of painting in his realm and the first Englishman to value paintings as art, instead of simply as likenesses or curios. King Charles II was of a more practical bent, but though he dabbled in chemistry, he achieved little of worth: *He had a Mathematicall genius*, Aubrey admitted, *but wanted early education*. Of James II, that lamentable monarch, however, Aubrey could find nothing better to say than that *he was acquainted fully with the State of our Naval Power, and knew as much, if not more than the meanest Sailor;* and his consort was distinguished by a single feat: *Colonel Popham's great tankard, the Dutches Y dranke it* (*almost*) *off at a draught.*

Even during these troublous times, the Court was still the cultural centre of the nation, and the circle of poets and playwrights who usually clustered round the King was augmented by the very fact of the war. Many men were in the same case as John Cleveland, the Cambridge poet, who, *being turned out of his Fellowship for a malignant, came to Oxford, where the King's Army was, and was much caressed by them.* And it was while the King was in residence at Christ Church that William Cartwright, the dramatist, was buried in the cathedral there at the early age of thirty-two. *Pitty 'tis so famous a bard should lye without an Inscription*, Aubrey thought, for his contemporaries had expected great things from him: *'Tis not to be forgott that King Charles 1st dropt a teare at the newes of his death.* In view of this sensibility, it is astounding to find that the manners of the Court were so foul. For in the next reign, Anthony Wood was to write: 'To give a further character of the court, though they were neat and gay in their apparell, yet they were very nasty and beastly, leaving at their departure their excrements in every corner, in chimneys, studies, cole-houses, cellars. Rude, rough, whoremongers; vaine, empty, careless.' With this attack Aubrey was in full agreement, for he himself pointed out that it was the lascivious King Charles II, and not the elegant Charles I, who *was the Patterne of Courtesie, and first brought good Manners into Fashion in England*, and in 1670 he said, *Till this time the Court itself was unpolished and unmannered. King James's Court was so far from being civill to woemen, that the Ladies, nay the Queen herself, could hardly pass by the King's apartment without receiving some Affront.*

Amidst all these excitements, calamity overtook John Aubrey. *In Aprill I fell sick of the Small pox at Trinity College*, he said, but as usual fate softened the blow for him. *William Radford, my good friend and old acquaintance and fellow collegiate, was so kind as to come to me every day and spend severall houres, or I think melancholy would have spoyled a scurvy Antiquary.* This illness was to mean the end of Aubrey's University career, all the same, for he goes on to say, *when I recovered, after Trinity weeke, my father sent for me into the Country again: where I conversed with none but servants and rustiques and soldiers quartred, to my great griefe, for in those dayes fathers were not acquainted with their children. It was a most sad life to me, then in the prime of my youth, not to have the benefitt of an ingeniose Conversation and scarce any good bookes – almost a consumption.* For a library was not yet considered to be an essential part of a gentleman's home: in fact, Lord Herbert of Cherbury was considered almost eccentric because *he had two Libraries, one at London, the other at Montgomery.*

The war itself seems to have made little stir in Wiltshire, and it must have been a great relief when *Major John Morgan fell sick of a malignant fever as he was marching with the King's Army into the West, and was brought to my fathers at Broad Chalke, where he was lodged secretly in a garret.* But though the war provided few diversions, it made the country round about even more unbearable. *Surely this tract of land enclines people to zeale,* exclaimed Aubrey despairingly. *Heretofore nothing but religious houses, now nothing but Quakers and Fanatiqs. A sourewood country,* he decided, *inclines people to contemplation, so that the Bible and ease (for it is all upon dayry grasing, or clothing) setts their witts a running and reforming.* And certainly the description which Aubrey left of his neighbours is most unprepossessing. *In North-wiltshire,* he said, (*a dirty, claeyy Country*) *they speak* (*I mean the Indigenies, or Aborigines only*) *drawning; they are Phlegmatiq; Skins pale and livid; slow, and dull, heavy of Spirit: here about is but little Tillage, or hard labour, they only milk the Cowes and make Cheese. They feed chiefly on Milke meates, which cooles their Braines too much, and hurts their Inventions. These Circumstances make them Melancholy, contemplative, and malicious: by consequence whereof more Lawsuites come out of North Wilts, at least double to the Southern Parts. And by the same reason they are generally more apt to be Fanatiques: (In Malmesbury Hundred, &c. – wett, clayy parts: Here have ever been reputed Witches). Their persons are generally plump and foggy: gallipot Eies, and some black: but they are generally handsome enough. On the Downes (sc. the South part) where 'tis all upon Tillage, or Shepherds: and labour hard, their flesh is hard, their bodies strong: being weary after their hard labour, they have not leisure to reade, and contemplate of Religion, but goe to Bed to their rest, to rise betimes the next morning to their labour. I remember (upon the foresayd reason) that Capt. John Graunt did say, it was observed that there were no Anchor Smyths Fanaticks: for it is a mighty laborious trade: and they must drinke strong drinke to keep up their Spirits: so they never troubled their Heads with curious Notions of Religion.*

To add to the miseries of his exile in the country, Aubrey got on extremely badly with his father, who had no sympathy at all with his son's newfangled learning. *My studies (geometry) were on horse back,* Aubrey confessed, *and in the house of office:* (*my father discouraged me*). For the relations between parents and children were very rigid in those days and the following passage, which Aubrey wrote in 1670, is plainly autobiographical. *From the time of Erasmus till about 20 years past, the learning was downright Pedantry,* he said. *The conversation and habitts of those times were as stiff and starcht as their bands and square beards: and Gravity was then taken for Wisdome. The very Doctors of those days were but old boies, when quibles past for wit, even in the pulpitts. The Gentry and the Citizens had little learning of any kind, and their way of breeding up their children was suitable to the rest: for wheras ones child should be ones nearest Friend, and the time of growing-up should be most indulged, they were as severe to their children as their schoolmaster; and their Schoolmasters, as masters of the House of correction. The child perfectly loathed the sight of his parents, as the slave his Torturor. Gentlemen of 30 or 40 years old, fitt for any employment in the common wealth, were to stand like great mutes and fools bare headed before their Parents; and the Daughters (grown woemen) were to stand at the Cupboards side during the whole time of the proud mothers visiit, unless (as the fashion was) 'twas desired that leave (forsooth) should be given to them to kneele upon cushions brought them by the servingman, after they had done sufficient Penance standing. The boys (growne young fellows) had their forheads turned up, and stiffened with spittle: they were to stand mannerly forsooth, thus, the foretop ordered as before, one hand at the band-string, the other on the breech or codpiece. The Gentlewoemen then had prodigious fannes, as is to be seen in old pictures, like that instrument which is used to drive Feathers: it had a handle at least half a yard long; with these the daughters were corrected oftentimes. (Sir Edw. Coke, Lord Chief Justice, rode the circuit with such a fan: Mr Dugdale sawe it, who told me of it. The Earl of Manchester used also a Fan.) But fathers and mothers slash't their daughters in the time of that Besome discipline when they were perfect woemen.*

No wonder, therefore, that Aubrey was depressed, and it was with obvious regret that he looked back upon the golden past, when *the Holy-mawle hung behind the Church dore, which when the father was seaventie the sonne might fetch to knock his father in the head, as effoete, & of no more use. This sad life I did lead in the country till 1646*, he said, *at which time I gott (with much adoe) leave of my father to let me goe to the Middle Temple, April the 6th, 1646. But my fathers sicknesse, and businesse, never permitted me to make any settlement to my studie.* Not that Aubrey had ever had any idea of making the Law his profession: the progression from University to the Temple was part of the normal education of a gentleman in those days, for only after a threefold training in the Classics, the Humanities, and the Law was a man considered competent to manage his estates.

24 June following, Aubrey records, *Oxon was surrendred, and then came to London many of the King's party, with whom I grew acquainted (many of them I knew before). I loved not debauches*, he was careful to explain, *but their martiall conversation was not so fitt for the Muses.*

As the Civil War dragged slowly on towards its close, the happiest period of Aubrey's life was dawning, for he announces: *Novemb. 6, I returned to Trinity College in Oxon again to my great joy; was much made of by the Fellowes; had their learned conversation, lookt on bookes, musique. Here and at Middle Temple (off and on) I (for the most part) enjoyd the greatest felicity of my life (ingeniose youths, like Rosebudds, imbibe the morning dew) till Dec. 1648 (Christmas Eve's eve) I was sent for from Oxon home again to my sick father, who never recovered. Where I was engaged to looke after his country businesse and solicite a lawe-suite*, and also incidentally to continue his delvings into the past, for within a month of his return, he had stumbled upon the greatest discovery of his lifetime.

Salisbury-plaines, and Stonehenge I had known from eight years old, he says, *but I never saw the Countrey about Marleborough, till Christmas 1648: being then invited to the Lord Francis Seymour's, by the Honourable Mr Charles Seymour (then of Allington near Chippenham, since Lord Seymour) with whom I had the honour to be intimately acquainted, and whose Friendship I ought to mention with a profound respect to his memorie.*

The morrow after Twelf day, Mr Charles Seymour and Sir William Button of Tokenham (a most parkely ground, and a Romancy-place) Baronet, mett with their packs of Hounds at the Greyweathers. These Downes looke as if they were Sow'n with great Stones, very thicke; and in a dusky evening they looke like a flock of Sheep: from whence it takes its name. One might fancy it to have been the Scene where the Giants fought with stones against the Gods. 'Twas here that our Game began: and the Chase led us (at length) through the Village of Aubury, into the Closes there: where I was wonderfully surprised at the sight of those vast stones, of which I had never heard before; as also at the mighty Banke and graffe (ditch) about it. I observed in the Inclosures some segments of rude circles, made with these stones, whence I concluded, they had been in old time complete. I left my Company a while, entertaining myself with a more delightfull indagation: and then (steered by the cry of the Hounds) overtooke the company, and went with them to Kynnet, where was a good Hunting dinner provided. Our Repast was cheerfull; which, being ended, we remounted, and beate over the Downes with our Grey-hounds. In this Afternoon's diversion I happened to see Wensditch and an old Camp, and two or three sepulchres. The evening put a period to our sport, he concluded, *and we returned to the Castle at Marleborough, where we were nobly entertained.*

Aubrey was rightly proud of his discovery, for Avebury had been completely ignored before. *It is very strange,* he thought, *that so eminent an Antiquitie should lye so long unregarded by our Chorographers.* And if Aubrey had not come upon it thus, by chance, it is possible that it would have gone unregarded for ever, for the villagers were even then engaged in breaking up the stones to build new houses.

One month later, with the execution of King Charles and the setting up of the Commonwealth, the break with the past was completed. And by a strange chance, in that very year, the modern world was born. For the idea of progress, a conception which differentiates modern civilization from everything that has preceded it, appeared quite suddenly, and mankind, abandoning its idea of a static world, was to become increasingly familiar with the idea of development and gradual change. *Till about the yeare 1649,* Aubrey says, *when Experimental Philosophy was first cultivated by a Club at Oxford, 'twas held a strange presumption for a Man to attempt an*

Innovation in Learnings; and not to be good Manners, to be more knowing than his Neighbours and Forefathers; even to attempt an improvement in Husbandry (though it succeeded with profit) was look'd upon with an ill Eie. Their Neighbours did scorne to follow it, though not to doe it, was to their own Detriment. 'Twas held a Sin to make a Scrutinie into the Waies of Nature; Whereas it is certainly a profound part of Religion to glorify God in his Workes: and to take no notice at all of what is dayly offered before our Eyes is grosse Stupidity.

The overwhelming importance of this change of attitude cannot be exaggerated, for this freeing of the mind was to cause a violent bound forward in every branch of thought. *In those times, to have had an inventive and enquiring Witt, was accounted Affectation*, Aubrey concludes, *which censure the famous Dr William Harvey could not escape for his admirable Discovery of the Circulation of the Blood.*

But it was not only the mind of England which had changed: the very face of the country altered as the mighty forests that had covered the island since time immemorial were consumed by the ironworks, until Shakespeare's Arden and *the Forests and Parks of Clarendon* were converted into the arable that we know today. *In England till even now since the resprit of these Warres, there were so many Forests, Chases, and Parkes, as were not to be match'd in any Kingdome. These were Vivaries for Beastes (the design of their Lords being to preserve Game) where they were safe not only by the Pale, or Wall; but under the Protection of many severe Laws: as if they had been naturaliz'd, enfranchis'd, and Citizens of our Commonwealth.* It was not always in this tone that Aubrey spoke of animals, however. *At Fausby (near Daintre) in Northamptonshire*, he said on another occasion, *a Raven did build her Nest on the Leads between the Tower and the Steeple. The oldest Peoples Grandfathers here, did never remember, but that this Raven yearly made her Nest here; and in the late Civil warre, the Soldiers killed her. I am sorry for the Tragical end of this old Church-Bird, that lived in so many changes of Government and Relegion.*

It is always hard for us to visualize the material life of our ancestors; to remember that Queen Elizabeth, in her jewelled dresses, had to walk through her palaces on straw-covered floors. But it is on their tables that the widest difference is noticeable, and as Aubrey describes the new foods that had come into England, it is almost impossible to imagine what the people lived on before. For it was Sir Walter Raleigh, more famous for his introduction of tobacco, who brought from the New World the potato, which was immediately impugned for erotic tendencies by the Elizabethans. *Cherries*, according to Aubrey, *were first brought into Kent tempore H. viii, who being in Flanders, and likeing the Cherries, ordered his Gardener, brought them hence and propagated them in England;* and it was not until Queen Elizabeth's time that that most English of plants, *Hoppes*, became common in Kent. Aubrey states that *about the 15th of Henry VIIIth divers things were newly brought into England, whereupon the Rhythme was made*

> *Greeke, Heresie, Turkey-cocks, and Beer,*
> *Came into England all in a yeare.*

England itself remained amazingly regional, mainly because of the difficulties of transport. *The Marquesse Hamilton (that was beheaded)*, Aubrey reports, *was a great Lover of Carpes, and was at great expense (but unsuccessfull) to Carry Carpes into Scotland from England in barrells: but their Noses did still gangrene, being bobb'd against the barrell*, and until someone thought of carrying the spawn, rather than the fish themselves, people in the outlying parts of the country had to content themselves with whatever nature provided, for there were no fishmongers inland and so, *by reason of the fasting dayes, all gentlemen's howses had anciently Fishponds, and fish in the motes about the howse.*

Within living memory, even, vast changes had taken place in the nation's diet. *Carrets*, says Aubrey, *were first sown at Beckington in Somersetshire. Some very old Man there (in 1668) did remember their first bringing thither*, and not only did *Mr Alexander James, Alderman of Bristoll*, tell him that *when he was a Boy, all the Turnips, that they had there, did come from Wales*, but *the Mother of Mr John Ashe remembred when all the Cabbages were brought from Holland. She was eighty yeares old, and upwards when she died.*

Agriculture, too, was improving, and Aubrey notes: *Limeing of ground began about 1590 or some time after the use of Tobacco, by Sir Walter Raleigh*, and it was Sir Richard Weston who *brought the first Clovergrass, about 1645, out of Brabant or Flandrs; at which time he also brought over the Contrivance of Locks, Turnpikes, and tumbling Boyes for Rivers*, while *Sir Isaac Wake was the first that planted Pines and Firres in England.*

Even tabby cats were once newfangled novelties. *W. Laud, A.B. Cant. was a great lover of Catts*, Aubrey reports, *He was presented with some Cyprus-catts, i.e. our Tabby-catts, which were sold, at first for 5 pounds a piece: this was about 1637, or 1638.* The fashion thus started resulted in a change which Aubrey strongly resented. *I doe well remember*, he says crossly, *that the common English Catt, was white with some blewish piednesse: sc. a gallipot blew. The race or breed of them are now almost lost.* But another change in the animal population of England at this time would probably not have aroused his anger had he noticed it and recognized its implications, for during Aubrey's lifetime the modern brown rat wiped out and replaced the medieval black rat, and it was this medieval rat which had been the carrier of the plague-flea.

Strange flowers, too, were reaching English shores. *Jessamines came into*

England with Mary, the Queen-Mother, he says, *and Laurell was first brought over by Alethea, Countesse of Arundell, grandmother to this Duke of Norfolke.* For *the Pleasure and Use of Gardens were unknown to our great Grandfathers: they were contented with Pot-herbs: and did mind chiefly their Stables. But in the time of King Charles II^{d} Gardening was much improved, and became common;* so common in fact that Aubrey could write in 1691, *especially since about 1683, there have been exotick Plants brought into England, no lesse than seven thousand.*

But to return to Aubrey's life: for the first three years of the Commonwealth he tried to alleviate the misery of his *sad life in the country*, by toying with the idea of travel abroad. *William Harvey, my she cosen Montague's physitian and friend, proved very communicative and willing to instruct any that were modest and respectfull to him and in order to my Journey, gave me, i.e. dictated to me, what to see, what company to keepe, what Bookes to read, how to manage my Studies: in short, he bid me goe to the Fountain head, and read Aristotle, Cicero, Avicenna, and did call the Neoteriques shitt-breeches.* These plans came to maturity in 1651, Aubrey continued, *when I made my will and settled my Estate on Trustees, intending to have seen the Antiquities of Rome and Italy, and then to have returned and married, but my mother, to my inexpressible griefe and ruine, hindred this designe, which was the procatratique cause of my ruine.*

His mother's importunities were no doubt caused by the illness of his father, who died at last in 1652, unregretted by his son, who ungratefully mentioned only that he was left *debts 1800 pounds*, and ignored the estates in Wiltshire, Surrey, Monmouth, Brecknock, Hereford, and Kent which also came to him, albeit they were well entangled with law suits.

Now that he was free from his father's disapproving gaze and master of his own purse, Aubrey embarked wholeheartedly on a career of dilettantism. His estates were left to look after themselves while he led the life of a wealthy young squire in London, which even under *the English Attila, Oliver*, was more congenial than the lonely farms of Wiltshire. For the condition of England *during Oliver's Triumphant Usurpation* is best summed up by an inn-sign near Oxford which, at the beginning of the Commonwealth, had been altered to read 'This was the King's Head'. And as Aubrey sought out *the merry men in the reigne of the Saintes*, he discovered that the main result of the Commonwealth was an increase in concealment, and hypocrisy, rather than a change of heart. The Presbyterians, as Anthony Wood was quick to notice, 'would not goe to ale-houses or taverns, but send for their liquors to their respective chambers and tiple it there. Some would goe in publick; but then, if overtaken, they were so cunning as to dissemble it in their way home by a lame leg or that some suddaine paine there had taken them.' A more unexpected result of Puritanism, however, was that 'Dr John Owen, the Deane of Christ Church, when Vice-Chancellor, had as much powder in his haire that would discharg eight cannons', as well as 'cambric band with larg costly band-strings, velvet jacket, his breeches set round at knee with ribbons, pointed, Spanish leather boots with Cambrig tops, etc. And all this was in opposition to a prelaticall cut.'

The death of his father had started Aubrey on a depressing train of thought, and after considering long and seriously what he was best fitted to do in life, he had to answer: *Truly nothing: only Umbrages. If ever I had been good for anything, 'twould have been a Painter, I could fancy a thing so strongly and had so cleare an idaea of it*, but to become a good painter would have been a laborious business, and so Aubrey decided that his real purpose in life was to be *a wheatstone* and to strike ideas from other people and sharpen their wits for work. He was not long, however, in finding his proper bent, for he mentions that *he began to enter into pocket memorandum bookes, philosophical and antiquarian remarques, Anno Domini 1654, at Llantrithid.*

In 1655, Aubrey says, *there was published by Mr Web a Booke intituled Stonehenge-restored (but writt by Mr Inigo Jones) which I read with great delight. There is a great deale of Learning in it: but having compared his Scheme with the Monument it self, I found he had not dealt fairly: but had made a Lesbian's rule, which is conformed to the stone; that is, he framed the monument to his own Hypothesis, which is much differing from the Thing it self. This gave me an edge to make more researches; and a farther opportunity was, that my honoured and faithfull Friend Colonell James Long of Draycot, since Baronet, was wont to spend a weeke or two every Autumne at Aubury in Hawking, where several times I have had the happiness to accompany him. I should now be both Orator and Soldier to give this honoured friend of mine, a Gentleman absolute in all numbers, his due Character*, said Aubrey, and therefore limited himself to giving a mere list of Sir James's capabilities. *In the Civill Warres, Colonel of Horse in Sir Francis Dodington's Brigade. Maried a most elegant Beautie and Witt. Good sword-man; horseman; admirable extempore Orator pro Harangue; Great Memorie; great Historian and Romancer; great Falkoner and for Horsemanship; for Insects; exceeding curious and searching long since, in naturall things.* And to show that he was not alone in appreciating his friend's charms, Aubrey mentions that *Oliver Protector, hawking at Hownslowe-heath, discoursing with him, fell in love with his company, and commanded him to weare his sword, and to meete him a Hawking, which made the strict Cavaliers look on him with an evill eye.*

Our Sport was very good, and in a Romantick countrey, Aubrey continues, *sc. the Prospects noble and vast, the Downes stock't with numerous Flocks of Sheep, the Turfe rich and fragrant with Thyme and Burnet. Nor are the Nut-brown Shepherdesses without their graces. But the flight of the Falcon was but a parenthesis to the Colonell's facetious discourse, who was tam Marti quam Mercurio; and the Muses did accompany him with his Hawkes and Spanniels.* Unfortunately Aubrey was so entertained by his friend's conversation that he never committed his arguments to paper, and so Inigo Jones went unrefuted.

Undaunted by his failure even to complete a pamphlet, Aubrey at once embarked on a much more elaborate task. *I am the first that ever made an Essay of this Kind for Wiltshire (and for ought I know in the Nation) having begun it in Ano 1656*, he said, and the work he was planning was indeed new. He had undertaken to write *The Naturall Historie of Wiltshire*, and although it was never published, he did in fact bring it nearer to completion than any of his other books.

The mere chapter headings show the vast scope of the work, for they range from *Air*, *Springs Medicinall*, *Rivers*, *Earths*, *Mineralls*, *Stones*, *Plantes*, *Beastes*, *Fishes*, *Birds*, *Insects and Reptiles*, *Men and Women*, to *Things Praeternatural*, *e.g. Witchcraft*, *Phantomes*, *&c.*, and *the Number of Attornies every 30 yeares since H. viii.* And there are numerous diversions into subjects like *The History of Cloathing and Cloathiers of Wilts*, *Faires and Markets: Their Rise and Decay*, and *Of the Grandure of the Herberts, Earles of Pembroke.*

In this book, Aubrey put forward many new theories, some absurd, some endorsed by time. *If you let fall a stone into the water*, he said, *immediately it makes a little Circle, then another bigger without that, and so forth, till it touches the Bank, and then it recoiles in a little Circle, which generates other bigger Circles; so sounds move by Sphaeres, in the same manner, which though obvious enough, I doe not remember to have seen in any Booke;* and this observation he counterbalanced by suggesting that it rains more often when the moon is full because *her Vicinity to the Earth gradually depresseth our amosphere.* This last idea is typical of the seventeenth century for, intoxicated by the possibilities of the scientific method, men were apt to put far more faith in it than it warranted. Aubrey measured the height of Salisbury spire by barometric pressure, for instance, and got the result to the nearest inch, and he says *to find the Proportion of the Downes of this Countrey to the Vales, I did divide Speeds Mappe of Wiltshire with a paire of Cizars, according to the respective Hundreds of Downes and Vale: And I weighed them in a Curious Ballance of a Goldsmith.*

On the whole, however, his observations were accurate and his deductions good. He noticed that the ground rose with age and also that the Roman remains at Silchester, though they were deep underground, were visible from a height, in the grass. Aubrey was the first archaeologist that England had produced, and he devoted himself to all the ramifications of that study: geology, heraldry, palaeography, numismatics, and comparative architecture: but being the first in the field, he was offered little help by his predecessors. *I have often times wish't for a Mappe of England coloured according to the colours of the Earth: with markes of the Fossils and Minerals*, he said, and he regretted that no one had ever found time to write *a Historie of the Weather*. His study of these archaeological remains, too, caused his fertile brain to throw out various ideas which were far in advance of his time. *That the World is much older, then is commonly supposed*, he said, *any man may be induced to believe from the finding Fossils so many Foot deep in the Earth*, and he foreshadowed the theory of evolution when he saw (*to use the Heralds terme*) *that Fishes are of the elder House*.

The work also contained a less learned side, which was so entertaining that John Ray felt obliged to issue a warning. 'I think (if you can give me leave to be free with you)', he wrote to Aubrey, 'that you are a little inclinable to credit strange relations. I have found men that are not skilfull in the history of nature very credulous, and apt to impose upon themselves and others, and therefore dare not give a firm assent to anything they report upon their own authority, but are ever suspicious that they may either be deceived themselves, or delight to teratologize (pardon ye word) and to make shew of knowing strange things.'

Luckily Aubrey ignored this well-meant advice and left in the 'strange relations', which nowadays provide the main interest of the work. Such complete irrelevancies as *the best way of dressing a Carpe* find their way into the *Naturall Historie*, besides a most useful hint for the cellar: *Dead Men's bones burn't to ashes and putt into drinke doe intoxicate exceedingly*. Then, too, he was ready with a most efficacious cure for anyone who happened to bang his head: *A Fellow in North-Wales, shrowding of a Tree fell downe on his head, and his Braine being turned, lay for dead: A Mason being thereby, advised that he should have a good strong coffin made, and his feete to come to the end of it, and his head not to touch the other end by two inches: He layeth the Man in the Coffin on a Table-board, and then with a huge Axe, gave a sound Knock at the feet, to turne by that contrary motion his braine right againe. After the blow was given the fellow gave a groane and spake: and he recovered.*

A whole treasure trove of words lies jumbled up together in this book. *In North Wilts*, Aubrey says, *the Milke mayds sing as shrill and cleare as any Swallow sitting on a Berne*, and the next minute he is telling us how *some Cow-stealers will make a hole in a hott loafe newly drawne out of the oven, and put it on an Oxes-horn for a convenient time, and then they can turn their softened hornes the contrary way: So that the owner cannot sweare to his own beast. Not long before the King's restauration, a fellow was hang'd at Tyburn for this Trick, and sayd, that he had never come thither, if he had not heard this Trick spoken of in a Sermon. Thought he, I will try this Trick.* After this salutary warning against the dangers of church-going, Aubrey flies off at a tangent again to report that *Isaac Selfe, a wealthy Cloathier of Milsham, died in the ninety second yeare of his Age, leaving behind him a numerous offspring; viz. eighty and three in number*, and this reminds him that *Mr Bonham's wife had two Children at one birth, the first time; and he being troubled at it, travelled: and was absent seven yeares. After his returne he got his wife with Child: and she was delivered of seven Children at one Birth.* What the moral of this story was, Aubrey omits to say, but he added that *Dr Wm. Harvey* (*Author of the Circulation of the Bloud*) *told me that one Mr Palmer's Wife in Kent did beare a Child every day for five daies together*, a tale which was capped by *Mris. Hine the Vicar's-wife of Kington St Michael* (*a very able Midwife*) who informed Aubrey that *Mris. Kath. H—* (*who was brought to bed at Dorchester*) (*Dorset*) *was delivered first of a Sonne* (*now liveing and the Heir*) *and afterwards for eight daies together, every day another Child: Some whereof had heads, and Armes, and no lower parts; others had lower, but no upper-parts; but she never had any Child afterwards.* Nor was this all, for *the said Mris. Hine did tell a storie* (*about 1649*) *which was confidently averred; that about Westerly, or Alderly, or that way in Glocestershire, there were two Children born in the grave.* Refusing to be outdone in this vein, William Harvey countered with the story of *a certain Knight in Kent, who having gott his Wives Mayd with Child, sent her to London to lie-in under pretence of seeing her friends: She was brought to bed there about Michaelmas; and after some convenient time she returned to her Lady: She found herselfe not well, and in December following, she fell in labour again, and was delivered of another Child.* It is unlikely that this untoward incident caused her neighbours much surprise, for when Mary Waterman, half an hour after bearing a normal child, *was delivered of a Monstrous-birth, haveing two Heades the one opposite to the other*, the seventeenth century coped with the matter with exemplary efficiency. *About four o Clock in the after-Noon the same day*, Aubrey records, *it was christened, by the name of Martha and Mary, having two pretty faces, and lived till fryday next.* And then he says, *I will whilst 'tis in my mind insert this Remarque, viz – about 1620 one Ricketts of Newberye, a Practitioner in Physick, was excellent at the Curing Children with swoln heads, and small legges: and the Disease being new, and without a name, He being so famous for the cure of it, they called the Disease the Ricketts: as the King's Evill from the King's cureing of it with his Touch; and now 'tis good sport to see how they vex their Lexicons, and fetch it from the Greek Ῥᾰχις, the back bone.*

It was no wonder, therefore, that when he presented a fair copy of his work to the Royal Society, it *gave them two or three dayes Entertainment, which they were pleased to like.* But though it circulated widely amongst his friends, and despite its hopeful dedication *to the Right Honourable Thomas Earle of Pembroke, my singular good Lord*, the *Naturall Historie* was never published; indeed it was never finished, for although Aubrey did his part, his *Advice to the Painter or Graver* was not carried out, and the list of the illustrations he desired went unnoticed, as he half suspected it would. *If these views were well donn*, he had said, *they would make a glorious Volume by itselfe, and like enough it might take well in the World. It were an inconsiderable charge to these Persons of Qualitie: and it would remaine to Posterity, when their Families are gonn, and their Buildings ruin'd by time, or Fire, as we have seen that stupendous Fabrick of Paul's Church, not a stone left on a stone, and lives now onely in Mr Hollar's Etchings in Sir William Dugdale's History of Pauls. I am not displeased with this Thought as a Desideratum*, he concluded, *but I doe never expect to see it donn: so few men have the hearts to doe publique good: to give 3, 4, or 5 pounds for a Copper Plate.*

It says a great deal for Aubrey's power of concentration that he was able to proceed as far with this work as he did, for in 1656 he also began *his chargeable and taedious Lawesuite about the Entaile in Brecknockshire and Monmouthshire, which lands*, he said rather hopefully, *now of right belong to me.* For his great-grandfather, the *little Doctor* of Queen Elizabeth's Court, had entailed *the Brecon estate on the Issue male of his eldest son, and in defailer, to skip the 2^d son (for whom he had well provided, and had married a good fortune) and to come to the third. Edward the eldest had seaven Sonnes: and his eldest son Sir Will had also seaven sonnes; and so I am heyre, being the 18th man in Remainder, which putts me in mind of Dr Donne:*

> *For what doeth it availe*
> *To be twentieth man in an Entaile?*

The tortuous descent of this land was further complicated by the fact that William Aubrey's executor *ran away into Ireland and cosened all the Legatees.* So Aubrey cannot really have been surprised when he lost the case. *It cost me 1200 pounds*, he noted sadly all the same, adding *this yeare, and the last, was a strange year to me, and full of Contradictions: – scilicet Love and Law-suites.*

For Aubrey's affairs were rapidly becoming desperate. *Then Debts and Law-suites*, he says, *opus et usus, borrowing of money and perpetuall riding*, which itself was not without complications, for he lists a whole chapter of accidents. *On Monday after Easter weeke*, he reports, *my uncle's nag ranne away with me, and gave me a very dangerous fall. Just before it I had an Impulse of the Briar under which I rode, which tickled him, at the Gap at the upper end of Bery Lane. Deo gratias! Then (I thinke) June 14, I had a fall at Epsam, and brake one of my ribbes and was afrayd it might cause an Apostumation*, and good antiquary that he was, he religiously preserved among his papers William Harvey's prescription for that treatment. *March or Aprill*, he wrote a few years later, *like to break my neck in Ely Minster, and the next day, riding a gallop there, my horse tumbled over and over, and yet (I thanke God) no hurt.* The next time, however, he was not to be so fortunate, for *Munday after Christmas, was in danger to be spoiled by my horse, and the same day received laesio in Testiculo which was like to have been fatall:* but was not: and ever afterwards he rode quietly.

To my prayse, he said, *I had wonderfull credit in the countrey for money. Sold Manor of Bushelton in Herefordshire to Dr T. Willis. Sold Manor of Stratford in the same county to Herbert, Lord Bishop of Hereford.* And so began the dissipation of his estates, so recently inherited, so soon to be squandered.

In 1659, Aubrey started a second work relating to Wiltshire, which was intended to form part of a County History of England. *At a Meeting of Gentlemen at the Devizes, for choosing of Knights of the Shire in March 1659*, he said, *it was wish'd by some that this County (wherein are many observable Antiquities) was survey'd, in Imitation of Mr Dugdale's Illustration of Warwickshire; but it being too great a Task for one Man, Mr William Yorke (Councellor at Law, and a Lover of this Kind of Learning) advis'd to have the Labour divided; he himself would undertake the Middle Division, I would undertake the North; T. Gore, Esq. Jeffrey Daniel, Esq. and Sir John Ernely, would be Assistants.* And so *An Essay towards the Description of the North Division of Wiltshire* was begun with high hopes, and was soon illustrated with armorial shields elaborately emblazoned and with facsimiles of old deeds and seals. But once again Aubrey malingered, and the work stopped just short of completion. *This good design vanished in fumo Tabaci, and was never thought of since*, he said hopelessly eleven years later. However he would not admit final defeat. *I have since that occasionally made this following Collection, which perhaps may sometime or other fall into some Antiquary's Hands, to make a handsom Work of it. I am heartily sorry*, he continued, *I did not set down the Antiquities of these parts sooner, for since the Time aforesaid (1659) many Things are irrecoverably lost.*

In former Daies the Churches and great Howses hereabouts did so abound with Monuments and Things remarquable that it would have deterred an Antiquarie from undertakeing it, he said. *But as Pythagoras did guesse at the vastnesse of Hercules Stature by the Length of his Foote, so amongst these Ruines are Remaines enough left for a Man to give a Guesse what noble Buildings &c. were made by the Piety, Charity and Magnanimity of our Fore-fathers.*

And as in Prospects, wee are there pleased most Where something keepes the Eie from being lost And leaves us roome to guesse; So here the Eie and Mind is no lesse affected with these stately Ruines, then they would have been when standing and entire. They breed in generous Minds a Kind of Pittie: and sett the Thoughts a-worke to make out their Magnifice as they were when in Perfection. But it was not only in buildings that Aubrey was interested, although he was so learned in architectural history: the countryside through which he wandered in search of his material entranced him quite as much. *This is a very noble seate*, he says of Down Ampney House, *and situated with great convenience for pleasure and profitt. By this house runnes a fine brooke, which waters these gallant meadowes on the west sides, where despasture a great number of cattle: – 30 milk-mayds singing.* And as he rode through Garesdon, he could not help recalling that *one Mody was a foote-man to King Henry the eighth who, falling from his horse as he was hawkeing (I think on Harneslow-heath) fell with his head in to mudde, with which, being fatt and heavie, he had been suffocated to death had he not been timely relieved by his footman Mody, for which service, after the dissolution of the Abbies, he gave him the manour of Garesdon.* After a regretful sigh at the easy preferment of the past, Aubrey's attention was distracted by a whip in a coat of arms, and the story he ferreted out was that *the Issue male of this Family being all extinct, except a brother who was a White-fryer, the Pope granted a Dispensation of his Vowes, and that he should quitt his Convent and marry to continue the name of the Family: which accordingly he did: and in such cases, the Brother that so departs, is to runne the Gauntlet as the Soldiers doe it, that is, all the fryers putt them selves into two rankes, having every one a Paenitentiall whip in his hand, and the dispensed fryer runnes through, every one giving him a lash.*

In the autumn of 1659, Aubrey was once again in London and was taking part in the debates at James Harrington's club, the Rota, where the principles of Republican government were debated and rotation by balloting was advocated as the cure of all its ills. *The Doctrine was very taking,* Aubrey admitted, *and the more because, as to human foresight, there was no possibility of the King's returne.* It must be remembered that the prime of Aubrey's youth and early manhood had coincided with the period of the Commonwealth and it seems clear from the vehemence of his defence of Milton's politics, that he had himself become a theoretical Republican. *Whatever he wrote against Monarchie,* Aubrey said, *was out of no animosity to the King's person, or owt of any faction or interest, but out of a pure Zeale to the Liberty of Mankind, which he thought would be greater under a fre state than under a Monarchiall goverment. His being so conversant in Livy and the Roman authors, and the greatness he saw donne by the Roman commonwealth, and the vertue of their great Commanders induc't him to.* And there could be no doubt that the prestige of England had increased under the Protectorate. Then too Aubrey had mixed constantly with the leaders of the Republic: *I heard Oliver Cromwell Protector tell the Lord Arundell of Wardour at Dinner at Hampton-Court 1657, that he had been in all the Counties of England, and that the Devonshire Husbandry was the best.* His membership of the Rota was, therefore, merely the logical outcome of his Republican leanings, but *in February 1660, upon the unexpected turne upon Generall Monke's comeing-in, all these aerie modells vanished,* and Aubrey was soon on the other side, involved in the thick of the negotiations for the restoration of the King. Thomas Mariett, who *every day was tampering with George Monk*, stayed with Aubrey during the parleying, and once again Aubrey's laziness caused him regret. *Every night late*, he said, *I had an account of all these Transactions in bed, which like a Sott as I was, I did not, while fresh in Memorie, committ to writing*. But he did find time to inform Thomas Hobbes of what was in the wind and to advise him to come to London at once, so as *to redintegrate his favour with his Majesty*, as soon as the King arrived.

Aubrey grew quite lyrical over the King's restoration, when it was accomplished, and it was left to Anthony Wood to see the ugly side of the business. The divines hurriedly putting on 'the most prelaticall garbe that could be' did not escape his jaundiced eye, and he watched with scorn while those 'that bore the faces of demure Saints, would now and then put out a wanton (in plaine terms, a baudy) expression, and, as occasion served, a pretty little Oath'. But even he had to admit that 'after the King came in I never heard of any that were troubled in conscience or that hung himself, as in Oliver's time, when nothing but praying and preaching was used'. For there was no doubt that life under the Commonwealth had been an appalling strain; and Aubrey says in his life of Wenceslas Hollar, *I remember he told me that when he first came into England (which was a serene time of Peace) that the people, both poore and rich, did looke cheerfully, but at his return, he found the Countenances of the people all changed, melancholy, spightfull, as if bewitched.*

When the excitements of the King's homecoming had begun to pall, Aubrey *accompanied A. Ettrick into Ireland for a moneth; and returning were like to be ship-wrackt at Holyhead, but no hurt donne*. Despite this narrow escape, Aubrey came back from his holiday refreshed in spirit and bubbling over with ideas for work – for other people to carry out. *From N. Wales I went into Ireland*, he wrote to Thomas Hobbes, *where I saw the manner of living of the natives, scorning industry and luxury, contenting themselves only with things necessary. That kingdom is in a very great distemper, and hath need of your advice to settle it; the animosities between the English and the Irish are very great, and will ere long, I am confident, break into war. Your brother I heare is well, whom I intend to see on Monday next, and shall with him sacrifice to your health in a glasse of sack.*

But Hobbes would not rise to this bait, although on another occasion Aubrey was more successful. *It was I.A.*, he says proudly, *that did putt Mr Hobbes upon writing his Treatise De Legibus, which is bound up with his Rhetorique that one cannot find it but by chance; no mention of it in the first Title*. Aubrey had learnt from his previous failure that a direct suggestion was not of much avail, and so this time he used a more roundabout way to achieve his desire. *In 1664 I sayd to him; Me thinkes 'tis pitty that you that have such a cleare reason and working head did never take into consideration the learning of the Lawes; and I endeavoured to perswade him to it. To which he was unwilling, telling me that 'twas a long, taedious, and difficult taske and he doubted he should not have dayes enough to left to doe it. Now all men will give the old Gent that right as to acknowledge he is rare for Definitions, and the Lawyers building on old-fashioned Maximes (some right, some wrong) must need fall into severall Paralogismes, for grand practisers have not the leisure to be analytiques. Upon this consideration I was earnest with him to consider these things. I then presented him the Lord Chancellor Bacon's Elements of the Lawe (a thin quarto) in order thereunto and to drawe him on; which he was pleased to accept, and perused; and the next time I came to him he showed me therein two cleare Paralogismes in the 2nd page (one, I well remember, was in page 2) which I am heartily sorry are now out of my remembrance. I desponded, for his reasons, that he should make any further attempt towards this Designe; but afterwards, it seemes, in the Countrey he writt his Treatise De Legibus. He drives on, in this, the King's Prerogative high. Judge Hales, who is no great Courtier, has read it and much mislikes it, and is his enemy. Judge Vaughan has perused it and very much commends it, but is afraid to license it for feare of giving displeasure.* Which explains very well the lack of any mention on the title page.

Although none of Aubrey's works had yet been published, they had circulated widely amongst his friends, and, founded upon the good word of Izaak Walton and Sir Thomas Browne, of Thomas Hobbes and John Locke, of Isaac Newton, Edmund Halley, Robert Boyle and Christopher Wren, of Samuel Butler and John Dryden, David Loggan and Nicholas Mercator, Wenceslas Hollar, Sir William Davenant, Edmund Waller, Andrew Marvell, John Evelyn, and Sir William Dugdale, Aubrey's reputation as an antiquary was so well established by 1662 that he was nominated as one of the Original Fellows of the Royal Society, an honour of which he was justifiably proud.

The ninety-eight Original Fellows were chosen rather for their interest in science than for their skill as scientists, and they included many of Aubrey's closest friends; there were poets like Denham and Dryden and Waller, Evelyn the diarist, Ashmole of Museum fame, Glisson the doctor, Christopher Wren the architect, as well as scientists proper like Hooke and Robert Boyle. Bishops, soldiers, and courtiers made up the number, and fourteen peers, including the Duke of Buckingham and the Marquess of Dorchester, were also members: while to complete the roll, King Charles II 'was pleased to offer himselfe to be entered one of the Society'.

The Royal Society 'for the promoting of Physico-Mathematicall-Experimentall Learning' had developed from that small *Philosophicall Clubbe* at Oxford which has been mentioned before and which had been transferred to London about 1658. *They mett*, says Aubrey, *at the Bull-head Taverne in Cheapside, till it grew to big for a Clubb. The first beginning of the Royal Society (where they putt discourse in paper and brought it to use) was in the Chamber of William Ball, Esqr., eldest son of Sir Peter Ball of Devon, in the Middle Temple. They had meetings at Taverns before, but 'twas here where it formally and in good earnest sett up: and so they came to Gresham Colledge parlour.*

The importance of this foundation cannot be over-emphasized. For the specialist was not yet born, and in the childhood of science it was still possible, as Aubrey has shown in his *Naturall Historie of Wiltshire*, to produce a new intellectual value without having to acquire skill and without troubling to acquaint oneself with a great deal of accumulated knowledge. *I have heard Sr Will Davenant say*, Aubrey noted, *that Witt did seem to be the easiest thing in the World, for when it is delivered, it appeares so naturall, that every one thinks he could have sayd the same: this of his, may also be applied to Inventions and Discoveries.*

The existing body of knowledge about trade and the sciences was so small in the seventeenth century that some of their discoveries do seem childishly simple. *Sir Paul Neale sayd, that in the Bishoprick of Durham is a Coalery, which by reason of the dampes ther did so frequently kill the Workemen (sometimes three or four in a Moneth) that he could make little or nothing out of it. It happened one time, that the workemen being merry with drink fell to play with fire-brands, and to throwe live-coales at one another by the head of the Pitt, where they usually have fires. It fortuned that a fire-brand fell into the bottome of the Pitt: where at there proceeded such a noise as if it had been a Gun: they likeing the Sport, threw down more fire-brands and there followed the like noise, for severall times, and at length it ceased. They went to work after, and were free from Damps, so having by good chance found out this Experiment, they doe now every morning throw-down some Coales, and they work as securely as in any other Mines.* But these improvements were not always accidental: *Before I leave this Towne*, Aubrey wrote of his friend Robert Hooke, *I will gett of him a catalogue of what he hath wrote; and as much of his Inventions as I can. But they are many hundreds; he believes not fewer than a thousand.* Nor were his other friends less ingenious: ruled copy books, mathematical symbols, even drogues (*Memorandum Dr Wilkins his notion of an Umbrella-like invention for retarding a ship when shee drives in a storme*), were invented by Aubrey's immediate circle, but perhaps the most fruitful suggestion of all was made by Sir Edward Ford, who *writt no Books, but two or three Pamphletts of a sheet or so. One was an ingeniose proposall of a publique Banke, as I remember, for the easy raysing of money and to avoyd the griping Usurers and to promote trade.* Aubrey himself was not behindhand in these matters: *Let a Ginne bee invented*, he said, *to shatter out Corne by jogging in stead of soweing or setting, the one being too wastfull, the other too troublesome and taking up too much time: and that the soweing and harroweing may bee but one and the same labour:* and besides this invention, he was working out a phonetic alphabet with Andrew Paschall (*which some persons looke upon as a Whim wham: but if it be so, the learned Verstergen was also liable to that severe censure*); and was also engaged in experiments with Francis Potter *to cure diseases, etc. by Transfusion of Bloud out of one man into another.*

Under these conditions, the Royal Society, with its regular Wednesday meetings, for the first time systematized scientific learning by allowing for the free interchange of ideas and the comparing of research, and this was all that was needed to produce the modern world. For, as H. G. Wells has said: 'The main difference of modern scientific research from that of the Middle Ages, the secret of its immense successes, lies in its collective character, in the fact that every fruitful experiment is published, every new discovery of relationship explained.'

A few months after the incorporation of the Royal Society, Aubrey says, *King Charles IId discoursing one morning with my Lord Brouncker and Dr Charleton concerning Stoneheng, they told his Majestie, what they had heard me say concerning Aubury, sc. that it did as much excell of Stoneheng as a Cathedral does a Parish Church. His Majestie admired that none of our Chorographers had taken notice of it: and commanded Dr Charleton to bring me to him the next morning. I brought with me a draught of it donne by memorie only: but well enough resembling it, with which his Majestie was pleased: gave me his hand to kisse, and commanded me to waite on him at Marleborough, when he went to Bath with the Queen (which was about a fortnight after) which I did: and the next day, when the Court were on their Journey, his Majestie left the Queen and diverted to Aubury, where I shewed him that stupendious Antiquity, with a view whereof, he and his Royal Highness the Duke of Yorke were very well pleased. His Majestie then commanded me to write a Description of it, and present it to him: and the Duke of Yorke commanded me to give an account of the Old Camps and Barrows on the Plaines.*

As his Majestie departed from Aubury to overtake the Queen he cast his eie on Silbury-hill, about a mile off: which he had the curiosity to see, and walkt up to the top of it, with the Duke of Yorke, Dr Charleton and I attending them, Aubrey continued proudly, and later he added this note, which reflects on the oddly public life of Royalty in those days. *When I had the honour to waite on King Charles and the Duke of Yorke to the top of Silbury-hill, his Royal Highnesse happened to cast his Eye on some of these small Snailes, not much bigger, or no bigger than small Pinnes-heads, on the Turfe of the Hill. He was surprised with the novelty; and commanded me to pick some up; which I did about a dozen or more, immediately; for they are in great abundance. The next Morning as he was abed with his Dutches at Bath, He told her of it: and sent Dr Charleton to me for them to shew Her as a Rarity.*

In September following (1663) I survey'd that old Monument of Aubury with a plaine table, and afterwards tooke a Review of Stonehenge, and then, I composed this following Discourse in obedience to his Majesties command: and presented it to Him: which he commanded me to put in print. This last command Aubrey ignored, despite the fact that his book was dedicated *to King Charles by His Majestie's most loyale and obedient Subject John Aubrey.* The thoroughness with which he had carried out the survey is proved by the fact that his plan of Stonehenge shows certain depressions in the ground which have since disappeared: *His Majestie commanded me to digge at the bottom of the stones marked with the fig. 1, to try if I could find any human bones,* he said, *but I did not doe it.* Because of his plan, these depressions, which are now known as 'Aubrey Holes', were located and excavated in 1921, and sure enough they were found to contain cremated remains, possibly of human sacrifices.

There have been several Books writt by learned men concerning Stoneheng, he continued, *much differing from one another, some affirming one thing, some another. Now I come in the Rear of all by comparative Arguments to give a clear evidence these monuments were Pagan Temples; which was not made-out before: and have also, with humble submission to better judgements, offered a probability, that they were Temples of the Druids.*

When a traveller rides along by the Ruines of a Monastery, Aubrey says, *he knows by the manner of building, sc., Chapell, Cloysters, &c., that it was a Convent, but of what Order, sc., Benedictine, Dominican, &c., it was, he cannot tell by the bare View. So it is clear that all the Monuments, which I have here recounted were Temples. Now my presumption is, That the Druids being the most eminent Priests, or Order of Priests, among the Britaines; 'tis odds, but that these ancient monuments, sc. Aubury, Stonehenge, Kerrig, Druidd &c., were Temples of the Priests of the most eminent Order, viz. Druids, and it is strongly to be presumed that Aubury, Stonehenge, &c., are as ancient as those times. This Inquiry, I must confess, is a gropeing in the Dark; but although I have not brought it into a clear light; yet I can affirm that I have brought it from an utter darkness to a thin mist, and have gonne further in this Essay than any one before me. These Antiquities are so exceeding old that no Bookes doe reach them, so that there is no Way to retrive them but by comparative antiquitie, which I have writt upon the spott, from the Monuments themselves. Historia quoquo modo scripta, bona est* [In whatever way history is written, it is good]; *and though this be writt, as I rode, a gallop; yet the novelty of it, and the faithfulness of the delivery, may make some amends for the uncorrectness of the Stile. The first draught,* he concludes, *was worn out with time and handling; and now, methinkes, after many years lying dormant, I come abroad like the Ghost of one of these Druids.* He felt sufficiently human, none the less, to preface the work with *A digression to obviate the scornfull smile*, for he was convinced that people would assume that he was interested in this monument only because it bore the same name as himself.

In the following year, Aubrey realized his lifelong desire to travel on the Continent. He had made ambitious plans to see *the Loyer, and the country of Brittany, and that about Geneva*, and after receiving Thomas Hobbes's best 'wishes for your safety and the continuance of your health, which is not to be despaired of in one that can temper himselfe from excesses, and especially in fruit, as you can', he set out. But as so often happens with one's fondest ambitions, the trip did not quite come up to his expectations. *June 11, landed at Calais*, he recorded. *In August following had a terrible fit of the Spleen, and Piles, at Orleans. I returned in October. Then Joan Sumner.*

The ominous ring of this last note proved fully justified, for poor Aubrey was as unfortunate in his dealings with women as he was incompetent with money. Since he had left Oxford, he had often been on the point of getting married, but always at the last moment he was foiled. *My Mother foll from her horse and brake her arme the last day of April (1649 or 50) when I was suitor to Mris. Jane Codrington*, he wrote, and never mentioned the lady's name again. Probably because in *1651 about the 16 or 18 April, I saw that incomparable good conditioned Gentlewoman, Mris. M. Wiseman, with whom at first sight I was in love – haeret lateri* [the deadly arrow sticks fast in the side], and indeed the wound did seem more permanent than usual, for five years later he was still attached to her, however insecurely, for he notes: *1656. This Yeare, and the last, was a strange year to me, and full of Contradictions: scilicet Love (M.W.) and Lawe-suites.* One of these *Contradictions* must have come from M.W., for in the next year he received a double blow, to his heart and his pocket: *1657: Novemb. 27, obiit Domina Katherina Ryves, with whom I was to marry; to my great Losse (2000 pounds or more, besides counting care of her brother, 1000 pounds per annum)*. Nothing daunted, however, he tried again: *1665, November 1, I made my first addresse (in an ill howre) to Joane Sumner*, and the catastrophe which then unrolled was to put a stop to his matrimonial adventures for ever.

1666: he said *this yeare all my business and affaires ran Kim Kam. Nothing tooke effect, as if I had been under an ill tongue. Treacheries and Enmities in abundance against me.* And an entry in the Salisbury Diocesan Registry this year shows how near he came to taking the fatal step. 'Awbry, John, of Easton Pierse,' it runs, 'and Mris. Joane Sumner of Sutton Benger, sp. Bondmen, William Browne of Sarum, tailor, and Joseph Gwynne of Easton Pierse, yeoman April 11th.'

1667: December, he continued, *arrested in Chancery lane, At Mrs Sumner's suite.*

1668: Febr. 24 a.m. about 8 or 9, Triall with her at Sarum. Victory and 600 pounds dammage, though divelish Opposition against me.

1668: July 26, was arrested by Peter Gale's malicious contrivance, the day before I was to goe to Winton for my 2[d] Triall, but it did not retain me above 2 howres; but did not then goe to Triall.

1669: March 5, was my Triall at Winton, from 8 to 9, the Judge being exceedingly made against me, by my Lady Hungerford. With much adoe, gott the Moiety of Sarum verdict, viz. 300 pounds.

Joan Sumner's decision to go to law with John Aubrey, instead of to the altar, was the *coup de grâce* to his tottering affairs, and with a sudden crash all his tangled estates tumbled about his ears. *Sold Easton-Pierse, and the farme at Broad Chalke*, he noted sadly, for his mother's family, *the Lytes, had Easton Piers in Lease and in Inheritance 249 years: sc. from Henry 6th. Lost 500 pounds + 200 pounds + goods + timber*, he continued, and the result was that *in 1669 and 1670 I sold all my Estates in Wilts. Absconded as a banished man. I was in as much affliction as a mortall could bee, and never quiet till all was gone, and I wholly caste myselfe on God's providence. Never quiett, nor anything of happiness till divested of all, 1670, 1671*, he repeats, *at what time Providence raysed me (unexpectedly) good Friends.*

For when all was sold, he found relief at last, and his next entry reads: *From 1670, to this very day (I thanke God) I have enjoyed a happy delitescency*, a statement which is rather belied by the succeeding paragraph, *1671: danger of Arrests.*

During this crisis, a meeting had taken place which was to give purpose to the remaining years of Aubrey's life and was also to provide him with the immortality which he so much desired. For on Thursday, 31 August 1667, Anthony Wood entered in his accounts 'Spent with Mr John Aubrey of Wilts, at Mother Web's and the Meremaid Tavern, 3s. 8d.', and it was not until nearly thirty years later that he returned to his Journal to make a fuller and more famous entry: 'Aug. 31 S.,' he then wrote, 'John Aubrey of Easton-Piers in the parish of Kingston S. Michael in Wiltsh. was in Oxon. with Edward Forest, a Book-seller living against Alls. Coll., to buy books. He then saw lying on the stall *Notitia Academiae Oxoniensis*; and asking who the Author of that book was, he answer'd the report was that one Mr Anthony Wood of Merton Coll. was the Author, but was not. Whereupon Mr Aubrey, a pretender to Antiquities, having been contemporary to A. Wood's elder brother in Trin. Coll. and well acquainted with him, he thought that he might be as well acquainted with A.W. himself. Whereupon repairing to his Lodgings, and telling him who he was, he got into his acquaintance, talk'd to him about his studies, and offer'd him what assistance he could make, in order to the completion of the work that he was in hand with. Mr Aubrey was then in a sparkish Garb, came to town with his Man and two Horses, spent high and flung out A.W. at all recknings. But his estate of 700 pounds per an. being afterwards sold, and he reserving nothing of it to himself, liv'd afterwards in a very sorry condition, and at length made shift to rub out by hanging on Edmund Wyld Esq. living in Blomesbury, near London, on James Bertie Earl of Abendon, whose first wife was related to him, and on Sir John Aubrey, his kinsman, living sometimes in Glamorganshire, and sometimes at Borstall neare Brill in Bucks. He was a shiftless person, roving and magotie-headed, and sometimes little better than crased. And being exceedingly credulous, would stuff his many letters to A.W. with fooleries, and misinformations, which sometimes would guid him into the pathes of error.'

As can be seen from the tone of this entry, Anthony Wood was an impossible man to get on with. An Oxford don, vain, touchy, spiteful and lacking in every social grace, he was impertinent to his superiors, rude to his equals, overbearing to his juniors, ungrateful to his benefactors, and unbearable to his family. The Warden of his own college he described as 'the very Lol-poop of the University, a most lascivious person, a great haunter of women's company and a common Fornicator', and the Warden's wife he despised for putting 'the College to unnecessary charges, and very frivolous expences, among which was a very larg Looking-Glass, for her to see hir ugly face, and body to the middle, and perhaps lower'. He quarrelled with John Fell, the great Dean of Christ Church, who at his own expense was publishing Wood's life work. He quarrelled with his fellow dons: 'Mr Roger Brent and I playing at cards, he fell out with me, called me all to nought and struck me. He looked like a rogue, like a whoring rascall, like a whoring rogue.'

The resultant unpopularity only increased his fury and loneliness until everything enraged him: 'Mr Davis looked red and jolly, as if he had been at a fish supper at C.C.C., and afterwards drinking – as he had been'; and a friend's criticism of his book was met with the comment 'the words as ugly as his face'.

But the climax was reached with his family, for it seems that his sister-in-law at last could stand no more. 'Cold meat, cold entertainment, cold reception, cold clownish woman', Wood noted in his Journal after one meal, and at last, on Easter Day, 1670, 'the melancholy, malitious and peevish woman slighted me and rose in the middle of dinner from the table. My brother Kit asked me whether I would be godfather and give a piece of plate to the childe in her belly. She said that she "would first see it rot, etc." with an envious eye and teeth.' After which scene he 'was dismist from his usual and constant diet by the rudeness and barbarity of a brutish woman' and 'was put to his shifts. This disaster A.W. look'd upon as the first and greatest misery of his life. It made him exceedingly melancholy and more retir'd.' But he soon justified this isolation to himself. 'He is so great an Admirer of a solitary and retired Life,' he says in the preface to one of his works, 'that he frequents no Assemblies of the said University, hath no companion in Bed or at Board, in his Studies, Walks or Journies, nor holds Communication with any, unless with some, and those very few, of generous and noble Spirits, that have in some measure been Promoters and Encouragers of this Work. And indeed all things considered he is but a degree different from an Ascetick, as spending all or most of his time, whether by Day or Night, in Reading, Writing, and Divine Contemplation.'

Such was his own view, but the truth of the matter was that Anthony Wood had been born in the wrong century. Suspicious, lonely, intolerant, envious, mean, he found himself isolated in that supremely social age: squeamish, disapproving, and obsessed with sex, he was revolted by the coarseness of the physical life around him: spiteful, snobbish, and pretentious, he flaunted his lack of social graces in the face of all, until his pompousness and prudery finally cut him off entirely from the life around him. And though he continued to look on himself as 'a universal Lover of Mankind', he was forced at length to admit that he was 'as 'twere Dead to the World, and utterly unknown in Person to the generality of the Scholars in Oxon'. 'As to the Author himself,' he finally confessed, 'he is a Person who delights to converse more with the Dead, than with the Living'; for being so ill at ease in his own times, he was at last driven to seek refuge in the past, for only there could he show the affection which he was unable to give to his contemporaries. 'Sweet chucks,' he wrote, 'beat not the bones of the buried: when he breathed, he was a man.' But even the dead were not spared his malignity, unless they had been long dead: 'March 31. F. died Ann, Duchess of York', he reported. 'She died with eating and drinking; died fast and fustie; salacious; lecherous.'

And so it says a great deal for Aubrey's charm that, after twenty-five years of friendship, Anthony Wood should merely call him 'roving and magotie-headed', an accusation, moreover, which was not altogether without justification, as we shall see.

That this was not Anthony Wood's original view is shown by the following letter, dated soon after the first meeting. 'You may remember when you were at Oxon,' he wrote to Aubrey on 11 November 1667, 'that you promised upon my enquirie &c., to obtaine some intelligence concerning Dr Joh. Hoskyns sometimes of New Coll. of his birth death and buriall, his bookes that he wrote and that might be worthie memorie of him. If you please to informe me as soone as you can, I shall take it for a verie great favour from your hands. 'Tis probable you might upon recollection informe me also of others that were Oxford men. The which, if you at your leisure can, you would alwaies oblige me to be, Sir, your most humble servant Anth. Woode.' And a few months later he again assured him, 'I am glad I have such a friend as you to stir in my business. I would by noe means have put you to this trouble, could I have reposed confidence in any other.'

Anthony Wood, at Dean Fell's suggestion, intended to follow up his 'Historia et Antiquitates Universitatis Oxoniensis' with an even more elaborate work entitled 'Athenae Oxoniensis: An Exact History of all the Writers and Bishops who have had their Education in the most ancient and famous University of Oxford from the Fifteenth Year of King Henry the Seventh Dom. 1500, to the end of the Year 1690'. But he soon found that his unpopularity was a great hindrance to him in gathering the information that he needed; and for this work, Aubrey's popularity and wide acquaintanceship were ideal. The offer of help, therefore, Wood accepted with alacrity, but Aubrey responded with such a will that Wood's tone soon changed towards him. For exactly four years after his original letter he was writing to Aubrey in this peremptory tone. 'Allington is not far from you. If you have occasion to goe that way, pray see whether Mr Nich. Fuller, the Critick have an Epitaph there. If not take the day and year of his buriall out of the Register. I have heard he died there. If you cannot goe, employ your brother and I shall be gratefull to him. If not buried there, perhaps at Salisbury, where he was prebend. He died about 1626.'

As time went on the commands became ever more direct. 'Quaere more of Mr Aubrew', Wood jotted down on his notes and sometimes one of these formidable lists of queries has survived. '1. Epitaph of Francis Potter; if none, then the day and yeare where buried. 2. Titles of Dr Pettie's books published, where borne (Rumney in Hampshire, quaere.) 3. When Dr John Godolphin died, where he died and where buried; quaere the bookseller that sold his books. 4. Title of books that John Davyes of Kidwelly translated. 7. Register of S. Pancrass Church. 8. Which daughter and heir of Carew Raleigh was married to Sir John Ellwes. 9. To send to Olor Iscanus to answer my letters. 10. To put John Dugdale in mind of John Davenport. 11. Mr Hook for the Christian name of . . . Oliver, glass paynter. 12. What is said of Father Simons in his collections. 13. Dr Walter Charlton, who he succeeded? 14. My letters to be returned. 15. Where Mr Robert Boyle lived and died.'

Faced with a list like this in an age when there were no books of reference to turn to, Aubrey set about gathering his information as best he could. Sometimes his friends helped him, but though Izaak Walton wrote part of the life of Ben Jonson, and Sir Thomas Browne contributed to John Dee's biography, they could not always be relied on, as that blank page shows which is headed *John Dryden, Esq. Poet Laureate. He will write it for me himselfe.* For as Aubrey was well acquainted with all the great figures of his time, it was mainly with the previous generation that he needed help, which meant that he had to appeal to his seniors for information, and his seniors were by now growing very old. *The Lives of John Dee, Dr Nepier, Sir William Dugdale, William Lilly, Elias Ashmole, Esq.*, he informed Anthony Wood, *Mr Ashmole has and will doe them himself; as he told me, but nowe he seems to faile.*

At other times, his information came in a far more roundabout way. Dr Bathurst was able to tell him about Lucius Cary, Lord Falkland, because *a mayd that lived with my Lord lived with his father:* nor was this backstairs method neglected by Aubrey himself: *Jack Sydenham was wont to carry me in his armes; a graceful servant*, he said, recalling his childhood, *he gave me this account;* and stone cutters and tradesmen were often pressed into use. Sermons, too, provided some amusing stories and contributed largely to the lives of the Great Earl of Cork, his daughter Mary, Countess of Warwick, and Colonel Charles Cavendish. Then again, church registers were searched, sometimes in vain, it is true: *My brother Tom searched the Register of Wilton from the beginning and talk't with old men. Philip Massinger was not buried there:* but at other times with unexpected results. *When I searched the Register of the Parish of St Saviours, Southwark in 1670, for the Obit of that eminent Dramatick Poet Mr John Fletcher*, Aubrey wrote to Anthony Wood, *the Parish-Clerk, aged above 80, told me that he was his Taylor, and that Mr Fletcher staying for a Suit of Cloaths before he retired into the Country in the great Plague, 1625, Death stopped his Journey and laid him low here.*

Tombstones were scanned for dates, and often proved fallible, for though Aubrey noticed that there was something wrong about the following: *Pray for the soul of Constantine Darrel Esq. who died Anno Domini 1400 and his wife, who died Anno Domini 1495:* he had no way of checking on Spenser's epitaph in Westminster Abbey, which, being forty-two years in error over his birth and three years over his death, made him eighty-six at his death, instead of forty-seven. Nevertheless tombstones had to be depended on for these facts, and often they yielded more: *Ellenor, wife of Sir John Denham was a beautiful woman*, he reported, *as appears by her Monument at Egham.* And every now and then he stumbled upon a veritable gold mine: *Did I tell you*, he wrote excitedly, *that I have met with old Mr Beeston who knew all the old English Poets, whose lives I am taking from him: his father was Master of the Playhouse*. And although *Mr Dryeden calles him the Chronicle of the Stage*, Aubrey had a virtual monopoly of his information, for he concludes *the more to be admired – he was not a company keeper; lived in Shoreditch; would not be debauched; and if invited to Court, was in pain.*

His fellow historians looked askance at some of these methods. *In my last I gave you some Memoirs of Cardinall Morton*, Aubrey wrote to Anthony Wood, *and that the Tradicion of the Countrey people in Dorset, when I was a Schooleboy there at Blandford, was that he was a Shoemaker's son of Bere: but Sir William Dugdale sayes 'by no means I must putt in writing Heare-Sayes'*. Despite this warning, the most fruitful source of all turned out to be casual conversation, and as Aubrey's taste for gossip was rather undiscriminating, mistakes would keep creeping in and were savagely resented by Anthony Wood, who made no allowances. *I remember*, Aubrey wrote apologetically after one such rebuke, *Sam. Butler (Hudibras) one time at the Tavern sayd, that 'twas this Earl of Dorset's father that translated the Comoedie called the Cid. writt by Corneille. Me thinkes he should not be mistaken: but the world is mighty apt to it you see.* And later he was to protest: *I heard an old Lawyer of the Middle Temple, 1646, who was Sir Edward Coke's country-man, say that he was born to 300 pounds land per annum, and I have heard some of his country say again that he was borne but to 40 per pounds per annum. What shall one beleeve?*

What indeed? For when Aubrey asked Randall Isaacson a simple question about his father, he was answered with this fantastic rigmarole: 'My father died in St Cathrin Coleman's parrish London, About the 7ᵉ of December, 1654, which is neare 34 yeares after my grandfather's death. I Calculate from the tyme of his Birth to my Grandfather's Death to bee 39 yeares: ad the 34 yeares after my Grandfather's death to the 39 before: 39+34 makes 73 years his age – which all the familie agree that hee was seaventy three yeares of age when hee died, soe that he was borne in anno 1581. Borne in anno 1581, dyed aged 73, makes 1654 the yeare when he dyed.'

Sometimes, too, he asked so many questions that his friends took pleasure in teasing him: *Dr John Newton – he told me he was borne in Bedfordshire, but would not tell me where;* while at other times his repeated queries seem to have exasperated them: *The Earle of Carnarvon does not remember Mr Brown, and I ask't his Lordship lately if any of his servants doe; he assures me NO.* That this was no isolated instance is proved by Aubrey's own sharpness with Anthony Wood: *On Sunday last I dined with Mr Ashmole, who bids me answer you POSITIVELY that Sir Richard Nepier never did write anything and sayes that he haz acquainted you thus much before by letter.*

But though he could extend his reach back to the Elizabethan age by this method – *Old Sergeant Hoskins the Poet (grandfather to this Sir John Hoskins, Baronet, my honoured friend) was well acquainted with Mr Nicholas Hill, by which meanes I have this tradicion which otherwise had been lost; as also his very name* – it had its disappointments too. *Mr Baron Brampton hath invited me to his chamber to give me a farther account of Generall Monk. I let slip the Opportunity, and my honoured friend is dead,* Aubrey said sadly on one occasion; and on another: *I thought to have taken Memoires of him; but deferring it Death took away Sir Jonas.* And ever after a loss like this, Aubrey nursed a secret regret, as he showed in his life of Edmund Waller: *Mr Thomas Big of Wickham haz been dead these 20 yeares, who could have told me the cause of his madness,* he said then. *I beleeve that I am right. You see how things become antiquated.*

Anything that could be checked was checked, however, with scrupulous care. *Thomas Hobbes, Malmesburiensis, Philosophus, was borne at his father's house in Westport,* Aubrey recorded, *being that extreme howse that pointes into, or faces, the Horse-fayre; the farthest howse on the left hand as you goe to Tedbury, leaving the Church on your right. To prevent mistakes, and that hereafter may rise no doubt what house was famous for this Famous man's Birth; I doe here testifie that in April, 1659, his brother Edmond went with me into this house, and into the Chamber where he was borne. Now things begin to be antiquated, and I have heard some guesse it might be at the howse where his brother Edmund lived and dyed. But this is so, as I here deliver it. This house was given by Thomas, the Vicar, to his daughter, whose daughter or granddaughter possessed it, when I was there. It is a firme house, stone-built and tiled, of one roome (besides a buttery, or the like, within) below, and two chambers above. 'Twas in the innermost where he first drew breath.*

Despite all this research for Anthony Wood, Aubrey still found time to carry on several projects of his own, for the distractions of the past had vanished when, at the age of forty-six, his financial ruin was complete. From 1670 onwards he enjoyed *a sweet otium,* because when he had his horoscope calculated, in 1671, he discovered a scapegoat for all his misfortunes. 'The nativity', said Henry Coley, the astrologer, 'is a most Remarkeable opposition, and 'tis much pitty the starres were not more favourable to the Native.' For, it seems, they 'threaten ruin to land and estate; give Superlative Vexations in Matters Relating to Marriag, besides wondrous Contests in Lawsuits: all of which vexations, I suppose the native hath had a Greater portion than ever was desired.' And even though another horoscope, cast this time by John Gadbury, an astrologer who was, unlike Coley, as yet unacquainted with Aubrey himself 'looks no more like Esq: Aubrey than an apple is like an Oyster', Aubrey seems to have found it a real relief to be able to blame his own incompetence upon the stars.

He was, in fact, so enthralled with the predictions that, not only did he make selections from the forty volumes of Nativities which William Lilly had assembled: *Mr Ashmole turnes and reads*, he said, *and I doe write;* but he also set about collecting, on his own account, the precise hours of the birth of most of his friends, which he entered in a little book entitled *A Collection of Genitures Well Attested. Walter Charleton M.D. borne at Shepton-Malet in com. Somerset, Feb. 2d, 1619, about 6 h. P.M. his mother being then at supper*, he notes, but not all confinements were as uneventful as this. *Sir William Dugdale was born September 12, 1605: That afternoon a Swarme of Bees pitch't under his Mother's chamber window, as it were an omen of his laborious Collections;* and worst of all perhaps was the case of Mris. Jane Smyth, for *when she was born it thundered and lightened and the house was on fire.* Anthony Ettrick, the friend with whom he had been in danger of drowning on his return from Ireland, was more fortunate: he came quietly into the world on a Sunday. *His mother would say he was a Sundaye's Bird.* But once again, Aubrey found himself baulked for lack of information: Christopher Wren had told him that *the bell rang VIII as his mother fell in Labour with him*, but Aubrey complained to Wood that *he hath putt a trick on us, as it seems; for he hath made him selfe a yeare younger then indeed he is, though he needs not be ashamed of his age, he hath made such admirable use of his time: 'tis a poore spirited thing, if he will not resolve me.* Anthony Wood's reply to this must have been interesting reading, for he had just tried to reduce his forty years to twenty-five, by writing to Aubrey: 'My Nativity I cannot yet retrive; but by talking with an ancient servant of my father's, I find I was born on the 17 of Decem, but the year when I am not certain: 'twas possibly about 1647'; and this from a man who had written an eyewitness account of King Charles I's entry into Christ Church in 1636.

But it was not birth alone that counted in astrology; every date was significant. If you fell ill, the time you took to your bed was of the utmost importance: *Sir Robert Henley, of Bramswell, Hants, Baronet, decubuit, Thursday, about 3 P.M., Feb. 14, Valentine's Day. He was taken ill a hunting about noon, I think the Tuesday before;* and Aubrey was always careful to transfer the leases of his fast-vanishing estates at the most propitious moment. *Eston-Pierse possession*, one horoscope is marked, and underneath is written: *25 March 1671, 1 P.M. possession given by Jonathan Rogers to Mr Sherwin.* The exact time at which an honour was granted was also most important and Aubrey several times repeated that *Sir Christopher Wren was Knighted at Whitehall on Friday, 14th November 1673, at 5 h A.M.* (*From Mr Robert Hooke, the next day*). Even a man's figure depended on the heavens, for Aubrey noted of Sir William Petty: *Jupiter in Cancer makes him fatt at heart. John Gadbury also sayes that Vomits would be excellent good for him;* and the stars had an even worse effect on poor William Marshall, the sculptor: *Conjunction of Mercury and Leo made him stutter*. It was no wonder, therefore, that Edward Davenant said *he thankt God his father did not know the houre of his birth; for that it would have tempted him to have studyed Astrologie, for which he had no esteeme at all.*

Throughout the nineteenth century, the pious clergymen who bowdlerized Aubrey's work fell particularly hard on him for this superstition. But in this they merely revealed their lack of historical knowledge, for though astrology had become gross superstition by their days, it was not always so. Until the publication of Newton's theory showed the fallacy of the beliefs on which the celestial scheme or horoscopes was founded, astrology had been one of the most serious attempts to explain the world scientifically. And it was in this scientific spirit that Aubrey approached the problem. *We have not that Science yet perfect*, he said, *'tis one of the Desiderata. The way to make it perfect is to gett a Supellex of true Genitures; in order wherunto I have with much care collected these ensuing, which the Astrologers may rely on, for I have sett doune none on randome, or doubtfull, information, but from their own Mouthes: quod N.B.* And when in 1673 *Sir Leoline Jenkins was sent with Sir Joseph Williamson, Plenipotentiaries to Nemeghen*, Aubrey gave striking proof of his empirical attitude: *I remember that very time they went away was opposition of Saturn and Mars. I sayd then to the Earl of Thanet that if that Ambassade came to any good I would never trust to Astrologie again.* It cannot be held against Aubrey that he at last decided, on the evidence before him, that astrology was the key to truth, for as Jeremy Bentham has said, 'He who thinks, and thinks for himself, will always have a claim to thanks; it is no matter whether it be right or wrong, so as it be explicit. If it is right, it will serve as a guide to direct: if wrong, as a beacon to warn.'

In those days a warning beacon was badly needed, for one of the first results of the Reformation had been a tremendous outburst of superstition, and the Puritans, encouraged by their literal acceptance of the truth of the Bible, soon spread their delusions throughout Europe. Aubrey realized this as well as anyone. *Though it was then the fashion to fall upon the church of Rome*, he said, *yet these men were as superstitious, but did not know it.* In Germany, Luther himself accused the Devil of having created flies purposely to distract him while writing good books, and in Calvin's Geneva several people went to the stake for the detestable crime of spreading the plague. It was not until the middle of Elizabeth's reign that the symptoms of this wild credulity began to appear in England, where, as the Puritan influence became dominant, it brought with it a renewed belief in witchcraft. Little action was taken by the State against those unfortunates during the Queen's reign, however, for Elizabeth disapproved most strongly of this particular superstition, very probably because her mother had not only been universally accounted to be a witch, but had also been sentenced 'to be beheaded or burned at the Kings pleasure'. No such family scruples held back the Stuarts, though, and on the accession of James I the prosecutions started which were to result in the execution of seventy thousand witches in England alone before 1680. Indeed King James himself, in his book on 'Daemonologie', gave a terrific fillip to the witch-trials, although he soon came up against so many frauds that he recanted his views. Aubrey tells two stories that must have contributed to the King's change of heart. First he says, *One Mris. Katharine Waldron (a Gentlewoman of good Family) pretended to be bewitched by a certain woman. She had acquired such a strange habit, that She would endure exquisite torments, as to have pinnes thrust into her flesh, nay under her Nailes. His Majesty being in these parts went to see her in one of her Fitts: she lay on a bed: and the King saw her endure the torments aforesayd. The Roome (as it is easily to be believed) was full of Company. His Majesty gave a sodain pluck to her Coates, and topt them over her head, and discovered ALL to the standers by: which surprise (it seemes she had some innate modesty in her) not imagining of such a thing made her immediately start, and detected the Cheate.* And then there was the case of *Richard Heydock, M.C. quondam Fellow of New College in Oxford, an Ingenious, and a learned Person: but much against the Hierachie of the Church of England. He had this Device to gaine Proselytes by preaching in his Dream: which was much noised abroad, and talk't of as a Miracle. But King James 1st being at Salisbury went to heare him: He observed that this Harangue was very methodicall &c. that he did but counterfeit a Sleep. He surprized the Doctor by drawing his sword, and swearing Gods waunes I will cutt-off his head: at which the Dr startled, and pretended to awake. So the Cheat was detected.*

But not all his subjects proved so astute as their sovereign, and although King James threw the whole weight of his influence and that of his Council, the Star Chamber, and the Episcopate, into the struggle against the growing mania, it was too late. Wherever the Puritans, and later the Parliament, held sway, the persecution broke out afresh, and books, pamphlets, and sermons poured from the press. It was, surprisingly, the educated class which was most obsessed by the belief in witchcraft, and it must be admitted that all the evidence available supported its existence; though perhaps Chief Justice Hale went somewhat too far in laying it down as a law that there must be such things as witches, since there were laws against witches, and it was not conceivable that laws had been made against something which did not exist. The witches themselves were never convicted without their voluntary confessions, usually under torture it is true, but even without this persuasion, many of the unfortunate creatures, like those present-day women who complain of non-existent sexual attacks, vociferously protested that they were in truth in league with the Devil. And the catalogue, which Aubrey has left, of the evils for which witches were held to be accountable, explains the astounding number of persons who suffered death for this crime. *Twisting of trees, tearing and turning up Oakes by the roots,* he listed. *Raysing tempests; wracking ships; throwing down steeples; blasting plantes; dwindle away young children. To overlooke and binde the spirits and phantasy; bewhattling and making men impotent, woemen miscarry* (*Countesse of Carlisle*). *Whirlewinds; haracanes; Spirits in 'em.* He went on to explain the organization of the witches' sabbath, which seems to have moved with the times, for they now held *the session, à la mode de Royal Society, with Balloting-box. Memorandum,* he concludes, *Sir Henry Billingsley said wise men alwaies saw that as some malicious woemen increased in years, increased also in malice: set howses on fire, mischiefe to children, etc. Thought it better to have them underground then above ground and raise storms: the familiars could not handsomely knock 'em in the head.* It was no wonder, therefore, that *when there was a Cabal of Witches detected at Malmesbury, they were examined by Sir James Long of Dracot-Cerne, and committed by him to Salisbury Gaole. I think there were 7 or 8 old women hanged. There were odd things sworne against them, as the strange manner of the dyeing of H. Dennys Horse: of flying in the Air on a staffe, etc. These examinations, &c. Sr James hath fairly written in a Book, which He promised to give to the Royall Society.* Despite this seeming support for the persecution amongst even the most scientific men, scepticism was slowly growing: *Mr Anth. Ettrick of the Middle Temple* (*a very judicious Gentleman*) *was a curious Observer of the whole Triall, and was not satisfied,* says Aubrey on another occasion. *The crowd of spectators made such a noise that the Judge could not heare the Prisoner, nor the Prisoner the Judge; but the words were handed from one to the other by Mr R. Chandler, and sometimes not truly reported.*

In the infancy of science, every theory, no matter how absurd it might seem superficially, had to be checked before it could be safely discarded; and nowadays Aubrey would not be maligned as a credulous fool, but would be praised as an anthropologist and a collector of folk-lore. *Old Customs and old wives fables are grosse things,* he admits, *but yet ought not to be buried in Oblivion; there may be some trueth and usefulnesse be picked out of them, besides 'tis a pleasure to consider the Errours that enveloped former ages: as also the present.* And the errors of the present were not confined to Aubrey, even though he noted them down with such a will. *William Lawd* (*Archbishop of Canterbury*) *in a Sermon Preached before the Parliament, about the beginning of the Reign of King Charles I affirms the power of Prayer to be so great, that though there be a Conjunction or Opposition of Saturn or Mars* (*as there was one of them then*) *it will overcome the malignity of it.* As the Church believed, so did the State: *A little before the Death of Oliver Protector, a Whale came into the River Thames and was taken at Greenwich. 'Tis said, Oliver was troubled at it.* Nor was Science itself free from the taint, for the astronomer Kepler was convinced that the planets, by their revolutions, produced 'a music of the spheres', which was audible only to the sun, which he believed to be the body of a divine spirit; while the great Newton himself accounted for the tangential velocities of the planets, which prevent them from falling into the sun, by supposing that, initially, they had been hurled by the hand of God.

Although he shared in some of the delusions of his time, Aubrey made many reservations in his beliefs. He says of *Phantomes: Though I myselfe never saw any such things, yet I will not conclude that there is no Truth at all in these reports. I believe that (extraordinarily) there have been such Apparitions; but where one is true, a hundred are Figments. There is a Lecherie in lyeing: and imposeing on the Credulous: And the Imagination of fearfull People is to admiration.*

Even though he sifted the mass of evidence which he had collected in this critical spirit, he was so much more of an antiquary than a scientist that he could never bring himself to discard any of the stories which he had so laboriously discovered. *It may seem nauseous to some*, he apologized, *that I have rakt up so many Western vulgar Proverbs; which I confess I disdeigne not to quote; Pliny himself being not afraid to call them Oracles. For Proverbes are drawn from the Experience and Observations of many Ages: and are the ancient Natural Philosophy of the Vulgar, preserved in old English and worse Rythmes, handed down to us for our curious moderne Philosophers to examine.* And many years later, in 1688, Aubrey gathered all these anecdotes and traditions into one volume, *The Remaines of Gentilisme and Judaisme*, in which he laboriously drew a parallel between the superstitions of his own country and those of Greece and Rome, and preserved for ever those meaningless customs that are so dear to the hearts of anthropologists. *In several parts of Oxfordshire*, he reports solemnly, *particularly at Lanton, it is the custom for the Maid Servant to ask the Man for Ivy to dress the Hous, and if the Man denies or neglects to fetch in Ivy, the Maid steals away a pair of his Breeches and nails them up to the gate in the yard, or highway.*

In these collections, he tried sincerely not to rely purely upon hearsay. *Mr Hierome Banks as he lay on his Death Bed in Bell-yard, said Three Days before he died, that Mr Jennings of the Inner-Temple (his great Acquaintance, Dead a Year or two before) gave Three Knocks, looked in, and said, Come away. He was as far from believing things as any man*, Aubrey said, and he reinforced the story by a similar experience of his own: *Three or four Dayes before my Father died*, he writes, *as I was in my Bed about Nine a Clock in the Morning perfectly awake, I did hear three distinct Knocks on the Beds-head, as if it had been with a Ruler or Ferula.* But even though Aubrey had experienced this case of haunting himself, he was not blind to the possibilities of charlatanry in other cases. *In the time of King Charles II*, he reports, *the Drumming at the House of Mr Monpesson of Tydworth made a great Talke over England. They did have some times Knockings: and if they sayd: Devill, knock so many knocks: so many knocks would be answered: But Mr Ettrick sometimes whispered the words: and it was then no returne. But*, says Aubrey with admirable common sense, *he should have spoken in Latin, or French, for the detection of this. Another time*, he adds, *Sir Christopher Wren went thither and lay there: He could see no strange things; but sometimes he should heare a drumming, as one may drumm with ones hand upon wainscot: But he observed that this drumming was not, but onely, when a certain Maid-servant was in the next Room: But all these remarqued, that the Devill kept no very unseasonable houres, sc. it seldom knock't after twelve at night: or before 6 in the morning.* This does not look like the writing of a grossly credulous man, especially when one considers the completely different state of mind of our ancestors.

For the habit of doubt is an extremely recent growth, almost wholly subsequent to Newton in fact, and Aubrey often showed a scepticism that was most praiseworthy in an age when any statement was accepted just because it was made. This completely uncritical state of mind is hard for us to visualize, because it has vanished almost entirely from the modern world; except in Ireland, where the people are still more likely to accept than to reject even the most obvious falsehood, and where, in consequence, the banshees and the fairies and the leprechauns have kept their last foothold in Europe. And in England in the seventeenth century critical thought was especially rare in connexion with religion. However much the various sects might differ in their interpretation of the Bible, not one of them doubted for an instant that every word in it was absolutely and literally true; and the Bible constantly mentioned witches and spectres and portents. So Aubrey's reservations with regard to the following story are very laudable. *Anno 1679*, he says, *After the Discovery of the Popish Plot, the Penal Laws were put in execution against the Roman Catholicks: So, that if they did not receive the Sacrament according to the Church of England in their Parish Church, they were to be severely proceeded against according to Law: Mr Ployden, to avoid the Penalty, went to his Parish Church at Lasham near Alton in Hampshire: when Mr Laurence (the Minister) had put the Chalice into Mr Ployden's hand, the Cup of it (wherein the Wine was) fell off. 'Tis true, it was out of order before; and he had a Tremor in his hand. The Communion was stopt by this accident.* Religion in those days being still very primitive, portents of this kind were expected: for although various pieces of *Priest-cheate* had been exposed at the Reformation, many of the rites of the Church were still attended by the grossest superstition. For instance, *Sinne-eaters* were still in existence in Aubrey's lifetime.

In the County of Hereford, he notes, *was an old Custome at Funeralls to hire poor people, who were to take upon them all the Sinnes of the party deceased. One of these (I remember) lived in a Cottage on Rosse-high way: He was a long, leane, ugly, lamentable poor raskal. The manner was that when the Corps was brought out of the house and layd on a Biere: a Loafe of bread was brought out, and delivered to the sinne-eater over the Corps, as also a Mazar-bowle of maple (Gossips bowle) full of beer, which he was to drinke up, and sixpence in money, in consideration whereof he tooke upon him (ipso facto) all the Sinnes of the Defunct, and freed him (or her) from Walking after they were dead. This custome alludes (me thinkes) something to the Scape goat in the old Lawe*. The cheapness of the price charged for the assumption of another man's sins is most surprising, for in the days before Hell was abolished by the Privy Council, its terrors were very real, as is shown by Queen Elizabeth's dreadful deathbed vision of herself ringed by flames. *In North-Wales, the Sinne-eaters are frequently made use of*, Aubrey adds, *but there, instead of a Bowle of Beere, they have a bowle of Milke.*

The throne also, like the Church, was surrounded by signs and portents, many of them so plausible that it is no wonder that they were believed. *An Old Man (like an Hermit) Second-sighted, tooke his Leave of King James the First, when he came into England*, Aubrey reports. *He took little notice of Prince Henry*, James's eldest son, who was to die at the age of eighteen, *but addressing himself to the Duke of York (since Charles I) fell a weeping to think what misfortunes he should undergo; and that he should be one of the miserablest unhappy Princes that ever was.* No one believed more firmly in such omens than Charles I himself, and to the very end of his life he was dogged by these coincidences. *The Head of King Charles I's Staff did fall off at his Tryal*, says Aubrey, *that is commonly known.*

It was at coronations, however, that superstition had the fullest play. *King Charles II was Crowned at the very conjunction of the Sun and Mercury*, Aubrey reports. *As the King was at Dinner in Westminster Hall, it Thundered and Lightned extreamly: The Canons and the Thunder played together.* But the second Charles was no superstitious man, and it was not until the crowning of his brother that the portents worried a King again. Aubrey was present at this ceremony and he carefully recorded the catastrophes, which foreshadowed so clearly the disastrous end of King James's troublous reign. *When King James II was Crowned (according to the Ancient Custom, the Peers go to the Throne, and kiss the King): The Crown was almost kiss'd off his Head. An Earl did sett it right: and as he came from the Abbey to Westminster-Hall, the Crown totter'd extreamly.*

The Canopy carried over King James IIs Head by the Wardens of the Cinque Ports, was torn by a puff of Wind as he came to Westminster-hall: It hung down very lamentably: I saw it. 'Twas of Cloath of gold & my strength (I am confident) could not have rent it and it was not a windy day.

The top of his Scepter (Flower de Lis) did then fall, which the Earl of Peterborough took up. Nor was this all. *Upon Saint Mark's day, after the Coronation of King James II, were prepared stately Fire-works on the Thames. It happened, that they took fire all together, and it was so dreadful, that several Spectators leap'd into the River, choosing rather to be drown'd than burn'd. In a Yard by the Thames was my Lord Powys's Coach and Horses: The Horses were so frightened by the Fire works, that the Coachman was not able to stop them, but ran over one who with great difficulty recovered.*

These accidents seemed to prove that the throne was once again of interest to the supernatural powers, for the profligacy of Charles II was so gross that, according to Anthony Wood, 'in the latter end of Nov. 1675, a pillion was set behind the statue of King Charles II on horseback at Stoks Market and on the horse's brest writ on paper: Hast, post-hast for a Midwife'; and serious doubts had begun to arise as to whether he could really be the instrument of God's healing. *Dr Ralph Bathurst, Dean of Wells and one of the Chaplains to King Charles, who is no Superstitious Man, protested to me that the curing of the King's Evill by the Touch of the King does puzzle his Philosophie: for whether they were of the House of Yorke, or Lancaster, it did. 'Tis true (indeed) there are Prayers read at the Touching, but neither the King minds them nor the Chaplains.* Nevertheless the belief in the King's miraculous power was still strong. *Arise Evans*, says Aubrey, *had a fungous Nose, and said, it was reveal'd to him, that the King's Hand would Cure him: And at the first coming of King Charles II into St Jame's Park he kiss'd the King's Hand, and rubb'd his Nose with it; which disturb'd the King, but Cured him.* But Aubrey was not deceived by this seeming proof. *In Somersetshire*, he added, *'tis confidently reported that some were Cured of the King's-evil, by the Touch of the Duke of Monmouth: The Lord Chancellor Bacon saith, That Imagination is next Kin to Miracle-working Faith.*

And so it seems that belief in the supernatural was not entirely pointless, when it could be turned to such excellent practical uses. Nor was it confined entirely to medical aid; advice about careers was sometimes given in this roundabout way: *Mr Brograve of Hamel near Puckbridge in Hertfordshire when he was a young Man, Riding in a Lane in that Country, had a blow given him on his Cheek (or Head): He look'd back, and saw that no body was near, behind him; anon, he had such another Blow: I have forgot if a Third. He turn'd back and fell to the Study of the Law; and was afterwards a Judge.* And the whereabouts of lost wills and buried treasure were so constantly being hinted at in dreams that it led occasionally to the most unfortunate results: *One Daniel Healy, of Donaghmore, in Ireland, having three different times dreamed that Money lay concealed under a large Stone in a field near where he lived, procured some Workmen to assist him in removing it, and when they had dug as far as the foundation, it fell suddenly and killed Healy on the spot.* However the best use of the gullibility of the time was made by *Mris. Abbott, the wife of a poor Cloathworker at Guildford,* who, by means of an elaborate confidence trick, procured *so good an education for her son that the child came, by degrees, to be Arch-Bishop of Canterbury.*

It can be seen, therefore, that a proper use of superstition could bring a rich reward; and it was also an admirable excuse for inefficiency. For instance, after a vast amount of money had been spent on boring for coal in Surrey, only to end in failure, *Mr William Lilly (Astrologer) was quick to blame the Subterranean Spirits: For as fast as the Irons were put in they would snap off.* It was this use which Aubrey made of astrology. *Thomas Morgan was unfortunate and idle,* he says of one of his friends, *seemed to have Saturne much his Enemie.* And having convinced himself that in like manner the loss of his own estates was due entirely to the stars being against him, Aubrey turned back to his life without repining *when all was gone.*

Only one regret still lingered. *I wished Monastarys had not been putt down,* he complained, *that the Reformers would have been more moderate as to that point. Nay, the Turkes have Monasteries. The Reformers in the Lutheran Countrys were more prudent then to destroy them: only altered the religion. Why should our Reformers be so severe?* For now that he was run out of his estates, Aubrey could have made good use of *the Convenience of Religious houses,* for he thought it *fitt there should be receptacles and provision for Contemplative men. What a pleasure 'twould have been to have travelled from Monastery to Monastery,* he sighed, and wished himself back in the old Catholic England, *before the Pope, with all his Authority, was clean banished the Realm.*

Then the Crusado's to the Holy-warres were most magnificent and glorious, Aubrey says, *and the rise I beleeve of the adventures of Knights Errants, and Romances. The solemnities of Processions in and about the Churches, and the Perambulations in the Fields, besides their convenience, were fine pleasing diversions. The Priestes went before in their Formalities, singing the Latin-service, and the people came after making their good-meaning-responses. The Reverence given to Holy-men was very great: then were the Churches open all day long, men and women going in and out hourely to and from their Devotions. Then were the Consciences of the people kept in so great awe by Confession: that Just dealing and vertue was habitual.*

This Countrey, he continues, speaking of his native Wiltshire, *was very full of Religious howses: a man could not have travelled but he must have mett*

Monkes, Fryars, Bonne Hommes, &c. in their several habits, black, white, gray, &c: and the tingle-tangle of the Convent-bells I fancie made very pretty musique, like College bells at Oxford.

Then were no Free-schooles: the boyes were educated at the Monasteries. The young mades (not at Hakney, Say schooles, &c. to learn pride and wantonnesse) but at the Nunneries, where they had examples of Piety, humilitie and modestie to imitate and practise. Here they learned Needle-worke, and the art of Confectionary: Surgery (anciently no apothecaries or Surgeons – the gentlewoemen did cure their poore neighbours: their hands are now too fine) Physicke, Writing, Drawing, etc.

Old Jacquer (who lived where Charles Hadnam did) could see from his House, the Nuns of the Priory of St Mary (juxta Kington) come into the Nymph-Hay with their Rocks and Wheels to spin, and with their Sowing Work. He would say that he hath told threescore and ten: tho' of Nuns there were not so many: but in all, with Lay-Sisters, as Widows, old Maids, and young Girles, there might be such a Number. This was a fine way of breeding-up young woemen, who are led more by Example, then Precept; and a good Retirement for Widows and grave single Women, to a civil, vertuous, and holy Life.

Plato saies that the foundation of Government is the Education of youth: by this meanes, it is most probable that this was a Golden-age.

And now Aubrey was well away on his reminiscences. *Let us imagine then what kind of Countrie this was in the time of the ancient Britons,* he says, *by the nature of the soile, which is a soure, woodsere land, very natural for the production of oaks especially. One may conclude that this North-division was a shady dismall wood; and the inhabitants almost as salvage as the Beasts, whose Skins were their only rayment. They were 2 or 3 degrees I suppose less salvage than the Americans.*

The Romans subdued and civilized them, however, but after they withdrew, *here was a mist of Ignorance for 600 years. They were so far from knowing Arts, that they could not build a wall with stone. They lived sluttishly in poor houses, where they eat a great deal of beef and mutton, and drank good Ale in a brown mazard; and their very Kings were but a Sort of Farmers.*

After the Christian Religion was planted here, it gave a great Shoote, and the Kings and great men gave vast revenues to the Church, who were ignorant enough in those Days. The Normans then came and taught them civility and building; which though it was Gothiq, as also their Policy (Feudalis Lex), yet they were magnificent.

For the Government, 'till the time of King Henry 8, it was like a nest of boxes; for Copy-holders (who till then were Villaines) held of the Lords of the Mannor, who held of a superior Lord, who held perhaps of another superior Lord or Duke, who held of the King. Upon any occasion of Bustling, or Tournaments in those Days, one of these great Lords sounded his Trumpets (the Lords then kept Trumpeters; even to King James) and summon'd those that held under them. Those again sounded their trumpetts, and so downward to the Copy-holders.

The Lords (then Lords in deed as well as Title) liv'd in their countries like petty Kings, had jura regalia belonging to their signories, had their Castles and Burroughes, and sent Burgesses to the Lower House; had Gallows within their Liberties where they could try, condemn, hang, and drawe; never went up to London but in Parliament-time, or once a yeare to do their homage and duty to the King.

No younger brothers then were, by the Custom and constitution of the Realme, to betake themselves to Trades, but were Church-men, or Retainers or Servants to great Men: rid good horses (now and then took a purse) and their bloud that was bred at the good Tables of their Masters was upon every occasion freely lett out in their Quarrels. It was then too common amongst their Masters to have Feuds with one another, and their servants at Market or where they met (in that slashing age) did commonly bang one anothers Bucklers.

The poor boyes did turn the Spitts, and lick't the dripping-pan, and grew to be huge lusty knaves.

In those dayes the Gentry begott their own servants and copyhold tenants (the custom of Lying with the Bride the first night).

No Ale-houses nor yet Innes then, unlesse upon great roades: when they had a minde to drinke they went to the Friaries; and when they travilled they had entertainement at the Religious howses for 3 dayes, if occasion so long required. The meeting of the Country was not then at tipling-howses, but in the Fields or Forests with their Hawkes or Howndes, with their bugle-hornes in silken baudries.

Such Joy and merriment was every Holiday; which dayes were kept with great Solempnitie and reverence. In Herefordshire and parts of the Marches of Wales, the Tabor and pipe were exceeding common. Many beggars begd with it: and the Peasants danced to it in the Churchyard on Holy dayes and Holy-day-eves. Now it is almost lost: the Drumme and Trumpet have putt that peaceable Musique to silence.

In those times (besides the jollities already mentioned) they had their Pilgrimages to several shrines, as chiefly hereabout, to St Joseph of Arimathea at his Chapil in Glastonbury-abby. In the roades thither were severall howses of entertaynment built purposely for them.

The disappearance of these *howses of entertaynement* was obviously a great blow to Aubrey, but he was not long in finding out their modern counterpart. Though he was by now divested of all, he was safe by means of his family connexions from actual want, for as he puts it *Providence raysed me (unexpectedly) good friends*, with one or other of whom he managed to spend the remainder of his days. There was *the Right Honourable Nicholas, Earl of Thanet, with whom I was delitescent at Hethfield in Kent neer a yeare: Sir Christopher Wren: Mr Ogilby: then Edmund Wyld Esq.* R.S.S. *tooke me into his Armes, with whom I most commonly take my Diet and sweet Otium's.* This latter was a man after Aubrey's own heart, as is shown by Roger North's description of him. 'One Mr Wyld, a rich Philosopher, lived in Bloomsbury. He was single, and his house a sort of knick-knack-atory. This gentleman was of a superior order, and valued himself upon new inventions of his own. He sowed salads in the morning to be cut for dinner; and claimed the invention of painted curtains, in varnish, upon silk; which would bend and not crack; and his house was furnished with them: and he delighted in nothing more than in showing his multifarious contrivances.' So it can be imagined that Aubrey was in his element in this place, helping in the experiments, wondering why in the autumn beads of sweat appeared on his host's patent curtains, and drinking and talking his fill. *Mr Wyld*, he says proudly, *will undertake to prepare an Earth ('twill be neare a halfe a yeare preparing) that shall produce Wheate without sowing: and he believes he can doe the like for Pease*. And so sure was his host of success that he was prepared to back his judgement with solid cash. *Edmund Wyld, Esq. R.S.S.*, Aubrey explained at greater length, *hath had a pott of Composition in his garden these 7 yeares, that beares nothing at all: not so much as grasse, or mosse. He makes this Challenge, if any Man will give him twenty pounds, he will give him an hundred if it doth not beare* Wheat spontaneously: *and the Party shall keep the Key: and he shall sift the Earth Composition with a fine Sieve; so that he may be sure, there are no graines of Wheat in it. He hath also a Composition for Pease: but that he will not warrant, not having tryed it*. But the wager found no takers, for Edmund Wyld was famous for his skill in gardening. *London. Bloomesbery. August 12, 1684*, Aubrey noted on another occasion, *my honoured Friend Edmund Wyld, Esq. did just before we sate down to dinner, sow in an Earthen Porringer of prepared Earth, Seeds of Parsley, Prunella, Balme, &c. The Porringer was sett on a chafing dish of Coales: and by the time we had ended Dinner (which was about an hower ½) seeds sprang visibly up, scilicet, nineteen, or 20 young plants. Their Leaves as big as common Pinnes heads: by and by appeared more, so that the Dish was full: Some of the Plants being drawn-out with a paire of pliers, the stalkes were about ½ inch long. About two or three houres after the Soweing, the Dish was exposed in the garden subdio: That night it happened to raine very hard all night, yet they all lived, and flourished till about the middle of September: and then they began to wither. Some of them lived till Michaelmass: and some till 8th or 10th of October following. I was one of the Four (besides Mr Wyld) that was an Eye-witnesse of this Experiment. The Dish remaines in the Garden to this day (Feb. 7, 16$\frac{89}{90}$)*, he concludes, *but no vegetable at all did ever growe in it since*. And to make this the ideal home for Aubrey 'most of the ingenious persons about town visited' his host; it is no wonder, therefore, that he sounded so complacent when he noted: *I now indulge my genius with my friends and pray for the young angels*.

Aubrey had now begun to reap the reward of his sensible recognition that *to be good and agreeable company is a vertue*. For though he had lost his fortune, he never lost a friend, and the warmth with which he continued to be regarded everywhere is shown by the following poem, which has been accidentally preserved amongst his papers. 'To his most honourd frend John Aubrey Esquire in imitation of Mr Greaves verses, etc.' runs the heading, but the author's name is missing:

If thou, my dearest Friend, in whose safe breast
I store my joys, and make my greifes take rest;
Who art alone to me instead of all
This World doth Wit, or Mirth, or Pleasure call:
If thou should'st ask, why I so little care
What interest or repute with most I beare?
Why with so very few my selfe I mate?
To th' rest regardless of their love or hate?
In short I'll tell thee, 'tis 'cause I would be
From noise of businesse and all troubles free.
Lies, False News, impertinence I hate,
And all things else which contradict my Fate,
With losse of Knowledge, truth and liberty
By affording every fool my company.
Yet what I love, with whom I would converse.
And freely consort, I'le unask'd rehearse:
One, whome by experience I truly find
To be my friend, and suited to my mind:
Reserv'd to others, but open unto me,
And has a Soul from base dissembling free,
And modest too; who thinks the greatest wit
Consists in the wise government of it:
Utters no secrets, constant to his friend,
Nor can his thoughts to wicked fallsehood bend:
One that Flies sadnesse, hates to be severe,
But with facetiousnesse unbends his care.
Yet one that's studious too, whose boundlesse mind
Scarce within Learning's limits is confin'd,
But chiefly Nature loves; and farre does pry
Into her secrets with his piercing eye.
These and like things I love; but to say true
I've all this while been but describing You.
You are the Man, my friend, whome I can love,
The love of others I do not much approve.

One disadvantage did arise, however, from Aubrey's dependence on his friends. *Edmund Wyld lives in the great square in Bloomsbery*, he wrote, *on the south side*, *next dore to the Blackmores head*, and by the most unfortunate chance his stomach, which he said *had been till then so tender that I could not drinke claret without sugar*, *nor white wine*, *but would disgorge*, chose this very moment to recover. And Aubrey was never one for half-measures, with the result that his writing became even more untidy and more inaccurate. *If I had but either one to come to me in a morning with a good Scourge*, came the familiar lament, *or did not sett-up till one or two with Mr Wyld*, *I could doe a great deal of businesse*.

That no blame really attaches to Edmund Wyld for his guest's incurable sociability is made only too clear by the Diaries of the period, where Aubrey constantly appears, drinking in taverns, talking in coffee-houses, or helping his friends in their work. 'Mr Aubery and I observed the Resistance of air to be duplicate to the velocity or rather in a musicall proportion', Robert Hooke wrote in 1674; and four years later he added, 'Observed with Aubery the Moon Eclipsed.' The same source provides us with more details of Aubrey's life in London. 'With Mr Aubery at Lord Brounkers, Mr Colwalls, Sir Jo. Moors, Cap. Sherbourns', Hooke says on one day, and nearly every night he notes: 'At Garways with Mr Hill, Mr Hoskins, Mr Wild, Mr Aubery, Godfry, Blackburn, Lodowick, &c.' Then there were frequent excursions to Knightsbridge to see the Bishop of Salisbury, or to visit his other friends. 'I dind with Boyle, it agreed well,' says Hooke, 'then with Aubery visited Harrington and Gadberry. Both mad but of Divers humours.' And every week there was the Royal Society to attend, with the promise of some drinking afterwards. 'Agreed upon new clubb to meet at Joes', wrote Robert Hooke on December the tenth, 1675. 'Mr Hill, Mr Lodowick, Mr Aubery, and I, and to joyn to us Sir Jo. More, Mr Wild, Mr Hoskins. We now began our New Philosophicall Clubb,' he added on New Year's Day, 'and Resolvd upon Ingaging ourselves not to speak of any thing that was then reveald *sub sigillo* to any one nor to declare that we had such a meeting at all. We began our first Discourse about light upon the occasion of Mr Newton's Late Papers.' And it was Aubrey who led off the discussion. All this activity cost money, though, and poor bankrupt Aubrey was soon reduced to borrowing from his friends. 'Lent Aubery 10sh. and before 20sh. and since 5: he promised to repay it', runs the entries, but when the time of reckoning came, no cash was forthcoming. 'Bought of Mr Aubery, Euclides Works Greek and Latin 10sh., Plunia *Purpur* 1s., Censorinus *de mensura Anni* 8d., Duret *Histoire des Langues*, and Scaliger *Contra Caldanum* 6s. 4d., Baytins *de re Navali* 2sh.,' wrote Robert Hooke, 'acquitted the former 20sh. lent.' But five days later another entry occurs in the Diary, 'Lent Aubery 20sh. more.'

Aubrey had hoped that the completion of his ruin would allow him to increase the work which he had been carrying on all through the crisis of his fortunes. *Notwithstanding all these embarassments*, he had said, *I did pian piano* (*as they occur'd*) *take notes of Antiquity; and having a quick draught, have drawne landskips on horse-back symbolically*. For Aubrey was still only forty-five when he lost his fortune, and being in the prime of life, he thought that he would be able to concentrate on his work at last, now that he was free from the continual distraction of trying to control his obstreperous accounts and to wriggle out of the lawsuits by which he had always been entangled in the past. *Anno 1671*, he says happily, *having sold all and disappointed as aforesaid of moneys I received, I had so strong an Impulse to* (*in good part*) *finish my Description of Wilts, two volumes in folio, that I could not be quiet till I had donne it, and that with danger enough, tanquam canis e Nilo* [like a dog at the Nile] *take a lap and away for feare of the Crocodiles, i.e. Catchpolls – And indeed all that I have donne and that little that I have studied have been just after that fashion, so that had I not lived long my want of Leisure would have afforded but a slender Harvest. My head was alwaies working; never idle, and even travelling* (*which from 1649 till 1670 was never off horseback*) *did gleane some observations, of which I have a collection in folio of 2 quiers of paper plus a dust basket, some whereof are to be valued.*

As if to disprove still further his theory that *a man's Spirit rises and falls with his fortunes: makes me lethargique*, Aubrey had branched off in yet another direction. In a letter to Anthony Wood at this time, he says: *I am writing a Comedy for Thomas Shadwell, which I have now almost finished since I came here. And I shall fit him with another, The Country Revell, both humours untoucht, but of this, Mum! for 'tis very satyricall against some of my mischievous enemies which I in my tumbling up and down have collected.* About the worth of his plays, Aubrey had no illusions, for he saw that the Civil War had utterly destroyed the English stage. By forbidding the performance of any play, the Puritans successfully broke the link with the great days of Shakespeare and Jonson, while the bigotry of their rule during the Commonwealth was largely responsible for the licentiousness of the early Restoration drama. As Professor Trevelyan has pointed out in his *English Social History*: 'These unhappy conditions were peculiar to England: the age of Wycherley over here was the age of Molière, Corneille and Racine in France. There the drama, comic as well as tragic, was decent and was serious, and the French have ever since taken their drama seriously, as the Elizabethan English took theirs, regarding it as a civilizing influence and a criticism of life.' But although Aubrey sadly noted: *Now our present writers reflect so much upon particular persons and coxcombeities, that twenty yeares hence they will not be understood*, he followed the popular model, and sketched (between the lines of some old legal documents) the design for a grossly obscene farce. For *The Countrey Revell* was written to expose both the coarseness of the simple country people (amongst whom was *Squeaker, a shee-Balladsinger*) and the vices of the gentry, and amongst the latter Aubrey included many thinly disguised portraits of his acquaintances. *Courtoise, a Knight of the Bath and Protector of distressed Ladies*, was really old Thomas Tyndale, Aubrey's Wiltshire neighbour, *Justice Wagstaffe* was Sir John Dunstable, and Aubrey's great enemy, Gwyn, the Earl of Oxford's secretary, appeared as *Sir Fastidious Overween. Sir Surly Chagrin, Captain Exceptious Quarrelsome, Squire Fitz-Ale* and *Sir Libidinous Gourmand* are also recognizable portraits of his contemporaries, and in the notes for these characters, Aubrey has left a scathing comment on the efficiency of his times. *Plato saies perpetuall drunkenness is the Reward of virtue*, says Squire Fitz-Ale at one point, and Sir Hugh the Vicar confesses to be *one of the old red-nosed Clergy, orthodox and canonicall. All the Parsons hereabout in Wiltshire*, Aubrey noted after this, *are Alehouse-hunters. James Long, Esq., hunted Sir Hugh driefoote to the Alehouse with his pack of hounds to the griefe of the revered Divine.* And of Sir John Dunstable, he says: *The Cellar he calls his Library*, and he continues, *Parliament men prepare themselves for the businesse of the Nation with Ale in the morning. Some Justices doe sleepe on the Bench every assizes.* One final note about this character shows that the Army was no less corrupt than the Church and the Law. *At Chippenham, the Deputye Lieutenants mett to see the Order of the Militia. After a taedious setting (at dinner, and drinking after dinner) the Drummes beate and the Soldiers began to march before the windowe to be seen by the Deputy Lieutenants. Justice Wagstaffe (Colonell) had not marcht before 'em many yardes but downe a falls all along in the dirt. His Myrmidons, multâ vi, heav'd him up, and then a cryed out, Some drinks, ho! and so there was an end of the Businesse.*

The plot deals with the fortunes of an adultress, who, pursued by her husband, is following her lover disguised in page's attire, and the play ends with most of the characters dead on the stage. *Raynes*, wrote Aubrey, who in his excitement seems to have inserted the real name of the injured husband, *comes and invades Sir Fastidious Overween, and is slayne by him; and then Sir Fastidious neglects her; she comes and stabbes him, and then herselfe.*

Naturally enough the play was never finished, for in 1672 Henry Coley wrote 'to his much honoured Freind Mr John Aubrey at the Right Honourable the Earle of Thanet's house at Hethfield in Kent', saying 'you are much wanted at London, and dayly expected and therefore I hope you will not be long absent. Interest calls for your appearance.' For at last a job was in prospect. *Dr Christopher Wren, my deare friend, without my knowledge contrived an employment for me, which he referred to me to consider of it,* Aubrey reported to Anthony Wood. *'Tis this – Mr Ogilby is writing the History of all England: the map is mending already. Now the Doctor told him that if that were all, it would be no very great matter. He was pleased to tell him that he could not meet with a fitter man for that turne than J.A. Now it's true it suites well enough with my Genius; but he is a cunning Scott, and I must deale warily with him, with the advice of my friends. It will be February next before I begin, and then between that and November followeing I must scurry all over England and Wales. The King will give me protection and letters to make enquiries.*

In the end Aubrey's task was limited to a single county only, and he *enter'd upon the Perambulation of the County of Surrey July 1 1673, and left off about the middle of September following.* In those two and a half months, he wandered about the county, noting with equal interest, *here a Ruinated Castle*, there a peculiarly ingenious automatic water closet. *Oatelands*, he says, *was formerly one of the Palaces belonging to the Crown of England. Here was a Fair Park, well stor'd with Deer, but dispark'd by the late Usurpers. In the Park was once a Paddock, with a Standing, where Queen Elizabeth was us'd to shoot with a Cross-Bow.* And in the parish of Godalming, he stumbled upon *a Mannour called Catteshulle, held from the King, as Master of his Concubines.*

His main task was the gathering of inscriptions from the parish churches. *This searching after Antiquities is a wearisome Taske. I wishe I had gonne through all the Church monuments*, he complained. *Though of all studies I take the least delight in this, yet methinkes I am carried on with a kind of divine aestrum: for nobody els hereabout hardly cares for it, but rather makes a scorne of it: But, me thinkes, it shewes a kind of gratitude and good nature, to revive the Memories and memorialls of the pious and charitable benefactors long since dead and gonne.* And a formidable array of inscriptions he has assembled; for, in his day, tombstones were not so stereotyped as they are now. Poems, jokes, advertisements even, found their place on the walls of the churches, but the design was most often to shock:

Thus Youth and Age and all Things pass away,
Thy Turn is now as His was Yesterday;
To morrow shall another take thy room,
The next day He a prey for Worms become,
And ore your dusty Bones shall others tread,
As you now walk and trample on the Dead;
'Till neither Stone nor Memory appear,
That ever you had Birth or Being here.

And life itself, which was so fleeting, was often held up to scorn:

This World to her was but a traged Play,
She came and saw't, dislikt, and pass'd away,

cries the epitaph on a ten-year-old child, Susanna Barford, and another answers:

Wealth, Honour, Bubbles are,
long life a Blast.
That Good this Virgin chose
shall everlast.

But the walls of the churches did not reflect only the melancholy side of seventeenth-century life: its prosperity and pride appeared too. For when they had made their fortunes, the newly enriched London merchants had begun to retire into the country, and the flamboyant tombstones, commemorating *Citizen and Fishmonger* or *Citizen and Haberdasher*, unselfconsciously reflect the prosperity they had attained. But the habits of a lifetime die hard, and some of the epitaphs were used to continue to drum up business even from the grave:

Here Lockyer lyes interred, enough his Name
Speakes one hath few Competitors in Fame;
A Name so great, so gen'ral, it may scorn
Inscriptions, which do vulgar Tombs adorn;
His Vertues and his Pills are so well known,
That Envy can't confine them under Stone;
This Verse is lost, his PILL embalmes him safe
To future Times without an Epitaph.

Another feature of Stuart life which stands out from the tombs is the incredible frequency with which both men and women married. At *Stretham*, Aubrey noted down this epitaph: *Here beneath Sleepe in the Lord Jesus, his gracefull Servantes (Wives of Thomas Hobbes, Esq);* and to have been just once wed was considered sufficiently startling to be recorded on one's tomb: *Dame Martha, 3d Daughter to Robert Wilson, Esqr. onely Wife to Sir Edward Grophy of Brendon in the County of Durham, Bart.* Nor was the humour of this situation missed by the citizens of that time:

That you have layd my Body here,
By that first Side I lov'd so deare,
I thank you Husband, runs one epitaph.
But yet I have another Boone,
When Fates shall come (as come full soon
It will and will not be deny'd)
That you would close my other Side.

Y'have thought it worthy to be Read,
You once were Second to my Bed;
Why may you not like Title have,
To this my Second Bed the Grave.
This Stone will cover us all Three,
And under it we shall be free,
From Love or Hate, or least Distrust
Of Jealousy to vex our Dust;
For here our Bodyes do but wayte
The Summons for their glorious State.

This sentiment would have been most unpopular with the occupant of a tomb at Barnes: *The best of Husbands, John Squier, late Faithful, and (oh! that for so short a Time) Painful Rector of this Parish.* And the following epitaph would have pleased him even less:

Here lies a Traveller old madam Besse,
Honest Charles Hales his wife I guesse.
She was his dear one, wee'le not belie her;
And so's mine too; wou'd she lay by her.

Aubrey's time, however, was not taken up wholly by *this wearisome Taske.* Wandering from church to church, he found time to visit the spas like Epsom, which were just then achieving popularity and were replacing the medieval pilgrimages as an excuse for holidays, and also to stay at the country houses on his way: *I must not forget my noble Friend, Mr Charles Howard's Cottage of Retirement (which he call'd his Castle) which lay in the Middle of a vast Heathy Country, where in the troublesome Times, he withdrew from the wicked World, and enjoy'd himself here, where he had only one Floor, his little Dining Room, a Kitchen, a Chapel and a Laboratory.* And in these places Aubrey heard many anecdotes which he was unable to resist introducing quite irrelevantly into his narrative. At Godalming, for instance, he met *Mr Samuel Speed (the famous and valiant Sea Chaplain and Sailor). In a Poem made by Sir John Birkenhead, on the Sea-fight with the Dutch, he takes Notice of our Vicar in this Manner.*

His Chaplain, he plyed his wonted Work,
He prayed like a Christian, and fought like a Turke,
Crying now for the King, and the Duke of York
With a thump, a thump, thump;

while at Dulwich College he noted that *the Tradition concerning the Occasion of the Foundation runs thus: That Mr Alleyne, being a Tragedian, and one of the Original Actors in the celebrated Shakespeare's Plays, in one of which he play'd a Daemon, with six others, and was in the midst of the Play surpris'd by an Apparition of the Devil, which so work'd on his Fancy, that he made a Vow, which he performed at this Place.* But it was at Croydon that Aubrey stumbled on a piece of information after his own heart. *There was one Oak*, he reports, *in the great Wood call'd Norwood, that had Miselto, a Timber Tree, which was felled about 1657. Some Persons cut this Misselto, for some Apothecaries in London, and sold them a Quantity for Ten Shillings, each time, and left only one Branch remaining for more to sprout out. One fell lame shortly after: Soon after, each of the others lost an Eye, and he that fell'd the Tree, about 1678 (tho' warned of these Misfortunes of the other Men) would not withstanding, adventure to do it, and shortly after broke his Leg; as if the Hamadryades had resolved to take an ample Revenge for the Injury done to that sacred and venerable Oak.* Aubrey mentions elsewhere that *When an Oake is felling (before it falles) it gives a kind of shriekes, or groanes, that may be heard a mile off, as if it were the Genius of the Oake lamenting. I cannot omit here taking Notice*, he continues excitedly, *of the great Misfortunes in the Family of the Earl of Winchelsea, who at Eastwell in Kent, felled down a most curious Grove of Oaks, near his noble Seat, and gave the First Blow with his own Hands. Shortly after, his Countess died in her Bed suddenly, and his eldest Son, the Lord Maidstone, was killed at Sea by a Cannon Bullet. It has been not unusually observed, that to cut Oak-Wood is unfortunate,* Aubrey concludes, and this family should have been particularly wary of flouting any superstition, for had not *My Lady Seymer dreamt, that she found a Nest, with Nine Finches in it. And so many Children she had by the Earl of Winchelsey, whose name is Finch.*

Coming to the end of his Perambulation, Aubrey returned to London, where he noted an interesting sidelight on the Reformation. *Robert de Wharton*, he says, *the last Prior of the Monastery dedicated to St Saviour at Bermondsey, surrendered this Convent into the King's Hands, 1 January 1538. He obtained a pension of £333. 6. 8d. per Annum.* That this generosity could have its disadvantages for the throne, however, is shown by the subtle revenge wreaked by another dispossessed pensioner. *The Last Lady Abbesse of Amesbury was a Kirton: who after the Dissolution married to one Appleton of Hampshire*, Aubrey reports. *She had during her life a Pension from King Henry IIX: she was one hundred and fourty yeares old when she dyed.*

Aubrey finished his tour with a description of the Surrey side of the Thames, directly opposite the City of London. *On the Bank Side were two Bear Gardens*, he says, *the Old and the New, wherein Bears, Bulls, Otters, &c. were kept to be baited by Dogs bred to that Sport, for the Diversion of the Spectators, the Destruction of the innocent Creatures, and the Gratification of a barbarous and savage Temper, which never more displays itself than in shewing a Complacency and Delight in these cruel Spectacles.*

Near this Garden was a Theatre, known by the name of the GLOBE Play-House, to which Beaumont, Fletcher, and Philip Massinger belonged and wrote for; and though the most eminent Place for Tragedies, Comedies, and Interludes, was, because of its Situation, only used in the hot Summer Months.

Not far from this Place were the Asparagus-Gardens, and Pimblico-Path, where were fine walks, cool Arbours, &c. much used by the Citizens of London and their Families, and both mentioned by the Comedians at the Beginning of 1600. 'To walk in Pimblico' became Proverbial for a Man handsomely drest; as these walks were frequented by none else.

Next the Bear-Garden on this Bank was formerly the Bordello, or Stewes, so called from the severall licensed Houses for the Entertainment of lewd Persons, in which were Women prepared for all Comers. The Knights Templars were notable wenchers; for whose convenience and use these Stewes on the Bankside (over against the Temple) were erected and constituted. They were subject to several Laws and Regulations (viz. No single Woman to take Money to lye with any Man, except she lye with him all Night, till the Morrow) and their Manner of Life and priviledged Places received several Confirmations from the Crown, as one in 1345 from King Edward III. In 1506, King Henry VII, for some Time shut up these Houses, which were in Number Eighteen; and not long after renewed their Licence, and reduced them to Twelve; at which Number they continued till their final Suppression by Sound of Trumpet in 1546, by King Henry VIII, whose tender Conscience startled at such scandalous and open Lewdness. The single women that were Retainers to, or Inmates in, these Houses, were Excommunicate, not suffered to enter the Church while alive, or if not reconciled before their Death, prohibited Christian Burial, and were interred in a Peice of Ground called the Single-Women's Church-Yard, set apart for their use only. These Houses were distinguished by several Signs painted on their Fronts, as, a Boar's Head, The Crane, the Cardinal's Hat, the Swan, the Bell, the Crosse-Keys, the Popes Head, and the Gun.

John Evelyn assured the author that 'with incredible satisfaction have I perus'd your Natural History of Surrey, &c; and greatly admire both your Industry in undertaking so profitable a Work, and your Judgement in the several Observations which you have made. It is so useful a Piece, and so obliging that I cannot sufficiently applaud it. Something I would contribute to it, if it were possible; but your Spicilegium is so accurate, that you have left nothing almost for those who come after you.' But now that the tour was over and the rough draft made, the inevitable happened, and eighteen years later Aubrey was to write, *In the Year 1673, it was my Intention to have describ'd the pleasant County of Surrey, which I am sorry I did not compleat.* The notes themselves would probably have disappeared completely, had not Anthony Wood seen them and desired Aubrey to *transcribe them fair, and to preserve them, there being many good Remarks that deserve not to be bury'd in Oblivion. I wish I had done it soon after my Perambulation, whilst the Idea of them was fresh and lively*, Aubrey lamented, *I should then have given it more Spirit. The Papers are like Sybillina Folia. I shall not take the Paines to digest them in better Order (which would require the Drudgery of another Transcribing) and I now set things down tumultuarily, as if tumbled out of a Sack, as they come to my Hand, Mixing Antiquities and Natural Things together, as I have here done them. They will be of some use to such as love Antiquities or Natural History; and on that Account I expose them to the View of the Candid Reader wishing him as much Pleasure in the Perusal of them, as I had in the Seeing of them. Vale.* Despite this hopeful ending, the book was not printed until Aubrey had been dead for twenty-two years, and even then the learned Dr Rawlinson had to put the work into some semblance of order; for it fell to him to collate it, as he said with justifiable exasperation, from two manuscripts 'both wrote with the Author's own Hand, and both huddled together in a very confused and immethodical Order'.

As soon as he had finished his Perambulation, Aubrey found himself surrounded by a multitude of jobs. First, a new edition of Camden's 'Britannia' was foreshadowed and a set of queries relating to it was printed and *considered at several meetings by Christ. Wren, John Hoskyns, R. Hooke, J. Ogilby, John Aubrey, Gregory King.* On top of this, Aubrey was assisting in the production of two more books, Dugdale's 'Monasticon' and the English version of Wood's 'Historia et Antiquitates Universitatis Oxoniensis'. His help with the latter work was so considerable that Anthony Wood, besides acknowledging it handsomely in the book itself, wrote Aubrey a special letter of thanks on its publication. 'I am verie glad that you have satisfied me in so many things and cease not to send into divers parts for further information of other men: I speake in my conscience (for I have told other men of it already) that I have had, and shall have more from you as to these things than all people besides whatsoever. What I have had hitherto besides has been for the most part by mine owne industry and purse.' And all this time Aubrey was busy collecting the anecdotes for Wood's other book 'Athenae Oxoniensis', and the two antiquaries were at the peak of their friendship. 'I am as carefull of your health and wellfare as any friend you have', Wood assured Aubrey, and the latter so delighted in his company that he wished to share him with all his acquaintances. *I sent you 2 lettres by my friend Mr George Ent, together with a bundle of bookes*, Aubrey wrote to Wood in August 1674. *He is a very honest gentleman and his Rhodomantades you will easily pardon.* And George Ent must have been prompt in his delivery of the letter of introduction which Aubrey had given him, for in November Aubrey wrote *I am very glad you two good folke are acquainted; according to my desire.* By March next year, however, matters were very different. *I am exceeding sorry for Mr Ent's strangenesse to you*, Aubrey wrote apologetically to Anthony Wood, *but 'tis confesst his friends must beare with him; and he being cholerique, &c: I read only that paragraph, where he introduced into your company two Boy-bachelors, and upbraided you of dotage.*

In the midst of all this work, moreover, disaster threatened. *1673, die Jovis, St Martin 9h.15+P.M.*, Aubrey noted with excusable exactness, *J.A. arrested by Gardiner, Sergeant, a lusty faire-haired solar Fellow, prowd, insolent, et omnia id genus.* For his financial difficulties were upon him again, and in his plight he enlisted the aid of his friends in the Royal Society to obtain a post for him, for he had been not unhelpful to them. 'They made him their drudge,' said one of his contemporaries, 'for when any curious experiment was to be donne, they would lay the task on him.' He therefore expected great things from *Mr Secretary Wren's indefinite Kindnesse*, and from Lord Brouncker, the President, and by now he was ready to accept any kind of job. *There are peaceable places among Souldiers*, he mused, *and now the navy offices thrive, and a man can nowhere so well hide himself in an office as there, 'cause 'tis out of the way.* This last idea was doubly attractive because another member of the Royal Society, Samuel Pepys, was already firmly entrenched there.

Nothing came of these projects, however, and by 1675 even Aubrey had begun to despair of ever recovering his fortunes in England, and so he turned his gaze towards the New World. But he was quite unable to make up his mind where to settle, for no sooner had Edmund Wyld offered to buy him an estate in New York, than the Earl of Thanet put him off it. 'I perceive that Mr Wild', the Earl had written, 'has a mind to buy some land in New-York, which place you suppose to be a Fine Country. You are the first that ever I heard terme that part a delicious Country. Corne, indeed I heare will grow there, and in the summer they may have fatt Beefe, and Mutton: But in the Winter, which is very long and tedious, They are like the Norvegians, that live upon Salt meates, and Fish, and have such vast Snowes, that they are forced to digge their wayes out of their houses else they will be stiffled.' Having by now thoroughly discouraged poor Aubrey, Lord Thanet continued: 'If he will by land in America, lett it be in the Bermudas, where health abounds, and safety is had, two chiefe things which a wise Man, as he, should looke after, and soe much with my humble service pray let him knowe.' The truth of the matter was that Lord Thanet owned land in Bermuda and had tried before to persuade Aubrey to go out there, and he was not alone in his desire to have so pleasant a companion on his estates. Only the previous year, Aubrey had appalled Anthony Wood by saying, *I am like to be spirited away to*

Jamaica by my Lord Vaughan, who is newly made Governor there, and mighty earnest to have me goe with him, and will look out some employment worth a Gentleman for me: an offer which Sir William Petty strongly advised Aubrey to accept. *In Jamaica,* he told him, *500 pounds gives 100 per annum: take a Chymist with me,* Aubrey noted, *for brandy, suger, etc. and goe halfe with him.*

Cecil Calvert, Lord Baltemore, Absolute Lord and Proprietary of Maryland and Avalon, who had been at Aubrey's college, made yet another offer and that the most tempting. *Now if I would be rich,* Aubrey day-dreamed, *I could be a prince. I could goe into Maryland, which is one of the finest countrys of the world; same climate with France; between Virginia and New England. I can have all the favour of my Lord Baltemore I could wish. His brother is his Lieutenant there; and a very good natured gentleman. Plenty of all things: ground there is 2000 miles westwards. I could be able I believe to carry a colony of rogues; another of ingenious Artificers; and I doubt not one might make a shift to have 5 or 6 ingeniose companions, which is enough.*

But somehow all these plans languished, probably from the very number of offers, and Aubrey made no move. For emigration was still a dangerous business, and as Professor Trevelyan has pointed out, 'more than three quarters of the first colonists died prematurely, succumbing to the miseries of the voyage, or to disease, famine, exposure, and Indian War'. *Sir John Dugdale saith that John Davenport was a Non-Conformist,* Aubrey told Anthony Wood, *and he hath enquired of his Relations, who know nothing of him, if dead or alive, but they believe he is dead. He went over sea; he thinkes to the Barbadoes, or some of these plantations, or to Holland:* whereas actually he was Pastor at New Haven in New England. And the sociable Aubrey was the last person to submit himself to an artificial death like this: if he had to be separated from his friends it would be by the grave, not by the sea. *For why,* he sensibly asked himself, *should I at this time of day, and being of a Monastic humour, make my selfe a slave and roast my self for Wealth?*

The expansion of the English race oversea was a comparatively recent development. Until Elizabeth's reign every English sovereign had tried to make England a great Continental power, and the titles which Mary Tudor accumulated on her marriage to Philip II show how near that ideal came to realization. A book that Aubrey mentions is dedicated *to the most mightie and most puissant Princess Marie, by the grace of God, Queen of England, Spaine, both Sicilies, France, Jerusalem, and Ireland: Defender of the Faith: Archduchesse of Austria: Duchess of Milaine, Burgundie and Brabant: Countesse of Haspurge, Flanders, Tyroll, etc.* But Mary died childless, and left England free to pursue her true destiny. In the next reign, England changed her national weapon, substituting the broadside for the long-bow, and this revolution in fighting tactics, and the consequent advantage in sea warfare which it gave her, caused England to turn towards the Western Ocean and the lands beyond it as her rightful domain. The other powers remained peculiarly blind to the possibilities of these floating batteries, and 'as late as 1511', Professor Trevelyan says, 'the Spaniards fought the Turks at Lepanto, by sea tactics the same as those by which the Greeks had defeated the Persians at Salamis'. The English, however, were fully conscious of the potentialities of the new weapons, and with them they laid the foundations of their sea power and their Empire.

Aubrey's continual hesitations had by now begun to irritate his friends. 'Weare not I a married man,' the Earl of Thanet told him crossly, 'and so consequently tyed by the Legg in England, or at the best my Chain being to reach noe further, then a voyage to Bourbon, or Provence; I would infallibly waite upon that noble kinsman of mine, my Cousin Charles Howard, in that Voyage for the Bermudas.' But Aubrey, though unmarried, was no less firmly 'tyed by the Legg' to London and Oxford, to the Royal Society and to his friends. For he had come now to dread even the suggestion of a job: *if I should have it*, he said on one occasion, *I should be like the weaned child, to leave Mr Wyld: who are inseparable, and dote together till 12 or 1, at night.*

Even when he had himself become a landowner in the colonies, Aubrey could not be tempted out of England. *Captain Poyntz (for service that I did him to the Earle of Pembroke and the Earl of Abingdon) did very kindly make me a Grant of a Thousand acres of Land in the Island of Tobago, anno Domini 1686, Febr. 2d. He advised me to send over people to plant and to gett Subscribers to come in for a share of these 1000 Acres, for 200 Acres would be enough for me.* But still he made no move, even though he knew that *in this delicate Island is Lac lunae (the mother of Silver).*

In the selfsame year, another windfall came his way. *William Penn, Lord Proprietor of Pennsylvania, did ex mero motu et ex gratia speciali* [from a genuine impulse and as a mark of his special favour] *give me a Graunt under his seale, of Six hundred acres in Pennsylvania, without my seeking or dreaming of it. He adviseth me to plant it with French Protestants for seaven yeares gratis and afterwards make them to pay such a Rent. Also he tells me, for 200 Acres ten pounds per annum Rent for ever, after three yeares.* This generous gift was Penn's last attempt to persuade Aubrey to join him in his experiment in the New World. But before making this grant he had tried both persuasion and direct invitations, and among Aubrey's papers is a letter, the intention of which is obvious, in which William Penn paints as alluring a picture as possible of his territory.

Dated 'Philadelphia, 13th of the 4th Month, called June, 1683', it runs as follows: 'Esteemed Friend, We are the wonder of our neighbours as in our coming and numbers, so to our selves in our health, Subsistence and Success: all goes well, blessed by God, and provision we shall have to spare, considerably, in a year or Two, unless very great quantitys of People croud upon us. The Aier, heat and Cold Resemble the heart of France: the Soyls good, the Springs many and delightfull, the fruits, roots, corns and Flesh, as good as I have commonly eaten in Europe, I may say most of them better. Strawberry's ripe in the woods in Aprill, and in the Last Month, Peas, beans, Cherrys, and mulberrys. Much black walnutt, Chesnutt, Cyprus, or white Cedar and mulberry are here. The Sorts of fish in these parts are excellent and numerous. Sturgeon leap day and night that we can hear them a bow Shot from the Rivers in our beds. We have Roasted and pickeled them, and they eat like veal one way, and Sturgeon the other way. Mineral here is great Store, I shall send some suddainly for Tryall. Vines are here in Abundance everywhere, some may be as bigg in the body as a man's thigh. I have begun a Vineyard by a French man of Languedock, and another of Poictou, near Santong. Severall people from other Colonys are retireing hither, as Virginia, Mary Land, New England, Road Island, New York &c: I make it my businesse to Establish vertuous Economy and therefore Sett twice in Councell every week, with good Success, I thank god. My Reception was with all the show of Kindness the rude State of the Country could yield; and after holding the Genrll Assemblys, I am not uneasy to the People. They to express their Love and gratitude gave me an Impost that might be worth 500 pounds per annum, and I returned it to them with as much Creditt. This is our present posture. I am Debtor to thy kindness for two Letters: wether this be pay or no, pray miss not to Continue to yield that Content And Liberality to Thy very True Freind William Penn.'

But to return to 1675. Aubrey, it seems, was once more hopeful of getting a place in England, for in that year Lord Thanet wrote to him: 'I am glad you have soe good an opportunity to make your addresses to that excellent Lady, the Younger Countess Dowager of Pembroke, who if yore Starrs be favourable, may, through the interest of the Dutches of Portsmouth, procure you some good imployment, if not neglected by a wonted trapishness incident in You. The freedom I take in menconing that you will, I hope, easily forgive, since I doe it not by way of check, but by a friendly advertisement to beware of it.' Aubrey's efficiency is well attested by the offers of emigration which he had received, for life was still so hard in the Plantations that no one but a fool, and the first colonists were far from that, would have suggested taking with them anyone who could not more than pull his own weight; and so it must have been his 'wonted trapishness' that caused this job, like all the others, to fall through.

The result was that Aubrey was immediately overwhelmed, yet again, by his financial difficulties (*upon a threatning of my brother to threw me in Gaole*) and in this predicament a strange letter arrived from the Earl of Thanet. 'J. Aubrey,' it began curtly, 'With this you will receive a Protection according to your desire, which when useless returne. I send it you under this provisoe, that yow are my Sollicitor to looke after my business in London; and for your Sallary that is agreed on. My mother hath lent me Thanet house garden, where I intend to fit up two or three chambers for my use when I come to London privately, and intend to stay not long there, one of which as my meniall Servant you may make use of when fitted up, and when it is you shall have notice. I would have you in future to take more time in writing your letters, for your last was soe ill writ that I had a great deale of trouble to read some part of it. Thanet.' Poor Aubrey must have been appalled to receive such a letter from a man whom he had always looked upon as one of his greatest friends, but the next post set his mind at rest. 'Sir,' wrote Lord Thanet then, 'I am not soe ignorant as not to knowe the Stile of myne of the third Instant is much unbefitting to writ unto a Gentleman of youre Birth. The reason why I make my selfe such a proud ill bread Fellowe in it, is the better to disguise the business You lately enjoyned me to doe for You. And on the same Score my Letters in the future shall be, by your permission, as little civill, then in case any thing should be questioned in the account you knowe of, in producing such, writ in soe imperious a manner, will induce all to believe that the business, although very unbefitting, of your belonging to me is noe otherwise then reall. Although this small service can hardly be inrolled under the notion of a Courtesy, yet I assure You 'tis the first Protection I ever gave: although I have been in this nature solicited by many. Weare there anything of moment that I could serve you in,' he concludes, 'you might freely command him who is in great reallity Your most affectionate and humble Servant: Thanet.'

Even armed with this powerful protection, however, Aubrey still felt unsafe (*if my brother should know of it*, he wrote, *he would fall upon me like a Tygre*), and to avoid any possibility of imprisonment for debt, he constantly changed his dwelling. 'Yor lodging,' Lord Thanet said, 'like an inchanted Castle, being never to be found out, I shall in the future direct my Letters to Mr Hookes chamber in Gressam Colledge as you desire.'

Matters had, in fact, become so serious that Aubrey was even toying with the idea of entering the Church. *Fough! The Cassock stinkes; it would be ridiculous*, he had said when the idea first came up two years before, but a letter to Anthony Wood shows that his objections were now taking a more practical turn. *I am stormed by my chiefest freinds afresh, viz. Baron Bertie*,

Sir William Petty, Sir John Hoskyns, Bishop of Sarum, etc. to turne Ecclesiastique; but the King of France growes stronger and stronger, and what if the Roman Religion should come-in againe? Why then, say they, cannot you turne too? You, I say, know well that I am no puritan, nor an enimy to the old Gentleman on the other side of the Alpes. Truly, if I had a good Parsonage of 2 or 300 pounds per annum (as you told me) it would be a shrewd temptation. That Aubrey was unlearned in theology and had a stutter caused not the slightest difficulty, for the standard was not high, and Aubrey himself said of one of the most learned divines, Robert Sanderson, Lord Bishop of Lincoln: *He had no great memorie: I am certain not a sure one: when I was a Fresh-man and heard him read his first Lecture, he was out in the Lord's Prayer.*

The question of his taking any services did not really arise. 'If the heasitation in your speech doth hinder,' one of his friends suggested, 'gett a Parsonage of 4 or 500 pounds per annum, and give a Curat 100 pounds per annum to officiate for you.'

This allotment of one-fifth of the revenue to the incumbent was very generous, for during his perambulation of Surrey, Aubrey had been so greatly shocked to find curates who received only sixteen or twenty pounds a year for doing the whole work of a parish that he was for once moved to anger. *I cannot here pass by without animadvertising on this poor mean Pittance, set aside for the Vicar, while the Lay Impropriator sacrilegiously fattens on the Revenue of the Church, and enjoys what neither in right Reason or Conscience was never design'd for, or belongs to the Laity,* he said. *Could Impropriators be once persuaded to set aside for the Service of the Altar a just Proportion (for the Age is too degenerate to expect a Surrender of the whole to the pious Uses first designed by the Donors) it might, in some measure, atone for the Rapine of their Ancestors.* But so frail is the human conscience that when Aubrey himself had the chance *to fatten on the Revenues of the Church*, he proposed to keep a mere four-fifths of the income for his own use.

This corruption was all the more serious when one considers the overwhelming importance of the Church in those days. 'Though it was an age of reading and writing in the conduct of the ordinary affairs of life,' says Professor Trevelyan, 'very little printed matter came in the way of the less educated. This gave all the greater importance to the sermon, which dealt as freely with political as with religious doctrines.' And though Charles II capped his aphorism about Presbyterianism being no religion for a gentleman by saying that Anglicanism was no religion for a Christian, there was no doubt about its entertainment value. For science had as yet had so little effect on the character of religious belief that the Church felt sure enough of itself to tolerate the kind of jesting that now seems irreverent. 'My Lord, my Lord,' cried one preacher to the dozing Lauderdale, 'you snore so loud, you will wake the King.' And it was with obvious satisfaction that Anthony Wood noted in his Journal: 'August 26, Sunday: a baudy Sermon at S. Marie's in the afternoon.' Though baudiness was a rare delight, jokes were common in church and preachers vied with each other in attracting the largest audiences for their performances. Some preached in their sleep, like that poor man who was so sadly discomfited by James I, and Meredith Lloyd told Aubrey that *when Dr Powell preacht, that a Smoake would issue out of his head; so great agitation of spirit he had*, which led Aubrey to ask in true scientific fashion: *Why might not such accidents heretofore be a Hint to the glories, which the Painters putt about the heads of canonized Saints*. As a final proof of the importance of the sermon in everyday life, Aubrey remarks that *Sir William Croftes, eldest brother to the now Bishop of Hereford, built a house in Leominster, to live there, to heare John Tombes preach*. Nor were the pleasures of religion confined to the actual service. *At Danby Wisk, in the North Riding of Yorkshire*, Aubrey says, *it is the custom for the parishioners, after receiving the Sacrament, to goe from church directly to the ale-house, and there drink together, as a testimony of charity and friendship*.

Aubrey still hesitated, though, very probably because he thought a parsonage was beneath him, for the clergy had not yet reached the pitch of gentility which they were to achieve in the next two centuries; and Clarendon, though he was a tireless supporter of the Anglican Church, noted with disgust that after the Civil War, 'the daughters of noble and illustrious Families bestowed themselves upon divines or other low and unequal matches'.

Aubrey's misgivings about the consequences of a change in religion were already growing out of date, as is shown by the tone in which he himself mentions the queasy consciences of the recent past. *John Barclay was in England tempore regis Jacobi*, he writes solemnly. *He was then an old man, white beard; and wore a hatt and a feather, which gave some severe people offence*. And there can be no doubt at all about the spirit in which he recorded that *in Sir Charles Scarborough's time (he was of Caius College) Dr Batchcroft, the Head of that House, would visit the boyes' Chambers, and see what they were studying; and Charles Scarborough's Genius let him to the Mathematics, and he was wont to be reading of Clavius upon Euclid. The old Dr had found in the title 'e Societate Jesu', and was much scandalized at it. Sayd he, By all meanes leave-off this author, and read Protestant Mathematicall bookes*. And when Aubrey mentioned the death, in 1671, of his friend, *Edward Bagshawe, a Prisoner to Newgate 22 weekes for refusing to take the Oath of Allegiance (he boggled at the word 'willingly' in the oath)* he hastened to add that *he was buried in the fanatique burying-place by the Artillery-ground in Moor-fields*.

The truth of the matter, as Aubrey realized perfectly well, was that the Wars of Religion had proved so disastrous that they had caused a definite reaction in favour of tolerance, and in the very next year after Aubrey had expressed his misgivings, the death penalty for heresy was finally abolished. 'Since their belief of their contrary truths is confessedly a work of divine revelation, why a man should be hanged because it has not yet pleased God to give him his spirit, I confess I am yet to understand', Robert Boyle had written when Parliament was trying to stamp out 'the spreading impostures of the sectaries' during the Commonwealth, and he was driven to the conclusion that 'it is strange that men should rather be quarrelling for a few trifling opinions, wherein they dissent, than to embrace one another for those many fundamental truths wherein they agree'. In this attitude Boyle was soon joined by most educated men, though not all of them would have agreed with Sir William Davenant, who confessed to Aubrey that *his private opinion was that Religion, at last, e.g. a hundred yeares hence, would come to Settlement, and that in a kind of ingeniose Quakerisme*. Aubrey himself was completely in sympathy with this civilized attitude: *George Webb, Bishop of Limrick*, he says, *dyed and was buried in Limerick about two or three daies before the Towne was taken by the Irish, who digged up the body again; it was about 1642. I confess I doe not like that super-zeale in the Canon Lawe, not to let alone there the bodys of Heretiques. It is too inhuman.*

Even Roman Catholicism was coming to be tolerated as a religion, although it was still hated as a political weapon, and Aubrey numbered among his personal friends *Capt. Pugh, a Rubroliterate gent, my acquaintance, a writer and a Poet. Bred up in Societate Jesu; but turn'd out because he was a Captaine in the late Warres. When his studie was searcht, his Orders were there found, and also a letter from the Queen-Mother (Whose Confessor he had sometimes been) to the King, that, if he should fall into any danger of the Lawe, upon sight of that lettre he should obtaine his Majesties pardon.* And very necessary this letter was to prove, for Aubrey continues: *All his bookes were seized on; amongst others his almanac, wherein he entred omnia Caroli II deliramenta et vitia* [all Charles II's follies and vices] *which was carried to the Council board.*

Despite outbursts of popular hysteria, like the one caused by Titus Oates, Catholicism had been looked on with sympathy by the upper classes ever since the Reformation. *When he lay dyeing*, Aubrey writes of his great-grandfather, *he desired them to send for a good man; they thought he meant Dr Goodman, Deane of St Paules, but he meant a Priest, as I have heard my cosen John Madock say. Capt. Pugh was wont to say that civilians (as most learned and Gent.) naturally incline to the Church of Rome; and the Common lawyers, as more ignorant and Clownish, to the church of Geneva.* And Aubrey had heard even

John Tombes, the Baptist, *who seemed to be a very pious and zealous Christian, say (though he was much opposite to the Romish Religion) that truly, for his part, should he see a poor zealous Friar goeing to preach, he should pay him respect.*

This attitude is the more surprising, when one realizes that Catholicism then appeared to the mass of Englishmen in very much the same light as Communism nowadays strikes the Americans. For by its immediate success, Luther's revolution was even more startling than Marx's; and it was no less violent. 'Whoso can strike, smite, strangle, or stab secretly or publicly,' enjoined Luther, 'such wonderful times are these that a prince can better merit Heaven with bloodshed than another with prayer', and in his political thought he showed himself a true German, the first in the lamentable procession of that nation's modern colossi. 'No one need think that the world can be ruled without blood,' he thundered, 'the civil sword shall and must be red and bloody.' Faced with this threat, it was no wonder that the Papacy reacted so violently: and with Christendom in danger, the Church adopted in self-defence a policy which had been outlined a century before by the Bishop of Verden. 'When the Church is threatened,' he had said, 'she is released from the commandments of morality; with unity as the end, the use of every means is sanctified, even cunning, treachery, violence, prison, death. For all order is for the sake of the community, and the individual must be sacrificed to the common good.' In pursuance of this totalitarian policy, the Papacy sided with every enemy of England for the next two hundred years, besides ceaselessly plotting revolution inside the country. Rebellion against a Protestant monarch was held to be the duty of every true Christian, and a procession of Jesuits passed between the Continent and the tightly organized and obedient Catholic families of England to foster this end. It was largely for these political reasons that Catholicism was excluded from all measures of toleration, long after they had been extended to every other sect. And it was because of this political danger that Aubrey was so alarmed when his own sympathies became too widely known. *When I was comeing one time out of All-souls,* he wrote to Anthony Wood in 1688, *the Gape-abouts, at the gate pointed at me, one sayd Romano-Catholicus: I pray God bless you and deliver you from effronts.*

But still Aubrey made no decision, even though he was reduced to such straits by 1677 that he had to sell the last of his possessions, his precious books. That he was still hopeful, however, is shown by a note: *I expect preferment through Sir Leoline Jenkins,* who was not only some *remote kin to* him, but also owed his rise entirely to the efforts of the Aubrey family. When this worthy was made *Principall Secretary of Estate,* therefore, Aubrey was quick to *wayte on him to congratulate for the Honour his Majestie had been pleased to bestowe on him*, but though he reported that *he recieved me with his usual courtesie, and sayd that it had pleased God to rayse-up a poore worme to doe his Majestie humble service*, he showed no sign of wishing to repeat the process and poor Aubrey went unsatisfied. And in 1683 the final blow fell: *It pleased God at Whitsuntide last*, he wrote, *to bereave me of a deare, usefull, and faithfull friend* (*Mr Johnson*) *who had the reversion of the place of Master of the Rolles; who generously, for friendship and neighbourhood sake* (*we were borne the same weeke and within 4 miles and educated together*) *gave me the Graunt to be one of his Secretaries. He was a strong lustie man and died of a malignant fever, infected by the Earl of Abingdons brother, making of his Will. It was such an Opportunity that I shall never have the like again*, Aubrey bewailed. *His death is an extraordinary losse to me, for that had he lived to have been Master of the Rolles I had been one of his Secretarys, worth 600 pounds or more.*

This disappointment seems to have brought Aubrey's age home to him, for he was now in his fifty-eighth year, and we hear no more of prospective jobs. But the habit of a lifetime dies hard, and in his *Faber Fortunae* he continued to jot down, as they occurred to him, ideas for recouping his fortunes. *Put somebody upon marrying the Thames and Avon, and gett a share in it*, he said hopefully, or *Gett a Patent to digge for the Coale that I have discovered in Slyfield-common in Surrey, near Gilford.* In all, sixty-two projects were noted down by him, but it is the last entry that is of the greatest interest, for Aubrey was far in advance of his time when he suggested *a Register Generall of People, Plantations, and Trade of England.* His idea was *to gett an Office for such a Registrie for the collecting the Accounts for the severall particulars following, viz:*

1. Of all the Births, Marriages, Burialls throughout all England: and to see them duly kept: that his Majestie may have a yearly account of the increase and decrease of his subjects.

2. An account of the Harths, and Houses in England: as also of the People, by their Age, Sex, Trade, Titles, and Office.

3. An account of the Trade is to be deduced from the Customs-house Bills, and Prices currant (*upon the Exchange*).

4. A particular account of the Excise, according to the last collections of subfarmes.

5. An account of the severall Payments that have been made by Land-taxes, Polls, Subsidies, Benevolence, and particular Imposts.

6. An account of all the Church Revenues.

7. A Villare Anglicanum, sc. an account of all the Cities, Townes, Villages, great Houses, Rodes, carriages, principal Innes and Families of England, with the Post-stages of the same.

8. An account of all the Scholars in the Universities: and public schooles.

9. An account of all the Prisoners from time to time, and of all Executions.

10. A particular account of the Shipping of England, and all Foreign parts: and the Sea-men resident in each Port.

11. The Prices currant of the principall Commodities in each Market of England.

12. The true number of Irish Cattle imported.

13. The number of Attorneys in each Countie: now: and what heretofore.

The design, he summed up, *is to have Abstracts of all the above particulars in order to compare them one with another, so as to give the King a true State of the Nation at all times.* And for his own advice Aubrey noted: *Be at Sir Leoline Jenkins to gett a Patent to authorize me to use all lawfull waies and means to procure accounts of the premisses, and that all the King's Officers be assistant to me therein gratis. Sir Wm Petty hath promised me, to assist me in it.*

The consideration of these ingenious projects was never allowed to interfere with his writing, however, and when Thomas Hobbes died in 1679, Aubrey, as his oldest friend, immediately set about preparing an informal biography to supplement the more impersonal Latin life which Hobbes had written at his request. *'Tis Religion to performe the Will of the Dead*, Aubrey says in the preface to his book, *which I here dischardge, with my Promise (1667) to my old friend, in setting forth his Life and performing the last Office to my honoured Friend Mr Thomas Hobbes, whom I have had the honour to know from my child-hood, being his Countryman and borne in Malmesbury Hundred and having both the same Schoolmaster.*

Since no body knew so many particulars of his Life as my selfe, Aubrey explained, *he desired that if I survived him, it should be handed to Posterity by my hands, which I declare and avow to do ingenuously and impartially, to prevent misreports and undeceive those who are scandalized.*

One sayes that when a learned man dyes, a great deal of Learning dyes with him. He was a flumen ingenii [a river of talent] *never dry. The recrementa* [*Remaines*] *of so learned a Person are valueable. Amongst innumerable Observables of him which had deserved to be sett downe, thus few (that have not scap't my Memory) I humbly offer to the Present Age and Posterity, tanquam tabulam naufragii* [like fragments of a shipwreck] *and as plankes and lighter thinges swimme, and are preserved, where the more weighty sinke and are lost. And as with the light after Sun-sett – at which time clear; by and by, comes the crepusculum* [dusk]*; then, totall darknes – in like manner is it with matters of Antiquitie. Men thinke, because every body remembers a memorable accident shortly after 'tis donne, 'twill never be forgotten, which for want of registring, at last is drowned in Oblivion; which reflection haz been a hint that by my meanes many Antiquities have been reskued and preserved (I myselfe now inclining to be Ancient) – or else utterly lost and forgotten.*

For that I am so minute, I declare I never intended it, but setting downe in my first draught every particular with purpose, upon review, to cutt off what was superfluous and trivall, I shewed it to some Friends of mine (who also were of Mr Hobbes's acquaintance) whose judgements I much value, who gave their opinion: and 'twas clearly their judgement, to let all stand; for though to soome at present it might appeare too triviall; yet hereafter 'twould not be scorned but passe for Antiquity.

And besides I have Precedents of Reverend writers to plead, who have in some Lives recited things as triviall, nay, the sayings and actions of good woemen. (Dean Fell hath recorded his Mother's jejune sayings and actions, and triviall remarques of Dr Hammond in his life, written by him.)

I am also to beg pardon of the Reader, he concludes, *for two long Digressions, viz. Malmesbury and Gorambery; but this also was advised as the only way to preserve them, and which I have donne for the sake of the Lovers of Antiquity. I hope its novelty and pleasantness will make compensation for its length.*

Anthony Wood, hearing that Aubrey was engaged on this task, was quick to warn him 'to have a care what he does, if he have a hand in it – that he write faire things or else sombody will be upon his back'. For it was on this very subject that Wood himself had come to grief just six years back. *Anno Domini 1674,* Aubrey noted, *Mr Anthony à Wood sett forth an elaborate Worke of eleven yeares study, intituled The History and Antiquities of the University of Oxford, wherin, in every respective Colledge and Hall, he mentions the Writers there educated and what Bookes they wrote. The Dean of Christ-church (Dr John Fell) having Plenipotentiary power of the Presse there, perused every sheet before 'twas to be sent to the presse; and maugre the Author and to his sore displeasure did expunge and inserted what he pleased in Mr Hobbes's life.*

Hereupon, the Author acquaints John Aubrey, Mr Hobbes's correspondent, with all that had passed; J.A. acquaints Mr Hobbes. Mr Hobbes takeing it ill, was resolved to vindicate himselfe in an Epistle to the Author. Accordingly an epistle dated Apr. 20, 1674, was sent to the Author in Manuscript, with an Intention to publish it when the History of Oxford was to be published. Upon the reciept of Mr Hobbes's Epistle by Anthony à Wood, he forthwith repaired, very honestly and without any guile, to the Deane of Christ Church to communicate it to him. The Deane read it over carelessly, and not without scorne, and when he had donne, bid Mr Wood tell Mr Hobbes, that he was an old man, had one foote in the grave, that he should mind his latter end, and not trouble the world any more with his papers, etc., or to that effect.

In the meane time Mr Hobbes meetes with the King in the Pall-mall, in St James's parke; tells him how he had been served by the Deane of Christ Church, and withall desires his Majestie to be pleased to give him leave to vindicate himself. The King seeming to be troubled at the dealing of the Deane, gave Mr Hobbes leave, conditionally that he touch no-body but him who had abused him, neither that he should reflect upon the Universitie.

Mr Hobbes understanding that this Historie would be published at the common Act at Oxon, about 11 July, the said yeare 1674, prints his Epistle at London, and sends downe divers Copies to Oxon, which being dispersed at Coffee-houses and Stationers shops, a Copie forthwith came to the Deane's hands, who upon the reading of it fretted and fumed at it as a most famous Libell, sent for the Author of the History and chid him, telling withall that he had corresponded with his Enemie (Hobbes). The Author replied that surely he had not forgot what he had donne, for he had communicated to him before what Mr Hobbes had sayd and written; whereupon the deane, recollecting himselfe, told him that Hobbes should suddenly heare more of him; so that the last sheete of paper being then in the presse and one leafe thereof being left vacant, the Deane supplied it with his answer.

To this scurrilous Answer the old Gentleman never made any Reply, but slighted the Dr's passion, and forgave it, Aubrey adds. *But 'tis supposed it might be the cause why Mr Hobbes was not afterwards so indulgent, or spared the lesse to speake his Opinion, concerning the Universities and how much their Doctrine and Method had contributed to the late Troubles.*

As Aubrey had been in the very centre of this controversy, he hardly needed reminding of the prejudice that a life of Hobbes was likely to arouse; even the King had to move warily when dealing with him, as Aubrey has recorded. For Hobbes had presented Charles II with his *History of England from 1640 to 1660, which the King has read and likes extreamely, but tells him there is so much Truth in it he dares not license for feare of displeasing the Bishops.* And Aubrey was naturally careful in these matters, as he had in his own family an excellent example of the perils of authorship. *In Queen Elizabeth's time*, he states, *one Penry of Wales wrote a booke called Martin-Mar-prelate. He was hanged for it. He was kin to my great-grandfather.* In Aubrey's own lifetime there had been the case of *George Withers, an easie rymer, and no good Poet whose witt was Satyricall. I thinke the first thing he wrote*, says Aubrey, *was 'Abuses Whipt and stript', for which he was committed to Newgate.* With examples like these before them, authors were very wary about printing their works. *This Earle of Clarendon told me*, says Aubrey, *he has his father's Life written by himselfe, but 'tis not fitt so soon to publish it;* and John Rushworth, the historian, wrote to him, 'I being neere of kin to Sir Thomas Fairfax, the Parliament's Generall, he made choice of me to be his secretary in the Wars, by which means I am beter inabled to give account of military affairs, both in the first Wars and in the second which hapened in the year 1648 – all of which I am now Perfeting the same, but the times favors not the Comeing of it forth.' Aubrey himself had been driven to a similar concealment, for in the year before his death he wrote to Thomas Tanner:

I gave my Holyoake's Dictionary to the Museum. Pray looke on the blanke leaves at the end of it, and you will find a thundering Copie of Verses that Henry Birkhead gave me in the praise of this King of France. Now he is dead, it may be look't-upon.

Whatever the reason was, Aubrey, without reading it over, sent the manuscript of his *Life of Hobbes* to Anthony Wood who, after he had extracted what he wanted, lent it to Richard Blackburne, *a generall scholar, prodigious memorie, sound judgement; but 30 yeares old now*, who promptly produced a Latin biography of the philosopher, founded largely on Aubrey's material; help which he acknowledged merely by including among a list of Hobbes's friends, 'John Aubrey of the Royal Society, Esq., a man born rather for the public good than his own, who chiefly encouraged me to the undertaking this work, and kindly supplied me with materials.'

Unlike Silas Taylor, who, in similar circumstances, ejaculated, *Soe I should have the fflitted milke for my entertainment and he goe away with the creame and all under his own name too*, Aubrey seemed to bear little resentment against the people who so ruthlessly stole the fruit of his labours. *In the meane time I suffer the grasse to be cutt under my feet, for Dr Blackbourne will have all the Glory*, Aubrey grumbled, but he busied himself, none the less, with collecting laudatory verses with which to preface Blackburne's edition. *I never yet knew a witt (unless he were a piece of an Antiquary) write a proper Epitaph, but have the reader ignorant, what countreyman, &c: only tickles his ears with Elogies*, Aubrey wrote to Anthony Wood in 1680. *I have engaged the Earle of Dorset, my Lord John Vaughan, to write verses, and they will engage my Lord Mowgrave, and the Earl of Rochester. I first engaged Mr Dreyden; and Mr Waller, who is willing he tells me (for they were old acquaintances) but he is something afrayd of the Ecclesiastiques.*

Towards Anthony Wood, Aubrey felt nothing but gratitude. *'Twill be a pretty thing and I am glad you putt me on it*, he wrote benevolently about the Brief Lives, *I doe it playingly:* and later he said, *my Memoires of Lives is now a booke of 2 quires, close written: and after I had begun it I had such an impulse in my spirit that I could not be at quiet till I had donne it. I beleeve never any in England were delivered so faithfully and with so good authority.* For Aubrey had become even more enthralled with this work since Anthony Wood had cunningly suggested to him that he might win fame by publishing his own version of the Lives at a later date: and it must have been encouraging, with this idea in mind, to see into what a lamentably pompous style Wood was translating his notes. Aubrey had written of Thomas Chaloner, *He was as far from a Puritan as the East from the West. He was of the Naturall Religion, and of Henry Martyn's Gang, and one who loved to enjoy the pleasures of this life:* whereas Wood's heavy-handed and self-righteous version ran, 'This Thomas Chaloner, who was as far from being a puritan or a presbyterian as the east is from the west, for he was a boon companion, was of Henry Martin's gang, was of the natural religion, and loved to enjoy the comfortable importances of this life, without any regard of laying up for a wet day, which at last he wanted.' Where Wood pointed a moral, Aubrey adorned a tale.

On Ascension Day, 1680, therefore, Aubrey sent the Minutes of his Lives to Anthony Wood at Oxford and for the next twelve years the volumes shuttled to and fro between them, growing ever more involved and more untidy. And now Aubrey felt free to work out a notion which he had first conceived in 1669: *An Idea of Education of Young Gentlemen, viz. From the Age of 9 or ten yeares, till 17, or 18;* and his views on this subject were so far in advance of his age, that it was not until this century that they were even given a trial.

The basic idea of his school he outlined as follows: *Plato saies, that the Education of Children is the Foundation of Government: it will follow, that the Education of the Nobless must be the Pillars and Ornaments of it: they are the Atlasses that beare-up the weight of it. 'Tis true, there is an ample provision made in both our Universities for the Education of Clerkes: but not care hath yet been taken for the right breeding-up of Gentlemen of Qualitie.*

The methods by which Aubrey wished to train the gentlemen of England for their task of government were astonishingly liberal. *The common way of teaching is so long, tedious, and praeposterous*, he said, *that it breakes the spirit of the fine tender ingeniose youths and causes 'em perfectly to hate learning*, and he attacked particularly *the ordinary schoolmasters' tyrannicall beating and dispiriting of children which many tender ingeniose children doe never recover again. Dr Busby*, he admits, *hath made a number of good Scholars, but I have heard several of his Scholars affirme, that he hath marred by his severity more than he hath made:* an awful accusation when one considers that, during his reign at Westminster, Busby not only produced the greatest architect of the age Sir Christopher Wren, the greatest poet John Dryden and the greatest philosopher John Locke, but that his pupils so monopolized the highest positions in the Church that the Bishop of Rochester thanked God 'that he was a Bishop although not a Westminster'. Aubrey nevertheless held to his doctrine that *Youth should be indulged as to all lawfull Pleasures*, and two hundred years before its time he produced the theory that *'Tis a very ill thing to cross children; it makes them ill-natured; wherefore let them not be cross'd in things indifferent.*

Aubrey had adopted the revolutionary idea that *a Schoole should be indeed the house of play and pleasure; and not of feare and bondage*, and his aim was to get his pupils to take *so great a delight in their Studies, that they would learn as fast as one could teach them*. He therefore decided *never to overcloude their tender memories: but let them, when they begin to be weary, turn the Globes and play with them.* Nor were more strenuous forms of exercise ignored. *Young men doe much want Ayring,* he thought, *especially those of a sulphurous complexion, they are apt to kindle a Feaver without it;* and so riding tours round the countryside were encouraged, and these expeditions had the added advantage of serving discipline as well as health. For the withdrawal of permission to share in these jaunts would serve as an adequate punishment for any breach of the lax discipline. For more serious misdemeanours, *Not to eat Tarts, and Fruit, or drinke Wine would be a penance,* Aubrey thought, but he had some doubts about the safety of this latter method: *It is observed, that those children who are too severely prohibited to drink wine, doe generally prove Drunkards,* besides which it was acknowledged to be *a good medicine against the Wormes.* Scrupulous in observing his rule *the scholars not to be beaten about the head,* he decided at last that thumb-screws would have to be employed to discourage the most serious naughtiness. From the health point of view, Aubrey also set special store in letting *the children sleep-out their full Sleep. No scholar to rise too early (especially in Winter),* runs one rule, *because it checks their Perspiration and so, dulls them; and it stints their growth. Some friends of mine,* he added, *impute their unluckiness to their too early rising at Westminster.* And in the garden, Aubrey intended to provide his pupils with *a noble Bassin to learn the Art of Swimming, and wash themselves in warme weather.*

His friend, Dr Ezreel Tonge (ever famous as *the inventor of the Way of teaching Children to write a good hand in twenty dayes' time, by writing over with black Inke, Copies printed from Copper-plates in red Inke, by which meanes Boyes learn to admiration) had,* according to Aubrey, *an excellent schoole, and followed precisely the Jesuites method of teaching; and boyes did profit wonderfully, as needes they must, by that method.* In imitation of his friend, therefore, Aubrey decided to limit his instruction to modern subjects, such as *Cookery, Chemistry, Cards (They may have a Banke for wine, of the money that is wonne at play every night), Merchants Accompts, the Mathematicks,* and *Dancing,* trusting that his pupils would be unconsciously forced into learning Latin by *the Ten or* 12 *Swisse, or Dutch, or Scotish Boyes of about fifteene years old (French boies will be naught,* he added curtly, *like the shearing of Hogges they make a great crie and little wool: their mindes do chiefly run on the propagation of their race)* whom he intended to educate free, in return for a promise to restrict their conversation to Latin. And the cook, the scullions, and the porter, *a lusty young Swiss with a long sword,* were likewise pledged to speak Latin only.

By these means, he hoped, the boys would pick up the classical tongues despite themselves, and another of his devices to this end was borrowed direct from Dr Tonge's school, *where was a long gallery, and he had severall printed heads of Caesar's, &c; verbes under such a head, governed by a Dative case;*

under another an Ablative. The boyes had it as readie as could be. Aubrey was convinced of the value of this pictorial method of education, even in later life: *Sir Ralph Hopton (since L*[d]*) was wont to say that he learn't more Philosophy once from a painted cloath in an Alehouse then in all the bookes he had read: sc.*

> *Never lament or make any mone*
> *For either ther's Remedy, or there is none.*

Another rule laid it down that *the Scholars were Not to be dressed à la mode till Dinner-time*, for Aubrey had been acutely aware that he was working against time ever since his friend, Mr J. Ward, had told him that he had found *by experience, that the only time of Learning is from nine to sixteen, afterwards Cupid beginns to Tyrannize.* And in case anyone should misunderstand exactly what Mr Ward meant by that, Aubrey mentioned that *Mr Hobbes told me, that G. Duke of Buckingham had at Paris when he was about twenty yeares old, desired Him to reade Geometrie to him: but his Grace had great naturall parts, and quicknesse of witt; Mr Hobbes read, and his Grace did not apprehend, which Mr Hobbes wondered at: at last, Mr Hobbes observed that his Grace was at mastrupation (his hand in his Codpiece). This is a very improper age; for that reason for learning.*

Aubrey was under no illusion about the opposition which his plan would meet, nor from what direction that opposition would come, for the book concludes: *But now (me thinkes) I see a black Squadron marching from Oxford led up by a Crosier Staffe (Jo. Fell, B*[p]*. Oxon) to discomfit this pretty Flock: and so my pleasing Dream*

is at an
END.

Although Aubrey headed this work, *A Private Essay only*, he took more trouble over it after its completion than over any of his other books. Not only did he choose the sites where he wished his schools to be, for he considered that half a dozen establishments would cover the needs of the whole country, but he continued for several years to make strenuous efforts to find a patron, or rather six patrons, who would put his schemes into practice. *Sir*, he wrote to Anthony Henley in 1694, *I hope this Child of mine will be presented to you in a lucky houre. I am much joy'd to heare that excellent character you give of the Earl of Leicester: He may be a meanes to promote this Designe: the Earl of Pembroke hath read it all over, and excerpted some things: he approves of it: but is not active. I have some hopes that the Marquess of Worcester (to whom my brother is well known) may propagate this Design in Wales: I am not over confident of my Lord Weymouth.* Unfortunately, however, he had overestimated the public spirit of all the other peers in whom he had placed such high hopes: for although they all admired the design, none took any practical steps to carry it out. *God's will be done*, was Aubrey's reaction. *If the Nobless have a mind to have their Children be put into the Clergie's pockets, much good may it do 'em.* And at last even he despaired of seeing his *Idea* take practical shape: *But I forsee that it will lie coffined up, and nobody have that Generosity to set affoote this noble Designe.*

Deare Friend, Aubrey wrote to Anthony Wood on 11 May 1686. *In January last, after a very great conflict of affliction, I rowsed up my spirits and writt a lettre to you, and immediately fell to worke with my Naturall History of Wilts, which I had just donne April 21, rough hewn, and finished the last chapter, when at the evening I heard of the sad news of the Decease of my deare and ever honoured mother: who died at Chalke, but my brother has buried her with my father in North Wilts (Kingston S. Michael). My head has been a fountain of teares, and this is the first lettre (except of businesse) that I have writt since my Griefe. I am now involved in a great deale of trouble, and Chalke must be sold; but I hope to make some reservations for my selfe, and I hope before I dye to be able to make an honourable present to you: for I am for the Spaniards way; sc. not to make my soule my Executor. I shall shortly goe to Chalke to see how matters goe there: and as soon as I can pick up a little money intend to see you at Oxon, and thinke the time very long till I am with you. God blesse you and comfort me, that I may but live to finish and publish my papers.*

Tuissimus, J.A.

Let me desire you to write to me by the next post, to let me know how you doe: yor letter will be a Cordial to me: therefore pray fail not. Fabian Philips is yours. I am sorry for the losse of our facetious friend Parson Hodges. I must make hast with my papers, for I am now 60.

Deborah Aubrey was 15 yeares old and as much as from January to June when she was married, John Aubrey says, and as he was her first child, there was less difference in years between them than there was between Aubrey and his brother, William. It was no wonder, therefore, that his mother's death brought home to him so forcibly his own age and the perilous condition of his works. *His Writings had the usual fate of those not printed in the Author's life-time*, Aubrey had written many years before about Nicholas Hill, and his *Minutes of Lives* are full of similar references. *George Herbert writt a folio in Latin*, he noted, *which because the Parson of Hineham could not read, his widowe condemned to the uses of good houswifry*, and he mentioned many other manuscripts besides which had *wrapt Herings by this time* or had *been putt under Pyes*. The examples were so unending: *George Sandys, Poet, had something in Divinity ready for the presse, which his niece my Lady Wyat lost in the Warres – the title of it shee does not remember:* and the Fire of London had caused such widespread destruction that even plagiarism was excusable in that age. *'Tis certaine*, Aubrey says, *that John Wallis is a person of reall worth, and may stand very gloriously upon his owne basis, and need not be beholding to any man for Fame, yet he is so extremely greedy of glorie, that he steales feathers from others to adorne his own cap; e.g. he lies at watch, at Sir Christopher Wren's discourse, Mr Robert Hooke's, Dr William Holder, &c; putts downe their notions in his Note booke, and then prints it, without owneing the Authors. This frequently, of which they complain. But though he does an injury to the Inventors, he does good to Learning, in publishing such curious notions, which the author (especially Sir Christopher Wren) might never have the leisure to write of himselfe.*

There was one example, however, which appalled Aubrey by its similarity in every detail to his own case. *One Mr Gerard of Castle Carey in Somerset, collected the Antiquities of that county, Dorset, and that of Devon,* he said, *which I cannot for my life retrive. His Executor had them, whose Estate was seized for debt; and they utterly lost.* And so, before setting out for Wiltshire to settle his mother's affairs, Aubrey made an elaborate will, although he had nothing to leave except instructions as to the fate of his manuscripts, and in it he charged Robert Hooke with the task of preparing his Wiltshire papers for the press. For to the men of the seventeenth century, their reputation after death was a matter of the utmost concern, and though few of them went so far as Machiavelli in believing that fame was the only immortality of which the individual was capable, the desire for a good and a lasting reputation was so general that Aubrey recorded with astonishment the reply Charles I made when Mr Ross endeavoured to persuade him to pay for the engraving of a manuscript by saying that *it would appeare glorious in historie after his Majestie's death. Pish, sayd He, I care not what they say of me in History when I am dead.*

Aubrey, however, cared most particularly and he eagerly accepted Elias Ashmole's suggestion that he should entrust his manuscripts to the newly founded Ashmolean Museum at Oxford; an idea with which his friends were not all in favour, as the following letter shows. *Mr Wood,* Aubrey begun coldly, *Last Teusday I went to see Mr Ashmole, whom I found ill. He lately received a letter from Dr Plot, about the things that I sent to Oxford; and says that he desired you to send to the Museum, but you denyed it, and would not let him see the Catalogue, that I sent. Mr Ashmole desired to speake with me about it, and is most outragiously angry; and charg'd me to write to you as soon as I could and to order you to putt the Box in the Museum; for he looks upon you as a Papist, and sayeth so does the whole Universitie, and there was present at this angry fitt of his, an Oxford scholar (I thinke his Kinsman) who owned, what Mr Ashmole sayd. Mr Ashmole saies that now there is such care and good method taken, that the Books in the Museum are more safe than those in the Librarie, or Archives; and he says he expects to heare of your being plunder'd, and papers burnt, as at the Spanish Ambassador's, at Wild house, where were burnt MSS and Antiquities invaluable, such as are not left in the world: and he further bids me tell you, that if you shall refuse to deliver the things sent downe by me, to Oxford, that he will never looke on you as Friend, and will never give a farthing more to the University of Oxford. Since therefore it is so ordered, I do desire and appoint you to send my Box forthwith (you may keep the Key) for feare that all my MSS &c. should be rifled by the Mobile (which God forbid, but Mr E. Ashmole and I doe much feare) besides my Guift will make a better shew, in the Museum; than when dispersed in 2 places. I have severall other MSS of my own and Mr Mercator's. That of mine that I most value is my Idea of Education of Young Gentlemen, which is in a Box as big as that sent to you; with choice Grammaticall bookes, ancient and modern, for the Informator to peruse and study. If I should die here, they will be lost or seized upon by Mr Kent's son: if I send them to the Museum, the Tutors would burn it, for it crosses their Interest exceedingly: if in your hands when you die your Nephew will stop gunnes with them. I intended the Earl of Abingdon, but he has now other Fish to fry. I think the Earl of Pembroke would do best, but had I money to pay an Amanuensis, I would leave a Copie in the hands of each of those 2 peeres. Tuissimus, J. Aubrey.*

All his works, therefore, were deposited in the Ashmolean, except for *The Minutes of Lives*, which Anthony Wood still kept, and *The Remaines of Gentilisme and Judaisme*, which Aubrey had finished that very year, and had dedicated *To His ever honoured Friend Edmund Wylde, Esqr as a small token of ancient Friendship*. As if to repay Aubrey for his sharpness to Anthony Wood, his bequest was no sooner settled than the museum was robbed, and there vanished among other things his *Picture in miniature, by Mr S. Cowper (which at an auction yields 20 Guineas) and Archbishop Bancroft's, by Hillyard, the famous Illuminer in Q. Elizabeth's time*. But his papers were untouched.

It was only fair that Aubrey should see his life-work settled safely before his death, for he had expended a great deal of energy in rescuing other people's libraries from dispersal. In 1683, he had attempted to get the Royal Society or the University of Oxford to purchase the mathematical collections of his old friend Sir Jonas Moore. Getting no response from either of these bodies, he had approached Isaac Newton, but with no more success, for Newton pointed out that Trinity College had incurred such heavy charges over its new buildings that the purchase was out of the question for them, and the University of Cambridge was likely to prove no better prospect, 'their chest being at present very low'.

Nor was it books alone that roused the easygoing Aubrey to such endeavours. When the havoc of the Civil War was succeeded by the disastrous Fire of London, he redoubled his efforts to preserve the dwindling number of antiquities that still remained. *'Tis pitty that in noblemen's galleries, the names are not writt on or behind the pictures,* he thought, and therefore in his life of Milton he made this note: *Write his name in red letters on his Pictures, with his widowe, to preserve.* In another case, he tried to kill two birds with one stone and failed in both attempts: *Mr Inigo Jones (Architect to King James I, and to King Charles I) was wont to wayte upon their Majesties when they went their Progress,* he said. *He design'd admirably well: and in these Progresses he drew a great many Prospects of the old Gothick, or ancient Castles, in sheetes of paper. He bought the Mannour of Burley neer Glastonbury (once belonging to it; but very unfortunate to the late Possessors) where in a large Parlour, I saw these Draughts of Castles: they did furnish the Roome round; one of them was falln downe, and in a childs hands, which I rescued: and hung it up my selfe. I have often intimated this to our Gravers to make them publick: but I cannot perswade them to it. But had the ingeniose Mr Wenceslaus Hollar lived, he would have donne it, upon my request. Of these once stately Castles, there is not now a stone left upon a stone.* In many other cases, too, Aubrey came too late to do anything but record the damage already done. *In the Abbey-church of Dowre are two remaynders of mayled and cross-legged monuments,* he reported, *one sayd to be of a Lord Chandois, th'other, the Lord of Eywas-lacy. A little before I sawe them a Mower had taken one of the armes to whett his syth.* This ignorant destruction was bad enough, but the thoughtlessness of the educated classes was even harder to bear: *Franciscus Linus made the Jesuits College at Liège the finest Dialls in the World. The like dialls he made (which resemble something of Candlesticks) in the garden at Whitehall, which were one night, Anno Domini 1674, broken all to pieces (for they were of glasse spheres) by the Earl of Rochester, Lord Buckhurst, Fleetwood Shephard, etc. comeing in from their Revells. What, said the Earl of Rochester, doest thou stand heer to marke time? Dash they fell to worke. Ther was a watchman alwayes stood there to secure it.*

Aubrey was no blind admirer of old things, however, for he said, *the old windowes of the Church of Clerken-well are of great antiquitie, as appears by their shape, and their uglinesse,* and he recorded with equal care vanishing legends: *The tradition is that the Bell of Lincoln's-Inne was brought from Cales* [Cadiz], *tempore Reginae Elizabethae, plundered in the expedition under the Earl of Essex:* and passing curiosities: *Mr Emanuel Decretz (Serjeant Painter to King Charles 1st) told me in 1649, that the Catafalco of King James at his funerall (which is a kind of Bed of State, erected in Westminster Abbey, as Robert Earl of Essex had, Oliver Cromwell, and General Monke) was very ingeniosely designed by Mr Inigo Jones, and that he made the 4 heades of the Cariatides (which bore up the Canopie) of playster of Paris, and made the drapery of them of white Callico, which was very handsome and very cheap, and shewed as well as if they had been cutt out of white marble.* Even the changes in the language were recorded by him, for his book *Villare Anglicanum* is subtitled: *Derivation of English Place names – A Collection of so many British words, as come to my memorie, that are endemized, and now current English: and have escaped the fury of the Saxon Conquest. How these curiosities would be quite forgott,* he added, *did not such idle fellowes as I am putt them downe!*

Now that his works were at last in safe custody, Aubrey set about revising them *so as to speed them to the Presse;* but as his revision consisted entirely of adding more haphazard notes, they came no nearer to publication until, in 1692, Thomas Tanner, afterwards Bishop of St Asaph, promised to arrange *The Naturall Historie of Wiltshire* for the printer. 'I shall go towards Lavington on Saturday next', the nineteen-year-old Tanner wrote to him. 'My principal business is to drive on our Common design, viz. the *Antiquities of Wiltshire,* which I hope will find encouragement. If it does not I will never undertake anything more for the publick. I am heartily sorry your *Monumenta* meets with no better incouragement in this age, but I like it never the worse for that. It hath been the ill fortune of the best books that they have not borne the Charges of their own impression. It is well known that no Bookseller would give Sir Henry Spelman five pounds in books for his incomparable Glossary, and you know that Sir Walter Raleigh burnt the latter part of his admirable History of the World, because the former had undone the printer. The Christian Scriptures and the Monasticon, volumes now worth old Gold, had never been printed had not the former been carried on by a publick fund, the other by the sole charges of the Editor. I hope to live to see the *Monumenta Britannica* in as good vogue as the best of them.' But though Tanner was to live for another forty years, he was not even to see Aubrey's book in print, let alone in vogue. For without a patron to pay for the publishing, few works came out in those days; and to have a patron often meant interference, as Anthony Wood had found to his cost in his dealings with John Fell. Nor was this the only disadvantage to be encountered, for Aubrey mentions the case of *Thomas Goodwyn, who was a generall Scholar, and had a delicate Witt; was a great Historian, and an excellent Poet. The Journey into France, crept in Bishop Corbet's poems, was made by him; by the same token it made him misse of preferment at Court, Mary the Queen-mother remembring how he had abused her brother, the King of France; which made him to accept of the place at Ludlowe, out of view of the World.* Aubrey, however, was to enjoy neither the advantages nor the disadvantages of the system, and his works remained unpublished for all the world as if he had lived in the days *when the Price of Writing of Manuscripts, before the use of Printing, was xxx shillings per quire.*

The *Monumenta Britannica,* which Tanner mentioned, had had its origin in the command given by Charles II to print an account of Avebury, but Aubrey had proceeded so slowly with the work and had added so many facts about other antiquities that five separate dedications of the book were made, as death took away one hoped-for patron after another, before it even got near the press. Now, however, 'Proposals for Printing Monumenta Britannica Written by Mr John Aubrey, Fellow of the Royal Society' were issued at long last. 'The whole Work will consist of about 160 Sheets, and will be Printed in Folio with abundance of Cuts' ran the advertisement, which gave the price as eighteen shillings, nine down and nine on delivery, and assured the public 'that the Booke will be printed by Candlemas next'. *In the Declension of the Roman Empire*, runs a sample page on the back of the prospectus, *the Britains being drawn away to defend other Provinces, their own Country lay open to the Incursion of the Invaders: In that miserable state of things, the Learned Men fled for Refuge into Ireland; upon which occasion Learning did flourish there a long time; but the memory of things* here *became obliterated. Books perish'd, and Tradition was forgot. The Saxon Conquerors ascribed Works great and strange to the Devil, or some Giants, and handed down to us only Fables. 'Twas in that Deluge of History, the Account of these British Monuments utterly perished; the Discovery whereof I do here endeavour (for want of written Record) to work out and restore after a kind of Algebraical Method, by compering them that I have seen, one with another and reducing them to a kind of Aequation: to (being but an ill Orator my self) to make the Stones give Evidence for themselves.* Although this extract sounds enticing, the plan seems to have languished, for the book never appeared. Edmund Gibson, who had seen the manuscript, probably gave the true reason, when he wrote to Thomas Tanner some years later. 'There is not in Mr Aubrey's books what I had expected', he said then. 'The accounts of things are so broken and short, the parts so much disordered, and the whole such a mere Rhapsody, that I cannot but wonder how that poor man could entertain any thoughts of a present Impression. They will be serviceable enough, however,' he admits, 'especially in Counties where Intelligence falls short; but in the rest, we shall not make much use of them.'

In the same year, 1692, another letter passed between John Aubrey and Anthony Wood. *Accidentally I spoke with Mr Gadbury, who is extremely incens't against you*, it ran. *He sayes that you have printed lyes concerning him.* For the first volume of 'Athenae Oxoniensis' had now appeared in London and in it Wood had raked up an old scandal about the astrologer's father, who, according to Aubrey, *when he was a taylor, takes the measure of a young Lady for a gowne, and clappes up a match. He tells me what you have wrote*, Aubrey's letter continues, *and I am sorry for it, for he was civil to you, and was an ingeniose loyall Person.* In October of the same year he wrote to Wood again: *I shewed your letter to Mr Gadbury, wherin you tell him that what he desires should be amended as to Himselfe shall be donne in the Appendix to be printed: but he huff't and pish't, saying that your Copies are flown abroad and the Scandalls are irrevocable and that he will have a fling at you in Print to vindicate himselfe.* But Wood remained blind to the indiscretion he had committed. 'I wonder at nothing more,' he said, 'then that Mr Gadbury should take it amiss of those things that I say of him: for whereas the generalitie of scholars did formerly take him to have been bred an Academician because he was borne at Oxon, and so, consequently, not to be much admired, now their eyes being opened and knowing that his education hath been mechanical they esteeme him a Prodigie of Parts and therefore are much desirous that his picture may hang in the public gallery at the Schooles.' This storm was but a foretaste of what was to follow, for with the appearance of Wood's second volume, disaster finally overwhelmed the long collaboration between the two antiquaries.

Now that Anthony Wood's work was published, Aubrey received back from him *The Minutes of Lives*, only to find that the manuscript had been mutilated. *INGRATITUDE*, wrote poor Aubrey on the first of the remaining pages. *This part the second, Mr Wood haz gelded from page 1 to page 44 and other pages too are wanting wherein are contained Truths, but such as I entrusted no body with the sight of, but himselfe: whom I thought I might have entrusted with my Life. There are severall papers that may cutt my throate. I find too late Memento diffidere* [Take care to distrust] *was a Saying worthy one of the Sages. He hath also embezilled the Index of it – quod N.B. It was stitch't up when I sent it to him. Novemb. 29, 1692.* Aubrey's anxiety was well founded: for Anthony Wood had cut out the lives of James I and the Duke of Monmouth amongst others, and his behaviour to his devoted assistant had been so bitter of late that Aubrey did well to have doubts about the safety of his throat.

The reason for Wood's unforgivable conduct soon became apparent, however, for the second volume of 'Athenae Oxoniensis' had no sooner appeared than he found himself surrounded by threats. 'Mr Henry Cruttenden told me', he confided to his Journal, 'that in New Coll. common-chamber severall of their fellowes said that I had abused their relations and that when dark nights come they would beat me.' Nor was this the worst, for a rumour floated down from London 'that the Presbyterians will raise a tax (two hundred thousand pounds) to give to the King that he will hang me'. For in his book Wood had not scrupled to tell the truth, particularly if it was unpleasant, and as ill luck would have it, it was a remark that he had copied from Aubrey that precipitated the storm. In his life of Judge Jenkins, Wood had foolishly repeated Aubrey's story about Lord Chancellor Hyde's corruption, and though Hyde had been banished for these very practices twenty-eight years before and had been dead for twenty years, his son, Lord Clarendon, issued a writ against Anthony Wood for libel.

It was this affair that finally changed Wood's attitude towards John Aubrey. Hearne has reported the humorous relationship of their early friendship: 'Anthony used to say of him, when he was at the same time in company: Look, yonder goes such a one, who can tell you such and such stories, and I'le warrant Mr Aubrey will break his neck downstairs rather than miss him.' This amiable attitude was now to disappear for ever and Aubrey became in Wood's view 'roving and magotie-headed, and sometimes little better than crased'.

One thing has always been said, though, in Anthony Wood's favour; that he confined his accusations of Aubrey to his Journal and never mentioned in court the source of the libellous statement, even though his whole defence rested on the fact that 'those things that are excepted against are not of the author's invention but what he found in letters sent to him from persons of knowne reputation, of which he is ready at any time to take his oath in any court of judicature. Which letters being at larg written, he for his own security did curtaile and contract them to what they now are without mentioning the name of the person. Yet notwithstanding this they are excepted against.' And notwithstanding this, Anthony Wood was fined forty pounds, was expelled from the University and, on the last day of July 1693, saw his book publicly burnt at Oxford by the common hangman.

But hidden amongst Tanner's papers there lies a letter that passed between Aubrey and Anthony Wood in December 1692. *All the last week I was ill*, it ran, *but on sunday I went to my Lord Abingdon, who saluted me with a sad aspect, and a sadder Intimation: sc. that he was exceedingly grieved for the Trouble that was comeing upon me: I was mightily surprized: sayd he, the Earl of Clarendon hath told me, that Mr Wood hath confessed to him, that he had the Libell from me: as also the other informations. I do admire that you should deale so unkindly with me, that have been so faithfull a friend to serve you ever since 1665, as to doe so by me. The Libell was printed, and not uncommon: Could not you have sayd, that you bought it: or had it of George Ent: or some body that is dead – To be short, my Lord is resolved to ruine me: pray let me know by the next post, what 'tis that you have donne against me, that I may be the better enabled to make my Defences. My heart is ready to breake: thus hoping to hear from you I rest, Yours J. Aubrey.* But no reply came: no reply for over eighteen months: and this biographer is confirmed in his opinion of Anthony Wood's treachery.

Early next year, Aubrey deposited his precious *Lives* in the Ashmolean, with special instructions that Anthony Wood was never to know about the bequest, for he still feared the vindictiveness of his late friend. But even so, his kindness of heart did not allow him to upbraid Wood for his shabby treatment of the *Lives* until over a year after the debacle which he had unwittingly caused; and then he took the edge off his complaint by suggesting the resumption of their friendship. *Mr Wood*, he wrote from Boarstall on 2 September 1694, *I thought I should have heard from you ere this time. I have been ill ever since I came from Oxford, till within these 5 days, of a Surfeit of Peaches, etc; so that I was faine to send to Kit White for a good Lusty Vomit. I could not eat a bitt of flesh for six days, but abstinence hath pretty well settled me again. Your unkindnes and choleric humour was a great addition to my ilnes. You know I have allwayes loved you, and never thought I tooke paines enough to serve you: and I was told by severall at Oxford, and so the last yeare, that you can never afford me a good word. You have cutt out a matter of 40 pages out of one of my volumnes, as also the Index: (Was ever any body so unkind?) and I remember you told me comeing from Hedington, that there were some things in it that would cutt my throat. I thought you so deare a friend that I might have entrusted my life in your hands, and now your unkindnes doth almost break my heart.* Having made this complaint, Aubrey was unable to carry his resentment any farther. *I would have you come the next week*, he continued, *for a fortnight hence Sir John Aubrey goes into Glamorganshire, and will have me with him. You cannot imagine how much your unkindnes vext and discomposed me. So God bless you. Tuissimus, J.A. I would have you come hither as early as you can*, Aubrey added in post-script, *because of perusing the MS and seeing the gardens, for the afternoon will be taken up with good fellowship.*

This letter at last stirred Anthony Wood into answering Aubrey's previous accusation. 'I must tell you', he wrote, 'that in your letter dated 3 Dec. 1692 you go forward to plague and disturb my thoughts without examination. At length when you came to towne an yeare after you told me it was a Banter. Now I appeal to all the world whither this was not an unworthy thing that you did never let me know it by letter to comfort my thoughts, only by word of mouth a yeare after and that by accident.' After which Anthony Wood upbraids Aubrey on many counts, referring again and again to 'your most wicked and silly letter', and proving himself to have been so kindly and faithful a friend that this biographer feels bound to reject Wood's version of the affair. Having Aubrey at a disadvantage, however, Wood seized the opportunity to bring up every grievance that had ever occurred to him. Aubrey had deserted him in his trouble, Aubrey had left a book to Trinity College Library that really belonged to him, and, worst of all, in 'that rascally letter that had been soaked in a pucket of ale', he had been unjustly accused of cutting up Aubrey's *Lives*. Not content with this written reprimand, Anthony Wood welcomed their suggested meeting as an opportunity to continue the quarrel. 'If you bring any body with you,' he said ominously, 'let him be only a servant, because I have several things to say to you.'

And on this note, this strange friendship ended, for no further letters passed between the two, and on November 28th, 1695, Anthony Wood died a solitary and painful death in his attic room at Oxford. *I am extreemely sorrowfull for the death of my dear Friend, and old Correspondent Mr Anthony Wood*, Aubrey wrote to Tanner when the news reached Llantrithid, *who (though his spleen used to make him chagrin, and to chide me) yet we could not be asunder, and he would alwayes seek me at my Lodgeings with his darke-Lanthorne, which should be a Relick. I hoped that he would have lived, to have given me a cast of his office, in naming the place of my obyt and grave; which I hope will be here: here is fine red earth, but not deep. I am glad you have all his papers, who will be faithfull to him, and finish what he left undone.*

Aubrey was now in his seventieth year, and having transferred his papers to Thomas Tanner, he at last had the leisure to complete a book for publication. 'John Aubrey talkes desperately of putting his *Monumenta Britannica* in the Press', wrote Edmund Gibson at this time, but it was a very different work that was eventually to appear. *My Lord*, runs the dedication to the Earl of Abingdon, *When I enjoyed the Contentment of Solitude in Your pleasant Walks and Gardens at Lavington the last Summer, I reviewed several scattered Papers which had lain by me for several Years; And then presumed to think, that if they were put together they might be somewhat entertaining: I therefore digested them there in this Order, in which I now present them to Your Lordship. It was my intention to have finished my Description of Wilts (half finished already) and to have Dedicated it to Your Lordship: but My Age is now too far spent for such Undertakings: I have therefore devolved that Task on my Countrey-man, Mr T. Tanner, who hath Youth to go through with it, and a Genius proper for such an Undertaking. Wherefore, I humbly beseech Your Lordship to accept of this small Offering, as a grateful Memorial of the profound Respect which I have for You, who have for many Years taken me into your Favour and Protection. My Lord, May the Blessed Angels be Your careful Guardians: such are the Prayers of Your Lordship's Most Obliged and Humble Servant, J. Aubrey.*

Aubrey's enduring reputation as a superstitious fool came from this book, the only publication of his long life. For although he said elsewhere, *I know that some will nauseate these old Fables: but I doe profess to regard them as the most considerable pieces of Antiquity, I collect: and that they are to be registred for Posterity, to let them understand the Encroachment of Ignorance on Mankind: and to see what strange Absurdity Man can by Custome and education be brought to believe:* he made no such reservation in regard to this work, which is a hotch-potch of myths and gullibility entitled:

MISCELLANIES

VIZ.

i. *Day-Fatality*	xii. *Marvels*
ii. *Local-Fatality*	xiii. *Magick*
iii. *Ostenta*	xiv. *Transportation in the Air*
iv. *Omens*	xv. *Visions in a Beril, or Glass*
v. *Dreams*	xvi. *Converse with Angels + Spirits*
vi. *Apparitions*	xvii. *Corps-Candles in Wales*
vii. *Voices*	xviii. *Oracles*
viii. *Impulses*	xix. *Extasie*
ix. *Knockings*	xx. *Glances of* { *Love* / *Envy* }
x. *Blows Invisible*	
xi. *Prophesies*	xxi. *Second-Sighted-Persons*

Collected by J. Aubrey, Esq.

Although Aubrey included too large a number of dreary coincidences under these enticing headings, he managed also to bring in many fascinating stories. Some are connected directly with the superstitions of the time: *At Paris, when it begins to Thunder and Lighten,* he says, *they do presently Ring out the great Bell at the Abbey of St German, which they do believe makes it cease. The like was wont to be done heretofore in Wiltshire; when it Thundred and Lightned, they did Ring St Adelm's at Malmesbury Abbey. The curious do say, that the Ringing of Bells exceedingly disturbs Spirits:* and again: *It is a thing very common to nail Horse-shoes on the Thresholds of Doors: Which is to hinder the power of Witches that enter into the House. Most Houses of the West-end of London have the Horse shoe on the Threshold. It should be a Horse-shoe that one finds.* Other passages are purely descriptive. *At Leghorn, and other Ports in Italie, when Shippes arrive, the Courtizans runne to the Mariners with their Lutes and Ghitarres, playing and singing, with their Haire dissheveld, and Breasts naked, to allure them. In like manner at Gosprit, neer Portsmouth, where the Seamen lye, the Towne is full of wanton wenches, and there is never a house but hath a Virginall in it: and (they say) scarce 3 honest women in the Town.*

Near Letterkenny in the County of Donegall, Aubrey says, reverting to superstition, *a party of the Protestants had been surpriz'd sleeping by the Popish-Irish, were it not for several Wrens that just wakned them by dancing and pecking on the Drums as the Enemy were approaching. For this reason the wild Irish mortally hate these Birds to this day, calling them Devils Servants, and killing them wher ever they catch them; They teach their Children to thrust them full of Thorns: You'll see sometimes on Holidays a whole Parish running like mad-men from Hedg to Hedg a Wren-hunting.* In the chapter on *Impulses*, Aubrey says, *Oliver Cromwell had certainly this Afflatus. One that I knew, that was at the*

Battle of Dunbar, told me that Oliver was carried on with a Divine Impulse; he did Laugh so excessively as if he had been drunk; his Eyes sparkled with Spirits. He obtained a great Victory; but the Action was said to be contrary to Human Prudence. The same fit of Laughter seiz'd Oliver Cromwell, just before the Battle of Naseby; as a Kinsman of mine, and a great Favourite of his, Colonel J.P. then present, testifi'd. Cardinal Mezarine said, that he was a lucky Fool.

In the *Miscellanies* Aubrey was not above showing how some superstitious beliefs could misfire: *I have seen some Rings made for sweet-hearts*, he said, *with a Heart enamelled held between two right hands. See an Epigramme of G. Buchanan on two Rings that were made by Q. Elizabeths appointment, which being layd one upon the other shewed the like figure. The Heart was 2 Diamonds, which joined made the Heart. Q. Eliz. kept one moeitie and sent the other as a Token of her constant Friendship to Mary Queen of Scotts; but she cutt off her Head for all that.* Nor is Aubrey's irrepressible sense of humour absent, as the following tales show. *This is an old piece of Priest-cheate*, he says. *The Image of the B. Virgin nodded at St Bernard, and said (id est, the Priests boy with a tube behind the statue) Good morrow Father Bernard. I thanke your Ladyship, qd he, but St Paul saieth that it is not lawfull for women to speake in the church.* And of his own time, Aubrey reported that *the second Lady of Sr Walter Long (whither voluntarily, or upon Sr Walter's desire I have forgott) did make a Solemn Promise to him, on his Death-bed, that she would not marry after his Decease. But not long after, one Sir Somerset Fox, a very Beautiful young Gentleman, did win her Love: so that notwithstanding her Promise aforesaid, she married him at South-wrax-hall. As he lead her by the hand from the Church into the Parlour, the Picture of Sr Walter, that then hung over the Parlour-dore (the String being eaten off with the rust of the naile) fell down upon her Ladyship, and crack'd in the fall: (it was painted on wood as the fashion was in those days). This made her Ladyship reflect on her Promise, and drew some Tears from her Eyes.*

It is reported concerning the Lord Duffus (in the Shire of Murray) his Predecessors, says Aubrey, *that upon a time, when he was walking abroad in the Fields near to his own House, he was suddenly carried away, and found the next Day at Paris in the French King's Cellar with a Silver Cup in his Hand; that being brought into the King's Prescence and question'd by him, Who he was? And how he came thither? He told his name, his Country, and the place of his Residence, and that on such a Day of the Month (which proved to be the Day immediately preceeding) being in the Fields, he heard the noise of a Whirl-wind, and of Voices crying Horse and Hattock (this is the Word which the Fairies are said to use when they remove from any place) whereupon he cried (Horse and Hattock) also, and was immediately caught up, and transported through the Air, by the Fairies to that place, where after he had drunk heartily he fell a sleep, and before he awoke, the rest of the Company were gone, and had left him in the posture wherein he was found. It's said, the King gave him the Cup which was found in his Hand, and dismiss'd him.* But not all *Transportation in the Air* was as uneventful as this, and Aubrey has left a record of one of the earliest air disasters, albeit an indirect one: *A Gentleman of my Acquaintance was in Portugal, Anno 1655*, he says, *when one was Burnt by the Inquisition for being brought thither from Goa in East India, in the Air, in an incredible short time.* This subject always fascinated Aubrey, and he mentioned many other cases of flying in the course of his works. Indeed he went further still, for amongst his inventions is the following note: *Fill or force in smoake into a Bladder and try if the Bladder will not be carryed up in the Ayre. If it is so, several bladders may drawe a man up into the ayre a certain hight, as the Holly-berrys arise to the middle of water in a glass. Memorandum try to what hight they will ascend in a deep vessell, and also try other Berryes if any will doe so.* He even proposed building a flying machine, but wise man that he was, he was going to take no risk without a parachute: *Memorandum to propose that Mr Packer sends to Norfolk or Suffolke to the gentleman that hath with much curiosity measured the feathers in the wings of severall Birds and taken the proportions of them and the weight of their bodies, and to send to Mr Francis Potter for his notions of Flying and of being safely delivered upon the ground from great Heights with a sheet, etc.*

This book being finished, or as nearly finished as anything Aubrey ever did (for even the printed book is full of gaps and references and hints for further research), he set out once more upon his travels. But in his seventy-second year he was growing very infirm: *January 5th 169$\frac{3}{4}$*, he had written three years before, *an apopletick fitt, circiter 4^{h}. P.M.:* and as he passed through his beloved Oxford on his way to Lady Long's in Wiltshire, death at last struck him down.

Aubrey had no dread of death: *If Solomon counts the day of ones death better than the day of ones birth*, he had said in his *Miscellanies*, *there can be no Objection why that also may not be reckoned amongst ones Remarkable and Happy days:* and his own sudden release from life would no doubt have pleased him, for he was ever concerned at the miseries of old age. Speaking of *Gideon de Laune, Apothecary to Mary the Queen mother, a very wise man, and as a signe of it left an estate of 80,000 pounds*, he said, *Sir William Davenant was his great acquaintance and told me of him, and that after his returne into England he went to visit him, being then octogenary, and very decrepit with the Gowt, but had his sight and understanding. He had a place made for him in the Kitchen chimney; and, non obstante he was master of such an estate, Sir William sawe him slighted not only by his daughter-in-lawe, but by the cooke-mayd, which much affected him – misery of old age.* And if the rich were treated thus, how much worse would be the case of a penniless gentleman, for Aubrey was haunted by the thought of John Rushworth, who like himself was an historian and something of a drunkard.

Yesterday I saw Mr Rushworth, he had written to Anthony Wood in 1689, *which was a great mortification. He hath quite lost his memory with drinking Brandy: remembred nothing of you, etc. His Landlady wiped his nose like a child. He was about 83, onwards to 84. He had forgot his children before he died.*

But however grateful Aubrey would have been to die while he was still vigorous, he would have grieved to know that his passing would go unnoticed. For though he was buried by his young friend Thomas Tanner, now Fellow of All Souls, no tomb was erected, despite the design and the instructions that he had prepared so carefully. *I would desire that this Inscription should be a stone about the bigness of a royal sheet of paper scilicet, about 2 foot square. Mr Reynolds of Lambeth, Stonecutter (Foxhall) who married Mr Elias Ashmole's Widow will help me to a Marble as square as an imperial sheet of paper for 8 shillings.*

Many years before, Aubrey had discovered a tomb called Gawen's Barrow on his farm at Broad Chalk. *I never was so sacralegious as to disturbe, or rob his urne*, he said. *Let his Ashes rest in peace: but I have oftentimes wish't, that my Corps might be interred by it: but the Lawes Ecclesiastick denie it. Our Bones in consecrated ground never lie quiet: and in London once in ten yeares (or thereabout) the Earth is carried to the Dung-wharf.* But though Aubrey was not buried in Wiltshire, at least his desire to lie undisturbed in his grave was granted. For the very time and place of his burial was forgotten, and not for one hundred and fifty years was an entry uncovered in the Register of the Church of St Mary Magdalene – '1697, JOHN AUBERY A Stranger was Buryed June 7th.'

And even now there is no memorial to this famous man at Oxford, save his life's work safely lodged in Sir Thomas Bodley's Library across the way.

*

These remains of his, which were then in the Ashmolean Museum, disprove once for all the accusation that John Aubrey frittered his life away. For even though several volumes of his manuscripts have vanished since his death, there still remain nine major works to his credit, besides innumerable others less substantial.

Many scholars, taking their cue from Anthony Wood, have none the less dismissed Aubrey as of little importance: but the fault lies much more in their misunderstanding of his talents than in his lack of them. For they have persisted in looking on Aubrey as an historian, and then running him down for his shortcomings in that field; whereas if one accepts James Bryce's dictum that 'the secret of historical composition is to know what to neglect', it is obvious that Aubrey cannot be considered as an historian, for his genius was for collection rather than selection. But a poor historian may be none the less a fine historical scholar, and the vividness of his stories and the pith of his quotations show the very real skill and scholarship that Aubrey applied to his task. For though he has often been condemned for his unreliability, the charge is once again based on muddled thinking: he was sometimes inaccurate, it is true, but he was never untruthful, and the distinction is a most important one. For Aubrey's belief in astrology in no wise affected his trustworthiness on other subjects, as Malone pointed out so clearly in the next century. 'If the representation attempted to be given of this ingenious and unfortunate gentleman were just and well founded,' he said, 'if it were true that every one who is weak in one place must necessarily be weak in all; that all those persons who in the last century were idle enough to put their faith in judicial astrology, and to give credit to preternatural appearances of the dead, were fools; and their judgement or testimony of no value on any subject whatever, however unconnected with these weaknesses: then, in this large list of ninnies, must we class, with Mr Aubrey, the accomplished and literate Charles the First; the grave and judicious Clarendon; the witty Duke of Buckingham; the fertile and ingenious Dryden; and many other names of equal celebrity; they must all "bench by his side", and must be set down as persons not capable of forming a true judgement on any matter whatsoever presented to them, and wholly unworthy of credit.' Aubrey summed up his own position perfectly when he wrote in his life of Hobbes: *But one may say of him, as one sayes of Jos. Scaliger, that where he erres, he erres so ingeniosely, that one had rather erre with him then hitt the mark with Clavius.*

No one, however, has tried to deny Aubrey's skill as a writer: and when he himself asked, *Is my English style well enough*? even Anthony Wood felt bound to answer ''Tis well' instead of falling hard upon him as he usually did for his queries. 'You should never ask these questions, but do them out of hand. You have time enough', was a more typical response.

Time, which is as kind to books as it is to wine, has even added to the quality of Aubrey's style; for the two and a half centuries that have passed since his death have caused Aubrey's work to mature in two separate ways. 'There is no beauty that hath not some strangeness in the proportion', Bacon has said, and it is in this direction that the years have had their first effect. Words, no less than men, have a history of their own, and in reading Aubrey after so great a lapse of time, the sharpness of every phrase and sentence is particularly striking. Unblunted by use, bare of acquired meanings and monotonous echoes, the words affect us with the freshness of a foreign tongue, and like a foreign language, they make everything seem doubly significant. The second effect of time is quite different. *It is said of Antiquaries, they wipe off the mouldinesse they digge, and remove the rubbish,*

Aubrey remarked disapprovingly, and the trivialities that he therefore insisted, against the advice of all his friends, on including in his works, have now become their greatest strength. As he moves slowly through the darkness of his vanished century, bringing one person after another into a ring of light, the contemporary details, which he had jotted down so casually, bring the very noise of the seventeenth century into our ears. Through him one gets the most vivid sense of the presence of the past, of that feeling which Rossetti summed up when he wrote:

> As much as in a hundred years she's dead
> Yet is today the day on which she died.

For Aubrey's writing was addressed not to the mind alone, but to the imagination, and the unerring skill with which he chose just that episode in a man's life when his personality was most extravagantly in bloom, gives even the shortest of his biographies a vividness which has never been excelled. *Thomas Fuller*, he says, *was of a middle stature; strong sett; curled haire; a very working head, in so much that, walking and meditating before dinner, he would eate-up a penny loafe, not knowing that he did it. His naturall memorie was very great, to which he added the Art of Memorie: he would repeat to you forwards and backwards all the signes from Ludgate to Charing-crosse.* And his technique was so perfect that he was able to render precisely the effect that he wished to produce, even in a single sentence. *William Cartwright's son having many children lives not handsomely and haz lost his Learning*, he says, and similar examples of his skill are unending. *Mr Philips, author of Montelion and Don Juan Lamberto, is very happy at Jiggish Poetry and Gypsies and Ballads – Mariana Morgan. She is a swidging lustie woman – Nicholas Mercator is of a soft temper, of great temperance (amat Veneram aliquantum): of a prodigious invention, and will be acquainted (familiarly) with no body – Mr Gore. He is a fidling peevish fellow – Thomas Willis, M.D. was middle stature: darke brindle haire (like a red pig) stammered much – the Duke of Monmouth's mother, Mrs Lucy Walters, who could deny no body – Robert Greville, Lord Brookes, was killed at the Siege of Lichfield, March the 2d (St Chad's day, to whom the Church is dedicated) 1643 by a Minister's sonne, born deafe and dumbe, out of the church. He was armed cap à pied; only his Bever was open – William Sanderson dyed at Whitehall (I was then there): went out like a spent candle: died before Dr Holder could come to him with the Sacrament – William Outram was a tall spare leane pale consumptive man; wasted himself much, I presume, by frequent preaching – Sir Francis Stuart was a Sea-captaine and (I thinke) he was one Summer, a Vice or Rere-Admirall. He was a learned Gentleman, and one of the Club at the Mermayd, in Fryday street, with Sir Walter Ralegh, etc, of that Sodalitie, Heroes and Witts of that time – Richard Martin, Recorder of London, was a very handsome man, a gracefull speaker, facetious, and well-beloved. I thinke he dyed of a merry Symposiaque with his fellow-Witts. He was Recorder but a moneth before his death – George Sandys, Poet, lies buried in the Chancel neer the dore on the south side, but without any remembrance or stone: which is pitty so sweet a Swan should lye so ingloriously.*

Aubrey's skill was so great, in fact, that he could conjure a living being out of a mere list of facts. *Mrs Abigail Sloper borne at Broad Chalke, near Salisbury, A.D. 1648. Pride; lechery; ungratefull to her father; married; runne distracted; recovered.* And again: *Richard Stokes, M.D. His father was Fellow of Eaton College. He was bred there and at King's College. Scholar to Mr W. Oughtred for Mathematiques (Algebra). He made himselfe mad with it, but became sober again, but I feare like a crackt-glasse. Became a Roman-catholique: maried unhappily at Liege, dog and catt, etc. Became a Sott. Dyed in Newgate, Prisoner for debt April 1681.*

As the stories lengthen, the impression becomes ever clearer. *John Partridge, the son of an honest waterman at Putney in Surrey. He was taught to read, and a little to write. He was bound Apprentice to a Shoemaker; where he was kept hard to his Trade. At 18 he gott him a Lillie's Grammar, and Goldman's Dictionary, and a Latin Bible, and Ovid's Metamorphoses. He is of indefatigable industrie and in a few yeares he made himself a competent master of the Latin tongue, well enough to reade any Astrologicall book, and quickly became a master of that Science. He then studyed the Greek tongue, and also the Hebrew, to neither of which he is a stranger. He then studyed good Authors in Physique, and intends to make that his Profession and Practyse: but is yet (1680) a shoemaker in Convent Garden – Mr Attorney Generall Noy was a great Lawyer and a great Humorist. There is a world of merry stories of him. A Countrey clowne asked for a good Inne, and he bids him ride into Lincoln's Inne, and asked if his Horse went to hay or to grasse. He caused the Breeches of a Bencher of Lincolne's Inne to be taken-in by a Tayler and made him believe that he had the Dropsie. Another time Noy and Pine of Lincolne's Inne went afoot to Barnet with clubbes in their hands, like countrey-fellowes. They went to the Red Lyon Inne; the people of the house were afrayd to trust them, fearing they might not pay – Richard Meriton: his true name was Head. He had been amongst the Gipsies. He looked like a knave with his gogling eies. He could transforme himselfe into any shape. Brake 2 or 3 times. Was at last a Bookeseller in Little Britaine, or towards his later end. He maintained himselfe by Scribbling: 20s. per sheet. He was drowned goeing to Plymouth by long Sea about 1676, being about 50 yeares of age – Saint Dunstan. He was a Somersetshire Gentleman. He was a great Chymist. The storie of his pulling the Devill by the nose with his tongues* [tongs] *in his Laboratorie, was famous in church-windowes. Meredith Lloyd had, about the biginning of the Civill Warres, a MS of this Saint's concerning Chymistrey, and sayes that there are severall MSS of his up and downe in England. He could make a fire out of Gold, with which he could sett any combustible matter on fire at a great distance. Meredith Lloyd tells me that, three or 400 yeares ago, Chymistry was in a greater perfection, much, then now; their proces was then more Seraphique and Universall: now they looke only after medicines.* The medieval hunt for the Philosopher's Stone had only recently been abandoned, however. Even in the previous century, Aubrey reported, *Thomas Charnock attained the secret from his master at Salisbury close, who dying left his worke with him. He lost it by fireing his Tabernacle on a New yeare's day. About this time being 28 yeares of Age, he learned the secret againe of the Prior of Bathe. He continued it nine monthes; was within a month of his reckoning; the crowe's head began to appear black.* But once again the elusive secret escaped his grasp, for a friend told Aubrey 'that he kept a fire in, divers yeares; that his daughter lived with him; that once he was gone forth, and by her neglect (whome he trusted it with in his abscence) the fire went out and so all his worke was lost: the Brazen head was very neare comeing to speake, but so was he disappointed'.

Sometimes Aubrey helped out one of his purely factual lives with a single story, and together they provide the complete portrait of a man. *Sir Mathew Hale, Judge,* he wrote, *1609, natus November 1st in the evening, his father then being at his prayers. 1640, maried the first time. (He was a great Cuckold.) 1656, his second mariage to his servant Mayd, Mary. 1660, made Lord Chief Baron. 1671, Lord Chiefe Justice of England, 18 May. 1676, Christmas day, he dyed. I remember,* Aubrey told Anthony Wood some years later, *about 1646 (or 1647) that Mr John Maynard (now Sir John, and serjeant) came into Middle Temple hall, from Westminster-hall, weary with business, and hungry, when we had newly dined. He sate-downe by Mr Bennet Hoskyns (the only son of Serjeant Hoskyns, the Poet) since Baronet, and some others; who having made an end of their Commons, fell unto various Discourse, and what was the meaning of the Text (Rom. v. 7.) 'For a just man one would dare to die; but for a good man one would willingly die.' They askt Mr Maynard what was the difference between a just man and a good man. He was beginning to eate, and cryed: Hoh! you have eaten your dinners, and now have leasure to discourse; I have not. He had eate but a Bitt or two when he reply'd: I'le tell you the difference presently* [now]*: serjeant Rolle is a just man, and Mathew Hale is a good man; and so fell to make an end of his dinner. And there could not be a better interpretation of this Text. For serjeant Rolle was just, but by nature penurious* [niggardly]*; and his wife made him worse: Mathew Hale was not only just, but wonderfully Charitable and open handed, and did not sound a trumpet neither, as the Hypocrites doe.*

The same Serjeant figures in one of Aubrey's other stories. *The Lady Hele gave by her Will 800 pounds per annum to be layd out for Charitable Uses and by the advice and prudence of Serjeant Maynard. He did order it according to the best of his understanding, and yet he sayd that he haz lived to see every one of these Benefactions abused.* Mankind, even then, was apt to treat a favour as a right, as the following unhappy tale shows only too clearly. *Madam Curtin, a good Fortune of 3000 pounds, daughter to Sir William Curtin, the great Merchant, lately married her footman, who, not long after marriage, beates her, getts her money, and ran away:* a double disaster for the poor lady, for even in those days servants were almost as hard to come by as another fortune. *The dayly concurse of Servants out of the Country to London, makes Servants Wages deare in the Countrey, and makes scarcity of Labourers,* Aubrey complained angrily. *Mr Fabian Philips affirmes to me that when he came first to London sc. 1619, an ordinary servant-mayds wages was but sixteen shillings per annum and now tis 3 or 4 pounds per annum.*

So unchanging are the troubles of the human race when looked at by a contemporary, a fact which Aubrey recognized only too well. *Mr William Prynne's advice to me for the reading of our English Historie,* he had recorded carefully, *was to read the Authors, that wrote of their owne Time.* Unless we look at the past through its own eyes, we can be hopelessly misled by the differences in emphasis. For the law of perspective seems to work contrariwise down the centuries: the figures grow larger as they walk away. But as Aubrey leads us amongst his friends, and we find bawdy verses written on Philip Sidney's famous death, or see Sir Walter Raleigh discomfited at dinner by his son, and catch the poet Suckling cheating at cards, the heroic figures lose their formal pose, and we see them once again as living men.

Aubrey's were the first biographies that did not point a moral; in fact, they were really a record of his unselfconscious gossip with his friends. For he would have agreed with Hazlitt, who liked 'a friend the better for having faults that one can talk about', and he had, like W. H. Mallock, 'the very highest opinion of scandal. It is founded on the most sacred of things – that is, Truth, and it is built up by the most beautiful of things – that is, Imagination.' But Aubrey was so kind a man that his gossip rarely turned to scandal, and his wit, in Disraeli's phrase, was excessively good-natured, and, like champagne, not only sparkled, but was sweet. *Will this not give offence?* Aubrey asked on more than one occasion, to be answered by Anthony Wood: 'Perhaps no.' John Ray, however, offered more detailed advice: 'Whatever you may conceive may give Offence, may by the wording of it be so softned and sweetned as to take off the Edge of it, as Pills are gilded to make them less ungrateful.'

In the letter which Aubrey attached to *the Minutes of Lives*, when he first sent them to Anthony Wood in 1680, he fully explained his aims and intentions. *Sir!* he said then, *I have, according to your desire, putt in writing these Minutes of Lives tumultuarily, as they occurr'd to my thoughts or as occasionally I had information of them. They may easily be reduced into order at your leisure by numbring them with red figures, according to time and place, &c. 'Tis a Taske that I never thought to have undertaken till you imposed it upon me, sayeing that I was fitt for it by reason of my generall acquaintance, having now not only lived above a halfe a Centurie of yeares in the world, but have also been much tumbled up and downe in it which hath made me much knowne; besides the moderne advantage of Coffee-howses in this great Citie, before which men knew not how to be acquainted, but with their owne Relations, or societies. I might add that I come of a longaevous race, by which meanes I have imped some feathers of the wings of Time, for severall Generations; which does reach high. When I first began, I did not thinke I could have drawne it out to so long a Thread.*

I here lay-downe to you (out of the conjunct friendship between us) the Trueth, and, as neer as I can and that religiously as a Poenitent to his Confessor, nothing but the trueth: the naked and plaine trueth, which is here exposed so bare that the very pudenda are not covered, and affords many passages that would raise a Blush in a young Virgin's cheeke. So that after your perusall, I must desire you to make a Castration (as Raderus to Martial) and to sowe-on some Figge-leaves – i.e. to be my Index expurgatorius.

What uncertainty doe we find in printed Histories! they either treading too neer on the heeles of trueth that they dare not speake plaine, or els for want of intelligence (things being antiquated) become too obscure and darke! I doe not here repeat any thing already published (to the best of my remembrance) and I fancy my selfe all along discourseing with you; alledgeing those of my Relations and acquaintance (as either you knew or have heerd of) ad faciendam Fidem: so that you make me to renew my acquaintance with my old and deceased Friends, and to rejuvenescere (as it were), which is the pleasure of old men. 'Tis pitty that such minutes had not been taken 100 yeares since or more: for want wherof many worthy men's Names and Notions are swallowd-up in oblivion; as much as these also would have been, had it not been through your Instigation: and perhaps this is one of the usefullest pieces that I have scribbeld.

I remember one sayeing of General Lambert's, that 'the best of men are but men at the best'; of this, you will meet with divers examples in this rude and hastie collection. Now these Arcana are not fitt to lett flie abroad, till about 30 yeares hence, he concludes, *for the author and the Persons (like Medlars) ought to be rotten first.*

*

The measure of his success is in the following pages, and is complete. For Aubrey had the rare gift of creating, and not just recording, life, and he has himself summed up his achievement in words that cannot be bettered:

These Remaines are tanquam Tabulata Naufragy [like fragments of a shipwreck] *that after the Revolution of so many Years and Govenments have escaped the Teeth of Time and (which is more dangerous) the Hands of mistaken Zeale. So that the retriving of these forgotten Things from Oblivion in some sort resembles the Art of a Conjuror, who makes those walke and appeare that have layen in their graves many hundreds of yeares: and to represent as it were to the eie, the places, Customes and Fashions, that were of old Times.*

Aubrey's Brief Lives

GEORGE ABBOT

Born 1562. Archbishop of Canterbury. Educated at Guildford Grammar School and Balliol College, Oxford. In 1592 he was appointed private chaplain to Lord Buckhurst, the Chancellor of the University, and in 1597 he became Master of University College, where he wrote for his pupils *A Briefe Description of the whole World*, which included an account of America. He was an extreme Puritan, and besides accusing Laud of Papacy and heresy, he burnt religious pictures in the market-place. His pamphleteering made him unpopular at Oxford when he was Vice-Chancellor, and in 1605 he committed one hundred and forty undergraduates to prison for sitting *with their hats on* in his presence at St Mary's Church. He revised the New Testament for the *Authorized Version*. Having won James I's approval by his efforts to re-establish episcopacy in Scotland, he was made Bishop of Coventry and Lichfield in 1609, and was translated to London in 1610. The next year, Secretary Calvert remarked: *By a strong north wind coming out of Scotland, Abbot was blown over the Thames to Lambeth.* As Archbishop of Canterbury, Abbot continued his struggle against Arminianism, burning two members of that faith and torturing another. He lost favour by his opposition to the Countess of Essex's divorce, but, having re-established his position in 1615 by the introduction of George Villiers (later Duke of Buckingham) at Court, he seized the opportunity to make his elder brother Bishop of Salisbury. In 1621, he accidentally shot a gamekeeper with a cross-bow while hunting, and though he settled £20 a year on the keeper's widow, *which soon procured her another husband*, and was also formally pardoned by the King, the Bishops Elect, of whom Laud was one, refused to be consecrated by him. In 1627 he was stripped of all authority by Charles I, and although, when he was restored to favour in 1628, the other prelates (who were *gaping after his Benefice*) were warned that *his Grace perhaps may eat the Goose which shall graze upon his grave*, he never again took any part in affairs of State, but lived in retirement until his death in 1633.

WHEN Arch-Bishop Abbot's Mother (a poor Cloath-worker's Wife in Gilford) was with Child of him, she did long for a Jack or Pike, and she dreamt that if she should Eat a Jack, her Son in her Belly should be a *great Man*. Upon this she was indefatigable to satisfy her Longing, as well as her Dream. She first enquir'd out for this Fish: but the next Morning, goeing with her Payle to the River-side (which runneth by the Howse, now an Ale-house, the Signe of the 3 Mariners) to take up some Water, a good Jack accidentally came into her Payle. She took up the much desir'd Banquet, dress'd it, and devour'd it almost all her selfe, or very neare. This odd Affair made no small Noise in the Neighbourhood, and the

Curiosity of it made severall People of Quality offer themselves to be Sponsors at the Baptismal Fount when she was deliver'd. This their Poverty accepted joyfully, and three were chosen, who maintained him at School, and University afterwards, his father not being able. This is generally recieved for a trueth.

It was Bred up a Scholar in the Town, and by degrees, came to be Arch-Bishop of Canterbury. Old Nightingale was his servant, and weepes when he talkes of him. Every one that knew, loved him. He was sometimes Cholerique.

THOMAS ALLEN

Born 1542. Mathematician. Educated at Trinity College, Oxford. Bachelor of Arts 1563. Fellow 1565. Master of Arts 1567. He obtained the patronage of the Earl of Northumberland, but refused the offer of a bishopric from the Earl of Leicester, as he preferred a life of retirement. He was described by Fuller as having succeeded to the skill and scandal of Friar Bacon. Died 1632.

Mr Allen was a very cheerfull, facetious man, and every body loved his company, and every Howse on their *Gaudie-dayes* were wont to invite him.

The great Dudley, Earle of Leicester, made use of him for casting of Nativities, for he was the best Astrologer of his time. Queen Elizabeth sent for him to have his advice about the new Star that appeared in the Swan or Cassiopeia (but I think the Swan) to which he gave his Judgement very learnedly.

In those darke times, Astrologer, Mathematician, and Conjurer were accounted the same things; and the vulgar did verily beleeve him to be a Conjurer. He had a great many Mathematicall Instruments and Glasses in his Chamber, which did also confirme the ignorant in their opinion, and his servitor (to impose on Freshmen and simple people) would tell them that sometimes he should meet the Spirits comeing up his staires like Bees. Now there is to some men a great Lechery in Lying, and imposing on the understandings of beleeving people, and he thought it for his credit to serve such a Master.

He was generally acquainted, and every long Vacation he rode into the Countrey to visitt his old Acquaintance and Patrones, to whom his great learning, mixt with much sweetnes of humour, rendred him very welcome.

One time being at Hom Lacy in Herefordshire, at Mr John Scudamore's (grandfather to the Lord Scudamor) he happened to leave his Watch in the Chamber windowe. (Watches were then rarities.) The maydes came in to make the Bed, and hearing a thing in a case cry *Tick*, *Tick*, *Tick*, presently concluded that that was his Devill, and tooke it by the String with the tongues [*tongs*], and threw it out of the windowe into the Mote (to drowne the Devill). It so happened that the string hung on a sprig of an elder that grew out of the Mote, and this confirmed them that 'twas the Devill. So the good old Gentleman gott his Watch again.

LANCELOT ANDREWES

Born 1555. Divine. Sometime Dean of Westminster and Chaplain-in-ordinary to Queen Elizabeth. Under James I, he rose into great favour and was made successively Bishop of Chichester, of Ely, and in 1618 of Winchester. He attended the Hampton Court Conference and was general editor of the Authorized Version of the Bible. Bishop Andrewes was a man of the very greatest learning, and it is said that the awe of his presence was wont to restrain King James from that unseemly levity in which he was rather too prone to indulge. Died 1626.

LANCELOT ANDREWES, Lord Bishop of Winton, was borne in London; went to Schoole at Merchant Taylors schoole. Mr Mulcaster was his schoolemaster, whose picture he hung in his Studie.

Old Mr Sutton, a very learned man in those dayes, of Blandford St Maries, Dorset, was his school fellow, and sayd that Lancelot Andrewes was a great long boy of 18 yeares old at least before he went to the University.

The Puritan faction did begin to increase in those dayes, and especially at Emanuel College. This party had a great mind to drawe in this learned young man, whom (if they could make theirs) they knew would be a great honour to them. They carried themselves outwardly with great sanctity and strictnesse. They preached up very strict keeping and observing the Lord's day: made, upon the matter, damnation to breake it, and that 'twas less Sin to kill a man. Yet these Hypocrites did bowle in a private green at their colledge every Sunday after Sermon; and one of the Colledge (a loving friend to Mr L. Andrewes) to satisfie him, one time lent him the Key of a Private back dore to the bowling green, on a Sunday evening, which he opening, discovered these zealous Preachers with their Gownes off, earnest at play. But they were strangely surprised to see the entrey of one that was not of the Brotherhood.

There was then at Cambridge a good fatt Alderman that was wont to sleep at Church, which the Alderman endeavoured to prevent but could not. Well! this was preached against as a signe of Reprobation. The good man was exceedingly troubled at it, and went to Andrewes his Chamber to be satisfied in point of Conscience. Mr Andrewes told him, that it was an ill habit of Body, not of Mind, and that it was against his Will; advised him on Sundays to make a more sparing meale, and to mend it at Supper. The Alderman did so, but Sleepe comes on again for all that, and was preached at; comes againe to be resolved with Teares in his eies. Andrewes then told him he would have him make a good heartie meal as he was wont to doe, and presently [*at once*] take out his full sleep. He did so, came to St Maries, where the Preacher was prepared with a Sermon to damne all who slept at Sermon, a certain signe of Reprobation. The good Alderman, having taken his full nap before, lookes on the Preacher all Sermon time, and spoyled the design. But I should have sayd that Andrewes was most extremely spoken against and preached against for offering to assoile or excuse a sleeper in sermon time. But he had learning and witt enough to defend himselfe.

His good learning quickly made him known in the University, and also to King James, who much valued him for it, and advanced him, and at last made him Bishop of Winchester: which Bishoprick he ordered with great Prudence as to government of the Parsons, preferring of ingeniose persons that were staked to poore livings and did *delitescere* [decline]. He made it his Enquiry to find out such men. Amongst severall others (whose names have escaped my memorie) Nicholas Fuller (he wrote *Critica Sacra*), Minister of Allington, neer Amesbury in Wilts, was one. The Bishop sent for him, and the poor man was afrayd and knew not what hurt he had donne. Makes him sitt downe to Dinner and, after the Desert, was brought in, in a dish, his Institution and Induction, or the donation of a Prebend; which was his way.

He dyed in Winchester house in Southwark, and lies buried in a Chapell at St Mary Overies, where his Executors have erected (but I beleeve according to his Lordship's will, els they would not have layed out 1000 pounds) a sumptuose Monument for Him.

He had not that smooth way of Oratory, as now. It was a shrewd and severe animadversion of a Scotish Lord, who, when King James asked him how he liked Bp A's sermon, said that he was learned, but he did play with his Text, as a Jack-an-apes does, who takes up a thing and tosses and playes with it, and then he takes up another, and playes a little with it. Here's a pretty thing, and there's a pretty thing!

FRANCIS BACON
VISCOUNT ST ALBANS

Born 1561. Philosopher and statesman. He went through the various steps of the legal profession, entered Parliament in 1584, and then wrote papers on public affairs, including *A Letter of Advice to Queen Elizabeth* urging strong measures against the Catholics. He made the acquaintance of the Earl of Essex, who treated him with generosity and endeavoured to advance him in his career; nevertheless, having been appointed to investigate the causes of Essex's revolt in 1601, he was largely responsible for the Earl's conviction. The accession of James I gave a favourable turn to Bacon's fortunes, and he was knighted in 1603; becoming Solicitor-General in 1607, Attorney-General in 1613, Lord Keeper in 1617, Lord Chancellor and Baron Verulam in 1618, and Viscount St Albans in 1621. In the same year, a Parliamentary Committee on the Administration of the Law charged him with corruption under twenty-three counts; and so clear was the evidence that he made no attempt at defence. He was sentenced to a fine of £40,000; to be committed to the Tower during the King's pleasure (which was that he should be released in a few days); to be perpetually banished from Court; and to be incapable of holding office or sitting in Parliament ever again. The remaining years of his life were spent in literary and philosophical work. It was Bacon's ambition to create a new system of philosophy, based on a right interpretation of nature, to replace that of Aristotle; and his development of inductive philosophy did in fact revolutionize future thought, for he did more than anyone else to free the intellect from preconceived notions and to direct it to the unbiased study of facts. He wrote *The Advancement of Learning*, *The History of Henry the Seventh*, *The New Atlantis*, *Maxims of the Law*, and his *Essays*. Bacon died in 1626, leaving debts of £22,000. Pope described him as *the wisest, brightest, meanest of mankind.*

In his Lordship's prosperity, Sir Fulke Grevil, Lord Brooke, was his great Friend and acquaintance; but when he was in disgrace and want, he was so unworthy as to forbid his Butler to let him have any more small Beer, which he had often sent for, his stomach being nice, and the small beere of Gray's Inne not liking his pallet. This has donne his memorie more dishonour then Sir Philip Sidney's friendship engraven on his monument hath donne him Honour.

Richard, Earle of Dorset, was a great admirer and friend of the Lord Chancellor Bacon, and was wont to have Sir Thomas Billingsley along with him, to remember and to putt downe in writing my Lord's sayings at Table.

Mr Ben Johnson was one of his friends and acquaintance, as doeth appeare by his excellent verses on his Lordship's birthday, and in his *Underwoods*, where he gives him a Character, and concludes that about his time and within his view were borne all the Witts that could honour a Nation or helpe studie.

The learned and great Cardinal Richelieu was a great admirer of the Lord Bacon.

He came often to Sir John Danvers at Chelsey. Sir John told me that when his Lordship had wrote *The History of Henry 7*, he sent the Manuscript copie to him to desire his opinion of it before 'twas printed. Qd. Sir John, Your Lordship knowes that I am no Scholar. 'Tis no matter, said my Lord: I knowe what a Schollar can say; I would know what you can say. Sir John read it, and gave his opinion what he misliked (which I am sorry I have forgott) which my Lord acknowledged to be true, and mended it; Why, said he, a Scholar would never have told me this.

Mr Thomas Hobbes was beloved by his Lordship, who was wont to have him walke with him in his delicate groves where he did meditate: and when a notion darted into his mind, Mr Hobbs was presently to write it downe, and his Lordship was wont to say that he did it better then any one els about him; for that many times, when he read their notes he scarce understood what they writt, because they understood it not clearly themselves.

In short, all that were great and good loved and honoured him. (Sir Edward Coke, Lord Chiefe Justice, alwayes envyed [*grudged at*] him, and would be undervalueing his Lawe, as you may find in my Lord's lettres, and I knew old Lawyers that remembred it.)

He was Lord Protector during King James's Progresse into Scotland, and gave Audiences in great State to Ambassadors in the Banquetting-house at Whitehall.

The Aviary at Yorke House was built by his Lordship; it did cost 300 pounds.

At every meale, according to the season of the yeare, he had his Table strewed with Sweet Herbes and Flowers, which he sayd did refresh his spirits and memorie.

When his Lordship was at his Country-house at Gorhambery, St Albans seemed as if the Court were there, so Nobly did He live. His servants had Liveries with his Crest (a Boare); his Watermen were more imployed by Gentlemen then any other, even the King's.

King James sent a Buck to him, and he gave the keeper fifty pounds.

He was wont to say to his servant Hunt (who was a notable thrifty man and loved this World, and the only servant he had that he could never gett to become bound for him) *The World was made for man, Hunt, and not man for the World.* Hunt left an estate of 1000 pound per annum in Somerset.

None of his servants durst appeare before him without Spanish leather bootes; for he would smelle the neates leather, which offended him.

The East India Merchants presented his Lordship with a Cabinet of Jewells, which his Page, Mr Cockaine, received, and deceived his Lord.

Three of his Lordship's servants kept their Coaches, and some kept Race-horses.

His Lordship would many times have Musique in the next roome where he meditated. I have now forgott what Mr Bushel sayd, whether his Lordship enjoyed his Muse best at night or in the Morning.

His Lordship was a good Poet, but conceal'd, as appeares by his Letters:

The world's a Bubble, and the life of man
Less than a span;
In his conception wretched, from the wombe
So to the tombe;
Curst from his cradle, and brought up to yeares
With cares and feares.
Who then to frail mortality shall trust
But limmes in water or but writes in dust.

Yet since with sorrow here we live opprest,
What life is best?
Courts are but onely superficiall scholes
To dandle fooles:
The rurall parts are turn'd into a den
Of savage men;
And wher's a city from all vice so free,
But may be term'd the worst of all the three?

Domestick cares afflict the husband's bed
Or paines his hed;
Those that live single take it for a curse,
Or doe things worse;
Some would have children; those that have them mone,
Or wish them gone.
What is it then to have, or have no wife,
But single thraldome or a double strife?

Our owne affections still at home to please
Is a disease;
To crosse the sea to any foreine soyle,
Perills and toyle;
Warres with their noise affright us; when they cease
W'are worse in peace.
What then remaines? but that we still should cry
Not to be borne, or, being borne, to dye.

He was a παιδεραστής [*pederast*]. His Ganimeds and Favourites tooke Bribes; but his Lordship alwayes gave Judgement *secundum aequum et bonum* [according as was just and good]. His Decrees in Chancery stand firme, i.e. there are fewer of his Decrees reverst then of any other Chancellor.

His Dowager married her Gentleman-usher Sir Thomas (I thinke) Underhill, whom she made deafe and blinde with too much of Venus. She was living since the beheading of the late King.

He had a uterine brother, Anthony Bacon, who was a very great statesman, and much beyond his brother Francis for the Politiques, a lame man; he was a Pensioner to [*too*], and lived with the Earle of Essex. And to him he dedicates the first Edition of his *Essayes*, a little booke no bigger then a Primer, which I have seen in the Bodlyan Library.

His sisters were ingeniose and well-bred; they well understood the Use of the Globes, as you may find in the preface of Mr Blundevill *Of the Sphaere: I began this Arithmetique more than 7 yeares since for that vertuous Gentlewoman Mris Elizabeth Bacon: and though at her request I had made this Arithmetique so plaine and easie as was possible (as to my seeming) yet her continuall sicknesse would not suffer her to exercise herself therin.*

He had a delicate, lively, hazel Eie; Dr Harvey tolde me it was like the Eie of a viper.

His Lordship being in Yorke-house garden, lookeing on Fishers as they were throwing their Nett, asked them what they would take for their Draught; they answered *so much*; his Lordship would only offer *so much*. They drew up their Nett and there were only 2 or 3 little fishes: his Lordship then told them it had been better for them to have taken his Offer. They replied, they hoped to have had a better Draught. But, sayd his Lordship, Hope is a good Breakfast but an ill Supper.

When his Lordship was in disfavour, his neighbours, hearing how much he was indebted, came to him with a Motion to buy Oake-wood of him. His Lordship told them, He would not sell his Feathers.

The Earle of Manchester being removed from his Place of Lord chiefe

Justice of the Common-Pleas to be Lord President of the Councell, told my Lord (upon his Fall) that he was sorry to see Him made such an Example. Lord Bacon replied *it did not trouble him, since he was made a President* [i.e. precedent].

The Bishop of London did cutte-downe a noble Clowd of Trees at Fulham. The Lord Chancellor told him that he was a good Expounder of darke places.

Upon his being in Dis-favour his Servants suddenly went away; he compared them to the flying of the Vermin when the Howse was falling.

One told his Lordship it was now time to looke about him. He replyed: I do not looke about me, I looke above me.

Sir Julius Caesar (Master of the Rolles) sent to his Lordship in his necessity a hundred pounds for a Present.

His Lordship would often drinke a good draught of strong Beer (March-beer) to-bedwards, to lay his working Fancy asleep, which otherwise would keepe him from sleeping great part of the night.

I remember Sir John Danvers told me, that his Lordship much delighted in his curious pretty garden at Chelsey, and as he was walking there one time he fell downe in a dead-sowne [*swoon*]. My Lady Danvers rubbed his face, temples, etc., and gave him cordiall water; as soon as he came to himselfe, sayde he, *Madam, I am no good footman.*

I will write something of Verulam, and his House at Gorhambery. At Verulam is to be seen, in some few places, some remaines of the Wall of this Citie. This magnanimous Lord Chancellor had a great mind to have made it a Citie again: and he had designed it, to be built with great uniformity: but Fortune denyed it Him, though she proved kinder to the great Cardinal Richelieu, who lived both to designe and finish that specious Towne of Richelieu, where he was borne; before, an obscure and small Vilage.

Within the bounds of the Walls of this old Citie of Verulam (his Lordship's Baronry) was Verulam-howse; which his Lordship built, the most ingeniosely contrived little pile, that ever I sawe. No question but his Lordship was the chiefest Architect; but he had for his assistant a favourite of his, a St Albans man, Mr Dobson, who was his Lordship's right hand, a very ingeniose person (Master of the Alienation Office); but he spending his estate upon woemen, necessity forced his son Will Dobson to be the most excellent Painter that England hath yet bred.

The howse did cost nine or ten thousand the building, and was sold about 1665 or 1666 by Sir Harbottle Grimston, Baronet, to two Carpenters for fower hundred poundes; of which they made eight hundred poundes.

I am sorry I measured not the front and breadth; but I little suspected it would be pulled downe for the sale of the Materials. There were good Chimney pieces; the roomes very loftie, and all were very well wainscotted. There were two Bathing-roomes or Stuffes [*stews*], whither his Lordship retired afternoons as he sawe cause. All the tunnells of the Chimneys were carried into the middle of the howse; and round about them were seates. The top of the howse was very well Leaded: from the Leads was a lovely Prospect to the Ponds, which were opposite to the East side of the howse, and were on the other side of the stately Walke of Trees that leades to Gorhambery-howse: and also over that Long Walke of Trees, whose topps afford a most pleasant variegated verdure, resembling the workes in Irish-stitch. In the middle of this howse was a delicate Staire-case of wood, which was curiously carved, and on the posts of every interstice was some prettie figure, as of a grave Divine with his booke and spectacles, a Mendicant Friar, etc., not one thing twice. On the dores of the upper storie on the outside (which were painted darke Umber) were the figures of the gods of the Gentiles, viz. on the South dore, 2d storie, was Apollo; on another, Jupiter with his Thunderbolt, etc., bigger then the life, and donne by an excellent hand; the heightnings were of hatchings of gold, which when the Sun shone on them made a most glorious shew.

The upper part of the uppermost dore on the East side had inserted into it a large Looking-glasse, with which the Stranger was very gratefully decieved, for (after he had been entertained a pretty while, with the prospects of the Ponds, Walks, and countrey, which this dore faced) when you were about to returne into the roome, one would have sworn (*primo intuitu* [at first glance]), that he had beheld another Prospect through the Howse: for, as soon as the Straunger was landed on the Balconie, the Conserge that shewed the howse would shutt the dore to putt this fallacy on him with the Looking-glasse. This was his Lordship's Summer-howse: for he sayes (in his essay) one should have seates for Summer and Winter as well as Cloathes.

From hence to Gorhambery in a straite line (about a little mile, the way easily ascending, hardly so acclive as a Deske) leade three parallel walkes: in the middlemost three coaches may passe abreast: in the wing-walkes two.

About the mid-way from Verolam-house to Gorambery, on the right hand, on the side of a Hill which faces the Passer-by, are sett in artificiall manner severall stately Trees of the like groweth and heighth, whose diversity of greens on the side of the hill are exceeding pleasant. These delicate walkes and prospects entertaine the Eie to Gorambery-howse, which is a large, well-built Gothique howse, built (I thinke) by Sr Nicholas Bacon, Lord Keeper, father to this Lord Chancellor, to whom it descended by the death of Anthony Bacon his middle brother, who died sans issue. The Lord Chancellor made an addition of a noble Portico, which fronts the Garden to the South; opposite to every arch of this Portico, and as big as the arch, are drawn by an excellent hand (but the mischief of it is, in water-colours) curious pictures, all Emblematicall, with Motto's under each. For example, one I remember is a ship tossed in a storm, the Motto, *Alter erit tum Tiphys* [There will come another Tiphys].

Over this Portico is a stately Gallerie, whose Glasse-windowes are all painted: and every pane with severall figures of beest, bird, or flower: perhaps his Lordship might use them as Topiques for Locall memorie. The windowes looke into the Garden: the side opposite to them no window; but is hung all with pictures at length, as of King James, his Lordship, and severall Illustrious persons of his time. At the end you enter is no windowe, but there is a very large picture, thus: In the middle on a Rock in the sea stands King James in armour with his regall Ornaments; on his right hand stands (but whether or no on a Rock I have forgott) King Hen. 4 of France, in armour; and on his left hand the King of Spaine in like manner. These figures are (at least) as big as the life: they are donne only with umbre and shell-gold; all the heightning and illuminated part being burnisht gold and the shadowed umbre, as in the pictures of the Gods on the dores of Verulam-howse. The roofe of this Gallerie is semi-cylindrique, and painted by the same hand and same manner, with heads and busts of Greek and Roman Emperours and Heroes.

In the Hall (which is of the auncient building) is a large storie very well painted of the Feastes of the Gods, where Mars is caught in a nett by Vulcan. On the wall, over the Chimney, is painted an Oake with Akornes falling from it, the Word, *Nisi quid potius* [Failing some better chance] and on the wall over the Table is painted Ceres teaching the Soweing of Corne, the Word, *Moniti meliora* [We now have better counsel].

The garden is large, which was (no doubt) rarely planted and kept in his Lordship's time. Here is a handsome Dore, which opens into Oake-wood; over this dore in golden letters on blew are six verses.

The Oakes of this wood are very great and shadie. His Lordship much delighted himselfe here: under every tree, he planted some fine flower, or flowers, some whereof are there still (1656) viz. Paeonies, Tulips.

From this Wood a dore opens into a place as big as an ordinary Parke, the west part whereof is Coppice-wood, where are Walkes cut-out as straight as a line, and broad enough for a coach, a quarter of a mile long or better. Here his Lordship much meditated, his servant Mr Bushell attending him with his pen and inke horne to sett downe his present Notions.

The east of this Parquet was heretofore, in his Lordship's prosperitie, a Paradise; now is a large ploughed field. The walkes, both in the Coppices and other Boscages, were most ingeniosely designed: at severall good Viewes, were erected elegant Sommer-howses well built of Roman-architecture, well wainscotted and cieled; yet standing, but defaced, so that one would have thought the Barbarians had made a Conquest here.

The figures of the Ponds were thus: they were pitched at the bottomes with pebbles of severall colours, which were work't in to severall figures, as of Fishes, etc., which in his Lordship's time were plainly to be seen through the cleare water, now over-grown with flagges and rushes. If a poore bodie had brought his Lordship half a dozen pebbles of a curious colour, he would give them a shilling, so curious was he in perfecting his Fish-ponds, which I guesse doe containe four acres. In the middle of the middlemost pond, in the Island, is a curious banquetting-house of Roman architecture, paved with black and white marble; covered with Cornish slatt, and neatly wainscotted.

His Lordship was wont to say, *I will lay my mannor of Gorambery on't*, to which one Judge made a spightfull reply, saying he would not hold a wager against that, but against any other Mannour of his Lordship's, he would. Now this Illustrious Lord Chancellor had only this Mannor of Gorambery.

In April, and the Springtime, his Lordship would, when it rayned, take his Coach (open) to receive the benefit of Irrigation, which he was wont to say was very wholsome because of the Nitre in the Aire and the *Universall Spirit of the World*.

Mr Hobbs told me that the cause of his Lordship's death was trying an Experiment; viz. as he was taking the aire in a Coach with Dr Witherborne (a Scotchman, Physitian to the King) towards High-gate, snow lay on the ground, and it came into my Lord's thoughts, why flesh might not be preserved in snow, as in Salt. They were resolved they would try the Experiment presently. They alighted out of the Coach and went into a poore woman's house at the bottom of Highgate hill, and bought a Hen, and made the woman exenterate it, and then stuffed the body with Snow, and my Lord did help to doe it himselfe. The Snow so chilled him that he immediately fell so extremely ill, that he could not returne to his Lodging (I suppose then at Graye's Inne) but went to the Earle of Arundel's house at High-gate, where they putt him into a good bed warmed with a Panne, but it was a damp bed that had not been layn-in in about a yeare before, which gave him such a colde that in 2 or 3 dayes as I remember Mr Hobbes told me, he dyed of Suffocation.

This October, 1681, it rang over all St Albans that Sir Harbottle Grimston, Master of the Rolles, had removed the Coffin of this most renowned Lord Chancellour to make roome for his owne to lye-in in the vault there at St Michael's church.

ISAAC BARROW

Born 1630. Mathematician. At the age of thirty he obtained the Greek Chair at Cambridge and, in 1662, the Gresham Professorship of Geometry, which he resigned on being appointed first Lucasian Professor of Mathematics in the same University. In 1669 he resigned in favour of his pupil, Isaac Newton. He was made a Doctor of Divinity by mandate in 1670, and having preached a celebrated sermon that lasted for three and a half hours, said he felt tired from *standing* so long. In 1672 he became Master of Trinity College, Cambridge, where he founded the library. Died 1677.

HIS Father, Thomas Barrow, was the second son of Isaac Barrow of Spinney abbey in the Countie of Cambridge, Esq., who was a Justice of the Peace there above fourtie yeares. The father of Thomas never designed him for a Tradesman, but he was so severe to him he could not endure to live with him, so he came to London and was apprentice to a Linnen-draper. He kept shoppe at the Signe of the White-Horse in Forster-Lane, near St Forster's Church, in St Leonard's parish; and his son was christened at St John Zacharie's in Forster Lane, for at that time St Leonard's Church was pulled downe to be re-edified.

He went to schoole, first to Mr Brookes at Charter-house, two yeares. His father gave to Mr Brookes 4 pounds per annum, whereas his pay was but 2 pound, to be carefull of him; but Mr Brookes was negligent of him, which the Captain of the school acquainted his father (his Kinsman) and sayd that he would not have him stay there any longer than *he* did, for that he instructed him.

Afterwards to one Mr Holbitch, about fower years, at Felton in Essex, from whence he was admitted of Peterhouse College in Cambridge first, and went to schoole a yeare after. Then he was admitted to Trinity College in Cambridge at 13 yeares old.

His father dealt in his Trade to Ireland, where he had a great losse, neer 1000 pounds; upon which he wrote to Mr Holbitch, a Puritan, to be pleased to take a little paines more than ordinary with him, because the times growing so bad, and such a losse then received, that he did not know how he might be able to provide for him; and so Mr Holbitch tooke him away from the Howse where he was boarded to his owne Howse, and made him Tutor to my Lord Viscount Fairfax, ward to the Lord Viscount Say and Seale, where he continued so long as my Lord continued.

This Viscount Fairfax, being a schooleboy, married a Gentleman's daughter in the towne there, who had but a thousand pounds. So leaving the schoole, would needs have Mr Isaac Barrow with him, and tolde him he would maintain him. But my Lord Say was so cruel to him that he would not allow anything; 'tis thought he dyed for want. The 1000 pounds could not serve him long.

During this time, olde Mr Thomas Barrow was shutt-up at Oxford, which was then a Garrison for the King, and could not heare of his Sonne. But young Isaac's Master, Holbitch, found him out in London, and courted him to come to his Schoole, and that he would make him his Heire: But he did not care to goe to schoole again.

When my Lord Fairfax faild, and that he saw he grewe heavy upon him, he went to see one of his Schoolefellowes, one Mr Walpole, a Norfolk Gent., who asked him what would he doe? He replyed he knew not what to doe; he could not goe to his father at Oxford. Mr Walpole then tolde him: I am goeing to Cambridge to Trinity College and I will maintaine you there; and so he did for halfe a yeare till the Surrender of Oxford; and then his Father enquired after him and found him at Cambridge. And the very next day after old Mr Barrow came to Cambridge, Mr Walpole was leaving the University and (hearing nothing of Isaac's father) resolved to take Isaac along with him to his Howse. His father then asked him what profession he would be of, a merchant or etc.? He begged of his father to lett him continue in the University. His father then asked what would maintain him. He told him 20 pounds per annum. I warrant you, sayd he, I will maintaine myselfe with it. His father replyed, I'le make a shift to allow you that. So his father then went to his Tutor and acquainted him. His Tutor, Dr Duport, told him he would take nothing for his Reading to him, for that he was likely to make a brave Scholar, and he would helpe him to halfe a chamber for nothing. And the next news his father heard of him was that he was chosen in to the Howse. Dr Hill was then Master of the College. He mett Isaac one day, and layd his hand upon his head, and sayd, Thou art a good boy, 'tis pitty thou art a Cavalier.

His Humour when a Boy, and after: merry and cheerfull, and beloved wherever he came. His grandfather kept him till he was seven yeares old; his father was faine to force him away, for he would have been good for nothing there.

A good Poet, English and Latin. He spake 8 severall Languages.

He was a strong and stowt man and feared not any man. He would fight with the Butchers boyes in St Nicholas shambles, and be hard enough for any of them.

He went to Travell three or four yeares after the King was beheaded, upon the Colledge account. He was a Candidate for the Greeke Professor's place and had the consent of the University, but Oliver Cromwell put in Dr Widrington, and then he travelled.

He was abroade about 5 yeares, viz. in Italie, France, Germany, Constantinople. As he went to Constantinople, two men of warre, Turkish Shippes, attacqued the Vessell wherin he was. In which engagement he shewed much valour in defending the vessell; which the men that were in that engagement often testifye, for he never told his father of it himself.

Upon his return, he came in Ship to Venice, which was stowed with Cotton-wooll, and as soon as ever they came on Shore the ship fell on fire and was utterly consumed, and not a man lost, but not any goods saved – a wonderfull preservation.

At Constantinople, being in company with the English Merchants, there was a Rhadamontade that would fight with any man and bragged of his Valour, and dared any man there to try him. So no man accepting, said Isaac (not then a Divine) Why, if none els will try you I will; and fell upon him and chastised him handsomly that he vaunted no more amongst them.

After he had been three years beyond sea, his Correspondent dyed, so that he had no more supply; yet he was so well beloved that he never wanted.

At Constantinople, he wayted on the Consul, Sir Thomas Bendish, who made him staye with him, and kept him there a yeare and a halfe, whether he would or no.

At Constantinople, Mr Dawes, a Turkey merchant, desired Mr Barrow to stay but such a time and he would returne with him, but when that time came he could not goe, some Businesse stayed him. Mr Barrow could stay no longer; so Mr Dawes would have had Mr Barrow have 100 pistolles. No, said Mr Barrow, I know not whether I shall be able to pay you. 'Tis no matter, said Mr Dawes. To be short, forced him to take fifty pistolls, which at his return he payd him again.

I have heard Mr Wilson say that when he was at study, was so intent at it when the bed was made, or so, he heeded it not nor perceived it, was so *totus in hoc* [absorbed]; and would sometimes be goeing out without his hatt on.

He was by no means a spruce man, not a Dr Smirke, but most negligent in his dresse. As he was walking one day in St James's parke, his hatt up, his cloake halfe on and halfe off, a gent. came behind him and clapt him on the Shoulder and sayd, Well goe thy wayes for the veriest scholar that ever I mett with.

He was a strong man, but pale as the Candle he studyed by.

His pill (an opiate, possibly Matthews his pil) which he was wont to take in Turkey, which was wont to doe him good, but he took it preposterously at Mr Wilson's, the Saddlers, neer Suffolk House, where he was wont to lye and where he dyed, and 'twas the cause of his death.

As he laye unravelling in the agonie of death, the Standers-by could hear him say softly, *I have seen the Glories of the world.*

FRANCIS BEAUMONT AND JOHN FLETCHER

Playwrights. Francis Beaumont was born in 1584 and collaborated with John Fletcher in the writing of plays from 1606 until his death in 1616. Dryden states that Beaumont was so accurate a judge of plays that Ben Jonson submitted all his writings to his censure. His superior faculty for the construction of plots is discernible in some of the plays that he wrote with Fletcher. Beaumont was educated at Oxford, and John Fletcher, who was born in 1579, was at Cambridge. Fletcher wrote fifty-two plays in all, fifteen of them with Beaumont, sixteen by himself, and the rest in collaboration with Rowley, Middleton, Massinger, Ben Jonson, and Shakespeare. He died in 1625.

MR FRANCIS BEAUMONT was the son of Judge Beaumont. There was a wonderfull consimility of phansey between him and Mr John Fletcher, which caused that dearnesse of frendship between them.

I thinke they were both of Queen's College in Cambridge.

I have heard Dr John Earles, since Bishop of Sarum, who knew them, say, that Mr Beaumont's maine Businesse was to lop the overflowings of Mr Fletcher's luxuriant Fancy and flowing Witt.

They lived together on the Banke side, not far from the Play-house, both batchelors; lay together; had one Wench in the house between them, which they did so admire; the same cloathes and cloake, &c. betweene them.

He writt (amongst many other) an admirable Elegie on the Countesse of Rutland. John Earles in his Verses on him, speaking of them,

A monument that will then lasting bee,
When all her Marble is more dust than shee.

Mr Edm. Waller on him:

> *I never yet the Tragick Scene assaid*
> *Deterr'd by thy inimitable* Mayd*:*
> *And when I striv'd to reach the Comick Stile*
> *Thy* Scornfull Lady *seem'd to mock my toile.*

John Fletcher, invited to goe with a Knight into Norfolke or Suffolke in the Plague-time 1625, stayd but to make himselfe a suite of Cloathes, and while it was makeing, fell sick of the Plague and dyed. This I had (1668) from his Tayler, who is now a very old man, and Clarke of St Mary Overy's in Southwark. Mr Fletcher had an Issue in his arm (I thought it had not used so long ago). The Clarke (who was wont to bring him Ivy-leaves to dresse it) when he came, found the Spotts upon him. Death stopped his Journey and laid him low here.

SIR JOHN BIRKENHEAD

Born 1616. Poet and journalist. Probationer Fellow of All Souls, Oxford, 1640. Devised and mostly wrote *Mercurius Aulicus*, the weekly journal of the Royalists at Oxford, 1642–5. He was imprisoned after the surrender of Oxford, and subsequently, according to Anthony Wood, *he lived by his wits in helping young gentlemen out at dead lifts in making poems, songs, and epistles to their respective mistresses, as also in translating and writing several little things and other petite employments.* In exile with the Prince of Wales 1648. Knighted at St Germains 1649. M.P. for Wilton 1661. Fellow of the Royal Society. His poems were mainly satirical. Died 1679.

SIR JOHN BIRKENHEAD, Knight, was borne at Nantwych, in Cheshire. His father was a Sadler there, and he had a brother a sadler, a Trooper in Sir Thomas Ashton's regiment, who was quartered at my father's, who tolde me so.

He went to Oxford University, and was first a Servitor of Oriall Colledge: he wrote an excellent hand, and, when William Laud, ABC [*Archbishop of Canterbury*], was last there, he had occasion to have some things well transcribed, and this Birkenhead was recommended to him, who performed his businesse so well, that the archbishop recommended him to All Soules College to be a Fellow, and he was accordingly elected. He was Scholar enough, and a Poet.

After Edgehill fight, when King Charles I first had his Court at Oxford, he was pitched upon as one fitt to write the Newes, which Oxford Newes was called *Mercurius Aulicus*, which he writt wittily enough, till the surrender of the Towne.

After the surrender of Oxford, he was putt out of his Fellowship by the Visitors, and was faine to shift for himselfe as well as he could. Most part of his time he spent at London, where he mett with severall persons of quality that loved his company, and made much of him.

He went over into France, where he stayed some time, I thinke not long. He received grace there from the Dutches of Newcastle, I remember he told me. He gott many a fourty shillings (I beleeve) by Pamphlets, such as that of *Col. Pride*, and *The Last Will and Testament of Philip Earle of Pembroke*, &c.

He was exceedingly bold, confident, witty, not very grateful to his benefactors; would Lye damnably. He was of midling stature, great goggli eies, not of sweet aspect.

He was chosen a Burghes of Parliament at Wilton in Wiltshire, anno Domini 1661, i.e. of the King's long parliament. Anno 1679 upon the choosing of *this* Parliament, he went downe to be elected, and at Salisbury heard how he was scorned and mocked at Wilton (whither he was goeing) and called *Pensioner*, etc: he went not to the Borough where he intended to stand; but returned to London, and tooke it so to heart that he insensibly decayed and pined away; and so dyed at his Lodgeings in Whitehall, and was buried Saturday, December 6, in St Martyn's churchyard-in-the-fields, neer the church, according to his Will and Testament; his reason was because he sayd they removed the bodies out of the Church.

I remember at Bristow (when I was a boy) it was a common fashion for the woemen to get a Tooth out of a Sckull in the Church yard; which they wore as a preservative against the Tooth-ach. Under the Cathedral-church at Hereford is the greatest Charnel-house for bones, that ever I saw in England. In A° 1650 there lived amongst those bones a poor old woman that, to help out her fire, did use to mix the deadmen's bones: this was thrift and poverty: but cunning alewives putt the Ashes of these bones in their Ale to make it intoxicateing.

SIR HENRY BLOUNT

Born 1602. Traveller. On 7 May 1634 he left Venice in a Venetian galley on his well-known voyage to the Levant. Sailing down the Adriatic, he landed at Spalatro in Dalmatia: thence he crossed the Dinaric Alps and descended into the plains of Bosnia, arriving at Sarajevo, the capital, after a journey of nine days. Departing thence with the Turkish troops proceeding to the war in Poland, he arrived at Valiero in Servia. Three days later he reached Belgrade and then proceeded by way of Nissa, Sofia in Bulgaria, and Philippolis [*Plovdiv*] to Adrianople, finally reaching Constantinople after a land journey of fifteen hundred miles in fifty-two days. He then sailed for Alexandria with the Turkish Fleet, visiting Rhodes on the way. Thence he reached Cairo by water in five days, from which he made an excursion to the interior of the great pyramid at Gizeh. Leaving Cairo in November, he took passage on board a French vessel at Alexandria, bound for Palermo. Re-embarking at Trepassi for Naples, he returned via Rome, Florence, and Bologna to Venice, where he arrived after eleven months, having journeyed about six thousand miles. Published *Voyage to the Levant*, 1636. Knighted 1640. Sided with the Royalists in the Civil War. Died 1682.

SIR HENRY BLOUNT, Knight, was borne (I presume) at Tittinghanger in the Countie of Hertford. It was heretofore the summer seate of the Lord Abbot of St Alban's.

He was pretty wild when young, especially addicted to common wenches. He was a second brother.

He was a Gentleman Pensioner to King Charles I, on whom he wayted (as it was his turne) to Yorke (when the King deserted the Parliament): was with him at Edgehill fight; came with him to Oxford; and so returned to London; walkt into Westminster Hall with his Sword by his side; the Parliamentarians all stared upon him as a Cavaleer, knowing that he had been with the King; was called before the House of Commons, where he remonstrated to them he did but his duty, and so they acquitted him.

In those dayes he dined most commonly at the Heycock's-ordinary, near the Pallzgrave head taverne, in the Strand, which was much frequented by Parliament men and gallants. One time Colonel Betridge being there (one of the handsomest men about the Towne) and bragged how much the woemen loved him. Sir H. Blount did lay a wager, that let them two goe together to a Bordello, he only without money, with his handsome person, and Sir Henry with a twenty-shilling piece on his bald croone, that the wenches should choose Sir Henry before Betridge; and Sir H won the wager. Edmund Wyld, Esq. was one of the witnesses.

There was a Pamphlet (writt by Henry Nevill, Esq.) called the *Parliament of Ladies*, wherin Sir Henry Blount was the first to be called to the Barre, for spreading abroad that abominable and dangerous Doctrine that it was far cheaper and safer to lye with Common Wenches then with Ladies of Quality.

His estate left him by his father was 500 pounds per annum, which he sold for an annuitie of 1000 pounds per annum; and since, his elder brother dyed.

He was made one of the Comittee for Regulating the Lawes. He was severe against Tythes, and for the abolishing them, and that every Minister should have 100 pounds per annum and no more.

Since he was — year olde he dranke nothing but water or Coffee. 1647, or therabout, he maryed to Mris Hester Wase, daughter of Christopher Wase, who dyed 1679, by whom he haz two sonnes, ingeniose young Gentlemen. Charles Blount (his second sonne) hath writt *Anima Mundi* (burnt by order of the Bishop of London) and of *Sacrifices*.

I remember twenty yeares since he inveighed much against sending youths to the Universities – *quaere* if his sons were there – because they learnt there to be debaucht, and that the learning that they learned there they were to unlearne againe, as a man that is buttond or laced too hard, must unbutton before he can be at his ease. Drunkeness he much exclaimed against, but wenching he allowed. When Coffee first came in he was a great upholder of it, and hath ever since been a constant frequenter of Coffee houses, especially Mr Farre at the Rainbowe, by Inner Temple Gate, and lately John's coffee house, at Fuller's rents.

The first Coffe howse in London was in St Michael's Alley in Cornehill, opposite to the church, which was sett up by one Bowman (Coachman to Mr Hodges, a Turkey merchant, who putt him upon it) in or about the yeare 1652. 'Twas about four yeares before any other was sett up, and that was by Mr Far. Jonathan Paynter, opposite to St Michael's Church, was the first apprentice to the Trade, viz. to Bowman. The Bagneo, in Newgate Street, was built and first opened in December 1679, built by Turkish Merchants.

He is a Gentleman of very cleare Judgement, great experience, much Contemplation, not of very much Reading, of great Foresight into Govenment. His conversation is admirable. When he was young, he was a great collector of Bookes, as his sonne is now.

He was heretofore a great Shammer, i.e. one that tells falsities not to doe any body any injury, but to impose on their understanding; e.g. at Mr Farre's, that at an Inne (nameing the signe) in St Albans, the Innekeeper had made a Hogs-trough of a free-stone coffin, but the pigges after that grew leane, dancing and skipping, and would run upon the topps of the houses like goates. Two young Gents., that heard Sir H tell this *sham* so gravely, rode the next day to St Albans to enquire; comeing there, nobody had heard of any such thing, 'twas altogether false. The next night as soon as they allighted, they came to the Rainbowe and found Sir H, looked louringly on him, and told him they wondered he was not ashamed as to tell such stories, etc. Why, Gentlemen, sayd Sir H, have you been there to make enquiry? Yea, sayd they. Why truly, gentlemen, sayd Sir H, I heard you tell strange things that I knew to be false. I would not have gonne over the threshold of the dore to have found you out in a Lye, at which all the Company laught at the two young Gents.

He was wont to say that he did not care to have his servants goe to Church, for there servants infected one another to goe to the Alehouse and learne debauchery; but he did bid them goe to see the Executions at Tyeburne, which worke more upon them than all the oratory in the Sermons.

He is now (1680) neer or altogether 80 yeares, his Intellectuals good still; and body pretty strong.

This last weeke of Sept. 1682, he was taken very ill at London, and his Feet swelled; and removed to Tittinghanger.

EDMUND BONNER

Born 1495. Divine. Chaplain to Cardinal Wolsey 1529. He appealed in person to Pope Clement VII against Henry VIII's ex-communication after his marriage to Anne Boleyn in 1533. Bishop of Hereford and Ambassador to the French Court 1538. Bishop of London 1539. Ambassador to the Emperor 1542. Bonner was three times imprisoned for his opposition to Edward VI's religious policy, and was deprived of his bishopric. Restored to his see on Mary's accession in 1553, he joined with such great severity in the Marian persecution that he became one of the chief villains in Foxe's Book of Martyrs, where he is referred to as the Bloody Bishop: he was said to have *delightedly followed the accusation and found means to indite Richard Mekins, a child not past his fifteenth year, who had heard folkes talke, and in his innocence had chanced to speake against the Sacrament of the Altar. The poore boy for the safeguard of his life would gladly have said that the twelve apostles taught it hym, for he had not cared whom he had named, such was his childish innocence and feare,* and had him burned to death at Smithfield. He refused the Oath of Supremacy to Elizabeth, and was again deprived of his bishopric. He died in prison in 1569, and although Foxe noted angrily that Bonner *had long feasted and banqueted in durance at the Marshalsea,* he held that his *stinking death* was a certain sign of God's wrath against *the children of the murdering mother church of Rome.*

BISHOP BONNER was of Broadgate hall; he came thither a poor boy, and was at first a skullion boy in the kitchin, afterwards became a Servitor, and so by his industry raysed to what he was.

When he came to his greatnes, in acknowledgement from whence he had his Rise, he gave to the Kitchin there a great brasse-pott, called Bonners-pott, which was taken away in the Parliament time. Mr Steevens has shewed the Pott to me, I remember. It was the biggest, perhaps, in Oxford.

CAISHO BOROUGH

MR CAISHO BURROUGHS was one of the most beautiful Men in England, and very Valiant, but very proud and blood-thirsty: There was then in London a very Beautiful Italian Lady, who fell so extreamly in Love with him, that she did let him enjoy her, which she had never let any Man do before: Wherefore, said she, I shall request this favour of you, never to tell anyone of it. The Gentlewoman died: and afterwards in a Tavern in London he spake of it: and there going to make water, the Ghost of the Gentlewoman did appear to him. He was afterwards troubled with the Apparition of her, even sometimes in company when he was drinking; but he only perceived it: Before she did appear he did find a kind of Chilness upon his Spirits.

Sir John Burroughes being sent Envoy to the Emperor by King Charles I, did take his Eldest Son Caisho Boroughes along with him, and taking his Journey through Italy, left his son at Florence to learn the Language; where he having an Intrigue with a beautiful Courtisan (Mistress of the Grand Duke) their Familiarity became so public, that it came to the Duke's Ear, who took a Resolution to have him Murdered, but Caisho having had timely notice of the Duke's design by some of the English there, immediately left the City without acquainting his Mistress with it, and came to England; whereupon the Duke being disappointed of his Revenge fell upon his Mistress in most reproachful Language, she on the other side resenting the sudden Departure of her Gallant of whom she was most passionately enamour'd, killed her self. At the same moment that she expired, she did appear to Caisho at his Lodgings in London. Collonel Remes was then in Bed with him, who saw her as well as he; giving him an account of her Resentments of his Ingratitude to her, in leaving her so suddenly, and exposing her to the Fury of the Duke, not omitting her own

Tragical EXIT, adding withall, that he should be slain in a Duell, which accordingly happened; and thus she appeared to him frequently, even when his younger Brother (who afterwards was Sir John) was a Bed with him. As often as she did appear, he would cry out with great shrieking, and trembling of his Body, as anguish of Mind, saying, *O God! here she comes, she comes*, and at this rate she appeared 'till he was killed; she appeared to him the morning before he was killed.

This Story was so common, that King Charles I sent for Caisho Burroughes's Father whom he examined as to the Truth of the Matter; who did (together with Collonel Remes) averr, the Matter of Fact to be true, so that the King thought it worth his while to send to Florence, to enquire at what time this unhappy Lady killed herself. It was found to be the same Minute that she first appeared to Caisho being a Bed with Colonel Remes. This Relation I had from my worthy Friend Mr Monson, who had it from Sir John's own Mouth, Brother of Caisho; he had also the same Account from his own Father, who was intimately acquainted with old Sir John Burroughes and both his Sons, and says, as often as Caisho related this, he wept bitterly.

JAMES BOVEY

JAMES BOVEY, Esq., was the youngest son of Andrew Bovey, Merchant, Cash-keeper to Sir Peter Vanore, in London. He was borne in the middle of Mincing-lane, in the parish of St Dunstan's in the East, London, anno 1622, May 7th, at six a clock in the morning. Went to schoole at Mercers Chapell, under Mr Augur. At 9 sent into the Lowe Countreys; then returned, and perfected himselfe in the Latin and Greeke. At 14, travelled into France and Italie, Switzerland, Germany, and the Lowe Countreys. Returned into England at 19; then lived with one Hoste, a Banquier, 8 yeares: was his cashier 8 or 9 yeares. Then traded for himselfe (27) till he was 31; then maried the only daughter of William de Vischer, a Merchant; lived 18 yeares with her, then continued single. Left off trade at 32, and retired to a Countrey life, by reason of his indisposition, the ayre of the Citie not agreeing with him. Then in these Retirements he wrote *Active Philosophy* (a thing not donne before) wherin are enumerated all the Arts and Tricks practised in Negotiation, and how they were to be ballanced by counter-prudentiall Rules.

Whilest he lived with Mr Hoste, he kept the Cash of the Ambassadors of Spaine that were here; and of the Farmers, called by them *Assentistes*, that did furnish the Spanish and Imperiall armies of the Low-Countreys and Germany; and also many other great Cashes, as of Sir Theodore Mayern, etc. (his dealing being altogether in money-matters) by which meanes he became acquainted with the Ministers of State both here and abroad.

When he was abroad, his chiefe employment was to observe the affaires of State and their Judicatures, and to take the Politique Surveys in the Countreys he travelled thorough, more especially in relation to Trade. He speakes the Low-Dutch, High-Dutch, French, Italian, Spanish, and Lingua Franco, and Latin, besides his owne.

When he retired from Businesse he studied the Lawe-Merchant, and admitted himselfe of the Inner Temple, London, about 1660. His Judgment haz been taken in most of the great Causes of his time in points concerning the Lawe Merchant.

For his health he never had it very well, but indifferently, alwaies a weake stomach, which proceeded from the agitation of the Braine. His Dyet was alwayes fine diet: much Chicken.

From 14 he began to take notice of all Prudentiall Rules as came in his way, and wrote them downe, and so continued till this day, Sept. 28, 1680, being now in his 59th yeare. He made it his businesse to advance the Trade of England, and many men have printed his Conceptions. He wrote a Table of all the Exchanges in Europe.

He hath writt (which is in his custodie, and which I have seen, and many of them read) these treatises, *viz*.

1. *The Characters, or Index Rerum:* in 4 tomes
2. *The Introduction to Active Philosophy*
3. *The Art of Building a Man: or Education*
4. *The Art of Conversation*
5. *The Art of Complyance*
6. *The Art of Governing the Tongue*
7. *The Art of Governing the Penn*
8. *The Government of Action*
9. *The Government of Resolution*
10. *The Government of Reputation*
11. *The Government of Power:* in 2 tomes
12. *The Government of Servients*
13. *The Government of Subserviency*
14. *The Government of Friendshipp*
15. *The Government of Enmities*

16. *The Government of Law-suites*
17. *The Art of Gaining Wealth*
18. *The Art of Preserving Wealth*
19. *The Art of Buying and Selling*
20. *The Art of Expending Wealth*
21. *The Government of Secresy*
22. *The Government of Amor Conjugalis:* in 2 tomes
23. *Of Amor Concupiscentiae*
24. *The Government of Felicity*
25. *The Lives of Atticus, Sejanus, Augustus*
26. *The Causes of the Diseases of the Mind*
27. *The Cures of the Mind, viz. Passions, Diseases, Vices, Errours, Defects*
28. *The Art of Discerning Men*
29. *The Art of Discerning a Man's selfe*
30. *Religion from Reason:* in 3 tomes
31. *The Life of Cum-fu-zu, soe farr wrote by J.B.*
32. *The Life of Mahomett, wrot by Sir Walter Raleigh's papers, with some small addition for methodizing the same.*

I have desired him to give these MSS to the library of the Royal Society.

As to his person, he is about 5 foot high, spare slender body, strait, haire exceeding black and curling at the end, a dark hazell eie, of a midling size, but the most sprightly that I have beheld, browes and beard of the colour as his haire. A person of great Temperance, and deepe Thoughts, and a working head, never Idle. From 14 he had a Candle burning by him all night, with pen, inke, and paper, to write downe thoughts as they came into his head; that he might not loose a Thought. Was ever a great Lover of Naturall Philosophie. His whole life has been perplex't in Lawe-suites (which haz made him expert in Humane affaires) in which he alwaies overcame. He had many Lawe-suites with powerfull Adversaries; one lasted 18 yeares. Red-haired men never had any kindnesse for him.

In all his Travills he was never robbed.

RICHARD BOYLE
EARL OF CORK

Born 1566. Statesman. Went to Ireland 1588. Escheator to James Crofton, the Escheator General 1590. Imprisoned on a charge of embezzling the records 1592. Later he was again accused of fraud, but this time was acquitted. Conveyed to Queen Elizabeth the news of the victory near Kinsale 1601. Purchased for £1,000 Sir Walter Raleigh's Irish estates, out of which he rapidly acquired a huge fortune. Knighted 1603. Privy Councillor for Munster 1606, and for Ireland 1612. Created Lord Boyle, Baron of Youghal 1616, and Viscount Dungarvan and Earl of Cork 1620. Lord Justice of Ireland 1629. Lord High Treasurer 1631. Died 1643.

RICHARD, the first Earle of Cork, being born a private Gentleman, and younger Brother of a younger Brother, to no other Heritage than is expressed in the Device and Motto, which his humble Gratitude inscribed on all the Palaces he built, *God's Providence, mine Inheritance*; by that Providence, and his diligent and wise Industry, raised such an Honour and Estate, and left such a Familie, as never any Subject of these three Kingdomes did, and that with so unspotted a Reputation of Integrity that the most invidious scrutiny could find no blott, though it winnowed all the methods of his Rising most severely.

Thomas, Earl of Strafford made him disgorge 1500 pounds per annum, which he restored to the Church.

Earl of Corke bought of Captaine Horsey fourtie Ploughlands in Ireland for *fourtie pounds*. (A. Ettrick assures me, I say againe fourtie ploughlands.)

Master Boyl, after Earle of Cork (who was then a Widdower) came one morning to waite on Sir Jeofry Fenton, at that time a great Officer of State in that Kingdome of Ireland, who being ingaged in business, and not knowing who it was who desired to speake with him, a while delayed him access; which time he spent pleasantly with his young Daughter in her Nurse's Arms. But when Sir Jeoffry came, and saw whom he had made stay somewhat too long, he civilly excused it. But Master Boyl replied, he had been very well entertayned; and spent his time much to his satisfaction, in courting his Daughter, if he might obtaine the Honour to be accepted for his Son-in-lawe. At which Sir Jeoffry, smiling (to hear one who had been formerly married, move for a Wife carried in Arms, and under two years old) asked him if would stay for her? To which he frankly answered him he would, and Sir Jeoffry as generously promised him he should then have his consent. And they both kept their words honourably.

And by this virtuous Lady he had thirteen Children, ten of which he lived to see honourably married, and died a grandfather by the youngest of them.

My Lady Petty sayes he had a wife or two before, and that he maried Mris Fenton without her father's consent.

This Noble Lord, by his prudent and pious Consort, no lesse an Ornament and Honour to their Descendants than himself, was blessed with five sonnes (of which he lived to see four Lords and Peeres of the Kingdome of Ireland, and a fifth, more than these Titles speak, a Soveraigne and Peerlesse in a larger Province, that of universall nature, subdued and made obsequious to his inquisitive mind) and eight Daughters.

THE HONOURABLE ROBERT BOYLE

Born 1627. Natural philosopher and chemist. He was the fourteenth child of the great Earl of Cork. His voluminous writings exhibit vividly the fruitfulness of the experimental method, and his observations added greatly to existing knowledge, especially in regard to pneumatics: his experimental proof of the proportional relation between the elasticity and pressure of gases is still known as *Boyle's Law*. It was Robert Boyle, in his *Skepticall Chymist* (1661), who destroyed the *Elements* of the Ancients and gave to the word its modern meaning. One of the founders of the Royal Society, he declined the presidency, from a scruple about oaths. His interest in religion was so intense that he taught himself *as much Greek and Hebrew as sufficed to read the Old and New Testaments*, so as not to have to rely on translations. *A Chaldee grammar I likewise took the pains of learning*, he continued, *to be able to understand that part of Daniel, and those few other portions of Scripture that were written in that tongue*; *and I have added a Syriac grammar purely to be able one day to read the divine discourses of our Saviour in His own language*. He was Governor of the Corporation for the Spread of the Gospel in New England from 1661 to 1689, and a Director of the East India Company. He died in 1691.

THE Honourable Robert Boyle, Esq., that profound Philosopher, accomplished Humanist, and excellent Divine, I had almost sayd Lay-Bishop, as one hath stiled Sir Henry Savil, was borne at Lismor in the County of Corke. He was nursed by an Irish Nurse, after the Irish manner, wher they putt the child into a pendulous Satchell (insted of a Cradle) with a slitt for the Child's head to peepe out.

When a boy at Eaton was verie sickly and pale. Went to the University of Leyden. Travelled France, Italy, Switzerland. I have oftentimes heard him say that after he had seen the Antiquities and architecture of Rome, he esteemed none any where els.

He speakes Latin very well, and very readily, as most men I have mett with. I have heard him say that when he was young, he read over Cowper's *Dictionary*: wherin I thinke he did very well, and I beleeve he is much beholding to him for his Mastership of that Language.

His father in his Will, when he comes to the Settlement and Provision for his son Robert, thus: *Item, to my son Robert, whom I beseech God to blesse with a particular Blessing, I bequeath, &c.* Mr Robert Hooke, who has seen the Rentall, sayes it was 3000 pounds per annum: the greatest part is in Ireland.

He is very tall (about six foot high) and streight, very temperate, and vertuouse, and frugall: a Batcheler; keepes a Coach; sojournes with his sister, the Lady Ranulagh. His greatest delight is Chymistrey. He haz at his sister's a noble Laboratory, and severall servants (Prentices to him) to looke to it. He is charitable to ingeniose men that are in want, and foreigne Chymists have had large proofe of his bountie, for he will not spare for cost to gett any rare Secret: *vide* Oliver Hill's book, where he is accused of grosse Plagiarisme.

At his owne costs and chardges he gott translated and printed the New Testament in Arabique, to send into the Mahometan countreys. He has not only a high renowne in England, but abroad; and when foreigners come to hither, 'tis one of their curiosities to make him a Visit.

His Works alone may make a Librarie.

HENRY BRIGGS

Born 1561. Mathematician. M.A. St John's College, Cambridge, 1585; Fellow 1588; first Professor of Geometry at Gresham College, London, 1596–1620. He succeeded Sir Henry Savile in the Professorship of Astronomy, which he had founded at Oxford. He visited Lord Napier in Scotland and the idea of tables of logarithms having 10 for their base, as well as the actual calculation of the first table of this kind, was due to Briggs. When the two great mathematicians met, says William Lilly, the astrologer, *almost one quarter of an hour was spent, each beholding the other almost with admiration* [amazement], *before one word was spoke.* Lilly goes on to say that Napier *was a great lover of astrology, but Briggs the most satirical man against it that hath been known.* He called it *a system of groundless conceits.*

He published and left in manuscript many works on mathematics and navigation, including *A Table to find the Height of the Pole* and *A tract on the North-west Passage to the South Sea through the Continent of Virginia.* He was a member of the company trading to Virginia. He died at Merton College, Oxford, on 26 January 1630, and a Greek epitaph that was written on him by Henry Jacob, one of the Fellows of Merton, ends by saying that *his soul still astronomises and his body geometrises.*

LOOKING one time on the mappe of England he observed that the two Rivers, the Thames and that Avon (which runnes to Bathe and so to Bristowe) were not far distant, *scilicet*, about 3 miles. He sees 'twas but about 25 miles from Oxford; getts a horse and viewes it and found it to be a levell ground and easie to be digged. Then he considered the chardge of cutting between them and the convenience of making a mariage between those Rivers which would be of great consequence for cheape and safe carrying of Goods between London and Bristow, and though the boates goe slowly and with meanders, yet considering they goe day and night they would be at their journey's end almost as soon as the Waggons, which often are overthrowne and liquours spilt and other goods broken. Not long after this he dyed and the Civill Warres brake-out.

It happened by good Luck that one Mr Matthewes of Dorset had some acquaintance with this Mr Briggs and had heard him discourse of it. He was an honest simple man, and had runne out of his Estate and this project did much run in his head. He would revive it (or els it had been lost and forgott) and went into the Country to make an ill survey of it (which he printed) but with no great encouragement of the Countrey or others.

Upon the restauration of King Charles II he renewed his designe and applyed himselfe to the King and Counsell. His Majestie espoused it more (he told me) then any one els. In short, for want of management and his non-ability, it came to nothing, and he is now dead of old age. But Sir Jonas Moore (an expert Mathematician and a practicall man) being sent to survey the mannor of Dantesey in Wilts (which was forfeited to the Crowne by Sir John Danvers his foolery) went to see these Streames and distances. He told me the streames were too small, unlesse in winter; but if some prince or the Parliament would rayse money to cutt through the hill by Wotton-Basset which is not very high, then there would be water enough and streames big enough. He computed the chardge, which I have forgott, but I thinke it was about 200,000 pounds.

Mr William Oughtred calls him the English Archimedes.

ELIZABETH BROUGHTON

MRIS ELIZABETH BROUGHTON was daughter of Edward Broughton of Herefordshire, an ancient Family. Her father lived at the Mannour-house at Cannon-Peon. Whether she was borne there or no, I know not; but there she lost her Mayden-head to a poor young fellow, then I beleeve handsome, but, in 1660, a pittifull poor old weaver, Clarke of the Parish. He had fine curled haire, but gray. Her father at length discovered her inclinations and locked her up in the Turret of the house, but she getts down by a rope; and away she gott to London, and did sett up for her selfe.

She was a most exquisite beautie, as finely shaped as Nature could frame; had a delicate Witt. She was soon taken notice of at London, and her price was very deare – a second Thais. Richard, Earle of Dorset, kept her (whether before or after Venetia I know not, but I guess before). At last she grew common and infamous and gott the Pox, of which she died.

I remember thus much of an old Song of those dayes, which I have seen in a Collection: 'twas by way of litanie, *viz*:

From the Watch at Twelve a Clock,
And from Bess Broughton's buttond smock,
Libera nos Domine.

In Ben Johnson's *Execrations against Vulcan*, he concludes thus:

Pox take thee, Vulcan. May Pandora's pox
And all the Ills that flew out of her Box
Light on thee. And if those plagues won't doe,
Thy Wive's Pox take thee, and Bess Broughton's too.

I see that there have been famous Woemen before our times.

I doe remember her father in 1646, neer 80, the handsomest shaped man that ever my eies beheld, a very wise man, and of an admirable Elocution. He was a Committee man in Herefordshire and Glocestershire; he was Commissary to Colonel Massey. He was of the Puritan Party heretofore, had a great guift in Praying, etc. His wife (I have heard my grandmother say, who was her neighbor) had as great parts as he. He was the first that used the Improvement of Land by Soape-ashes when he lived at Bristowe, where they then threw it away, and the Haven being like to be choaked up with the Soape-ashes (for which severall Complaints and

Indictments) considering that grounds were improved by Compost, he made an experiment of improving by soape-ashes, having land neer the City; and mightily emproved it. This I had from himselfe.

THOMAS BUSHELL

Born 1594. Speculator and mining engineer. Page and seal bearer to Francis Bacon, who *imparted to him many secrets in discovering and extracting minerals*. When Bacon became Lord Chancellor, Bushell accompanied him to Court, where he attracted the notice of James I by the gorgeousness of his attire. His walks and fountains at Enstone in Oxfordshire were visited by Charles I and Henrietta Maria in 1636, and though the King's visit was unexpected, his ingenious host managed to improvise for him *an entertainment of artificial thunders and lightnings, rain, hail-showers, drums beating, organs playing, birds singing, waters murmuring all sorts of tunes*, &c. Farmed the Royal Mines in Wales 1636. Master of the Mint at Aberystwyth 1637, at Shrewsbury 1642, and at Oxford 1643. Held Lundy Island for the King till 1647, and then lived in concealment. Gave Parliament security for his good behaviour, and leased the Crown Mines from the State Council 1652. Died 1674.

MR THOMAS BUSHELL was one of the Gentlemen that wayted on the Lord Chancellour Bacon. 'Twas the fashion in those dayes for Gentlemen to have their Suites of Clothes garnished with Buttons. My Lord Bacon was then in Disgrace, and his Man Bushell having more Buttons than usuall on his Cloake, etc, they sayd that his Lord's breech made Buttons and Bushell wore them: from whence he was called Buttond Bushell.

He was only an English Scholar, but had a good witt and a working and contemplative head. His Lord much loved him.

His Genius lay most towards naturall philosophy and particularly towards the Discovery, drayning, and improvement of the Silver mines in Cardiganshire, etc. He wrote a stich't Treatise of Mines and improving the adits [*entrances*] to them and Bellowes to drive-in Wind.

Mr Bushell was the greatest Master of the Art of running in Debt (perhaps) in the world: and lived so long that his depts were forgott, so that they were the great-grandchildren of the creditors. He died one hundred and twenty thousand pounds in dept. He had so delicate a way of making his Projects alluring and feazible, profitable, that he drewe to his Baits not only rich men of no designe, but also the craftiest Knaves in the countrey, such who had cosened and undon others; e.g. Mr Goodyeere, who undid Mr Nicholas Mees' father, etc.

He had the strangest bewitching way to drawe-in people (yea, discreet and wary men) into his projects that ever I heard of. His tongue was a Charme, and drewe in so many to be bound for him, and to be ingaged in his Designes, that he ruined a number.

As he had the art of running in dept, so sometimes he was attacqued and throwen into Prison; but he would extricate himselfe again straingely.

After his master the Lord Chancellor dyed, he maried, and lived at Enston, Oxon; where having some land lyeing on the hanging of a hill facing the South, at the foot wherof runnes a fine cleare stream which petrifies, and where is a pleasant Solitude, he spake to his servant, Jack Sydenham, to gett a Labourer to cleare some Boscage which grew on the side of the Hill, and also to dig a Cavity in the hill, to sitt and read, or contemplate. The Workman had not worked an hower before he discovers not only a Rock, but a rock of an unusuall figure with Pendants like Icecles as at Wokey Hole, Somerset, which was the occasion of making that delicate Grotto and those fine Walkes.

The Grotto belowe lookes just South; so that when it artificially raineth, upon the turning of a cock, you are enterteined with a Rainbowe. In a very little pond (no bigger then a Basin) opposite to the rock, and hard by, stood a Neptune, neatly cutt in wood, holding his Trident in his hand, and ayming with it at a Duck which perpetually turned round with him, and a Spanniel swimming after her – which was very pretty, but long since spoyled.

Here in fine weather he would walke all night. Jack Sydenham sang rarely: so did his other servant, Mr Batty. They went very gent. in cloathes, and he loved them as his children.

He did not encumber him selfe with his wife, but here enjoyed himselfe thus in this Paradise till the War brake out, and then retired to Lundy isle.

Anno 1647 or 8, he came over into England, and when he landed at Chester, and had but one Spanish three pence (this I had from some-one of Great Tew to whom he told it) and, sayd he, I could have been contented to have begged a penny like a poor man. At that time he sayd he owed, I forgett whether it was 50 or sixty thousand pounds: but he was like Sir Kenelm Digby, if he had not 4d., wherever he came he would find Respect and Credit.

He had donne something (I have now forgott what) that made him obnoxious to the Parliament or Oliver Cromwell, about 1650; would have been hang'd if taken; printed severall letters to the Parliament, etc, dated from beyond Sea, and all that time laye privately in his Howse in

Lambeth marsh, where the pointed pyramis is. In the garret there is a long Gallery, which he hung all with black, and had some death's heads and bones painted. At the end where his Couch was, was in an old Gothique Nich (like an old Monument) painted a Skeleton recumbent on a Matt. At the other end, where was his pallet-bed, was an emaciated dead man stretched out. Here he had severall mortyfying and divine Motto's (he imitated his Lord as much as he could) and out of his windowes a very pleasant prospect. At night he walked in the garden and orchard. Only Mr Sydenham, and an old trusty woman, was privy to his being in England.

He was a handsome proper Gentleman when I sawe him at his house aforesayd at Lambith. He was about 70, but I should not have guessed him hardly 60. He had a perfect healthy constitution: fresh, ruddy face, hawke-nosed, and was temperate.

Mr Edmund Wyld sayes that he tap't the mountaine of Snowdon in Wales, which was like to have drowned all the countrey; and they were like to knock him and his men in the head.

In the time of the Civill Warres his Hermitage over the Rocks at Enston were hung with black-bayes; his bed had black Curtaines, etc, but it had no bed posts but hung by 4 Cordes covered with blak-bayes instead of bed-postes. When the Queen-mother came to Oxon to the King, she either brought (as I thinke) or somebody gave her, an entire Mummie from Egypt, a great raritie, which her Majestie gave to Mr Bushell, but I beleeve long ere this time the dampnesse of the place haz spoyled it with mouldinesse.

SAMUEL BUTLER

Born 1612. Satirist. The son of a farmer. In early youth he was page to the Countess of Kent, and thereafter Clerk to various Puritan Justices. After the Restoration he became Secretary to the Lord President of Wales. At this time he married a widow of means, which however were soon dissipated. In 1663 the first part of *Hudibras* appeared, and the other two in 1664 and 1678. *Hudibras*, which stands at the head of the satirical literature of England, is the most remarkable document of the reaction against Puritanism at the Restoration, and might be taken as the seamy side of *The Pilgrim's Progress*, being directed not against righteousness but against self-righteousness. This book was immensely popular, and King Charles II always carried a copy with him. Nevertheless, Butler died in extreme poverty in 1680.

HIS father was a man but of slender fortune, and to breed him at schoole was as much education as he was able to reach to. When but a Boy he would make observations and reflections on every Thing one sayd or did, and censure it to be either well or ill. He was never at the University, for the reason alledged.

He came when a young man to be a servant to the Countesse of Kent, whom he served severall yeares: she gave her Gentlemen 20 pounds per annum a-piece. Here, besides his Study, he employed his time much in painting and drawing, and also in Musique. He was thinking once to have made painting his Profession. His love to and skill in painting made a great friendship between him and Mr Samuel Cowper (the Prince of Limners of this Age.)

He was Secretarie to the Duke of Bucks, when he was Chancellor of Cambridge. He might have had Preferments at first; but he would not accept any but very good ones, so at last he had none at all, and dyed in want.

He then studyed the Common Lawes of England, but did not practise. He maried a good Jointuresse, the relict of one Morgan, by which meanes he lived comfortably.

John Cleveland was a fellow of St John's Colledge in Cambridge, where he was more taken notice of for his being an eminent Disputant, then a good Poet. Being turned out of his Fellowship for a malignant he came to Oxford, where the King's Army was, and was much caressed by them. After the King was beaten out of the field, he came to London, and retired in Grayes Inne. He, and Sam Butler, &c. of Grayes Inne, had a Clubb every night.

In my fathers time, they had a Clubb (*fustis*) at the school-dore: and when they desired leave *exeundi foras* (two went together still) they carried the Clubbe. I have heard that this was used in my time in Country-schooles before the Warres. When Monkes or Fryars goe out of their Convent, they always are licensed by couples; to be witnesses of one anothers actions or behaviour. We use now the word Clubbe for a Sodality at a Taverne or Drinking-house.

He printed a witty Poeme called *Hudibras*, which tooke extremely; so that the King and Lord Chancellor Hyde (who haz his picture in his Library over the Chimney) would have him sent for, and accordingly he was sent for. They both promised him great matters, but to this day he haz got *no* Employment, only the King gave him 300 pounds.

After the restauration of his Majestie when the Court at Ludlowe was againe sett-up, he was then the King's Steward at the castle there.

He haz often sayd, that way (e.g. Mr Edmund Waller's) of Quibling with Sence will hereafter growe as much out of fashion and be as ridicule as quibling with words.

His verses on the Jesuites, not printed:

No Jesuite ever took in hand,
To plant a church in barren Land;
Or ever thought it worth his while
A Swede or Russe to reconcile;
For where there is not store of wealth,
Souls are not worth the charge of health.
Spaine on America had 2 designes
To sell their Ghospell for their mines;
For had the Mexicans been poore,
No Spaniard twice had landed on their shore.
'Twas Gold the Catholick Religion planted,
Which, had they wanted Gold, they still had wanted.

Satyricall Witts disoblige whom they converse with; and consequently make to themselves many Enemies and few Friends; and this was his manner and case. He was of a leonine-coloured haire, sanguino-cholerique, middle sized, strong; a severe and sound judgement, high coloured; a good fellowe. He haz been much troubled with the Gowt, and particularly 1679, he stirred not out of his chamber from October till Easter.

He dyed of a Consumption, September 25; and buried 27, according to his Appointment, in the Church-yard of Convent Garden; *scil.* in the north part next the church at the east end. His feet touch the wall. His grave, 2 yards distant from the Pillaster of the Dore, (by his desire) 6 foot deepe.

About 25 of his old acquaintance at his Funerall. I myself being one of the eldest, helped to carry the Pall. His coffin covered with black Bayes.

WILLIAM BUTLER

Born 1535. Physician. Licensed to practise medicine. He attended Henry, Prince of Wales, who died in 1612 in his eighteenth year. Died 1618.

WILL BUTLER, physitian; he was of Clare-hall in Cambridge, never tooke the Degree of Doctor, though he was the greatest Physitian of his time.

The occasion of his first being taken notice of was thus: About the comeing in of King James, there was a Minister a few miles from Cambridge, that was to preach before his Majestie at Newmarket. The parson heard that the King was a great Scholar, and studyed so excessively that he could not sleepe, so somebody gave him some opium, which had made him sleep his last, had not Doctor Butler used this following remedy. He was sent for by the Parson's wife. When he came and sawe the Parson, and asked what they had donne, he told her that she was in danger to be hanged for killing her husband, and so in great choler left her. It was at that time when the Cowes came into the Backside to be milkt. He turnes back and asked whose Cowes those were. She sayd, her husband's. Sayd he, Will you give one of those Cowes to fetch your husband to life again? That she would, with all her heart. He then causes one presently to be killed and opened, and the parson to be taken out of his Bed and putt into the Cowes warme belly, which after some time brought him to life, or els he had infallibly dyed.

He was a man of great Moodes, a humorist. One time King James sent for him to Newmarket, and when he was gonne halfe-way left the Messenger and turned back; so then the messenger made him ride before him.

I think he was never maried. He lived in an Apothecary-shop in Cambridge, Crane's, to whom he left his estate, and he in gratitude erected the Monument for him at his own chardge, in the fashion he used. He was not greedy of money, except choice Pieces of Golde, or Rarities.

Once, on the rode from Cambridge to London, he took a fancy to a chamberlayne or tapster in his Inne, and took him with him and made him his favourite, by whom only accession was to be had to him, and thus enriched him.

He would many times (I have heard say) sitt among the Boyes at St Maries' Church in Cambridge (and just so would the famous attorney general Noy in Lincoln's Inne, who had many such froliques and humours).

He kept an old mayd whose name was Nell. Dr Butler would many times go to the Taverne, but drinke by himself. About 9 or 10 at night old Nell comes for him with a candle and lanthorne, and sayes, Come you home, you drunken Beast. By and by Nell would stumble; then her Master calls *her* drunken beast; and so they did drunken beast one another all the way till they came home.

A Serving man brought his Master's water to Doctor Butler, being then in his Studie (with turn'd Barres) but would not bee spoken with. After much fruitlesse importunity the man tolde the doctor he was resolved he should see his Master's water; he would not be turned away, threw it on the Dr's head. This humour pleased the Dr, and he went to the Gent. and cured him.

A gent. lying a-dyeing, sent his Servant with a horse for the doctor. The horse, being exceeding dry, ducks downe his head strongly into the water, and plucks downe the Dr over his head, who was plunged in the water over head and ears. The Dr was madded, and would return home. The man swore he should not; drewe his sword, and gave him ever and anon (when he would returne) a little prick, and so drove him before him.

The Dr lyeing at the Savoy in London next the water side, where there was a Balcony look't into the Thames, a Patient came to him that was grievously tormented with an Ague. The Dr orders a boate to be in readinesse under his windowe, and discoursed with the patient (a Gent.) in the Balcony, when, on a signall given, two or three lusty Fellowes came behind the Gentleman and threwe him a matter of 20 feete into the Thames. This surprize absolutely cured him.

A Gent. with a red ugly, pumpled face came to him for a cure. Said the Dr, I must hang you. So presently he had a device made ready to hang him from a Beame in the roome, and when he was e'en almost dead, he cutt the veines that fed these pumples and lett out the black ugley Bloud, and cured him.

That he was chymical I know by this token, that his mayd came running in to him one time like a slutt and a Furie; with her haire about her eares, and cries, Butler! come and looke to your Devilles your selfe, and [*an*, i.e. *if*] you will; the stills are all blowne up! She tended them, and it seems gave them too greate a heate. Old Dr Ridgely knew him, and I thinke was at that time with him.

He was much addicted to his humours, and would suffer persons of quality to wayte sometimes some hours at his dore, with Coaches, before he would receive them. Dr Gale, of Paule's School, assures me that a French man came one time from London to Cambridge, purposely to see him, whom he made staye two howres for him in his Gallery and then he came out to him in an old blew gowne. The French gentleman makes him 2 or 3 very lowe Bowes to the ground. Dr Butler whippes his Legge over his head, and away goes into his chamber, and did not speake with him.

WILLIAM CAMDEN

Born 1551. Antiquary and historian. He was appointed Headmaster of Westminster School in 1593. He made tours of antiquarian investigation up and down England, and published his *Britannia* in 1586. In 1597 he was made Clarencieux King-at-Arms, which freed him from his academic duties and enabled him to devote more time to his historical work. His other principal books are *Annals of the Reign of Elizabeth*, *Monuments and Inscriptions in Westminster Abbey*, and a collection of *Ancient English Historians*. He wrote principally in Latin, but his *Britannia* was translated into English by Philemon Holland in 1610. Died 1623.

DR NICHOLAS MERCATOR has Stadius's *Ephemerides*, which had been one of Mr Camden's; his name is there (I knowe his hand) and there are some notes by which I find he was Astrologically given.

In his *Britannia* he haz a remarkable Astrologicall observation, that when Saturn is in Capricornus a great Plague is certainly in London. He had observed it all his time, and setts downe the like made by others before his time. Saturn was so posited in the great plague 1625, and also in the last great plague 1665. He likewise delivers that when an Eclipse happens in Scorpio that 'tis fatall to the Towne of Shrewsbury.

Mr Camden told Sir Robert Filmore that he was not suffered to print many things in his *Elizabetha*, which he sent over to his acquaintance and correspondent Thuanus, who printed it all faithfully in his *Annalls* without altering a word.

He was basted by a Courtier of the Queene's in the Cloysters at Westminster for denigrating Queen Elizabeth in his History.

When my grandfather went to schoole at Yatton-Keynell (neer Easton-Piers) Mr Camden came to see the church, and particularly tooke notice of a little painted-glasse-windowe in the chancell, which (ever since my remembrance) haz been walled-up, to save the parson the chardge of glazing it.

'Tis reported, that he had bad Eies (I guesse Lippitude) which was a great inconvenience to an Antiquary.

Mr Camden much studied the Welch language, and kept a Welsh servant to improve him in that language, for the better understanding of our Antiquities.

Sir William Dugdale tells me that he haz Minutes of King James's life to a moneth and a day, written by Mr William Camden (those memoires were continued within a fortnight of his death) as also his owne life, according to yeares and daye, which is very briefe, but 2 sheetes, Mr Camden's owne hand writing. Sir William Dugdale had it from John Hacket, Bishop of Coventry and Lichfield, who did filch it from Mr Camden as he lay a dyeing.

He lies buried in the South Cross-aisle of Westminster Abbey, his effigies ½ on an Altar; in his hand a Booke, on the leaves wherof is writt BRITANNIA.

I have heard Sir Wm. Dugdale say, that though Mr Camden had the Name, yet Mr Glover was the best Herald that did ever belong to the Office. He tooke a great deale of paines in searching the Antiquities of severall Counties. He wrote a most delicate hand, and pourtrayed finely.

There is (or late was) at a Coffee house at the upper end of Bell-yard (or Shier-lane) under his owne hand, a Vistation of Cheshire, a most curious piece, which Sir Wm. Dugdale wish't me to see; and he told me that at York, at some ordinary house (I thinke a house of entertainment) he sawe such an elaborate piece of Yorkshire. But severall Counties he surveyd, and that with great exactnes, but after his death they were all scattered abroad, and fell into ignorant hands.

WILLIAM CARTWRIGHT

Born 1611. Dramatist and divine. He was educated at the Free School at Cirencester and afterwards, as a King's Scholar, at Westminster, whence he was chosen in 1628 Student of Christ Church, Oxford. Having taken the degree of M.A. in 1635, he entered into holy orders and became, according to Anthony Wood, *the most florid and seraphical preacher in the University.* On 1 September 1642 he was nominated one of the Council of War and on 16 September he was imprisoned by the Lord Say, but was released on bail and next April was chosen Junior Proctor of the University. He died at Oxford on 29 November 1643 of a malignant fever (called the camp-disease) and was buried on 1 December at the upper end of the north aisle of Christ Church Cathedral. His reputation amongst his contemporaries was enormous, and Fell said of him: *Cartwright was the utmost man could come to.* Lloyd is still more enthusiastic in his praise: *To have the same person cast his net and catch souls as well in the pulpit as on the stage! A miracle of industry and witt, sitting sixteen hours a day at all manner of knowledge, an excellent preacher in whom hallowed fancies and reason grew visions, and holy passions, raptures and extasies, and all this at thirty years of age!* When *The Royal Slave, a Tragi-Comedy* was performed before the King and Queen by the students of Christ Church in 1636, the Court *unanimously acknowledg'd that it did exceed all things of that nature which they had ever seen*, and his early death was felt to deal a mortal blow to the stage. The King, who was then at Oxford, being asked why he wore black on the day of Cartwright's funeral, replied that *since the Muses had so much mourned for the loss of such a son, it would be a shame for him not to appear in mourning for the loss of such a subject.*

GLOCESTERSHIRE is famous for the birth of William Cartwright at a place called Northway neer Tewksbury. Were he alive now he would be sixty-one. (This I have from his brother, who lives not far from me, and from his sisters whom I called upon in Glocestershire at Leckhampton. His sister Howes was 57 yeares old the 10 March last: her brother William was 4 yeares older.)

His father was a gentleman of 300 pounds per annum. He kept his Inne at Cirencester, but a year or therabout, where he declined and lost by it too. He had by his wife 100 pounds per annum, in Wiltshire, an impropriation, which his son has now (but having many children, lives not handsomely and haz lost his Learning: he was by the second wife, whose estate this was).

He writt a Treatise of Metaphysique, as also Sermons, particularly the Sermon that by the King's command he preached at His return from Edgehill fight.

William Cartwright was buried in the south aisle in Christ Church, Oxon. Pitty 'tis so famous a Bard should lye without an Inscription.

'Tis not to be forgott that King Charles 1st dropt a teare at the newes of his death.

LUCIUS CARY VISCOUNT FALKLAND

Born 1610. Poet, statesman, courtier. Imprisoned in the Fleet to prevent him fighting a duel 1630. Vainly sought service in Holland before serving as a volunteer against the Scots 1639. Member of the Short and Long Parliaments. Spoke against Laud's ecclesiastical tyranny and for Strafford's attainder, but opposed the abolition of Episcopacy 1641. Secretary of State 1642. Accompanied Charles I to York and was sent to negotiate with Parliament 1642. Present at the siege of Gloucester. Despairing of peace, he threw away his life at Newbury fight in September 1643. His verses and philosophical tractates were published posthumously.

HE maried Letice, the daughter of Sir Richard Morison, by whom he had two sonnes; the eldest lived to be a man, died *sine prole* [without issue], the second was father to this Lord Falkland now living.

This Lady Letice was a good and pious Lady, as you may see by her Life writt about 1649 or 50, by John Duncomb D.D. But I will tell you a pretty story from William Hawes, of Trin. Coll., who was well acquainted with the Governor aforesaid, who told him that my Lady was (after the manner of woemen) much governed by, and indulgent to, the Nursery: when she had a mind to beg any thing of my Lord for one of her mayds, nurses, etc, she would not doe it by herselfe (if she could helpe it) but putt this Gentleman upon it, to move it to my Lord. My Lord had but a small estate for his Title; and the old gentleman would say, Madam, this is so unreasonable a motion to propose to my Lord that I am certaine he will never grant it; e.g. one time to lett a Farme twenty pound per annum: under value. At length, when she could not prevaile on him, she would say that, I warrant you, for all this, I will obtaine it of my Lord: *it will cost me but the expence of a few Teares*. Now she would make her words good: and this great Witt, the greatest master of Reason and Judgement of his time, at the long runne, being stormed by her *Teares* (I presume there were kisses and secret embraces that were also ingredients), would this pious Lady obtain her unreasonable desires of her poor Lord.

My Lord in his Youth was very wild, and also mischievous, as being apt to stabbe and doe bloudy mischiefs; but 'twas not long before he tooke up to be serious, and then grew to be an extraordinary hard student. I have heard Dr Ralph Bathurst say that, when he was a boy, my Lord lived at Coventrey (where he had then a House) and that he would sett up very late at nights at his study, and many times came to the Library at the Schoole there.

The Studies in fashion in those dayes (in England) were Poetrey; and Controversie with the Church of Rome. My Lord's Mother was a Zealous Papist, who being very earnest to have her son of her Religion, and her son upon that occasion, labouring hard to find the Trueth, was so far at last from setling on the Romish church, that he setled and rested in the Polish (I meane Socinianisme). He was the first Socinian in England; and Dr Hugh Crescy, of Merton Coll. (Dean of Leighlin in Ireland, afterwards a Benedictin Monke) told me that he himselfe was the first that brought Socinus's bookes; shortly after, my Lord comeing to him, and casting his eie on them, would needs presently borrow them, to peruse; and was so extremely taken and satisfied with them, that from that time was his Conversion.

My Lord much lived at Tue [*Great Tew*], which is a pleasant seat, and about 12 miles from Oxford; his Lordship was acquainted with the best Witts of that University, and his House was like a Colledge, full of Learned men. Mr William Chillingworth, of Trinity College in Oxford (afterwards D.D.) was his most intimate and beloved favourite, and was most commonly with my Lord. His chaplaine Charles Gataker was an ingeniose young Gentleman, but no Writer. For learned Gentlemen of the Country, his acquaintance was Mr Sandys, the Traveller and Translator; Ben. Johnson; Edmund Waller, Esq.; Mr Thomas Hobbes, and all the excellent of that peacable time.

In the Civill-warres he adhered to King Charles I, who after Edge-hill fight made him Principall Secretary of Estate (with Sir Edward Nicholas) which he dischardged with a great deal of Witt and Prudence, only his advice was very unlucky to his Majestie, in perswading him (after the victory at Rowndway-downe, and the taking of Bristowe) to sitt-downe before Glocester, which was so bravely defended by that incomparably vigilant Governor, Col. Massey, and the diligent and careful soldiers and citizens (men and woemen) that it so broke and weakened the King's Army, that 'twas the procatractique cause of his ruine. After this, all the King's matters went worse and worse. At the fight at Newbery, my Lord Falkland being there, and having nothing to doe to chardge; as the two armies were engageing, rode in like a mad-man (as he was) between them, and was (as he needs must be) shott. Some that were your superfine discoursing politicians and fine Gentlemen, would needs have the reason of this mad action of throwing away his Life so, to be his discontent for the unfortunate advice given to his master as aforesaid; but, I have been well enformed, by those who best knew him, and knew intrigues behind the curtaine (as they say) that it was the griefe of the death of Mris Moray, a handsome Lady at Court, who was his Mistresse, and whom he loved above all creatures, was the true cause of his being so madly guilty of his own Death, as afore mentioned.

The next day, when they went to bury the dead, they could not find his Lordship's body; it was stript and trod-upon and mangled, so there was one that wayted on him in his chamber would undertake to know it from all other bodyes, by a certaine Mole his Lordship had in his Neck, and by that marke did finde it. He lies interred at Great Tue, but, I thinke, yet without any monument.

In the dining roome, there is a picture of his at length, and like him ('twas done by Jacob de Valke, who taught me to paint). He was a little man and of no great strength of body; he had blackish haire, something flaggy, and I thinke his eies black. Dr Earles would not allow him to be a good poet, though a great Witt; he writt not a smoth verse, but a great deal of Sense.

SIR CHARLES CAVENDISH

Born 1591. Mathematician. Brother of the first Duke of Newcastle. Accompanied Sir Henry Wotton to France 1612. Knighted 1619. M.P. for Nottingham 1624, 1628, and 1640. On the outbreak of the Civil War he served for the King, under his brother, as lieutenant-general of horse 1642. Despairing of the Royal cause, he went to Hamburg with his brother in 1644 and remained on the Continent until 1651. He then returned to London, where he lived in relative poverty as most of the family estates had been confiscated. He was, however, admitted to compound, on making submission to Parliament, and bought back Welbeck and Bolsover, which had been confiscated from his brother. Died 1654.

SIR CHARLES CAVENDISH was the younger Brother to William, Duke of Newcastle. He was a little, weake, crooked man, and nature having not adapted him for the Court nor Campe, he betooke himself to the Study of the Mathematiques, wherin he became a great Master. His father left him a good Estate, the revenue wherof he expended on bookes and on learned men.

He had collected in Italie, France, &c, with no small chardge, as many Manuscript Mathematicall bookes as filled a Hoggeshead, which he intended to have printed; which if he had lived to have donne, the growth of Mathematicall Learning had been 30 yeares or more forwarder then 'tis. But he died of the Scurvey, contracted by hard study, about 1652, and left an Attorney of Clifford's Inne, his Executor, who shortly after died, and left his Wife Executrix, who sold this incomparable Collection aforesaid, by weight to the past-board makers for Wast-paper. A good Caution for those that have good MSS to take care to see them printed in their lifetimes.

He writt severall things in Mathematiques for his owne pleasure.

CHARLES CAVENDISH

Born 1620. Royalist general. Travelled in the East 1638–40. Served under the Prince of Orange 1641. At the beginning of the Civil War he became a volunteer in the Guards. He was given a troop after Edgehill. He raised a regiment of horse and was given command in Nottinghamshire and Lincoln. He was victorious at Grantham, Ancaster, and Burton-on-Trent, but was defeated and slain at Gainsborough in 1643, at the age of twenty-three.

CHARLES CAVENDISH, Colonel, was second son to the Right Honourable Earle of Devonshire, brother to this present Earle, William.

He was well educated, and then travelled into France, Italie, &c; but was so extremely delighted in travelling, that he went into Greece, all over; and that would not serve his turne but he would goe to Babylon, and then his Governour would not adventure to goe any further with him; but to see Babylon he was to march in the Turks armie.

Upon his returne into England the Civill Warres brake-out, and he tooke a Commission of a Colonel in his Majestie's Cause, wherin he did his Majestie great service, and gave signall proofs of his Valour.

He was the Souldiers' Mignion, and his Majestie's Darling, designed by him Generall of the Northern Horse (and his Commission was given him) a great marke of Honour for one of about five and twenty: *Thus shall it be donne to the man whom the King delights to Honour*.

Col. Cavendish was a Princely person, and all his actions were agreable to that character: he had in an eminent degree the semblance and appearance of a man made to governe. Methinkes he gave cleare this indication, the King's Cause lived with him, the King's Cause died with him; when Cromwell heard that he was Slaine, he cried upon it *We have donne our Businesse*.

And yet two things (I must confess) this Commander knew not, pardon his ignorance, he knew not to Flie away – he knew not how to aske quarter – though an older did, I meane Henderson; for when this bold person entred Grantham on the one side, that wary Gentleman, who should have attaqued it, fled away on the other. If Cato thought it Usurpation in Caesar to give him his Life, Cavendish thought it a greater for Traytors and Rebells of a common Size to give him his. This brave Hero might be opprest (as he was at last by numbers) but he could not be conquered.

What wonders might have been expected from a Commander so Vigilant, so Loyall, so Constant, had he not dropt downe in his blooming age? But though he fell in his green yeares, he fell a prince, and a great one too; one whose Loyaltie to his great Master nothing could shake.

An high Extraction to some persons is like the Dropsie, the greatnesse of the man is his disease, and renders him unwieldlie: but here is a Person of great Extract free from the swelling of Greatness, as brisk and active as the lightest Horseman that fought under him. In some parts of India, they tell us, that a Nobleman accounts himselfe polluted if a Plebeian touch him; but here is a person of that rank who used the same familiaritie and frankness amongst the meanest of his Souldiers, the poorest miner, and amongst his equalls; and by stooping so low, he rose the higher in the common account, and was valued accordingly as a Prince, and a Great one.

Sir Robert Harley, an ingeniose Gent. and expert Soldier, haz often sayd, that (generally) the Commanders of the King's Army would never be acquainted with their Soldiers, which was an extraordinary Prejudice to the King's Cause. A Captaine's good look, or good word (some times) does infinitely winne them and oblige them; and he would say 'twas to admiration how Souldiers will venture their Lives for an obligeing Officer.

Consider Abner in the Manner of his Fall, that was by a treacherous hand, and so fell Cavendish. *And when Abner was returned to Hebron, Joab tooke him aside in the Gate to speake with him quietly, and smote him there under the fifth Rib, that he died, for the bloud of Asahel his brother.* Thus fell Abner; and thus Cavendish – the Colonell's horse being mired in a bog at the Fight before Gainsborough, 1643, the Rebels surround him, and take him Prisoner; and after he was so, a base raskall comes behind him, and runs him through. Thus fell two great men by treacherous handes.

And lastly, the place of his Fall, that was in Israel. Here Abner fell in his, and Cavendish fell in our Israel – the Church of England. In this Church brave Cavendish fell, and what is more then that, in this Churches quarrel.

Thus I have compared Colonel Cavendish with Abner, a fighting and a famous man in Israel; you see how he does equal, how he does exceed him.

THOMAS CHALONER

Born 1595. Regicide. M.P. for Richmond in Yorkshire 1645–53. Commissioner in Munster 1647. He was one of Charles I's judges, and although he was absent on the last day, when sentence was given, he signed the death warrant. Councillor of State 1651. In 1653, at the forcible dissolution of the Long Parliament, Cromwell called him a drunkard. M.P. for Scarborough 1659. Excluded from Indemnity 1660. Died 1661.

THOMAS CHALONER, Esq., was a well bred Gentleman, and of very good naturall parts, and of an agreable Humor. He had the accomplishments of Studies at home, and Travells in France, Italie, and Germanie.

Riding a-hunting in Yorkshire (where the Allum Workes now are) on a Common, he tooke notice of the soyle and herbage, and tasted the water, and found it to be like that where he had seen the Allum workes in Germanie. Wherupon he gott a Patent of the King (Charles I) for an Allum-worke (which was the first that ever was in England) which was worth to him two thousand pounds per annum, or better; but some Courtiers did thinke the Profitt too much for him, and prevailed so with the King, that, notwithstanding the Patent aforesayd, he graunted a Moietie, or more, to another (a courtier) which was the reason that made Mr Chaloner so interest himselfe for the Parliament-cause, and, in revenge, to be one of the King's Judges.

He was as far from a Puritan as the East from the West. He was of the Naturall Religion, and of Henry Martyn's Gang, and one who loved to enjoy the pleasures of this life. He was (they say) a good Scholar, but he wrote nothing that I heare of, onely an anonymous pamphlett *An Account of the Discovery of Moyses's Tombe*; which was written very wittily. It was about 1652. It did sett the Witts of all the Rabbis of the Assembly then to worke, and 'twas a pretty while before the Shamme was detected.

He had a trick sometimes to goe into Westminster-hall in a morning in Terme-time, and tell some strange story (Sham) and would come thither again about 11 or 12 to have the pleasure to heare how it spred; and sometimes it would be altered, with additions, he could scarce know it to be his owne. He was neither proud nor covetous, nor a hypocrite: not apt to doe injustice, but apt to revenge.

After the restauration of King Charles the Second, he kept the Castle at the Isle of Man, where he had a pretty Wench that was his Concubine; where when Newes was brought him that there were some come to the Castle to demaund it for his Majestie, he spake to his Girle to make him a Possett, into which he putt, out of a paper he had, some Poyson, which did, in a very short time, make him fall a-vomiting exceedingly; and after some time vomited nothing but Bloud. His Retchings were so violent that the Standers by were much grieved to behold it. Within three howres he dyed. The Demandants of the Castle came and sawe him dead: he was swoln so extremely that they could not see any eie he had, and no more of his nose than the tip of it, which shewed like a Wart, and his Coddes were swoln as big as one's head.

WILLIAM CHILLINGWORTH

Born 1602. Divine. Educated at Oxford. Falling into theological doubts, he became a convert to Roman Catholicism and studied at the Jesuit College at Douai in 1630. In the following year he returned to Oxford and, after further consideration of the points at issue, he rejoined the Church of England. This exposed him to violent attacks by the Romanists, in reply to which he published in 1637 *The Religion of the Protestants a Safe Way to Salvation.* He was regarded as one of the ablest controversialists of the Anglican Church. Died 1644.

WILLIAM CHILLINGWORTH, D.D., was borne in Oxford. His father was a Brewer.

About anno 1630, he was acquainted with one who drew him and some other scholars over to Doway, where he was not so well entertained as he thought he merited for his great Disputative Witt. They made him the porter (which was to trye his temper, and exercise his obedience), so he stole over and came to Trinity College again, where he was fellowe.

William Laud, ABC [*Archbishop of Canterbury*], was his Godfather and great friend. He sent his Grace weekly intelligence of what passed in the University. Sir William Davenant (poet laureat) told me that notwithstanding this Doctor's great Reason, he was guilty of the detestable Crime of Treacherie. Dr Gill, Filius Dris. Gill (Schoolmaster of Paules-schoole) and Chillingworth held weekely intelligence one with another for some yeares, wherein they used to nibble at states-matters. Dr Gill in one of his letters calles King James and his sonne, *the old foole and the young one*, which letter Chillingworth communicates to W. Laud, AB Cant. The poore young Dr Gill was seised, and a terrible storme pointed towards him, which, by the eloquent intercession and advocation of Edward, Earle of Dorset, together with the Teares of the poore old Doctor, his father, and supplications on his knees to his Majestie, were blowne-over. I am sorry so great a witt should have such a *naeve* [blemish].

He was a little man, blackish haire, of a Saturnine complexion. He never swore to all the points of the Church of England.

The Lord Falkland and he had such extraordinary clear reasons, that they were wont to say at Oxon that if the great Turke were to be converted by naturall reason, these two were the persons to convert him.

When Doctor Kettle (the president of Trin. Coll. Oxon.) dyed, which was in anno 1643, Dr Chillingworth was Competitor for the Presidentship, with Dr Hannibal Potter and Dr Roberts. Dr Han. Potter had been formerly Chaplain to the Bishop of Winton, who was so much Dr Potter's friend, that though (as Will Hawes haz told me) Dr Potter was not lawfully elected, upon referring themselves to their visitor (Bishop of Winton), the Bishop (Curle) ordered Dr Potter possession; and let the fellowes gett him out if they could. This was shortly after the Lord Falkland was slaine, who had he lived, Dr Chillingworth assured Will. Hawes, no man should have carried it against him: and that he was so extremely discomposed and wept bitterly for the losse of his deare Friend, yet notwithstanding he doubted not to have an astergance for it.

My tutor, W. Browne, haz told me, that Dr Chillingworth studied not much, but when he did, he did much in a little time. He much delighted in Sextus Empeiricus. He did walke much in the College grove, and there contemplate, and meet with some *cod's-head* or other, and dispute with him and baffle him. He thus prepared himselfe before-hand. I thinke it was an Epidemick evill of that time, which I thinke is growne out of fashion, as unmannerly and boyish. He was the readiest and nimblest Disputant of his time in the university, perhaps none haz equalled him since.

I have heard Mr Thomas Hobbes, Malmsb. (who knew him) say, that he was like a lusty fighting fellow that did drive his enimies before him, but would often give his owne party smart back-blowes.

He lies buried in the south side of the Cloysters at Chichester, where he dyed of the *morbus castrensis* (siphylis) after the taking of Arundel castle by the Parliament: wherin he was very much blamed by the King's soldiers for his Advice in military affaires there, and they curst *that little Priest* and imputed the Losse of the Castle to his advice. In his sicknesse he was inhumanely treated by Dr Cheynell, who, when he was to be buryed, threw his booke into the grave with him, saying, *Rott with the rotten; let the dead bury the dead.*

GEORGE CLIFFORD EARL OF CUMBERLAND

Born 1558. Courtier and adventurer. Succeeded his father as third Earl 1570. Having run through a great part of his very handsome property, he seized on the opportunity offered by the war with Spain to re-establish himself. In 1588 he commanded the *Elizabeth Bonaventure*, a Queen's ship of 600 tons, against the Spanish Armada and, after the decisive action off Gravelines, carried the news of the victory to the camp at Tilbury. The reports of his gallantry so pleased the Queen that she lent him the *Golden Lion*, and later the *Victory*, to undertake expeditions to the South Seas. At his own expense, he fitted out ten privateering expeditions against Spain and Spanish America between 1586 and 1598, sailing personally with those of 1589, 1591, 1593, and 1598. At Court he was in high favour with the Queen, whose glove, set with diamonds, he wore as a plume in his hat. But want of fortune or management attended all his expeditions, and his loss seemed greater than his gain. Having at his majority inherited a large property, he was nearly a thousand pounds in debt when he died in 1605.

THIS George, Earl of Cumberland, built the greatest Fleet of shipping that ever any Subject did. The Armada of the Argonautes was but a trifle to this. He was the greatest Navigator and did the most prodigious things at sea that ever any subject did at his own cost: he had a little fleet of (I thinke 20) brave ships of his own building and manning: for doing whereof he sold the Inheritance of above sixteen thousand pounds per annum; did great things against the Spaniard, etc: in the West Indies, whose atchievements would have much more compensated his chardges. But the Queen and councell when he had donne these things, seised on all his prizes and kept his ships, saying it was not to the safety of State to have any subject doe such great things.

He had a vast Estate, and could then ride in his owne lands from Yorkeshire to Westmorland.

The best account of his Expedition with his Fleet to America is to be found in Purchas's *Pilgrim*. He tooke from the Spaniards to the value of seaven or 8 hundred thousand poundes. When he returned with this rich Cargo (the richest without doubt that ever Subject brought) the Queene's Councell (where he had some that envyed him – *Virtutis comes Invidia*: [Envy is the attendant of Greatness]) layed their heads together and concluded 'twas too much for a Subject to have, and confiscated it all to the Queen, even the Shippes and all, and to make restauration to the Spaniard, that he was forced to sell fifteene thousand pounds per annum.

This was the breaking of that ancient and noble Family; but Robert, Earl of Salisbury (who was the chiefest Enemie) afterwards maried his Daughter, as he might well be touch't in conscience, to make some recompence after he had donne so much mischiefe.

As I take it, Sir Walter Ralegh went this brave Voyage with his Lordship; and Mr Edmund Wright, the excellent Navigator; and, not unlikely, Mr Harriot too.

SIR EDWARD COKE

Born 1552. Judge and law writer. Educated at Norwich Free School and Trinity College, Cambridge. Went to reside in Clifford's Inn in 1571, where he soon obtained a good practice. He married Bridget Paston, who brought him £30,000, besides a considerable property in land, and throughout his life he steadily added to his possessions. Advanced by Burghley's influence, he became Recorder of London and Solicitor-General in 1592, Speaker of the House of Commons in 1593, and Attorney-General in 1594. To spite Bacon, he married Burghley's granddaughter in 1598. Began publishing his *Law Reports* 1600. He showed great rancour in the trials of Essex, Raleigh, and the Gunpowder Plotters. Decided against the King's authority to make law by proclamation 1610. Compelled, through Bacon's influence and against his own wish, to become Chief Justice of the King's Bench 1613. Suspended, partly through Bacon's representations to James I, and then dismissed from this office 1616. Though he returned to power later, his chief fame rests on his *Reports*, which established the supremacy of the Common Law in England. Died 1634.

WHEN I was first of the Middle Temple, I heard an old Lawyer, who was his country-man affirme that Sir Edward Coke, Knight, Lord Chief Justice of the King's Bench, was borne but to 300 pounds a yeare land, and I have heard some of his country say again that he was borne but to 40 pounds per annum. What shall one beleeve?

He was of Clifford's Inne before he was of the Inner Temple, as the fashion then was first to be of an Inne of Chancery.

Old John Tussell (that was my attorney) haz told me that he gott a hundred thousand pounds in one yeare, viz. 1° Jacobi, being then Attorney Generall. His advice was that every man of Estate (right or wrong) should sue-out his Pardon, which cost 5 pounds which belonged to him.

He left an estate of eleaven thousand pounds per annum. Sir John Danvers, who knew him, told me that he had heard one say to him, reflecting on his great scraping of wealth, that his sonnes would spend his Estate faster than he gott it; he replyed, They cannot take more delight in the spending of it then I did in the getting of it.

His second wife, Elizabeth, the relickt of Sir William Hatton, was with Child when he maried her: laying his hand on her belly (when he came to bed) and finding a Child to stirre, What, sayd he, Flesh in the Pott. Yea, quoth she, or els I would not have maried a Cooke.

He shewed himselfe too clownish and bitter in his carriage to Sir Walter

Ralegh at his Triall, where he sayes, *Thou Traytor*, at every word, and *thou lyest like a Traytor*.

He will play with his Case as a Cat would with a mouse and be so fulsomely Pedantique that a Schoole boy would nauseate it. But when he comes to matter of Lawe, all acknowledge him to be admirable.

When Mr Cuff, secretary to the Earle of Essex, was arraigned, he would dispute with him in Syllogismes, till at last one of his brethern said, Prithee, brother, leave off: thou doest dispute scurvily. Cuff was a smart man and a great Scholar and baffeld him. Said Cooke, *Dominum cognoscite vestrum* [Know your own Master] Cuff replied, *My Lord, you leave out the former part of the verse, which you should have repeated*, *Acteon ego sum*, reflecting on his being a Cuckold.

After he was putt out of his place of Lord Chief Justice of the King's Bench, to spite him, they made him Sheriff of Buckinghamshire; at which time he caused the Sheriff's oath to be altered, which till that time was, amongst other things, to enquire after and apprehend all Lollards. He was also chosen, after he was displaced, a Burghesse to sitt in Parliament.

He was of wonderfull painstaking, as appeares by his Writings. He was short-sighted but never used spectacles to his dyeing day, being then 83 yeares of age. He was a very handsome proper man and of a curious compexion, as appeares by his Picture at the Inner Temple, which his grandson gave them about 1668, at length, in his Atturney generall's fusted gowne, which the House haz turned into Judge's robes.

The world expected from him a Commentary on Littleton's *Tenures*; and he left them his Common-place book, which is now so much made use of.

Memorandum: when the Play called *Ignoramus* (made by one Ruggles of Clare-hall) was acted with great applause before King James, they dressed Sir Ignoramus like Chief Justice Coke and cutt his beard like him and feigned his voyce. This drollery did sett all the Lawyers against the Clergie, and shortly upon this Mr Selden wrote of Tythes not *jure divino*.

JEAN BAPTISTE COLBERT

Born 1619. Statesman. Louis XIV made it a rule to work in person at what he called *his business as king*. He carried on his operations regardless of the great dignitaries of the land, closeting himself with three or four confidential ministers, and himself deciding all the important business of government in accordance with the reports they made to him. Since these ministers were men of bourgeois origin, Louis XIV imagined himself to be dealing with mere clerks who were the instruments of his will. But as a matter of fact, since they possessed experience of affairs and were acquainted with the details of administration, they were able to suggest to the King whatever decisions they desired him to make. The most active of these ministers was Colbert, for whom was created the new office of Controller-General of Finance, with which he combined two other Secretaryships of State so as to concentrate in his own hands all business except the army and diplomacy. Colbert had no new ideas to contribute: in his view the most important thing was to keep the greatest possible quantity of money in the kingdom; he therefore tried to discourage imports and to hamper the maritime trade of other countries, while encouraging the manufacture of industrial products in France by creating trading companies, each of which enjoyed a monopoly in a certain field. But all these companies went bankrupt, leaving only a few traces behind them, such as the Gobelins and Beauvais tapestry works, the mirror manufactory of Saint-Gobain and the lace of Chantilly and Alençon. While he was responsible for the navy, Colbert tried in vain to revive the galleys in the Mediterranean, but his influence produced effects on the Atlantic fleet which have lasted until the present day, for he imposed registration and compulsory service on all the sailors and fishermen of France, and he founded the Naval Pensions Fund, the most ancient insurance fund in France. He died in 1683.

MONSIEUR COLBERT was a Merchant and an excellent Accomptant, i.e. for Debtor and Creditor. He is of Scottish extraction and that obscure enough, his grandfather being a Scotish bag-piper to the Scotch regiment.

Cardinal Mezarin found that his Stables were very chardgeable to him, and was imposed upon in his Accompts. He hearing of this merchant Colbert to be a great master in this Art, sends for him and desires him to make inspection into his accounts and putt him into a better method to avoyd being abused. Which he did, and that so well that he imployed him in ordering the accounts of all his Estate and found him so usefull that he also made use of him to methodize and settle the Accompts of the King. This was his Rise.

JOHN COLET

Born 1467. Scholar and theologian. He was the son of a wealthy citizen, who was twice Lord Mayor of London. The only survivor of a family of twenty-two, he went to Oxford and Paris, and thence to Italy, where he learned Greek and probably met Savonarola. Deciding to enter the Church, several livings were conferred on him by his family in 1485, while he was still a minor and long before he was ordained: for it was not until 1497 that he became a deacon, and the year after that a priest. He continued to follow his studies, devoting himself chiefly to St Paul's Epistles, on which he lectured in Latin at Oxford. He was outspoken against the corruptions of the Church, and would have been called to account but for the protection of Archbishop Warham: he was, in fact, later accused of heresy and treason. He had the spirit of a scientific inquirer, holding that the first four chapters of Genesis should be considered as poetry rather than fact, and that we should love God rather than know Him. He became friendly with Erasmus in 1498, and Sir Thomas More called him his *spiritual director*. In 1504 he was appointed Dean of St Paul's. He inherited a vast fortune on his father's death in 1505, and spent £40,000 of it on the foundation of St Paul's School. It is rather for his learning and his attitude to the advancement of knowledge, than for his own writings, that he has such a high place in the history of English literature. He died in 1519.

JOHN COLET, D.D., Deane of St Paule's, London. After the Conflagration (his Monument being broken) somebody made a little hole towards the upper edge of his Coffin, which was closed like the coffin of a Pye and was full of a Liquour which conserved the body. Mr Wyld and Ralph Greatorex tasted it and 'twas of a kind of insipid tast, something of an Ironish tast. The Coffin was of Lead, and layd in the Wall about 2 foot ½ above the surface of the Floore.

This was a strange rare way of conserving a Corps: perhaps it was a Pickle, as for Beefe, whose Saltness in so many years the Lead might sweeten and render insipid. The body felt, to the probe of a stick which they thrust into a chinke, like boyld Brawne.

THOMAS COOPER

Born 1517. Divine and scholar. The son of an Oxford tailor. It had been Cooper's intention to take Orders, but having adopted Protestant views, he found himself checked by the accession of Queen Mary. He therefore changed his pursuit, took a degree in Physic, and began to practise in Oxford. In 1545 Thomas Lanquet died while writing a *Chronicle of the World*: he had brought it down from the Creation to A.D. 17, and Cooper undertook to carry it on to the reign of Edward VI. *Cooper's Chronicle A.D. 17–1547* was published in 1549. In 1548 he had published a *Latin Dictionary*. On the death of Mary he was ordained, and in 1565 he published his *Thesaurus Linguae Romanorum*, which delighted Queen

Elizabeth so much that she expressed her determination to promote the author as far as lay in her power. Cooper was therefore made Dean of Christ Church and Vice-Chancellor of Oxford in 1567, Dean of Gloucester in 1569, Bishop of Lincoln in 1570, and of Winchester in 1584. His wife was utterly profligate, but he refused to be divorced, even when the heads of the University offered to arrange it for him, declaring that he would not charge his conscience with such a scandal. He was lampooned by Martin Mar-Prelate in 1588 and 1589, and published an *Admonition* in his own defence in the latter year. He died in 1594.

DR EDWARD DAVENANT told me that this learned man had a shrew to his wife: who was irreconcileably angrie with him for sitting-up late at night so, compileing his *Dictionarie*.

When he had halfe-donne it, she had the opportunity to gett into his studie, tooke all his paines out in her lap, and threw it into the fire, and burnt it. Well, for all that, the good man had so great a zeale for the advancement of learning, that he began it again, and went through with it to that Perfection that he hath left it to us, a most usefull Worke. He was afterwards made Bishop of Winton.

RICHARD CORBET

Born 1582. Divine. He was friendly with the powerful Duke of Buckingham, who procured the Deanery of Christ Church for him in 1620. In 1628 when the Deanery was required by the Earl of Dorset for Brian Duppa, Corbet was elected to the vacant see of Oxford, and was translated to Norwich in 1632. He was acknowledged the best poet of all the bishops of England, and though his verse was usually in a rollicking satiric vein, he wrote one extremely bitter poem *Upon Mrs Mallet, an unhandsome gentlewoman that made love to him*. He died in 1635.

RICHARD CORBET, D.D., was the son of Vincent Corbet, who was a Gardner at Twicknam. He was a Westminster scholar; old Parson Bussey, of Alscott in Warwickshire, went to schoole with him. He would say that he was a very handsome man, but something apt to abuse, and a Coward.

He was a Student of Christ Church in Oxford. He was very facetious, and a good Fellowe. One time, he and some of his acquaintance being merry at Fryar Bacon's study (where was good liquor sold) they were drinking on the Leads of the house, and one of the scholars was a sleepe, and had a paire of goode silke stockings on. Dr Corbet (then M.A. if not B.D.) gott a paire of Cizers and cutt them full of little Holes, but when the other awaked, and perceived how and by whom he was abused, he did chastise him, and made him pay for them.

After he was Doctor of Divinity, he sang Ballads at the Crosse at Abingdon on a market-day. He and some of his Camerades were at the Taverne by the Crosse (which, by the way, was then the finest of England; I remember it when I was a Freshman; it was admirable curious Gothique Architecture, and fine Figures in the niches; 'twas one of those built by King Edward I for his Queen). The Ballad-singer complayned he had no custome; he could not putt-off his Ballads. The jolly Dr putts-off his Gowne, and putts-on the Ballad-singer's Leathern jacket, and being a handsome man, and had a rare full Voice, he presently vended a great many, and had a great Audience.

He was made Deane of Christ Church. He had good Interest with great men, as you may find in his Poems, and with the then great Favourite, the Duke of Bucks. His excellent Witt was lettres of recommendation to him. I have forgott the story, but at the same time that Dr Fell thought to have carried it, Dr Corbett putt a pretty trick on, to lett him take a journey on purpose to London for it, when he had already the Graunt of it. His Poems are pure naturall Witt, delightfull and easie.

He preached a Sermon before the King at Woodstock (I suppose King James) and no doubt with a very good grace; but it happened that he was out, on which occasion there were made these verses:

A reverend Deane,
With his Ruffe starch't cleane,
Did preach before the King:
In his Band-string was spied
A Ring that was tyed,
Was not that a pritty thing?
The Ring without doubt
Was the thing putt him out,
So oft hee forgot what was next;
For all that were there,
On my conscience dare sweare
That he handled it more than his Text.

His conversation was extreme pleasant. Dr Stubbins was one of his Cronies; he was a jolly fatt Dr and a very good house-keeper; parson in Oxfordshire. As Dr Corbet and he were riding in Lob Lane in wett weather ('tis an extraordinary deepe, dirty lane) the coach fell; and Dr

Corbet sayd that Dr Stubbins was up to the elbowes in mud, he was up to the elbowes in Stubbins.

He was made Bishop of Oxford, and I have heard that he had an admirable, grave and venerable aspect.

One time, as he was Confirming, the country-people pressing in to see the Ceremonie, sayd he, *Beare off there, or I'le confirm yee with my Staffe.* Another time, being to lay his hand on the head of a man very bald, he turns to his chaplaine, Lushington, and sayd, *Some Dust, Lushington*, (to keepe his hand from slipping). There was a man with a great venerable Beard: sayd the Bishop, *You, behind the Beard.*

His Chaplain, Dr Lushington, was a very learned and ingeniose man, and they loved one another. The Bishop sometimes would take the key of the wine-cellar, and he and his Chaplaine would goe and lock themselves in and be merry. Then first he layes downe his Episcopall hat – *There lyes the Doctor.* Then he putts off his gowne – *There lyes the Bishop.* Then 'twas, *Here's to thee, Corbet*, and *Here's to thee, Lushington.*

He married Alice Hutton, whom 'twas sayd he bigott. She was a very beautifull woman, and so was her mother. He had a son that went to schoole at Westminster, with Ned Bagshawe: a very handsome youth, but he is run out of all, and goes begging up and downe to Gentlemen.

His Antagonist, Dr Price the Anniversarist, was made Deane of Hereford. Dr Watts, Canon of that church, told me that this Deane was a mighty Pontificall proud man, and that one time when they went in Procession about the Cathedral church, he would not doe it the usually way in his surplice, hood, etc, on foot, but rode on a mare thus habited, with the Common prayer booke in his hand, reading. A stone horse [*stallion*] happend to breake loose, and smelt the mare, and ran and leapt her, and held the Reverend Deane all the time so hard in his Embraces, that he could not gett off till the horse had done his bussinesse. But he would never ride in procession afterwards.

The last words he sayd were, *Good night, Lushington.*

ABRAHAM COWLEY

Born 1618. Poet. In childhood he was greatly influenced by reading Spenser, a copy of whose poems was in the possession of his mother. This, he said, made him a poet. His first book, *Poetic Blossoms*, was written when he was only ten and published when he was fifteen. At Cambridge he was distinguished for his graceful translations. On the outbreak of the Civil War he joined the Royalists, was turned out of his College, and in 1646 followed the Queen to Paris, where he remained for twelve years, during which time he rendered unwearied service to the royal family and was employed on delicate diplomatic missions. At the Restoration he wrote some loyal odes, but was disappointed by being refused the Mastership of the Savoy, and retired to the country. Cowley's fame among his contemporaries was much greater than that which posterity has accorded to him. He is said by Pope to have died of a fever brought on by lying in the fields after a drinking-bout in 1667.

MR ABRAHAM COWLEY: he was borne in Fleet-street, London, neer Chancery-lane; his father a Grocer.

He writ when a Boy at Westminster Poems and a Comedy called *Love's Riddle*, dedicated to Sir Kenelme Digby.

A.C. discoursed very ill, and with hesitation.

In December 1648, King Charles the first, being in great trouble, and prisoner at Caeresbroke, or to be brought to London to his Triall; Charles Prince of Wales being then at Paris, and in profound sorrow for his father, Mr Abraham Cowley went to wayte on him; his Highnesse asked him whether he would play at Cards, to diverte his sad thoughts. Mr Cowley replied, he did not care to play at cards; but if his Highness pleasd, they would use *Sortes Virgilianae* (Mr Cowley always had a Virgil in his pocket). The Prince accepted the proposal, and prick't his pinne in the fourth booke of the *Æneids*. The Prince understood not Latin well, and desired Mr Cowley to translate the verses, which he did admirably well, and Mr George Ent (who lived in his house at Chertsey, in the great plague 1665) shewed me Mr Cowley's owne hand writing.

By a bold people's stubborn arms opprest,
Forced to forsake the land he once possess't,
Torn from his dearest sonne, let him in vaine
Seeke help, and see his friends unjustly slain.
Let him to base unequal termes submit,
In hope to save his crown, yet loose both it
And life at once, untimely let him dy,
And on an open stage unburied ly.

Now as to the last part, I well remember it was frequently and soberly affirmed by officers of the army, &c. Grandees, that the body of King Charles the First was privately putt into the Sand about White-hall; and the coffin that was carried to Windsor and layd in King Henry 8th's vault was filled with rubbish, or brick-batts. Mr Fabian Philips, who adventured his life before the King's Tryall, by printing, assures me, that the Kings Coffin did cost but six shillings: a plain deale coffin.

He was Secretarie to the Earle of St Albans (then Lord Jermyn) at Paris. When his Majestie returned, George, Duke of Bucks, hearing that at Chertsey was a good Farme belonging to the Queene-mother goes to the Earl of St Alban's and the commissioners to take a Lease of it. Said the Earle to him, That is beneath your Grace, to take a Lease. That is all one, qd. he, I desire to have the favour to buy it for my money. He payd for it, and had it, and freely and generously gave it to his deare and ingeniose friend, Mr Abraham Cowley, for whom purposely he bought it: which ought not to be forgotten.

He lies interred at Westminster Abbey, next to Sir Jeffrey Chaucer, where the Duke of Bucks has putte a neate Monument of white marble; above that a very faire Urne, with a kind of Ghirland of Ivy about it. His Grace the Duke of Bucks held a tassell of the Pall.

Vide his Will, *scilicet*, for his true and lasting Charity, that is, he settles his Estate in such a manner that every yeare so much is to be payd for the enlarging of poor Prisoners cast into Gaole by cruel Creditors for small Debts. I doe think this memorable Benefaction is not mentioned in his life in print before his Workes; it is certainly the best method of Charity.

SIR CHARLES DANVERS

Born 1568. Soldier. His brothers were Henry, Earl of Danby and Sir John Danvers. Charles Danvers was elected a Member of Parliament in 1586, when he was eighteen. He served under Lord Willoughby in the Netherlands and was knighted by his commander in 1588. He and his brother Henry were outlawed for killing a neighbour, Henry Long, in a quarrel in 1593, and they took refuge in France, where Henri IV received them kindly and interceded with Queen Elizabeth in their behalf. However, it was not until 1598 that they were pardoned. In 1599 Charles Danvers was given a colonel's commission in the army that accompanied Essex to Ireland, and later joined in Essex's abortive rising in 1601. He made a full confession, admitting his guilt, and was beheaded the same year.

Sommerford magna – the Assassination of Harry Long was contrived in the parlour of the Parsonage here: R. Wisdome was then Lecturer and preacht that day, and Henry Long expired in his armes. My great-grandfather, R. Danvers, was in some trouble about it, his Horses and Men being in that Action. His Servants were hanged.

Sir John Danvers, the father, was a most beautifull and good and even-tempered person. He was of a mild and peacable nature, and his sonnes' sad accident brake his heart.

George Herbert's verses pinned on the Curtaine of the picture of old Sir John:

Passe not by: search and you may
Find a Treasure worth your stay.
What makes a Danvers would you find?
In a faire Bodie, a faire Minde.
Sir John Danvers' earthly part
Here is copyed out by Art:
But his heavenly and divine
In his Progenie doth shine.
Had he only brought them forth
Know that much had been his Worth.
Ther's no Monument to a Sonne:
Reade him there, and I have donne.

His picture is yet extant: my Cosen John Danvers (his Son) haz it.

Sir Henry Danvers, Knight, Earle of Danby and Baron of Dauntesey, was second sonn of old Sir John Danvers of Dauntesey Knight. He was of a magnificent and munificent spirit: and made that noble Physick-garden at Oxford, and endowed it with I think 30 pounds per annum.

Henry, Earl of Danby, was page to Sir Philip Sydney. He perfected his Latin when a man by parson Oldham of Dodmerton; was a perfect master of the French; a Historian; Tall and spare; Temperate; sedate and solid; a very great favorite of Prince Henry. He bred up severall brave young Gentlemen, and preferred them, e.g. Colonel Leg, since Earl of Dartmouth, and severall others; lived most at Cornbury; a great Improver of his Estate, to eleaven thousand pounds per annum at the least, neer twelve. A great Oeconomist: He allowed three thousand pounds per annum only for his Kitchin. All his servants were sober and wise in their respective places.

He was made a Knight of the Garter A.D. 1633. For many years before St Georges Feast had not been more magnificently kept, then when this Earle with the Earle of Morton were installed Knights of the Garter. One might then have beheld the abridgment of English, and Scotish in their Attendance. The Scotish Earle (like Zeuxis his Picture) adorned with all art and costlinesse: whilst our English Earle (like to the plaine sheet of

Apelles) by the gravity of habit, gott the advantage of the Gallantry of his Corrival with judicious beholders.

He never maried; and by his Will made 1639, setled his Estate on his hopefull Nephew Henry D'Anvers (only sonne of Sr John Danvers) snatch't away (before fully of age) to the great griefe of all good men.

Full of Honour, Wounds, and Dayes, he dyed Anno Domini 1643, and lies buried in a little Chapel made for his Monument, on the north side of Dantesey-church; near to the Vault where his father and ancestors lie.

Elizabeth Danvers, his mother, an Italian, prodigious parts for a Woman. I have heard my father's mother say that she had Chaucer at her fingers' ends. A great Politician; great Witt and spirit, but revengefull: knew how to manage her estate as well as any man; understood Jewels as well as any Jeweller. Very Beautifull, but only short-sighted.

To obtain Pardons for her Sonnes she maryed Sir Edmund Carey, cosen-german to Queen Elizabeth, but kept him to hard meate.

Sir Charles Danvers advised the Earle of Essex, either to treat with the Queen (but Sir Ferdinando Gorges did let the Hostages goe) or to make his way through the gate at Essex-house, and then to hast away to High-gate, and so to Northumberland (the Earl of Northumberland maried his mother's sister) and from thence to the King of Scots, and there they might make their Peace; if not, the Queen was old and could not live long. But the Earle followed not his advice, and so they both lost their heads on Tower-hill, February the 6th, 1600.

His familiar acquaintance were the Earl of Oxon; Sir Francis and Sir Horace Vere; Sir Walter Raleigh, etc – the Heroes of those times.

With all their faylings, Wilts cannot shew two such Brothers.

SIR JOHN DANVERS

Born 1588. Regicide. Brother of Sir Charles Danvers and the first Earl of Danby. Knighted by James I, he was Member of Parliament for Oxford University in 1625, 1626, 1628, and 1639. A colonel in the Parliamentary Army, he sat as M.P. for Malmesbury in 1645. He signed the death-warrant of Charles I in 1649, and from that date until 1653 he was a member of the Council of State. He died in 1655.

THE Mannor of Dantesey in Wilts was forfeited to the Crowne by Sir John Danvers his foolery.

At Dantesey was a robbery committed at the Mannour howse, on the family of the Stradlings: Sir Edward, and all his servants, except one plowboy who hid himselfe, were murthered: by which meanes, this whole Estate came to Anne his sister, and heire. She married after to Sir John Danvers (the father) a handsome gentleman, who clapt up a match with her before she heard the newes, he, by good fortune lighting upon the Messenger first. She lived at that time in Paternoster-Rowe at London, and had but an ordinary portion.

This Robbury was donne on a Satterday night; the next day the neighbors wondered none of the family came to Church; they went to see what was the matter, and the Parson of the parish very gravely went along with them, who, by the boy was proved to be one of the company, and was, I thinke, hanged for his paines.

Sir John Danvers told me that when he was a young man, the principall reason of sending their sons to Travell, was to weane them from their acquaintance and *familiarity* with the *Servingmen*: for then Parents were so austere and grave, that the Sonnes must not be company for their father, and *some* company men must have: so they contracted a familiarity with the Serving men, who got a *hank* upon them they could hardly after clawe off. Nay, Parents would suffer their Servants to domineer over their Children: and some in what they found their child to take delight, in that would be sure to crosse them.

This young Sir John's first wife was the Lady Herbert, a widowe, mother of the Lord Edward Herbert of Cherbury and George Herbert, Orator. By her he had no issue; she was old enough to have been his Mother. He maried her for love of her Witt. The Earl of Danby was greatly displeased with him for this disagreable match.

Sir John was a great friend of the King's partie and a Patron to distressed and cashiered Cavaliers. But to revenge himselfe of his sister, the Lady Gargrave, and to ingratiate himself more with the Protector to null his brother, Earl of Danby's, Will, he, contrary to his owne naturall inclination, did sitt in the High Court of Justice at the King's Triall.

The Pleasure and Use of Gardens were unknown to our great Grandfathers: They were contented with Pot-herbs: and did mind chiefly their Stables. But in the time of King Charles II^{d} Gardening was much improved, and became common. 'Twas Sir John Danvers of Chelsey (Brother and Heir to Henry Danvers Earle of Danby) who first taught us the way of Italian Gardens: He had well travelled France & Italy, and made good Observations: He had in a faire Body an harmonicall Mind: In his Youth his Complexion was so exceedingly beautifull and fine that Thomas Bond Esqr. (who was his Companion in his Travells) did say, that the People would come after him in the Street to admire Him. He had a very fine Fancy, which lay (chiefly) for Gardens, and Architecture. The Garden at Chelsey in Middlesex (as likewise the House there) doe remaine Monuments of his Ingenuity. He was a great acquaintance and Favorite of the Lord Chancellour Bacon, who took much delight in that elegant Garden.

Sir John, being my Relation and faithfull Friend, was wont in fair mornings in the Summer to brush his Beaver-hatt on the Hysop and Thyme, which did perfume it with its naturall Spirit; and would last a morning or longer.

EDWARD DAVENANT

EDWARD DAVENANT, S. Theol. Dr, was the eldest son of Edward Davenant, Merchant of London, who was the elder brother to the Right Reverend Father in God, the learned John Davenant Bishop of Sarum.

I will first speake of the father, for he was an incomparable man in his time, and deserves to be remembred. He was of a healthy complexion (except the gout), rose at 4 or 5 in the morning, so that he followed his Studies till 6 or 7, the time that other merchants goe about their Businesse; so that, stealing so much and so quiet time in the morning, he studied as much as most men. He understood Greeke and Latin perfectly, and was a better Grecian than the Bishop: he writt a rare Greeke character as ever I sawe. He was a great Mathematician, and understood as much of it as was knowen in his time. He understood Trade very well, was a sober and good menager, but the winds and seas cross'd him. He had so great losses that he broke, but his Creditors knowing it was no fault of his, and also that he was a person of great Vertue and justice, used not extremity towards him; but I thinke gave him more Credit, so that he went into Ireland, and did sett up a Fishery for Pilchards at Wythy Island, in Ireland, where in 20 yeares he gott 10,000 pounds; satisfied and payd his Creditors; and over and above left a good estate to his son. His picture bespeakes him to be a man of judgement, and parts, and gravity extraordinary. He slipt comeing down the stone stayres at the Palace at Sarum, which bruise caused his death.

His brother, the Bishop, hung the Choire of Sarum with purple velvet, which was plundered in the Sacrilegious Times.

Dr Edward Davenant was borne at his Father's howse at Croydon in Surrey (the farthest handsome great howse on the left hand as you ride to

Bansted Downes). I have heard him say, he thankt God his father did not knowe the houre of his birth; for that it would have tempted him to have studyed Astrologie, for which he had no esteeme at all.

He went to school at Merchant Taylors' school, from thence to Queen's Colledge in Cambridge, of which house his uncle John Davenant (afterwards Bishop of Sarum) was head, where he was Fellowe. 'Twas no small advantage to him to have such a learned Father to imbue arithmeticall knowledge into him when a boy, night times when he came from schoole.

I remember when I was a young Oxford Scholar, that he could not endure to heare of the *New* (Cartesian) *Philosophy*: For, sayd he, if a new Philosophy is brought-in, a new Divinity will shortly follow; and he was right.

When his uncle was preferred to the church of Sarum, he made his nephew Treasurer of the Church, which is the best Dignity, and gave him the Vicaridge of Gillingham in com. Dorset, and then Paulsholt parsonage, neer the Devises, which last in the late troubles he resigned to his wive's brother William Grove.

He was to his dyeing day of great diligence in study, well versed in all kinds of Learning, but his Genius did most strongly encline him to the Mathematiques, wherin he has written (in a hand as legible as print) MSS in 4to a foot high at least. I have often heard him say (jestingly) that he would have a man knockt in the head that should write anything in Mathematiques that had been written of before. I have heard Sir Christopher Wren say that he does beleeve he was the best Mathematician in the world about 30 or 35+ yeares agoe. But being a Divine he was unwilling to print, because the world should not know how he had spent the greatest part of his time.

I have writt to his Executor, that we may have the honour and favour to conserve his MSS in the Library of the Royal Societie, and to print what is fitt. I hope I shall obtaine my desire. He had a noble Library, which was the aggregate of his Father's, the Bishop's, and his owne.

He was of middling stature, something spare; and weake, feeble leggs; he had sometimes the Goute; was of great temperance, he always dranke his beer at meales with a Toast, winter and summer, and sayd it made the beer the better.

He was very ready to teach and instruct. He did me the favour to informe me first in Algebra. His daughters were Algebrists.

He had an excellent way of improving his children's memories, which was thus: he would make one of them read a chapter or &c, and then they were (*sur le champ*) to repeate what they remembred, which did exceedingly profitt them; and so for Sermons, he did not let them write notes (which jaded their memorie) but gave an account vivâ voce. When his eldest son, John, came to Winton-schoole (where the Boyes were enjoyned to write Sermon-notes) he had not wrote; the Master askt him for his Notes – he had none, but sayd, If I doe not give you as good an account of it as they doe, I am much mistaken.

He was heire to his uncle, John Davenant, Bishop of Sarum. When Bishop Coldwell came to this Bishoprick, he did lett long Leases, which were but newly expired when Bishop Davenant came to this sea; so that there tumbled into his coffers vast summes. His predecessor, Dr Tounson, maried John Davenant's sister, continued in the see but a little while, and left severall children unprovided for, so the King or rather Duke of Bucks gave Bishop Davenant the Bishoprick out of pure charity: 'twas the only Bishoprick that he disposed of without symony, all others being made merchandise of for the advancement of his kindred. Bishop Davenant being invested, maried all his nieces to Clergie-men, so he was at no expence for their preferment. He granted to his nephew (this Dr) the lease of the great Mannour of Poterne, worth about 1000 pounds per annum; made him Threasurer of the church of Sarum, of which the corps is the parsonage of Calne, which was esteemed to be of the like value. He made severall purchases, all of which he left him; insomuch as the churchmen of Sarum say, that he gained more by this Church then ever any man did by the Church since the Reformation, and take it very unkindly that, at his death, he left nothing (or but 50 pounds) to that Church which was the source of his Estate. How it happened I know not, or how he might be workt-on in his old age, but I have heard severall yeares since, he hadd sett downe 500 pounds in will for the Cathedral Church of Sarum.

He was not only a man of vast learning, but of great goodnes and charity; the parish and all his friends will have a great losse in him. He took no use for money upon bond. He was my singular good friend, and to whom I have been more beholding then to any one beside; for I borrowed five hundred pounds of him for a yeare and a halfe, and I could not fasten any interest on him.

SIR WILLIAM DAVENANT

Born 1606. Dramatist. One of the founders of the Classical school of English poetry. He wrote twenty-five plays. Poet Laureate 1637. Knighted 1643. A Royalist in the Civil War, he was three times imprisoned by the Parliamentarians in the Tower, from which he was once released at the intercession of Milton. He had the satisfaction of repaying in kind these good offices when Milton, in his turn, was in danger in 1660. He owned the theatre where movable scenery and female actors were first habitually used, during the Interregnum. Died 1668.

SIR WILLIAM DAVENANT, Knight, Poet Laureate, was borne in the City of Oxford, at the Crowne Taverne. He went to schoole at Oxon to Mr Sylvester, but I feare he was drawne from schoole before he was ripe enough.

His father was John Davenant, a Vintner there, a very grave and discreet Citizen; his mother was a very beautifull woman and of a very good witt, and of conversation extremely agreable.

Mr William Shakespeare was wont to goe into Warwickshire once a yeare, and did commonly in his journey lye at this house in Oxon, where he was exceedingly respected. (I have heard Parson Robert say that Mr William Shakespeare haz given him a hundred kisses.) Now Sir William would sometimes, when he was pleasant over a glasse of wine with his most intimate friends – e.g. Sam Butler, author of *Hudibras*, etc, say, that it seemed to him that he writt with the very spirit that did Shakespeare, and seemed contented enough to be thought his Son. He would tell them the story as above, in which way his mother had a very light report, whereby she was called a Whore.

He was preferred to the first Dutches of Richmond to wayte on Her as a Page. I remember he told me, she sent him to a famous Apothecary for some Unicornes-horne, which he resolved to try with a Spider which he incircled in it, but without the expected successe; the Spider would goe over, and thorough and thorough, unconcerned.

He was next a servant (as I remember, a Page also) to Sir Fulke Grevil, Lord Brookes, with whom he lived to his death, which was that a servant of his (that had long wayted on him, and his Lordship had often told him that he would doe something for him, but did not, but still putt him off with delayes) as he was trussing up his Lord's pointes comeing from Stoole (for then their breeches were fastned to the doubletts with points; then came in hookes and eies; which not to have fastened was in my boy-hood a great crime) stabbed him. This was at the same time that the Duke of Buckingham was stabbed by Felton, and the great noise and report of the Duke's, Sir William told me, quite drowned this of his Lord's, that 'twas scarce taken notice of. This Sir Fulke G. was a good witt, and had been a good Poet in his youth. He wrote a Poeme in folio which he printed not till he was old, and then (as Sir W. said) with too much judgement and refining, spoyled it, which was at first a delicate thing.

He writt a Play or Playes, and verses, which he did with so much sweetnesse and grace, that by it he got the love and friendship of his two Mecaenasses, Mr Endymion Porter and Mr Henry Jermyn (since Earl of St Albans) to whom he has dedicated his Poeme called *Madegascar*. Sir John Suckling was also his great and intimate friend.

After the death of Ben Johnson he was made in his place Poet Laureat.

He gott a terrible clap of a Black handsome wench that lay in Axe-yard, Westminster, whom he thought on when he speakes of Dalga in *Gondibert*, which cost him his Nose, with which unlucky mischance many witts were too cruelly bold: e.g. Sir John Menis, Sir John Denham, etc.

In the Civill Warres in England he was in the Army of William, Marquess of Newcastle (since Duke) where he was Generall of the Ordinance. I have heard his brother Robert say, for that service there was owing to him by King Charles the First 10,000 pounds. During that warre, 'twas his Hap to have two Alderman of Yorke his Prisoners, who were something stubborne, and would not give the Ransome ordered by the Councell of Warr. Sir William used them civilly and treated them in his Tent, and sate them at the upper end of his Table *à la mode de France*, and having donne so a good while to his chardge, told them (privately and friendly) that he was not able to keepe so chargeable Guests, and bad them take an opportunity to escape, which they did: but having been gon a little way they considered with themselves that in gratitude they ought to goe back and give Sir William their Thankes; which they did, but it was like to have been to their great danger of being taken by the Soldiers, but they happened to gett safe to Yorke.

After the King was beaten out of the field, Sir William Davenant (who received the honour of Knighthood from the Duke of Newcastle by Commission) went into France; resided chiefly in Paris, where the Prince of Wales then was. He then began to write his Romance in Verse called *Gondibert*, and had not writt above the first booke, but being very fond of it, prints it (before a quarter finished) with an Epistle of his to Mr Thomas Hobbes, and Mr Hobbes excellent Epistle to him printed before it. The Courtiers with the Prince of Wales could never be at quiet about this piece, which was the occasion of a very witty but satericall little booke of Verses writt by George Duke of Bucks, Sir John Denham, etc:

That thou forsak'st thy sleepe, thy Diet,
And which is more then that, our quiet.

This last word Mr Hobs told me was the occasion of their writing.

Here he layd an ingeniose Designe to carry a considerable number of Artificers (chiefly Weavers) from hence to Virginia; and by Mary the queen-mother's meanes, he got favour from the King of France to goe into the Prisons and pick and choose. So when the poor dammed wretches understood what the designe was, they cryed *uno ore* [with one voice] *Tout tisseran*, i.e. We are all weavers. Will picked 36, as I remember, if not more, shipped them, and as he was in his voyage towards Virginia, he and his Tisseran were all taken by the Shippes then belonging to the Parliament of England. The Slaves, I suppose, they sold, but Sir William was brought Prisoner to England. Whether he was first a Prisoner at Caresbroke Castle in the Isle of Wight or at the Tower of London, I have forgott; he was a Prisoner at Both. His *Gondibert* was finished at Caresbroke Castle. He expected no mercy from the Parliament, and had no hopes of escaping his life. It pleased God that the two Aldermen of Yorke aforesayd, hearing that he was taken and brought to London to be tryed for his life, which they understood was in extreme danger, they were touched with so much Generosity and goodness, as, upon their owne accounts and meer motion, to try what they could to save Sir William's life, who had been so civill to them and a meanes to save theirs, to come to London: and acquainting the Parliament with it, upon their petition, etc., Sir William's life was saved.

'Twas Harry Martyn that saved Sir William Davenant's life in the Howse. When they were talking of sacrificing one, then said Henry that in Sacrifices they always offered pure and without blemish: now yee talke of making a Sacrifice of an old rotten rascall. *Vide* H. Martyn's life, where by this very jest, then forgott, the Lord Falkland saved H. Martyn's life.

Being freed from imprisonment, because Playes (*scil.* Tragedies and Comoedies) were in those Presbyterian times scandalous, he contrives to set up an Opera *stylo recitativo*, wherein Serjeant Maynard and severall Citizens were engagers. It began at Rutland howse in Charter-house-yard; next at the Cock-pitt in Drury-Lane, where were acted very well, *stylo recitativo*, *Sir Francis Drake*, and *the Siege of Rhodes*. It did affect the Eie and eare extremely. This first brought Scenes in fashion in England; before, at playes, was only a Hanging.

Anno Domini 1660 was the happy restauration of his Majestie Charles II. Then was Sir William made, and the Tennis-Court in Little Lincolnes-Inne-fielde was turn'd into a Play-house for the Duke of Yorke's Players, where Sir William had Lodgeings, and where he dyed.

I was at his funerall. He had a coffin of Walnutt-tree; Sir John Denham sayd 'twas the finest coffin that ever he sawe. His body was carried in a Herse from the Play-house to Westminster-abbey, where, at the great West dore, he was received by the Singingmen and Choristers, who sang the Service of the Church (I am the Resurrection, etc.) to his Grave, which is in the South crosse aisle, on which, on a paving stone of marble, is writt, in imitation of that on Ben Johnson: *O rare Sir Will. Davenant.*

But me thought it had been proper that a Laurell should have been sett on his Coffin – which was not donne.

JOHN DEE

Born 1527. Mathematician and astrologer. Fellow of Trinity College, Cambridge, where the clever stage effects he introduced into a performance of Aristophanes' *Peace* procured him his lifelong reputation of being a magician. Studied at Louvain 1548. Lectured on Euclid at Paris 1550. Rector of Upton-upon-Severn 1553. Acquitted by the Star Chamber of a charge of practising sorcery against Queen Mary's life, but put under the surveillance of Bishop Bonner as a possible heretic. Suggested to Queen Mary the formation of a Royal Library of Ancient Manuscripts 1556. Visited Venice 1563. Made a voyage to St Helena. Travelled to Hungary to present his *Monas Hieroglyphica* to Maximilian II 1563. Explained the appearance of a new star 1572. At her request, he gathered descriptions of newly discovered countries for Queen Elizabeth 1580. Made calculations to facilitate the adoption in England of the Gregorian Calendar 1583. Went to Prague and interviewed the Emperor Rodolph II and Stefan Batory of Poland (1584) but was compelled to leave by the representations of the Bishop of Piacenza 1585. He headed a small confraternity, which dissolved in 1589, for seeking the Philosopher's Stone and invoking the angels. Warden of Manchester College 1595–1604. Fruitlessly petitioned James I to be formally cleared of the imputation of being a magician 1604. Wrote *A Treatise of the Rosie Crucean Secrets.* He invented the phrase 'The British Empire'. Died 1608.

HEE had a very faire cleare rosie complexion; a long beard as white as milke; he was tall and slender; a very handsome man. His Picture in a wooden cutt is at the end of Billingsley's *Euclid.* He wore a Gowne like an Artist's gowne, with hanging sleeves, and a slitt; a mighty good man he was.

My great Grandfather, Will. Aubrey, and he were Cosins, and intimate acquaintance. Mr Ashmole hath letters between them, under their owne hands, viz. one of Dr W.A. to him (ingeniosely and learnedly written) touching the *Sovraignty of the Sea*, of which J.D. writt a booke which he dedicated to Queen Elizabeth and desired my great grandfather's advice upon it. Dr A's countrey-house was at Kew, and J. Dee lived at Mortlack, not a mile distant. I have heard my grandmother say they were often together.

Among the MSS in the Bodlean library of Doctor Gwyn, are severall letters between him and John Dee, of Chymistrey and Magicall Secrets.

Meredith Lloyd sayes that John Dee's printed booke of *Spirits*, is not above the third part of what was writt, which were in Sir Robert Cotton's Library; many whereof were much perished by being buryed, and Sir Robert Cotton bought the field to digge after it. He told me of John Dee, etc, conjuring at a poole in Brecknockshire, and that they found a wedge of Gold; and that they were troubled and indicted as Conjurors at the Assizes; that a mighty storme and tempest was raysed in harvest time, the countrey people had not knowen the like.

Old Goodwife Faldo (a Natif of Mortlak in Surrey) did know Dr Dee, and told me that he did entertain the Polonian Ambassador at his howse in Mortlak, and dyed not long after; and that he shewed the Eclipse with a darke Roome to the said Ambassador. She beleeves that he was eightie years old when he dyed. She sayd, he kept a great many Stilles goeing. That he layd the storme. That the Children dreaded him because he was accounted a Conjurer. He recovered the Basket of Cloathes stollen, when she and his daughter (both Girles) were negligent: she knew this.

He used to distill Egge-shells, and 'twas from hence that Ben. Johnson had his hint of the *Alkimist*, whom he meant.

He was a great Peace-maker; if any of the neighbours fell out, he would never lett them alone till he had made them friends. He told a woman (his neighbour) that she laboured under the evill tongue of an ill neighbour (another woman) which came to her howse, who he sayd was a Witch.

He was sent Ambassador for Queen Elizabeth (Goody Faldo thinkes) into Poland. The Emperour of Muscovia, upon report of the great learning of the Mathematician, invited him to Mosco, with offer of two thousand pound a yeare, and from Prince Boris one thousand markes; to have his Provision from the Emperor's Table, to be honourably received, and accounted as one of the chief men in the Land. All of which Dee accepted not.

His regayning of the Plate for a friend's Butler, who comeing from London by water with a Basket of Plate, mistooke another basket that was like his. Mr J. Dee bid them goe by water such a day, and looke about, and he should see the man that had his basket, and he did so; but he would not gett the lost horses, though he was offered severall angells.

Arthur Dee, his sonne, a Physitian at Norwych and intimate friend of Sir Thomas Browne, M.D., told Dr Bathurst that (being but a Boy) he used to play at Quoits with the Plates of Gold made by Projection in the Garret of Dr Dee's Lodgings in Prague and that he had more than once seen the Philosopher's Stone.

SIR JOHN DENHAM

Born 1615. Poet and architect. Son of the Chief Baron of the Exchequer in Ireland. He began his literary career with a tragedy, *The Sophy* (1641), which seldom rises above mediocrity. His poem *Cooper's Hill* (1642) is the work by which he is remembered. It is the first example in English of a poem devoted to local description and was extravagantly praised by Dr Johnson; but the place now assigned to Denham is a much more humble one. In his earlier years he suffered for his Royalism, but after the Restoration he enjoyed prosperity. Died 1669.

SIR JOHN DENHAM was unpolished with the smallpox: otherwise a fine complexion. He was of the tallest, but a little incurvetting at his shoulders, not very robust. His haire was but thin and flaxen, with a moist curle. His gate was slow, and was rather a Stalking (he had long legges). His Eie was a kind of light goose-gray, not big; but it had a strange Piercingness, not as to shining and glory, but (like a Momus) when he conversed with you he look't into your very thoughts.

He was admitted of Trinity Colledge in Oxford: I have heard Mr Josias Howe say that he was the dreamingst young fellow; he never expected such things from him as he haz left the world. When he was there he would Game extremely; when he had played away all his money he would play away his Father's wrought rich gold Cappes. He was as good a Student as any in the House. Was not suspected to be a Witt.

He was much rooked by Gamesters, and fell acquainted with that unsanctified Crew, to his ruine. His father had some suspition of it, and chid him severely, wherupon his son John (only child) wrot a little Essay, *Against Gameing, and to shew the Vanities and Inconveniences of it*, which he presented to his father to let him know his detestation of it. But shortly after his Father's death (who left 2000 or 1500 pounds in ready money, 2 houses well furnished, and much plate) the money was played away first, and next the plate was sold. I remember about 1646 he lost 200 pound one night at New-cutt.

He was generally temperate as to drinking; but one time when he was a Student of Lincolne's-Inne, having been merry at the Taverne with his Camerades, late at night, a frolick came into his head, to gett a playsterer's brush and a pott of Inke, and blott out all the Signes between Temple-barre and Charing-crosse, which made a strange confusion the next day, and 'twas in Terme time. But it happened that they were discovered, and it cost him and them some moneys. This I had from R. Estcott, Esq, that carried the Inke-pott.

At last, viz. 1640, his Play of The Sophy came out, which did take extremely. Mr Edmund Waller sayd then of him, that he *broke-out like the Irish Rebellion: three score thousand strong*, before any body was aware.

At the beginning of the Civill Warre he was made Governor of Farnham Castle for the King, but he was but a young Soldier, and did not keepe it. In 1643, after Edgehill fight, his Poeme called *Cowper's-hill* was printed at Oxford, in a sort of browne paper, for then they could gett no better.

1647 he conveyed, or stole away the two Dukes of Yorke and Glocester from St James's (from the Tuition of the Earle of Northumberland) and conveyed them into France to the Prince of Wales and Queen-mother.

Anno 1652, he returned into England, and being in some straights was kindly entertayned by the Earle of Pembroke at Wilton, where I had the honour to contract an acquaintance with him. He was, as I remember, a yeare with my Lord of Pembroke at Wilton and London; he had then sold all the Lands his Father had left him.

The parsonage-house at Egham (vulgarly called The Place) was built by Baron Denham; a house very convenient, not great, but pretty, and pleasantly scituated, and in which his son, Sir John, (though he had better seates) did take most delight in. He sold it to John Thynne, Esq. In this parish is a place called Cammomill-hill, from the Cammomill that growes there naturally; as also west of it is Prune-well-hill (formerly part of Sir John's possessions) where was a fine Tuft of Trees, a clear Spring, and a pleasant prospect to the East, over the levell of Middlesex and Surrey. Sir John tooke great delight in this place, and was wont to say (before the troubles) that he would build there a Retiring-place to entertaine his muses; but the warres forced him to sell that as well as the rest. He sold it to Mr Anstey. In this parish W. and by N. (above Runney-Meade) is Cowper's Hill, from whence is a noble prospect, which is incomparably well described by that Sweet Swan, Sir John Denham.

In the time of the Civill-warres, George Withers, the Poet, begged Sir John Denham's Estate at Egham of the Parliament, in whose cause he was a Captaine of Horse. It happened that G.W. was taken prisoner, and was in danger of his Life, having written severely against the King, &c. Sir John Denham went to the King, and desired his Majestie not to hang him, for that *whilest G.W. lived, he should not be the worst Poet in England*.

He was much beloved by King Charles the first, who much valued him for his ingenuity. He graunted him the reversion of the Surveyor of His Majestie's buildings, after the decease of Mr Inigo Jones; which place, after the restauration of King Charles II he enjoyed to his death, and gott seaven thousand pounds, as Sir Christopher Wren told me of, to his owne knowledge. Sir Christopher Wren was his Deputie.

He burlesqued Virgil, and burnt it, sayeing that 'twas not fitt that the best Poet should be so abused. In the verses against *Gondibert*, most of them are Sir John's. He was satyricall when he had a mind to it.

His first wife was the daughter and heire of Mr Cotton of Glocestershire, by whom he had 500 pounds per annum, one son, and two daughters.

He maried his 2nd wife, Margaret Brookes, a very beautifull young lady: Sir John was ancient and limping. The Duke of Yorke fell deepely in love with her (though I have been morally assured he never had any carnall knowledge of her). This occasioned Sir John's distemper of madness, which first appeared when he went from London to see the famous Freestone quarries at Portland in Dorset, and when he came within a mile of it, turned back to London again, and did not see it. He went to Hounslowe, and demanded rents of Lands he had sold many yeares before; went to the King, and told him he was the Holy Ghost. But it pleased God that he was cured of this distemper, and writt excellent verses (particularly on the death of Mr Abraham Cowley) afterwards. His 2nd lady had no child: was poysoned by the hands of the Countess of Rochester, with Chocolatte.

RENÉ DESCARTES

Born 1596. Philosopher, mathematician, and scientist. Descartes was the founder of modern philosophy, for his outlook was profoundly affected by the new physics and astronomy. He was the first philosopher since Aristotle not to accept the foundations laid by his predecessors, but to attempt to construct a complete philosophic edifice *de novo*. To obtain complete quiet, he enlisted in the Dutch army 1617. On the outbreak of the Thirty Years War he transferred to the Bavarian army 1619. In Bavaria, during the winter of 1619, the weather being cold, he got into a stove in the morning, and stayed there all day meditating; by his own account his philosophy was half-finished when he came out. In 1621 he gave up fighting, but his meditation was so constantly interrupted in civilian life that, in 1628, he joined the army that was besieging La Rochelle. From 1629 until 1649, he lived in Holland to escape persecution, but even so he himself suppressed his book, *Le Monde*, which maintained two heretical doctrines: the earth's rotation and the infinity of the universe. In September 1649, Queen Christina of Sweden sent a warship to fetch Descartes as she wanted daily lessons from him, but it turned out that she could not spare the time except at five in the morning, and this unaccustomed early rising in the cold of a Scandinavian winter was too much for Descartes, who fell ill and died in 1650.

THE Societie of Jesus glorie in that theyr order had the educating of him.

He was too wise a man to encomber himselfe with a Wife; but as he was a man, he had the desires and appetities of a man; he therefore kept a good conditioned hansome woman that he liked, and by whom he had some Children (I thinke 2 or 3.) 'Tis pity but comeing from the Braine of such a father, they should be well cultivated.

He was so eminently learned that all learned men made visits to him, and many of them would desire him to shew them his Instruments (in those dayes mathematicall learning lay much in the knowledge of Instruments, and, as Sir Henry Savile sayd, in doeing of tricks) he would drawe out a little Drawer under his Table, and shew them a paire of Compasses with one of the Legges broken; and then, for his Ruler, he used a sheet of paper folded double.

Mr Hobbes was wont to say that had Des Cartes kept himselfe wholy to Geometrie that he had been the best Geometer in the world but that his head did not lye for Philosophy. He did very much admire him, but sayd that he could not pardon him for writing in the Defence of Transubstantiation, which he knew to bee absolutely against his judgement, and donne meerly to putt a compliment on the Jesuites.

SIR EVERARD DIGBY

Born 1578. Conspirator. His father died when he was fourteen and his wardship was purchased from the Crown by Roger Manners, who sold it at an advanced price to young Digby's mother. The heir to large estates and connected with many of the greatest families in England, he soon appeared at Court, where he was appointed to an office in the Household. But he spent the greater part of his time in the country, hunting and hawking. In 1596 he married a great heiress. He was converted to Catholicism at Court by John Gerard in 1599, and his wife and mother soon followed his example. When James I came to England, Digby was among the gathering which welcomed the King at Belvoir Castle, and he received the honour of knighthood there; but the Catholics were disappointed by James I, and Digby joined the Gunpowder Plot. His task was to prepare for a rising in the Midlands, when the catastrophe should have been brought about, and it was settled that he should invite a large number of the disaffected gentry to meet him at Dunchurch in Warwickshire to join in a hunt, when, it was rumoured, strange news might be expected. This gathering was fixed for 5 November 1605, but was not a success, and quickly dissolved when some of the plotters arrived from London with news of their failure. Fleeing to Holbeach House in Gloucestershire, the conspirators determined to sell their lives dearly, but Sir Everard deserted them, only to be captured some days later. He was tried in Westminster Hall and was executed on Thursday, 30 June 1606.

SIR EVERARD DIGBY was a most gallant Gentleman and one of the handsomest men of his time.

'Twas his ill fate to suffer in the Powder-plott. When his heart was pluct out by the Executioner (who, *secundum formam*, cryed, Here is the heart of a Traytor!) it is credibly reported, he replied, Thou liest!

SIR KENELM DIGBY

Born 1603. Author, naval commander, and diplomatist. After leaving Oxford he travelled a great deal. While in France, the Queen-Mother, Marie de Medicis, whom he met at a masked ball, made immodest advances to him: to avoid her importunities, he spread a report of his death and went to Italy by sea. During the ceremony of knighthood, James I turned his face away from the naked sword, owing to constitutional nervousness, and would have thrust the point into Digby's eye had not Buckingham interposed. He was engaged in sea-fighting and conquered the French and Venetian fleets in the Mediterranean in 1627. Digby was imprisoned by the Parliament in 1642 at *The Three Tobacco Pipes nigh Charing Cross*, where his charming conversation made the prison *a place of delight*. During the Civil War he was active on the side of the King, and on the failure of his cause he was banished for a time. He was the author of several religious and quasi-scientific books, including one *On the Cure of Wounds* by means of a sympathetic powder which he imagined he had discovered: this powder was to be rubbed on the weapon causing the wound, not on the wound itself. Died 1665.

SIR KENELME DIGBY, Knight, a Gentleman absolute in all Numbers, was the eldest son of Sir Everard Digby, who was accounted the handsomest Gentleman in England. Sir Everard sufferd as a Traytor in the

Gun-powder-Treason; but King James restored his estate to his son and heire.

He was borne at Gotehurst, Bucks on the eleventh of June: see Ben Johnson, 2d volumne:

Witnesse thy Actions done at Scanderoon
Upon thy Birthday, the eleaventh of June.

(Mr Elias Ashmole assures me, from two or 3 Nativities by Dr Nepier, that Ben. Johnson was mistaken and did it for the ryme-sake.)

Sir Kenelme Digby was held to be the most accomplished Cavalier of his time. He went to Glocester Hall in Oxon, anno 1618. The learned Mr Thomas Allen (then of that house) was wont to say that he was the *Mirandula* of his age.

He was such a goodly handsome person, gigantique and great voice, and had so gracefull Elocution and noble addresse, etc, that had he been drop't out of the Clowdes in any part of the World, he would have made himself respected. But the Jesuites spake spitefully, and sayd *'twas true, but then he must not stay there above six weekes*. He was Envoyé from Henrietta Maria (then Queen-mother) to the Pope, where at first he was mightily admired; but after some time he grew high, and Hectored with his Holinesse, and gave him the Lye. The pope sayd he was mad.

Tempore Caroli Imi he received the Sacrament in the Chapell at White-hall, and professed the Protestant Religion, which gave great scandal to the Roman Catholiques; but afterwards *he looked back*.

In the Times of Confusion, the Bishop of Winchester's Lodging in Southwark, being a large Pile of Building, was made a Prison for the Royalists; and here Sir Kenelm Digby wrote his Book *of Bodies*, and diverted himself in Chymistry, and used to make artificial precious Stones, as Rubies, Emeralds, &c out of Flint, as Sir Francis Dodington, Prisoner with him at the same Time, told me.

He was well versed in all kinds of Learning. And he had also this vertue, that no man knew better how to abound and to be abased, and either was indifferent to him. No man became Grandeur better; sometimes again he would live only with a Lackey, and Horse with a foote-cloath.

He was very generous, and liberall to deserving persons. When Abraham Cowley was but 13 yeares old, he dedicated to him a Comedy, called *Love's Riddle*, and concludes in his Epistle – *The Birch that whip't him then would prove a Bay*. Sir K. was very kind to him.

He was of undaunted courage, yet not apt in the least to give offence. His conversation was both ingeniose and innocent.

Sir John Hoskyns enformes me that Sir Kenelme Digby did translate Petronius Arbiter into English.

He maried, much against his Mother's consent, that celebrated Beautie and Courtezane, Mrs Venetia Stanley, whom Richard Earle of Dorset kept as his Concubine, and had children by her, and setled on her an Annuity of 500 pounds per annum, which after Sir K.D. maried was unpayd by the Earle; and for which Annuity Sir Kenelme sued the Earle, after marriage, and recovered it. He would say that a handsome lusty man that was discreet might make a vertuose wife out of a Brothell-house. This Lady carried herselfe blamelessly, yet (they say) he was jealous of her. Richard, Earle of Dorset, invited her and her husband once a yeare, when with much desire and passion he beheld her, and only kissed her hand, Sir Kenelme being still by. She dyed suddenly, and hard-hearted woemen would censure him severely.

After her death, to avoyd envy and scandall, he retired into Gresham Colledge at London, where he diverted himselfe with his Chymistry, and the Professors good conversation. He wore there a long mourning cloake, a high crowned hatt, his beard unshorne, look't like a Hermite, as signes of sorrowe for his beloved wife, to whose memory he erected a sumptuouse monument, now quite destroyed by the great Conflagration.

He was borne to three thousand pounds per Annum. What by reason of the Civil-warres, and his generous mind, he contractedst great Debts, and I know not how (there being a great falling out between him and his then only son, John) he settled his Estate upon Cornwalleys, a subtile sollicitor, and also a Member of the House of Commons, who did put Mr John Digby to much charge in Lawe.

Mr John Digby brought me a great book, as big as the biggest Church Bible that ever I sawe, and the richliest bound, bossed with silver, engraven with scutchions and crest (an ostrich) it was a curious velame. It was the History of the Family of the Digbyes, which Sir Kenelme either did, or ordered to be donne. There was inserted all that was to be found any where relating to them, out of Records of the Tower, Rolles, &c. All ancient Church monuments were most exquisitely limmed by some rare Artist. He told me that the compileing of it did cost his father a thousand pound. Sir Jo. Fortescue sayd he did beleeve 'twas more. When Mr John Digby did me the favour to shew me this rare MS, This booke, sayd he, is all that I have left me of all the Estate that was my Father's.

Sir Kenelm Digby, that renowned Knight, great Linguist, and Magazen of Arts, was born and died on the Eleventh of June, and also fought fortunately at Scanderoon the same day. Hear his Epitaph, composed by Mr Farrer:

Under this Stone the Matchless Digby lies,
Digby the Great, the Valiant, and the Wise:
This Age's Wonder, for his Noble Parts;
Skill'd in six Tongues, and learn'd in all the Arts.
Born on the day he died, th'Eleventh of June,
On which he bravely fought at Scanderoon.
'Tis rare that one and self-same day should be
His day of Birth, of Death, of Victory.

VENETIA DIGBY

Born 1600. She was secretly married to Sir Kenelm Digby in the spring of 1625 and their first child was born in the October of that year: but the marriage was not acknowledged until 1627. Absurd reports were circulated that Digby had killed her by insisting on her drinking viper-wine to preserve her beauty. At the time of her death in 1633, Ben Jonson, Thomas May, Joseph Ruther, Owen Feltham, William Habington, Lord George Digby, and Aurelian Townsend commemorated her loss in verse.

VENETIA STANLEY was the daughter of Sir Edward Stanley. She was a most beautifull desireable Creature, and being maturo viro was left by her father to live with a tenant and servants at Enston Abbey in Oxfordshire: but as private as that place was, it seemes her Beautie could not lye hid. The young Eagles had espied her, and she was sanguine and tractable, and of much Suavity (which to abuse was great pittie).

In those dayes, Richard, Earle of Dorset (eldest son and heire to the Lord Treasurer) lived in the greatest splendor of any nobleman in England. Among other pleasures that he enjoyed, Venus was not the least. This pretty creature's fame quickly came to his Lordship's eares, who made no delay to catch at such an opportunity.

I have now forgott who first brought her to Towne, but I have heard my uncle Danvers say (who was her contemporary) that she was so commonly courted, and that by Grandees, that 'twas written over her lodging one night *in literis uncialibus*:

PRAY COME NOT NEER,
FOR DAME VENETIA STANLEY LODGETH HERE.

The Earle of Dorset aforesayd was her greatest Gallant, who was extremely enamoured of her, and had one, if not more children by her. He setled on her an Annuity of 500 pounds per annum.

Among other young Sparkes of that time, Sir Kenelme Digby grew acquainted with her, and fell so much in love with her that he maried her, much against the good will of his mother, but he would say that a wise man, and lusty, could make an honest woman out of a Brothell-house.

Sir Edmund Wyld had her picture (and you may imagine was very familiar with her) which picture is now at Droitwych, in Worcestershire, at an Inne in an entertayning-roome, where now the Towne keepe their Meetings. (She was first a Miss to Sir Edmund Wyld.) Also at Mr Rose's, a Jeweller in Henrietta-Street in Convent Garden, is an excellent piece of hers, drawne after she was newly dead.

She had a most lovely and sweet turn'd face, delicate darke-browne haire. She had a perfect healthy constitution; strong; good skin; well-proportioned; much enclining to a *Bona Roba* (near altogether.) Her face, a short ovall; darke-browne eie-browe about which much sweetness, as also in the opening of her eie-lidds. The colour of her cheekes was just that of the Damaske rose, which is neither too hott nor too pale. She was of a just stature, not very tall.

Sir Kenelme had severall Pictures of her by Vandyke, &c. He had her hands cast in playster, and her feet and Face. See Ben Johnson's 2d. volumne, where he hath made her live in Poetrey, in his drawing of her both Body and Mind:

> *Sitting, and ready to be drawne,*
> *What makes these Tiffany, silkes, and lawne,*
> *Embroideries, feathers, fringes, lace,*
> *When every limbe takes like a Face! etc.*

When these Verses were made she had three children by Sir Kenelme, who are there mentioned, viz. Kenelme, George, and John.

She dyed in her bed, suddenly. Some suspected that she was poysoned. When her head was opened there was found but little braine, which her husband imputed to her drinking of viper-wine; but spitefull woemen would say 'twas a viper husband who was jealous of her that she would steale a leape. I have heard some say, e.g. my cosen Elizabeth Falkner, that after her mariage she redeemed her Honour by her strick't living. Once a yeare the Earle of Dorset invited her and Sir Kenelme to dinner, where the Earle would behold her with much passion, and only kisse her hand.

About 1676 or 5, as I was walking through Newgate-street, I sawe Dame Venetia's Bust from off her tombe standing at a Stall at the golden Crosse, a Brasier's shop. I perfectly remembred it, but the fire had gott-off the Guilding; but taking notice of it to one that was with me, I could never see it afterwards exposed to the street. They melted it downe. How these curiosities would be quite forgott, did not such idle fellowes as I am putt them downe.

DESIDERIUS ERASMUS

Born 1466. The leader of the Northern Renaissance, he was the illegitimate son of a priest [see Reade's *The Cloister and the Hearth*]. His guardians, having embezzled his money, cajoled him into becoming a monk, a step which he regretted all his life. In 1493 he became secretary to the Bishop of Cambrai, which enabled him to leave the monastery and travel. Though he hated scholasticism, he was for a time at the University of Paris. In 1499 he made his first visit to England, where he liked the fashion of kissing girls. Here he made friends with Colet and More, who persuaded him to undertake serious work rather than literary trifles. He therefore started to learn Greek in 1500, and brought out a Greek Testament, with a new Latin translation, in 1516. He also tried to learn Hebrew, but gave it up. He lived in England from 1509 until 1514, where he wrote his most famous book, *The Praise of Folly*, illustrated by Holbein, which contained a scathing attack on the abuses of the Church. However, he was so disgusted by the violence of the Protestant revolt that he sided with the Catholics, and a controversy on Free Will with Luther forced him further and further into reaction. His timidity unfitted him for the intolerance which the Reformation had engendered; he sank into obscurity, and died in 1536.

HIS name was *Gerard Gerard*, which he translated into *Desiderius Erasmus*. Of Roterdam: he loved not Fish, though borne in a Fish-towne.

He was *begot* (as they say) *behind dores*. His father tooke great care to send him to an excellent Schoole, which was at Dusseldorf, in Cleveland. He was a tender Chitt, and his mother would not entruste him at board, but tooke a house there, and made him cordialls.

He was of the order of Augustine, whose habit was the same that the Pest-house-master at Pisa in Italie wore; and walking in that Towne, people beckoned him to goe out of the way, taking him to be the master of the Pest-house; and he not understanding the meaning, and keeping on his way, was there by one well basted. He made his complaint when he came to Rome, and had a dispensation for his habit.

He studied sometime in Queens Colledge in Cambridge: his chamber was over the water. He mentions his being there in one of his *Epistles*, and blames the Beere there.

Sir Charles Blount, of Maple-Durham, in Com. Oxon. (neer Reding) was his Scholar (in his *Epistles* there are some to him) and desired Erasmus to doe him the favour to sitt for his Picture, and he did so, and it is an excellent piece: which picture my cosen John Danvers, of Baynton (Wilts), haz: his wive's grandmother was Sir Charles Blount's daughter or grand-daughter. 'Twas pitty such a rarity should have been aliend from the Family, but the issue male is lately extinct. I will sometime or other endeavour to gett it for Oxford Library.

He had the Parsonage of Aldington in Kent, which is about 3 degrees perhaps a healthier place then Dr Pell's parsonage in Essex. I wonder they could not find for him better preferment; but I see that the Sun and Aries being in the second house, he was not borne to be a rich man.

John Dreyden, Esq, Poet Laureat, tells me that there was a great friendship between his great grand-father's father and Erasmus Roterodamus, and Erasmus was Godfather to one of his sonnes, and the Christian name of Erasmus hath been kept in the family ever since. The Poet's second sonne is Erasmus.

They were wont to say that Erasmus was Interdependent between Heaven and Hell, till, about the year 1655, the Conclave at Rome damned him for a Heretique, after he had been dead 120 yeares.

His deepest divinity is where a man would least expect it: viz. in his *Colloquies* in a Dialogue between a Butcher and a Fishmonger.

Julius Scaliger contested with Erasmus, but gott nothing by it, for, as Fuller sayth, he was like a Badger, that never bitt but he made his teeth meet.

He was the *Πρόδρομος* [*forerunner*] of our knowledge, and the man that made the rough and untrodden wayes smooth and passable.

THOMAS FAIRFAX LORD FAIRFAX

Born 1612. Soldier. Knighted 1640. Became a general for the Parliament 1642. Recaptured Leeds and captured Wakefield 1643. Commander-in-Chief of the Parliamentary Army 1645. Defeated Charles I at Naseby, where he captured a standard with his own hands, and stormed Bristol, 1645. Reduced Oxford and received the thanks of Parliament 1646. Seized Charles I against his will 1647. Transmitted to the Commons the Army's demand for the King's punishment

1648. He was one of the King's judges, but endeavoured to stop his execution, 1649. State Councillor and Commander-in-Chief 1649. He resigned his command from unwillingness to invade Scotland 1650. He headed the Commission sent to Charles II at The Hague in 1660, to arrange his restoration. Died 1671.

THOMAS, Lord Fairfax of Cameron, Lord Generall of the Parliament-armie. When Oxford was surrendred, the first thing General Fairfax did was to sett a good Guard of Soldiers to preserve the Bodleian Library. 'Tis said there was more hurt donne by the Cavaliers (during their Garrison) by way of Embezilling and cutting off chaines of bookes, then there was since. He was a lover of Learning, and had he not taken this speciall care, that noble Library had been utterly destroyed, for there were ignorant Senators enough who would have been contented to have had it so.

CARLO FANTOM

CAPTAIN CARLO FANTOM, a Croatian, spake 13 languages; was a Captain under the Earle of Essex. He was very quarrelsome and a great Ravisher. He left the Parliament Party, and went to the King Ch. the first at Oxford, where he was hanged for Ravishing.

Sd. he, I care not for your Cause: I come to fight for your halfe-crowne, and your handsome woemen: my father was a R. Catholiq; and so was my grandfather. I have fought for the Christians against the Turkes; and for the Turkes against the Christians.

Sir Robert Pye was his Colonel, who shot at him for not returning a horse that he tooke away before the Regiment. This was donne in a field near Bedford, where the Army then was, as they were marching to the relief of Gainsborough. Many are yet living that sawe it. Capt. Hamden was by: The bullets went through his Buff-coat, and Capt. H sawe his shirt on fire. Capt. Carl. Fantom tooke the Bullets, and sayd he, Sir Rob. Here, take your bullets again. None of the Soldiers would dare to fight with him: they sayd, they would not fight with the Devil.

Edmund Wyld, Esq, was very well acquainted with him, and gave him many a Treat, and at last he prevailed with him so far, towards the knowledge of this secret, that Fantom told him, that the Keepers in their Forests did know a certain herb, which they gave to Children, which made them to be shott-free (they call them Hard-men).

In a Booke of Trialls by Duell in foli (writ by Segar, I thinke) before the Combatants fight, they have an Oath administered to them by the Herald; where is inserted (among other things) that they have not about them either Charme or Herb.

Martin Luther in his Commentaries on the First (or second Commandment, I thinke the First) saies that a Hard-man was brought to the Duke of Saxonies Court: he was brought into the great Hall and was commanded to be shott with a Musquet: the bullet drop't downe and he had only a blew Spott on his Skin, where he was struck. Martin Luther was then by, and sawe the Bullet drop-downe.

They say that a silver bullet will kill any Hardman, and can be beaten to death with cudgels. The Elector Palatine, Prince Robert's [*Rupert's*] Brother, did not believe at all, that any man could make himself hard.

Robert Earl of Essex, General for the Parliament had this Capt. Fantom in high esteeme: for he was an admirable Horse-officer, and taught the Cavalry of the army the way of fighting with Horse: the General saved him from hanging twice for Ravishing; once at Winchester, 2nd at St Albans: and he was not content only to ravish himselfe, but he would make his soldiers doe it too, and he would stand by and look on.

He met (comeing late at night out of the Horse-shoe Tavern in Drury lane) with a Liuetenant of Col. Rossiter, who had great jingling Spurres on. Qd. he, the noise of your Spurres doe offend me, you must come over the Kennel and give me satisfaction. They drew and parted at each other and the Lieuetenant was runne thorough and died within a hour or two: and 'twas not known, who killed him.

SIR WILLIAM FLEETWOOD

Born 1535. Recorder of London. Member of the Parliaments of 1572, 1584, 1586, and 1588. By the Earl of Leicester's influence, he was elected Recorder of London in 1571, and soon became famous for vigorously and successfully enforcing the laws against vagrants, thieves, priests, and papists. In 1576 he was committed to the Fleet Prison for a short time for breaking into the Portuguese Ambassador's chapel under cover of the law against Popish recusants. In 1580 he was made Serjeant-at-Law, and in 1583 a Commissioner for the Reformation of Abuses in Printing. In the same year, he drafted a scheme for housing the poor and preventing the plague in London by maintaining open spaces. In 1588 he reported on the proceedings to be taken against Jesuits, and in 1589 on the right of sanctuary for criminals attaching to Saint Paul's Cathedral. He resigned his office in 1591, on receipt of a pension of £100 per annum, and died in 1594.

He was a very severe Hanger of Highwaymen, so that the Fraternity were resolved to make an example of him: which they executed in this manner. They lay in wayte for him not far from Tyburne, as he was to come from his House in Bucks; had a Halter in readinesse; brought him under the Gallowes, fastned the rope about his neck and on the Tree, his hands tied behind him (and servants bound) and then left him to the Mercy of his Horse, which he called Ball. So he cryed, Ho Ball. Ho, Ball – and it pleased God that his horse stood still till somebody came along, which was halfe a quarter of an hour or more. He ordered that this Horse should be kept as long as he would live, and it was so; he lived till 1646.

One day goeing on foote to Guild-hall with his Clarke behind him, he was surprised in Cheapside with a sudden and violent Loosenesse, neer the Standard. He turned up his breech against the Standard and bade his man hide his face; For they shall never see my Arse again, sayd he.

JOHN FLORIO

Born 1545. Author. His father, who was in 1550 preacher to a congregation of Italian Protestants in London, was forced to leave the country after charges of gross immorality had been brought against him. Florio matriculated at Magdalen, Oxford, in 1581, and according to Anthony Wood was *a teacher and instructor of certain scholars in the University*. His first patron was the Earl of Leicester, after whose death *he lived some years in the pay and patronage* of Southampton, while to the Earl of Pembroke he was soon under heavy obligations. At the close of the sixteenth century Florio was living in London on intimate terms with all the chief literary men and their patrons. It is possible that Shakespeare modelled Holofernes in *Love's Labour's Lost* on Florio, and it is certain that his translation of Montaigne's *Essays* (which was licensed to Edward Blount in 1599, but was not published until 1603) formed the basis of Gonzago's description of an ideal state in *The Tempest*. *Montaigne speaks now good English*, wrote Sir William Cornwallis in 1600. *It is done by a fellow less beholding to nature for his fortunes than wit, yet lesser for his face than his fortune. The truth is he looks more like a good fellow than a wise man, and yet he is wise beyond either his fortune or education.* Florio died in 1625.

JOHN FLORIO was borne in London in the beginning of King Edward VI, his father and mother flying from the Valtolin ('tis about Piedmont or Savoy) to London for Religion: Waldenses. – The family is originally of Siena, where the name is to this day.

King Edward dying, upon the persecution of Queen Mary, they fled back again into their owne countrey, where he was educated.

Afterwards he came into England, and was by King James made Informator to Prince Henry for the Italian and French tongues, and clarke to the closet to Queen Anne.

Scripsit: First and Second Fruits, being two books of the Instruction to learne the Italian tongue: Dictionary; and translated Montagne's Essayes.

He dyed of the great plague at Fulham anno 1625.

FRANCIS FRY

Transportation by an Invisible Power. A Letter from the Reverend Mr Andrew Paschal, B.D., Rector of Chedzoy in Somerset, To John Aubery, Esq; at Gresham College.

ABOUT November last, in the Parish of Spreyton, in the County of Devon, there appeared in a Field near the Dwelling-house of Phil. Furze, to his Servant Francis Fry, being of the age of 21 next August, an aged Gentleman with a Pole in his Hand, and like that he was wont to carry about with him when living, to kill Moles withall, who told the Young Man not to be afraid of him; but should tell his Master, i.e. his Son, That several legacies that he had bequeathed were unpaid, naming 10s. to one, 10s. to another, &c. Fry replied, that the party he last named was Dead. The Spectrum replied, he knew that, but said it must be paid to (and named) the next Relation. These things being performed, he promised he would trouble him no further. These small Legacies were paid accordingly. But the young Man having caried 20s. order'd by the Spectrum to his Sister Mrs Furze of the Parish of Staverton near Totness, which Money the Gentlewoman refus'd to receive, being sent her, as she said, from the Devil. The same Night Fry lodging there, the Spectrum appear'd to him again, whereupon Fry challenged his promise not to trouble him, and said he had done all he had desir'd him; but that Mrs Furze would not receive the Money. The Spectrum replied, that's true indeed. But bid him ride to Totness and buy a Ring of that value, and that she would take! Which was provided for her, and receiv'd by her.

Then Fry rode homewards attended by a Servant of Mrs Furze. But having come into Spreyton Parish, or rather a little before, he seem'd to carry an old Gentlewoman behind him, that often threw him off his Horse, and hurried him with such violence, as astonished all that saw him, or heard how horridly the Ground was beaten; and being come into his Master's Yard, Fry's Horse (a mean Beast) sprung at once 25 foot.

The trouble from the Man-Spectre ceased from this time. But the old Gentlewoman, Mrs Furze, Mr Furze's second Wife, whom the Spectre at his first appearance to Fry called, That Wicked Woman my Wife (though I knew her, and took her for a very good Woman) presently after appears to several in the House, viz. to Fry, Mrs Thomasin Gidley, Anne Langdon born in my Parish, and to a little Child which was forced to be remov'd from the House; sometimes in her own shape, sometimes in shapes more horrid, as of a Dog belching Fire, and of an Horse, and seeming to ride out at the Window, carrying only one pane of Glass away, and a little piece of Iron.

After this Fry's Head was thrust into a narrow space, where a Man's Fist could not enter, between a Bed and a Wall; and forced to be taken thence by the strength of Men, all bruised and bloody; upon this it was thought fit to Bleed him, and after that was done, the Binder was remov'd from his Arm, and convey'd about his Middle, and presently was drawn so very straight, it had almost killed him, and was cut asunder, making an ugly uncouth noise. Several other times with Handkerchiefs, Cravats, and other things he was near strangled, they were drawn so close upon his Throat.

He lay one Night in his Periwig (in his Master's Chamber, for the more safety) which was torn all to pieces. His best Periwig he inclosed in a little Box on the inside, with a Joind-stool and other weight upon it; the Box was snapp'd asunder, and the Wig torn all to flitters. His Master saw his Buckles fall all to pieces on his Feet: But, first I should have told you the Fate of his Shoe-strings, one of which a Gentlewoman greater than all exception, assured me that she saw it come out of his Shoe, without any visible Hand, and fling itself to the farther end of the Room; the other was coming out too, but that a Maid prevented and help'd it out, which crisp'd and curl'd about her Hand like a living Eel. The Cloathes worn by Anne Langdon and Fry (if their own) were torn to pieces on their backs. The same Gentlewoman, being the Daughter of the Minister of the Parish, Mr Roger Specott, showed me one of Fry's Gloves, which was torn in his Pocket while she was by. I did view it near and narrowly, and do seriously confess that it is torn so very accurately in all the Seams and in other places, and laid abroad so artificially, and it is so dexterously tattered (and all done in the Pocket in a Minute's time) as nothing Human could have done it; no Cutler could have made an Engine to do it so.

Other fantastical Freeks have been very frequent, as, the marching of a great Barrel full of Salt out of one Room to another; an Andiron laying itself over a Pan of Milk that was scalding on the Fire, and two Flitches of Bacon descending from the Chimney where they hung, and laid themselves over that Andiron. The appearing of the Spectrum (when in her own shape) in the same Cloathes to seeming, which Mrs Furze her daughter-in-law has on. The intangling of Fry's Face and Legs, about his Neck, and about the Frames of the Chairs, so as they have been with great difficulty disengaged.

But the most Remarkable of all happened in that Day that I passed by the Door in my return hither, which was Easter-eve, when Fry, returning from Work (that little he can do) he was caught by the Woman Spectre by the Skirts of his Doublet, and carried into the Air; he was quickly mist by his Master and the Workmen, and great enquiry was made for Fran. Fry, but no hearing of him; but after half an Hour after, Fry was heard Whistling and Singing in a kind of Quagmire. He was now affected [*supposed*] as he was wont to be in his Fits, so that none regarded what he said; but coming to himself an Hour after, he solemnly protested, That the Daemon carried him so high that he saw his Master's House underneath him no bigger than a Hay-cock, that he was in perfect sense and prayed God not to suffer the Devil to destroy him; that he was suddenly set down in that Quagmire. The Workmen found one Shoe on one side of the House, and the other Shoe on the other side; his Periwig was espied next Morning hanging on the Top of a tall Tree.

It was soon observ'd, that Fry's part of his Body that had laid in the Mud, was much benum'd, and therefore the next Saturday, which was the eve of Low-Sunday, they carried him to Crediton to be let Blood; which being done, and the Company having left him for a little while, returning they found him in a Fit, with his Fore-head all bruised and swoln to a great Bigness, none being able to guess how it came, till he recover'd himself, and then he told them, That a Bird flew in at the Window with a great force, and with a Stone in its Mouth flew directly against his Forehead. The People looked for it, and found on the Ground just under where he sat, not a Stone, but a weight of Brass, or Copper, which the People were breaking, and parting it among themselves. He was so very ill that he could not ride but one Mile or little more that Night, since which time I have not heard of him, save that he was ill handled the next Day, being Sunday.

Indeed Sir you may wonder that I have not Visited that House, and the poor afflicted People; especially, since I was so near, and passed by the very Door: But, besides that they have called to their assistance none but Nonconforming Ministers, I was not qualified to be welcome there, having given Mr Furze a great deal of trouble the last Year about a Conventicle in his House, where one of this Parish was the Preacher. But I am very well assured of the truth of what I have written, and (as more appears) you shall hear from me again.

I had forgot to tell you that Fry's Mother came to me, grievously bewailing the miserable condition of her Son. She told me that the Day before he had five Pins thrust into his Side. She ask'd, and I gave her the best Advice I could. Particularly, that her Son should declare all that the Spectre, especially the Woman, gave him in Charge, for I suspect, there is *aliquid latens* [something concealed]; and that she should remove him thence by all means. But I fear that she will not do it. For I hear that Anne Langdon is come into my Parish to her Mother, and that she is grievously troubled there. I might have written as much of her, as of Fry, for she had been as ill treated, saving the Aerial Journey. Her Fits and Obsessions seem to be greater, for she Scrieches in a most Hellish tone. Thomasin Gidley (though removed) is in trouble, as I hear.

THOMAS GOFFE

Born 1591. Divine and poet. Three of his tragedies were acted at Christ Church, Oxford, and his play *The Careless Shepherdess* was performed before the King and Queen at Salisbury. He was a woman-hater and a bachelor, until he was inveigled into marrying a parishioner at East Clandon, of which he was the incumbent from 1620 until his death. This lady was the widow of his predecessor, and she and her children by her first husband so persecuted poor Goffe that he died shortly after his marriage in 1629.

THOMAS GOFFE the Poet was Rector here; he was buried in the Middle of the Chancel, but there is nothing in Remembrance of him; his Wife, it seems, was not so kind. I find by the Register-Book, that he was buried, July 27, 1629. His Wife pretended to fall in Love with him, by hearing him preach: Upon which, said one Thomas Thimble (one of the Squire Bedell's in Oxford, and his Confident) to him: Do not marry her: if thou dost, she will break thy Heart. He was not obsequious to his Friend's sober Advice, but for her Sake altered his Condition, and cast Anchor here.

One time some of his Oxford Friends made a Visit to him. She look'd upon them with an ill Eye, as if they had come to eat her out of her House and Home (as they say). She provided a Dish of Milk, and some Eggs for Supper, and no more: They perceived her Niggardliness, and that her Husband was inwardly troubled at it (she wearing the Breeches), so they resolv'd to be merry at Supper, and talk all in Latin, and laugh'd exceedingly. She was so vex'd at their speaking Latin, that she could not hold, but fell out a Weeping, and rose from the Table. The next Day, Mr Goffe order'd a better Dinner for them, and sent for some Wine: They were merry, and his Friends took their final Leave of him.

'Twas no long Time before this Xantippe made Mr Thimble's Prediction good; and when he died, the last Words he spake were: *Oracle*, *Oracle*, *Tom Thimble*, and so he gave up the Ghost.

JOHN GRAUNT

Born 1620. Statistician. He gained such esteem by his integrity as a merchant that he was able, when he was only thirty years old, to procure the Professorship of Music in Gresham College for his friend Dr William Petty. In 1662 appeared the first *Natural and Political Observations made upon the Bills of Mortality by John Graunt, Citizen of London. With reference to the Government, Religion, Trade, Growth, Ayre, Diseases, and the several Changes of the said City*. This work laid the foundation of the science subsequently styled Political Arithmetic by Sir William Petty. Charles II specially recommended Graunt to be chosen an original member of the Royal Society, advising the Society that *if they found any more such tradesmen, they should be sure to admit them all without any more adoe*. After his retirement, Graunt was admitted into the management of the New River Company, and was rumoured, because of his Catholicism, to have cut off the supply of water to the city the night before the Fire of London. He died in 1674.

CAPTAINE JOHN GRAUNT (afterwards, major) was borne *24º die Aprilis*, at the 7 Starres in Burchin Lane, London, in the parish of St Michael's Cornhill, ½ an houre before eight a clock on a munday morning, the signe being in the 9 degree of Gemini that day at 12 a clock, Anno Domini 1620.

He was bred-up (as the fashion then was) in the Puritan way; wrote Short-hand dextrously; and after many yeares constant hearing and writing sermon-notes, he fell to buying and reading of the best Socinian bookes, and for severall yeares continued of that Opinion. At last, he turned a Roman Catholique, of which Religion he dyed a great Zealot.

To give him his due prayse, he was a very ingeniose and studious person, and generally beloved, and rose early in the morning to his Study before shop-time. He understood Latin and French. He was a pleasant facetious Companion, and very hospitable.

He was by Trade, Haberdasher of small-wares, but was free of the Drapers-Company. A man generally beloved; a faythfull friend. Often chosen for his prudence and justnes to be an Arbitrator; and he was a great Peace-maker. He had an excellent working head, and was very facetious and fluent in his conversation.

He had gonne thorough all the Offices of the City as far as Common-councill-man. He was Common-councill-man two yeares. Captaine of the Trayned Band, severall yeares: Major of it, two or three yeares, and then layd downe trade and all other publique Employment for his Religion, being a Roman Catholique.

He wrote *Observations on the bills of Mortality* very ingeniosely, but I beleeve, and partly know, that he had his Hint from his intimate and familiar friend Sir William Petty, to which he made some *Additions*, since printed. And he intended (had he lived) to have writt more on the subject.

He wrott some *Observations on the Advance of the Excise*, not printed; and also intended to have written something of Religion.

Major John Graunt dyed on Easter-eve 1674, and was buryed the Wednesday followeing in St Dunstan's church in Fleetstreet in the body of the said church under the piewes towards the gallery on the north side, i.e. under the piewes (alias hoggsties) of the north side of the middle aisle (what pitty 'tis so great an Ornament of the Citty should be buryed so obscurely!) *aetatis anno 54°.*

His death is lamented by all Good men that had the happinesse to knowe him; and a great number of ingeniose persons attended him to his grave. Among others (with Teares) was that ingeniose great Virtuoso, Sir William Petty, his old and intimate Acquaintance, who was sometime a student at Brasenose College.

He had one son, a man, who dyed in Persia; one daughter, a Nunne at (I thinke) Gaunt. His widowe yet alive.

He was my honoured and worthy Friend – *cujus animae propitietur Deus, Amen.*

EDMUND GUNTER

Born 1581. Mathematician. Educated at Westminster and Christ Church. He took Holy Orders in 1615, and became Professor of Astronomy in Gresham College and vicar of St George's, Southwark, in 1619. He published in 1620 a *Table of Artificial Sines and Tangents, to a radius of 100,000,000 parts to each minute of the Quadrant*, and assisted in the invention of Logarithms. He discovered by experiments at Deptford the variation of the magnetic needle, but this discovery seemed so strange that he suspected an error and dropped his investigations in 1622. He originated Gunter's Chain, which is still constantly used in land surveying, and first used the words cosine and cotangent, as well as inventing the decimal separator. He died in 1626.

CAPTAIN RALPH GRETOREX, Mathematical-Instrument Maker in London, sayd that he was the first that brought Mathematicall Instruments to perfection. His *Booke of the Quadrant, Sector, and Crosse-staffe* did open men's understandings and made young men in love with that Studie. Before, the Mathematicall Sciences were lock't-up in the Greeke and Latin tongues; and so lay untoucht, kept safe in some Libraries. After Mr Gunter published his Booke, these Sciences sprang up amain, more and more to that height it is at now (1690).

When he was a Student at Christchurch, it fell to his lott to preach the Passion Sermon, which some old divines that I knew did heare, but 'twas sayd of him then in the University that our Saviour never suffered so much since his Passion as in that sermon, it was such a lamentable one – *Non omnia possumus omnes* [all things are not possible to all men]. The world is much beholding to him for what he hath donne well.

JOHN HALES

Born 1584. Theologian. He was one of the best Greek scholars of his day and lectured on that language at Oxford. In 1616 he became chaplain to Sir Dudley Carleton, the English Ambassador at The Hague, and attended the Synod of Dort, where he was converted from Calvinism to Arminianism. A lover of quiet and learned leisure, he declined all high and responsible ecclesiastical preferment, and chose and obtained scholarly retirement in a Fellowship of Eton, of which his friends, Sir Henry Savile and Sir Henry Wotton, were successively Provost. His treatise on *Schism and Schismatics* gave offence to Laud, but Hales defended himself so well that Laud made him a Prebendary of Windsor. Refusing to acknowledge the Commonwealth, he was deprived of his fellowship and fell into poverty. Died 1656.

WENT to School, at Bath (as I take it). Fellow of Merton Colledge: afterwards fellow of Eaton College.

He was a generall Scolar, and I beleeve a good poet: for Sir John Suckling brings him into the *Session of the Poets*:

Little Hales all the time did nothing but smile,
To see them, about nothing, keepe such a coile.

When the Court was at Windsor, the learned Courtiers much delighted in his company, and were wont to grace him with their company.

Mr Hales was the common Godfather there, and 'twas pretty to see, as he walked to Windsor, how his Godchildren fell on their Knees. When he was Bursar, he still gave away all his Groates for the Acquittances to his Godchildren; and by that time he came to Windsor bridge, he would have never a Groate left.

He had a noble Librarie of bookes, and those judicially chosen, which cost him not lesse then 2500 pounds; and which he sold to Cornelius Bee, Bookeseller, in Little Britaine, (as I take it, for 1000 pounds) which was his maintenance after he was ejected out of his Fellowship at Eaton-College. Mris Powney told me that she was much against the sale of 'em, because she knew it was his Life and joy. He had then only reserved some few for his private use, to wind-up his last dayes withall.

I have heard his nephew, Mr Sloper, say, that he much loved to read Stephanus, who was a Familist, I thinke that first wrote of that Sect of the Familie of Love: he was mightily taken with it, and was wont to say that sometime or other those fine Notions would take in the world. He was one of the first Socinians in England, I thinke the first.

The Ladie Salter (neer Eaton) was very kind to him after his Sequestration; he was very welcome to her Ladyship and spent much of his time there: (from her Nephew).

He lodged (after his Sequestration) at Mris Powney's house, a widowe-woman, in Eaton, opposite to the churchyard, adjoyning to the Christopher Inne southwards. She is a very good woman and of a gratefull spirit. She told me that when she was maried, Mr Hales was very bountifull to them in setting them up to live in the world. She was very gratefull to him and respectfull to him: a woman primitively good, and deserves to be remembred. She has been handsome: a good understanding, and cleanlie. I wish I had her Christian name.

She has a handsome darke old-fashioned howse. The hall, after the old fashion, above the wainscot, painted cloath, with godly sentences out of the Psalmes, etc, according to the pious custome of old times; a convenient garden and orchard.

'Tis the howse where I sawe him, a prettie little man, sanguine, of a cheerfull countenance, very gentile, and courteous; I was recieved by him with much humanity: he was in a kind of violet-colourd cloath Gowne, with buttons and loopes (he wore not a black gowne) and was reading Thomas à Kempis; it was within a yeare before he deceased. He loved Canarie; but moderately, to refresh his spirits.

He had a bountifull mind. I remember in 1647, a little after the Visitation, when Thomas Mariett, Esq, Mr William Radford, and Mr Edward Wood (all of Trinity College) had a frolique from Oxon to London, on foot, having never been there before; they happened to take Windsore in their way, made their addresse to this good Gentleman, being then Fellow. Mr Edward Wood was the Spookes-man, remonstrated that they were Oxon Scholars: he treated them well, and putt into Mr Wood's hands Ten shillings.

This Mris Powney assures me that the poor were more relievable (that is to say) that he recieved more kindnesse from them than from the Rich. That that I putt downe of my Lady Salter is false. She had him to her house indeed, but 'twas to teach her sonne, who was such a blockhead he could not read well.

He might have been restored to his Fellowship again, but he would not accept the offer. He was not at all Covetous, and desired only to leave X pounds to bury him.

He lies buried in the Church yard at Eaton, under an altar monument of Black marble, erected at the sole chardge of Mr Curwyn, with a too long Epitaph. He was no Kiff or Kin to him.

EDMUND HALLEY

Born 1656. Astronomer. Elected a Fellow of the Royal Society at the age of twenty-two. But for Halley, Newton's *Principia* would not have existed; his suggestions originated it and, although his father's death had left him in poor circumstances, he printed Newton's work at his own expense and averted the threatened suppression of the third book. In 1691 Halley was refused the Savilian Professorship of Astronomy at Oxford, owing to a suspicion of his being a materialist. Assistant Secretary to the Royal Society 1685–93. Deputy Controller of the Mint at Ipswich 1696. William III gave him command of a war-sloop, the *Paramour Pink*, in 1698, with orders to study the variation of the compass and to attempt to discover what land lay to the south of the Western Ocean. Halley penetrated to the Antarctic, and explored the Atlantic from shore to shore until 1700. The following year he published a general chart of the variation of the compass shown by Halleyan lines. He then made a thorough survey of the tides and coasts of the English Channel, of which he published a map in 1702. In 1703 he was made Savilian Professor of Geometry at Oxford. He was also elected Secretary of the Royal Society in 1713, and became Astronomer Royal in 1721. At the age of sixty-four, he began the process of observing the moon through its complete cycle of eighteen years, and in 1729 was elected a foreign member of the Paris Academy of Sciences. Peter the Great admitted him familiarly to his table, and at Vienna he was presented with a diamond ring from the Emperor's own finger. Halley worked out the Law of Inverse Squares, the first detailed description of a circulatory theory of the Trade Winds and Monsoons, and a new method of finding the roots of equations. He discovered the law connecting elevation in the atmosphere with its density, and first measured height by barometric readings. He improved diving apparatus, experimented on the dilatation of liquids by heat, and by his scientific voyages laid the foundations of physical geography. But his most enduring fame was caused by his accurate prediction of the return in 1758 of the comet (named after him) of 1531, 1607, and 1682. He died in 1742 after drinking a glass of wine against his doctor's orders.

MR EDMUND HALLEY, Artium Magister, the eldest son of Edmund Halley, a Soape-boyler, a wealthy Citizen of the City of London, of the Halleys, of Derbyshire, a good family. He was born in Shoreditch parish, at a place called Haggerston, the backside of Hogsdon.

At 9 yeares old, his father's apprentice taught him to write, and arithmetique. He went to Paule's schoole to Dr Gale: while he was there he was very perfect in the caelestiall Globes in so much that I heard Mr Moxton (the Globe-maker) say that if a star were misplaced in the Globe, he would presently find it. He studyed Geometry, and at 16 could make a dyall, and then, he said, thought himselfe a brave fellow.

At 16 went to Queen's Colledge in Oxon, well versed in Latin, Greeke, and Hebrew: where, at the age of nineteen, he solved this useful Probleme in Astronomie, never donne before, viz. *from 3 distances given from the Sun, and Angles between, to find the Orbe*, for which his name will be ever famous.

He went to Dantzick to visit Hevelius. December 1st, 1680, went to

Paris: Cardinal d'Estrée caressed him and sent him to his brother the Admirall with a lettre of Recommendation. He hath contracted an acquaintance and friendship with all the eminentst Mathematicians of France and Italie, and holds a correspondence with them.

He gott leave and a *viaticum* of his father to goe to the Island of *Sancta Hellena*, purely upon account of advancement of Astronomy, to make the globe of the Southerne Hemisphere right, which before was very erroneous, as being donne only after the observations of ignorant seamen. There he stayed some moneths. There went over with him (amongst others) a woman, and her husband, who had no child in several yeares; before he came from the Island, she was brought to bed of a Child. At his returne, he presented his Planisphere, with a short description, to his Majesty who was very well pleased with it; but received nothing but Prayse.

THOMAS HARCOURT

Born 1618. Jesuit. His real name was Whitbread, and he was born in Essex. He entered the Society of Jesus at Watten in 1635. He spent thirty-two years as a missioner in England. Upon Titus Oates's revelation of an alleged Popish Plot, he was tried and executed in June 1679.

PETRIFICATION of a Kidney. – When Father Harcourt suffered at Tyburne, and his bowells, etc, throwne into the fire, a butcher's boy standing by was resolved to have a piece of his Kidney which was broyling in the fire. He burn't his fingers much, but he got it; and one Roydon, a Brewer in Southwark, bought it, a kind of Presbyterian. The wonder is, 'tis now absolutely petrified. But 'twas not so hard when he first had it. It being alwayes carried in the pocket hardened by degrees, better then by the fire – like an Agate polished. I have seen it. He much values it.

THOMAS HARIOT

Born 1560. Mathematician. He was mathematical tutor to Sir Walter Raleigh, who sent him to survey Virginia in 1585; his *Brief and True Report* appears in Hakluyt's *Voyages*. He made inventions which gave algebra its modern form, and used telescopes simultaneously with Galileo. Through them he observed sun-spots and the comets of 1607 and 1618. Died 1621.

Mr Hariot went with Sir Walter Ralegh into Virginia, and haz writt the *Description of Virginia*, which is printed. Dr Pell tells me that he finds amongst his papers, an Alphabet that he had contrived for the American Language, like Devills.

When the Earle of Northumberland and Sir Walter Ralegh were both Prisoners in the Tower, they grew acquainted, and Sir Walter Raleigh recommended Mr Hariot to him, and the Earle setled an Annuity of two hundred pounds a yeare on him for his life, which he enjoyed. But to Hues (who wrote *de Usu Globorum*) and to Mr Warner he gave an Annuity but of sixty pounds per annum. These 3 were usually called the Earle of Northumberland's three Magi. They had a Table at the Earle's chardge, and the Earle himselfe had them to converse with him, singly or together.

Sir Francis Stuart had heard Mr Hariot say that he had seen nine Cometes, and had predicted Seaven of them, but did not tell them how. 'Tis very strange: *excogitent Astronomi*.

He did not like (or valued not) the old storie of the Creation of the World. He could not beleeve the old position; he would say *ex nihilo nihil fit* [nothing comes of nothing]. But a *nihilum* killed him at last: for in the top of his Nose came a little red speck (exceeding small) which grew bigger and bigger, and at last killed him. I suppose it was that which the Chirurgians call a *noli me tangere* [touch me not].

He made a Philosophical Theologie, wherin he cast-off the Old Testament, and then the New-one would (consequently) have no Foundation. He was a Deist. His Doctrine he taught to Sir Walter Raleigh, Henry Earle of Northumberland, and some others. The Divines of those times look't on his manner of death as a Judgement upon him for nullifying the Scripture.

JAMES HARRINGTON

Born 1611. Political theorist. He left Oxford without taking a degree, and travelled to Holland, where he joined the Court of the Elector Palatine. Later he travelled through France to Rome, where he refused to kiss the Pope's toe, excusing himself afterwards to Charles I by saying that he would not kiss the foot of any prince, after kissing the King's hand. He also visited Venice, where he was greatly impressed by the system of government. In 1656 he published *Oceana*, his model of a commonwealth. Harrington's main principle is that power depends upon the balance of property, and normally of landed property. The senate prepares laws, which are voted upon by the people, and the magistrates carry them out. Elaborate systems of rotation and balloting are worked out in detail, and the permanence of the system is secured by the equilibrium of all interests. His republic is a moderate aristocracy. Harrington died in 1677.

HIS Genius lay chiefly towards the Politiques and Democraticall Government.

Anno 1647, if not 6, he was by Order of Parliament made one of his Majestie's Bedchamber. Mr Harrington and the King often disputed about Government. The King loved his company; only he would not endure to heare of a Commonwealth: and Mr Harrington passionately loved his Majestie. He was on the Scaffold with the King when he was beheaded; and I have oftentimes heard him speake of King Charles I with the greatest zeale and passion imaginable, and that his death gave him so great a griefe that he contracted a Disease by it; that never any thing did goe so neer to him.

He made severall Essayes in Poetry, viz. love-verses, &c; but his Muse was rough, and Mr Henry Nevill, an ingeniose and well-bred Gentleman, a member of the House of Commons, and an excellent (but concealed) Poet, was his great familiar and Confident friend, and disswaded him from tampering in Poetrie which he did *invita Minervâ* [against Minerva's will], and to improve his proper Talent, viz. Politicall Reflections.

Whereupon he writ his *Oceana*, printed London 1656. Mr T. Hobbes was wont to say that Henry Nevill had a finger in that pye; and 'tis like enough. That ingeniose Tractat, together with his and H. Nevill's smart discourses and inculcations, dayly at Coffe-houses, made many Proselytes.

In so much that, anno 1659, the beginning of Michaelmas-terme, he had every night a meeting at the (then) Turke's head, in the New Pallace-yard, where was made purposely a large ovall-table, with a passage in the middle for Miles to deliver his Coffee. About it sate his Disciples, and the Virtuosi. The Discourses in this Kind were the most ingeniose, and smart, that ever I heard, or expect to heare, and bandied with great eagernesse: the Arguments in the Parliament howse were but flatt to it.

Here we had (very formally) a *Balloting-box*, and balloted how things should be caried, by way of *tentamens* [experiment]. The room was every evening full as it could be cramm'd. One time Mr Stafford and his Gang came in, in drink, from the Taverne, and affronted the Junto (Mr Stafford tore their Orders and Minutes). The Soldiers offerd to kick them downe stayres, but Mr Harrington's moderation and persuasion hindred it.

The Doctrine was very taking, and the more because, as to human foresight, there was no possibility of the King's returne. But the greatest part of the Parliament-men perfectly hated this designe of *Rotation by Ballotting*; for they were cursed Tyrants, and in love with their Power, and 'twas death to them, except 8 or 10, to admitt of this way, for H. Nevill proposed it in the Howse, and made it out to them, that except they embraced that Modell of Government they would be ruind.

Pride of Senators-for-Life is insufferable; and they were able to grind any one they owed ill will to to powder; they were hated by the armie and the countrey they represented, and their name and memorie stinkes – 'twas worse then Tyranny. Now this Modell upon Rotation was that the third part of the Senate should rote out by ballot every yeare, so that every ninth yeare the Howse would be wholly alterd; no Magistrate to continue above 3 yeares, and all to be chosen by Ballot, then which manner of Choice, nothing can be invented more faire and impartiall.

Well: this Meeting continued Novemb., Dec., Jan., till Febr. 20 or 21; and then, upon the unexpected turne upon Generall Monke's comeing-in, all these aerie modells vanished. Then 'twas not fitt, nay Treason, to have donne such; but I well remember, he severall times (at the breaking-up) sayd, Well, the King will come in. Let him come-in, and call a Parliament of the greatest Cavaliers in England, so they be men of Estates, and let them sett but 7 yeares, and they will all turn Common-wealthe's men.

Anno Domini 1660, he was committed prisoner to the Tower; then to Portsey castle. His durance in these Prisons (he being a Gentleman of a high spirit and a hot head) was the procatractique [*originating*] cause of his deliration or madnesse; which was not outragious, for he would discourse rationally enough and be very facetious company, but he grew to have a phancy that his Perspiration turned to Flies, and sometimes to Bees; and he had a versatile timber house built in Mr Hart's garden (opposite to St James's parke) to try the experiment. He would turne it to the sun, and sitt towards it; then he had his fox-tayles there to chase away and massacre all the Flies and Bees that were to be found there, and then shut his *Chassees* [window]. Now this Experiment was only to be tryed in Warme weather, and some flies would lye so close in the cranies and cloath (with which it was hung) that they would not presently shew themselves. A quarter of an hower after perhaps, a fly or two, or more, might be drawen-out of the lurking holes by the warmeth; and then he would crye out, Doe not you see it apparently that these come from me? 'Twas the strangest sort of madnes that ever I found in any one: talke of any thing els, his discourse would be very ingeniose and pleasant.

He was wont to find fault with the constitution of our Government, that 'twas *by jumps*, and told a story of a Cavaliero he sawe at the Carnival in Italie, who rode on an excellent managed horse that with a touch of his toe would jumpe quite round. One side of his habit was Spanish, the other French; which sudden alteration of the same person pleasantly surprized the spectators. Just so, said he, 'tis with us. When no Parliament, then absolute Monarchie; when a Parliament, then it runnes to a Commonwealth.

He was wont to say that Right Reason in Contemplation, is Vertue in Action, et vice versa. Vivere secundum naturam is to live vertuously, the Divines will not have it so; and that when the Divines would have us be an inch above Vertue, we fall an ell belowe it.

He married to his old sweet-heart Mris Dayrell, a comely and discreete ladie. It happening so, from some private reasons, that he could not enjoy his deare in the flower and heate of his youth, he would never lye with her, but loved and admired her dearly: for she was *vergentibus annis* [sloping towards old age] when he maried her, and had lost her sweetenesse.

For above twenty yeares before he died (except his imprisonment) he lived in the Little-Ambry (a faire house on the left hand) which lookes into the Deanes-yard in Westminster. In the upper story he had a pretty gallery, which looked into the yard, where he commonly dined, and meditated, and tooke his Tobacco.

Henry Nevill, Esq, never forsooke him to his dyeing day. Though neer a whole yeare before he died, his memorie and discourse were taken away by a disease ('twas a sad sight to see such a sample of Mortality, in one whom I lately knew, a brisque, lively cavaliero) this Gentleman, whom I must never forget for his constant friendship, payd his visits as duly and respectfully as when his friend was in the prime of his Understanding – a true friend.

WILLIAM HARVEY

Born 1578. Anatomist and physiologist. Educated at Caius College, Cambridge, and the University of Padua, then the most famous school of physic. His theory of the circulation of the blood was expounded to the College of Physicians in 1616, but his treatise on the subject was not published until 1628. He died in 1657.

WILLIAM HARVEY, Dr of Physique and Chirurgery, Inventor of the Circulation of the Bloud, was borne at the house which is now the Post-house, a faire stone-built-house, which he gave to Caius college in Cambridge, with some lands there. His brother Eliab would have given any money or exchange for it, because 'twas his father's, and they all borne there; but the Doctor (truly) thought his memory would better be preserved this way, for his brother has left noble seates, and about 3000 pounds per annum, at least.

William Harvey, was always very contemplative, and the first that I heare of that was curious in Anatomie in England. I remember I have heard him say he wrote a booke *De Insectis*, which he had been many yeares about, and had made dissections of Frogges, Toades, and a number of other Animals, and had made curious Observations on them, which papers, together with his goods, in his Lodgings at Whitehall, were plundered at the beginning of the Rebellion, he being for the King, and with him at Oxon; but he often sayd, That of all the losses he sustained, no griefe was so crucifying to him as the losse of these papers, which for love or money he could never retrive or obtaine.

When Charles I by reason of the Tumults left London, he attended him, and was at the fight of Edge-hill with him; and during the fight, the Prince and Duke of Yorke were committed to his care. He told me that he withdrew with them under a hedge, and tooke out of his pockett a booke and read; but he had not read very long before a Bullet of a great Gun grazed on the ground neare him, which made him remove his station.

He told me that Sir Adrian Scrope was dangerously wounded there, and left for dead amongst the dead men, stript; which happened to be the saving of his Life. It was cold, cleer weather, and a frost that night; which staunched his bleeding, and about midnight, or some houres after his hurte, he awaked, and was faine to drawe a dead body upon him for warmeth-sake.

I first sawe him at Oxford, 1642, after Edgehill fight, but was then too young to be acquainted with so great a Doctor. I remember he came severall times to Trinity College to George Bathurst, B.D., who had a Hen to hatch Egges in his chamber, which they dayly opened to discerne the progres and way of Generation. I had not the honour to be acquainted with him till 1651, being my she cosen Montague's physitian and friend. I was at that time bound for Italy (but to my great griefe disswaded by my mother's importunity). He was very communicative, and willing to instruct any that were modest and respectfull to him. And in order to my Journey, gave me, i.e. dictated to me, what to see, what company to keepe, what Bookes to read, how to manage my Studies: in short, he bid me goe to the Fountain head, and read Aristotle, Cicero, Avicenna, and did call the Neoteriques shitt-breeches.

He wrote a very bad hand, which (with use) I could pretty well read. He understood Greek and Latin pretty well, but was no Critique, and he wrote very bad Latin. The *Circuitis Sanguinis* [Circulation of the Blood] was, as I take it, donne into Latin by Sir George Ent.

At Oxford, he grew acquainted with Dr Charles Scarborough, then a young Physitian (since by King Charles II Knighted) in whose conversation he much delighted; and wheras before, he marched up and downe with the Army, he tooke him to him and made him ly in his Chamber, and said to him, Prithee leave off thy gunning, and stay here; I will bring thee into practice.

His Majestie King Charles I gave him the Wardenship of Merton Colledge in Oxford, as a reward for his service, but the Times suffered him not to recieve or injoy any benefitt by it.

After Oxford was surrendred, which was 24 July 1646, he came to London, and lived with his brother Eliab a rich Merchant in London, who bought, about 1654, Cockaine-house, now (1680) the Excise-office, a noble house, where the Doctor was wont to contemplate on the Leads of the house, and had his severall stations, in regard of the sun, or wind.

He did delight to be in the darke, and told me he could then best contemplate. He had a house heretofore at Combe, in Surrey, a good aire and prospect, where he had Caves made in the Earth, in which in Summer time he delighted to meditate.

Ah! my old friend Dr Harvey – I knew him right well. He made me sitt by him 2 or 3 hours together in his meditating apartment discoursing. Why, had he been stiffe, starcht, and retired, as other formall Doctors are, he had known no more than they. From the meanest person, in some way, or other, the learnedst man may learn something. Pride has been one of the greatest stoppers of the Advancement of Learning.

He was far from Bigotry.

He was wont to say that man was but a great, mischievous Baboon.

He had been physitian to the Lord Chancellour Bacon, whom he esteemed much for his witt and style, but would not allow him to be a great Philosopher. Said he to me, *He writes Philosophy like a Lord Chancellor*, speaking in derision; *I have cured him.*

When Doctor Harvey (one of the Physitians College in London) being a Young Man, went to Travel towards Padoa: he went to Dover (with several others) and shewed his Pass, as the rest did, to the Governor there. The Governor told him, that he must not go, but he must keep him Prisoner. The Doctor desired to know for what reason? how he has transgrest. Well, it was his Will to have it so. The Pacquet Boat Hoised Sail in the Evening (which was very clear) and the Doctor's Companions in it. There ensued a terrible Storme, and the Pacquet-Boat and all the Passengers were Drown'd: The next day the sad News was brought to Dover. The Doctor was unknown to the Governor, both by Name and Face; but the Night before, the Governor had a perfect Vision in a Dream of Doctor Harvey, who came to pass over to Calais; and that he had a Warning to stop him. This the Governor told to the Doctor the next day. The Doctor was a pious good Man, and has several times directed this Story to some of my Acquaintance.

Dr Harvy told me, and any one if he examines himself will find it to be true, that a man could not fancy – truthfully – that he is imperfect in any part that he has, *verbi gratiâ*, Teeth, Eie, Tongue, Spina dorsi, etc. Natura tends to perfection, and in matters of Generation we ought to consult more with our sense and instinct, then our reason, and prudence, fashion of the country, and Interest. We see what contemptible products are of the prudent politiques; weake, fooles, and ricketty children, scandalls to nature and their country. The Heralds are fooles: *tota errant via* [they are on completely the wrong track]. A blessing goes with a marriage for love upon a strong impulse.

He that marries a widdowe makes himself Cuckold. *Exempli gratia*, if a good Bitch is first warded with a Curre, let her ever after be warded with a dog of a good straine and yet she will bring curres as at first, her wombe being first infected with a Curre. So, the children will be like the first Husband (like raysing up children to your brother). So, the Adulterer, though a crime in Law, the children are like the husband.

He would say that we Europeans knew not how to order or governe our Woemen, and that the Turks were the only people used them wisely.

I remember he kept a pretty young wench to wayte on him, which I guesse he made use of for warmeth-sake as King David did, and tooke care of her in his Will, as also of his man servant.

He was very Cholerique; and in his young days wore a dagger (as the fashion then was) but this Dr would be to apt to draw-out his dagger upon every slight occasion.

I have heard him say, that after his Booke of the *Circulation of the Blood* came-out, that he fell mightily in his Practize, and that 'twas beleeved by the vulgar that he was crack-brained; and all the Physitians were against his Opinion, and envyed [*grudged against*] him; many wrote against him. With much adoe at last, in about 20 or 30 yeares time, it was recieved in all the Universities in the world; and, as Mr Hobbes sayes in his book *De Corpore* [Of the Body], *he is the only man, perhaps, that ever lived to see his owne Doctrine established in his life-time.*

He was Physitian, and a great Favorite of the Lord High Marshall of England, Thomas Howard Earle of Arundel and Surrey, with whom he travelled as his Physitian in his Ambassade to the Emperor at Vienna. In his Voyage, he would still be making of excursions into the Woods, makeing Observations of strange Trees, and plants, earths, etc, naturalls, and sometimes like to be lost, so that my Lord Ambassador would be really angry with him, for there was not only danger of Thieves, but also of wild beasts.

He was much and often troubled with the Gowte, and his way of Cure was thus; he would then sitt with his Legges bare, if it were a Frost, on the leads of Cockaine-house, putt them into a payle of water, till he was almost dead with cold, and betake himselfe to his Stove, and so 'twas gone.

He was hott-headed, and his thoughts working would many times keepe him from sleepinge; he told me that then his way was to rise out of his Bed and walke about his Chamber in his Shirt till he was pretty coole, i.e. till he began to have a horror, and then returne to bed, and sleepe very comfortably.

He was not tall; but of the lowest stature, round faced, olivaster complexion; little Eie, round, very black, full of spirit; his haire was black as a Raven, but quite white 20 yeares before he dyed.

I remember he was wont to drinke Coffee; which he and his brother Eliab did, before Coffee-houses were in fashion in London.

His practise was not very great towards his later end; he declined it, unlesse to a speciall friend, e.g. my Lady Howland, who had a cancer in her Breast, which he did cutt-off and seared, but at last she dyed of it. He rode on horseback with a Footcloath [*ornamental saddle-cloth*] to visitt his Patients, his man following on foote, as the fashion then was, which was very decent, now quite discontinued. (The Judges rode also with their Foote-cloathes to Westminster-hall, which ended at the death of Sir Robert Hyde, Lord Chief Justice. Anthony Earl of Shafton, would have revived, but severall of the judges being old and ill horsemen would not agree to it.)

All his Profession would allow him to be an excellent Anatomist, but I never heard of any that admired his Therapeutique way. I knew severall practisers in London that would not have given 3d. for one of his Bills; and that a man could hardly tell by one of his Bills what he did aime at. (He did not care for Chymistrey, and was wont to speake against them with an undervalue.)

He had, towards his latter end, a preparation of Opium and I know not what, which he kept in his study to take, if occasion should serve, to putt him out of his paine, and which Sir Charles Scarborough promised to give him; this I beleeve to be true; but doe not at all beleeve that he really did give it him.

Not but that, had he laboured under great Paines, he had been readie enough to have donne it; I doe not deny that it was not according to his Principles upon certain occasions. But the manner of his dyeing was really, and *bonâ fide*, thus, viz. the morning of his death about 10 a clock, he went to speake, and found he had the dead palsey in his Tongue; then he sawe what was to become of him, he knew there was then no hopes of his recovery, so presently sends for his brother and young nephewes to come-up to him, to whom he gives one his Watch ('twas a minute watch with which he made his experiments), to another another thing, etc, as remembrances of him; made a signe to Sambroke, his Apothecary, to lett him blood in the Tongue, which did little or no good; and so ended his dayes. The Palsey did give him an easy Passe-port.

For 20 yeares before he dyed he tooke no manner of care about his worldly concernes, but his brother Eliab, who was a very wise and prudent menager, ordered all not only faithfully, but better then he could have donne himselfe. He dyed worth 20,000 pounds, which he left to his brother Eliab. In his Will he left his old friend Mr Thomas Hobbes 10 pounds as a token of his Love.

He lies buried in a Vault at Hempsted in Essex, which his brother Eliab Harvey built; he is lapt in lead, and on his brest in great letters:

DR WILLIAM HARVEY

I was at his Funerall, and helpt to carry him into the Vault.

EDWARD HERBERT
LORD HERBERT OF CHERBURY

Born 1583. Philosopher and historian. At the age of sixteen, he married a kinswoman four years his senior, while he was at the University. At his coronation in 1603, James I made him a Knight of the Bath and, in 1608, he went to the Continent, where for some years he was engaged in military and diplomatic affairs, not without his share of troubles. In 1624 he was created an Irish and a few years later an English peer, as Baron Herbert of Cherbury. It was in 1624 also that he wrote his treatise *De Veritate*, in which truth is distinguished from (i) revelation, (ii) the probable, (iii) the possible, and (iv) the false. This was the first purely metaphysical work written by an Englishman and gave rise to much controversy. His other chief philosophical work was *De Religione Gentilium* (1663) which has been called the charter of the Deists, and was intended to prove that all religions recognize the same five main articles. He also wrote a *Life of Henry VIII* (1649), and his *Autobiography*, besides some poems of a metaphysical cast. On the outbreak of the Civil War he sided, though somewhat half-heartedly, with the Royalists, but in 1644 he surrendered to the Parliament, received a pension, and held various offices. Died 1648.

I HAVE seen him severall times with Sir John Danvers; he was a black [*dark*] man.

The Castle of Montgomery was a most Romancy seate: It stood upon a high Promontory, the north side 30+ feete high. From hence is a most delightsome prospect, 4 severall wayes. Southwards, without the Castle, is Prim-rose-hill: vide Donne's Poem:

Upon this Prim-rose-hill,
Where, if Heaven would distill
A Showre of raine, each severall drop might goe
To his owne Prim-rose, and grow Manna so;
And where their forme, and their infinitie
Make a terrestiall Galaxie,
As the small starres doe in the Skie:

In this pleasant Solitude did this noble Lord enjoy his Muse.

This stately Castle was demolished since the late Warres at the Chardge of the Countrey.

Mr Fludd tells me he had constantly prayers twice a day in his howse, and Sundayes would have his Chaplayne, Dr Coote (a Cambridge scholar and a learned) read one of Smyth's Sermons.

James Usher, Lord Primate of Ireland, was sent for by him, when in his death-bed, and he would have received the sacrament. He sayd indifferently of it that *if there was good in any-thing 'twas in that*, or *if it did no good 'twould doe no hurt*. The Primate refused it, for which many blamed him. He then turned his head to the other side and expired very serenely.

GEORGE HERBERT

Born 1593. Poet. He was educated at Westminster School and Trinity College, Cambridge, where he took his degree in 1616 and was public orator from 1619 until 1627. He became the friend of Sir Henry Wotton, Donne, and Bacon, the the last of whom is said to have held him in such high esteem as to submit his writings to him before publication. He acquired the favour of James I, who conferred upon him a sinecure worth £120 a year, and having powerful friends, he attached himself for some time to the Court in the hope of preferment. The death of two of his patrons, however, led him to change his views, and coming under the influence of Nicholas Ferrar, the quietist of Little Gidding, and of Laud, he took orders in 1626, becoming in 1630 Rector of Bemerton in Wiltshire, where he passed the remainder of his life, discharging the duties of a parish priest with conscientious assiduity. His chief works are *The Temple, or Sacred Poems and Private Ejaculations* (1634), *The Country Parson* (1652), and *Jacula Prudentium*, a collection of pithy proverbial sayings, the two last in prose. *The Temple*, which was published posthumously, had immediate acceptance, and according to Izaak Walton, who wrote his life, twenty thousand copies were sold in a few years. Among its admirers were Charles I, William Cowper, and Coleridge. Herbert wrote some of the most exquisite sacred poetry in the language, although his style, influenced by Donne, is at times characterized by artificiality and conceits. He was an excellent classical scholar and an accomplished musician. He died in 1633.

In Brecknockshire, about 3 miles from Brecknock, is a village called Penkelly, where is a little Castle. It is an ancient Seate of the Herberts. Mr Herbert, of this place, came, by the mother's side, of Wgan. The Lord Cherbery's ancestor came by the second venter, who was a Miller's daughter. The greatest part of the estate was settled on the issue by the 2d venter, viz. Montgomery castle, and Aberystwith. Upon this Match with the Miller's daughter are to this day recited, or sung, by the Welsh, verses to this sence: *O God! Woe is me miserable, my father was a Miller, and my mother a Milleresse, and I am now a Ladie.*

In a Buriall-place in the Church at Montgomery (belonging to the Castle) is a great freestone monument of Richard Herbert, Esq (father to the learned Lord Herbert of Cherbery, and Mr George Herbert, who wrote the Sacred Poëms) where are the effigies of him and Magdalene his wife, who afterwards was maried to Sir John Danvers of Wilts, and lies interred at Chelsey church but without any monument. Dr Donne, Dean of St Paul's, preached her funerall sermon, to which are annexed severall verses, Latin and Greeke, by Mr George Herbert, in Memorie of her. She was buryed, as appeares by the sermon, July 1, 1627.

Mr George Herbert was kinsman (remote) and Chapelaine to Philip, Earl of Pembroke and Montgomery, and Lord Chamberlayn. His Lordship gave him a Benefice at Bemmarton (between Wilton and Salisbury) a pittifull little chappell of Ease to Foughelston. The old house was very ruinous. Here he built a very handsome howse for the Minister, of Brick, and made a good garden and walkes. He lyes in the Chancell, under no large, nor yet very good, marble grave-stone, without any Inscription.

In the Chancell are many apt sentences of the Scripture. At his Wive's Seate, *My life is hid with Christ in God* (he hath verses on this Text in his Poems). Above, in a little windowe-blinded, with a Veile (ill painted) *Thou art my hideing place.*

He maried Jane, the third daughter of Charles Danvers, of Bayntun, in com. Wilts, Esq, but had no issue by her. He was a very fine complexion and consumptive. His mariage, I suppose, hastened his death. My kinswoman was a handsome *bona roba* and ingeniose.

When he was first maried he lived a yeare or better at Dantesey house. H. Allen, of Dantesey, was well acquainted with him, who has told me that he had a very good hand on the Lute, and that he sett his own Lyricks or sacred poems.

Scripsit: Sacred Poems, called *The Church*, printed, Cambridge, 1633; a Booke entituled *The Country Parson*, not printed till about 1650, 8vo. He also writt a folio in Latin, which because the parson of Hineham could not read, his widowe (then wife to Sir Robert Cooke) condemned to the uses of good houswifry. (This account I had from Mr Arnold Cooke, one of Sir Robert Cooke's sonnes, whom I desired to aske his mother-in-lawe for Mr G. Herbert's MSS.)

He was buryed (according to his owne desire) with the singing service for the buriall of dead, by the singing men of Sarum. Francis Sambroke (attorney) then assisted as a Chorister boy; my uncle, Thomas Danvers, was at the Funerall.

'Tis an honour to the place, to have had the heavenly and ingeniose contemplation of this good man, who was pious even to prophesie; e.g.

Religion now on tip-toe stands,
Ready to goe to the American strands.

MARY HERBERT
COUNTESS OF PEMBROKE

Born 1561. She spent her childhood chiefly at Ludlow Castle, where her father, Sir Henry Sidney, resided as President of Wales, and she was carefully educated, acquiring a knowledge of Latin, Greek, and Hebrew. Her brother Philip was her constant childhood companion. On Queen Elizabeth's suggestion she became a member of the Royal Household in 1575, and accompanied the Queen on her progresses round the country. In 1577 she became the third wife of Henry, Earl of Pembroke, and the Earl of Leicester advanced a part of her dowry, owing to her father's poverty. She suggested the composition of her brother's *Arcadia*, which she revised and added to. For in 1586 she lost her mother, her father, and her brother and, when she had recovered from these blows, she applied herself to the literary tasks which Sir Philip Sidney had left unfinished or had contemplated, and took under her protection the many men of letters to whom he had acted as patron: Edmund Spenser, Samuel Daniel, Nicholas Breton, Thomas Moffat, Thomas Nashe, Gabriel Harvey, John Donne, and Ben Jonson. Her poetry, according to Sir John Harrington, should *outlast Wilton's walls*. Died 1621.

MARY, Countesse of Pembroke, was sister to Sir Philip Sydney: maried to Henry, the eldest son of William Earle of Pembroke; but this subtile old Earle did see that his faire and witty daughter-in-lawe would horne his sonne, and told him so, and advised him to keepe her in the Countrey and not to let her frequent the Court.

She was a beautifull Ladie and had an excellent witt, and had the best breeding that that age could afford. Shee had a pritty sharpe-ovall face. Her haire was of a reddish yellowe.

She was very salacious, and she had a Contrivance that in the Spring of the yeare, when the Stallions were to leape the Mares, they were to be brought before such a part of the house, where she had a *vidette* (a hole to peepe out at) to looke on them and please herselfe with their Sport; and then she would act the like sport herselfe with *her* stallions. One of her great Gallants was Crooke-back't Cecill, Earl of Salisbury.

In her time, Wilton House was like a College, there were so many learned and ingeniose persons. She was the greatest Patronesse of witt and learning of any Lady in her time. She was a great Chymist, and spent yearly a great deale in that study. She kept for her Laborator in the house Adrian Gilbert (vulgarly called Dr Gilbert) halfe-brother to Sir Walter Raleigh, who was a great Chymist in those dayes and a Man of excellent naturall Parts; but very Sarcastick, and the greatest Buffoon in the Nation; cared not what he said to man or woman of what quality soever. 'Twas he that made the curious wall about Rowlington-parke, which is the parke that adjoynes the howse at Wilton. Mr Henry Sanford was the Earle's Secretary, a good scholar and poet, and who did penne part of the *Arcadia* dedicated to her (as appeares by the preface). He haz a preface before it with the two letters of his name. She also gave an honourable yearly Pension to Dr Mouffet, who hath writt a Booke *De Insectis*. Also one Boston, a good Chymist, a Salisbury man borne, who did undoe himselfe by studying the Philosophers-stone, and she would have kept him, but he would have all the golde to himselfe, and so dyed, I thinke, in a Gaole. And I cannot imagine that Mr Edmund Spencer could be a stranger here.

At Wilton is a good Library, which was collected in this learned Ladie's time. There is a Manuscript very elegantly written, viz. all the *Psalmes of David* translated by Sir Philip Sydney, curiously bound in crimson velvet. There is a MS writt by Dame Marian *Of Hunting and Hawking*, in English verse, written in King Henry 8th's time. There is the Legier book of Wilton, one page Saxon and the other Latin, which Mr Dugdale perused. There was a Latin Poeme, a Manuscript, writt in Julius Caesar's time; wherein amongst the Dogges, was mention of Tumblers, and that they were found no where, but in Britaine.

This curious seate of Wilton and the adjacent countrey is an Arcadian place and a Paradise. Sir Philip Sydney was much here, and there was so great love between him and his faire sister that I have heard old Gentlemen say that they lay together, and it was thought the first Philip Earle of Pembroke was begot by him, but he inherited not the witt of either brother or sister.

This Countesse, after her Lord's death, maried to Sir Matthew Lister, Knight, one of the colledge of Physitians, London. Jack Markham saies they were not maried. He was, they say, a learned and handsome Gentleman. She built then a curious house in Bedfordshire called Houghton Lodge, neer Ampthill. The architects were sent for from Italie. It is built according to the Description of Basilius's house in the firste booke of

Arcadia. It is most pleasantly situated, and has fower Visto's; each prospect 25 or 30 miles. This was sold to the Earle of Elgin. The house did cost 10,000 pounds the building.

An epitaph on the Lady Mary, Countesse of Pembroke (in print somewhere) by William Browne, who wrote the *Pastoralls*:

Underneath this sable Herse
Lies the Subject of all Verse:
Sydney's Sister, Pembroke's Mother –
Death! ere thou Kill'st such another
Fair, and good, and learnd as SHEE,
Time will throw his Dart at thee.

WILLIAM HERBERT
EARL OF PEMBROKE

Born 1501. Esquire of the Body of Henry VIII. Married a sister of Queen Catharine Parr. Gentleman of the Privy Chamber 1546. Appointed one of Henry VIII's executors and a member of Edward VI's Council. Knight of the Garter and Master of the Horse 1548. Helped to quell Cornish Rising 1549. President of Wales 1550. Took part in Somerset's trial (1551) and obtained his Wiltshire estates. Created Earl of Pembroke 1551. Joined Northumberland in proclaiming Lady Jane Grey as Queen, but declared for Mary in time. Intimate with King Philip. Envoy to France 1555. Governor of Calais 1556. Lord Steward under Elizabeth 1568. Died 1570.

HE was (as I take it) a younger brother, a mad fighting young Fellow. 'Tis certaine he was a servant to the house of Worcester, and wore their blew-coate and Badge. My cosen Whitney's great aunt gave him a golden angell when he went to London. One time, being at Bristowe, he was arrested, and killed one of the Sheriffes of the City. He made his escape through Back-street, through the (then great) Gate, into the Marsh, and gott into France.

Upon this action of Killing the Sheriffe, the City ordered the Gate to be walled-up, and only a little posterne gate or dore, with a Turnestile for a foot-passenger, which continued so till Bristowe was a Garrison for the King, and the great Gate was then opened. He was called *black Will Herbert*.

In France he betooke himselfe into the Army, where he shewd so much courage, and readinesse of witt in Conduct, that in short time he became Eminent, and was favoured by the King, who afterwards recommended him to Henry the VIII of England, who much valued him, and heaped favours and honours upon him.

He maried Anne Par, sister of Queen Katharine Par, by whom he had 2 sonnes, Henry Earl of Pembroke and Edward, the ancestor of the Lord Powys.

He was made Privy Councellor and conservator of King Henry the Eight's Will. He could neither write, nor read, but had a Stamp for his name. He was of good Naturall; but very Cholerique. He was strong sett, but bony, reddish-favoured, of a sharp eie, sterne looke.

Upon the Dissolution of the Abbeys, he gave him the Abbey of Wilton, and a country of Lands and Mannours there about belonging to it. He gave him also the Abbey of Remesbury, in Wilts, with much lands belonging to it. He gave him Cardiff-Castle, in Glamorganshire, with the ancient Crowne-lands belonging to it.

In Queen Mary's time, upon the return of the Catholique Religion, the nunnes came again to Wilton Abbey, and this William, Earl of Pembroke, came to the gate (which lookes towards the court by the street, but now is walled up) with his cappe in hand, and fell upon his knee to the Lady Abesse and the Nunnes, crying *peccavi* [I have sinned]. Upon Queen Mary's death, the Earle came to Wilton (like a Tygre) and turned them out, crying, out, ye Whores, to worke, to worke, ye Whores, goe spinne.

He, being a stranger in our Country, and an upstart, was much envyed. And in those days (of sword and buckler) noblemen (and also great Knights, as the Longs) when they went to the Assizes or Sessions at Salisbury, etc, had a great number of Retainers following them; and there were (you have heard) in those dayes, Feudes, i.e. quarrels and animosities, between great neighbours. Particularly this newe Earle was much envyed by the then Lord Sturton of Sturton (which is a most parkely ground and Romancy pleasant place: heretofore all horrid, and woody) who would when he went or returned from Sarum (by Wilton was his rode) sound his Trumpets and give reproachfull challenging words; 'twas a relique of Knighthood Errantry.

These Lord Stourtons were possessed of a great Estate in the West till in Queen Maries dayes, the Lord Stourton was attainted by his murthering of Mr Hargill his Steward, whom he killed and buryed in his Cellar, for which he was hanged in a silken halter at Salisbury.

There was a great Feud between this Lord Stourton and William Herbert the first Earle of Pembroke of that Family, who was altogether a

Stranger in the West, and from a private Gentleman, and of no Estate, but only a Soldier of Fortune becoming a Favourite of King Henr. 8, at the dissolution of the Abbeys, in few years from nothing slipt into a prodigiouse Estate of the Church Lands: Which brought great Envy on him, from this Baron of an ancient Family and great Paternall Estate, besides the Difference in Religion. This Lord Stourton aforesayd was a person of great Spirit and Courage, and kept in his Retinew the stoutest fellowes he could heare of: Amongst others, he heard of one Hargill, a mighty, stowt fellowe, who had lately killed a man, who was recommended to his Lordship for his valour: who when he came in to his family, the Lord Stourton gave the next Sunday ten groates to the Priest of the parish to say a Masse for him at Church, for the expiation of his (Hargill) sin in killing the man. A surley, dogged, crosse fellowe it seemes he was, whom at last when his Lordship had advanced to be Steward of his Estate, cosined his Lord of the Mannour of Kilmanton (the next parish). I thinke it was a Trust: Which the Lord Stourton, who also had a good spirit, seeing his servant Hargill had so ensnared him in lowe tricks, as that he could not possibly be relieved: not able to beare so great and ungratefull an abuse, murthered him as aforesayd.

In Queen Elizabeth's time, some Bishop (I have forgott who) that had been his chaplain, was sent to the Earl of Pembroke from the Queen and Council, to take Interrogatories from him. So he takes out his pen and inke, examines and writes. When he had writt a good deale, sayd the Earle, Now lett me see it. Why, quoth the Bishop, Your Lordship cannot read it? That's all one: I'le see it, quoth he, and takes it, and teares it to pieces. Zounds, you rascall, quoth he, d'ee thinke I will have my Throate cutt with a pen-knife? It seems they had a minde to have pick't a hole in his Coate, and to have gott his Estate.

'Tis reported that he caused himselfe to be lett bloud, and bled so much that it was his death, and that he should say as he was expiring, *They would have Wilton, they would have Wilton*, and so gave up the Ghost.

This William (the founder of the Family) had a little reddish picked nosed Cur-dog: none of the Prettiest: which loved him, and the Earle loved the dog. When the Earle dyed, the dog would not goe from his Master's dead body, but pined away, and dyed under the hearse; the picture of which Dog is under his picture in the Gallery at Wilton.

WILLIAM AND PHILIP HERBERT EARLS OF PEMBROKE

William Herbert (1580–1630) succeeded his father as third earl in 1601. He was *immoderately given up to women*, and was committed to the Fleet Prison and banished from Court for refusing to marry Mary Fitton, a Maid of Honour and a favourite of Queen Elizabeth, who was with child by him. On the accession of James I, Pembroke secured a high position at Court, becoming a Knight of the Garter, Keeper of the Forest of Clarendon, and Lord Lieutenant of Cornwall. In 1604 he married Lady Mary Talbot, a great heiress, and the wedding was celebrated by a tournament at Wilton, but Clarendon said *he paid much too dear for his wife's fortune by taking her person into the bargain.* He attended the death-bed of James I, who entreated him to testify publicly that he had died a Protestant. Pembroke carried the crown at Charles I's coronation, and was made a member of the committee which advised the King on foreign affairs, and of the Permanent Council of War. He was deeply interested in the New World, becoming a Member of the King's Council for the Virginia Company in 1609, the North West Passage Company in 1612, the Bermudas Company in 1615, the New England Company in 1620, and the Guiana Company in 1627. He was also a member of the East India Company. He was a patron of many poets, including Massinger and Chapman, and every New Year's Day he sent Ben Jonson £20 to buy books. Inigo Jones visited Italy at his expense, and he was the friend of Donne and Shakespeare, the First Folio of whose plays is dedicated *To the Most Noble and Incomparable Pair of Brethren, William and Philip Herbert*. Philip, who succeeded his brother as fourth Earl of Pembroke, was born in 1584 and was named after Sir Philip Sidney. In the early years of the reign he was the chief favourite of James I, who created him Earl of Montgomery and made him lavish grants of land. In 1628 he received the grant of Trinidad, Tobago, and the Barbadoes. He was foul-mouthed and quarrelsome, and took the Parliamentary side in the Civil War. Died 1650.

'TIS certain, the Earles of Pembroke were the most popular Peers in the West of England; but one might boldly say, in the whole Kingdome. The Revenue of this Family was till about 1652, 16,000 pounds per annum. But with his Offices and all he had thirty thousand Pounds per annum. And, as the Revenue was great, so the greatnesse of his Retinue, and Hospitality were answerable. One hundred and twenty Family uprising and down lyeing: whereof you may take out six or seven, and all the rest Servants, and Retayners.

William 2d & Philip 3d Earles were gallant and handsome persons:

they espoused not Learning, but were addicted to Field sports and Hospitality. Earle William entertained at Wilton, at his own Cost, King James the first, during the space of many moneths.

King Charles 1st did love Wilton above all places: and came thither every Sommer. It was HE, that did put Philip (1st) Earle of Pembroke upon makeing this magnificent Garden and Grotto, and to new-build that side of the House that fronts the Garden with two stately Pavilions at Each end, all al Italiano. Wilton-garden was the third garden of the Italian mode. But in the time of King Charles IId, Gardening was much improved and became common: I doe beleeve, I may modestly affirm, that there is now (1691) ten times as much gardning about London as there was in A° 1660: and we have been since that time much improved in foreign plants: especially since about 1683, there have been exotick Plants brought into England, no lesse than seven thousand.

William Herbert, Earl of Pembroke, was a most noble Person, and the Glory of the Court in the Reignes of King James and King Charles. He was handsome, and of an admirable presence. He was the greatest Maecenas to learned Men of any Peer of his time: or since. He was very generous and open handed: he gave a noble Collection of choice Bookes, and Manuscripts to the Bodlaean Library at Oxford, which remain ther as an honourable Monument of his Munificence. 'Twas thought, had he not been suddenly snatcht away by Death (to the grief of all learned, and good men) that he would have been a great Benefactor to Pembroke Colledge in Oxford; whereas there remains only from him a great piece of Plate, that he gave there.

His Nativity was calculated by old Mr Thomas Allen: his death was foretold, which happened true at the time praedicted, at his House at Baynards Castle in London. He was very well in health; but because of the Fatal Direction which he lay under, he made a great Entertainment (a Supper) for his Friends: ate and dranke plentifully; went well to bed, and died in his sleep.

Earl William was a most magnificent and brave Peer, and loved learned men. He was a good Scholar, and delighted in Poetrie: and did sometimes (for his Diversion) write some Sonnets and Epigrammes, which deserve Commendation: some of them are in print. He was of an Heroiq, and publick Spirit, Bountiful to his Friends, and Servants, and a great Encourager of Learned Men.

Philip Earle of Pembroke (his Brother) did not delight in Books, or Poetry: but exceedingly loved Painting and Building, in which he had singular Judgement, and had the best Collection of any Peer in England, and was the great Patron to Sir Anthony van Dyck: and had most of his

Painting. His Lordship's chiefe delight was in Hunting and Hawking, both which he had to the greatest perfection of any Peer in the Realm.

Wilton will appeare to have been an Academie, as well as Palace, and was (as it were) the Apiarie, to which Men, that were excellent in Armes, and Arts, did resort, and were carress't; and many of them received honourable Pensions.

As aforesaid, Philip the first Earle of that name, did not love Bookes, as his elder Brother William did: but when he was young, he had a wonderfull Sagacity or faculty of discerning Men: i.e. to espie the reality or deceit of Ambassadours and Ministers of Estate, which did render Him the more acceptable to King James the first.

Philip Earle of Pembroke (sonne of Philip aforesayd) had an admirable Witt, and was contemplative but did not much care for reading. His chiefest Diversion was Chymistrie, which his Lordship did understand very well and he made Medicines, that did great Cures.

It was the right hon. Philip (1st) Earle of Pembroke, that was the great Hunter. It was in his Lordship's time (*sc. tempore Jacobi I and Caroli I*) a serene calme of Peace, that Hunting was at its greatest Heighth that ever was in this Nation. The Roman Governours had not (I thinke) the leisure; the Saxons were never at quiet; and the Baron's Warres, and these of Yorke and Lancaster, took up the greatest part of the time since the Conquest: So that the Glory of the English Hunting breath'd its last with this Earle: who deceased about 1644, and shortly after the Forests and Parkes were sold, and converted into Arable.

'Twas after his Lordship's Decease, that I was a Hunter: that is to say with the right honble William, Lord Herbert of Cardiff, the aforesaid Philip's Grandson.

This present Earl of Pembroke (1680) has at Wilton, 52 Mastives and 30 Grey-hounds, some Beares, and a Lyon, and a matter of 60 fellowes more bestiall then they.

THOMAS HOBBES

Born 1588. Philosopher. For a great part of his life he was in the service of the Cavendish family and in 1647 was appointed mathematical tutor to the exile Prince of Wales in Paris. When the Parliament of 1628 drew up the Petition of Right, Hobbes published a translation of Thucydides, with the expressed intention of showing the evils of democracy. It was not the actual occurrence of the

Civil War that caused his opinions, but the prospect of it; naturally, however, his convictions were strengthened when his fears were realized and in 1651, from exile, he published the *Leviathan*, which stressed the comfort of firm government. At the Restoration, Charles II awarded him a pension of £100 a year – which, however, His Majesty forgot to pay. Hobbes's agnosticism soon got him into fresh trouble, and he was refused leave to print anything in England on controversial subjects. He continued to produce important works nevertheless, and they were printed at Amsterdam. His last book was published when he was eighty-seven. Died 1679.

THE day of his Birth was April the fifth, Anno Domini 1588, on a Fryday morning, which that yeare was Good Fryday. His mother fell in labour with him upon the fright of the Invasion of the Spaniards.

Mr Hobbes' father was Minister of Westport juxta Malmesbury, to which Brokenborough and Charlton doe belong as Chapells of Ease: the Vicaridge of Malmesbury is but xx nobles per annum=£6 13s. 4d. He was one of the Clergie of Queen Elizabeth's time – a little Learning went a great way with him and many other ignorant Sir Johns in those days; could only read the prayers of the Church and the homilies; and disesteemed Learning (his son Edmund told me so) as not knowing the Sweetnes of it.

Westport is the Parish without the West-gate (which is now demolished) which Gate stood on the neck of land that joines Malmesbury to Westport. Here was, before the late Warres, a very pretty church, consisting of 3 aisles, or rather a nave and two aisles, dedicated to St Mary; and a fair spire-steeple, with five tuneable Bells, which, when the Towne was taken by Sir W. Waller, were converted into Ordinance, and the church pulled-downe to the ground, that the Enemie might not shelter themselves against the Garrison. The Steeple was higher then that now standing in the Borough, which much adorned the Prospect. The Windowes were well painted, and in them were Inscriptions that declared much Antiquitie; now is here rebuilt a Church like a Stable.

The old vicar Hobs was a good Fellow and had been at cards all Saturday night, and at church in his sleep he cries out *Trafells is troumps*, viz. clubs. Then quoth the Clark, *Then, Master, he that have Ace doe rub*.

He was a collirice [*choleric*] man, and a parson (which I thinke succeeded him at Westport) provoked him (a purpose) at the church doore, soe Hobs stroke him and was forcd to fly for it and died in obscurity beyound London, about 80 yeares since.

As to his Father's ignorance and clownery, 'twas as good metal in the Oare which wants excoriating and refineing. A witt requires much cultivation, much paines, and art and good conversation to perfect a man.

Thomas, the Father, had an elder Brother whose name was Francis, a wealthy man, and had been Alderman of the Borough; by Profession a Glover, which is a great Trade here, and in times past much greater. (Shall I expresse or conceale this *glover*? The philosopher would acknowledge it.) Having no child, he contributed much to, or rather altogether maintained, his Nephew Thomas at Magdalen-hall in Oxon; and when he dyed gave him an *agellum* (a moweing-ground) called the Gasten-ground, lyeing neer to the Horse-faire, worth 16, or 18 poundes per annum; the rest of his Landes he gave to his nephew Edmund. Edmund was neer two yeares elder then his brother Thomas, and something resembled him in aspect, not so tall, but fell much short of him in his Intellect: though he was a good plain understanding countrey-man. He had been bred at Schoole with his brother; could have made Theme, and verse, and understood a little Greek to his dyeing day. He dyed about 13 yeares since, aetat. circiter 80.

At fower yeer old Mr Thomas Hobbes (Philosopher) went to Schoole in Westport church till 8 – then the church was painted. At 8 he could read well and number a matter of 4 or 5 figures. After, he went to Malmesbury to Parson Evans. After him, he had for his Schoolemaster, Mr Robert Latimer, a young man of about nineteen or twenty, newly come from the University, who then kept a private schoole in Westport. This Mr Latimer was a good Graecian, and the first that came into our Parts hereabout since the Reformation. He was a Batchelour and delighted in his Scholar, T.H.'s company, and used to instruct him, and two or three ingeniose youths more, in the evening till nine a clock.

When he was a Boy he was playsome enough, but withall he had even then a contemplative Melancholinesse; he would gett him into a corner, and learn his Lesson by heart presently [*at once*]. His haire was black, and his schoolfellows were wont to call him *Crowe*.

At fourtenn yeares of age, he went away a good Schoole-scholar to Magdalen-hall, in Oxford. It is not to be forgotten that before he went to the University, he had turned Euripidis *Medea* out of Greeke into Latin Iambiques, which he presented to his Master. Mr H told me that he would faine have had them, to see how he did grow. Twenty odde yeares agoe I searcht all old Mr Latimer's papers, but could not find them; the Oven had devoured them.

At Oxford Mr T.H. used, in the Summer time especially, to rise very early in the Morning, and would tye the leaden-counters with Pacthreds, which he did besmere with birdlime, and bayte then with parings of cheese, and the Jack-dawes would spye them a vast distance up in the aire, and as far as Osney-abbey, and strike at the Bayte, and so he harled in the String, which the wayte of the counter would make cling about their Wings.

(This story he happened to tell me, discoursing of the Optiques, to instance such sharpnes of sight in so little an eie.) He did not much care for Logick, yet he learnd it, and thought himself a good Disputant. He tooke great delight there to goe to the Booke-binders shops, and lye gaping on Mappes.

After he had taken his Batchelor of Arts degree, the than principall of Magdalen-hall (Sir James Hussee: a great encourager of towardly youths) recommended him to his yong Lord (the Earl of Devonshire) when he left Oxon, who had a conceit that he should profitt more in his learning if he had a Scholar of his owne age to wayte on him then if he had the information of a grave Doctor. He was his Lordship's page, and rode a hunting and hawking with him, and kept his privy-purse.

By this way of life he had almost forgott his Latin. He therefore bought him bookes of an Amsterdam print that he might carry in his pocket (particularly Caesar's *Commentarys*) which he did read in the Lobbey, or Ante-chamber, whilest his Lord was making his Visits.

He spent two yeares in reading romances and playes, which he haz often repented and sayd that these two yeares were lost of him – wherin perhaps he was mistaken too. For it might furnish him with copie of words.

The Lord Chancellour Bacon loved to converse with him. He assisted his Lordship in translating severall of his *Essayes* into Latin, one, I well remember, is that *Of the Greatnes of Cities*: the rest I have forgott. His Lordship was a very Contemplative person, and was wont to contemplate in his delicious walkes at Gorambery, and dictate to Mr Thomas Bushell, or some other of his Gentlemen, that attended him with inke and paper ready to sett downe presently his Thoughts. His Lordship would often say that he better liked Mr Hobbes's taking his thoughts, then any of the other, because he understood what he wrote, which the others not understanding, my Lord would many times have a harde taske to make sense of what they writt.

1634: this summer – I remember 'twas in Venison season (July or August) – Mr T.H. came into his Native Country to visitt his Friends, and amongst others he came then to see his old school-master, Mr Robert Latimer, at Leigh-de-la-mer, where I was then a little youth at Schoole in the church, newly entred into my Grammar by him. Here was the first place and time that ever I had the honour to see this worthy, learned man, who was then pleased to take notice of me, and the next day visited my relations. He was then a proper man, briske, and in very good habit. His hayre was then quite black. He stayed at Malmsbury and in the neighborhood a weeke or better. His conversation about those times was much about

Ben. Jonson, Mr Ayton, etc. 'Twas the last time that ever he was in Wiltshire.

He was 40 yeares old before he looked on Geometry; which happened accidentally. Being in a Gentleman's Library, Euclid's Elements lay open, and 'twas the *47 El. libri 1*. He read the Proposition. *By G—*, sayd he (he would now and then sweare an emphaticall Oath by way of emphasis) *this is impossible!* So he reads the Demonstration of it, which referred him back to such a Proposition; which proposition he read. That referred him back to another, which he also read. *Et sic deinceps* [and so on] that at last he was demonstratively convinced of that trueth. This made him in love with Geometry.

I have heard Mr Hobbes say that he was wont to draw lines on his thigh and on the sheetes, abed, and also multiply and divide.

He would often complain that Algebra (though of great use) was too much admired, and so followed after, that it made men not contemplate and consider so much the nature and power of Lines, which was a great hinderance to the Groweth of Geometrie; for that though algebra did rarely well and quickly, and easily in right lines, yet 'twould not *bite* in *solid* (I thinke) Geometry. Quod N.B.

'Twas pitty that Mr Hobbs had not began the study of the Mathematics sooner, els he would not have layn so open. But one may say of him, as one sayes of Jos. Scaliger, that where he erres, he erres so ingeniosely, that one had rather erre with him then hitt the marke with Clavius.

After he began to reflect on the Interest of the King of England as touching his affaires between him and parliament, for ten yeares together his thoughts were much, or almost altogether, unhinged from the Mathematiques; which was a great putt-back to his Mathematicall improvement; for in ten yeares (or better) discontinuance of that Study (especially) one's Mathematiques will become very rusty.

When the Parliament sate that began in April 1640 and was dissolved in May following, and in which many pointes of the Regall Power, which were necessary for the Peace of the Kingdome and Safety of his Majestye's Person, were disputed and denyed, Mr Hobbes wrote a little Treatise in English, wherin he did sett-forth and demonstrate, that the sayd Powers and Rights were inseparably annexed to the Soveraignty, which soveraignty they did not then deny to be in the King; but it seemes understood not, or would not understand, that Inseparability. Of this Treatise, though not printed, many Gentlemen had copies, which occasioned much talke of the Author; and had not his Majestie dissolved the Parliament, it had brought him in danger of his life.

Bp Manwaring (of St David's) preach'd *his Doctrine*; for which, among others, he was sent prisoner to the Tower. Then thought Mr Hobbes, 'tis time now for me to shift for my selfe, and so withdrew into France, and resided at Paris. This little MS treatise grew to be his Booke *De Cive*, and at last grew there to be the so formidable LEVIATHAN; the manner of writing of which booke (he told me) was thus. He sayd that he sometimes would sett his thoughts upon researching and contemplating, always with this Rule that he very much and deeply considered one thing at a time (*scilicet*, a weeke or sometimes a fortnight). He walked much and contemplated, and he had in the head of his Staffe a pen and inke-horne, carried always a Note-book in his pocket, and as soon as a notion darted, he presently entred it into his Booke, or els he should perhaps have lost it. He had drawne the Designe of the Booke into Chapters, etc, so he knew whereabout it would come in. Thus that booke was made.

He wrote and published the *Leviathan* far from the intention either of disadvantage to his Majestie, or to flatter Oliver (who was not made Protector till three or four yeares after) on purpose to facilitate his returne; for there is scarce a page in it that he does not upbraid him.

His Majestie was displeased with him (at Paris) for a while, but not very long, by means of some's complayning of and misconstruing his writing. But his Majestie had a good Opinion of him, and sayd openly, That he thought Mr Hobbes never meant him hurt.

Anno 1650 or 1651, he returned into England, and lived most part in Fetter-lane, where he writt, or finished, his booke *de Corpore*, in Latin and then in English.

He was much in London till the restauration of his Majesty, having here convenience not only of Bookes, but of learned Conversation. I have heard him say, that at his Lord's house in the Countrey there was a good Library, and bookes enough for him, and that his Lordship stored the Library with what bookes he thought fitt to be bought; but he sayd, the want of learned Conversation was a very great inconvenience, and that though he conceived he could order his thinking as well perhaps as another man, yet he found a great defect. Methinkes in the country, for want of good conversation, one's Witt growes mouldy.

1660. The winter-time of 1659 he spent in Derbyshire. In March following was the dawning of the coming in of our gracious Soveraigne, and in April the Aurora. I then sent a letter to him in the Countrey to advertise him of the Advent of his Master the King and desired him by all meanes to be in London before his Arrivall; and knowing his Majestie was a great lover of good Painting I must needs presume he could not but suddenly see Mr Cowper's curious pieces, of whose fame he had so much heard abroad and seene some of his worke, and likewise that he would sitt to him for his Picture, at which place and time he would have the best convenience of renewing his Majestie's graces to him. He returned me thankes for my friendly intimation and came to London in May following.

It happened, about two or three dayes after his Majestie's happy returne, that, as he was passing in his coach through the Strand, Mr Hobbes was standing at Little Salisbury-house gate (where his Lord then lived). The King espied him, putt of his hatt very kindly to him, and asked him how he did. About a weeke after, he had orall conference with his Majesty at Mr S. Cowper's, where, as he sate for his picture, he was diverted by Mr Hobbes pleasant discourse. Here his Majestie's favours were redintegrated to him, and order was given that he should have free accesse to his Majesty, who was always much delighted in his witt and smart repartees.

The witts at Court were wont to bayte him. But he feared none of them, and would make his part good. The King would call him *the Beare*: Here comes the Beare to be bayted: (this is too low witt to be published).

He was marvellous happy and ready in his replies, and that without rancor (except provoked) but now I speake of his readinesse in replies as to witt and drollery. He would say that he did not care to give, neither was he adroit at, a present answer to a serious *quaere*: he had as lieve they should have expected an extemporary solution to an Arithmeticall probleme, for he turned and winded and compounded in philosophy, politiques, etc, as if he had been at Analyticall worke. He alwayes avoided, as much as he could, to conclude hastily.

1665. This yeare he told me that he was willing to doe some good to the Towne where he was borne; that his Majestie loved him well, and if I could find out something in our Countrey that was in his Guift, he did beleeve he could beg it of his Majestie, and seeing he was bred a Scholar, he thought it most proper to endowe a Free-schoole there; which is wanting now (for, before the Reformation, all Monasteries had great Schooles appendant to them; e.g. Magdalen schoole and New College schoole). After enquiry I found out a piece of land in Bradon-forest (of about 25 pounds per annum value) that was in his Majesties guift, which he designed to have obtained of his Majestie for a salary for a Schoolmaster; but the Queen's Priests smelling-out the Designe and being his Enemies, hindred this publique and charitable Intention.

Mr Samuel Cowper (the Prince of Limners of this last Age and my ever honoured Friend, who besides his Art was an ingeniose person and of great humanity) drew his Picture as like as art could afford, and one of the best pieces that ever he did: which his Majesty, at his returne, bought of him, and conserves as one of his rarities in his Closet at Whitehall.

His Lord who was a waster, sent him up and downe to borrow money, and to gett Gentlemen to be bound for him, being ashamed to speake him selfe.

In his youth he was unhealthy; of an ill complexion (yellowish): he tooke colds, being wett in his feet (there were no hackney coaches to stand in the streetes) and trod both his Shoes aside the same way. Notwithstanding he was well beloved: they lov'd his company for his pleasant facetiousness [*amiability*] and good-nature.

From forty, or better, he grew healthier, and then he had a fresh, ruddy, complexion. He was *Sanguineo-melancholicus*; which the physiologers say is the most ingeniose complexion. He would say that there might be good witts of all compexions; but good-natured, impossible.

In his old age he was very bald (which claymed a veneration) yet within dore, he used to study, and sitt bare-headed, and sayd he never tooke cold in his head, but that the greatest trouble was to keepe-off the Flies from pitching on the baldnes.

Face not very great; ample forehead; whiskers yellowish-redish, which naturally turned up – which is a signe of a brisque witt. Belowe he was shaved close, except a little tip under his lip. Not but that nature could have afforded a venerable Beard, but being naturally of a cheerfull and pleasant humour, he affected not at all austerity and gravity to looke severe. He desired not the reputation of his wisdome to be taken from the cutt of his beard, but from his reason.

He had a good eie, and that of a hazell colour, which was full of Life and Spirit, even to the last. When he was earnest in discourse, there shone (as it were) a bright live-coale within it. He had two kinds of lookys: when he laugh't, was witty, and in a merry humour, one could scarce see his Eies; by and by, when he was serious and positive, he open'd his eies round (i.e. his eie-lids). He had midling eies, not very big, nor very little.

There was a good Painter at the Earl of Devonshire's in Derbyshire not long before Mr Hobbes dyed, who drew him with the great decayes of old age.

Though he left his native countrey at 14, and lived so long, yet sometimes one might find a little touch of our pronunciation. – Old Sir Thomas Malette, one of the Judges of the King's Bench, knew Sir Walter Ralegh, and sayd that, notwithstanding his great Travells, Conversation, Learning, etc, yet he spake broade Devonshire to his dyeing day.

He had very few Bookes. I never sawe (nor Sir William Petty) above halfe a dozen about him in his chamber. Homer and Virgil were commonly on his Table; sometimes Xenophon, or some probable historie, and Greek Testament, or so.

He had read much, if one considers his long life; but his contemplation was much more then his reading. He was wont to say that if he had read as much as other men, he should have knowne no more then other men.

He was wont to say that he had rather have the advice, or take Physique from an experienced old Woman, that had been at many sick people's Bed-sides, then from the learnedst but unexperienced Physitian.

'Tis not consistent with an harmonicall soule to be a woman-hater, neither had he an Abhorrescence to good wine but he was, even in his youth (generally) temperate, both as to wine and women. I have heard him say that he did beleeve he had been in excesse in his life, a hundred times; which, considering his great age, did not amount to above once a yeare. When he did drinke, he would drinke to excesse to have the benefitt of Vomiting, which he did easily; by which benefit neither his witt was disturbt longer then he was spuing nor his stomach oppressed; but he never was, nor could not endure to be, habitually a good fellow, i.e. to drinke every day wine with company, which, though not to drunkennesse, spoiles the Braine.

For his last 30+ yeares, his Dyet, etc, was very moderate and regular. He rose about seaven, had his breakefast of Bread and Butter; and tooke his walke, meditating till ten; then he did putt downe the minutes of his thoughts, which he penned in the afternoon. He thought much and with excellent method and stedinesse, which made him seldom make a False step.

He had an inch thick board about 16 inches square, whereon paper was pasted. On this board he drew his lines (schemes). When a line came into his head, he would, as he was walking, take a rude Memorandum of it, to preserve it in his memory till he came to his chamber. He was never idle; his thoughts were always working.

His dinner was provided for him exactly by eleaven, for he could not now stay till his Lord's howre – *scil.* about two: that his stomach could not beare.

After dinner he tooke a pipe of tobacco, and then threw himselfe immediately on his bed, with his band off, and slept (tooke a nap of about halfe an howre).

In the afternoon he penned his morning Thoughts.

Besides his dayly Walking, he did twice or thrice a yeare play at Tennis (at about 75 he did it) then went to bed there and was well rubbed. This he did believe would make him live two or three yeares the longer.

In the countrey, for want of a tennis-court, he would walke up-hill and downe-hill in the parke, till he was in a great sweat, and then give the servant some money to rubbe him.

He had alwayes bookes of prick-song lyeing on his table: which at night, when he was abed, and the dores made fast, and was sure nobody heard him, he sang aloud (not that he had a very good voice) but for his health's Sake: he did beleeve it did his Lunges good, and conduced much to prolong his life.

He had the shaking Palsey in his handes; which began in France before the year 1650, and haz growne upon him by degrees, ever since, so that he haz not been able to write very legibly since 1665 or 1666, as I find by some letters he hath honoured me withall. Mr Hobbs wase for severall yeares before he died so Paralyticall that he wase scarce able to write his name, and that in the abscence of his Amanuensis not being able to write anything, he made Scrawls on a piece of paper to remind him of the conceptions of his Mind he design'd to have committed to writing.

His extraordinary Timorousnes Mr Hobs doth very ingeniosely confess and atributes it to the influence of his Mother's Dread of the Spanish Invasion in 88, she being then with child of him: it is very prodigious that neither the timorousness of his Nature from his Infancy, nor the decay of his Vital Heat in the extremity of old age, accompanied with the Palsy to that violence, shou'd not have chilled the briske Fervour and Vigour of his mind, which did wonderfully continue to him to his last.

His work was attended with Envy [*spite*], which threw severall aspersions and false reports on him. For instance, one (common) was that he was afrayd to lye alone at night in his Chamber; I have often heard him say that he was not afrayd of *Sprights*, but afrayd of being knockt on the head for five or ten pounds, which rogues might think he had in his chamber; and severall other tales, as untrue.

When Mr T. Hobbes was sick in France, the Divines came to him, and tormented him (both Roman Catholic, Church of England, and Geneva). Sayd he to them, Let me alone, or els I will detect all your Cheates from Aaron to yourselves.

Mr Edmund Waller sayd to me, when I desired him to write some Verses in praise of him, that he was afrayd of the Churchmen: that, what was chiefly to be taken notice of in his Elogie was that he, being but *one*, and a private Person, pulled-downe all their Churches, dispelled the mists of Ignorance, and layd-open their Priest-craft.

There was a report (and surely true) that in Parliament, not long after the King was setled, some of the Bishops made a Motion to have the good old Gentleman burn't for a Heretique. Which, he hearing, feared that his papers might be search't by their order, and he told me he had burnt part of them; among other things, a Poeme, in Latin Hexameter and Pentameter, of the Encroachment of the Clergie (both Roman and Reformed) on the Civil Power.

That he was a Christian 'tis cleare, for he recieved the Sacrament of Dr Pierson, and in his confession to Dr John Cosins, on his (as he thought) death-bed, declared that he liked the Religion of the Church of England best of all other.

He dyed worth neer 1000 pounds, which (considering his charity) was more than I expected: for he was very charitable to those that were the true objects of his Bounty. One time, I remember, goeing in the Strand, a poore and infirme old man craved his Almes. He, beholding him with eies of pitty and compassion, putt his hand in his pocket and gave him 6d. Sayd a Divine that stood by, Would you have donne this, if it had not been Christ's command? Yea, sayd he. Why? quoth the other. Because, sayd he, I was in paine to consider the miserable condition of the old man; and now my almes, giving him some reliefe, doth also ease me.

Thomas Hobbs said that if it were not for the gallowes, some men are of so cruell a nature as to take a delight in killing men more than I should to kill a bird. I have heard him inveigh much against the Crueltie of Moyses for putting so many thousands to the Sword for Bowing to the Golden Calf.

Mr Benjamin Johnson, Poet-Laureat, was his loving and familiar Friend and Acquaintance.

His nephew Francis pretty well resembled his uncle Thomas, especially about the eie; and probably had he had good Education might have been ingeniose; but he drowned his Witt in Ale.

When he was at Florence, he contracted a friendship with the famous Galileo Galileo, whom he extremely venerated and magnified; and not only as he was a prodigious Witt, but for his sweetnes of nature and manners. They pretty well resembled one another as to their countenances, as by their Pictures doeth appear; were both cheerfull and melancholique-sanguine; and had both a consimilitie of Fate, to be hated and persecuted by the Ecclesiastiques.

Mr Robert Hooke loved him, but was never but once in his company.

William Harvey, Dr Of Physique and Chirurgery, Inventor of the Circulation of the Bloud, left him in his Will ten poundes, as a token of his love.

Mr John Dreyden, Poet Laureat, is his great admirer, and oftentimes makes use of his Doctrine in his Playes – from Mr Dreyden himselfe.

Sir Jonas Moore, Mathematicus, Surveyor of his Majestie's Ordinance, who had a great veneration for Mr Hobbes, and was wont much to lament he fell to the study of the Mathematiques so late.

Lucius Carey, Lord Falkland was his great friend and admirer, and so was Sir William Petty; both which I have here enrolled amongst those friends I have heard him speake of, but Dr Blackburne left 'em both out (to my admiration [*amazement*]). I askt him why he had donne so? He answered because they were both ignote to Foreigners.

Des Cartes and he were acquainted and mutually respected one another. He would say that had he kept himself to Geometry he had been the best Geometer in the world but that his head did not lye for Philosophy.

I have heard him say that Aristotle was the worst Teacher that ever was, the worst Politician and Ethick – a Countrey-fellow that could live in the World would be as good: but his *Rhetorique* and *Discourse of Animals* was rare.

He had a high esteeme for the Royall Societie, having sayd that Naturall Philosophy was removed from the Universities to Gresham Colledge, meaning the Royall Societie that meetes there; and the Royall Societie (generally) had the like for him: and he would long since have been ascribed a Member there, but for the sake of one or two persons, whom he tooke to be his enemies: viz. Dr Wallis (surely their Mercuries are in opposition) and Mr Boyle. I might add Sir Paul Neile, who disobliges everybody.

1675, he left London *cum animo nunquam revertendi* [with the intention of never returning] and spent the remaynder of his dayes in Derbyshire with the Earl of Devonshire at Chatsworth and Hardwyck, in Contemplation and study.

These love verses he made not long before his death:

Tho' I am now past ninety, and too old
T' expect preferment in the Court of Cupid,
And many Winters made mee ev'n so cold
I am become almost all over stupid,

Yet I can love and have a Mistresse too,
As fair as can be and as wise as fair;
And yet not proud, nor anything will doe
To make me of her favour to despair.

To tell you who she is were very bold;
But if i' th' Character your Selfe you find
Thinke not the man a Fool tho he be old
Who loves in Body fair, a fairer mind.

He fell sick about the middle of October 1679. His disease was the Strangury, and the Physitians judged it incurable by reason of his great age and naturall decay. About the 20th of November, my Lord being to remove from Chatsworth to Hardwick, Mr Hobbes would not be left behind; and therefore with a fetherbed laid into the Coach, upon which he lay warme clad, he was conveyed safely, and was in appearance as well after that little journey as before it. But seven or eight days after, his whole right side was taken with the dead palsy, and at the same time he was made speechlesse. He lived after this seven days, taking very little nourishment, slept well, and by intervals endeavoured to speake, but could not. In the whole time of his sickness he was free from fever. He seemed therefor to dye rather for want of the Fuell of Life (which was spent in him) and meer weaknesse and decay, then by the power of his disease, which was thought to be onely an effect of his age and weaknesse. He was put into a Woollen Shroud and Coffin, which was covered with a white Sheet, and upon that a black Herse cloth, and so carryed upon men's shoulders, a little mile to Church. The company, consisting of the family and neighbours that came to his Funerall, and attended him to his grave, were very handsomely entertained with Wine, burned and raw, cake, biscuit, etc.

A true copy of Mr Hobbes's will

Item, whereas it hath pleased my good Lord the Earle of Devonshire, to bid me oftentimes heretofore, and now at the making of this my last Will, to dispose therein of one hundred pounds, to be paid by his Lordship, for which I give him most humble thanks; I doe give and dispose of the same in this manner: There be five grand-children of my Brother Edmund Hobbes, to the eldest whereof whose name is Thomas Hobbes, I have heretofore given a peece of Land, which may and doth I think content him, and therefore to the other four that are younger, I dispose of the same 100 pounds the gift of my Lord of Devonshire, to be divided equally amongst them, as a furtherance to bind them Apprentices.

My Lord of Devonshire has paid the hundred pounds to Mr Hobbes's kinred, which he bid Mr Hobbes dispose of in his Will.

WILLIAM HOLDER

Born 1616. Divine. Fellow of the Royal Society 1663. Canon of St Paul's 1672. Sub-Dean of the Chapel Royal (1674) where he became so famous a disciplinarian that he was known as Mr Snub-Dean. He published *Elements of Speech* in 1669, and various treatises on harmony and the Julian Calendar. Died 1698.

HE is a handsome, gracefull person, and of a delicate constitution, and of an even and smooth temper; so that, if one would goe about to describe a perfect good man, would drawe this Doctor's Character. He is very Musicall, both theoretically and practically, and he had a sweet voyce: gracefull Elocution; his discourse so Gent. and obligeing; cleer reason; is a good Poet. He is extremely well qualified for his place of the Sub-Almoner of the King's Chapell, being a person abhorring covetousness, and full of Pitty.

The only Son of Edward Popham, Admirall for the Parliament, being borne deafe and dumbe, was sent to him to learne to speake, which he taught him to doe: by what method, and how soon, you may see in the Appendix concerning it to his *Elements of Speech*. It is a most ingeniose and curious Discourse, and untouched by any other; he was beholding to no Author; did only consult with Nature. This Gentleman's son afterwards was a little while (upon Dr Holder's preferment to Ely) a scholar of Dr Wallis, (a most ill-natured man, an egregious lyer and backbiter, a flatterer and fawner on my Lord Brouncker and his Miss, that my Lord may keepe up his reputation) under whom he forgott what he learnt before, the child not enduring his morose pedantique humour. Not long since in one of the *Philosophical Transactions* is entered a long mountebanking panegyrique of the Doctor's prayse for doeing so strange a thing and never makes any mention of Dr Holder at all. Dr H questioning Oldenburgh (I happened to be then present) Mr Oldenburgh (though a great friend of Dr Wallis) acknowledged that the Doctor himselfe penned it every word; which occasioned Dr Holder to write against him in a pamphlet in 4to.

Mr Thomas Hobbes writes to me, I wonder not if Dr Wallis, or any other, that have studyed Mathematicks onely to gaine Preferment, when his ignorance is discovered, convert his study to jugling and to the gaining of a reputation of conjuring, decyphering, and such Arts. As for the matter it selfe, I meane the teaching of a man borne deafe and dumbe to speake, I thinke it impossible. But I doe not count him deafe and indocible that can heare a word spoken as loud as is possible at the very entrance to his Eare; and he that could make him heare (being a great and common good) would well deserve both to be honoured and to be enriched. He that could make him speake a few words onely deserved nothing. But he that brags of this and cannot doe it, deserves to be whipt.

But to returne to this honest worthy Gentleman – Anno about 1646, he went to Bletchington to his parsonage, where his hospitality and learning, mixt with great courtesie, easily conciliated the love of all his neighbours to him.

He was very helpfull in the Education of his brother-in-law, Mr Christopher Wren (now Knighted), a youth of a prodigious inventive Witt, and of whom he was as tender as if he had been his owne Child, who gave him his first Instructions in Geometrie and Arithmetique, and when he was a young Scholar at the University of Oxford, was a very necessary and kind friend.

The parsonage-house at Bletchington was Mr Christopher Wren's home, and retiring-place; here he contemplated, and studied, and found-out a great many curious things in Mathematiques. About this house he made severall curious Dialls, with his owne handes, which are still there to be seen. Which see, as well worthy to be seen.

It ought not to be forgott the great and exemplary love between this Doctor and his vertuose wife, who is not lesse to be admired, in her sex and station, then her brother Sir Christopher; and (which is rare to be found in a woman) her excellences doe not inflate her. Amongst many other Guifts she haz a strange sagacity as to curing of wounds, which she does not doe so much by presedents and Reciept bookes, as by her owne excogitancy, considering the causes, effects, and circumstances. His Majestie King Charles II had hurt his hand, which he intrusted his Chirurgians to make well; but they ordered him so that they made it much worse, so that it swoll, and pained him up to his shoulder; and pained him so extremely that he could not sleep, and began to be feaverish. Then one told the King what a rare shee-surgeon he had in his house; she was presently [*at once*] sent for at eleven clock at night. She presently made ready a Pultisse, and applyed it, and gave his Majestie sudden ease, and he slept well; next day she dressed him, and in a short time perfectly cured him, to the great griefe of all the Surgeons, who envy [*grudge at*] and hate her.

WENCESLAS HOLLAR

Born 1607. Engraver. He lived in Frankfort, Cologne, and Antwerp and had difficulty enough to subsist, until Thomas Howard, Earl of Arundel, brought him to England. Teacher of drawing to the Prince of Wales 1640. He fought in the ranks for the King, but was captured by Parliament and escaped to Antwerp. In 1652 he returned to England. He was appointed His Majesty's Designer in 1660. Before the introduction of photography, picture painting and engraving were important professions, and Hollar charged fourpence an hour for his work, of which 2,733 examples are enumerated. Besides making copies of famous paintings and illustrating books, Hollar executed a fine map of London after the Fire, illustrated the coronation of Charles II, and engraved a series of pictures of women's costumes, which have proved invaluable to historians. Died 1677.

WINCESLAUS HOLLAR, Bohemus, was borne at Prague. His father was a Knight of the Empire and a Protestant, and either for keeping a conventicle, or being taken at one, forfeited his Estate, and was ruined by the Roman Catholiques.

He told me that when he was a Schoole-boy he tooke a delight in draweing of Mapps; which draughts he kept, and they were pretty. He was designed by his father to have been a Lawyer, and was putt to that profession, when his father's troubles, together with the Warres, forced him to leave his countrey. So that what he did for his delight and recreation only when a boy, proved to be his livelyhood when a man.

I thinke he stayd sometime in Lowe Germany, then he came into England, wher he was very kindly entertained by that great Patron of Painters and draughts-men, Thomas Howard Lord High Marshall, Earl of Arundell and Surrey, where he spent his time in draweing and copying rarities, which he did etch (i.e. eate with *aqua fortis* in copper plates). When the Lord Marshall went Ambassador to the Emperor of Germany to Vienna, he travelld with much grandeur; and among others, Mr Hollar went with him (very well clad) to take viewes, landskapes, buildings, etc, remarqueable in their Journey, which wee see now at the Print-Shopps.

He hath donne the most in that way that ever any one did, insomuch that I have heard Mr John Evelyn, RSS, say that at sixpence a print his Labour would come to . . . pounds (*quaere* JE). He was very short-sighted, and did worke so curiously that the curiosity of his Worke is not to be judged without a magnifying-glasse. When he tooke his Landskapes, he, then, had a glasse to helpe his Sight.

At Arundel-house he maried with my Ladie's wayting woman, Mrs Tracy, by whom he haz a daughter, that was one of the greatest Beauties I have seen; his son by her dyed in the Plague, an ingeniose youth, drew delicately.

When the Civil Warres brake-out, the Lord Marshall had leave to goe beyond the sea. Mr Hollar went into the Lowe-Countries where he stayed till about 1649.

I remember he told me that when he first came into England (which was a serene time of Peace) that the people, both poore and rich, did looke cheerfully, but at his returne, he found the Countenances of the people all changed, melancholy, spightfull, as if bewitched.

He was a very friendly good-natured man as could be, but Shiftlesse to the World, and dyed not rich. I have sayd before that his father was ruined upon the account of the Protestant religion. Winceslaus dyed a Catholique, of which religion, I suppose, he might be ever since he came to Arundel-howse. Had he lived till the 13th of July following, he had been just 70 yeares old.

ROBERT HOOKE

Born 1635. Experimental philosopher. Curator of Experiments at the Royal Society 1662. Fellow (1663) and Secretary of the Royal Society 1677–82. Gresham Professor of Geometry 1665. Designed Bethlehem Hospital, Montague House, and the College of Physicians. He helped Newton by hints in Optics, and his anticipation of the Law of Inverse Squares was admitted by Newton. He pointed out the real nature of combustion 1665; proposed to measure the force of gravity by the swinging of a pendulum 1666; discovered the fifth star in Orion 1664; inferred the rotation of Jupiter; first observed a star by daylight; and made the earliest attempts at telescopic determination of the parallax of a fixed star. He also first applied the spiral spring to regulate watches; expounded the true theory of the elasticity and the kinetic hypothesis of gases 1678; constructed the first Gregorian telescope 1674; described a system of telegraphy 1684; first asserted the true principle of the arch; and invented the marine barometer and other instruments. Died 1703.

Mr Robert Hooke, curator of the Royall Societie at London, was borne at Freshwater in the Isle of Wight; his father was Minister there, and of the family of the Hookes of Hooke in Hants, in the road from London to Saram, a very ancient Family and in that place for many (3 or more) hundred yeares. His father died by suspending him selfe.

John Hoskyns, the Painter, being at Freshwater, to drawe pictures, Mr Hooke observed what he did, and, thought he, Why cannot I doe so too? So he gitts him Chalke, and Ruddle, and coale, and grinds them, and putts them on a Trencher, gott a pencill, and to worke he went, and made a picture: then he copied (as they hung up in the parlour) the Pictures there, which he made like. Also, being a boy there, at Freshwater, he made a Diall on a round trencher; never having had any instruction. His father was not Mathematicall at all.

When his father died, his Son Robert was but 13 yeares old, to whom he left one Hundred pounds, which was sent up to London with him, with an intention to have bound him Apprentice to Mr Lilly the Paynter, with whom he was a little while upon tryall; who liked him very well, but Mr Hooke quickly perceived what was to be donne, so, thought he, why cannot I doe this by my selfe and keepe my hundred pounds?

He went to Mr Busby's the Schoolemaster of Westminster, at whose howse he was; and he made very much of him. With him he lodged his hundred pounds. There he learnd to play 20 lessons on the organ. He there in one weeke's time made himselfe master of the first VI books of *Euclid*, to the Admiration of Mr Busby. At Schoole here he was very mechanicall, and (amongst other things) he invented thirty severall wayes of Flying.

He was never a King's Scholar, and I have heard Sir Richard Knight (who was his school-fellow) say that he seldome saw him in the schoole.

Anno Domini 1658 he was sent to Christ Church in Oxford, where he had a Chorister's place (in those dayes when the Church Musique was putt-downe) which was a pretty good maintenance. He lay in the chamber in Christ Church that was Mr Burton's, of whom 'tis whispered that, *non obstante* all his Astrologie and his booke of *Melancholie*, he ended his dayes in that chamber by hanging him selfe.

He was there Assistant to Dr Thomas Willis in his Chymistry; who afterwards recommended him to the Hon'ble Robert Boyle, Esqre, to be usefull to him in his Chymicall operations. Anno Domini 1662 Mr Robert Boyle recommended Mr Robert Hooke to be Curator of the Experiments of the Royall Society, wherin he did an admirable good worke to the Commonwealth of Learning, in recommending the fittest person in the world to them.

Anno Domini 1666 the great Conflagration of London happened, and then he was chosen one of the two Surveyors of the Citie of London; by which he hath gott a great Estate. He built Bedlam, the Physitians' College, Montague-house, the Piller on Fish-street-hill, and Theatre there; and he is much made use of in Designing Buildings.

He is but of midling stature, something crooked, pale faced, and his face but little belowe, but his head is lardge; his eie full and popping, and not quick; a grey eie. He haz a delicate head of haire, browne, and of an excellent moist curle. He is and ever was very temperate, and moderate in dyet, etc.

As he is of prodigious inventive head, so is a person of great vertue and goodnes. Now when I have sayd his Inventive faculty is so great, you cannot imagine his Memory to be excellent, for they are like two Bucketts, as one goes up, the other goes downe. He is certainly the greatest Mechanick this day in the World.

'Twas Mr Robert Hooke that invented the Pendulum-Watches, so much more usefull than the other Watches. He hath invented an Engine for the speedie working of Division, etc, or for the speedie and immediate finding out the Divisor.

Before I leave this Towne, I will gett of him a Catalogue of what he hath wrote; and as much of his Inventions as I can. But they are many hundreds; he believes not fewer than a thousand. 'Tis such a hard matter to get people to doe themselves right.

Mr Robert Hooke did in Anno 1670, write a Discourse, called, *An Attempt to prove the Motion of the Earth*, which he then read to the Royal Society; wherein he haz delivered the Theorie of explaining the coelestial motions mechanically: his words are these: I shall explaine a systeme of the world, differing in many particulars from any yet known, answering in all things to the common rules of mechanicall motions. This depends upon 3 suppositions; first, that all coelastiall bodys whatsoever have an attractive or gravitating power towards their own centers, whereby they attract not only their own parts, and keep them from flying from them, as we may observe the Earth to doe, but that they doe also attract all the other coelestiall bodys that are within the sphere of their activity, and consequently that not only the Sun and the Moon have an influence upon the body and motion of the Earth, and the Earth upon them, but that Mercury also, Venus, Mars, Saturne, and Jupiter, by their attractive powers have a considerable influence upon its motion, as, in the same manner, the corresponding attractive power of the Earth hath a considerable influence upon every one of their motions also. The second supposition is this, that all bodys whatsoever, that are putt into direct and simple motion will soe continue to move forwards in a straight line, till they are by some other effectuall powers deflected and bent into a motion describing a circle, ellipsis, or some other uncompounded curve line. The third supposition is, that these attractive powers are soe much the more powerfull in operating, by how much nearer the body wrought upon is to their own centers.

About 9 or 10 years ago, Mr Hooke writt to Mr Isaac Newton, of Trinity College, Cambridge, to make a Demonstration of this theory, not telling him, at first, the proportion of the gravity to the distance, nor what was the curv'd line that was thereby made. Mr Newton, in his Answer to the letter, did expresse that he had not thought of it; and in his first attempt about it, he calculated the Curve by supposing the attraction to be the same at all distances: upon which, Mr Hooke sent, in his next letter, the whole of his Hypothesis, *scil.* that the gravitation was reciprocall to the square of the distance: which is the whole coelastiall theory, concerning which Mr Newton haz made a demonstration, not at all owning he receiv'd the first Intimation of it from Mr Hooke. Likewise Mr Newton haz in the same Booke printed some other Theories and experiments of Mr Hooke's, without acknowledgeing from whom he had them.

This is the greatest Discovery in Nature that ever was since the World's Creation. It never was so much as hinted by any man before. I wish he had writt plainer, and afforded a little more paper.

JOHN HOSKYNS

Born 1566. Lawyer. Fellow of New College, Oxford, 1586. M.P. for Hereford 1614. Serjeant-at-Law 1623. Welsh judge. According to tradition, he revised the *History of the World* by Sir Walter Raleigh, with whom he became very intimate during his confinement in the Tower, and *polished* the verses of Ben Jonson so zealously as to be called Ben's *father*. Died 1638.

HE had a brother, John, D.D., a learned man, Rector of Ledbury and canon of Hereford, who was designed to be a Scholar, but this John (the Serjeant) would not be quiet, but he must be a Scholar too. In those dayes boyes were seldome taught to read that were not to be of some learned profession. So, upon his instant importunity, being then ten years of age, he learned to reade, and, at the yeare's end, entred into his Greeke grammar. Charles Hoskyns was brother to the Serjeant and the Doctor; a very ingeniose man, who would not have been inferior to either but killed himself with hard Study.

He was a yeare at Westminster; and not speeding there, he was sent to Winton Schole, where he was the Flower of his time. He was of a strong constitution, and had a prodigious memorie. I remember I have heard that one time he had not made his exercise (verse) and spake to one of his Forme to shew him his, which he sawe. The Schoolmaster presently calles for the Exercises, and Hoskyns told him that he had writ it out but lost it, but he could repeate it, and repeated the other boye's exercise (I think 12 or 16 verses) only at once reading over. When the boy who really had made them shewed the Master the same, and could not repeate them, he was whipped for stealing Hoskyn's Exercise. There were many pretty stories of him when a schooleboy, which I have forgott.

The Latin verses in the quadrangle at Winton-colledge, at the Cocks where the Boyes wash their hands, where there is the picture of a good Servant, with asses eares and Hind's feet, a padlock on his Lippes, etc, very good hieroglyphick, with a hexastique in Latin underneath (which I doe not remember). It was done by the Serjeant when he went to school there; but now finely painted.

When he came to New College, he was *Terrae filius* [the scholar appointed to declaim]; but he was so bitterly Satyricall that he was expelled and putt to his shifts.

He went into Somersetshire and taught a Schole for about a yeare at Ilchester. He compiled there a Greeke Lexicon as far as M, which I have seen. He maried (neer there) a rich widowe, by whome he had only one sonne and one daughter.

After his mariage he admitted himselfe at the Middle Temple, London. He wore good Cloathes, and kept good company. His excellent Witt gave him letters of Commendacion to all ingeniose persons. At his first comeing to London he gott acquainted with the Under-Secretaries at Court, where he was often usefull to them in writing their Latin letters.

He was a close-prisoner in the Tower, *tempore Regis Jacobi*, for speaking too boldly in the Parliament-house of the King's profuse liberality to the Scotts. He made a Comparison of a Conduit, whereinto water came, and ran-out afarre-off. Now, said he, this pipe reaches as far as Edinborough. He was kept a *close prisoner* there, i.e. his windowes were boarded up. Through a small chinke he sawe once a crowe, and another time, a Kite; the sight whereof, he sayd, was a great pleasure to him.

He, with much adoe, obtained at length the favour to have his little son Bennet to be with him; and he then made a Latin Distich, thus englished by him:

My little Ben, whils't thou art young,
And know'st not how to rule thy Tongue,
Make it thy Slave whil'st thou art free,
Least it as mine imprison thee.

I have heard that when he came out of the Tower, his Crest was graunted him (I believe) for his bold Spirit, and (I suppose) contrived by himselfe, viz. a Lyon's head couped or, breathing fire. The Serjeant would say jocosely that it was the only Lyon's head in England that tooke Tobacco.

His great Witt quickly made him be taken notice of. Ben. Johnson called him *father*. Sir Benet told me that one time desiring Mr Johnson to adopt him for his sonne, No, said he, I dare not; 'tis honour enough for me to be your Brother: I was your Father's sonne, and 'twas he that polished me. In shorte, his acquaintance were all the Witts then about the Towne; e.g. Sir Walter Raleigh (who was his Fellow-prisoner in the Tower, where he was Sir Walter's *Aristarchus* to review and polish Sir

Walter's stile); John Donne, D.D.; Sir Benjamin Ruddyer, with whom it was once his fortune to have a quarrel and fought a Duell with him and hurt him in the Knee, but they were afterwards friends again; Sir Henry Wotton, Provost of Eaton College; *cum multis aliis* [with many others].

His verses on the fart in the Parliament house are printed in some of the *Drolleries*. He had a booke of Poemes, neatly written by one of his Clerkes, bigger then Dr Donne's Poemes, which his sonn Benet lent to he knowes not who, about 1653, and could never heare of it since.

Was wont to say that all those that came to London were either Carrion or Crowes.

His conversation was exceedingly pleasant, and would make verses on the Roade, where he was the best Company in the world. He was a great master of the Latin and Greke languages; a great Divine; made the best Latin Epitaphs of his time. He understood the Lawe well, but worst at that.

He wrote his owne Life, which was to shew that wheras Plutarch had wrote the Lives of many Generalles, etc., Grandees, that he, or an active man might, from a private fortune by his witt and industrie attain to the Dignity of a Serjeant at Lawe – but he should have said that they must have parts like his too.

He was a very strong man, and valiant, and an early riser in the morning (*scil.*, at four in the morning). He was black-eyed and had black hayre.

I will now describe his Seate at Morhampton (Hereff.). At the Gatehouse is the Picture of the old fellowe that made the fires, with a Block on his back, boytle and wedges and hatchet. In the Chapelle, over the Altar, are two Hebrewe words and underneath a distich. Here is an Organ that was Queen Elizabeth's. In the gallery, the picture of his Brother Doctor in the Pulpit, Serjeant in his Robes, the Howse, Parke, etc; and underneath are verses. In the first leafe of his Fee-booke he drew the picture of a Purse.

In the Garden, the picture of the Gardiner, on the Wall of the Howse, with his Rake, Spade, and water-pott in his left hand. Under severall venerable and shady Oakes in the Parke, he had seates made; and where was a fine purling Spring, he did curbe it with stone.

Not many moneths before his death (being at the Assises or Sessions at Hereford) a massive countrey fellowe trod on his toe, which caused a Gangrene which was the cause of his death. One Mr Dighton of Glocester, an experienced Chirurgian who had formerly been chirurgian in the Warres in Ireland, was sent for to cure him; but his Skill and care could not save him. His Toes were first cutt-off. The Minister of his Parish had a clubbe-foote, or feete (I think his name was Hugh). Said he, *Sir Hugh* (after his toes were cutt off) *I must be acquainted with your shoemaker*.

I remember, before the late Warres, the Ministers in Herefordshire, etc. (Counties that way) had the Title of Sr, as the Bachalours of Art have at Oxon, as Sir Richard, of Stretford; Sir William, of Monkland. And so it was in Wilts, when my grandfather Lyte was a boy; and anciently everywhere. In all old Wills before the Reformation it is upon Record.

Sir Robert Pyle, Attorney of the Court of Wardes, was his neighbour, but there was no great goodwill between them – Sir Robert was haughty. He happened to dye on Christmas day: the newes being brought to the Serjeant, said he, The devill haz a Christmas-pye.

HENRY ISAACSON

Born 1581. Theologian and chronologer. Master of Arts of Pembroke Hall, Cambridge. Friend of Bishop Andrews. Published *Tabula Historico-Chronologica* 1633; a *Life of Bishop Andrews* 1650; and other works. Died 1654.

MR HENRY ISAACSON was Secretary to Lancelot Andrews, Lord Bishop of Winton. Thomas Bourman, Dr of Divinity, of Kingston upon Thames, did know Mr Isaacson, and told me that he was a learned man, which I easily believed when I heard he was Secretary to that learned Prelate, who made use of none but for merit.

The Dr told me that when he presented his *Chronologie* to his Majestie King Charles the first, 'twas in the matted Gallery at White-hall. The King presently discerned the purpose of the Treatise, and turned to his owne Birth; sayd the King, *And here's one Lye to begin with*. It seemes that Mr Isaacson had taken it out of a foreigner, who used the other Account. Poor Mr Isaacson was so ashamed at this unlucky rencounter, that he immediately sneak't away and stayd not for prayse or reward, both which perhaps he might have had, for his Majestie was well pleased with it.

'Twas presented in an ill Hower. An Astrologer would give something to know *that day and hower*.

DAVID JENKINS

Born 1586. Welsh judge. Judge of Great Sessions for Carmarthen, Cardigan, and Pembrokeshire 1643. An ardent Royalist, he was captured at Hereford in 1645, and steadfastly contested the right of Parliament to try him. Imprisoned until the Restoration. He published several Royalist treatises, as well as *8 Centuries of Reports* 1661. He was a patron of the Welsh Bards in Glamorganshire, where he died in 1663.

HE was of very good courage. Rode in the Lord Gerard's Army in Pembrokeshire, in the forlorne-hope, with his long rapier drawne holding it on-end. He was taken prisoner at Hereford. Long time prisoner in the Tower, Newgate, Wallingford, and Windsore. Never submitted to the Usurping power (I thinke, the only man). All his Estate was confiscated; and was always excepted by the Parliament in the first Ranke of delinquents.

In his Circuit in Wales at the beginning of the Warres, he caused to be Indicted severall men of those parts (that were Parliament, etc, engaged against the King) for highe Treason; and the grand jury indicted them. Afterwards, when he was prisoner in Newgate, some of these Grandees came to him to triumph over him, and told him that if they had been thus in his power, he would have hanged them. *God forbid els!* replied he: which undaunted returne they much admired [*wondered at*].

The Parliament intended to have hanged him; and he expected no lesse, but resolved to be hangd with the Bible under one arme and Magna Charta under the other. And hangd he had been, had not Harry Martyn told them in the House that *Sanguis martyrum est semen ecclesiae* [the blood of martyrs is the seed of the Church] and that that way would doe them more mischiefe. So his life was saved, and they removed him out of the way to Wallingford Castle.

'Twas pitty he was not made one of the Judges of Westminster-hall for his long sufferings; and he might have been he told me, if he would have given money to the Chancellor Hyde: but he scornd it. He needed it not, for he had his estate againe (1500 pounds per annum), and being old and *carceribus confractus* [broken with imprisonment]. Mr T. Hobbes, Malmesburiensis, told him one day at dinner that *that hereafter would not shew well for somebodie's Honour in History.*

SIR LEOLINE JENKINS

Born 1623. Civilian and diplomatist. In May 1651 he was indicted *for a seminary of rebellion and sedition*. In 1655 he anticipated a threatened *bannition* by the Parliament by retiring to the Continent with his pupils. Fellow of Jesus College, Oxford, 1660; Principal 1661–73; Deputy-Professor of Civil Law 1662; he was also accustomed to conduct the foreign correspondence of the University and was appointed to receive foreign visitors of distinction. Judge of the Admiralty Court (1665) and of the Prerogative Court of Canterbury 1669. He was knighted in 1670, after he had obtained the setting aside in favour of Charles II of his sister the Duchess of Orleans's claims to Henrietta Maria's personalty. M.P. for Hythe (1673–8) and for Oxford University 1679–85. He represented England at the Congress of Cologne in 1673, and on his voyage home, while still in the Meuse at Brielle, he fired on a Dutch man-of-war for neglecting to lower her flag, upon which the Dutchman obeyed under protest. He was also Plenipotentiary at Nymegen from 1676–9, and he marked his resentment at the bad faith displayed by Louis XIV during the negotiations by rejecting a present of his miniature, set in diamonds, though Colbert urged its acceptance to the point of importunity. Roger North calls him *the most faithful drudge of a Secretary that ever the Court had*. Despite his exemplary life, he was *inclined to laugh immoderately at a jest, especially if it were coarse*, which Charles II discovering, *failed not, after the tendency of his own fancy, to ply his Secretary with conceits of that complexion*. He died in 1685.

SIR LLEUELLIN JENKINS, Knight, was borne at Llantrithid in the countie of Glamorgan. His father (whom I knew) was a good plaine Countrey-man, a Copyholder of Sir John Aubrey, Knight and Baronet (eldest son of Sir Thomas) whose Mannour it is.

He went to Schoole at Cowbridge, not far off.

David Jenkins, that was prisoner in the Tower (maried a sister of Sir John Aubrey) was some remote kin to him; and, looking on him as a boy towardly, diligent, and good, he contributed something towards his Education.

Anno Domini 1641, he was matriculated of Jesus College in Oxford, where he stayed till (I thinke) he tooke his Degree of *Bac. Artium*.

About that time Sir John Aubrey sent for him home to enforme his eldest sonne Lewis Aubrey (since deceased, 1659) in Grammar; and that he might take his learning the better, he was taught in the Church-house where severall boyes came to schoole, and there were 6 or 7 Gentlemen's sonnes (Sir Francis Maunsell, Bart; Mr Edmund Thomas; etc) boarded in the Towne. The young Gentlemen were all neer of an age, and ripe for the University together, and to Oxford they all went under Mr Jenkin's care about anno 1649 or 50, but by reason of the Disturbances of those Times, Sir John would not have his sonne of any College. But they all studyed at Mr (now Sir) Sampson White's house, a Grocer, opposite to University College. Here he stayed with my Cosen about 3 yeares or better, and then, in *anno* 1655, he travelled with my Cosen and two or 3 of the other Gentlemen into France, where they stayd about 3 yeares and made themselves Masters of that Language.

He first began the Civill Lawe, viz. bought Vinnius on Justinian, 1653.

When he brought home Mr Lewis Aubrey, he returned to Jesus College. After his Majestie's restauration Dr Maunsell was restored to his Principallship of that house, but being very old and wearie of worldly cares, he kept it not long, before he resigned it to Mr Jenkins.

Gilbert Sheldon, Archbishop of Canterbury, and Sir John Aubrey were *co-etanei* [fellow-students], and contracted a great friendship at Oxon in their youth, which continued to their deaths. In the Troublesome times after Dr Sheldon was expelled, he was a yeare (I thinke) or two with Sir John at Llantrithid, where he tooke notice of the vertue and assiduity of the young man Mr Jenkins. After the King's restauration Sir John Aubrey recommended Mr Jenkins to him; made him. Anno 1668, he [Sheldon] was Archbishop of Canterbury: Sir William Meyric, LL.D. and Judge of the Prerogative Court of Canterbury, dyed, and the Archbishop conferred that place on Mr Jenkins.

When Mary the Queen-Mother dyed at Paris, the King of Fraunce caused her Jewells and Treasures to be locked up and sealed. His Majestie of Great Britaine sent Sir Llewellin (which is Leoline in Latin) to Paris concerning the Administration. Anno 1670, he had the Honour of Knighthood.

Anno 1673, he was sent with Sir Joseph Williamson, Plenipotentiaries, to Nemeghen: I remember that very time they went away was opposition of Saturn and Mars. I sayd then to the Earl of Thanet that if that Ambassade came to any good I would never trust to Astrologie again.

March 25, 1680, he was made Principall Secretary of Estate. When I came to wayte on him to congratulate for the Honour his Majestie had been pleased to bestowe on him, he received me with his usuall courtesie, and sayd that *it had pleased God to rayse-up a poore worme to doe his Majestie humble service*.

He haz a strong body for study, indefatigable, temperate and vertuous. God blesse him.

BEN JONSON

Born 1573. Actor, poet and playwright. Educated at Westminster School. Began to work for the Admiral's Company of Players both as player and playwright in 1597. Killed a fellow-actor in a brawl, but escaped death, by benefit of clergy, 1598: he became a Roman Catholic during his imprisonment, but abjured twelve years later. His *Every Man in his Humour*, with Shakespeare in the cast, was performed by the Lord Chamberlain's Company at the Globe 1598. His first tragedy *Sejanus* was given at the same theatre by Shakespeare's Company in 1603. His masques, for which Inigo Jones designed the scenery, became popular at Court, but Jonson was nevertheless imprisoned in 1605 for libelling the Scots. Although Drummond described him *as a great lover and praiser of himself, a contemner and scorner of others, given rather to lose a friend than a jest, jealous of every word and action of those about him, especially after drink*, he was the friend of Shakespeare, Donne, Bacon, Selden, Chapman, Beaumont, Fletcher, Herrick, Suckling, Sir Kenelm Digby, and Lord Falkland, and among his patrons were the Sidneys, the Earl of Pembroke, and the Earl and Countess of Newcastle. He was the first Poet Laureate and died in 1637.

MR BENJAMIN JOHNSON, Poet Laureat, was a Warwyckshire man. 'Tis agreed that his father was a Minister; and by his Epistle dedicat. of *Every Man* . . . to Mr William Camden that he was a Westminster Scholar and that Mr W. Camden was his School-master.

His mother, after his father's death, maried a Bricklayer; and 'tis generally said that he wrought sometime with his father-in-lawe (and particularly on the Garden-wall of Lincoln's Inne next to Chancery Lane) and that a Knight, a Bencher, walking thro', and hearing him repeate some Greeke verses out of Homer, discoursing with him and finding him to have a Witt extraordinary, gave him some Exhibition to maintaine him at Trinity College in Cambridge.

Then he went into the Lowe-countreys, and spent some time (not very long) in the armie, not to disgrace, as you may find in his *Epigrammes*.

Then he came over into England, and acted and wrote, but both ill, at the Green Curtaine, a kind of Nursery or obscure Play-house, somewhere in the Suburbes (I thinke towards Shoreditch or Clarkenwell).

He killed Mr Marlow, the Poet, on Bunhill, comeing from the Green-curtain play-house.

Then he undertooke again to write a Playe, and did hitt it admirably well, viz. *Every Man* . . . , which was his first good one.

Serjeant John Hoskins of Herefordshire was his *Father*. I remember his sonne (Sir Bennet Hoskins, Baronet, who was something Poetical in his youth) told me, that when he desired to be adopted his [Jonson's] *Son*: No, sayd he, 'tis honour enough for me to be your Brother; I am your father's son: 'twas he that polished me, I doe acknowledge it.

He was (or rather had been) of a clear and faire skin; his habit was very plaine. I have heard Mr Lacy, the Player, say that he was wont to weare a coate like a coachman's coate, with slitts under the arme-pitts. He would many times exceed in drinke (Canarie was his beloved liquor) then he would tumble home to bed, and, when he had thoroughly perspired, then to studie. I have seen his studyeing chaire, which was of strawe, such as olde woemen used, and as Aulus Gellius is drawen in.

At riper yeares, after he had studied at Cambridge he came of his owne accord to Oxon and there entred himselfe in Christ Church and tooke his Master's degree in Oxon (or conferred on him) anno 1619. When I was in Oxon, Bishop Skinner of Oxford, who lay at our college, was wont to say that he understood an Author as well as any man in England.

Long since, in King James's time, I have heard my uncle Danvers say (who knew him) that he lived without temple Barre, at a Combe maker's shop, about the Elephant and Castle. In his later time he lived in Westminster, in the house under which you passe as you goe out of the Church yard into the old Palace; where he dyed.

'Twas an ingeniose remarque of my Lady Hoskins, that B.J. never writes of Love, or if he does, does it not naturally.

Ben Johnson had one eie lower than t'other, and bigger, like Clun the Player; perhaps he begott Clun. He mentions in his *Epigrammes*, a Sonne that he had, and his Epitaph.

He tooke a Catalogue from Mr Lacy (the Player) of the Yorkshire Dialect. 'Twas his Hint for Clownery to his Comoedy called *The Tale of a Tub*. This I had from Mr Lacy.

King James made him write against the Puritans, who began to be troublesome in his time.

A Grace by Ben Johnston, extempore, Before King James:

Our King and Queen the Lord-God blesse,
The Paltzgrave and the Lady Besse,
And God blesse every living thing
That Lives, and breath's, and loves the King.
God bless the Councell of Estate,
And Buckingham the fortunate.
God Blesse them all, and keepe them safe:
And God Blesse me, and God blesse Raph.

The King was mighty enquisitive to know who this Raph was. Ben told him 'twas the Drawer at the Swanne Tavernne by Charing-crosse, who drew him good Canarie. For this Drollery his Majestie gave him an hundred poundes.

B. Jonson had 50 pounds per annum for many yeares together to keepe off Sir W. Wiseman of Essex from being Sheriff. At last King James prick't him, and Ben came to his Majestie and told him he had prick't him to the heart, and then explayned himselfe: *innuendo* Sir W.W. being prick't Sheriffe: and gott him struck off.

Ben Johnson, riding through Surrey, found the Women weeping and wailing, lamenting the Death of a Lawyer, who lived there: He enquired why so great Grief for the Losse of a Lawyer? Oh, said they, we have the greatest Loss imaginable; he kept us all in Peace and Quietness, and was a most charitable good Man: Whereupon Ben made this Distich:

God works Wonders now and then,
Behold a Miracle, deny't who can,
Here lies a Lawyer *and an* honest *man.*

'Tis Pity that good Man's Name should not be remember'd.

This account I received from Mr Isaac Walton (who wrote Dr John Donne's &c Life) Decemb. 2, 1680, he being then eighty-seaven years of age. This is his owne hand writing. I only knew Ben Johnson: but my Lord of Winton knew him very well, and says he was in the 6th, that is the upermost fforme in Westminster Schole. At which time his father dyed, and his mother marryed a brickelayer, who made him (much against his will) to help him in his trade. But in a short time, his scole maister, Mr Camden, got him a better imployment, which was, to atend or accompany a son of Sir Walter Rauleyes in his travills. Within a short time after their returne, they parted (I think not in cole bloud) and with a love sutable to what they had in their travills (not to be comended) and then Ben began to set up for himself in the trade by which he got his subsistance and fame. Of which I nede not give any account. He got in time to have 100 pounds a year from the King, also a pention from the Cittie, and the like from many of the nobility, and some of the gentry, which was well payd for love or fere of his raling in verse or prose, or boeth. My Lord of Winton told me, he told him he was (in his long retyrement and sickness, when he saw him, which was often) much afflickted that hee had profain'd the scripture in his playes; and lamented it with horror; yet, that at that time of his long retyrement, his pentions (so much as came yn) was given to a woman that govern'd him, with whom he livd and dyed nere the Abie in West mimster; and that nether he nor she tooke much care for next weike, and wood be sure not to want wine; of which he usually tooke too much before he went to bed, if not oftner and soner. My Lord tells me he knowes not, but thinks he was borne in Westminster. So much for brave Ben.

When B.J. was dyeing King Charles sent him but x pounds.

He lies buryed in the north aisle in the path of square stone (the rest is Lozenge) opposite to the Scutcheon of Robertus de Ros, with this Inscription only on him, in a pavement square of blew marble, about 14 inches square,

O RARE BENN JOHNSON

which was donne at the charge of Jack Young, afterwards knighted, who, walking there when the grave was covering, gave the fellow eighteen pence to cutt it.

RALPH KETTELL

Born 1563. Don. Scholar of Trinity College, Oxford, 1579; Fellow 1583; Master of Arts 1586; Doctor of Divinity 1597; third President 1599. He was vigilant in dealing with College estates and discipline, and he rebuilt Trinity College Hall. Died 1643.

RALPH KETTELL, D.D., was borne in Hartfordshire. The Lady Elizabeth Pope brought him in to be a Scholar of the House at eleaven yeares of age (as I have heard Dr Ralph Bathurst say).

I have heard Dr Whistler say that he wrote good Latin, and Dr Ralph Bathurst (whose grandmother he maried) that he scolded the best in Latin of any one that ever he knew. He was of an admirable healthy Constitution.

He dyed a year after I came to the Colledge, and he was then a good deal above 80, and he had then a fresh ruddy complexion. He was a very tall well-growne man. His gowne and surplice and hood being on, he had a terrible gigantique aspect with his sharp gray eies.

Mr Edward Bathurst of Trinity College, Oxon, drew a Picture of Dr Kettle some three Years after his Death, by sole Strength of Memory, he having so strong an Idea of him impressed on his Mind, that it well resembled him.

He was, they say, white very soon; he had a very venerable presence and was an excellent Governour. One of his maximes of Governing was to keepe-downe the *Juvenilis Impetus*. He was chosen President, the second after the foundation of the College.

He was a right Church of England man, and every tuesday in Terme-time, in the morning, the Undergraduates (I have forgott if Baccalaurs) were to come into the Chapell and heare him expound on the 36 Articles of the Church of England. I remember he was wont to talk much of the Rood-loft, and of the wafers; he remembred those times. On these dayes, if anyone had committed a fault, he should be sure to heare of it in the Chapell before his fellow Collegiates.

He'd have at any him that had a white Cap on; for he concluded him to have been drunke, and his head to ake. Sir John Denham had borrowed money of Mr Whistler, the Recorder, and after a great while the Recorder askt him for it again. Mr Denham laught at it, and told him he never intended that. The Recorder acquainted the President, who, at a Lecture in the Chapell, rattled him, and told him, Thy father (Judge) haz hanged many an honester man. In my time, Mr Anthony Ettrick and some others frighted a poor young freshman of Magd. Hall with conjuring, which when the old Dr heard of: on the next Tuesday, sayd he, *Mr Ettrick* (who is a very little man) *will conjure up a Jackanapes to be his Great-grandfather.*

He sawe how the Factions in Religion in those dayes drew, and he kept himselfe unconcerned. W. Laud, Archbishop of Canterbury, sent him one time a servant of his with Venison, which the old Dr with much earnest-ness refused, and sayd he was an old man, and his Stomach weake, and he had not eaten of such Meate in a long time, and by no meanes would accept of it; but the servant was as much pressing it on him on the other side, and told the President that he durst not carry it back againe. Well, seeing there was no avoyding it, the President asked the Servant seriously, if the Archbishop of Canterbury intended to putt in any Scholars or Fellowes into his College?

One of the Fellowes (in Mr Francis Potter's time) was wont to say that Dr Kettel's braine was like a Hasty-pudding, where there was Memorie, Judgemente, and Phancy all stirred together. He had all these Faculties in great measure, but they were all just so jumbled together. If you had to doe with him, taking him for a Foole, you would have found in him great Subtility and reach; *è contra*, if you treated him as a Wise man you would have mistaken him for a Foole. A neighbour of mine, Mr St Low, told me heard him preach once in St Marie's Church at Oxon. I know not whether this was the only time or no that he used this following way of conclusion: *But now I see it is time for me to shutt up my Booke, for I see the Doctor's men come-in wiping of their beardes from the Ale-house.* He could from the pulpit plainly see them, and 'twas their custom in Sermon to go there, and about the end of Sermon to returne to wayte on their masters.

He had two wives, if not three, but no child. His second wife was a Villiers (or rather I thinke the Widow of Edward Villers, Esq) who had two beautifull daughters, co-heires. The eldest, whom severall of good estate would gladly have wedded, he would needs dispose of himselfe, and he thought nobody so fitt a husband for this Angelique creature as one Mr Bathurst, of the College, a second brother, and of about 300 pounds per annum, but an indifferent Scholar, red fac'd, not at all handsome. But the Doctor's fashion was to goe up and downe the College, and peepe in at the Keyholes to see whether the Boyes did follow their books or no. He seldome found Bathurst minding of his Booke, but mending of his old doublet or breeches. He was very thrifty and penurious, and upon this reason he carried away this curious [*rare*] creature. But she was very happy in her Issue; all her children were very Ingeniose and prosperous in the world, and most of them beautifull.

One Mr Isham (elder brother to Sir Justinian Isham) a gentleman-commoner of this Howse, dyed of the small-pox. He was a very fine Gentleman and very well-beloved by all the Colledge, and severall of the Fellowes would have preacht his Funerall Sermon, but Dr Kettel would not permitt it, but would doe it himselfe; which the Fellowes were sorry for, for they knew he would make a ridiculous piece of worke of it. But preach the Dr did; takes a Text and preaches on it a little while; and then takes another Text for the satisfaction of the young Gentleman's Mother and anon takes another Text for the satisfaction of the young Gentleman's Grandmother. When he came to the Panegyrique, sayd he: He was the finest swet young Gentleman; it did my heart good to see him walke along the Quadrangle. We have an olde Proverbe that *Hungry Dogges will eate dirty puddings*, but I must needes say for this young Gentleman that he always loved *Sweet*, he spake it with a squeaking voice, *things*, and there was end.

He observed that the Howses that had the smallest beer had the most drunkards, for it forced them to goe into the towne to comfort their stomachs, wherefore Dr Kettel alwayes had in his College excellent beere, not better to be had in Oxon, so that we could not goe to any other place but for the worse, and we had the fewest drunkards of any howse in Oxford.

He was irreconcileable to long haire; called them hairy Scalpes, and as for Perriwigges (which were then very rarely worne) he beleeved them to be the Scalpes of men cutte off after they were hang'd, and so tanned and dressed for use. When he observed the Scolars haire longer than ordinary (especially if they were Scholars of the Howse) he would bring a paire of Cizers in his Muffe (which he commonly wore) and woe be to them that sate on the outside of the Table. I remember he cutt Mr Radford's haire with the knife that chipps the bread on the Buttery Hatch, and then he sang (this is in the old play of *Gammer Gurton's needle*):

And was not Grim the Collier finely trimm'd?
Tonedi, Tonedi.

Mr Lydall, sayd he, how doe you decline tondeo? Tondeo, tondes, Tonedi?

He was constantly at Lectures and Exercises in the Hall, to observe them, and brought along with him his Hower-glasse; and one time, being offended with the Boyes, he threatened them that if they did not doe their excercise better he would bring an Hower-glasse two howers long.

One time walking by the Table where the Logick Lecture was read, where the Reader was telling the Boyes that a Syllogisme might be true *quoad formam*, but not *quoad materiam*; said the President (who would putt-in sometimes) There was a Fox that spyed a Crowe upon a tree, and he had a great mind to have him, and so getts under the tree in a hope, and layes out his tayle crooked like a Horne, thinking the Crowe might come and peck at it, and then he would seise him. Now come we (this was his word) I say the foxe's tayle is a horne: is this a true proposition or no? (to one of the boyes). Yes, sayd he (the Dr expected he should have sayd No; for it putt him out of his designe); *Why then*, sayd he, *take him and toot him*; and away he went.

As they were reading of inscribing and circumscribing Figures, sayd he, I will shew you how to inscribe a Triangle in a Quadrangle. Bring a pig into the quadrangle, and I will sett the colledge dog at him, and he will take the pig by the eare, then come I and take the Dog by the tayle and the hog by the tayle, and so there you have a Triangle in a quadrangle; *quod erat faciendum*.

He dragg'd with one foot a little, by which he gave warning (like a rattlesnake) of his comeing. Will Egerton (Major General Egerton's younger brother) a good witt and mimick, would goe so like him that sometimes he would make the whole Chapell rise up imagining he had been entring in.

He preach't every Sunday at his parsonage at Garsington, about five miles off. He rode on his bay gelding, with his boy Ralph before him, with a leg of mutton (commonly) and some colledge bread. He did not care for the countrey Revells because they tended to debauchery. Sayd he, at Garsington revell, Here is, *Hey for Garsington!* and *hey for Cuddesdon!* and *hey Hockley!* but here's nobody cries, *hey for God Almighty!*

Upon Trinity Sunday (our Festival day) he would commonly preach at the Colledge, whither a number of the scholars of other howses would come, to laugh at him. In his prayer (where he was, of course, to remember Sir Thomas Pope, our founder, and the Lady Elizabeth, his wife, deceased) he would many times make a willfull mistake, and say, *Thomas Pope, our confounder*, but then presently recall himselfe.

He sang a thin shrill high Treble, but there was one J. Hoskyns who had a higher, and was wont to playe the wag with the Doctor, to make him straine his voyce up to his.

He was a person of great Charity. In his College, where he observed diligent boys that he ghessed had but a slender exhibition from their Friends, he would many times putt money in at their windowes; that his right hand did not know what his left did. Servitors that wrote good hands he would sett on worke to transcribe for him, and reward them generosely, and give them good advise.

The Parsonage of Garsington belongs to the College, and this good old Doctor, when one of his parish, that was an honest industrious man, happened by any accident to be in decay and lowe in the World, would let his Parsonage to him for a yeare, two or three, fourty pounds a yeare under value.

You must knowe that there was a great Faction between Dr Kettle and the Fellowes; and one time at a Scrutiny, the Doctor upbraiding them for their direspect to Him: Qd, Oh! you are brave gallant Gentlemen, and *learned* men, you dispise, and snort and fart at your poor President: I am an old blind-sincks: but who was it proposed you to be fellows from poor raskall-Jacks, and Servitors: Was it not your President? and yet none of your Friends were ever so gratefull to present me with so much as a wrought Night-cap. I cry you mercy (Mr Dr Hobbs!) indeed. I remember, your Mother sent me once a Gammon of Bacon.

Mris Howe, of Grendon, sent him a present of Hippocris, and some fine cheese-cakes, by a plain countrey fellow, her servant. The Dr tastes the wine: *What*, sayd he, *didst thou take this drinke out of a Ditch?* and when he saw the cheese-cakes – *What have we here, Crinkum, Crankum?* The poor fellow stared on him, and wondered at such a rough reception of such a handsome present, but he shortly made him amends with a good dinner and halfe-a-crowne.

(Dr Thomas Batchcroft did out-doe Dr Kettle. One sent this Doctor a Pidgeon-pye from New-market or thereabout, and he askt the bearer whither 'twas hott, or cold?)

In August 1642, the Lord Viscount Say and Seale came (by order of the Parliament) to visit the Colleges to see what of new Popery they could discover in the chapells. In our Chapell, on the backside of the Skreen, had been two Altars (of painting well enough for those times, and the Colours were admirably fresh and lively). That on the right hand as you enter the Chapell was dedicated to St Katharine, that on the left was of the taking our Saviour off from the crosse. My Lord Say sawe that this was done of old time, and Dr Kettel told his Lordship: *Truly, my Lord, we regard them no more then a dirty Dish-clout*; so they remained untoucht till Harris's time, and then were coloured over with green.

'Tis probable this venerable Doctor might have lived some yeares longer, and finisht his Century, had not those civill warres come on; which much grieved him, that was wont to be absolute in the colledge, to be affronted and disrespected by rude soldiers. I remember being at the Rhetorique Lecture in the hall; a foot soldier came in and brake his hower-glasse. The Dr indeed was just stept out, but Jack Dowch pointed at it.

Our Grove was the Daphne for the Ladies and their gallants to walke in, and many times my Lady Isabella Thynne (who lay at Balliol College) would make her entry with a Theorbo or Lute played before her. I have heard her play on it in the Grove myself, which she did rarely; for which Mr Edmund Waller hath in his *Poems* for ever made her famous. She was most beautifull, most humble, charitable, etc, but she could not subdue one thing. I remember one time this Lady and fine Mris Fenshawe (her great and intimate friend, who lay at our College) would have a frolick to make a visit to the President. The old Dr quickly perceived that they came to abuse him: he addresses his discourse to Mris Fenshawe, saying, Madam, your husband and father I bred up here, and I knew your grandfather. I know you to be a gentlewoman, I will not say you are a Whore; but gett you gonne for a very woman.

Mris Fenshawe was wont, and my Lady Thynne, to come to our Chapell, mornings, halfe dressd, like Angells [*loose women*]. The dissoluteness of the times, as I have sayd, grieving the good old Doctor, his dayes were shortened, and dyed and was buried at Garsington.

Seneca's scholar Nero found fault with his style, saying 'twas *arena sine calce* [mortar without lime] now Dr Kettel was wont to say that Seneca writes as a Boare does pisse, *scilicet* by jirkes.

I cannot forget a story that Robert Skinner, Lord Bishop of Oxford, haz told us: One Slymaker, a Fellow of this College long since, a fellow of great impudence, and little learning – the fashion was in those dayes to goe, every Satterday night (I thinke) to Joseph Barnes shop, the booke-seller opposite to the west end of St Mary's, where the Newes was brought from London, etc. This impudent clowne would alwayes be hearkning to people's whisperings and overlooking their letters, that he was much taken notice of. Sir Isaac Wake, who was a very witty man, was resolved he would putt a Trick upon him, and understood that such a Sunday Slymaker was to preach at St Mary's. So Sir Isaac, the Saterday before, reades a very formall lettre to some person of quality, that Cardinal Baronius was turned Protestant, and was marching with an Army of 40,000 men against the Pope. Slymaker hearkned with greedy Eares, and the next day in his prayer before his Sermon, beseeched God *of his infinite mercy and goodnesse to give a blessing to the Army of Cardinal Baronius, who was turnd Protestant, and now marching with an Army of forty thousand men*, and so runnes on: he had a Stentorian voice, and thunderd it out. The Auditors all stared and were amazed: George Abbot (afterwards Bishop of Sarum) was then Vice-cancellor, and when Slymaker came out of the Pulpit, sends for him, and asked his name: Slymaker, sayd he; No, sayd the Vice-canc, 'tis *Lyemaker*.

Dr Kettel, when he scolded at the idle young boies of his colledge, he used these names, viz. Turds, Tarrarags (these were the worst sort, rude Rakills) Rascal-Jacks, Blindcinques, Scobberlotchers (these did no hurt, were sober, but went idleing about the Grove with their hands in their pocketts, and telling the number of the trees There, or so).

To make you merry, I'le tell you a story that Dr Henry Birket told us t'other day at his cosen Mariet's, *scilicet* that about 1638 or 1640, when he was of Trinity College, Dr Kettel, preaching as he was wont to doe on Trinity Sunday, told 'em that they should keepe their Bodies chast and holy; but, said he, you Fellows of the College here eate good Commons, and drinke good double Beer, and breede Seed, and that will gett-out. How would the good old Dr have raunted and beate-up his Kettle-Drum, if he should have seen such Luxury in the College as there is now! *Tempora mutantur* [times change].

RICHARD KNOLLES

Born 1550. Historian. Headmaster of the Grammar School at Sandwich in Kent, where he was engaged for twelve years on his *Generall Historie of the Turkes from the first beginning of that Nation*, which was published in 1603 and ran through many editions. Dr Johnson said that the book showed *all the excellencies that narration can admit*, explaining Knolles's limited reputation by the fact that he wrote of a subject *of which none desires to be informed*. Byron said of the book: *I believe it had much influence on my future wishes to visit the Levant, and gave perhaps the oriental colouring which is observed in my poetry*. Southey and Coleridge also greatly admired the work, which is a fine example of the English of its time. Knolles died in 1610.

THE Lord Burleigh, when he read Knolls *Turkish history* was particularly extremely pleased at the discription of the Battail of Lepanto; sent for Knolles, who told him an ingeniose young man came to him, hearing what he was about, and desired that he might write that, having been in that Action.

My Lord hunted after him, and traced him from place to place, and at last to Newgate; he was reduced to such necessity. He was hanged but a 14 night before. He unluckily lost a good opportunity of being preferred.

SIR HENRY LEE

Born 1530. Courtier. He was educated by his uncle, Sir Thomas Wyatt the elder, and entered the service of Henry VIII in 1545. Clerk of the Armoury 1549. Knighted 1553. M.P. for Buckinghamshire 1558 and 1572. Personal Champion to Queen Elizabeth from 1559 to 1590. Master of the Ordnance 1590. He was visited by Queen Elizabeth at his country house in 1592. Knight of the Garter 1597. He was a great builder and sheep farmer, and died in 1610.

OLD Sir Henry Lee, of Ditchley, in Oxon, Knight of the Garter, was a Gentleman of a good estate, and a strong and valiant person; and was supposed brother of Queen Elizabeth. He ordered that all his Family should be christned *Harry's*.

He was a raunger of Woodstocke Parke, and (I have heard my old cosen Whitney say) would many times in his younger yeares walke at nights in the Parke with his Keepers.

This Sir Henry Lee's Nephew and Heire (whom I remember very well: he often came to Sir John Danvers) was called *Whip and Away*. The occasion of it was this: The old Hero declining in his strength by age, and so not being able to be a Righter of his owne Wronges as heretofore, some person of quality had affronted him. So he spake to Sir Henry Lee, his heire, to lie in wayte for him about the Bell Inne, in the Strande, with halfe a dozen or more lustie fellowes at his back, and as the partie came along to give him a good Blow with his Cane and *Whip and away*; the tall fellowes should finish the revenge. Whether 'twere nicety of conscience, or Cowardice, but Sir Henry the younger absolutely refused it. For which he was disinherited and the whole estate settled on a keeper's sonne of Whitchwood forest of his owne name, a one-eied young man, no kinne to him, from whom the Earle of Lichfield now is descended, as also the Lady Norris and Lady Wharton.

He was never maried, but kept woemen to reade to him when he was a-bed. One of his Readers was parson Jones, his wife, of Wotton. I have heard her daughter (who had no more Witt) glory what a brave reader her mother was, and how Sir Harry's Worship much delighted to heare her. But his dearest deare was Mris Anne Vavasour. He erected a noble altar monument of marble wheron his effigies in armour lay; at the feet was the *Effigies* of his mistresse, Mris Anne Vavasour. Which occasioned these verses:

Her lies the good old Knight Sir Harry,
Who loved well, but would not marry;
While he lived, and had his feeling,
She did lye, and he was kneeling,
Now he's dead and cannot feele
He doeth lye and shee doeth kneele.

Some Bishop did threaten to have this Monument defaced; at least, to remove Mris A. Vavasour's *effigies.*

WILLIAM LEE

Inventor. Educated at Christ's and St John's Colleges, Cambridge. He acquired an aversion to hand-knitting, because a young woman to whom he was paying his addresses seemed, when he visited her, to be always more mindful of her knitting than of his presence. He therefore invented the Stocking Frame, which Queen Elizabeth came to see in action. But she was disappointed by the coarseness of the work, having hoped it would make silk stockings, and refused to grant the monopoly he asked for. Lee altered the machine, and produced a pair of silk stockings in 1598, which he presented to the Queen, but Elizabeth now feared that the invention would prejudice hand-knitters, and it was consequently discouraged. As King James took up a similar attitude, Lee went to France, where he had been promised great rewards by King Henri IV, but the latter's assassination disappointed these hopes, and Lee died of grief at Paris in 1610.

He was the first Inventor of the Weaving of Stockings by an Engine of his contrivance. He was a Sussex man borne, or els lived there. He was a poor Curate, and, observing how much paines his Wife tooke in knitting a payre of Stockings, he bought a Stocking and a halfe, and observed the contrivance of the Stitch, which he designed in his Loome, which (though some of the appendent Instruments of the Engine be altered) keepes the same to this day. He went into France, and dyed there before his Loome was made there. So the Art was, not long since, in no part of the world but England. Oliver Protector made an Act that it should be Felonie to transport this Engine. This Information I tooke from a Weaver (by this Engine) in Pear-poole lane, 1656. Sir John Hoskyns, Mr Stafford Tyndale, and I, went purposely to see it.

It ought never to be forgott, what our ingenious Countrey-Man Sir Christopher Wrenn proposed to the Silke-Stocking-Weavers of London, viz. a way to weave seven pair or nine paire of stockings at once (it must be an odd Number). He demanded four hundred pounds for his Invention: but the weavers refused it, because they were poor: and besides, they sayd, it would spoile their Trade; perhaps they did not consider the Proverb, That Light Gaines, with quick returnes, make heavy Purses. Sir Christopher was so noble, seeing they would not adventure so much money, he breakes the Modell of the Engine all to pieces, before their faces.

RICHARD LOVELACE

Born 1618. Cavalier and poet. He was the heir to great estates in Kent, and was educated at Oxford, where he was described by Anthony Wood as *the most amiable and beautiful person that eye ever beheld.* Leaving Oxford, he repaired in great splendour to the Court, and served in the Scottish expeditions of 1639. For presenting the Kentish Petition in favour of the King in 1642, he was thrown into the Gatehouse Prison, where he wrote the poem *Stone walls do not a prison make, nor iron bars a cage.* He rejoined Charles I in 1645, and served with the French King in 1646. It being reported that he was killed, his betrothed Lucy Sacheverell (Lucasta) married another man. Lovelace was again imprisoned in 1648, and while in prison he prepared his poems for the press. He had by now spent his whole fortune in support of the Royalist cause, whereupon he grew, says Wood, *very melancholy (which brought him at length into a consumption) became very poor in body and person, was the object of charity, went in ragged cloaths (whereas when he was in his glory he wore cloth of gold and silver) and mostly lodged in obscure and dirty places, more befitting the worst of beggars and poorest of servants.* He died in 1658.

RICHARD LOVELACE, Esq; he was a most beautifull Gentleman.

Obiit in a Cellar in Long Acre, a little before the Restauration of his Majestie. Mr Edmund Wyld, etc, have made collections for him, and given him money. George Petty, Haberdasher, in Fleet Street, carried xxs. to him every Monday morning from Sir John Many and Charles Cotton, Esq, for many moneths, but was never repayd.

One of the handsomest men in England. He was an extraordinary handsome Man, but prowd. He wrote a Poem called *Lucasta.*

HENRY MARTEN

Born 1602. Regicide. Member of the Short and Long Parliaments, where he was the leader of anti-Royalist feeling, saying that *he did not think one man wise enough to govern all.* Charles I demanded that Marten should be tried for High Treason, and excepted him from pardon. When the Civil War broke out, Marten subscribed £1,200 to the Parliamentary cause, and undertook to raise a regiment of horse. He was made Parliamentary Governor of Reading, but he was committed to the Tower in 1643 for saying that *it were better one family should be destroyed than many.* He was readmitted to Parliament in 1646, however, and became the leader of the extreme party. He was one of the King's judges, and it is said that when it came to Cromwell's turn to affix his name to the warrant of King Charles's execution, he wrote his signature hurriedly and then, in a burst of mirth, he smeared the ink of his pen across the face of Henry Marten, the secretary. On Charles II's return, Marten gave himself up, but was excepted from Indemnity and imprisoned until his death in 1680.

HENRY MARTIN, esq, son and heir of Sir Henry Martin, Knight, Judge of the Arches, was of the University of Oxford, travelled France, but never Italie. His staturc was but middling; his habit moderate; his face not good. Sir Edward Baynton was wont to say that his company was incomparable, but that he would be drunke too soone.

His father found out a rich Wife for him, whom he married something unwillingly. He was a great lover of pretty girles, to whom he was so liberall that he spent the greatest part of his estate. When he had found out a maried woman that he liked (and he had his Emissaries, male and female, to looke out) he would contrive such or such a good bargain, 20 or 30 pounds per annum under rent, to have her neer him. He lived from his wife a long time. If I am not mistaken, shee was sometime distempered by his unkindnesse to her.

King Charles I had a complaint against him for his Wenching. It happened that Henry was in Hyde parke one time when his Majestie was there, goeing to see a Race. The King espied him, and sayd aloud, Let that ugly Rascall be gonne out of the Parke, that whore-master, or els I will not see the sport. So Henry went away patiently, *sed manebat alta mente repostum* [but it lay stored up deep in his heart]. That Sarcasme raysed the whole Countie of Berks against him. He was as far from a Puritane as light from darknesse. Shortly after (1641) he was chosen Knight of the Shire of that Countie, *nemine contradicente* [no contrary votes], and proved a deadly Enemy to the King.

He was a great and faithfull lover of his Countrey, and never gott a farthing by the Parliament. He was of an incomparable Witt for Repartes; not at all covetous; humble, not at all Arrogant, as most of them were; a great cultor of Justice, and did always in the House take the part of the oppressed.

His speeches in the House were not long, but wondrous poynant, pertinent, and witty. He was exceedingly happy in apt instances. He alone haz sometimes turned the whole House. Makeing an invective speech one time against old Sir Henry Vane; when he had don with him, he said, But for young Sir Harry Vane; and so sate him downe. Severall cryed out, What have you to say to young Sir Harry? He rises up: Why! if young Sir Harry lives to be old, he will be old Sir Harry! and so sate downe, and set the House a-laughing, as he oftentimes did. Oliver Cromwell once in the House called him, jestingly or scoffingly, Sir Harry Martin. H.M. rises and bowes; I thanke your *Majestie*. I always thought when you were a *King* I should be Knighted. A godly member made a Motion to have all profane and unsanctified persons expelled the Houses. H.M. stood up and moved that all Fooles might be putt out likewise, and then there would be a thin House. He was wont to sleepe much in the House (at least dog-sleepe). Alderman Atkins made a Motion that such scandalous members as slept, and minded not the businesse of the House, should be putt out. H.M. starts up: Mr Speaker, a motion has been to turne out the Nodders, I desire the Noddees [*noddies, noodles*] may also be turnd out.

His short lettre to his cosen Stonehouse of Radley by Abingdon that *if his Majestie should take advice of his Gunsmiths and powder-men, he would never have peace* – from Sir John Lenthall: as also of his draweing the Remonstrance of the Parliament when 'twas formed a Commonwealth –

within five or six lines of the beginning he sayes *restored to it's auncient Goverment of a Commonwealth*. When 'twas read Sir Henry Vane stood up and repremanded and wondred at his impudence to affirme such a notorious Lye. H.M., standing up, meekely replied that *there was a Text had much troubled his spirit for severall dayes and nights of the man that was blind from his mother's womb whose sight was restored at last*, i.e. was restored to the sight which he should have had.

Henry Martin made a Motion in the House to call the Addressers to account (viz. those that addressed to Richard Cromwell, Protector, to stand by him with their lives and fortunes) and that all the addressers that were of it (of the House) might be turned out as enemies to the Commonwealth of England and betrayers of their Trust to bring in Government by a single person. Had not Dick Cromwell sneak't away then, it is certain that the Rump would have cutt off his Head, as I am well assured from a deare friend of mine.

H.M. sayd that he had seen the Scripture fulfilled: *Thou hast exalted the humble and meeke; thou hast filled the emptie, and the rich hast thou sent emptie away.*

Anno 1660 he was obnoxious for having been one of the late King's Judges, and he was in very great danger to have suffred as the others did (he pleaded only the King's Act of Proclamation at Breda which he shewd in his hand) but (as he was a Witte himselfe) so the Lord Falkland saved his life by Witt, saying, Gentlemen, yee talke here of makeing a Sacrifice; it was the old Lawe, all Sacrifices were to be without spott or blemish; and now you are going to make an old Rotten Rascall a Sacrifice. This Witt tooke in the House, and saved his life.

He was first a prisoner at the Tower; then at Windsore (removed from thence because he was an eie-sore to his Majestie) from thence to Chepstowe, where he is now (1680). During his imprisonment, his wife relieved him out of her joincture, but she dyed.

When his study was searcht they found letters to his Concubine, which was printed 4to. But 'tis not to his disgrace; there is Witt and good nature in them.

ANDREW MARVELL

Born 1621. Poet and satirist. He travelled on the Continent for four years. In 1653 he became tutor to Cromwell's ward, William Dutton, and in 1657 was made Milton's assistant in the Latin secretaryship to the Council. After the Restoration he entered Parliament, became a violent politician with strong Republican leanings, and wrote satires and pamphlets, attacking first the ministers but afterwards Charles II himself. Despite this he remained a favourite with the King, who offered him a place at Court and a present of £1,000, which were both declined. From 1660 to 1678 he wrote a series of newsletters to his constituents at Hull, chronicling the debates in the House of Commons. But his fame rests upon his poems written in praise of gardens and country life. He died in 1678.

He was of middling stature, pretty strong sett, roundish faced, cherry cheek't, hazell eie, browne haire. He was in his conversation very modest, and of very few words: and though he loved wine he would never drinke hard in company, and was wont to say that, he would not play the good-fellow in any man's company in whose hands he would not trust his life. He had not a generall acquaintance.

In the time of Oliver the Protector he was Latin Secretarie. He was a great master of the Latin tongue; an excellent poet in Latin or English: for Latin verses there was no man could come into competition with him.

I remember I have heard him say that the Earle of Rochester was the only man in England that had the true veine of Satyre.

His native towne of Hull loved him so well that they elected him for their representative in Parliament, and gave him an honourable pension to maintaine him.

He kept bottles of wine at his lodgeing, and many times he would drinke liberally by himselfe to refresh his spirits, and exalt his Muse. (I remember I have been told that the learned Goclenius (an High-German) was wont to keep bottells of good Rhenish-wine in his studie, and, when his spirits wasted, he would drinke a good Rummer of it.)

Obiit Londini, Aug. 18, 1678; and is buried in St Giles church in-the-fields about the middle of the south aisle. Some suspect that he was poysoned by the Jesuites, but I cannot be positive.

THOMAS MAY

Born 1595. Poet and historian. The son of Sir Thomas May, he went to Cambridge and thence to Gray's Inn, but soon discarded law for literature. In 1622 he produced his first comedy, *The Heir*, and also a translation of Virgil's *Georgics*. Six years later appeared his translation of *Lucan*, which gained him the favour of Charles I, at whose command he wrote two poems, each in seven books, *The Reigne of King Henry II* and *The Victorious Reigne of King Edward III*. But when the Civil War broke out, May took the side of the Parliament and was made Secretary to the Long Parliament, the historian of which he became. *The History of the Parliament of England, which began Nov. 3, 1640*, was published in 1647: the narrative closes with the Battle of Newbury (1643) and is prefaced with a short review of the preceding reigns from that of Elizabeth. May was also the author of several tragedies, which exhibit either featureless mediocrity or pretentious extravagance. He died in 1650.

As to Tom May, Mr Edmund Wyld told me that he was acquainted with him when he was young, and then he was as other young men of this Towne are, *scil.* he was debaucht *ad omnia*: but doe not by any meanes take notice of it; for we have all been young. But Mr Marvel in his Poems upon Tom May's death falls very severe upon him.

A great acquaintance of Tom Chaloner. Would, when *inter pocula* [in his cups], speake slightingly of the Trinity.

He stood Candidate for the Laurell after B. Jonson; but Sir William Davenant caried it.

Amicus: Sir Richard Fanshawe. Mr Emanuel Decretz (Serjeant Painter to King Charles Ist) was present at the debate at their parting before Sir Richard went to the King, where both Camps were most rigorously banded.

His translation of Lucan's excellent Poeme made him in love with the Republique, which Tang stuck by him.

Came of his death after drinking with his chin tyed with his cap (being fatt); suffocated.

SIR HUGH MIDDLETON

Born 1560. Merchant. He traded as a goldsmith, banker, and cloth-maker. Alderman of Denbigh 1597. M.P. for Denbigh 1603, 1614, 1620, 1623, 1625, and 1628. He built the New River from Chadwell to London: this canal, which was about thirty-eight miles long, ten feet wide, and four feet deep, was completed in 1613. King James paid half the cost in return for half the profits. Middleton also obtained large profits from the lead and silver mines in Cardiganshire 1617. Began reclaiming Brading Harbour 1620. Created baronet 1622. Died 1631.

MR INGELBERT was the first Inventer or Projector of bringing the water from Ware to London called *Middleton's water*. He was a poore-man, but Sir Hugh Middleton, Alderman of London, moneyed the businesse; undertooke it; and gott the profit and also the Credit of that most usefull Invention, for which there ought to have been erected a Statue for the memory of this poore-man from the City of London.

A Country Fellow seeing them digging the Channel for the new River said, that he would save them 2000 pounds, that is, he would turn up the Earth with a Plough; and had strong Ploughs and Harness made purposely, which was drawn by 17 Horses, and sav'd a vast deal of Expence.

This Sir Hugh Middleton had his Picture in Goldsmyth's hall with a Waterpott by him, as if he had been the Sole Inventor. Mr Fabian Philips sawe Ingolbert afterwards, in a poore Rug-gowne like an Almes-man, sitting by an apple-woman at the Parliament-stayres.

Memorandum: that now (1682) London is growne so populous and big that the New River of Middleton can serve the pipes to private houses but twice a weeke.

JOHN MILTON

Born 1608. Poet and statesman. He first struck a distinctive note in the stately ode *On the Morning of Christ's Nativity*. Having given up the idea of entering the Church, for which his father had intended him, he lived at Horton in Bucks with his father until 1637, reading the classics and preparing himself for his vocation as a poet. Here he wrote *L'Allegro* and *Il Penseroso* in 1632, *Comus* in 1634, and *Lycidas* in 1637. From 1637 to 1639, he travelled abroad and visited Grotius and Galileo. In June 1642 he married Mary Powell and next year published his pamphlet on *The Doctrine and Discipline of Divorce*, which made him notorious. In 1645 he published his *Tractate of Education* and the *Areopagitica* on the liberty of the press: but within five years Milton himself was working as Censor of Publications for the Commonwealth. After the execution of Charles I, he was appointed Latin Secretary to the newly formed Council of State and retained this post until the Restoration, when he was arrested and fined, losing the greater part of his fortune. He was soon released from custody, however, and returned to his poetry, completing *Paradise Lost* in 1664. In 1663, being now totally blind and somewhat helpless, he asked his friend Dr Paget to recommend a wife to him: the lady chosen was Elizabeth Minshull, aged twenty-five, who survived him for fifty-three years. In 1671 *Samson Agonistes* and *Paradise Regained* were published. In Milton the influences of the Renaissance and of Puritanism met. To the former he owed his wide culture and his profound love of everything noble and beautiful, to the latter his lofty and austere character, and both these elements meet in his writings. Leaving Shakespeare out of account, he holds an indisputable place at the head of English poets. He died in 1674.

MR JOHN MILTON was of an Oxfordshire familie. His Grandfather was a Roman Catholic of Holton, in Oxfordshire, near Shotover.

His father was brought-up in the University of Oxon, at Christ Church, and his grandfather disinherited him because he kept not to the Catholique Religion (he found a Bible in English, in his Chamber). So therupon he came to London, and became a Scrivener (brought up by a friend of his; was not an Apprentice) and gott a plentifull estate by it, and left it off many yeares before he dyed. He was an ingeniose man; delighted in musique; composed many Songs now in print, especially that of *Oriana*. I have been told that the Father composed a Song of fourscore parts for the Lantgrave of Hess, for which his Highnesse sent a meddall of gold, or a noble present. He dyed about 1647; buried in Cripple-gate-church, from his house in the Barbican.

His son John was borne the 9th of December, 1608, *die Veneris* [Venus Day, i.e. Friday], half an hour after 6 in the morning, in Bread Street, in London, at the Spread Eagle, which was his house (he had also in that street another howse, the Rose; and other houses in other places). Anno Domini 1619, he was ten yeares old; and was then a Poet. His school-master then was a Puritan, in Essex, who cutt his haire short.

He went to Schoole to old Mr Gill, at Paule's Schoole. Went at his owne Chardge only, to Christ's College in Cambridge at fifteen, where he stayed eight yeares at least. Then he travelled into France and Italie (had Sir H. Wotton's commendatory letters). At Geneva he contracted a great friendship with the learned Dr Deodati of Geneva. He was acquainted with Sir

Henry Wotton, Ambassador at Venice, who delighted in his company. He was severall yeares beyond Sea, and returned to England just upon the breaking-out of the Civill Warres.

From his brother, *Christopher Milton:* when he went to Schoole, when he was very young, he studied very hard, and sate-up very late, commonly till twelve or one a clock at night, and his father ordered the mayde to sitt-up for him, and in those yeares (10) composed many Copies of Verses which might well become a riper age. And was a very hard student in the University, and performed all his exercises there with very good Applause. His first Tutor there was Mr Chapell; from whom receiving some unkindnesse (whipt him) he was afterwards (though it seemed contrary to the Rules of the College) transferred to the Tuition of one Mr Tovell, who dyed Parson of Lutterworth. He went to travell about the year 1638 and was abroad about a year's space, chiefly in Italy.

Immediately after his return he took a lodging at Mr Russell's, a Taylour, in St Bride's Churchyard, and took into his tuition his [Milton's] sister's two sons, Edward and John Philips, the first 10, the other 9 years of age; and in a yeare's time made them capable of interpreting a Latin authour at sight. And within three years they went through the best of Latin and Greek Poetts – Lucretius and Manilius, of the Latins (and with him the use of the Globes, and some rudiments of Arithmetic and Geometry). Hesiod, Aratus, Dionysius Afer, Oppian, Apollonii *Argonautica*, and Quintus Calaber. Cato, Varro and Columella *De re rustica* were the very first Authors they learn't. As he was severe on the one hand, so he was most familiar and free in his conversation to those to whome most sowre in his way of education. N.B. he mad his Nephews Songsters, and sing, from the time they were with him.

His first wife (Mrs Powell, a Royalist) was brought up and lived where there was a great deale of company and merriment, dancing, etc. And when she came to live with her husband, at Mr Russell's, in St Bride's Churchyard, she found it very solitary; no company came to her; oftimes heard his Nephews beaten and cry. This life was irkesome to her, and so she went to her Parents at Fost-hill. He sent for her, after some time; and I thinke his servant was evilly entreated: but as for matter of wronging his bed, I never heard the least suspicions; nor had he, of that, any Jealousie.

Two opinions doe not well on the same Boulster; she was a Royalist, and went to her mother to the King's quarters, neer Oxford. I have perhaps so much charity to her that she might not wrong his bed: but what man, especially contemplative, would like to have a young wife environ'd and storm'd by the Sons of Mars, and those of the enemi partie? He parted from her, and wrote the Triplechord about divorce.

He had a middle wife, whose name was Katharin Woodcock. No child living by her.

He maried his third wife, Elizabeth Minshull, the year before the Sicknesse: a gent. person, a peacefull and agreable humour.

Hath two daughters living: Deborah was his amanuensis (he taught her Latin, and to reade Greeke to him when he had lost his eie-sight).

His sight began to faile him at first upon his writing against Salmasius, and before 'twas full compleated one eie absolutely faild. Upon the writing of other bookes, after that, his other eie decayed. His eie-sight was decaying about 20 yeares before his death. His father read without spectacles at 84. His mother had very weake eies, and used spectacles presently [*very soon*] after she was thirty yeares old.

His harmonicall and ingeniose Soul did lodge in a beautifull and well proportioned body. He was a spare man. He was scarce so tall as I am (*quaere*, quot feet I am high: *resp.*, of middle stature).

He had abroun hayre. His complexion exceeding faire – he was so faire that they called him *the Lady of Christ's College*. Ovall face. His eie a darke gray.

He was very healthy and free from all diseases: seldome tooke any physique (only sometimes he tooke manna): only towards his latter end he was visited with the Gowte, Spring and Fall.

He had a delicate tuneable Voice, and had good skill. His father instructed him. He had an Organ in his howse; he played on that most. Of a very cheerfull humour. He would be chearfull even in his Gowte-fitts, and sing.

He had a very good Memorie; but I believe that his excellent Method of thinking and disposing did much to helpe his Memorie.

His widowe haz his picture, drawne very well and like, when a Cambridge-schollar, which ought to be engraven; for the Pictures before his bookes are not at all like him.

His exercise was chiefly walking. He was an early riser (*scil.* at 4 a clock *manè*) yea, after he lost his sight. He had a man to read to him. The first thing he read was the Hebrew bible, and that was at 4 h. *manè*, ½ h. plus. Then he contemplated.

At 7 his man came to him again, and then read to him again, and wrote till dinner; the writing was as much as the reading. His daughter, Deborah, could read to him in Latin, Italian and French, and Greeke. Maried in Dublin to one Mr Clarke (sells silke, etc) very like her father. The other sister is Mary, more like her mother.

After dinner he used to walke 3 or four houres at a time (he always had a Garden where he lived) went to bed about 9.

Temperate man, rarely dranke between meales. Extreme pleasant in his conversation, and at dinner, supper, etc; but Satyricall. (He pronounced the letter R (*littera canina*) very hard – a certaine signe of a Satyricall Witt – *from John Dreyden.*)

All the time of writing his *Paradise Lost*, his veine began at the Autumnall Aequinoctiall, and ceased at the Vernall or thereabouts (I believe about May) and this was 4 or 5 yeares of his doeing it. He began about 2 yeares before the King came-in, and finished about three yeares after the King's restauracion.

In the 4th booke of *Paradise Lost* there are about six verses of Satan's Exclamation to the Sun, which Mr E. Philips remembers about 15 or 16 yeares before ever his Poem was thought of, which verses were intended for the Beginning of a Tragoedie which he had designed, but was diverted from it by other businesse.

He was visited much by the learned; more then he did desire. He was mightily importuned to goe into France and Italie. Foraigners came much to see him, and much admired [*wondered at*] him, and offer'd to him great preferments to come over to them; and the only inducement of severall foreigners that came over into England, was chiefly to see Oliver Protector, and Mr John Milton; and would see the hous and chamber wher he was borne. He was much more admired abrode then at home.

His familiar learned Acquaintance were Mr Andrew Marvell, Mr Skinner, Dr Pagett, M.D.

John Dreyden, Esq, Poet Laureate, who very much admires him, went to him to have leave to putt his *Paradise Lost* into a Drame in rythme. Mr Milton recieved him civilly, and told him *he would give him leave to tagge his Verses.*

His widowe assures me that Mr T. Hobbs was not one of his acquaintance, that her husband did not like him at all, but he would acknowledge him to be a man of great parts, and a learned man. Their Interests and Tenets did run counter to each other.

Whatever he wrote against Monarchie was out of no animosity to the King's person, or owt of any faction or interest, but out of a pure Zeale to the Liberty of Mankind, which he thought would be greater under a fre state than under a Monarchiall government. His being so conversant in Livy and the Roman authors, and the greatness he saw donne by the Roman commonwealth, and the vertue of their great Commanders induc't him to.

Mr John Milton made two admirable Panegyricks, as to Sublimitie of Witt, one on Oliver Cromwel, and the other on Thomas, Lord Fairfax, both which his nephew Mr Philip hath. But he hath hung back these two yeares, as to imparting copies to me for the Collection of mine. Were they made in commendation of the Devill, 'twere all one to me: 'tis the *ὕψος* [*ethos*] that I looke after. I have been told that 'tis beyond Waller's or anything in that kind.

GEORGE MONK
DUKE OF ALBEMARLE

Born 1608. Soldier. He served against the Irish Rebels, in command of a foot regiment, and returned with his Irish troops to help Charles I on the outbreak of the Civil War, but he was taken prisoner by Fairfax in 1644 and was imprisoned in the Tower. He was offered command in Ireland by Parliament on condition of taking the negative oath, after which he became Adjutant-General and Governor of Ulster. In 1650 he accompanied Cromwell to Scotland, becoming Commander-in-Chief the next year and completing the conquest of that country in 1652. He was then appointed Admiral and fought in the three great battles which practically ended the Dutch War, before resuming command of the Army in Scotland in 1654. In 1655 he greatly extended the powers of civil government which had been granted to him and his Council. He was implicitly trusted by Oliver Cromwell, on whose death he sent Richard Cromwell a letter of valuable advice. In 1659 he received Royalist overtures and marched slowly towards London, demanding the issue of writs for a new Parliament and ordering the guards to admit the secluded members. He was elected head of a new Council, General-in-Chief of the Land Forces, and Joint Commander of the Navy in February 1660, but he refused the offer of supreme power for himself. He then received from the King a commission as Captain-General, authorizing him to appoint a Secretary of State, and letters for the City, the Council, and the Parliament, which voted the restoration of the monarchy in May. On the King's arrival, Monk was knighted, and in July he was made a Knight of the Garter and created Baron Monck, Earl of Torrington, and Duke of Albemarle. Monk had great influence with the new government in military matters (his own regiments being retained by the King as his Household Guard), but less influence in political matters and none in ecclesiastical questions. He remained in London throughout the Plague of 1665, maintaining order and superintending preventive measures. In 1666 he was beaten by the Dutch in a naval battle off the North Foreland, but was immediately recalled to restore order in the City after the great Fire of London. He became First Lord of the Treasury in 1667, but retired in 1668 and died in 1670.

GEORGE MONK was borne in Devon, a second son of an ancient familie, and which had about Henry 8's time 10,000 pounds per annum (as he himselfe sayd).

He was a strong, lusty, well-sett young fellow; and in his youth happened to slay a man, which was the occasion of his flying into the Low-countries, where he learned to be a Soldier.

At the beginning of the late Civill-warres, he came over to the King's side, where he had command.

He was a prisoner in the Tower, where his semstress, Nan Clarges, a Blacksmith's daughter was kind to him; in a double capacity. It must be remembered that he then was in want, and she assisted him. (The trueth was, he was forgotten and neglected at Court, that they did not thinke of Exchanging him.) Here she was gott with child. She was not at all handsome, nor cleanly. Her mother was one of the *five Woemen-Barbers*.

There was a maried woman in Drury Lane that had clapt (i.e. given the pox to) a woman's husband, a neighbour of hers. She complained of this to her neighbour gossips: so they concluded on this Revenge, viz. to gett her and whippe her and to shave all the haire off her pudenda; which severities were executed and put into a Ballad. 'Twas the first Ballad I ever cared for the reading of; the Burden of it was thus:

Did yee ever heare the like
Or ever heard the same
Of five Woemen-Barbers
That lived in Drewry-lane?

Her brother, Thomas Clarges, came a ship-board to G.M. and told him his sister was brought to bed. *Of what?* sayd he. *Of a Son. Why then*, sayd he, *she is my Wife*. He had only this Child.

I have forgott by what meanes he gott his Libertie, and an Employment under Oliver (I thinke) at Sea, against the Dutch, where he did good service; he had courage enough. But I remember the Seamen would laugh, that instead of crying *Tack about*, he would say *Wheele to the right*, or *left*.

He had command in Scotland, where he was well-beloved by his Soldiers, and, I thinke, that countrie (for an Enemie). Oliver, Protector, had a great mind to have him home, and sent him a fine complementall letter, to come into England to advise with him. He sent his Highnesse word, that if he pleased he would come and wayte on him at the head of 10,000 men. So that designe was spoyled.

Anno 1659/60 (as I remember) he came into London with his Army, about one a clock P.M., being then sent for by the Parliament to disband Lambert's Armie. Shortly after he was sent for to the Parliament House; where, in the howse, a Chaire was sett for him, but he would not in modestie sitt downe in it. The Parliament (the Rumpe of a Howse: 'twas the wooden invention of Generall Browne, a woodmonger) made him odious to the Citie, purposely, by pulling downe and burning their gates (which I myselfe sawe). The Rumpe invited him to a great Dinner, shortly after, from whence it was never intended that he should have returned (of this I am assured by one of that parliament). The members stayed till 1, 2, 3, 4 a clock, but at last his Excellency sent them word he could not come. I beleeve he suspected some treacherie.

You must know that long before these dayes, Colonel Massey, and Thomas Mariett, of Whitchurch in Warwickshire, Esqre, held correspondence with his Majestie, who wrote them letters with his owne hand, which I have seen. Both these were now in London privately. Tom Mariett laye with me (I was then of the Middle Temple), G.M. lay at Drapers Hall in Throckmorton Street. Col. Massey (Sir Edward afterwards) and T. Mariett every day were tampering with G.M. as also Col. Robinson (afterwards Liewtenant of the Tower) whom I remember they counted not so wise as King Salomon, and they could not find any inclination or propensity in G.M. for their purpose, *scil.* to be instrumentall to bring in the King. Every night late, I had an account of all these Transactions in bed, which like a Sott as I was, I did not, while fresh in Memorie, committ to writing, as neither has T.M., but I remember in the maine, that they were satisfied he no more intended the King's restauration, when he came into England, or first came to London, then his Horse did. But shortly after, finding himselfe at a Losse; and that he was purposely made Odious to the Citie, as aforsayd – and that he was a lost man – by the Parliament; and that the generality of the Citie and countrey were for the restoring the King, having long groaned under the Tyranny of other Governments; he had no way to save himselfe but to close with the citie, etc, again.

Thredneedle Street was all day long, and late at night, crammed with multitudes, crying out, *A free Parliament*, *a free Parliament*, that the aire rang with their clamours. One evening, he comeing out on horseback, they were so violent that he was almost afrayd of himselfe, and so, to satisfie them (as they used to doe to importunate children), *Pray be quiet, yee shall have a free Parliament*. This about 7, or rather 8, as I remember, at night. Immediately, a Loud Holla and shout was given, all the Bells in Citie ringing and the whole Citie looked as if it had been in a flame by the Bonfires, which were prodigiously great and frequent and ran like a Traine over the Citie, and I saw some Balcones that began to be kindled. They made little Gibbetts and roasted Rumpes of mutton: nay, I sawe some very good Rumpes of Beefe. Healths to the King, Charles II, were drank in the streets by the Bonfires, even on their Knees, and this humor ran by the next night to Salisbury; where there was like Joy: so to Chalke, where they made a great Bonfire on the top of the hill; from hence to

Blandford and Shaftesbury, and so to Land's End, and perhaps it was so all over England. So that the return of his most gracious Majestie was by the hand of God, but as by this person meerly accidental, whatever the pompous history in 8vo sayes.

Well! a free-Parliament was chosen, and mett; Sir Harbottle Grimston, Knight and Baronet, was chosen Speaker. The first thing he putt to the Question was, Whether Charles Steward should be sent for, or no? Yea, yea, *nemine contradicente* [no one denying]. Sir John Greenvill (now Earle of Bathe) was then in Towne, and posted away to Bruxells, found the King at Dinner, little dreaming of so good Newes, rises presently from Dinner, had his Coach immediately made readie, and that night gott out of the King of Spaine's Dominions, into the Prince of Orange's country, I thinke, Breda.

Now, as the Morne growes lighter and lighter, and more glorious, till it is perfect day, so it was with the Joy of the People. Maypoles, which in the Hypocriticall times 'twas sin to sett up, were now sett up in every crosse way; and at the Strand, neer Drury Lane, was sett up the most prodigious one for height that (perhaps) was ever seen; they were faine, I remember, to have the assistance of the Sea-men's art to elevate it; that which remaines, being broken with a High Wind, I think about 1672, is but two parts of three of the whole height from the grownd, besides what is in the earth. The Juvenile and rustique folkes at that time had so much their fullnesse of desires in this kind that I think there must have been very few sett-up since. The Honours conferred on G.M. every one knowes.

His sence might be good enough, but he was slow, and heavie. He dyed and had a magnificent Funerall, suitable to his Greatnesse. His figure in his robes was very artificially donne, which laye in a Catafalco under a Canopie, in or neer the East End of Westminster Abbey, a moneth or six weekes. Seth Ward, Lord Bishop of Sarum (his great acquaintance) preached his Funerall Sermon.

His eldest Brother dyed *sine prole* [without issue], about the time of the King's returne. His other Brother was made Bishop of Hereford. G.M. and his Duchess dyed within a day or two of each other. The Bishop of Sarum told me that he did the last office of a Confessor to his Grace; and closed his Eies (as his Lordship told me himselfe).

Some moneths before G.M.'s comeing into England, the King sent Sir Richard Grenvill (since Earl of Bath) to him to negotiate with him that he would doe him service, and to correspond with him. Said he, If opportunity be, I will doe him service, but I will not by any meanes have any correspondence with him; and he did like a wise man in it, for he would certainly have been betrayed.

'Twas shrewd advice which Wyld, then Recorder of London, gave to the Citizens, i.e. to keep their purse-strings fast, els, the Parliament would have payd the Army, and kept out the King.

He was first an Ensigne, and after a Captain, in the Lowe-countreys, and for making false musters was like to have been . . . , which he afterwards did not forget.

This underneath was writt on the Dore of the House of Commons:

Till it be understood
What is under Monke's hood,
The Citizens putt in their hornes,
Until the ten days are out,
The Speaker haz the Gowt,
And the Rump, they sitt upon Thornes.

SIR JONAS MOORE

Born 1617. Mathematician. Tutor to the Duke of York 1647, from which post he was ousted by what he called *the malicious and cunning subtlety* of Anthony Ascham. Surveyor of the Fen Drainage System 1649. Sent to report on the fortification of Tangier 1663. Knighted and Surveyor-General of the Ordnance 1663. Published *Arithmetick* and *A New System of Mathematicks*. Died 1679.

SIR JONAS MOORE was borne at Whitelee in Lancashire, towards the Bishoprick of Durham. He was inclined to Mathematiques when a boy, which some kind friends of his putt him upon, and instructed him in it, and afterwards Mr Oughtred more fully enformed him; and then he taught Gentlemen in London, which was his livelyhood.

He was one of the most accomplisht Gentlemen of his time; a good Mathematician, and a good Fellowe.

When the great Levell of the Fennes was to be surveyed, Mr Wyld who was his Scholar and a Member of Parliament was very instrumentall in helping him to the employment of Surveying it, which was his Rise, which I have heard him acknowledge with much gratitude before severall persons of quality, since he was a Knight, and which evidenced an excellent good nature in him.

When he surveyed the Fennes, he observed the Line that the Sea made on the Beach, which is not a straight line, by which meanes he gott great

Credit in keeping-out the sea in Norfolke; so he made his Bankes against the sea of the same line that the sea makes on the Beach; and no other could doe it, but that the sea would still breake-in upon it.

He made a Modell of a Citadell for Oliver Cromwell, to bridle the City of London, which Mr Wyld has; and this Citadell was to have been the Crosse building of St Paule's church.

Sciatica: he cured it by boyling his Buttock.

The Duke of Yorke said that: Mathematicians and Physicians had no Religion: which being told to Sir Jonas More, he presented his duty to the D.Y. and wished, with all his heart that his Highnesse *were a Mathematician too*: this was since he was supposed to be a Roman Catholic.

He dyed at Godalmyng, and was buried at the Tower Chapell, with sixty peices of Ordinance (equall to the number of his yeares). He alwayes intended to have left his Library of Mathematicall bookes to the Royall Societie, of which he was a Member; but he happened to dye without making a Will, wherby the Royal Societie have a great Losse.

His only Sonne, Jonas, had the honour of Knighthood conferred upon him, August 9, 1680, at Windsor; his Majestie being pleased to give him this Marke of his Favour *as well in consideration of his owne abilities, as of the faithfull service of his father deceased* – but young Sir Jonas, when he is old, will never be *old Sir Jonas*, for all the Gazette's elogie.

I remember Sir Jonas told us that a Jesuite (I think 'twas Grenbergerus, of the Roman college) found out a way of Flying, and that he made a youth performe it. Mr Gascoigne taught an Irish boy that way, and he flew over a River in Lancashire (or therabout) but when he was up in the ayre, the people gave a shoute, wherat the boy being frighted, he fell downe on the other side of the river, and broke his legges, and when he came to himselfe, he sayd that he thought the people had seen some strange apparition, which fancy amazed him. This was anno 1635, and he spake it in the Royall Societie, upon the account of the Flyeing at Paris, two yeares since.

SIR ROBERT MORAY

He was the son of Sir Mungo Moray. He served in the French Army, where he was highly favoured by Cardinal Richelieu. He returned to England at the outbreak of the Civil War and was knighted by Charles I at Oxford in 1643. He then returned to France, where he became on good terms with Cardinal Mazarin. In 1645 he was captured in Bavaria, but was released in order to negotiate a treaty secretly between France and Scotland, by which it was proposed to attempt the restoration of Charles I. Moray recommended Charles's surrender to the Scots and was with him at both Newark and Newcastle. A plan for the King's escape from Scottish custody was frustrated only by the royal captive's timidity. Moray resumed his career in France, in command of the Scots Regiment, after the downfall of the monarchy in England, and the Scottish Parliament sent cargoes of prisoners to him to recruit his corps. He later joined Charles II in Paris, in 1654, after the collapse of the Highland rising. In 1663 Moray was appointed Lord of the Exchequer for Scotland and Deputy Secretary: thenceforward down to 1670, the government of that country was mainly carried on by Lauderdale, the King, and himself. He was devoid of ambition and the King used to say, in illustration of Moray's independence of character, that *he was head of his own church*. He died in 1673.

SIR ROBERT MORAY, Knight, was of the ancient family of the Morays in Scotland. He was borne (as I take it) in the Highlands. The Highlanders (like the Swedes) can make their owne Cloathes; and I have heard Sir Robert say that he could doe it. I have heard some of Ol. Cromwels army say, that the Highlanders ate only oate-meale and water and milk: that their Rivers did abound with Trowtes but they had not the witt to take them till the English taught 'em.

He spent most of his time in France. After his juvenile education at Schoole and the University he betooke himselfe to military employment in the service of Lewis the 13th. He was at last a Lieuetenant-Colonel. He was a great master of the Latin tongue and was very well read. They say he was an excellent soldier.

He was far from the rough humour of the Camp-breeding, for he was a person the most obliging about the Court and the only man that would doe a kindnesse *gratis* upon an account of Friendship. A Lacquey could not have been more obsequious and diligent. What I doe now averre I know to be true upon my owne score as well as others. He was a most humble and good man, and as free from Covetousness as a Carthusian. He was abstemious and abhorred woemen. His Majesty was wont to teaze at him. 'Twas pitty he was a Presbyterian.

He was the chiefe appuy of his Countreymen and their good Angel. There had been formerly a great friendship between him and the Duke of Lauderdale, till, about a yeare or two before his death, he went to the Duke on his returne from Scotland and told him plainly that he had betrayed his Countrey.

He was one of the first Contrivers and Institutors of the Royall Societie and was our first President, and performed his charge in the Chaire very well.

He was my most honoured and obligeing friend, and I was more obliged to him then to all the Courtiers besides. I had a great losse in his death, for, had he lived, he would have got some employment or other for me before this time. He had the King's eare as much as any one, and was indefatigable in his undertakings. I was often with him. I was with him three houres the morning he dyed; he seemed to be well enough. I remember he dranke at least ½ pint of faire water, according to his usuall custome.

His lodgeing where he dyed was the leaded pavillion in the garden at Whitehall. He dyed suddenly July 4th about 8 hours P.M. A.D. 1673. Had but one Shilling in his pocket, i.e. *in all*. The King buryed him. He lyes by Sir William Davenant in Westminster abbey.

He was a good Chymist and assisted his Majestie in his Chymicall operations.

SIR THOMAS MORE

Born 1478. Statesman and author. While practising the law, he won the favour of Henry VIII. He was knighted in 1514 and employed on various embassies. The King kept inviting him to Court, but More would not come; at last the King came uninvited to dine with him at his house in Chelsea. More had no illusions as to Henry VIII; when complimented on the King's favourable disposition, he replied: If my head should win him a castle in France it should not fail to go. He published *Utopia* (in Latin) in 1516. When Wolsey fell, the King appointed More as Lord Chancellor in his stead. Contrary to the usual practice, he refused all gifts from litigants. He soon fell into disfavour, because the King was determined to divorce Catherine of Aragon in order to marry Anne Boleyn, and More was unalterably opposed to the divorce. His incorruptibility when in office is shown by the fact that after his resignation he had only £100 a year. In spite of his opinions, the King invited him to his wedding with Anne Boleyn, but More refused the invitation. For refusing to take the Oath of Supremacy to Henry as head of the Church of England, More was beheaded on 7 July 1535. He was canonized in 1935.

SIR THOMAS MORE, Lord Chancellour: his Countrey-howse was at Chelsey, in Middlesex, where Sir John Danvers built his howse. Where the gate is now, adorned with two noble Pyramids, there stood anciently a Gate-house, which was flatt on the top, leaded, from whence there is a most pleasant prospect of the Thames and the fields beyond. On this place the Lord Chancellour More was wont to recreate himselfe and contemplate. It happened one time that a Tom of Bedlam came up to him, and had a Mind to have throwne him from the battlements, saying Leap, Tom, leap. The Chancellour was in his gowne, and besides ancient and not able to struggle with such a strong fellowe. My Lord had a little dog. Sayd he, Let us first throwe the dog downe, and see what sporte that will be. So the dog was throwne over. This is very fine sport, sayd my Lord, Let us fetch him up, and try once more. While the mad man was goeing downe, my Lord fastned the dore, and called for help, but ever after kept the dore shutt.

(Till the breaking-out of the Civil-warre, Tom o Bedlam's did travell about the Countrey: they had been poore distracted men that had been putt into Bedlam, where recovering to some sobernesse they were truncated to goe a begging, e.g. they had on their left arme an Armilla or Tinne printed in some workes: about 4 inches long: they could not gett it off. They wore about their necks a great Horne of an Oxe, in a string or Bawdrie, which, when they came to an house for Almes, they did sound; and they did putt the drinke given them into this Horne, whereto they did putt a stopple. Since the Warres I doe not remember to have seen anyone of them.)

In his *Utopia* his lawe is that the young people are to see each other stark-naked before marriage. Sir William Roper, of Eltham, in Kent, came one morning, pretty early, to my Lord, with a proposall to marry one of his daughters. My Lord's daughters were then both together abed in a truckle-bed in their father's chamber asleep. He carries Sir William into the chamber and takes the Sheete by the corner and suddenly whippes it off. They lay on their Backs, and their smocks up as high as their armepitts. This awakened them, and immediately they turned on their bellies. Quoth Roper, I have seen both sides, and so gave a patt on the buttock, he made choice of, sayeing, Thou art mine. Here was all the trouble of the wooeing. This account I had from my honoured friend old Mris Tyndale, whose grandfather, Sir William Stafford, was an intimate friend of this Sir W. Roper, who told him the story.

His discourse was extraordinary facetious [*amusing*]. Riding one night, upon the suddaine he crossed himselfe *majori cruce* [with the great sign of the cross] crying out Jesu Maria! doe not you see that prodigious Dragon in the skye? They all lookt up, and one did not see it, and nor the tother did not see it. At length one had spyed it, and at last all had spied. Whereas there was no such phantome, only he imposed on their phantasies.

After he was beheaded, his trunke was interred in Chelsey church, neer the middle of the South wall, where was some slight Monument erected. His head was upon London bridge. There goes this story in the family, viz. that one day as one of his daughters was passing under the Bridge, looking on her father's head, sayd she, That head haz layn many a time in my Lapp, would to God it would fall into my Lap as I passe under. She had her wish, and it did fall into her Lappe, and is now preserved in a vault in the Cathedral Church at Canterbury.

The Descendant of Sir Thomas, is Mr More, of Chilston, in Herefordshire, where, among a great many things of value plundered by the Soldiers, was his Chap [*jawbone*], which they kept for a Relique. Methinks 'tis strange that all this time he is not Canonised, for he merited highly of the Church.

SIR THOMAS MORGAN

Soldier. He served in the Low Countries and, under the command of Fairfax, in the Thirty Years War. Parliamentary Governor of Gloucester 1645. Captured Chepstow Castle and Monmouth 1645. Assisted General Monk in Scotland, and rose to the rank of Major-General 1651–7. Appointed second in command in Flanders 1657. Knighted on his return to England 1658. Morgan then rejoined Monk in Scotland and played a conspicuous part in the Restoration in Edinburgh. Governor of Jersey 1665. Died 1679. His alleged autobiography was published in 1699.

LITTLE Sir Thomas Morgan, the great soldier, was of meane Parentage in Monmouthshire. He went over to the Lowe-Countrie warres about 16, being recommended by some friend of his to some Commander there, who, when he read the letter, sayd, What! has my cosen recommended a *Rattoon* to me? at which he tooke pett, and seek't his fortune (as a soldier) in Saxon Weymar.

He spake Welch, English, French, High Dutch, and Low Dutch, but never a one well. He seated himself at Cheuston, in Herefordshire.

Sir John Lenthall told me that at the taking of Dunkyrke, Marshall Turenne, and, I thinke, Cardinall Mezarine too, had a great mind to see this famous Warrior. They gave him a visitt, and wheras they thought to have found an Achillean or gigantique person, they saw a little man, not many degrees above a dwarfe, sitting in a hutt of Turves, with his fellowe soldiers, smoaking a Pipe about 3 inches (or neer so) long, and did cry-out to the Soldiers, when angry with them, *Sirrah, I'le cleave your skull!* as if the wordes had been prolated by an Eunuch.

ROBERT MURRAY

Born 1635. Writer on trade. Took up his freedom in the Clothworkers' Company 1660. Invented ruled copy-books. Originated the idea of the Penny Post in London 1681. Appointed Paymaster of the 1714 Lottery. He published various proposals for the advancement and improvement of trade and the raising of revenue. Died 1725.

MR ROBERT MURRAY is a Citizen of London, a Milliner, of the Company of Cloathworkers. His father, a Scotchman; mother, English. Borne in the Strand.

Mr Murray was formerly clarke to the generall Company for the Revenue of Ireland, and afterwards clark to the Committee of the grand Excise of England; and was the first that invented and introduced into this city the Club of Commerce consisting of one of each Trade, whereof there were after very many erected and are still continued in this city. And also continued and sett-up the office or Banke of Credit at Devonshire house in Bishopsgate Street without, where men depositing their goods and merchandize were furnished with bills of current credit on $\frac{2}{3}$ or $\frac{3}{4}$ of the value of the said Goods answering to the intrinsique value of money, whereby the deficiency of coin might be fully subplyed: and for rendring the same current, a certain or competent number of traders (viz. 10 or 20 of each trade, wherof there be 500 severall trades within the citty) were to be associated or formed into such a society or Company of traders as might amongst them compleat the whole body of Commerce, whereby any possest of the said current credit might be furnisht amongst themselves with any kind of goods or merchandise as effectually as for money could do elsewhere.

The Penny-Post was sett up anno Domini 1680, Our Lady day, being Fryday, a most ingeniose and usefull Project. Invented by Mr Murray first, and then Mr Dockery joined with him.

RICHARD NAPIER

Born 1559. Astrologer. Matriculated from Exeter College, Oxford, 1577. Rector of Great Linford 1590. Studied astrology under Simon Forman, an astrologer and quack doctor, who claimed miraculous powers and obtained a large and disreputable practice, chiefly among Court ladies, for which he was frequently imprisoned at the instance of medical and other authorities. Forman *was used to say he would be a Dunce*, but Napier ultimately developed so much skill that Forman on his death in 1611 bequeathed him all his manuscripts. Licensed to practise medicine 1604. Died 1634.

MR ASHMOLE told me, that a Woman made use of a Spell to cure an Ague, by the Advice of Dr Nepier. A Minister came to her and severely repremanded her, for making use of a Diabolical help, and told her, she was in danger of Damnation for it, and commanded her to burn it. She did so, and her Distemper returned severely; insomuch that she was importunate with the Doctor to use the same again. She used it, and had ease. But the Parson hearing of it, came to her again, and thundred Hell and Damnation, and frighted her so, that she burnt it again. Whereupon she fell extremely Ill, and would have had it a Third time, but the Doctor refused, saying, *That she had contemned and slighted the power and goodness of the Blessed Spirits* (*or Angels*), and so she died. The cause of the Lady Honywoods Desparation, was that she had used a Spell to Cure her.

In Dr Bolton's *Sermons* is an Account of the Lady Honywood, who despaired of her Salvation. Dr Bolton endeavour'd to comfort her: Said she (holding a Venice-glass in her Hand) I shall as certainly be Damned, as this Glass will be broken: And at that word, threw it hard on the Ground; and the Glass remained sound; which did give her great comfort. The Glass is yet preserved among the *Cimelia* of the Family. This Lady lived to see descended from her (I think) Ninety, which is mentioned by Dr Bolton.

Dr Napier was uncle and Godfather to Sir Richard Napier: he was no Doctor, but a Divine and practised Physick; but gave most to the Poor that he got by it. When a Patient, or Querant came to him, he presently went to his Closet to Pray: It appears by his Papers, that he did converse with the Angel Raphael, who gave him the Responses, and told to admiration the Recovery or Death of the Patient. His knees were horny with frequent Praying. 'Tis certain, he foretold his own Death to a Day and Hour: he dyed Praying upon his Knees; being of a very great Age, 1634 April the First.

Sir Richard Napier is buryed at Lindford, but died at Besels-leigh; but before he came thither he laye at an Inne, where, when the Chamberlain brought him up to his Chamber, and the Dr look't on the bed and sawe a dead man lye in or on the bed – *What!* sayd he, *do you lodge me where a dead man lies?* Said the Chamberlain, *Sir, here is no dead man.* The Dr look't at it again, and sawe it was himselfe. And from thence he went (ill) to Besil's-leigh, and died.

JOHN OGILBY

Born 1600. Dancing master, author, and publisher. He was entrusted with *the poetical part* of Charles II's coronation in 1661. He later became a publisher, printing many splendid books, mostly in folio, *adorned with sculpture* by Hollar and other eminent engravers; and the King issued a proclamation in 1665 forbidding anyone to represent or *counterfeit the sculpture* in them for fifteen years. To facilitate the sale of these luxurious volumes, Ogilby established a lottery under Royal patronage, in which all the prizes were books of his own editing and publishing, and Pepys was successful in one of the draws; but Ogilby complained that the losing subscribers would not pay. John Ogilby was ridiculed by Dryden and Pope, and his name has become almost proverbial for a bad poet. He died in 1676.

MR JOHN OGILBY would not tell where in Scotland he was borne. He sayd drollingly that he would have as great contests hereafter for the place of his Birth, as was of Homer's.

He was of a Gentleman's family, and bred to his Grammar. His father had spent his Estate, and fell to decay, and was a Prisoner of the King's Bench, whom, together with his Mother, his son relieved by his own Industry (Spangles, needles), being then but about the age of 12 or 13 yeares. By the advantage of his Sonne's industry, he raysed a small summe of Money, which he adventured in the Lottery for the advancement of the Plantation in Virginia; and he gott out of prison by this meanes. His motto (of his lott) was,

I am a poor prisoner, God wott,
God send me a good Lott,
I'le come out of prison, and pay all my debt.

It so happened that he had a very good Lott, that did pay his Debts.

John (the Son) bound himself Apprentice to one Mr Draper, who kept a dancing-schoole in Grayes-Inne-lane, and in short time arrived to so great excellence in that art, that he found meanes to purchase his time of his Master and sett up for himselfe. Mr John Lacy, the Player, from whom I take this Information, was his apprentice.

When the Duke of Buckingham's great Masque was represented at Court, he was chosen (among the rest) to performe some extraordinary part in it; and high-danceing, i.e. vaulting and cutting capers being then in Fashion, he, endeavouring to doe something extraordinary, by misfortune of a false step when he came to the ground, did spraine a veine on the inside of his Leg, of which he was lame for ever after, which gave an occasion to say that *he was an excellent Dancing master*, *but never a good Leg.*

He taught 2 of the Lord Hopton's (then Sir Ralph) sisters to dance; and Sir Ralph taught him to handle the pike and Musket, *scil.* all the Postures.

He went over into Ireland to Thomas, Earle of Strafford, Lord Liuetenant there. Mr J.O. was in the Lord Lieutenant's Troope of Guards, and taught his Lady and Children to dance; that was his Place. And here it was that first he gave proofe of his inclination to Poetry, by Paraphrasing upon some of Aesop's *fables.*

Upon this Mr Chantrel putt him upon learning the Latin tongue (in the 40 aetat, plus) and taught him himself and tooke a great deale of paines with him. This was the first time he began his Latin. He printed Virgill, translated by himselfe into English verse, 8vo, dedicated to the Right Honourable William, Lord Marquesse of Hertford, who loved him very well. Aesop, in 4to, next. He writt a fine hand.

He had a warrant from the Lord Livetenant to be Master of the Ceremonies for that Kingdome; and built a little theatre in St Warburgh street, in Dublin. It was a short time before the Rebellion brake out, by which he was undon, and ran thorough many hazards, and particularly being like to have been blow'n-up at the Caste of Refarnum [Rathfarnham] neer Dublin.

He stayed in Ireland a good while after the Warres broke-out: came into England about the yeare 1648. He was wreckt at Sea, and came to London very poor, and went on foot to Cambridge.

After he had translated Virgil, he learnt Greeke in 1653 of Mr Whitfield, a Scotch Bishop's son, and grew so great a proficient in it that he fell-to to translate Homer's *Iliads*, 1660.

Next, as if by a prophetique spirit, foreseeing the restauration of King Charles II, and also the want there might be of Church Bibles, he printed the fairest Impression, and the most correct of English Bibles, in Royall and Imperiall paper, that ever was yet donne.

1662, he went into Ireland again, being then *by Patent* (before, but *by Warrant*) Master of the Revells (having disputed his Right with Sir William

Davenant, who had gott a Graunt) and built a noble theatre at Dublin, which cost 2000 pounds, the former being ruind and spoyled in the Troubles, and a cowhouse made of the stage.

His *Odysses* came out in 1665. People did then suspect, or would not beleeve that 'twas he was the Author of the paraphrase upon Æsop, and to convince them he published a 2nd volume, which he calles his *Æsopiques*, which he did during the Sicknesse, in his retirement at Kingston upon Thames.

His *History of China*, in folio, before the Fire; then his *History of Japan*. The generall and dreadfull Conflagration burn't all that he had, that he was faine to begin the world again, being then at best worth 5 pounds.

Being thus utterly undon again by the Fire, he made his Proposalls for the printing of a faire English *Atlas*, of which he lived to finish the Historys of Africa, America, and part of Asia. And then, being encouraged by the King and the Nobility to make an actuall Survey of England and Wales, he proceeded in it so far as to an actuall Survey of the Roads both in England and Wales, which composed his Volume of his *Britannia*.

He had such an excellent and prudentiall Witt, and master of so good addresse, that when he was undon he could not only shift handsomely (which is a great mastery) but he would make such rationall proposalls that would be embraced by rich and great men, that in a short time he could gaine a good Estate again, and never failed in any thing he evr undertooke but allwayes went through with profits and glorie.

WILLIAM OUGHTRED

Born 1574. Mathematician. Educated at Eton and King's College, Cambridge. Ordained 1603. Vicar of Albury in Surrey 1610. Published *Clavis Mathematicae* 1631. Wrote *Circles of Proportion* and other works. He invented trigonometrical abbreviations and introduced the multiplication and proportion signs. Died 1660.

His Father taught to write at Eaton, and was a Scrivener; and understood common Arithmetique, and 'twas no small helpe and furtherance to his son to be instructed in it when a schoole-boy. His Grandfather came from the North for Killing a man. The last Knight of the Family was one Sir Jeffrey Oughtred. I thinke a Northumberland family.

Anno Domini 1610 he was instituted and inducted into the Rectory or

Parsonage of Albury, in com. Surrey, worth a hundred pounds per annum: he was Pastor of this place fifty yeares.

William Oughtred, that was an Honour to the English Nation, maried Mrs Caryl (an ancient Family in those parts) by whom he had nine sonnes (most lived to be men) and four daughters. None of his sonnes he could make scholars.

He was a little man, had black haire, and blacke eies (with a great deal of spirit). His head was always working. He would drawe lines and diagrams on the Dust.

His oldest son Benjamin, who lives with my cosen Boothby (who carresses him, and gives him his Dyet, and a little House near to lie in) and now an old man, he bound Apprentice to a Watchmaker; who did worke pretty well, but his sight now failes for that fine worke. He told me that his father did use to lye a bed till 11 or twelve a clock, with his Doublet on, ever since he can remember. Studyed late at night; went not to bed till eleaven a clock; had his tinder box by him; and on the top of his Bed-staffe, he had his Inke horne fix't. He slept but little. Sometimes he went not to bed in two or three nights, and would not come downe to meales till he had found out the *quaesitum*.

He was more famous abroad for his learning, and more esteemed, then at home. Severall great Mathematicians came over into England on purpose to converse with him. His countrey neighbours (though they understood not his worth) knew that there must be extraordinary worth in him, that he was so visited by Foreigners.

When Mr Seth Ward, M.A. and Mr Charles Scarborough, D.M. came as in Pilgrimage, to see him and admire him, Mr Oughtred had against their comeing prepared a good dinner, and also he had dressed himselfe, thus: an old red russet cloath-cassock that had been black in dayes of yore, girt with a old leather girdle, an old fashion russet hatt, that had been a Bever, *tempore Reginae Elizabethae*. When learned Foraigners came and sawe how privately he lived, they did admire and blesse themselves, that a person of so much worth and learning should not be better provided for.

Seth Ward, M.A., a Fellow of Sydney Colledge in Cambridge (now Bishop of Sarum) came to him, and lived with him halfe a yeare (and he would not take a farthing for his diet) and learned all his Mathematiques of him. Sir Jonas More was with him a good while, and learn't; he was but an ordinary Logist before. Sir Charles Scarborough was his Scholar; so Dr John Wallis was his Scholar; so was Christopher Wren his scholar; so was Mr Smethwyck, R.S.S. But he did not so much like any as those that tugged and tooke paines to worke out Questions. He taught all free.

One Mr Austin (a most ingeniose man) was his scholar, and studyed so much that he became mad, fell a laughing, and so dyed, to the great griefe of the old Gentleman. Mr Stokes, another scholar, fell mad, and dream't that the good old Gentleman came to him, and gave him good advice, and so he recovered, and is still well.

He could not endure to see a Scholar write an ill hand; he taught them all presently [*immediately*] to mend their hands. Amongst others Mr Thomas Henshawe, who when he came to him wrote a lamentable hand, he taught to write very well. He wrote a very elegant hand, and drew his Schemes most neatly, as they had been cut in copper. His father (no doubt) was an ingeniose artist at the Pen and taught him to write so well.

He was an Astrologer, and very lucky in giving his Judgements on Nativities; he confessed that he was not satisfied how it came about that one might foretell by the Starres, but so it was that it fell out true as he did often by his experience find; he did beleeve that some genius or spirit did help.

The Countrey people did beleeve that he could conjure, and 'tis like enough that he might be well enough contented to have them thinke so.

He has told Bishop Ward, and Mr Elias Ashmole (who was his neighbour) that on this spott of ground (or leaning against this Oake, or that ashe) the Solution of such or such a Probleme came into my head, as if infused by a Divine Genius, after I had thought on it without Successe for a yeare, two, or three.

Ben Oughtred told me that he had heard his father say to Mr Allen (the famous Mathematicall Instrument-maker) in his shop, that he had found out the Longitude: *sed vix credo* [but I scarcely believe it].

I have heard Mr Hobbes say, and very truely, that with all his great skill in Algebra, he did never add one Proposition to Geometrie: he could bind up a Bundle well.

He was a great lover of Chymistry, which he studyed before his son Ben can remember, and continued it; and told John Evelyn, of Detford, Esq, R.S.S., not above a yeare before he dyed, that if he were but five yeares (or three yeares) younger, he doubted not to find out the Philosopher's stone. It was made of the harshest cleare water that he could gett, which he lett stand to putrify, and evaporated by cimmering.

His wife was a penurious woman, and would not allow him to burne candle after Supper, by which meanes many a good notion is lost, and many a Probleme unsolved; so that Mr Henshawe, when he was there, bought candle, which was a great comfort to the old man.

The right hon'ble Thomas Howard, Earle of Arundel and Surrey, Lord High Marshall of England, was his great Patron, and loved him intirely. One time they were like to have been killed together by the fall at Albury of a grott, which fell downe but just as they were come out. My Lord had many Grotts about his house, cutt in the Sandy sides of hills, wherin he delighted to sitt and discourse.

In the time of the Civill Warres the Duke of Florence invited him over, and offered him 500 pounds per annum; but he would not accept of it, because of his religion.

Notwithstanding all that has been sayd of this excellent man, he was in danger to have been Sequestred, and one Onslowe that was a great Stickler against the Royalists and a Member of the House of Commons and living not far from him – he translated his *Clavis* into English and dedicated it to him to clawe with him, and it did doe his businesse and saved him from Sequestration.

I have heard his neighbour Ministers say that he was a pittiful Preacher; the reason was because he never studyed it, but bent all his thoughts on the Mathematiques; but when he was in danger of being Sequestred for a Royalist, he fell to the study of divinity, and preacht (they sayd) admirably well, even in his old age.

He was a good Latinist and Graecian, as appears in a little Treatise of his against one Delamaine, a Joyner, who was so sawcy to write against him (I thinke about his *circles of Proportion*).

Nicolaus Mercator went to see him a few yeares before he dyed. 'Twas about Midsommer, and the weather was very hott, and the old gentleman had a good fire, and used Mr Mercator with much humanity (being exceedingly taken with his excellent Mathematicall Witt) and one piece of his courtesie was, to be mighty importunate with him to sett on his upper hand next the fire; he being cold (with age) thought he had been so too.

Before he dyed he burned a world of Papers, and sayd that the world was not worthy of them; he was so superb [*proud*]. He burned also severall printed bookes, and would not stirre, till they were consumed. His son Ben was confident he understood Magique.

He dyed the 13th day of June, 1660, in the yeare of his age eighty-eight plus odde dayes. Ralph Greatrex, his great friend, the Mathematicall Instrument-maker, sayed he conceived he dyed with joy for the comeing-in of the King, which was the 29th of May before. *And are yee sure he is restored? Then give me a glasse of Sack to drinke his Sacred Majestie's health.* His spirits were then quite upon the wing to fly away.

The 15th of June he was buried in the chancell at Albury. I had much adoe to find the very place where the bones of this learned and good man lay (and 'twas but 16 yeares after his death). When I first ask't his son Ben, he told me that truly the griefe for his father's death was so great, that he did not remember the place – now I should have thought it would have made him remember it the better – but when he had putt on his considering cap (which was never like his father's) he told as aforesaid, with which others did agree.

I have desired Mr John Evelyn, etc, to speake to our Patrone, the Duke of Norfolk, to bestowe a decent Inscription of marble on him, which will also perpetuate his Grace's fame.

JOHN OVERALL

Born 1560. Divine. Regius Professor of Theology at Cambridge 1596–1607. Master of Catherine Hall 1598–1607. Dean of St Paul's 1602. Took part in the Hampton Court Conference and the enlargement of the Church Catechism 1604. One of the Revisers of the Old Testament 1611. Bishop of Coventry and Lichfield 1614, and of Norwich 1618. He was not given to preaching, because *he found he had spoken Latin so long it was troublesome to him to speak English in a continued oration*. Died 1618.

I KNOW not what he wrote or whether he was any more than a common-prayer Doctor: but most remarqueable by his Wife, who was the greatest Beautie of her time in England. That she was so, I have it attested from the famous Limmer Mr Hoskins, and other old Painters, besides old Courtiers. She was not more beautifull than she was obligeing and kind, and was so tender-hearted that (truly) she could scarce denie any one. She had (they told me) the loveliest Eies that were ever seen, but wondrous wanton. When she came to Court, or to the Play-house, the Gallants would so flock about her. Richard the Earle of Dorset, and his brother Edward, since Earle, both did mightily adore her. And by their report he must have had a hard heart that did not admire her. Bishop Hall sayeth in his *Meditations* that there is none so old, that a beautifull person loves not; nor so young, whom a lovely feature moves not.

The good old Deane, notwithstanding he knew well enough that he was horned, loved her infinitely: in so much that he was willing she should enjoy what she had a mind to.

Among others who were charmed by her was Sir John Selby, of Yorkshire. Old Mris Tyndale (who knew her) remembres a song made of her and Sir John, part whereof was this, viz:

The Deane of Paule's did search for his wife,
and where d'ee thinke he found her?
Even upon Sir John Selbye's bed,
as flatte as any Flounder.

Of these two Lovers was made this following copie of Pastorall verses:

Downe lay the Shepherd Swaine
so sober and demure
Wishing for his wench againe
so bonny and so pure
With his head on hillock lowe
and his armes akimboe,
And all was for the losse of his
hye nonny nonny noe.

His Teares fell as thinne
as water from the still,
His haire upon his chinne
grew like Thyme upon a hill,
His cherry cheekes pale as snowe
did testify his mickle woe
And all was for the losse of his
hye nonny nonny noe.

Sweet she was, as kind a Love
as ever fetter'd Swayne;
Never such a daynty one
shall man enjoy again.
Sett a thousand on a rowe
I forbid that any showe
Ever the like of her
hye nonny nonny noe.

Face she had of Filberd hue
and bosom'd like a Swan
Back she had of bended Ewe,
and wasted by a span.
Haire she had as black as Crowe
from the head unto the toe
Downe downe all over her
hye nonny nonny noe.

With her Mantle tuck't up high
she foddered her flock
So bucksome and alluringly
her knee upheld her smock
So nimbly did she use to goe
so smooth she danc't on tip-toe,
That all the men were fond of her
hye nonny nonny noe.

She smiled like a Holy-day,
she simpred like the Spring,
She pranck't it like a Popingaie,
and like a Swallow sing:
She trip't it like a barren Doe,
she strutted like a gor-crowe,
Which made the men so fond of her
hye nonny nonny noe.

To sport it on the merry downe
to daunce the Lively Haye;
To wrastle for a green gowne
in heate of all the day
Never would she saye me no
yet me thought I had thô
Never enough of her
hye nonny nonny noe.

But gonne she is the prettiest Lasse
that ever trod on plaine.
What ever hath betide of her
blame not the Shepherd Swayne
For why? she was her owne Foe,
and gave herselfe the overthrowe
By being so franke of her
hye nonny nonny noe.

FINIS

JOHN PELL

Born 1611. Mathematician. M.A. of Trinity College, Cambridge, 1630. Professor of Mathematics at Amsterdam 1643, and at Breda 1646. Returned to England in 1652, and was employed by Cromwell as a diplomat in Switzerland 1654–8. Rector of Fobbing 1661–85. Vicar of Laindon 1663–85. D.D. Lambeth 1663. His mathematical reputation was great, but he accomplished little, and left nothing of moment. He died in poverty in 1685.

JOHN PELL, S.T. Dr, was the son of John, who was the son of John. His father dyed when his son John was but 5 yeares old and six weekes, and left him an excellent Library.

He went to Schoole at the Free-schoole at Stenning, a Burrough towne in Sussex, at the first Founding of the schoole. At 13 yeares and a quarter old he went as good a scholar to Cambridge, to Trinity Colledge, as most Masters of Arts in the University (he understood Latin, Greek, and Hebrew) so that he played not much (one must imagine) with his school-fellowes, for, when they had play-dayes, or after schoole-time, he spent his time in the Library aforesaid.

Before he went first out of England, he understood these Languages (besides his mother-tongue) viz. Latin, Greek, Hebrue, Arabique, Italian, French, Spanish, High-Dutch, and Low-Dutch.

Anno Domini 1632 he maried Ithamara Reginalds, second daughter to Mr Henry Reginalds of London. He had by her 4 sonnes and 4 daughters borne in this order S, D, D, S, D, S, D, S.

In the year 1638 Mr Theodore Haake came first to be acquainted with Mr Pell by Mr S. Hartlib's meanes, who having heard of his extraordinarie parts in all kinde of learning, especially the Mathematics, perswaded that the same might be farre more usefully employed and improoved for the publick advancement of Learning, he never left soliciting and engaging frends heer to perswade Mr Pell instead of keeping Scool, as he then did in Sussex, to come up to London, where he soon got into great esteem among the most learned, both Natives and Forreigners, with whom he conversed. But he so minded and followed still the Cultivating of his more abstracting Studies, and naturally averse from suing or stooping much for what he was worthy of, it was a good while before he obtained any suteable place or settlement.

Mr Haake recommended him once to my Lord Bishop of Lincoln (*quondam* Lord Keeper of England) who became very desirous to see the

Man, inviting them of purpose to dine once with his Lordship for the freer discourse of all sorts of literature and Experiments, to get a touch and taste that satisfaction Mr Pell could give him. Which proved so pertinent and abundant that my Lord put the question to him whether he would accept of a Benefice which he was ready, glad, and willing to bestow on him for his Encouragement. Mr Pell thankd his Lordship, saying he was not capacitate for that, as being no Divine and having made the Mathematics his main studie, for the great publick need and usefullnesse therof, which he had in a manner devoted himself to improve and advance to the uttmost of his reach and abilities. Which answer pleased my Lord so well that he replyed, Alasse! what a sad case it is that in this great and opulent kingdome there is no publick encouragement for the excelling in any Profession but that of the Law and Divinity. Were I in place as once I was, I would never give over praying and pressing his Majesty till a noble Stock and Fund might be raised for so fundamentall, universally usefull, and eminent Science as Mathematicks. And therupon his Lordship requested Mr Pell to befriend him with his visits as often as he could spare time, promising him always a very hearty welcome. Yet Mr Pell who was no Courtier came there no more.

In the mean time he communicated to his friends his excellent *Idea Matheseos* in half a sheet of paper, which got him a great deal of repute, both at home and abroad, but no other special advantage, till Mr John Morian, a very learned and expert Gentleman, gave Mr Haake notice that Hortensius, Mathematical Professor at Amsterdam, was deceased, wishing that their friend Mr Pell might succeed. Sir William Boswell, his Majestie's ambassador in Holland, being here then, Theodore Haake conferred with him about it, who promised all his assistance; and between them, and by these two, a call was procured from Amsterdam for Mr Pell, in 1643: and in May 1644 T.H. met him settled there on his return out of Denmarke. Where he was, among others, dearly welcome to Gerardus Joannes Vossius.

And soon after his fame was much augmented by his refuting a large book of Longomontanus *Quadratura*, which caused the Prince of Orange (Henry Frederick) being about to erect an Academie at Breda, to borrow Mr Pell from the Magistrate of Amsterdam, to grace his new Academe with a man of that fame for a few years. And there being comfortably stayed, the most learned of the then Parliament heer, jealous that others should enjoy a countryman of their own, they never left offers and promises till they got him hither to be – they gave out – Professor Honorarius heer. But the successe prov'd soon deficient, and reduced him to much inconvenience, as having now a charge of a pretty large Family, viz. his wife with 4 or 5 children. And this continued till in 1654 Oliver, Lord Protector, sent him Envoyé to the Protestant Cantons of Switzerland; resided chiefly at Zurich. He was sent out with the Title of Ablegatus, but afterwards he had order to continue there with the Title of Resident.

In 1658 he returned into England, and so little before the death of Oliver Cromwell that he never sawe him since he was Protector.

Memorandum that in his Negociation he did no disservice to King Charles IId, nor to the church, as may appeare by his letters which are in the Secretarie's Office.

Richard Cromwell, Protectoı, did not fully pay him for his business in Piedmont, wherby he was in some want; and so when King Charles II had been at home ten months, Dr Sanderson, Bishop of Lincoln, perswaded him to take Holy Orders.

Gilbert Sheldon, Lord Bishop of Lundon, gave Dr Pell the scurvy Parsonage of Lanedon cum Basseldon in the infamous and unhealthy (aguesh) Hundreds of Essex (they call it Kill-priest sarcastically) and King Charles the Second gave him the Parsonage of Fobing, 4 miles distant.

At Fobbing, seven curates dyed within the first ten yeares; in sixteen yeares, six of those that had been his Curates at Laindon are dead; besides those that went away from both places; and the death of his Wife, servants, and grandchildren.

Gilbert Sheldon being made Archbishop of Canterbury, John Pell was made one of his Cambridge Chapleines (he haz 2 Oxford Chaplaines and 2 Cambridge) and complaining one day to his Grace at Lambith of the unhealthinesse of his Benefice as abovesayd, sayd my Lord, I doe not intend that you shall live there. No, sayd Pell, but your Grace does intend that I shall die there.

Lord Brereton was sent to Breda to recieve the Instruction of this worthy Person, by his grandfather (George Goring, the Earle of Norwich) anno 1647, where he became a good proficient, especially in Algebra to which his Genius most inclined him and which he used to his dyeing day, which was 17 March, 1680: lies buried in St Martin's church in the Fields. I cannot mention this Noble Lord but with a great deale of Passion, for a more vertuous person (besides his great learning) I never knew. I have had the honour of his acquaintance since his comeing from Breda into England. Never was there greater love between Master and Scholar then between Dr Pell and this Scholar of his, whose death hath deprived this worthy Doctor of an ingeniose Companion and a usefull Friend.

Now by this time (1680) you doubt not but this great, learned man, famous both at home and abroad, haz obtained some considerable Dignity in the Church. You ought not in modestie to ghesse at lesse then a

Deanery. Why, truly, he is stak't to this poor preferment still! For though the parishes are large, yet (Curates, etc, discharged) he cleares not above 3-score pound per annum (hardly fourscore) and lives in an obscure lodging, three stories high, in Jermyn Street, next to the signe of the Ship, wanting not only bookes but his proper MSS which are many.

He could not cringe and sneake for preferment though otherwise no man more humble nor more communicative. He was cast into King's Bench prison for Debt Sept 7, 1680.

In March 1682 he was very kindly invited by Daniel Whistler, M.D., to live with him at the Physitians College in London, where he was very kindly entertained; which the Dr likt and accepted of, loving good cheer and good liquour, which the other did also; where eating and drinking too much, was the cause of shortning his daies. About the middle of June he fell extreme sick of a Cold and removed to a grandchild of his maried to one Mr Hastings in St Margaret's Churchyard, Westminster, neer the tower, who now (1684) lives in Brownlow Street in Drury Lane, where he was like to have been burnt in his bed by a candle. Nov 26, fell into convulsion fitts which had almost killed him.

Dr Pell haz often sayd to me that when he solves a Question, he straines every nerve about him, and that now in his old age it brings him to a Loosenesse.

Dr J. Pell was the first inventor of that excellent way or method of the marginall working in Algebra. He haz sayd to me that he did believe that he solved some questions *non sine Divino auxilio* [not without divine aid].

Dr Pell had a brother a Chirurgian and Practitioner in Physick, who purchased an Estate of the Natives of New-York and when he died left it to his Nephew John Pell, only son of the Doctor, who is a Justice of the Peace in New Yorke, and lives well. It is a great estate 8 miles broad and several miles long. Dr Pell thought to have gonne over to him.

Both his Parsonages are of the value of two hundred pounds per annum (or so accounted) but the Doctor was a most shiftless man as to worldly affaires, and his Tenants and Relations cousin'd him of the Profits and kept him so indigent that he wanted necessarys, even paper and Inke, and he had not 6d in his purse when he dyed, and was buried by the Charity of Dr Richard Busby and Dr Sharp, Rector of St Giles-in-the-fields and Dean of Norwich, who ordered his Body to lye in a Vault belonging to the Rector (the price is X pounds).

He dyed of a broaken heart.

WILLIAM PENN

Born 1644. Quaker and founder of Pennsylvania. Educated at Christ Church, Oxford, where he became a Quaker and was in consequence expelled from the University. For attacking the doctrines of the Trinity, the Atonement, and Justification by Faith, he was imprisoned in the Tower in 1668, where he wrote *No Cross, No Crown*. He was again imprisoned for preaching in 1671, and used his enforced leisure to write *The Great Cause of Liberty of Conscience*, an able defence of religious toleration. In 1681 he was granted the territory now forming the state of Pennsylvania by Charles II, and he determined to found there a community based upon the principles of toleration. But his later years were embittered by troubles in Pennsylvania, and by the dishonesty of one of his agents, who nearly ruined him and who was the cause of his being imprisoned for debt. He died soon after his release in 1718.

WILLIAM PENN was the eldest son of Sir William Penn, Knight, Admirall both of the English Navy before the Restauration of the King, and commanded as Captain-Generall under the Duke of York in 1665 against the Dutch Fleet. His father was a very good man, but no Quaker; was very much against his sonne.

He was mighty lively but with Innocence, and extremely tender under rebuke; and very early delighted in retirement; much given to reading and meditating of the Scriptures, and at 14 had marked over the Bible. Oftentimes at 13 or 14 in his meditations ravisht with joy, and dissolved into teares.

The first Sense he had of God was when he was 11 yeares old at Chigwell, being retired in a chamber alone; he was so suddenly surprized with an inward comfort and (as he thought) an externall glory in the roome that he has many times sayd that from thence he had the Seale of divinity and Immortality, that there was a God and that the Soule of man was capable of enjoying his divine communications. His schoolmaster was not of his Perswasion.

About the Plague, growing entirely solitary, was employed by his father in a Journey into Ireland to the Duke of Ormond's court: the diversions of which not being able to keepe downe the stronger motions of his Soule to a more religious and retired life, upon the hearing of one Thomas Lowe, a Tradesman, of Oxon at Cork, 1667, was so thoroughly convinced of the simplicity and selfe-deniall of the way of the people called Quakers that from thence he heartily espoused that Judgement and Beliefe.

Since which time he has passed a life of great variety of circumstances, both with respect to good and evill report, divers controversies orall and written, severall Imprisonments; one in Ireland, one in the Tower, 3rd in Newgate.

Notwithstanding those many odd adventures of his Life, he hath severall times found favour from his Majestie and also the D.Y., with divers of the Nobilitye, and men of Quality and learning in this Kingdome.

Travelled into Germany, Upper and Lower, annis 1671 and 1677, where severall were affected with his way. Did he gaine any to him in France? *Negat.*

His Majestie owing to his father 10,000 pounds (which, with the interest of it, came not to lesse than 20,000 pounds) did in consideration therof grant to him and his heirs a province in America which his Majesty was pleased to name Pennsylvania, the 4th day of March 1681. His Patent for Transylvania is from the beginning of the 40th degree to 43 degrees in Latitude, and 5 degrees in Longitude from Chisapeak-bay.

August 26, 1682, Saturday. This day about 4 a clock P.M., W. Penne, Esq, went towards Deale to launch for Pensylvania. God send him a prosperous and safe Voyage.

He speaks well the Latin and the French tongues, and his owne with great mastership. He was chosen, *nemine contradicente*, Fellow of the Royal Societie, London, with much respecte. He often declares in the Assemblies of his Friends, and that with much eloquence and fervency of spirit: by which, and his perpetuall attendances on King and Prince for the reliefs of his Friends, he often exposes his health to hazard.

W. Penn, Esq, married Gulielma Maria Springet, daughter of Sir William Springet, of the Springets of the Broyles in Sussex. She was a *posthuma* of her father, a young Gent. of Religion and courage who dyed at the Siege of Arundel. His daughter was his Image in person and qualities, virtuous, generous, wise, humble, plaine [*frank*]; generally beloved for those good qualities and one more – the great cures she does, having great skill in physic and surgery, which she freely bestows.

She early espoused the same way, about anno 1657. She was a great fortune to her husband, being worth *de claro* above 10,000 pounds. Her fortune, quality, and good humour gave her the importunity of many suitors of extraordinary condition, e.g. Lord Brookes and Lord John Vaughan, etc; but valueing the Unity of beliefe and selfe deniall of her profession above the glories of the World, resisted their motions till Providence brought a man of equall condicion and fortune to herself to the syncere embracing of the same Fayth, whose mariage haz been crowned with a continued affection.

Sir William Penn, Knight, his father, was a man of excellent naturall abilities, not equalled in his time for the knowledge of navall affayres; and instrumentall to the raysing of many families. Bred his son religiously; and, as the times grew loose, would have his sonn of the fashion, and was therfore extreme bitter at his sonne's retirement. But this lasted not alwayes; for, in the conclusion of his life, he grew not only kind, but fonde; made him the judge and ruler of his Family; was sorry he had no more to leave him (and yet, in England and Ireland, he left him 1500 pounds per annum). But, which is most remarkeable, he that opposed his sonne's way because of the crosse that was in it to the world's Latitude, did himselfe embrace this faith, recommending to his son the plainesse and selfe deniall of it, sayeing, *Keep to the plainesse of your way, and you will make an end of the Priests to the ends of the Earth*. And so he deceased, desiring that none but his son William should close his eies (which he did).

SIR WILLIAM PETTY

Born 1623. Political economist. He went to sea at an early age, but his precocious talents so excited the envy of his fellow-seamen that they deserted him on the coast of France with a broken leg. Instead of returning home, he studied on the Continent. He published economic treatises, the most important of which were entitled *Political Arithmetic* (collected edition 1690), a term signifying what we now call statistics. He died in 1687.

HIS father was by profession a clothier, and also did dye his owne cloathes: he left little or no estate to Sir William. About 12 or 13, i.e. before 15, he haz told me, happened to him the most remarkable *accident of life* (which he did not tell me) and which was the foundation of all the rest of his greatnes and acquiring riches. He haz told me that he never gott by Legacies, but only x pounds, which was not payd.

He enformed me that, about 15, in March, he went over into Normandy, to Caen, in a vessell that went hence, with a little stock, and began to play the merchant, and had so good successe that he maintained himselfe, and also educated himselfe; this I guessed was that most remarkable *accident* that he meant. Here he learn't the French tongue, and perfected himselfe in the Latin (before, but a competent smattering) and had Greeke enough to serve his turne. Here (at Caen) he studyed the Arts: he was sometime at

La Flesshe in the college of Jesuites. At 18, he was (I have heard him say) a better Mathematician then he is now; but when occasion is, he knows how to recurre to more mathematicall Knowledge. At Paris he studyed Anatomie, and read Vesalius with Mr Thomas Hobbes, who loved his company. Mr H then wrot his *Optiques*; Sir W.P. then had a fine hand in drawing and limning, and drew Mr Hobbes Opticall schemes for him, which he was pleased to like. At Paris, one time, it happened that he was driven to a great streight for money, and I have heard him say, that he lived a weeke on two peniworth (or 3, I have forgott which, but I thinke the former) of Walnutts.

He came to Oxon, and entred himselfe of Brasen-nose college. Here he taught Anatomy to the young Scholars. Anatomy was then but little understood by the university, and I remember he kept a body that he brought by water from Reding a good while to read upon some way soused or pickled. About these times Experimentall Philosophy first budded here and was first cultivated by these Vertuosi in that darke time.

Anno Domini 1650 happened that memorable accident and experiment of the reviving Nan Green a servant maid, who was hang'd in the castle of Oxon for murdering her bastard-child. After she had suffer'd the law, she was cut downe, and carried away in order to be anatomiz'd by some yong physitians, but Dr William Petty finding life in her, would not venter upon her, only so farr as to recover her life. Which being look'd upon as a great wonder, there was a relation of her recovery printed, and at the end several copies of verses made by the young poets of the Universitie were added.

He was about 1650 elected Professor of Musique at Gresham Colledge, by, and by the Interest of his Friend Captaine John Graunt (who wrote the Observations on the Bills of Mortality) and at that time was worth but fourtie pounds in all the world.

Shortly after, he was recommended to the Parliament to be one of the Surveyors of Ireland, to which employment Capt John Graunt's interest did also help to give him a Lift, and Edmund Wyld, Esq, also, then a Member of Parliament, and a good fautor of Ingeniose and good men, for meer meritt sake (not being formerly acquainted with him) did him great service, which perhaps he knowes not of.

Severall made offers to the Parliament to survey it (when the Parliament ordered to have it surveyed) for 4000 pounds, 5000 pounds, 6000 pounds; but Sir William (then Dr) went *lower* then them all and gott it. Sir Jonas More contemnd it as dangerous, loving to sleepe in a whole skin: he was afrayd of the Tories [*Irish bandits*].

By this Surveying Employment he gott an Estate in Ireland (before the restauration of King Charles II) of 18,000 pounds per annum, the greatest part wherof he was forced afterwards to refund, the former owners being then declared Innocents. He hath yet there 7 or 8000 pounds per annum and can, from the Mount Mangorton in the com. of Kerry, behold 50,000 Acres of his owne land. He hath an Estate in every province of Ireland.

The Kingdome of Ireland he hath surveyed, and that with that exactnesse, that there is no Estate there to the value of threscore pounds per annum but he can shew, to the value, and those that he employed for the Geometricall part were ordinary fellowes, some (perhaps) foot-soldiers, that circumambulated with their *box and needles*, not knowing what they did, which Sir William knew right well how to make use of.

I remember about 1660 there was a great difference between him and Sir Hierome Sanchy, one of Oliver's knights. They printed one against the other: this knight was wont to preach at Dublin. The Knight had been a Soldier, and challenged Sir William to fight with him. Sir William is extremely short sighted, and being the challengee it belonged to him to nominate place and weapon. He nominates, for the place, a darke Cellar, and the weapon to be a great Carpenter's Axe. This turned the knight's challenge into Ridicule, and so it came to nought.

Before he went into Ireland, he sollicited, and no doubt he was an admirable good Sollicitor. I have heard him say that in Sollliciting (with the same paines) he could dispatch severall businesses, nay, better than one alone, for by conversing with severall he should gaine the more knowledge, and the greater Interest.

In the time of the Warre with the Dutch, they concluded at the Councell-board at London, to have so many sea men out of Irland (I think 1500). Away to Irland came one with a Commission, and acquaints Sir William with it; sayes Sir William, You will never rayse this number here. Oh, sayd the other, I warrant you, I will not abate you a man. Now Sir William knew 'twas impossible, for he knew how many Tunne of shipping belongd to Ireland, and the rule is, to so many tunnes so many men. Of these shipps halfe were abroad, and of those at home so many men unfit. In fine, the Commissioner with all his diligence could not possibly rayse above 200 seamen there. So we may see how statesmen may mistake for want of this Politique Arithmetique.

Another time the Councell at Dublin were all in a great racket for the prohibition of Coale from England and Wales, considering that all about Dublin is such a vast quantity of Turfe; so they would improve their rents, sett poor men on worke, and the City should be served with Fuell cheaper. Sir William prima facie knew that this project could not succeed. Sayd he, If you will make an order to hinder the bringing-in of Coales by foreigne vessells, and bring it in Vessells of your owne, I approve of it very well: But for your supposition of the cheapnesse of the Turfe, 'tis true, 'tis cheape on the place, but consider carriage, consider the yards that must contayn such a quantity for respective houses, these yards must be rented; what will be the chardge? They supputated, and found that (every thing considered) 'twas much dearer then to fetch coale from Wales, or etc.

Sir W. Petty was a Rota man [*member of republican Rota Club*], and troubled Mr James Harrington with his Arithmeticall proportions, reducing Politie to Numbers.

Anno 1660 he came into England, and was presently [*at once*] recieved into good grace with his Majestie, who was mightily pleased with his discourse. He can be an excellent Droll (if he haz a mind to it) and will preach *extempore* incomparably, either the Presbyterian way, Independent, Cappucin frier, or Jesuite.

I remember one St Andrewe's day (which is the day of the Generall Meeting of the Royall Society for Annuall Elections) I sayd, Methought 'twas not so well that we should pitch upon the Patron of Scotland's day, we should rather have taken St George or St Isidore (a Philosopher canonized). No, said Sir William, I would rather have had it on St Thomas day, for he would not beleeve till he had seen and putt his fingers into the Holes, according to the Motto *Nullius in verba* [not bound to swear obedience to any man's dogma].

Anno Domini 1663 he made his double-bottom'd Vessell (launched about New-yeare's tide) of which he gave a Modell to the Royall Societie made with his owne hands, and it is kept in the Repository at Gresham College. It did doe very good service, but happned to be lost in an extraordinary storme in the Irish sea. About 1665 he presented to the Royall Societie a Discourse of his (in manuscript, of about a Quire of paper) of Building of Shippes, which the Lord Brounker (then President) tooke away, and still keepes, saying, 'Twas too great an Arcanum of State to be commonly perused; but Sir William told me that Dr Robert Wood, M.D. has a copie of it, which he himselfe haz not.

Anno Domini 1667 he maried on Trinity Sunday the relict of Sir Maurice Fenton, of Ireland, Knight, daughter of Sir Hasdras Waller of Ireland, a very beautifull and ingeniose Lady, browne, with glorious Eies, by whom he hath some sonnes and daughters, very lovely children, but all like the Mother. He has a naturall Daughter that much resembles him, no legitimate child so much, that acts at the Duke's Playhouse.

He is a proper handsome man, measured six foot high, good head of browne haire, moderately turning up. His eies are a kind of goose-gray, but very short sighted, and, as to aspect, beautifull, and promise sweetnes of nature, and they doe not decieve, for he is a marvellous good-natured person. Eie-browes thick, darke, and straight (horizontall).

He is a person of an admirable inventive head, and practicall parts. He hath told me that he hath read but little, that is to say, not since 25 aetat., and is of Mr Hobbes his mind, that had he read much, as some men have, he had not known so much as he does, nor should have made such Discoveries and improvements.

He had his patent for Earle of Kilmore and Baron of Shelbrooke, which he stifles during his life to avoyd Envy, but his Sonne will have the benefit of the Precedency. (I expected that his Sonne would have broken-out a Lord or Earle: but it seemes that he had enemies at the Court at Dublin, which out of envy obstructed the passing of his Patent.)

Monday, 20th March, he was affronted by Mr Vernon: Tuesday following Sir William and his Ladie's brother (Mr Waller) Hectored Mr Vernon and caned him.

He has told me, that wheras some men have accidentally come into the way of preferment, by lying at an Inne, and there contracting an Acquaintance; on the Roade; or as some others have donne; he never had any such like opportunity, but hewed out his Fortune himselfe. To be short, he is a person of so great worth and learning, and haz such a prodigious working witt, that he is both fitt for, and an honour to, the highest preferment.

Sir William Petty had a boy that whistled incomparably well. He after wayted on a Lady, a widowe, of good fortune. Every night this boy was to whistle his Lady asleepe. At last shee could hold out no longer, but bids her chamber-mayd withdrawe: bids him come to bed, setts him to worke, and marries him the next day. This is certeyn true.

Sir William Petty died at his house in Peccadilly-street (almost opposite to St James church) on fryday, 16th day of December, 1687, of a Gangrene in his foot, occasioned by the swelling of the Gowt, and is buried with his father and mother in the church at Rumsey, a little Haven towne in Hampshire.

KATHERINE PHILIPS

Born 1631. Poet. The daughter of John Fowler, a London merchant, she married James Philips in 1647. She adopted the pseudonym Orinda, to which her contemporaries prefixed the epithet Matchless. Her earliest verses were prefixed to the *Poems of Henry Vaughan* in 1651, and her collected verses appeared in 1667. She instituted a Society of Friendship, a literary salon for the discussion of poetry and similar topics. Her translation of Corneille's *Pompée* was acted in Dublin with great success. Cowley, in an elegy, mourned her death from small-pox in 1664.

SHE was very religiously devoted when she was young; prayed by herself an hower together, and tooke Sermons verbatim when she was but 10 yeares old. (At the age of nine yeares, Thomas Randolph wrot the History of our Saviour's Incarnation in English verse, which his brother John haz to shew under his owne handwriting – never printed, kept as a Raritie.)

She was when a Child much against the Bishops, and prayd to God to take them to him, but afterwards was reconciled to them. Prayed aloud, as the hypocriticall fashion then was, and was overheared.

From her cosen Blacket, who lived with her from her swadling cloutes to eight, and taught her to read: When a child she was mighty apt to learne, and she assures me that she had read the Bible thorough before she was full four yeares old; she could have sayd I know not how many places of Scripture and chapters. She was a frequent Hearer of Sermons; had an excellent Memory and could have brought away a sermon in her memory. Very good-natured; not at all high-minded; pretty fatt; not tall; read pumpled face; wrote out Verses in Innes, or Mottos in windowes, in her table-booke.

Mr J. Oxenbridge, her uncle, is now Prisoner in the Fleet on her account for a Dept of her husband, bound for him 28 yeares since.

SIR WILLIAM PLATERS

Born 1590. Knighted 1623. Succeeded to his father's Baronetcy 1638. The loyal and gallant achievements of this gentleman and his son are recorded on his wife's tomb at Dickleburgh in Norfolk:

> Here under lyeth buried the body of Dame Frances Platers, the daughter and heir of Charles le Grys, of Billingford, in Norff., Esq. She married Sir William Playters, of Sotterley, in Suffolk, Knt. and Bart.; sometimes one of the deputie Lieuetenants and Vice-Admiral of the said countie, and Justice of the Peace and Coram; and Collonel of a regiment of foot, till turn'd out of all by the then rebellious Parliament; and in fine out of that Hous of Parliament, whereof he had the misfortune to be a member. She had issue by him only Thomas, who married with Rebecka, the daughter and co-heir of Tho. Chapman, of Woormly, in the county of Hartford, Esq., which said Sir Tho. was a great traveller before and after marriage, his ladie sometimes beyond the seas with him: a learned schollar; an exact linguist, expert in all arts and knowledge; of rare temper and courage; and of great esteem in most courts in Christendom; High Sheriff for the countie of Suffolk, by commission from His Majestie of blessed memory, 1646, till forc'd by that fatal Parliament to flee to the King at Oxford, where, by commission from his Majesty, he raised a regiment of Hors, wherewith he performed remarkable service, till his Majesties forces were totally ruin'd; and then he departed the Kingdome, arriving in Cicilia, where, by commission from that Viceroy, he had command of a squadron of six shipps against all enemies to the crown of Spain, which being prepared, he put to sea, and performed many gallant services, much to the honour of the Spanish flagg. In July, 1651, he put into the port of Messina with a very rich prize and posted to the court at Palermo, where he met with an honourable reception for the several good services he had performed; but at 4 days end he there fell ill of a violent fever, whereof within 8 days he died, aged about 35 years; and by the Princes ordir had an honourable interment, and much lamented there, but much greater cause at home, leaving no issue, but a sorrowful widow and sad childless parents.

Sir William died in 1668.

SIR WILLIAM PLATER, Knight, was a Cambridgeshire Gentleman. He had a good Estate, about 3000 pounds per annum. He was a very well bred Gentleman, as most was of those times; had travelled France, Italie, etc, and understood well those languages. He was one of the Long Parliament in the time of the late Warres.

He was a merry man in the raigne of the Saints.

He was a great admirer and lover of handsome woemen, and kept severall. Henry Martyn and he were great Cronies, but one time (about 1644) there was some difference between them: H.M. invited him to a Treat, where Sir William fell in love with one of his Misses and slockst her away, and Sir John Berkinhead inserted in his *Mercurius Aulicus* how the Saintes fell out. He was temperate and thriftie as to all other things.

He had onely one Sonne, who was handsome and ingeniose, and whome he cultivated with all imaginable care and Education, and, knowing that he was flesh and bloud, tooke care himselfe to provide sound and agreeable females for him. He allowed his son liberally, but enjoyned him still temperance, and to sett downe his expences.

His Sonne made a very good returne of his Education. He was a Colonel in the King's Army, and was killed in his service, which his father tooke so to heart that he enjoyed not himselfe afterwards.

SIR JOHN POPHAM

Born 1531. Lawyer. Educated at Balliol College, Oxford. M.P. for Bristol 1571–83. Privy Councillor 1571. He drafted a Bill for preventing idleness by setting the poor to work (1572) and later drafted the Act for transporting vagabonds. Solicitor-General 1579. Speaker of the House of Commons 1580; on being asked by Queen Elizabeth, shortly after the prorogation of Parliament, what had passed in the House, he replied: 'If it please your Majesty, seven weeks.' Attorney-General 1581. Lord Chief Justice and knighted 1592. He presided at the trials of Essex, Raleigh, and the Gunpowder Plotters. He died in 1607.

HE for severall yeares addicted himselfe but little to the Studie of the Lawes, but profligate company, and was wont to tak a purse with them. His wife considered her and his condition, and at last prevailed with him to lead another life, and to stick to the Studie of the Lawe; which upon her importunity he did, being then about thirtie yeares old. He spake to his wife to provide a very good Entertainment for his Camerades, to take his Leave of them, and after that day fell extremely hard to his Studie, and profitted exceedingly. He was a strong, stout man, and could endure to sit at it day and night, became eminent in his calling, had good practise; called to be a serjeant, and a Judge.

Sir John Dayrell of Littlecote in Com. Wilts having gott his Ladie's waiting woman with child, when her travell came sent a servant with a horse for a midwife, whom he was to bring hood-winked [*blindfolded*]. She was brought and layd the woman, but as soon as the child was borne, she saw the Knight take the Child and murther it, and burn it in the fire in the chamber. She having donne her businesse was extraordinarily rewarded for her paines, and sent blinfold away. This horrid Action did much run in her mind, and she had a desire to discover it, but knew not where 'twas. She considerd with her selfe the time that she was riding, and how many miles might be rode at that rate in that time, and that it must be some great person's house, for the roome was twelve foot high; and she could knowe the chamber if she sawe it. She went to a Justice of peace, and search was made. The very chamber found. The Knight was brought to his Tryall, and, to be short, this Judge had this noble Howse, parke and mannor, and (I thinke) more for a Bribe to save his life: Sir John Popham gave Sentence according to Lawe; but being a Great person, and a Favourite, he procured a *Noli prosequi*.

I have seen his picture; he was a huge, heavie, ugly man. He left a vast estate to his son, Sir Francis (I thinke ten thousand pounds per annum), he lived like a hog, but his sonne John was a great waster, and dyed in his father's time. He was the greatest Howse-keeper in England; would have at Littlecote four or five or more Lords at a time. His wife (Harvey) was worth to him I thinke 60,000 pounds, and she was as vaine as he, and she sayd that she had brought such an estate, and she scorned but she would live as high as he did, and in her husband's abscence would have all the woemen of the countrey thither, and feast them and make them drunke; as she would be herselfe. They both dyed by excesse; and, by Luxury, and cosonage by their servants, when he dyed there was, I thinke, a hundred thousand pound debt.

Old Sir Francis he lived like a hog at Hownstret in Somerset all this while with a moderate pittance.

Mr John would say that his wive's estate was ill gott, and that was the reason they prospered no better. She would say that the old Judge gott the estate unjustly, and thus they would twitt one another, and that with matter of trueth.

I remember this Epitaph was made on Mr John Popham:

Here lies he who not long since
Kept a Table like a Prince,
Till Death came, and tooke away.
Then ask't the old man, what's to pay?

Lord Chief Justice Popham first brought in (i.e. revived) Brick building in London (*scil.* after Lincolne's Inne and St James's) and first sett-afoote the Plantations, e.g. Virginia, which he stockt or planted out of all the Gaoles of England.

At the Hall in Wellington, in the Countie of Somerset (the ancient seate of the Popham's) and which was this Sir John's, Lord Chiefe Justice, hang Iron Shackells: of which the Tradicion of the Countrey is, that long agoe, one of the Pophams (Lord of this place) was taken and kept a slave by the Turkes, for a good while, and that by his Ladie's great pietie and continuall prayers he was brought to this place by an invisible power with these Shackells on his legges, which were hung-up as a memoriall, and continued till the Howse (being a Garrison) was burn't. All the Countrey people steadfastly beleeve the trueth thereof.

FRANCIS POTTER

Born 1594. Divine and mechanician. Master of Arts at Trinity College, Oxford, 1616. Bachelor of Divinity 1625. Rector of Kilmington 1628–78. Fellow of the Royal Society 1663. His book *The Number of the Beast* was commended by Joseph Mead as *a wonderful discovery, the happiest that ever yet came into the world*, and as calculated *to make some of your German speculatives half wild*. Died 1678.

ANNO AETATIS 15 he went to Trinity Colledge in Oxon, where his brother Hannibal was his Tutor. Here he was a Commoner twenty-seaven yeares, and was senior to all the house, but Dr Kettle and his brother.

His Genius lay most of all to the Mechanicks; he had an admirable mechanicall Invention, but in that darke time wanted encouragement, and when his father dyed, he succeeded him in the Parsonage of Kilmanton, worth, per annum, about 140 pounds.

Anno Domini 1625, goeing into his chamber, the notion of 25, the roote of 666, for the roote of the number of the Beast in the Revelation, came into his head; so he opposed 25 to 12, the roote of 144.

He published nothing but his *Interpretation of the number 666*, in 4to, printed at Oxford, 1642, which haz been twice translated into Latin, into French, and other languages. Mr Launcelot Moorhouse, a very learned man, and a solid and profound Mathematician, wrote against Mr Francis Potter's booke of 666, and falls upon him, for that 25 is not the true roote, but the propinque root; to which Mr Potter replied with some sharpnes, and that it ought not to be the true roote, for this agrees better with his purpose.

When he tooke his Degree of Batchelaur in Divinity, his Question was *An Papa sit Anti-Christus?* [Whether the Pope be Anti-Christ?] In his younger yeares he was very apt to fall into a Swoune, and so he did when he was disputing in the Divinity-schoole upon that Question. I remember he told me that one time reading Aristotle *De Natura Animalium*, where he describes how that the Lionesses, when great with young, and neer their time of parturition, doe goe between two trees that growe neer together, and squeeze out their young ones out of their bellies; he had such a strong Idea of this, and of the paine that the lionesse was in, that he fell into a Swoune.

He was of a very tender constitution, and sickly most of his younger yeares. His manner was, when he was beginning to be sick, to *breath strongly* a good while together, which he sayed did emitt the noxious vapours. As he was never a strong man, so in his later times he had his health best; only about four or five yeares before his death his eie-sight was bad, and before he dyed quite lost.

He look't the most like a Monk, or one of the Pastours of the old time, that ever I saw one. He was pretty long visagd and pale cleare skin, gray eie. His discourse was admirable, and all new and unvulgar. His house was as undeckt as a Monke's cell; yet he had there so many ingeniose inventions that it was very delightfull. I never have enjoyed so much pleasure, nor ever was so much pleased with such Philosophicall and heartie Entertainment as from him.

On the buttery-dore in his Parlour he drew his father's picture at length, with his booke (fore-shortned) and on the spectacles in his hand is the reflection of the Gothique South windowe. I mention this picture the rather, because in processe of time it may be mistaken by tradition for his son Francis's picture, author of the booke aforesayd. He was from a Boy given to draweing and painting. The Founder's (Sir Thomas Pope's) picture in Trinity colledge hall is of his copying.

He was alwayes much Contemplative, and had an excellent Philosophicall head. He was no great read man; he had a competent knowledge in the Latin, Greeke, and Hebrue tongues, but not a Critique. Greeke he learn'd by Montanus's *Interlineary Testament*, after he was a man, without a Grammar, and then he read Homer. He understood only common Arithmetique, and never went farther in Geometrie then the first six bookes of Euclid; but he had such an inventive head, that with this foundation he was able to doe great matters in the Mechaniques, and to solve *phaenomena* in naturall philosophy. He had but few bookes, which when he dyed were sold for fifty-six shillings, and surely no great bargaine.

He invented and made with his owne handes a pair of beame Compasses, which will divide an inch into a hundred or a thousand parts. I have heard him say that he had never seen a water-house-engine, but that he could invent a better.

At the Epiphanie, 1649, when I was at his house, he then told me his notion of curing diseases, etc, by Transfusion of Bloud out of one man into another, and that the hint came into his head reflecting on Ovid's story of Medea and Jason, and that this was a matter of ten yeares before that time. About a yeare after, he and I went to trye the experiment, but 'twas on a Hen, and the creature to [*too*] little and our tooles not good: I then sent him a Surgeon's Lancet. Anno 1652, I recieved a letter from him concerning this Subject, which many yeares since I shewed, and was read and entred in the bookes of the Royall Societie, for Dr Lower would have arrogated the Invention to himselfe, and now one R. Griffith, Dr of Physique, of Richmond, is publishing a booke of the transfusion of bloud. (Mr Meredith Lloyd tells me that Libavius speakes of the Transfusion of Bloud, which I dare sweare Mr F. Potter never sawe in his life.)

In the troublesome times 'twas his happinesse never to bee sequestred. He was once maliciously informed against to the Committee at Wells (a thing very common in those times). When he came before them, one of them (I have forgot his name) gave him a pint of wine, and gave him great prayse, and bade him goe home, and feare nothing.

He haz told me that he had oftentimes dream't that he was at Rome, and being in fright that he should be seised on and brought before the Pope, did wake with the feare. (Pope Innocent IV, against whom Robert Grotest, Bishop of Lincolne, wrote, dreamt that the Bishop of Lincolne came to him, and gave him a great blowe over the face with his Staffe.)

'Twas pitty that such a delicate inventive Witt should be staked to a private preferment in an obscure corner where he wanted ingeniose conversation, from whence men rarely emerge to higher preferment, but contract a mosse on them like an old pale in an Orchard for want of ingeniose conversation, which is a great want even to the deepest thinking men (as Mr Hobbes haz often sayd to me).

The last time I sawe this honoured friend of mine, Octob 1674, I had not seen him in 3 yeares before, and his lippitude then was come even to blindnesse, which did much grieve me to behold. He had let his beard be uncutt, which was wont to be but little. I asked him why he did not get some kinswoman or kinsman of his to live with him, and looke to him now in his great age? He answer'd me that he had tryed that way, and found it not so well; for they did begrudge what he spent that 'twas too much and went from them, whereas his servants (strangers) were kind to him and tooke care of him.

WILLIAM PRYNNE

Born 1600. Controversial writer. Educated at Oxford, he studied law at Lincoln's Inn until he became immersed in writing controversial pamphlets, the best known of which was his *Histrio-Mastix, or a Scourge for Stage Players* (1633), a bitter attack on most of the popular amusements of the day. For writing it, Prynne was brought before the Star Chamber, fined £5,000, pilloried, and had both his ears cut off, besides being sentenced to imprisonment for life. Undeterred by this, he issued from his prison a fierce attack on Laud and the hierarchy, for which he was again fined, pilloried, and branded on both cheeks with the letters S.L. for Seditious Libeller. Removed to Caernarvon Castle, he remained there until liberated in 1641 by the Long Parliament. He soon after became a Member of the House, and joined with extreme rancour in the prosecution of Laud. He then turned his attacks on to the Independents, the Army, and the Protectorate, and was among those expelled from the House of Commons by Cromwell, whom he had opposed in regard to the execution of the King with such asperity that he again suffered imprisonment, from which he was released in 1652. He supported the Restoration, and was by Charles II appointed Keeper of the Records in the Tower, where he did good service by compiling the *Calendar of Parliamentary Writs and Records*. He published altogether about two hundred books and pamphlets, dying in 1669.

ANNO 1637 he was stigmatized in the Pillorie, and then Banished to Cornet-castle in Guernsey, where he was very civilly treated by the Governour Carteret, a very ancient familie in that Island. His Eares were not quite cutt off, only the upper part, his tippes were visible. Bishop William Lawd, A.B. Cant., was much blamed for being a Spectator, when he was his Judge. Anno 1641 he was, with Burton and Bastwyck, called home by the Parliament, and hundreds mett him and them out of London some miles.

He was a learned man, of immense reading, but is much blamed for his unfaithfull quotations. He was of a strange Saturnine complexion. Sir C.W. sayd once, that he had the countenance of a Witch.

His manner of Studie was thus: he wore a long quilt cap, which came 2 or 3, at least, inches over his eies, which served him as an Umbrella to defend his Eies from the light. About every three houres his man was to bring him a roll and a pott of Ale to refocillate his wasted spirits: so he studied and dranke, and munched some bread; and this maintained him till night, and then, he made a good Supper: now he did well not to dine, which breakes of one's fancy, which will not presently be regained: and 'tis with Invention as a flux, when once it is flowing, it runnes amaine: if it is checked, flowes but *guttim* [drop by drop]: and the like for perspiration, check it, and 'tis spoyled.

He endured severall Imprisonments for the King's cause, and was (really) very instrumentall in his restauracion.

Upon the opening of the Parliament, viz. letting in the Secluded Members, he girt on his old long rustie Sword (longer then ordinary). Sir William Waller marching behind him (as he went to the Howse) W. Prynne's long sword ranne between Sir William's short legges, and threw him downe, which caused laughter.

ELEANOR RADCLIFFE COUNTESS OF SUSSEX

Wife of Edward Radcliffe, who became the sixth Earl of Sussex on the death of his cousin in 1629. He died without issue in 1641 and his widow died in 1666.

COUNTESS OF SUSSEX, a great and sad example of the power of Lust and Slavery of it. She was as great a beautie as any in England, and had a good Witt. After her Lord's death (he was jealous) she sends for one (formerly her Footman) and makes him groom of the chamber. He had the Pox and shee knew it; a damnable Sott. He waz not very handsom, but his body of an exquisite shape (*hinc sagittae* [hence the arrows, i.e. love]). His Nostrils were stufft and borne out with corkes in which were quills to breath through. About 1666 this Countesse dyed of the Pox.

SIR WALTER RALEIGH

Born 1552. Military and naval commander and author. He served as a soldier in France and Ireland. Became a favourite of Queen Elizabeth, who vastly enriched him. Founded the first Virginia colony, explored Guiana, led an attack on the Spanish navy at Cadiz 1596, besides other naval ventures. The death of Elizabeth in 1603 was the turning-point in Raleigh's fortunes. Thenceforward disaster clouded his days. He was unjustly sentenced to death for treason in 1603, and though he was reprieved, spent thirteen years in the Tower. Released in 1615, he set out on his last voyage to Guiana, which proved a failure and in which he lost his eldest son. He returned a broken and dying man, but met with no pity from his ungenerous King, who (urged, it is believed, by the King of Spain) had him beheaded on 29 October 1618.

In his youth for several yeares he was under streights for want of money. I remember that Mr Thomas Child, of Worcestershire, told me that Sir Walter borrowed a Gowne of him when he was at Oxford (they were both of the same College) which he never restored, nor money for it.

He went into Ireland, where he served in the Warres, and shewed much courage and conduct, but he would be perpetually differing with (I thinke) Gray, then Lord Deputy, so that at last the Hearing was to be at councell table before the Queen, which was what he desired; where he told his Tale so well, and with so goode a Grace and Presence, that the Queen tooke especiall notice of him, and presently preferred him. So that it must be before this that he served in the French warres.

Queen Elizabeth loved to have all the Servants of her Court proper men, and as beforesaid Sir W.R.'s gracefull presence was no meane recommendation to him. I thinke his first preferment at Court was, Captaine of her Majestie's Guard. There came a countrey gentleman (or sufficient yeoman) up to Towne, who had severall sonnes, but one an extraordinary proper handsome fellowe, whom he did hope to have preferred to be a Yeoman of the Guard. The father (a goodly man himselfe) comes to Sir Walter Raleigh, a stranger to him, and told him that he had brought up a boy that he would desire (having many children) should be one of her Majestie's guard. Quod Sir Walter Raleigh, had you spake for yourselfe I should readily have graunted your desire, for your person deserves it, but I putt in no boyes. Said the father, Boy come in. The Son enters, about 18 or 19, but such a goodly proper young Fellow as Sir Walter had not seen the like: He was the tallest of all the Guard. Sir

Walter Raleigh sweares him immediately; and ordered him to carry up the first Dish at Dinner, where the Queen beheld him with admiration, as if a beautiful young Giant had stalked in with the service.

Sir Walter Raleigh was a great Chymist, and amongst some MSS receipts I have seen some secrets from him. He studyed most in his Sea-Voyages, where he carried always a Trunke of Bookes along with him, and had nothing to divert him. He made an excellent Cordiall, good in Feavers, etc; Mr Robert Boyle haz the recipe, and makes it and does great Cures by it.

A person so much immerst in action all along, and in fabrication of his owne Fortunes (till his confinement in the Tower) could have but little time to study but what he could spare in the morning. He was no Slug; without doubt he had a wonderfull waking spirit, and a great judgment to guide it.

Durham House was a noble palace; after he came to his greatness he lived there or in some apartment of it. I well remember his study, which was a little turret that looked into and over the Thames, and had the prospect which is pleasant perhaps as any in the World, and which not only refreshes the eie-sight but cheeres the spirits, and (to speake my mind) I beleeve enlarges an ingeniose man's thoughts.

Shirburne castle, parke, mannor, etc, did belong (and still ought to belong) to the Church of Sarum. Sir W.R. begged it as a Bôn from Queen Elizabeth: where he built a delicate Lodge in the Park of Brick; not big: but very convenient for the bignes, a place to retire from the Court in Summer time, and to contemplate, etc. Upon his attainder it was begged by the favorite Carr, Earl of Somerset, who forfeited it (I thinke) about the poysoning of Sir John Overbury. Then John, Earl of Bristowe, had it given him for his good service in the Ambassade in Spaine, and added two Wings to Sir Walter Raleighs Lodge. In short and indeed, 'tis a most sweet and pleasant place and site as any in the West: perhaps none like it.

He was a tall, handsome and bold man; but his *naeve* [blemish] was that he was damnable proud. Old Sir Robert Harley, of Brampton Brian Castle, who knew him, would say it was a great question who was the proudest, Sir Walter or Sir Thomas Overbury, but the difference that was, was judged on Sir Thomas's side.

Old John Long, who then wayted on Sir W. Long, being one time in the Privy-garden with his master, saw the Earle of Nottingham wipe the dust from Sir Walter R.'s shoes with his cloake in compliment. He was a second to the Earle of Oxford in a Duell. Was acquainted and accepted with all the Hero's of our Nation in his time.

He had a most remarkeable aspect, an exceeding high forehead, long-faced and sour eie-lidded, a kind of pigge-eie. His Beard turnd up naturally.

In the great parlour at Downton, at Mr Raleghs, is a good piece (an originall) of Sir W. in a white sattin doublet, all embrodered with rich pearles, and a mighty rich chaine of great Pearles about his neck, and the old servants have told me that the pearles were neer as big as the painted ones.

Old Sir Thomas Malett, one of the Justices of the King's bench *tempore Caroli I et II*, knew Sir Walter, and I have heard him say, that notwithstanding his so great Mastership in Style and his conversation with the learnedest and politest persons, yet he spake broad Devonshire to his dying day. His voice was small, as likewise were my schoolfellowes his grand-nephewes.

In his youth his Companions were boysterous blades, but generally those that had witt; except otherwise uppon designe, to gett them engaged for him, e.g. Sir Charles Snell, of Kington Saint Michael in North Wilts, my good neighbour, an honest young gentleman but kept a perpetuall Sott. He engaged him to build a ship, the *Angel Gabriel*, for the Designe for Guiana, which cost him the mannor of Yatton Keynell, the farme at Easton Piers, Thornhill, and the church-lease of Bishops Cannings; which ship, upon Sir Walter Raleigh's attainder, was forfeited.

In his youthful time was one Charles Chester, that often kept company with his acquaintance: he was a bold, impertenent fellowe, and they could never be at quiet for him; a perpetuall talker, and made a noyse like a drumme in a roome. So one time at a taverne, Sir W.R. beates him and seales up his mouth, i.e. his upper and neather beard, with hard wax. From him Ben Jonson takes his Carlo Buffono (i.e. Jester) in *Every Man out of his Humour*.

He loved a wench well; and one time getting up one of the Mayds of Honour up against a tree in a Wood ('twas his first Lady) who seemed at first boarding to be something fearfull of her Honour, and modest, she cryed, sweet Sir Walter, what doe you me ask? Will you undoe me? Nay, sweet Sir Walter! Sweet Sir Walter! Sir Walter! At last, as the danger and the pleasure at the same time grew higher, she cryed in the extasey, Swisser Swatter Swisser Swatter. She proved with child, and I doubt not but this Hero tooke care of them both, as also that the Product was more than an ordinary mortal.

My old friend James Harrington, Esq, was well acquainted with Sir Benjamin Ruddyer, who was an acquaintance of Sir Walter Raleigh's. He told Mr J.H. that Sir Walter Raleigh, being invited to dinner with some great person, where his son was to goe with him: He sayd to his Son, Thou art such a quarrelsome, affronting creature that I am ashamed to have such a Beare in my Company. Mr Walt humbled himselfe to his Father, and promised he would behave himselfe mightily mannerly. So away they went, and Sir Benjamin, I thinke, with them. He sate next to his Father and was very demure at leaste halfe dinner time. Then sayd he, I this morning, not having the feare of God before my eies, but by the instigation of the devill, went to a Whore. I was very eager of her, kissed and embraced her, and went to enjoy her, but she thrust me from her, and vowed I should not, *For your father lay with me but an hower ago*. Sir Walt, being so strangely supprized and putt out of his countenance at so great a Table, gives his son a damned blow over the face; his son, as rude as he was, would not strike his father, but strikes over the face of the Gentleman that sate next to him, and sayed, *Box about, 'twill come to my Father anon*. 'Tis now a common used Proverb.

His intimate Acquaintance and Friends were: Edward de Vere, Earle of Oxford, Sir Francis Vere, Sir Horatio Vere, Sir Francis Drake, Nicholas Hill, Thomas Cavendish, Mr Thomas Hariot, Sir Walter Long, of Dracot in Wilts, Cavaliero Surff, Ben Johnson, etc.

Sir Walter was the first that brought Tobacco into England and into fashion. In our part of North Wilts, e.g. Malmesbury hundred, it first came into fashion by Sir Walter Long.

I have heard my grandfather Lyte say that one pipe was handed round from man to man about the Table. They had first silver pipes, the ordinary sort made use of a walnute-shell and a strawe.

It was sold then for its wayte in Silver. I have heard some of our old yeomen neighbours say, that when they went to Malmesbury or Chippenham market, they culled out their biggest shillings to lay in the Scales against the Tobacco.

Sir W.R., standing in a Stand at Sir Robert Poyntz parke at Acton (which was built by Sir Robert's Grandfather to keep his Whores in) tooke a pipe of Tobacco, which made the Ladies quitt it till he had donne.

Within these 35 yeares 'twas scandalous for a Divine to take Tobacco. Now, the Customes of it are the greatest his Majestie hath.

I have now forgott whether Sir Walter Raleigh was not for the putting of Mary Queen of Scotts to death; I thinke, yea: but besides that, at a consultation at Whitehall after Queen Elizabeth's death, how matters were to be ordered and what ought to be donne, Sir Walter Raleigh declared his opinion, 'twas the wisest way for them to keepe the Government in their owne hands and sett up a Commonwealth, and not to be subject to a needy, beggarly nation. It seems there were some of this caball who kept this not so secret but that it came to King James' eare, who, where the English Noblesse mett and received him, being told upon presentment to his Majesty their names, when Sir Walter Raleigh's name was told (Ralegh) said the King, O my soule, mon, I have heard rawly of thee.

It was a most stately sight, the glory of that Reception of his Majesty, where the Nobility and Gentry were in exceeding rich equippage, having enjoyed a long peace under the most excellent of Queens: and the Company was so exceeding numerous that their obedience carried a secret dread with it. King James did not inwardly like it, and, with an inward envy, sayd that he doubted not but that he should have been able on his owne strength (should the English have kept him out) to have dealt with them, and get his Right. Sayd Sir Walter Raleigh to him, Would to God that had been putt to the tryall: Why doe you wish that sayd the King. Because, sayd Sir Walter; that then you would have known your friends from your foes. But that reason of Sir Walter was never forgotten nor forgiven.

He was such a person (every way) that (as King Charles I sayes of Lord Strafford) a Prince would rather be afrayd of then ashamed of. He had that awfulness and ascendency in his Aspect over other mortalls.

Old Major Stansby of Hants, a most intimate friend and neighbour and coetanean of the late Earle of Southampton (Lord Treasurer) told me from his friend, the Earle, that as to the plott and businesse about the Lord Cobham, he being then Governor of Jersey, would not fully doe things unless they would goe to his island, and there advise and resolve about it; and that really and indeed Sir Walter's purpose was when he had them there, to have betrayed them and the plott, and to have them delivered up to the King and made his Peace.

As for his noble Design in Guiana; *vide* a Latin voyage which John, Lord Vaughan, showed me, where is mention of Captaine North (brother to the Lord North) who went with Sir Walter, where is a large account of these matters. Mr Edmund Wyld knew him, and sayes he was a learned and sober Gentleman and good Mathematician, but if you happened to speake of Guiana he would be strangely passionate and say 'twas the blessedst countrey under the Sun, etc, reflecting on the spoyling that brave Designe.

Captain Roger North was a most accomplished Gentleman: he was a great Algebrist, which was rare in those dayes; but he had the acquaintance of his fellow-Traveller Mr Hariot. He had excellent Collections and Remarques of his Voyages, which were all unfortunately burnt in Fleet Street at the great Conflagration of the City. This Family speakes not well of Sir Walter Raleigh, that Sir Walter designed to breake with the Spanyard, and to make himselfe popular in England. When he came to Guiana, he could not show them where the Mines of Gold were. He would have then gonne to the King of France (Lewis XIII), but his owne men brought him back.

When Sir Walter Raleigh was carried prisoner from the West to

London, he lay at Salisbury, where, by his great Skill in Chimistry, he made himself like a Leper: by which meanes he thought he might retard his journey to a Prison: and study his escape. Dr Heydock was sent for to give his opinion, if the Prisoner might be carried to London without danger of his life. The Dr feeles Sr Walters Pulses, and found they did beat well: and so detected the Imposture.

I have heard old Major Cosh say that Sir W. Raleigh did not care to goe on the Thames in a Wherry-boate; he would rather goe round about over London bridg.

When he was attached by the Officer about the business which cost him his head, he was carried in a whery, I thinke only with two men. King James was wont to say he was a Coward to be so taken and conveyed, for els he might easily have made his escape from so slight a guard.

I have heard my cosen Whitney say that he saw him in the Tower. He had a velvet cap laced, and a rich Gowne and trunke-hose.

He there (besides compiling his *History of the World*) studyed Chymistry. The Earle of Northumberland was prisoner at the same time, who was Patrone to Mr Harriot and Mr Warner, two of the best Mathematicians then in the world, as also Mr Hues, who wrote *De Globis*. Serjeant Hoskins (the Poet) was a prisoner there too: he was Sir Walter's Aristarchus.

At the end of his *History of the World*, he laments the Death of the most noble and most hopefull Prince Henry, whose great Favorite he was: and who, had he survived his father, would quickly have enlarged him; with rewards of Honour. So upon the Prince's death ends his first part of his *History of the World*, with a gallant Eulogie of Him, and concludes: *Versa est in Luctum Cithara mea; at cantus meus invocem flentium* [my lyre is changed into the sound of mourning; and my song into the voices of people weeping].

His Booke sold very slowly at first, and the Booke-seller complayned of it, and told him that he should be a looser by it, which put Sir W into a passion, and sayd that since the world did not understand it, they should not have his second part, which he tooke and threw into the fire, and burnt before his face.

He was scandalised with Atheisme; but he was a bold man, and would venture at discourse which was unpleasant to the Church-men. I remember my Lord Scudamour sayd, 'twas basely sayd of Sir W.R. to talke of the Anagramme of Dog. In his speech on the Scaffold, I have heard my cosen Whitney say (and I thinke 'tis printed) that he spake not one word of Christ, but of the great and incomprehensible God, with much zeale and adoration, so that he concluded that he was an a-christ, not an atheist.

He tooke a pipe of Tobacco a little before he went to the scaffold, which some formall persons were scandalised at, but I thinke 'twas well and properly donne, to settle his spirits.

I remember I heard old father Symonds say that a father was at his execution, and that to his knowledge he dyed with a Lye in his mouth: I have now forgott what 'twas. The time of his Execution was contrived to be on my Lord Mayers day (viz. the day after St Simon and St Jude) 1618, that the Pageants and fine shewes might drawe away the people from beholding the Tragoedie of one of the gallantst worthies that ever England bred. Buryed privately under the high altar at St Margaret's Church in Westminster, in which grave (or neer) lies James Harrington, Esq, author of *Oceana*.

Mr Elias Ashmole told me that his son Carew Ralegh told him that he had his father's Skull; that some yeares since, upon digging up the grave, his skull and neck bone being viewed, they found the bone of his Neck lapped over, so that he could not have been hanged.

Even such is tyme that takes in Trust
Our Youth, our Joyes, our all we have,
And payes us but with Earth and Dust;
Who, in the darke and silent Grave,
When we have wandered all our wayes
Shutts up the Story of our Dayes.
But from this Earth, this Grave, this Dust,
My God shall rayse me up I trust.

These Lines Sir Walter Raleigh wrote in his Bible, the night before he was beheaded, and desired his Relations with these words, viz. *beg my dead body, which living is denyed you; and bury it either in Sherbourne or Exeter Church.* He was somtimes a Poet, not often.

A Scaffold was erected in the old Palace yard, upon which after 14 yeares reprivement [*stay of execution*], his head was cutt off: at which time, such abundance of bloud issued from his veines, that shewed he had stock of nature enough left to have continued him many yeares in life, though now above three score yeares old, if it had not been taken away by the hand of Violence. And this was the end of the great Sir Walter Raleigh: great sometimes in the favour of Queen Elizabeth, and next to Sir Francis Drake, the great Scourge and hate of the Spaniard, who had many things to be commended in his life, but none more than his constancy at his death, which he tooke with so undaunted a resolution that one might perceive that he had a certain expectation of a better life after it, so far he was from holding those Atheisticall opinions, an Aspersion whereof some had cast upon him.

On the famous Sir Walter Rawleigh, who fell a Sacrifice to Spanish Politicks:

Here lieth, hidden in this Pitt,
The Wonder of the World for Witt.
It to small purpose did him serve;
His Witt could not his Life preserve.
Hee living, was belov'd of none,
Yet in his death all did him moane.
Heaven hath his Soule, the world his Fame,
The grave his Corps; Stukley his shame.

MARY RICH
COUNTESS OF WARWICK

Born 1625. She was the seventh daughter and thirteenth child of Richard Boyle, first Earl of Cork, and sister of Robert Boyle the chemist. At the age of fourteen, she expressed *a very high averseness and contradicon* to the suitor chosen for her by her father: *Being refused in marriadge by my unrewly daughter Mary*, the old Earl noted angrily in his Journal, *he departed my hows the second of September to the Bathe*. His daughter later gave her own explanation. *Living so much at my ease*, she said, *I was unwilling to change my condition*, for the Earl of Cork had recently moved to the Savoy and *when we were once settled there, my father living extraordinarily high, drew a very great resort thither*. Amongst other visitors was Charles Rich, second son of the Earl of Warwick, a poverty-stricken young man *with £1300 or £1400 a year at the most*. A young man in such straitened circumstances had little hope of gaining the hand of the great Earl's daughter, and yet for two years he proved *a most diligent gallant to me*, Mary reported, *applying himself, when there were no other beholders in the room but my sister, to me; but if any other person came in he took no more than ordinary notice of me*. However, Mary caught measles when she was sixteen, and Charles Rich's anxiety was so marked that the family's suspicions were at last aroused. Mary Boyle was therefore packed off into the country in disgrace, but not before she had accepted Charles Rich, *so handsome did he express his passion*. After several weeks the Earl of Cork relented, and gave his daughter permission to marry and a dowry of £7,000; whereupon Mary Boyle, who had been *always a great enemy to a public marriage*, insisted on eloping. Five years later, her only son, *which I then doated on with great fondness*, fell seriously ill and his mother vowed to God that she would become *a new creature*, if her child recovered. He did get better, and Mary Rich, who had always been *stedfastly set against being a Puritan*, and had particularly delighted in *constant crowds of company*, now *began to find in myself a greate desire to go into the country, which I never remember before to have had, thinking it allways the saddest thing that could be when we were to remove.* Her home in Essex thereafter became the resort of pious Puritan ministers and Bishops from London, and her new faith stood her in good stead when her only child finally died of smallpox in his twenty-first year: *I was dumb*, she says, *and held my peace, because God did it.* Her husband became fourth Earl of Warwick on his brother's death in 1659, and died himself in 1673, leaving his entire estate at his wife's disposal for her lifetime. She became widely known for her charity, and died in 1678.

SHEE needed neither borrowed Shades, nor reflexive Lights, to set her off, being personally great in all naturall Endowments and accomplishments of Soul and Body, Wisdome, Beautie, Favour, and Virtue;

Great in the honour of her Birth, being born a Lady and a Virtuosa both;

Great by her Tongue, for never woman used one better, speaking so gracefully, promptly, discreetly, pertinently, holily, that I have often admired the edifying words that proceeded from her mouth;

Great by her Pen, as you may discover by that little tast of it the world hath been happy in, the hasty fruit of one or two interrupted houres after Supper, which she professed to me, with a little regret, when she was surprised with its sliding into the world without her knowledge, or allowance, and wholly beside her expectation;

Great by being the greatest Mistresse and Promotress, not to say the Foundress and Inventress, of a new Science – the Art of obliging; in which she attain'd that Sovereign Perfection, that she reigned over all their hearts with whom she did converse;

Great in her nobleness of Living and Hospitality;

Great in the unparallelld sincerity of constant, faithfull, condescending Friendship, and for that Law of Kindness which dwelt in her Lips and Heart;

Great in her dexterity of Management;

Great in her quick apprehension of the difficulties of her Affaires, and where the stress and pinch lay, to untie the Knot, and loose and ease them;

Great in the conquest of her selfe;

Great in a thousand things beside, which the world admires as such: but she despised them all, and counted them but loss and dung in comparison of the feare of God, and the excellency of the Knowledge of Christ Jesus.

CHARLES ROBSON

Born 1598. Divine. Fellow of Queen's College, Oxford, 1620. Owing to his lax habits the College gladly gave him three years' leave of absence in 1623, and he was appointed preacher to the colony of English merchants at Aleppo at a salary of £50 a year. This leave was extended and Robson did not return to England until 1630, when he became a Bachelor of Divinity. However, in 1631 he was deprived of his Fellowship on account of his dissolute haunting of taverns and brothels and his neglect of study and divine worship, and the University appointed him to a vicarage in Cumberland. He died in 1638.

ROBSON was the first that brought into England the Art of making Venice-glasses, but Sir Edward Zouche (a Courtier and a drolling Favourite of King James) oppressed this poor man Robson, and forc't it from him, by these four verses to King James, which made his Majestie laugh so that he was ready to beshitt his Briggs. The verses are these:

Severn, Humber, Trent, and Thames,
And thy great Ocean, and her Streames,
Must putt downe Robson, and his Fires
Or downe goes Zouche and his desires.

The King granted this ingeniose manufacture to Zouch, being tickled as aforesayd with these Rythmes; and so poor Robson was oppressed and utterly undon: and came to that low degree of Poverty that Mr Philips told me that he swept the Yard at Whitehall and that he himselfe saw him doe it.

WALTER RUMSEY

Born 1584. Lawyer. He was called to the Bar in 1608. Judge of Great Sessions for the Counties of Brecknock, Glamorgan, and Radnor from 1631 till he was removed by Parliament in 1647. At the Restoration he was made Keeper of the Judicial Seal for the same counties, and was nominated to be a Knight of the Royal Oak. He died in 1660.

HE was so excellent a lawyer, that he was called *The Pick-lock of the Lawe.*
He was an ingeniose man, and had a Philosophicall head; he was most

curious for graffing, inocculating, and planting, and ponds. If he had any old dead plumbe-tree or apple-tree, he lett them stand, and planted Vines at the bottome, and lett them climbe up, and they would beare very well.

He was one of my Councell in my Law-suites in Breconshire about the Entaile: he had a kindnesse for me and invited me to his house, and told me a great many fine things, both naturall and antiquarian.

He was very facetious [*amusing*], and a good Musitian, playd on the organ and lute. He could compose.

He was much troubled with Flegme, and being so one winter at the Court at Ludlowe (where he was one of the councesellors) sitting by the fire, spitting and spawling, he tooke a fine tender sprig and tied a ragge at the end, and conceited [*contrived*] he putt it downe his throat and fetch-up the Flegme, and he did so. Afterwards he made this instrument of Whale-bone. I have oftentimes seen him use it. I could never make it goe downe my throat, but for those that can 'tis a most incomparable engine. If troubled with the wind, it cures you immediately, with a blast as when a Bottle is un-stopp't. It makes you vomit without any paine, and besides, the Vomits of Apothecaries have *aliquid veneni* [some poison] in them. He wrote a little booke of this way of medicine, called *Organon Salutis* (An Instrument to cleanse the stomach). I had a young fellow, Marc Collins, that was my servant, that used it incomparably, more easily than the Judge: he made of them. In Wilts, among my things, are some of his making still. The Judge sayd he never sawe any one use it so dexterously in his life. It is no paine, when downe your throate; he would touch the bottome of his Stomach with it.

THOMAS SACKVILLE EARL OF DORSET

Born 1536. Poet and statesman. He was a cousin of Queen Elizabeth and studied at both Oxford and Cambridge, before removing to the Inner Temple. He was created Lord Buckhurst in 1566. His father had amassed so great a fortune that he was known as *Sir Richard Fill Sack*, but his son was extravagant beyond all bounds and soon fell into considerable difficulties, but he was so humiliated by being kept waiting by one of his creditors that he embraced a *magnificent economy*. Queen Elizabeth sent him on an embassy to Paris in 1570 to treat of the marriage then proposed between herself and the Duke of Anjou, and appointed him one of the Commissioners for the trial of Mary Queen of Scots; he had to announce to her the sentence of death, and to superintend her execution. In 1587 he was imprisoned for a year after a quarrel with Leicester, but in 1588 he was made a Knight of the Garter, and in 1591 he became Chancellor of the University of Oxford. He was selected to negotiate peace with Spain in 1598, and on the death of Burghley he was appointed Lord High Treasurer, in which office he was confirmed by James I, who created him Earl of Dorset in 1604. At the age of seventy-two he was seriously ill and the King sent him a ring set with twenty diamonds, hoping *that he might live as long as the dyamonds of that ring did endure.* However, he died soon after, in 1608, in the presence of the King, and *on opening his head, they found in it certain little bags of water, which, falling upon his brain, caused his death.* In his poetry, Sackville is the connecting link between Chaucer and Spenser. In conjunction with Thomas Norton, he wrote *Gorboduc*, the first regular English tragedy, which rid the theatre of the rigid conventions of its infancy and cleared the stage for the genius of Marlowe and Shakespeare.

EPIGRAM on the Earle of Dorset, who dyed suddenly at the Council-Boord:

Uncivil Death! that would'st not once conferre,
Dispute, or parle with our Treasurer,
Had He been Thee, or of thy fatall Tribe,
He would have spar'd thy life, and ta'ne a Bribe.
He that so often had, with gold and witt,
Injur'd strong Lawe, and almost conquer'd it,
At length, for want of evidence to shewe,
Was forc't himselfe to take a deadly blowe.

The Tryall was with this Sir Richard Temple's great Grandfather. The Lord Treasurer had in his Bosome some writings, which as he was pulling-out to give in evidience, sayed *Here is that will strike you dead!* and as soon as he had spoken these words, fell downe starke dead in the place.

Richard, Earle of Dorset, (eldest grandson and heire to the Lord Treasurer) lived in the greatest grandeur of any nobleman of his time in England. He had 30 Gentlemen, and gave to each 50 pounds per annum, besides keeping and his horse. G. Villiers (after Duke of Bucks) was a Petitioner to have had a Gentleman's place under him, and miss't it, and within 12 moneth was a greater man himselfe; but the Duke ever after bore a grudge to the Earl of Dorset. 'Twas he that translated *the Cid* (a French Comoedie) into English, about 1640. His eldest sonne is Richard, Earl of Dorset and Middlesex, a most noble Lord and my most kind friend.

SIR HENRY SAVILE

Born 1549. Scholar. Fellow of Merton College, Oxford, at the age of sixteen. Lectured in mathematics. Warden of Merton 1585–1622. Translated *Histories of Tacitus* 1591. Secretary of Latin tongue to Queen Elizabeth. Provost of Eton 1596. Knighted 1604. He was one of the scholars commissioned to prepare the authorized translation of the Bible. He assisted Sir Thomas Bodley in founding his library. Founded the Savile Professorships of Geometry and Astronomy at Oxford. Died 1622.

SIR HENRY SAVILL, Knight was a younger (or son of a younger) brother, not borne to a foot of land.

He was a learned gentleman as most was of his time; he would faine have been thought (I have heard Mr Hobbes say) to have been as great a scholar as Joseph Scaliger. But as for Mathematiques, I have heard Dr Wallis say that he look't on him to be as able a Mathematician as any of his time. He was an extraordinary handsome and beautifull man; no lady had a finer complexion.

Queen Elizabeth favoured him much; he read I thinke Greeke and Politiques to her. He was also preferred to be Provost of Eaton colledge.

He was a very severe Governour, the scholars hated him for his austerity. He could not abide Witts: when a young Scholar was recommended to him for a good Witt, *Out upon him, I'le have nothing to doe with him; give me the ploding student. If I would look for witts, I would goe to Newgate: there be the Witts*; and John Earles (afterwards Bishop of Sarum) was the only scholar that ever he tooke as recommended for a Witt, which was from Dr Goodwyn, of Christ Church.

He was not only a severe Governor, but old Mr Yates (who was fellow in his time) would make lamentable complaints of him to his dyeing day, that he did oppresse the fellows grievously, and he was so great and a favourite to the Queen, that there was no dealing with him; his *naeve* [blemish] was that he was too much inflated with his learning and riches.

He was very munificent, as appeares by the two Lectures he has given to Astronomy and Geometry. Bishop Seth Ward, of Sarum, has told me that he first sent for Mr Gunter, from London (being of Oxford University) to have been his Professor of Geometrie: so he came and brought with him his Sector and Quadrant, and fell to resolving of Triangles and doeing a great many fine things. Said the grave Knight, *Doe you call this reading of Geometrie? This is shewing of tricks, man!* and so dismisst him with scorne, and sent for Henry Briggs, from Cambridge.

I have heard Dr Wallis say, that Sir H. Savill has sufficiently confuted Joseph Scaliger *de Quadratura Circuli*, in the very margent of the booke: and that sometimes when J. Scaliger sayes AB=CD ex constructione, Sir H. Savill writes sometimes in the margent, *Et Dominatio vestra est Asinus ex constructione* [and your rule is an ass by construction]. One sayes of Jos Scaliger, that where he erres, he erres so ingeniosely, that one had rather erre with him then hit the mark with Clavius.

He had travelled very well, and had a generall acquaintance with the Learned men abroad; by which meanes he obtained from beyond sea, out of their Libraries, severall rare Greeke MSS, which he had copied by an excellent Amanuensis for the Greeke character. He gave his Collection of Mathematicall Bookes to a peculiar little Library belonging to the Savilian Professors.

SYLVANUS SCORY

The son of John Scory, Bishop of Hereford. He fought in the Low Countries. Prebendary of Hereford 1565–9. Member of Parliament for Newton in Hampshire in 1597. Died 1617.

HE was a very handsome Gentleman, and had an excellent Witt, and his father gave him the best Education, both at home and beyond the Seas, that that age would afford, and loved him so dearly that he fleeced the Church of Hereford to leave him a good estate: and he did let such long and so many leases, that, as Mris Masters told me, they were not out till about these 60 yeares. To my best remembrance she told me that the estate left him was 1500 pounds per annum, which he reduced to nothing (allowing himselfe the libertie to enjoy all the pleasures of this World) and left his sonne so poor, that when he came among gentlemen, they would fancy a crowne or ten shillings for him.

I have heard Sir John Denham saye that he haz been well enformed that he was the most accomplished Gentleman of his time: 'tis a good testimoniall of his worth, that Mr Benjamin Johnson (who ever scorned an unworthy Patrone) dedicated to him. I have heard Sir John Denham also say, that he was the greatest confident and intimate Favourite of Monsieur of France (brother to the French King) who was a suitor to Queen

Elizabeth, and whom her Majestie entirely loved; and as a Signalle of it, one time at St Paules church London, openly kissed him in time of divine Service; and would have had him for her Husband, but only for reasons of State.

When her Majestie dismissed him 'twas donne with all passion and respecte imaginable. She gave him royall presents: he was attended to Dover by the flower of the Court; among others by this Sparke of whom I now write. When Monsieur tooke his leave of him, he told him that though 'twas so that her Majestie could not marie him (as aforesayd) yet he knew that she so much loved him that she would not deny him any request, wherby he might honour and benefit a Friend: and accordingly writes his love-letter to his Mistresse the Queen of England, and in it only begs that single favour to looke upon Mr Scorie (the bearer) with a particular and extraordinary grace for his sake: delivered him the letter (and, as I take it, gave him a jewell).

As Sylvanus returned to London through Canterbury, the Mayer there (a Shoemaker) a pragmaticall fellow, examined him, who and whence, etc, and what his business was, and if he had a Passe? Yes, quod he, I have a Passe, and produces Monsieur's letter, superscribed to her Majestie, which, one would have thought, had been enough to have shewen. The Mayor presently breakes open the Love-letter, and reades it. I know not how, this action happened to take wind; and 'twas brought to Court, and became so ridicule, that Sylvanus Scory was so laughed at and jeer'd that he never delivered the letter to the Queen; which had been the easiest and most honourable step to preferment that mortall man could have desired.

JOHN SELDEN

Born 1584. Jurist. His first work, written in 1606, was *Analecton Anglo-Britannicon*, a chronological collection of English records down to the Norman invasion. In 1610 appeared a treatise on the *Duello, or Single Combat*; in 1614 he wrote *Titles of Honour*, which is full of profound learning and is still a high authority; and three years later he gained a European reputation as a scholar through his book *De Deis Syris* (On the Gods of Syria), an inquiry into Polytheism. He was forced, before the High Commission Court, to recant the doctrines he had put forward in his *History of Tithes* in 1618, and in 1621 he was imprisoned for opposition to James I's prerogative. He was Member of Parliament for Lancaster in 1623, and his moderate views brought him under suspicion from both sides, so that he was imprisoned in the Tower from 1630 until 1634. After the execution of the King, to which he was strongly opposed, he took little part in public affairs, and died in 1654.

HIS father was a yeomanly man, of about fourty pounds per annum, and played well on the violin, in which he tooke delight, and at Christmas time, to please him selfe and his neighbours, he would play to them as they danced.

He was of Hart-hall in Oxon, and Sir Giles Mompesson told me that he was then of that house, and that he was a long scabby-pold boy, but a good student.

Thence he came to the Inner-Temple. He was quickly taken notice of for his learning, and was Sollicitor and Steward to the Earle of Kent, whose Countesse, being an ingeniose woman and loving men, would let him lye with her, and her husband knew it. After the Earle's death he maried her. He did lye with Mris Williamson (one of my Lady's woemen), a lusty bouncing woman, who robbed him on his death-bed. I remember in 1646, or 1647, they did talk also of my Lady's Shee Blackamore.

I remember my Sadler (who wrought many years to that Family) told me that Mr Selden had got more by his Prick then he had done by his practise. He was no eminent practiser at Barre.

He never owned the mariage with the Countesse of Kent till after her death, upon some Lawe-account.

He kept a plentifull Table, and was never without learned company: he was temperate in eating and drinking. He had a slight stuffe, or silke, kind of false carpet, to cast over the table where he read and his papers lay, when a stranger came-in, so that he needed not to displace his bookes or papers.

His treatise that Tythes were not *jure divino* drew a great deale of Envy upon him from the Clergie. W. Laud, Archbishop of Canterbury, made him make his Recantation before the High Commission Court. After, he would never forgive the Bishops, but did still in his writings levell them with Presbyterie.

After he had got a *dulce ocium* [*otium*, rest] he chiefly addicted himselfe to his more ingeniose studies and Records. He was one of the Assembly of Divines and was like a Thorne in their sides: he was wont to mock the Assembly-men about their little gilt Bibles, and would baffle and vexe them sadly: sayd he, *I doe consider the original*: for he was able to runne them all downe with his Greeke and Antiquities.

He was very tall, I guesse about 6 foot high, sharp ovall face, head not very big, long nose inclining to one side, full popping Eie (gray). He was a Poet.

In his younger yeares he affected obscurity of style, which, after, he quite left off, and wrote perspicuously. 'Twill be granted that he was one of the greatest Critiques of his time.

Mr J. Selden writt a 4to booke called *Tabletalke*; which will not endure the Test of the Presse.

Sir Robert Cotton (the great Antiquary, that collected the Library) was his great Friend, whose son Sir Thomas Cotton was obnoxious to the Parliament and skulked in the Countrey. Mr Selden had the Key and command of the Library, and preserved it, being then a Parliament-man.

He intended to have given his owne Library to the University of Oxford, but received disobligation from them, for that they would not lend him some MSS; wherfore by his Will he left it to the disposall of his Executors (viz. Lord Chiefe Justice Hales, Lord Chief Justice Vaughan, Rowland Jukes, and his flatterer) who gave it to the Bodleian Library, at Oxon.

He would tell his intimate friends, Sir Bennet Hoskyns, etc, that he had no body to make his heire, excepte, it were a Milke-mayd: and that such people did not know what to doe with a great estate. (Bishop Grostest, of Lincoln, told his brother, who asked him to make him a grate man; Brother, said he, if your Plough is Broken, I'le pay the mending of it; or if an Oxe is dead, I'le pay for another: but a Plough-man I found you, and a Plough-man I'le leave you.)

He dyed of a Dropsey; he had his Funerall Scutcheons all ready moneths before he dyed. When he was neer death, the Minister was comeing to him to assoile him: Mr Hobbes happened then to be there, sayd he, What, will you that have wrote like a man, now dye like a woman? So the Minister was not let in.

Mr Johnson, Minister of the Temple, buryed him, the Directory way [*i.e. by Baxter's 'General Directory of Worship', not the Book of Common Prayer*], where, amongst other things, he quoted the sayeing of a learned man (he did not name him) that *when a learned man dies, there dyes a great deale of learning with him*, and that *if Learning could have kept a man alive our Brother had not dyed.*

WILLIAM SEYMOUR
DUKE OF SOMERSET

Born 1588. Great-grandson of Protector Somerset. Courtier and soldier. There were some doubts about his legitimacy. Against James I's wishes, he secretly married Arabella Stuart, great-granddaughter of Henry VII, in 1610, and when the marriage was discovered they were committed to the Tower. Having made a plan to join Arabella Stuart on the Continent, his barber, Batten, helped him to escape. Batten, who was well known to the guards, presented himself at the Tower completely disguised, and asked for Mr Seymour's barber, whom he professed to know was within. On being admitted, he transferred the disguise to Seymour and then boldly sallied forth with him. The barber was committed to the Tower next day, and Seymour fled to the Continent, but his wife was prevented from joining him. After her death in the Tower in 1615, he made his peace with the King and returned to England. Knight of the Bath 1616. He adopted the title of Baron Beauchamp 1618. On his grandfather's death, he became Earl of Hertford in 1621; Privy Councillor and created Marquis of Hertford 1640; Governor to Charles, Prince of Wales, 1641. In the Civil Wars he became a Royalist Commander, capturing Hereford, Cirencester, and Bristol and being victorious at Lansdown in 1643. In 1645 he was put in charge of Oxford, and on its surrender next year, he compounded for his estates and attended Charles I during his imprisonment. He joined with the Duke of Richmond and the Earl of Southampton in praying the King's Judges to lay upon them, as Charles's advisers, the exclusive responsibility for his acts, and when this plea failed, he obtained permission to bury the King's body at Windsor. He received the Garter, the Barony of Seymour, and the Dukedom of Somerset at the Restoration, but died the same year.

CONCERNING Furze-cutters: Brianston by Blandford in Dorset was, *tempore Henr. 8*, belonging to Sir John (I thinke) Rocklington: he had a faire Estate, and no child; and there was a poor cottager whose name was Rogers that had a pretty wife whom this Knight did visit and had a mind to have a child by her. As he did suppose he afterwards had; and in consideration of affection, etc, settled his whole estate on this young Rogers. William, Lord Marquesse Hartford, Duke of Somerset, was son of the grand-daughter of this Rogers.

This present Lord Roberts of Truro (now Earl of Radnor) his grandfather (or great-grandfather) was a Furze-cutter in Cornwall; which I have heard old Parson Wodenot of Linkenhorne in Cornwall say many times.

WILLIAM SHAKESPEARE

Born 1564. Actor, poet, theatre manager, and playwright. Died 1616.

MR WILLIAM SHAKESPEARE was borne at Stratford upon Avon in the County of Warwick. His father was a Butcher, and I have been told heretofore by some of the neighbours, that when he was a boy he exercised his father's Trade, but when he kill'd a Calfe he would doe it in a high style, and make a Speech. There was at this time another Butcher's son in this Towne that was held not at all inferior to him for a naturall witt, his acquaintance and coetanean, byt dyed young.

This William, being inclined naturally to Poetry and acting, came to London, I guesse about 18: and was an Actor at one of the Play-houses, and did acte exceedingly well: now B. Johnson was never a good Actor, but an excellent Instructor.

He began early to make essayes at Dramatique Poetry, which at that time was very lowe; and his Playes tooke well.

He was a handsome, well-shap't man: very good company, and of a very readie and pleasant smoothe Witt.

The Humour of the Constable in Midsomernight's Dreame, he happened to take at Grendon, in Bucks (I thinke it was Midsomer night that he happened to lye there) which is the roade from London to Stratford, and there was living that Constable about 1642, when I first came to Oxon. Ben Johnson and he did gather Humours of men dayly where ever they came. One time as he was at the Tavern at Stratford super Avon, one Combes, an old rich Usurer, was to be buryed. He makes there this extemporary Epitaph:

Ten in the Hundred the Devill allowes,
But Combes will have twelve he sweares and vowes:
If anyone askes who lies in this Tombe,
Hoh! quoth the Devill, 'Tis my John o' Combe.

He was wont to goe to his native Countrey once a yeare. I thinke I have been told that he left 2 or 300 pounds per annum there and thereabout to a sister.

I have heard Sir William Davenant and Mr Thomas Shadwell (who is counted the best Comoedian we have now) say that he had a most prodigious Witt, and did admire his naturall parts beyond all other Dramaticall writers.

His Comoedies will remaine witt as long as the English tongue is understood, for that he handles *mores hominum* [the ways of mankind]. Now our present writers reflect so much on particular persons and coxcombeities that twenty yeares hence they will not be understood.

Though, as Ben Johnson sayes of him, that he had little Latine and lesse Greek, he understood Latine pretty well: for he had been in his younger yeares a schoolmaster in the countrey.

He was wont to say that he never blotted out a line in his life. Sayd Ben Johnson, I wish he had blotted-out a thousand.

OLIVE SHERINGTON

She was the daughter and co-heir of Sir Henry Sherington, who in his turn had succeeded to the vast estates left by his brother, Sir William, whose third wife was the mother of his brother Henry's wife. This Sir William was one of the chief officers of the Mint under Henry VIII, and by malpractices, carried to an enormous extent, obtained the means of speculating on a vast scale in the purchase of Abbey lands, but his frauds were discovered in 1548 and he was locked up in the Tower. On his own confession he was convicted of having counterfeited twelve thousand pounds' worth of coinage in a single year, besides having defrauded the King of clippings and shearings of coin to the amount of several thousand pounds more, and of having falsified indentures and books: all this to such an extent that he was quite unable to declare the whole amount of his profits. For these offences he was attainted and his lands forfeited. The fact of his confession showed, according to Bishop Latimer, that *he is a chosen man of God, and one of his elected*, and within three years he had amassed another fortune sufficiently large to enable him to buy back all his estates for £13,000. Olive Sherington, after the death of John Talbot, her first husband, was married to Sir Robert Stapylton of Yorkshire, and after her second widowhood lived at Lacock Abbey until her death.

DAME OLAVE, a Daughter and coheir of Sir Henry Sharington of Lacock being in Love with John Talbot (a younger Brother of the Earle of Shrewsbury) and her Father not consenting that she should marry him: discoursing with him one night from the Battlements of the Abbey-Church; said shee, *I will leap downe to you*: her sweet Heart replied, he would catch her then: but he did not believe she would have done it: she leap't downe and the wind (which was then high) came under her coates: and did something breake the fall: Mr Talbot caught her in his armes, but she struck him dead; she cried out for help, and he was with great difficulty brought to life again: her father told her that since she had made such a leap she should e'en marrie him. She was my honoured friend Col. Sharington Talbot's Grand Mother: and died at her house at Lacock about 1651, being about an hundred years old.

SIR PHILIP SIDNEY

Born 1554. Soldier, statesman, and poet. His father was three times Lord Deputy of Ireland and President of Wales. He was at the French Court on the fateful 24 August 1572, the Massacre of Saint Bartholomew, but left Paris soon after and went to Germany, Poland, Hungary, and Italy. On his return he became a friend of Spenser, who dedicated his *Shepheard's Calendar* to him. In 1580 he lost the favour of the Queen by remonstrating against her proposed marriage with the Duke of Anjou, and in 1583 he was married himself to the daughter of Sir Francis Walsingham. His writings consist of his famous pastoral romance *Arcadia*, his sonnets *Astrophel and Stella*, and his *Defence of Poesie*. Sidney has always been considered as the type of English chivalry; and his extraordinary contemporary reputation, resting on his personal qualities of nobility and generosity (for none of his works was published in his lifetime), is shown by the inscription on the tomb of Fulke Greville, Lord Brooke: *Here lies the body of Sir Fulke Grevile, Knight, Servant to Queen Elizabeth, Counsellor to King James, and Friend to Sir Philip Sidney*. In 1585 Sidney was engaged in the war in the Low Countries and was fatally wounded at Zutphen.

SIR PHILIP SYDNEY, Knight, whose Fame will never dye, whilest Poetrie lives, was the most accomplished Cavalier of his time. He was not only of an excellent witt, but extremely beautifull: he much resembled his sister, but his Haire was not red, but a little inclining, viz a darke ambor colour. If I were to find a fault in it, methinkes 'tis not masculine enough; yett he was a person of great courage.

He travelled France, Italie, Germany; he was in the Poland warres, and at that time he had to his Page (and as an excellent accomplishment) Henry Danvers (afterwards Earle of Danby) then second son of Sir John Danvers of Dantesey in Wilts, who accounted himselfe happy that his son was so bestowed. He makes mention, in his *Art of Poesie*, of his being in Hungarie (I remember).

He was a reviver of Poetry in those darke times, which was then at a very low ebbe: there is not 3 lines but there is *by God*, or *by God's wounds*.

He was much at Wilton with his sister, and at Ivy-church (which adjoyns to the parke pale of Clarindon Parke) situated on a hill that overlookes all the Country westwards, and North over Sarum and the plaines, and into that delicious parke (which was accounted the best of England) Eastwards. It was anciently a pleasant Monasterie (the Cloysters remayne still).

My great Uncle Mr Thomas Browne remembred him; and sayd that he was wont, as he was hunting on our pleasant plaines, to take his Table booke out of his pocket, and write downe his notions as they came into his head, when he was writing his *Arcadia* (which was never finished by him): he made it young, and Diying desired his folies might be burnt. These Romancy Plaines, and Boscages did no doubt conduce to the heightening of Sir Philip Sidneys Phansie.

He was of a very munificent spirit, and liberall to all Lovers of Learning, and to those that pretended to any acquaintance with Parnassus: in so much that he was cloyed and surfeited with the Poetasters of those dayes. Among others, Mr Edmund Spenser made his addresse to him, and brought his *Faery Queen*. Sir Philip was busy at his Study, and his servant delivered Mr Spencer's booke to his master, who layd it by, thinking it might be such kind of Stuffe as he was frequently troubled with. Mr Spencer stayed so long that his patience was wearied, and went his way discontented, and never intended to come again. When Sir Philip perused it, he was so exceedingly delighted with it that he was extremely sorry he was gonne, and where to send for him he knew not. After much enquiry he learned his lodgeing, and sent for him, mightily caressed him, and ordered his servant to give him so many pounds in gold. His servant sayd that that was too much. No, sayd Sir Philip, and ordered an addition. From this time there was a great friendship between them, to his dying day.

Tilting was much used at Wilton in the times of Henry Earle of Pembroke, and Sir Philip Sydney. At the Solemnization of the great Wedding of William the 2d Earle of Pembroke to one of the Co-heires of the Earle of Shrewsbury, here was an extraordinary Shew: at which time a great many of the Nobility, and Gentry, exercised: and they had Shields of Pastboard painted with their Devices, and Emblemes: which were very pretty and ingenious: and I believe they were most of them contrived by Sir Philip Sidney. There are some of them hanging in some houses at Wilton to this day; but I did remember many more. Most (or all of them) had some relation to Marriage. One (I remember) was a Hawke lett of the hand, with her Leashes hanging at her Legges, which might hang her wher 'ere she pitch't: And is an Embleme of Youth, that is apt to be ensnared by their own too plentiful Estates.

I have heard Dr Pell say, that he haz been told by ancient gentlemen of those dayes of Sir Philip, so famous for men at Armes, that 'twas then held as a great disgrace for a young Cavalier to be seen riding in the street in a Coach, as it would now for such a one to be seen in the streetes in a Petticoate and Wastcoate. So much in the fashion of the times nowe altered.

He maried the daughter of Sir Francis Walsingham, Principall Secretary of Estate (I thinke his only child) whom he loved very well: in so much that having received some shott or wound in the Warres in the Lowe-countreys (where he had command of the Ramikins, I thinke) he would not (contrary to the injunction of his Physitians and chirurgions) forbeare his carnall knowledge of her, which cost him his life; upon which occasion there were some roguish verses made.

His body was putt in a leaden coffin (which, after the firing of Paule's, I myselfe sawe) and with wonderful greate state was caried to St Paules church, where he was buried in our Ladie's Chapell. There solempnized this Funerall all the Nobility and great Officers of Court; all the Judges and Serjeants at Lawe; all the Soldiers and Commanders and Gentry that were in London; the Lord Mayer and Aldermen, and Liverymen. His body was borne on men's shoulders (perhaps 'twas a false coffin).

When I was a boy 9 yeares old, I was with my father at one Mr Singleton's an Alderman and Wollen-draper in Glocester, who had in his parlour over the Chimney, the whole description of the Funerall, engraved and printed on papers pasted together, which at length was, I beleeve, the length of the room at least; but he had contrived it to be turned upon two Pinnes, that turning one of them made the figures march all in order. It did make such a strong impression on my tender Phantasy that I remember it as if it were but yesterday. I could never see it elsewhere. The house is in the great long street, over against the high steeple, and 'tis likely it remaines there still. 'Tis pitty it is not re-donne.

SIR HENRY SPELMAN

Born 1562. Historian and antiquary. He wrote many valuable works on legal and ecclesiastical antiquities, including *A History of Sacrilege* (published 1698); *Glossarium Archaeologicum*, a dictionary of obsolete law terms, which landed him in trouble with Archbishop Laud for including Magna Carta and Magnum

Consilium Regis under the M's (1626); *A History of the English Councils* (1639); and *Tenures by Knight-Service* (1641). He sat in Parliament and on various Commissions, as a reward for which he was voted a grant of £300. He died in 1641.

WHEN he was about 10 or 12 he went to schoole to a curs't Schoolmaster, to whom he had an Antipathie. His Master would discountenance him, and was very severe to him, and to a dull boy he would say, *as very a dunce as H. Spelman.* He was a boy of great spirit, and would not learne there. He was (upon his importunity) sent to another Schoolmaster and profited very well. I have heard his grandson say, that the Spelmans' Witts open late: Sir Henry did not understand Latin perfectly till he was fourty years old.

He was much perplexed with Lawe-suites and worldly troubles, so that he was about 40 before he could settle himselfe to make any great progresse in learning, which when he did, we find what great Monuments of Antiquarian knowledge he haz left to the World.

When his daughter-in-lawe (Sir John's wife) returned home from visitting her Neighbours, he would alwaies aske her what of Antiquity she had heard or observed, and if she brought home no such account, he would chide her (jestingly). He said to Sir William Dugdale, We are beholding to Mr Speed and Stowe for *stitching up* for us our English History. It seemes they were both Taylers.

He was a handsome Gentleman (as appeares by his picture in *Bibliotheca Cottoniana*) strong and valiant, and wore allwayes his Sword, till he was about 70 or more, when, finding his legges to faulter through feebleness as he was walking, *Now*, said he, *'tis time to leave off my Sword.*

EDMUND SPENSER

Born 1552. Poet. He was educated at Merchant Taylors School, then newly opened, and at Pembroke Hall, Cambridge. Through his college friend, Gabriel Harvey, he obtained in 1578 a place in the Earl of Leicester's household, and became acquainted with Sir Philip Sidney, with whom he formed a literary club styled the *Areopagus*, chiefly for the purpose of naturalizing the classical metres in English verse. In 1579 he began *The Faerie Queene* and published his *Shepheard's Calender*, which was enthusiastically received. In 1580 he was appointed secretary to Lord Grey de Wilton, then going to Ireland as Lord Deputy. Spenser acquired Kilcolman Castle in County Cork, a former possession of the Earls of

Desmond, with three thousand acres attached. Here he settled, and occupied himself with literary work, writing his elegy *Astrophel* on Sir Philip Sidney, and preparing *The Faerie Queene* for the press, three books of which he entrusted to the printer on his visit to London in 1589, during which Sir Walter Raleigh presented him to Queen Elizabeth, who awarded him a pension of fifty pounds. He reluctantly returned to Kilcolman, which he regarded as a place of exile, in 1591, and wrote *Colin Clouts come home againe*. In 1594 Spenser celebrated his marriage to Elizabeth Boyle in his splendid *Epithalamion*, and two years later published the second part of *The Faerie Queene*. His castle of Kilcolman was burnt in October 1598, in a sudden insurrection, and his youngest child perished in the flames. Spenser and his wife escaped with difficulty, and he died in destitution in London in 1599 and was buried near Chaucer in Westminster Abbey.

MR BEESTON sayes, he was a little man, wore short haire, little band and little cuffs.

Mr Edmund Spencer was of Pembroke-hall in Cambridge; he misst the Fellowship there, which Bishop Andrewes gott. He was an acquaintance and frequenter of Sir Erasmus Dreyden: His Mistris Rosalind was a kinswoman of Sir Erasmus Ladys. The chamber there at Sir Erasmus' is still called Mr Spencers chamber. Lately, at the college takeing-downe the Wainscot of his chamber, they found an abundance of Cards, with stanzas of the *Faerie Queen* written on them.

Mr Samuel Woodford (the Poet who paraphras'd the Psalmes) lives in Hampshire neer Alton, and he told me that Mr Spenser lived sometime in these parts, in this delicate sweet ayre: where he enjoyed his Muse: and writt good part of his Verses. He had lived some time in Ireland, and made a description of it, which is printed.

I have said before that Sir Philip Sidney, and Sir Walter Ralegh were his acquaintance. Sir John Denham told me, that ABp. Usher, Lord Primate of Armagh, was acquainted with him; by this token: when Sir William Davenant's *Gondibert* came forth, Sir John askt the Lord Primate if he had seen it. Said the Primate, Out upon him, with his vaunting Preface, he speakes against my old friend Edmund Spenser.

In the South crosse-aisle of Westminster abbey, next the Dore, is this Inscription:

Heare lies (expecting the second comeing of our Saviour Christ Jesus) the body of Edmund Spencer, the Prince of Poets of his tyme, whose divine spirit needs no other witnesse, then the workes which he left behind him. He was borne in London, in the yeare 1510 [*1552*], and dyed in the yeare 1596 [*1599*].

THOMAS STREET

Born in Ireland 1622. Astronomer. He was a clerk in the Excise Office. He published *Astronomia Carolina* 1661; *The Planetary Systeme* 1670; and *The Tables of the Moon and Mercury*; besides carrying forward the study of Trigonometry. He died in 1689.

ANNO 1661 he printed that excellent piece of *Astronomia Carolina*, which he dedicated to King Charles II, and also presented it well bound to Prince Rupert and the Duke of Monmouth; but never had a farthing of any of them.

He had the true motion of the Moon by which he could discover and demonstrate the never yet discovered Art and Science of finding the true Longitude, yet 2 of his familiar acquaintance tell me that he did not committ this Discovery to paper: so it is dead with him.

He made attempts to be introduced to King Charles II and also to King James II, but Courtiers would not doe it without a good gratuitie.

He was of a rough and cholerique humour. Discoursing with Prince Rupert, his Highnesse affirmed something that was not according to Art: sayd Mr Street, Whoever affirmes that, is no Mathematician. So they would point at him afterwards at Court and say *there's the man that huff't Prince Rupert*.

He dyed in Chanon-row at Westminster, the 17th of August 1689, and is buried in the church yard of the New Chapell there towards the East window of the Chancel, within twenty or 30 foot of the wall. His acquaintance talke of clubbing towards an Inscription. No man living haz deserved so well of Astronomie.

THOMAS STUMP

Born 1616. Soldier. His great-great-grandfather *Stump, was a wealthy Cloathier at Malmesbury, tempore Henrici VIII: at the Dissolution of the Abbeys he bought a great deal of the Abbey lands thereabout. When King Henry 8th hunted in Bradon forest, he gave his Majesty and the Court a great entertainment at his House (the Abbey). The King told him, He was afraid he had undone himself, he replied, that his own Servants should only want their supper for it.* His eldest son, Sir James Stump, was High

Sheriff and from him *are descended severall of our greatest Nobility, the Earles of Suffolk and Lincoln, etc.*

CAPTAIN THOMAS STUMP of Malmesbury. 'Tis pity the strange Adventures of him should be forgotten. He was the eldest Sonn of Mr Will. Stump, Rector of Yatton Keynell: was a Boy of most daring Spirit; he would climb Towers and Trees most dangerously: nay he would walke on the Battlements of the Tower there.

He had too much Spirit to be a Scholar, and about at 16 went in a Voyage with his Uncle (since Sir Thomas) Ivy to Guyana in Anno 1633, or 1632. When the Ship put in somewhere there 4 or 5 of them straggled into the Countrey too far: and in the interim the wind served, and the Sailes were hoist, and the Stragglers left behind.

It was not long before the wild People seized on them, and stript them: and those that had beards, they knocked their braines out: And (as I remember) did eat them: but the Queen saved T. Stump and the other boy. T. Stump threw himself into the River (Oronoque) to have drowned himself, but could not sinke; he is very full chested. The other youth shortly after died. Thomas Stump lived with them till 1636 or 1637.

His Narrations are very strange and pleasant; but so many yeares have made me almost forgett all. He sayes there is incomparable Fruits there: and that it may be termed the Paradise of the World. He says that the Spondyles of the back-bones of the huge Serpents there are used, to sit on, as our Women sitt upon Butts. He taught them to build Hovills: and to thatch and wattle. I wish I had a good account of his abode there: he is *fide dignus* [worthy of belief]. I never heard of any man that lived so long among those Salvages.

A Ship then sayling by (a Portughese) he swam to it; they took him up and made use of him for a Sea-boy. As he was sayling near Cornwall, he stole out of a Port-hole, and swam to shore; and so beg'd to his Fathers in Wiltshire. When he came home, no body knew him: and they would not own him: only Jo. Harris the Carpenter knew him: At last he recounted so many Circumstances, that he was owned, and in 1642 had a Commission for a Captain of Foot in King Charles Ist army.

SIR JOHN SUCKLING

Born 1609. Poet. His father was Secretary of State and Comptroller of the Household to James I. After travelling on the Continent, he served for a short time under Gustavus Adolphus and, on his return to England, he was knighted and went to Court, where his wealth, generosity, and wit made him a general favourite. He became a leader of the Royalist party in the early troubles, but he got into trouble in connexion with a plot to rescue Strafford from the Tower, and fled to the Continent. He wrote four plays: *Aglaura*, which he provided with two fifth acts, one tragic, the other not; *Brennoralt*; *The Goblins*; and *The Sad One*; but his chief fame rests on his songs and ballads. He also wrote *The Session of the Poets*, which is mainly of antiquarian interest. Died 1642.

I HAVE heard Mris Bond say that Sir John's father was but a dull fellow (her husband Mr Thomas Bond knew him) the witt came by the mother.

By 18 he had well travelled France and Italie, and part of Germany, and (I thinke also) of Spaine.

He returned to England an extraordinary accomplished Gent., grew famous at Court for his readie sparkling witt; which was envyed, and he was (Sir William Davenant sayd) the Bull that was bayted. He was incomparably readie at repartying, and his Witt most sparkling when most sett-upon and provoked.

He was the greatest gallant of his time, and the greatest Gamester, both for Bowling and Cards, so that no Shopkeeper would trust him for 6d, as today, for instance, he might, by winning, be worth 200 pounds, and the next day he might not be worth half so much, or perhaps sometimes be *minus nihilo*. He was one of the best Bowlers of his time in England. He played at Cards rarely well, and did use to practise by himselfe a-bed, and there studyed how the best way of managing the cards could be. His Sisters would come to the Peccadillo-bowling-green, crying for feare he should loose all their Portions.

Sir John Suckling invented the game of Cribbidge. He sent his Cards to all Gameing places in the countrey, which were marked with private markes of his; he gott twenty thousand pounds by this way.

Sir William Davenant (who was his intimate friend and loved him intirely) would say that Sir John, when he was at his lowest ebbe in gameing, I meane when unfortunate, then would make himselfe most glorious in apparell, and sayd that it exalted his spirits, and that he had then best Luck when he was most gallant, and his Spirits were highest.

Sir William would say that he did not much care for a Lord's converse, for they were in those dayes damnably Proud and arrogant, and the French would say that *My Lord d'Angleterre look't comme un Mastif-dog.* But now the age is more refined, and much by the example of his gracious Majestie who is the Patterne of Courtesie.

There happened, unluckily, a difference between Sir John Suckling and Sir John Digby (brother to Sir Kenelme) about a Mistresse or Gameing, I have now forgott. Sir John was but a slight timberd man, and of midling stature; Sir John Digby was a proper person of great strength and courage answerable, and yielded to be the best swordsman of his time. Sir John, with two or three of his party, assaults Sir John Digby goeing into a Play-house. Sir J.D. had only his Lacquey with him, but Sir J.D. flew on them like a Tigre, and made them run. 'Twas pitty that this accident brought the blemish of Cowardise to such an ingeniose young Sparke. Sir J.D. was such a Hero that there were very few but he would have served in like manner.

Mr Snowdon tells me that after Sir John's unluckie rencounter, or Quarrel with Sir John Digby, wherin he was baffled, 'twas strange to see the envie and ill-nature of people to trample, and Scoffe at, and deject one in disgrace; inhumane as well as unchristian. The Lady Moray had made an entertainment for severall persons of quality at Ashley, in Surrey, near Chertsey, whereat Mr Snowdon then was. There was the Countess of Middlesexe, whom Sir John had highly courted, and had spent on her, and in treating her, some thousands of pounds. At this entertainment she could not forbeare, but was so severe and ingrate as to upbraid Sir John of his late recieved Baffle; and some other Ladys had their flirts. The Lady Moray (who invited them) seeing Sir John out of Countenance, for whose worth she alwaies had a respect: Well, sayd shee, I am a merry Wench, and will never forsake an old friend in disgrace, so come, sitt downe by me, Sir John (said she) and seated him on her right hand, and countenanced him. This raysed Sir John's dejected spirites that he threw his Reparties about the Table with so much sparklingnesse and Gentilenes of Witt, to the admiration of them all.

When the Expedition was into Scotland, Sir John Suckling, at his owne chardge raysed a Troope of 100 very handsome young proper men, whom he clad in white doubletts and scarlett breeches, and scarlet Coates, hatts, and feathers, well horsed and armed. They say 'twas one of the finest sights in those days. But Sir John Menis made a Lampoon of it:

The Ladies opened the Windows to see,
So fine and goodly a sight-a . . . etc.

I thinke the Lampoon sayes he made an inglorious chardge against the Scotts.

He was of middle stature and slight strength, brisque round eie, reddish fac't and red nose (ill liver) his head not very big, his hayre a kind of sand colour, his beard turnd-up naturally, so that he had a briske and gracefull looke. He died a Batchelour.

He made a magnificent entertainment in London for a great number of Ladies of Quality, all beauties and young, which cost him many hundreds of poundes, where were all the rarities that this part of the world could afford, and the last service of all was Silk Stockings and Garters, and I thinke also Gloves.

Anno Domini 1637, Sir John Suckling, William Davenant, Poet Laureate (not then knighted) and Jack Young, came to Bathe. Sir John came like a young Prince for all manner of Equipage and convenience, and Sir W. Davenant told me that he had a Cart-load of Bookes carried downe; and 'twas there, at Bath, that he writt the little Tract in his Booke about Socinianism. 'Twas as pleasant a journey as ever men had; in the height of a long Peace and luxury, and in the Venison Season. The second night they lay at Marlborough, and walking on the delicate fine downes at the Backside of the Towne, whilest supper was making ready, the maydes were drying of cloathes on the bushes. Jack Young had espied a very pretty young Girle, and had gott her consent for an assignation, which was about midnight, which they happened to overheare on the other side of the hedge, and were resolved to frustrate his designe. They were wont every night to play at Cards after supper a good while: but Jack Young pretended wearinesse, etc, and must needes goe to Bed, not to be perswaded by any meanes to the contrary. They had their landlady at supper with them; said they to her, Observe this poor Gentleman, how he yawnes: now is his mad fit comeing uppon him. We beseech you that you make fast his doores, and gett somebody to watch and looke to him, for about midnight he will fall to be most outragious. Gett the Hostler, or some strong fellow, to stay-up, and we will well content him, for he is our worthy friend, and a very honest Gent., only, perhaps, twice in a yeare he falls into these fitts.

Jack Young slept not, but was ready to goe out as the clocke struck to the houre of appointment, and then going to open the Dore he was disappointed, knocks, bounces, stampes, calls *Tapster! Chamberlayne! Hostler!* sweares and curses dreadfully; nobody would come to him. Sir John and W. Davenant were expectant all this time, and ready to dye with laughter. I know not how, he happened to gett open the Dore, and was comeing downe the stayres. The Hostler, a huge lusty fellow, fell upon him, and held him, and cryed, Good Sir, take God in your mind, you shall not goe out to destroy yourself. J. Young struggled and strived, insomuch that at last he was quite spent and dispirited, and was faine to goe to bed to rest himselfe.

In the morning the Landlady of the House came to see how he did, and brought him a Cawdle; Oh, Sir, sayd she, You had a heavy fitt last night; pray, Sir, be pleased to take some of this to comfort your heart. Jack Young thought the woman had been mad, and being exceedingly vexed, flirted the porrenger of Cawdle in her face. The next day his Camerades told him all the plott, how they crosse-bitt him. That night they went to Bronham House, Sir Edward Baynton's (then a noble seate, since burnt in the Civill Warres) where they were nobly entertained severall dayes. From thence, they went to West Kington to Parson Davenant, Sir William's eldest brother, where they stayd a weeke – mirth, witt and good cheer flowing. From thence to Bath, six or seven miles.

My Ladye Southcott, whose husband hanged himselfe, was Sir John Suckling's sister. At her house in Bishopsgate-Street, London, is an originall of her brother Sir John of Sir Anthony van-Dyke, all at length, leaning against a rock, with a play-booke, contemplating. It is a piece of great value.

When his *Aglaura* was put on, he bought all the Cloathes himselfe, which were very rich; no tinsell, all the lace pure gold and silver, which cost him . . . I have now forgott. He had some scaenes to it, which in those dayes were only used at Masques.

He went into France, where after sometime, being come to the bottome of his Found, reflecting on the miserable and despicable condition he should be reduced to, having nothing left to maintaine him, he (having a convenience for that purpose, lyeing at an apothecarie's house in Paris) tooke poyson, which killed him miserably with vomiting. He was buryed in the Protestants Churchyard. This was (to the best of my remembrance) 1646.

His Picture, which is like him, before his Poemes, says that he was about 28 yeares old when he dyed.

THOMAS SUTTON

Born 1532. Usurer. Student of Lincoln's Inn. Surveyor of the Ordnance in the Northern Parts 1570. Obtained leases of land rich in coal in Durham, and made an enormous fortune, which was further increased by his marriage with Elizabeth, widow of John Dudley. He settled in London 1580. Purchased the Charterhouse 1611, where he established a hospital of eighty inmates and a school of forty boys. He was estimated the richest commoner in England, his estates being reckoned at £5,000 a year and his personalty at £60,410. Died 1611.

THOMAS SUTTON, Founder of the Hospitall, was first a Garrison-soldier at Barwick. He was a lusty, healthy, handsome fellowe, and there was a very rich Brewer that brewed to the Navy, etc, who was ancient and he had maried a young buxome wife, who enjoyed the embraces of this more able performer as to that point. The old brewer doted on his desirable wife and dies and left her all his Estate, which was great.

Sutton was a man of good understanding, and improved it admirably well: But the particular wayes by which he did it I have now forgott. But he was much upon mortgages, and fed severall with hopes of being his Heire. The Earle of Dorset (I thinke Richard) mightily courted him and presented him, hoping to have been his Heire; and so did severall other great persons.

The later end of his dayes he lived in Fleetstreet at a Wollen draper's shop, opposite to Fetter-lane; where he had so many great Chests full of money, that his chamber was ready to groane under it; and Mr Tyndale, who knew him and I thinke had money of him on mortgage during his Lawe-suite, was afrayd the roome would fall. He lived to establish his Hospitall, and was Governor there himselfe.

'Twas from him that B. Johnson tooke his hint of the Fox: and by Seigneur Volpone is meant Sutton.

SILAS TAYLOR

Born 1624. Historian. Educated at Westminster School and New Inn Hall, Oxford. Captain in the Parliamentary Army. Commissary for Ammunition under Sir Edward Harley at Dunkirk 1660. He published *The History of the Gavelkind*, 1663, and left in manuscript a collection for *The History of Herefordshire*. He died in 1678.

HE was a Captaine in the Parliamentary Army, under Col. Massey. He was a Sequestrator in Herefordshire: and had in those times great power: which power he used civilly and obligeingly, that he was beloved by all the King's party.

He was very musicall, and hath composed many things, and I have heard Anthemes of his sang before his Majestie, in his Chapell, and the King told him he liked them. He had a very fine chamber organ in those unmusicall dayes.

His father left him a pretty good estate, but he bought Church Lands and had the moeity of the Bishop's palace, at Hereford, where he leyd out much money in building and altering. The times turning, he was faine to disgorge all he had gott, and was ruined, but Sir Paul Neile got for him the Keeper of the King's Stores at Harwich, worth about 1000 pounds per annum.

He was a great lover of Antiquities, and ransackt the MSS of the Church of Hereford (there were a great many that lay uncouth and unkiss [*neglected*]).

He had severall MSS by him of great Antiquity: one thin 4to of the Philosopher's Stone, in Hieroglyphicks, with some few Latin verses underneath; the most curiously limned that ever I sawe. His Majesty offered him 100 pounds for it, but he would not accept it.

Capt. Taylor searched the Records in the Tower, and retrived some Privileges that the Borough of Harwich had lost, for which the Borough ought ever to have his remembrance in esteeme: and tho' he dyed above 100 pounds in their debt, yet the Towne lost not by him, for the reason aforesaid.

The History or Collection of this Ancient Borough he pawned a little before his death to Mr Baker, the Print-seller by the Old Exchange, for 4 pounds 15s. I acquainted Sir Philip Parker, whom the Borough uses to choose for their Burghesse, to buy it for his Borough. He would not lay out so much money, which would doe them more service then all his roast-beefe, wine, and ale at an Election.

He also garbled [*sifted*] the Library of the Church of Worcester, and Evidences, where he had the originall Grant of King Edgar (θαλασσιαρχης [*thalassiarchis*]) whence the Kings of England derive their right to the Soveraignty of the Sea. 'Tis printed in Mr Selden's *Mare Clausum*. I have seen it many times, and it is as legible as but newly written (Roman character). He offered it to the King for 120 pounds but his Majesty would not give so much. Since his death, I acquainted the Secretary of Estate that he dyed in debt and his Creditors seised on his goods and papers. He told me that it did of right belong to Worcester Church. I told one of their Prebends, and they cared not for such things. I beleeve it haz wrapt Herings by this time.

JOHN TOMBES

Born 1603. Divine. Educated at Magdalen Hall, Oxford. Being a Presbyterian, he refused to baptize infants, and appealed to the Westminster Assembly on the subject and published tracts. Master of the Temple 1645–7. In 1646 he had an interview with Cromwell. He organized the Baptist Church, and wrote tracts against Paedobaptists (infant baptizers), Quakers, and Papists. Died 1676.

HE was a great Master of the Greeke Tongue, and the Hebrue he understood well. He alwaies carried a little Greeke Testament about with him: he had it almost *memoriter*.

He was soon taken notice of for his curious, searching, piercing witt: he preached somewhere Eastwards from Oxon, and had a Sect followed him; and 'twas predicted he would doe a great deale of mischiefe to the Church of England, reflecting that the greatest Witts have donne the most mischiefe to the Church, introducing new opinions, etc.

He was Vicar of a market-towne in Herefordshire, where he was very well beloved by his parish, and Sir William Croftes, eldest brother to the now Bishop of Hereford, built a house at Leominster, to live there, to heare him preach.

Then he went into his owne country, to Beaudley a market Towne, at which time Mr Baxter, his Antagonist, preacht at Kitterminster, the next market towne, two miles distant. They preacht against one another's Doctrines, and printed against each other. Mr Tombes was the Coryphaeus of the Anabaptists: both had great audience; they went severall miles on foot to each Doctor. Once (I thinke oftner) they disputed face to face; and the followers were like two armies, about 1500 of a party; and truly, at last they fell by the eares, hurt was donne, and the civill magistrates had much adoe to quiet them.

About Anno 1664 he came to the Act at Oxford, and did there *in Vesperiis* sett up a Challenge to maintaine *contra omnes gentes* [against all comers] the Anabaptisticall doctrine; but not a man would grapple with him. Now, though *primâ facie* this might seeme very bold to challenge a whole University, 'twas not so strange neither, for he came throughly prepared, after 30 yeares' study and thoughts, and most of them surprised.

He was thought to be as great a Divine as most we had after Bishop Sanderson dyed. I remember he never, or seldome, was wont to say Our Saviour Christ, but *my Lord Christ*. He seemed to be a very pious and zealous Christian. Putting aside his Anabaptisticall positions, he was comformable enough to the Church of England.

I have heard him say (though he was much opposite to the Romish Religion) that truly, for his part, should he see a poor zealous Friar goeing to preach, he should pay him respect.

NICHOLAS TOWES

To one Mr Towes, who had been School-fellow with Sir George Villers, the Father of the first Duke of Buckingham (and was his Friend and Neighbour) as he lay in his bed awake (and it was Day-light) there came into his Chamber the Phantome of his dear Friend Sir George Villers: Said Mr Towes to him, Why, you are Dead, what make you here? Said the Knight, I am Dead, but cannot rest in peace for the Wickedness and Abomination of my Son George at Court. I do appear to you, to tell him of it, and to advise and dehort him from his Evil ways. Said Mr Tows, the Duke will not believe me, but will say, that I am Mad, or Doat. Said Sir George, Go to him from me, and tell him by such a Token (some Mole) that he had in some secret place, which none but himself knew of. Accordingly Mr Towes went to the Duke, who Laugh'd at his Message. At his return home, the Phantome appeared again; and told him, that the Duke would be Stab'd (he drew out a Dagger) a quarter of a Year after: And you shall outlive him half a Year; and the Warning that you shall have of your Death will be, that your Nose will fall a-bleeding: All which accordingly fell out so.

This Account I have had (in the main) from two, or three; but Sir William Dugdale affirms what I have here taken from him to be true, and that the Apparition told him of several things to come, which proved true, e.g. of a Prisoner in the Tower, that should be honourably delivered. This Mr Towes had so often the Ghost of his old Friend appear to him, that it was not at all terrible to him. He was Surveyor of the Works at Windsor (by the favour of the Duke): Being then sitting in the Hall, he cried out, The Duke of Buckingham is stabb'd: He was stabb'd that very moment.

Sir William Dugdale did farther inform me that Major General Middleton (since Lord) went into the Highlands of Scotland, to endeavour to make a Party for King Charles the First. An Old Gentleman (that was second-sighted) came and told him that his endeavour was good; but he would be unsuccessful, and moreover, That they would put the King to Death: and that several other Attempts would be made, but all in vain: But that his Son would come in, but not Reign; but at last would be Restored.

This Lord Middleton had a great Friendship with the Laird Bocconi, and they had made a Sacrament, That the first of them that Died should appear to the other in extremity. The Lord Middleton was taken Prisoner at Worcester Fight, and was Prisoner in the Tower of London under Three Locks. Lying in his Bed pensive, Bocconi appeared to him; my Lord Middleton asked him if he were dead or alive? He said, Dead, and that he was a Ghost, and told him, that within Three Days he should escape, and he did so in his Wive's Cloaths. When he had done his Message, he gave a Frisk, and said,

Givenni givanni 'tis very strange,
In the World to see so sudden a Change.

And then gathered up and vanished.

Anno 1670, not far from Cyrencester, was an Apparition: Being demanded, whether a good Spirit, or a bad? returned no answer, but disappeared with a curious Perfume and most melodious Twang. Mr W. Lilly believes it was a Farie.

THOMAS TRIPLETT

Born 1603. Divine. Educated at St Paul's School and Christ Church, Oxford. Vicar of Woodburn, Northumberland, 1630; Rector of Whitburn in Durham 1631; and of Washington in the same county 1640. Canon of York 1641; collated to Canonries at Salisbury 1645, and Durham 1649, but was sequestrated by Parliament and was not installed till 1660. Sub-Dean and Canon of Westminster 1662. In his will he left £20 a year *in trust for Foure of the most worthy Schollers of the Free Schoole of Westminster that want means to subsist att the university*. He died in 1670.

HE went to schoole to Dr Gill, as appears by his Ballad, which will last longer than any Sermon that ever he made.

Dr Gill was a very ingeniose person, as may appeare by his Writings. Notwithstanding, he had moodes and humours, as particularly his whipping fitts:

As Paedants out of the schoole-boies breeches
doe clawe and curry their owne itches.

This Dr Gill whipt Sir John Duncomb (who was not long after a Colonel of Dragoons at Edgehill-fight) taken pissing against the wall. He had his sword by his side, but the boyes surprized him: somebody had throwen a stone in at the windowe; and they seised on the first man they lighted on. He would have cutt the Doctor, but he never went abroad but to church, and then his army went with him. He complained to the Councill, but it became ridicule, and so his revenge sank.

Dr Triplet came to give his Master a Visit, and he whip't him. The Dr gott Pitcher of Oxford, who had a strong and sweet Base, to sing this Song under the schoole windowes, and gott a good guard to secure him with swords, etc, and he was preserved from the examen of the little myrmidons which issued-out to attach him; but he was so frighted that he beshitt himselfe most fearfully:

A French man voyd of English
Enquiring for Paul's steeple
His Pardonnez-moy
He counted a toy,
For he whip't him before all the people.

For a piece of Beef and Turnip,
Neglected, with a Cabbage,
He took up the Pillion
Of his bouncing Mayd Jillian,
And sowc't her like a Baggage.

After his Sequestration, Dr Triplett kept a Schoole at Dublyn, when the King was beheaded. Afterwards at Hayes, Surrey, 12 miles from London. 'Twas here our common friend George Ent went to schoole to him, who told me that he had forgott the smart of his old master Gill. He was very severe.

I'le tell you a story of our old friend. His Master Triplett was a great lover of Honey, and one of his Schoole-fellowe's mothers having sent a pott of honey to the Doctor, G. Ent putt his schoole-fellow to beg a little of his Master, and he had gott a manchet and so they would have a *Regalio*. The Doctor was in his study; and the boy takes the confidence to approach with his *Quaeso, Praeceptor, da mihi Mel* [Please, Sir, give me some Honey]. G. Ent was sneaking behind. Quoth the disturbed doctor, You audacious raskall, and gave him a good cuff on the eare, How dare you be thus impudent? Sirrah, who putt you on? The boy answered, whiningly, G. Ent. The enraged Doctor flies out of his study (he was a very strong man) gives poor George a kick in the breech, and made him fly downe a flight of 7 or 8 staires to the landing place, where his head first came to. He was stunn'd, but 'twas well his neck was not broken. 'Twas a most cruel and inhumane act to use a poore child so. It so happened that a day or two before G.E. had shaled a Tooth. He writes a letter to his father (now Sir George Ent) and incloses the tooth in it; relates the story, and that he lost the tooth by that meanes. The next day the grave and learned Dr Ent comes to Hayes (the fame of whose learning and Testimonie did give great credit and reputation to this schoole) expostulates with the Doctor about his sonne. To be short, tooke him away, and placed him with Mr William Radford (an honest sequestred fellow of Trinity College, Oxon, and an excellent schoolmaster, having been bred at Thame under Dr Birt and afterwards sent to Winton). This accident well-nigh did breake Dr Triplett's schoole. But shortly after this time, happened the Restauration of his Majestie, and then he was also restored to his former preferments.

WILLIAM TWISSE

Born 1578. Puritan divine. Probationer Fellow of New College, Oxford, 1596. Chaplain to Elizabeth, Queen of Bohemia, at Heidelberg 1613. Rector of Newington Longueville 1613. Vicar of Newbury 1620. He then refused all further preferment, as *lacking music in singing and rhetoric for the preaching, and not skilled to stroke a cathedral beard canonically*. He became Prolocutor of the Westminster Assembly in 1643, but was opposed to the alienation of Church property. He died in 1646 and was buried in Westminster Abbey, but in 1661 his remains were, by royal command, disinterred and thrown into a common pit in St Margaret's Churchyard.

His sonne Dr Twisse, Minister of the New-church neer Tothill-street Westminster, told me, that he had heard his father say, that when he was a schoole-boy at Winton-colledge, that he was a rakell; and that one of his Schoolefellowes and camerades (as wild as himselfe) dyed there; and that, his father goeing in the night to the House of office, the phantome or Ghost of his dead schoolefellow appeared to him, and told him *I am damn'd*: and that this was the Beginning of his Conversion.

Memorandum: the Dr had a melancholique and Hypocondriaque temperament.

THOMAS TYNDALE

Born 1588. Son of Thomas Tyndale of Eastwood Park, Thornbury, by Oriane, sister and co-heir of Claudius le Bon, Seigneur de Fourneau in Normandy. In 1620 he married Dorothy, the daughter of William Stafford, author of *A Brief Concert of English Polity*, who in 1587 had revealed a plot against Queen Elizabeth, only to find himself implicated, for which he was imprisoned in the Tower. Thomas Tyndale sold Eastwood Park in 1619 and bought the site and demesne of the Priory of Kington St Michael, where he lived until his death in 1672. His widow told Aubrey many of the more scandalous stories about the Elizabethan Court.

THOMAS TYNDALE, an old Gentleman that remembers Queen Elizabeth's raigne and Court, one of true Gravity and prudence, not one that depends upon the grave cutt of his beard to be thought so. He hath seen much in his time both at home and abroade; and with much choler inveighes against things now: Alas! O' God's will! Now-a-dayes every one, forsooth! must have coaches, forsooth! In those dayes Gentlemen kept horses for a man-at-Armes, besides their Hackney and hunting horses. This made the Gentry robust and hardy and fitt for service; were able to be their owne guides in case of a rout or so, when occasion should so require. Our Gentry forsooth in these dayes are so effeminated that they know not how to ride on horseback.

The advantage that King Charles I had: Gentlemen tho [*then*] kept good horses, and many horses for a man-at-Armes, and men that could ride them; hunting horses. Now we are come all to our Coaches forsooth! Now young men are so farre from managing good horses, they know not how to ride a hunting nag or handle their weapons. So God help the King if, etc.

In Sir Philip Sydney's time 'twas as much disgrace for a Cavalier to be seen in London rideing in a Coach in the street as now 'twould be to be seen in a petticoate and wastcoate. In those days when a Senator went to the Parliament-house a-foote, or a horse-back with his rich Footcloath, he had at his heeles ½ a dozen or 10 tall fellowes with blew coates and badges and long basket-hilt swords. Now forsooth only a laquey and a little spitt-pig.

Tho [*then*] when the Gentry mett, it was not at a poor blind sordid ale-house, to drinke up a barrell of drinke and lie drunke there two or three dayes together; fall together by the eares. They mett tho [*then*] in the fields, well-appointed, with their Hounds or their Hawkes; kept up good Hospitality; and kept a good retinue, that would venture that bloud and spirit that filled their vaines which their Masters tables nourisht; kept their Tenants in due respect of them. We had no depopulacion in those dayes.

You see in me the Ruines of Time. The day is almost at end with me, and truly I am glad of it: I desire not to live in this corrupt age. I foresawe and foretold the late changes, and now easily foresee what will follow after. Alas! O' God's will! It was not so in Queen Elizabeth's time: then youth bare Respect to old Age.

Tho [*then*] the elders and better sort of the Parish sate and beheld the pastimes of the young men, as wrastling, shooting at Butts, bowling, and dancing. All this is now lost; and pride, whoreing, wantonnesses, and drunkennesses. Their servants like clownes too, drunkards too: breeches of one sort, Doublet of another, drabled with the teares of the Tankard and greasie. Dick Pawlet built an alehouse for his Servants, without the Gate, for convenience sake, because the servants should be within call.

In those dayes Hunting and Falconery were at the height. Good cheere was then much in use; but to be wiser then one's neighbours, scandalous and to be envyed at. And the Nobility and Gentry were, in that soft peace, damnable prowd and insolent.

HENRY AND THOMAS VAUGHAN

Born 1622. Poets and physicians. Henry was known as the *Silurist* because of his love for the County of Brecknockshire, the county of his birth, which was anciently inhabited by the Silures. He was at Jesus College, Oxford, and studied law in London, before settling as a physician at Brecon and Newton-by-Usk. In his youth he was a decided Royalist, and was imprisoned along with his twin brother Thomas. His first book, which appeared in 1646, was *Poems, with the Tenth Satire of Juvenal Englished. Olor Iscanus* (The Swan of Usk), a collection of poems and translations, was surreptitiously published in 1651. About this time he had a serious illness which led to deep spiritual impressions, and thereafter his writings were almost entirely religious. *Silex Scintillans* (Sparks from the Flint) is his best known work and contains the magnificent *They are all gone into the world of light. Flores Solitudinis* (Flowers of Solitude) and *The Mount of Olives* are devout meditations in prose. The two brothers were joint authors of *Thalia Rediviva: the Pastimes and Diversions of a Country Muse*, a collection of translations and original poems, 1678. Thomas Vaughan died in 1666 and Henry in 1695.

THERE were two Vaughans (Twinnes) both very ingeniose, and writers. One writt a Poeme called *Olor Iscanus* (Henry Vaughan, the first-borne) and another booke of divine meditations. He is ingeniose, but prowd and humorous [*moody*]. His brother wrote severall Treatises, whose names I have now forgott, but names himself *Eugenius Philalethes*.

They were borne at Llansanfraid in Brecknockshire, by the river Uske (Isca). Their grandmother was an Aubrey: their father, a coxcombe and no honester then he should be – he cosened me of 50s. once.

Eugenius Philalethes was of Jesus College. Whither Henry was I have forgotten; but he was a Clarke sometime to Judge Sir Marmaduke Lloyd.

This Account I had from Mr Henry Vaughan, whose handwriting it is:

Honoured Cousin.

Yours of the 10th June I received att Breckon, where I am still attendinge our Bishops Lady in a tertian feaver, and cannot as yet have the leasure to step home; butt lest my delayings of tyme here should bringe the account (you expect) too late into your hands: I shall now in part give you the best I can, and be more exact in my next.

My brother and I were borne att Newtin, in Brecknockshire, in the parish of St Bridget's, in the year 1621.

I stayed not att Oxford to take my degree, butt was sent to London, beinge then designed by my father for the study of the Law, which the sudden eruption of our late civil warres wholie frustrated.

My brother continued there for 10 or 12 yeares, and I thinke he could be noe lesse than Master of Arts. He died upon an imployment for his majesty, within 5 or 6 miles of Oxford, in the yeare that the last great plague visited London. He was buried by Sir Robert Murrey, his great friend (and then Secretary of Estate for the Kingdome of Scotland) to whom he gave his bookes and MSS.

My brothers imployment was in physic and Chymistrie: he was ordayned minister by bishop Mainwaringe and presented to the Rectorie of St Brigets by his kinsman, Sir George Vaughan.

My profession allso is physic, which I have practised now for many years with good successe (I thanke god!) and a repute big enough for a person of greater parts than my selfe.

My brother died in the seaven and fortieth year of his age, upon the 27th of Februarie in the yeare 1666, and was buried upon the first of March.

Dear Sir, I am highly obliged to you that you would be pleased to remember and reflect upon such low and forgotten thinges as my brother and my selfe. I shall be ever ready to acknowledge the honour you have done us, and if you have any Concerne in these parts that I may be serviceable in: I humblie beg, that you would call upon and Command,

Honoured Cousin,

Your most affectionate and most faithfull humble servant, H. Vaughan.

June the 15th —73

Sir Robert Moray the morning he dyed told me he buryed my cosen Thomas Vaughan at Albery neer Ricot within three miles of Oxford. He dyed at Mr Kem's howse, the minister.

EDWARD DE VERE EARL OF OXFORD

Born 1550. He was a courtier of Queen Elizabeth, who lost his friends by his insolence and pride, and his fortune by his extravagance. He married a daughter of Lord Burghley, who had to support his family after his death. He had some reputation as a writer of short pieces, many of which are in *The Paradise of Dainty Devices*. He was the seventeenth holder of the title, and died in 1604.

THIS Earle of Oxford, making of his low obeisance to Queen Elizabeth, happened to let a Fart, at which he was so abashed and ashamed that he went to Travell, 7 yeares. On his returne the Queen welcomed him home, and sayd, My Lord, I had forgott the Fart.

Mr Nicholas Hill was one of the most learned men of his Time: a great Mathematician and Philosopher, and a Poet and Traveller. But no writer (that I ever heard of) or, if he was, his writings had the usuall fate of those not printed in the Author's life-time. He was (or leaning) a Roman Catholiq. He was so eminent for knowledge, that he was the favourite of the great Earle of Oxford, who had him to accompanie him in his Travells (he was his Steward) which were so splendid and sumptuous, that he lived at Florence in more grandeur than the Duke of Tuscany. This Earle spent fourty thousand pounds per annum in seaven yeares Travell.

In his Travells with his Lord (I forget whither Italy or Germany, but I thinke the former) a poor man begged him to give him a penny. A penny! said Mr Hill, what dost say to ten pound? Ah! ten pound! said the Beggar, that would make a man happy. N. Hill gave him immediately

10 pounds and putt it downe upon account – Item, to a Beggar ten pounds, to make him happy, which his Lordship allowed and was well pleased at it.

As I have heard, it was that great Antiquary King Charles the First his observation, that the three ancientist Families of Europe for Nobility, were the *Veres* in England, Earls of Oxford, and the *Fitz-Geralds* in Ireland, Earls of Kildare, and *Momorancy* in France.

Surlinesse and inurbanitie too common in England: Chastise these very severely. A better instance of a squeamish and disobligeing, slighting, insolent, proud fellow, perhaps cannot be found then in Gwin, the Earle of Oxford's Secretary. No reason satisfies him, but he overweenes and cutts some sower faces that would turne the milke in a faire ladie's breast.

WILLIAM DE VISSCHER

Born 1595. Merchant. His family came from Emden, where he was born, which was then a Hanseatic Port and so one of the main trading centres in Europe. He died in 1668.

At two yeares old was brought into England by his father, an eminent Merchant; lived 55 yeares in one house at St Mary Hill, and dyed in the 74th yeare of his age. He lived there till the Fire of London; he dyed about 3 yeares after – he did not enjoy himselfe afterwards.

In the last great Dearth of Corne in England, when there was a great complaint and Cry of the Poore, he bade them bee of good comfort for they should not starve, for he would give them his labour and the use of his Estate for that yeare. He (being a man of vast Credit) gave his Factors order that what corne they could buy at such and such rates beyond sea, to hire flye-boates and send them over to the Port of London, of which he bought in one yeare two thousand five hundred sayle. The Corne that cost him 12s. per bushell beyond sea, he sold here for 14s.; and some of the places from whence he had corne (they selling it by reason of the greatnesse of the price) afterwards wanted it themselves and were faine to be supplied from hence; for which they were faine to pay halfe value more then the first cost, or els must have starved.

Many Disasters happened to many of the Shippes that were bound for London (some that never arrived were destroyed by foule weather; some wind-bound so long till their Corne fired for want of ayering, and was faine to be throwne overboard) that in the whole matter, after all the adventures runne, he did not gaine five and twenty hundred pounds. The Fly-boates caryed 800 tunne, and some more.

He was a very eminent Merchant, as most was of his time; and was valued by common reputation (when he maried his daughter) to be worth sixscore thousand pounds.

He stayed in London during the whole time of the Plague, and had not all that time one sick in his family. He was a temperate man, and had his house very cleanly kept.

EDMUND WALLER

Born 1606. Poet. He belonged to an old and wealthy family, and though he was related to John Hampden and was distantly connected with Oliver Cromwell, he was a staunch Royalist. At the age of sixteen he became a Member of Parliament, in which he sat for various constituencies for the rest of his life. In 1631 he added still further to his fortune by marrying Anne Banks, a London heiress, who died three years later. In 1643 he was detected in a Royalist plot and was expelled from the House, fined £10,000, and banished. On this occasion he showed cowardice and treachery, humiliating himself in the most abject manner and betraying all his associates. Returning to England by permission in 1652, he addressed some laudatory verses to Cromwell. Nevertheless, at the Restoration he was ready with a congratulatory address to Charles II, and when the King pointed out its inferiority to the Ode on Cromwell, Waller is said to have replied, *Poets, Sire, succeed better in fiction than in truth*. The poem, however, succeeded in its object, and the poet became a favourite at Court and sat in Parliament until his death in 1687.

I HAVE heard Mr Thomas Bigge, of Wickham, say (who was his schoolefellow, and of the same forme) that he little thought then he would have been so rare a Poet; he was wont to make his Exercise for him.

About 23, or between that and 30, he grew (upon I know not what occasion) mad; but 'twas (I thinke) not long ere he was cured. He was proud: to such, a Check often gives that distemper. He was passionately in love with Dorothea, the eldest daughter of the Earle of Leicester, whom he haz eternized in his Poems: and the Earle loved him, and would have been contented that he should have had one of the youngest daughters; perhaps *this* might be the Check.

One of the first refiners of our English language and poetrey. When he was a brisque young sparke, and first studyed Poetry; me thought, sayd he, I never sawe a good copie of English verses; they want smoothness; then I began to essay. I have severall times heard him say that he cannot versify when he will: but when the Fitt comes upon him, he does it easily, i.e. in plaine terms, when his Mercurius and Venus are well aspected.

He told me he was not acquainted with Ben Johnson (who dyed about 1638) but familiarly with Lucius Lord Falkland, Sydney Godolphin, Mr Hobbes, etc.

I have heard Mr Edmund Waller say that the Lord Marquisse of Newcastle was a great Patron to Dr Gassendi, and M. DesCartes, as well as Mr Hobbes, and that he hath dined with them all three at the Marquiss's Table at Paris.

He was very much admired at Court before the late Civill Warres. 1643, he being then a Member of the house of Commons, he was committed prisoner to the Tower for the Plott with Tomkins (his cosen germane) and Chaloner, for firing the City of London and delivering the Parliament, etc, to the King's partie. He had much adoe then to save his life, and in order to do it, sold his Estate in Bedfordshire, about 1300 pounds per annum, to Dr Wright, M.D., for about 10,000 pounds (much under value) which was procured in 24 hours time or els he had been hanged: With which money he Bribed the whole House, which was the first time a house of Commons was ever bribed. His excellent rhetoricall speech to the House to save his life, as also his Panegyrique to Oliver, Lord Protector, he would not suffer to be inserted in the edition of his *Poems* since the restauration of King Charles II.

When King Charles II returned, he received Mr Waller very kindly, and no man's conversation is more esteemed at Court now then his. The Dutches of Yorke (daughter to the Duke of Modena) very much delights in his company, and hath layd her commands on him to write, which he hath dedicated to her Highnes.

His Intellectuals are very good yet (1680) and he makes verses, but he growes feeble. He wrote verses of the Bermudas 50 yeares since, upon the information of one who had been there; walking in his fine woods the poetique spirit came upon him.

He is of somewhat above a middle stature, thin body, not at all robust; fine thin skin, his face somewhat of an olivaster, his hayre frizzd, of a brownish colour; full eye, popping out and working; ovall faced, his forehead high and full of wrinckles: his head but small, braine very hott, and apt to be cholerique. He is something magisteriall, and haz a great mastership of the English Language. He is of admirable and gracefull Elocution and exceeding ready.

He has spent most of his time in London; especially in Winter; but oftentimes in the Summer he enjoyes his Muse at Beconsfield in Bucks, which is incomparable Aire, and where are delicious walkes in the woods. Now I speake of Woods, I remember he told us there, that he cutt downe and grubbed-up a Beech wood of his, at Beconsfield in Bucks, and without soweing, but naturally, there sprang up a wood all of Birch.

He haz but a tender weake body, but was alwayes very temperate. They made him damnable drunke at Somerset-house, where, at the water stayres, he fell downe, and had a cruell fall. 'Twas pitty to use such a sweet swan so inhumanely.

I have heard him say that he so much admired Mr Thomas Hobbes booke *De Cive*, when it came forth, that he was very desirous to have it donne into English, and Mr Hobbes was most willing it should be done by Mr Waller's hand, for that he was so great a Master of our English language. Mr Waller freely promised him to doe it, but first he would desire Mr Hobbes to make an Essaye; he (T.H.) did the first booke, and did it so extremely well, that Mr Waller would not meddle with it, for that nobody els could doe it so well.

Mr Christopher Wase repeating to him the bitter satyricall verses made on Sir Carre Scroop, viz:

> *Thy Brother murdred, and thy Sister whor'd,*
> *Thy Mother too, and yet thy Penne's thy Sword;*

Mr Waller replyed sur le champ, That men write ill things well, and good things ill; that Satyricall writing was downe-hill, most easie and naturall; that at Billingsgate one might hear great heights of such witt; that the cursed earth naturally produces briars and thornes and weeds, but roses and fine flowers require cultivation. All his writings are free from offence.

Mr Edm. Waller sayd to Eliz. Countess of Thanet, That Poetrie was abused, when 'twas turned to any other way, than hymnes.

He hath a great memory: and remembers a History best when read to him: yet, notwithstanding his great Witt and mastership in rhetorique, he will oftentimes be guilty of mispelling in English. He writes a lamentably poor hand, as bad as the scratching of a hen.

He was borne in the parish of Agmundesham, in Buckinghamshire, at a place called Winchmore-hill, which was sold by his father, and which he had a very great desire to have bought again, not long before his death, but the Owner would not sell it. Said he, to his cosen Hamden, *A Stagge, when he is hunted, and neer spent, alwayes returnes home.*

He made some verses of his owne dyeing, but a fortnight, or a little more before his Decease. He dyed at 83, and his Witt was as florid then as at any time of his Life. He derived his Poetick witt from the Hamdens; severall of them have been Poets.

SETH WARD

Born 1617. Divine. At Cambridge he was *Terrae filius*, that is, he had to make a satirical speech at the Act, but his contribution was so alarmingly witty that he nearly lost his degree. Prebendary 1660, Dean 1661, and Bishop 1662, of Exeter. Translated to Salisbury 1667. Chancellor of the Garter 1671. He was extremely severe with dissenters. He published his sermons and some theological and mathematical treatises. Died 1689.

SETH WARD, Lord Bishop of Sarum, was borne at Huntingford, a small market-towne in Hartfordshire, anno Domini 1618 (when the great blazing Starre appeared). His Father was an Attorney there, and of very honest repute. (Dr Guydos, physician of Bath, says that anciently there was but One Attorney in Somerset, and he was so poor, that he went a foot to London; and now, 1689, they swarme there like Locusts: they go to Market and breed Contention.) His father taught him common arithmetique, and his Genius lay much to the Mathematiques, which being naturall to him, he quickly and easily attained.

At sixteen yeares old he went to Sydney colledge in Cambridge; he was Servitour to Dr Ward (Master of the Colledge, and Professor of Divinity) who being much taken with his ingenuity and industry, as also with his suavity of nature, quickly made him Scholar of the Howse, and after, Fellowe. Though he was of his name, he was not at all akinne to him (which most men imagined because of the great kindnesse to him) but the consimility of their dispositions was a greater tye of Friendship then that of blood, which signifies but little, as to that point.

Sir Charles Scarborough, M.D. (then an ingeniose young student, and Fellowe of Caius Colledge in Cambridge) was his great acquaintance; both students in mathematiques; which the better to perfect, they went to Mr William Oughtred, at Albury in Surrey, to be enformed by him in his *Clavis Mathematica*, which was then a booke of *Aenigmata*. Mr Oughtred treated them with exceeding humanity, being pleased at his heart when an ingeniose young man came to him that would ply his Algebra hard. When they returned to Cambridge, they read the *Clavis Mathematica* to their

Pupills, which was the first time that that booke was ever read in a University. Mr Laurence Rooke, a good mathematician and algebrist (and I thinke had also been Mr Oughtred's disciple) was his great acquaintance.

Anno Domini 1644, at the breaking out of the Civill-warres, he was a Prisoner, together with Dr Ward, Dr Collins, Sir Thomas Hatton, &c for the King's Cause, in St John's Colledge in Cambridge, and was put out of his Fellowship at Sydney Colledge. Being gott out of Prison, he was very civilly and kindly received by his friend and neighbour, Ralph Freeman, of Apsten, Esq, a vertuous and hospitable Gentleman.

Anno Domini 1648, the Visitation of the Parliament was [*at*] Oxford, and turned out a great many Professors and Fellowes. The Astronomy Reader, Dr Greaves, being sure to be ejected, was unwilling to be turned out of his place, but desired to resigne it rather to some worthy person, wherupon Dr Charles Scarborough and William Holder, D.D. recommended to Dr Greaves, their common friend, Mr Seth Ward. Seth Ward, A.M. was invited to succeed him, and came from Mr Freeman's to Oxford, had the Astronomy Professor's place, and lived at Wadham Colledge, where he conversed with the Warden, Dr John Wilkins.

Anno Domini 1656, he had from Brownrigg, Bishop of Exon, the grant of the Chantor's place of the Church of Exon (which then signified nothing).

Anno Domini 1659, William Hawes, then President of Trinity Colledge in Oxford, having broken in his lunges a vein (which was not curable) Mr Ward being very well acquainted and beloved in that colledge; by the consent of all the Fellowes, William Hawes resigned up his Presidentship to him, and dyed some few days after. Anno 1660, upon the restauration of King Charles II, Dr Hannibal Potter (the President sequestred by the Parliamentary Visitors) re-enjoyed the Presidentship again.

He then enjoyed his Chanters place at Excester, and, I thinke, was certainly minister of St Laurence church in London.

Anno Domini 1661, the Deane of Exon dyed, and then it was his right to step-in next to the Deanry.

Anno Domini 1663, the Bishop of Exon dyed: Dr Ward, the Deane, was in Devonshire at that time, at a Visitation, where were a great number of the Gentrey of the Countrey. Deane Ward was very well knowne to the Gentry, and his learning, prudence, and Comity had wonne them all to be his Friends. The newes of the death of the Bishop being brought to them, who were all very merry and rejoycing with good entertainment, with great Alacrity the Gentlemen cryed all, *uno uno*, Wee will have Mr Deane to be our Bishop. This was at that criticall time when the House of Commons were the King's darlings. The Deane told them that for his part he had no interest or acquaintance at Court; but intimated to them how much the King esteemed the Members of Parliament (and a great many Parliament men were then there) and that his Majestie would deny them nothing. If 'tis so, Gentlemen (sayd Mr Deane) that you will needes have me to be your bishop, if some of you will make your addresse to his Majestie, 'twill be donne. With that they dranke the other Glasse, a health to the King, and another to their wished-for Bishop; had their horses presently made ready, putt foot in Stirrup, and away they rode merrily to London; went to the King, and he immediately graunted them their request. This is the first time that ever a Bishop was made by the House of Commons.

Now, though Envy cannot deny, that this worthy Person was very well worthy any Preferment could be conferred on him, Yet the old Bishops were exceedingly disgruntled at it, to see a briske young Bishop that could see through all their formall gravity, but 40 yeares old, not come in at the right dore but leape over the pale. It went to their very hearts. Well, Bishop of Excester he was, to the great joy of all the Diocese. Being Bishop he had then free accesse to his Majestie, who is a lover of ingenuity and a discerner of ingeniose men, and quickly tooke a liking to him.

He is (without all manner of flattery) so prudent, learned, and good a man, that he honours his Preferment as much as the Preferment does him: and is such a one that cannot be advanced too high. My Lord (Lucius) Falkland was wont to say that he never knew any one that a paire of Lawne sleeves had not altered from himselfe, but only Bishop Juxon; had he knowne this excellent Prelate, he would have sayd he had knowne one more. As he is the pattern of humility and courtesie, so he knowes when to be severe and austere; and he is not one to be trampled or worked upon. He is a Batchelour, and of a most magnificent and munificent mind.

He hath been a Benefactor to the Royall Societie (of which he was one of the first Members and Institutors: the beginning of Philosophical Experiments was at Oxon, 1649, by Dr Wilkins, Seth Ward, Ralph Bathurst, &c). He also gave a noble pendulum Clock to the Royall Societie (which goes a weeke) to perpetuate the memory of his deare and learned friend, Mr Laurence Rooke, who tooke his sicknesse of which he dyed by setting up so often for Astronomicall Observations.

He haz perused all the Records of the Church of Sarum, which, with long lyeing, had been conglutinated together; read them all over, and taken abridgements of them, which haz not been donne by any of his predecessors I beleeve for some hundreds of yeares.

Anno 1669, Dr Christopher Wren was invited by the Bishop of Sarum (Seth Ward) where he made a particular Survey of the Cathedrall Church.

He was at least a weeke about it, and a curious discourse it was: it was not above two sheetes. Upon my writing *The Natural History of Wilts*, I had occasion to insert it there: I asked the Bishop for it, and he told me he had lent it, to whome he could not tell, and had no copy of it. 'Tis great pity the paines of so great an artist should be lost. Sir Christopher tells me he hath no copie of it neither.

The black malice of the Deane of Sarum – he printed sarcasticall Pamphletts against him – was the cause of his disturbd spirit, wherby at length, he quite lost his memorie. For about a moneth before he dyed he tooke very little Sustenance, but lived on the Stock, and died a Skeleton.

I searcht all Seth, Episcopus Sarum's, papers that were at his house at Knightsbridge neer London where he dyed. The custome is, when the Bishop of Sarum dies, that the Deane and Chapter lock-up his Studie and put a Seale on it. His scatterd papers I rescued from being used by the Cooke since his death; which was destinated with other good papers and letters to be put under pies.

WALTER WARNER

While William Harvey may have read Warner's manuscript treatise about the circulation of the blood, it is obvious that Warner's views were based on the current knowledge of the period, correct in certain details, but ignorant of the implications of the whole. Professor Rolleston said in the Harveian Oration of 1873: 'What was left for Harvey to discover was nothing less than *the circulation itself*. His predecessors had but impinged, and that by guesswork, upon different segments of the circle, and then gone off at a tangent into outer darkness, whilst he worked and proved and demonstrated round its entire periphery.' Warner died in 1640.

THIS Walter Warner was both Mathematician and Philosopher, and 'twas he that putt-out Thomas Hariot's *Algebra*, though he mentions it not.

Walter had but one hand (borne so): Dr John Pell thinks a right hand; his mother was frighted, which caused this deformity, so that instead of a left hand, he had only a Stump with five warts upon it, instead of a hand and fingers. He wore a cuffe on it like a pockett. The Doctor never sawe his stump, but Mr Warner's man told him so.

This account I received from Mr Isaac Walton: this is his owne hand writing – Mr Warner did long and constantly lodg nere the Water-stares or market in Woolstable (Woolstable is a place or lane not far from Charing Crosse, and nerer to Northumberland howse). My Lord of Winchester tells me he knew him, and that he saide he first fownd out the cerculation of the blood, and discover'd it to Dor Harvie (who said that 'twas he (himselfe) that found it) for which he is so memorably famose.

Mr Warner did tell Dr Pell, that when Dr Harvey came out with his *Circulation of the Blood*, he did wonder whence Dr Harvey had it: but comeing one day to the Earle of Leicester, he found Dr Harvey in the Hall, talking very familiarly with Mr Prothero, to whom Mr Warner had discoursed concerning this Exercitation of his *De Circulatione Sanguinis*, and made no question but Dr Harvey had his Hint from Prothero. Dr Pell sayes that Mr Warner rationated demonstratively by Beates of the Pulses that there must be a Circulation of the Blood.

Warner had a pention of 40 pounds a yeare from that Earle of Northumberland that lay so long a prisner in the Towre, and som alowance from Sir Tho. Alesbery with whome he usually spent his sumer in Windesor park, and was welcom, for he was harmless and quet. His winter was spent at the Wolstable, where he dyed in the time of the Parliament of 1640, of which, or whome, he was no louer.

Mr Walter Warner made an Inverted Logarithmicall Table, i.e. whereas Briggs' table fills his Margin with Numbers encreasing by Unites, and over-against them setts their Logarithms, which because of incommensurability must needs be either abundant or deficient; Mr Warner (like a Dictionary of the Latine before the English) fills the Margin with Logarithmes encreasing by Unites, and setts to every one of them so many continuall meane proportionalls between one and 10, and they for the same reason must also have the last figure incompleat. These, which, before Mr John Pell grew acquainted with Mr Warner, were ten thousand, and at Mr Warner's request were by Mr Pell's hands, or direction, made a hundred-thousand.

Quaere Dr Pell, what is the use of those Inverted Logarithmes? for W. Warner would not doe such a thing in vaine.

JOHN WHITSON

Born 1557. Merchant adventurer. When Philip II of Spain laid an embargo on English ships in 1585, Whitson fitted out the *Mayflower* to make reprisals. He took an active part in the early voyages for the settlement of North America. He was four times married, and was John Aubrey's godfather. Died 1629.

JOHN WHITSON, Alderman of the City of Bristol, was borne at Cover in the Forest of Deane in the Countie of Gloucester: he went to schoole at Bristow, where he made a good proficience in the Latin tongue. He was bound Apprentice to Alderman Vawr, a Spanish Merchant of this City. He was a handsome young fellow; and his old Master (the Alderman) being dead, his Mistress one day called him into the Wine-cellar and bad him broach the best Butt in the Cellar for her; and truly he broach't his Mistrisse, who after maried him. This story will last perhaps as long as Bristol is a City.

He had a very good healthy constitution, and was an early Riser; wrote all his Letters and dispatched his businesse betime in the Morning. He had a good naturall Witt, and gaind by the Spanish trade a fair Estate.

He lived nobly; kept a plentifull Table; and was the most popular magistrate in the City, alwaies chosen a Member of Parliament. He kept a noble house, and did entertain and treat the Peers and great Persons that came to the City. He kept his Hawkes.

He was charitable in his Life in breeding-up of poor Scholars: I remember five that had been bred-up under him, but not one of them came to good, they lived so luxuriously.

His second Wife was a very beautifull Dame, as by her picture (at length) in the Dining rome, doeth appear. By her he had a Daughter, his only child, who was counted the Flower of Bristol, who was maried to Sir Thomas Trenchard of Dorsetshire. His beloved and only Daughter dyeing (together with her child), Richard Wheeler, his Nephew, who was bred a Merchant under him with others, was his Heir; but he proving a Sott and a capricious Coxcombe, he setled all his Estate upon the City of Bristow for pious Uses, and was, I doe believe, the greatest Benefactor that ever the City had.

He dyed about the seaventy-sixth yeare of his age by a fall from his horse; his head pitching on a nail that stood on its head by a Smyth's shop. He was buried very honourably; besides all his Relations in mourning, he had as many poor old men and woemen as he was yeares old in mourning gownes and hoodes, the Mayor and Aldermen in Mourning; all the Trained Band (he was their Colonel) attended the Funerall and their Pikes had black Ribons and Drummes were covered with Black cloath.

JOHN WILKINS

Born 1614. Divine. Though he had been private chaplain to Charles I's nephew, the Prince Palatine (elder brother of Prince Rupert), he adhered to the Parliamentary side in the Civil War, and took the Covenant. Warden of Wadham College, Oxford, 1648. Master of Trinity College, Cambridge, 1659. Deprived of the Mastership at the Restoration, he became a Prebendary of York. First Secretary of the Royal Society 1662. Dean of Ripon 1663. Bishop of Chester 1668. Died 1672.

HIS father was a Goldsmith in Oxford. Mr Francis Potter knew him very well, and was wont to say that he was a very ingeniose man, and had a very Mechanicall head. He was much for Trying of Experiments, and his head ran much upon the *perpetuall motion*. He maryed a daughter of Mr John Dod (who wrote on the Commandments) at whose house, at Fawlsley, she laye-in with her son John, of whome we are now to speake.

He had his Grammar learning in Oxford (I thinke from Mr Sylvester, over the meadowes). He was admitted of Magdalen-hall in Oxford, 1627; his Tutor there was the learned Mr John Tombs (Coryphaeus of the Anabaptists).

He has sayd oftentimes that the first rise, or hint of his Rising, was from goeing accidentally a courseing of a Hare: where an ingeniose Gentleman of good quality falling into discourse with him, and finding him to have very good partes, told him that he would never gett any considerable preferment by continuing in the University; and that his best way was to betake himselfe to some Lord's or great persons' House that had good Benefices to conferre. Sayd Mr J. Wilkins, I am not knowne in the world; I know not to whom to addresse myselfe upon such a designe. The Gentleman replied, I will recommend you myselfe, and did so, to (as I thinke) Lord Viscount Say and Seale, where he stayed with very good likeing till the late Civill warres, and then he was Chaplain to his Highnesse Charles Louis, Prince Elector Palatine of the Rhine, with whom he went (after the Peace concluded in Germany) and was well preferred there by his Highnesse.

After the Visitation at Oxon by the Parliament, he gott to be Warden of Wadham Colledge. Anno 1656 he maried to Robina, the Relict of Dr French, Canon of Christchurch, Oxon, and sister to Oliver, (then) Lord Protector, who made him Master of Trinity colledge in Cambridge (in which place he revived Learning by strickt examinations at elections: he was much honoured there, and heartily loved by all) where he continued till 1660 (the Restauration of his Majestie). Then he was Minister of Saint Laurence church in London. His friend, Seth Ward, D.D., being made Bishop of Excester, he was made there Deane, and anno 1668 by the favour of George, Duke of Buckingham, was made Bishop of Chester; and was extremely well beloved in his Diocese. Anno Domini 1672 he dyed of the stone.

He left a Legacy of four hundred pounds to the Royall Society, and had he been able would have given more. He was no great read man; but one of much and deepe thinking, and of a working head; and a prudent man as well as ingeniose. He was one of Seth, Lord Bishop of Sarum's most intimate Friends. He was a lustie, strong growne, well sett, broad shoulderd person, cheerfull, and hospitable.

He was the principall Reviver of Experimentall Philosophy at Oxford, where he had weekely an experimentall philosophicall Clubbe, which began 1649, and was the *Incunabula* of the Royall Society. When he came to London, they mett at the Bullhead taverne in Cheapside (e.g. 1658, 1659, and after) till it grew to big for a Clubb. The first beginning of the Royal Society (where they putt discourse in paper and brought it to use) was in the Chamber of William Ball, Esqr, eldest son of Sir Peter Ball of Devon, in the Middle Temple. They had meetings at Taverns before, but 'twas here where it formally and in good earnest sett up: and so they came to Gresham Colledge parlour.

Scripsit: *The Discovery of a World in the Moone* (long since); *A Discourse tending to prove that 'tis probable our Earth is one of the Planets*; *Art of Praying and Preaching*; *Mathematicall Magique*, dedicated to the Prince Elector; *Reall Character* – This last was his Darling, and nothing troubled him so much when he dyed, as that he had not compleated it; which will now in a yeare more be donne by the care and studies of Mr Robert Hooke, of Gresham College; Mr Andrew Paschall, B.D. of Chedzoy, in com. Somerset; Mr Francis Lodwyck, of London, merchant; Mr John Ray, R.S.S., of Essex; and Mr Thomas Pigott, M.A. (Wadham College).

JOHN WILMOT
EARL OF ROCHESTER

Born 1647. Poet and libertine. Master of Arts at Oxford when little more than fourteen. He travelled abroad and, on his return, 1664, he identified himself with the most dissolute set of Charles II's Courtiers, soon excelling them all in profligacy. In 1666 he was made a Gentleman of the King's Bedchamber and, in 1674, he received a special mark of the royal favour by being appointed Keeper of Woodstock Park. Towards the end of his life he declared that he was under the influence of drink for five consecutive years. At the same time he cultivated a brilliant faculty for amorous lyrics, obscene rhymes, and mordant satires in verse, which more than once caused his dismissal from Court. However, he was always taken back into favour and although he quickly ruined his physical health by his excesses, his intellect retained all its vivacity until his death in 1680.

About 18, he stole his Lady, Elizabeth Malet, a daughter and heir, a great fortune; for which I remember I sawe him a Prisoner in the Tower about 1662 [*in 1665*].

His youthly spirit and oppulent fortune did sometimes make him doe extravagant actions, but in the country he was generally civill enough. He was wont to say that when he came to Brentford the Devill entred into him and never left him till he came into the Country again.

He was Raunger of Woodstock-parke and lived often at the Lodge at the west end, a very delightfull place and noble prospect westwards. Here his Lordship had severall lascivious Pictures drawen.

His Lordship read all manner of bookes. Mr Andrew Marvell (who was a good Judge of Witt) was wont to say that he was the best English Satyrist and had the right veine. 'Twas pitty Death tooke him off so soon.

In his last sicknesse he was exceedingly paenitent and wrote a letter of his repentance to Dr Burnet, which is printed.

He sent for all his servants, even the piggard- [*pig-yard*] boy, to come and hear his Palinode [*repentance*].

THOMAS WOLSEY

Born 1475. Cardinal and statesman. Rector of Lymington; Prebendary of Lincoln and Hereford: Canon of Windsor: Dean of Lincoln, Hereford, York, and St Stephen's, Westminster: Precentor of London: Bishop of Tournay, Lincoln, Bath and Wells, Durham, and Winchester: Archbishop of York: Cardinal. Chaplain to Henry VII 1507. Almoner to Henry VIII 1509. Lord Chancellor 1515. He accompanied Henry VIII to the Field of the Cloth of Gold in 1520. Wolsey displayed on a colossal scale the pride and power of the medieval Church, and was almost as rich a man as the King himself. For his natural son he obtained four arch-deaconries, a deanery, five prebends, and two rectories. Wolsey reluctantly supported Henry in his divorce from Catherine of Aragon 1527. Owing to the delay in the divorce proceedings, he incurred the dislike of Anne Boleyn, who influenced the King against him, with the result that a Bill of Indictment was preferred against him in 1529. After receiving a General Pardon, he retired to Cawood, but he was again arrested for High Treason, on information given by his physician Dr Agostini, who accused the Cardinal of bringing *the King's Majesty into marvellous danger, for knowing himself to have the foul and contagious disease of the great pox, broken out upon him in divers parts of his body, he had come daily to His Grace, blowing upon him with his perilous and infective breath.* He died at Leicester, on his way to London to answer these charges, in 1530.

THOMAS WOLSEY, Cardinal, was a Butcher's son, of Ipswych, in Suffolke. He was Baccalaur of Arts so young, that he was called the Boy-Bacchalaur.

He was a Fellowe of Magdalen Colledge in Oxford, where he was Tutor to a young Gentleman of Limmington, near Ilchester, in whose guift the presentation of that church is, worth the better part of 200 pounds per annum, which he gave to his Tutor Wolsey. He had committed hereabout some debauchery (I thinke, drunke: no doubt he was of a high rough spirit) and spake derogatorily of Sir Amias Paulet (a Justice of Peace in the neighbourhood) who putt him into the Stockes, which, when he came to be Cardinall, he did not forget; he layed a Fine upon Sir Amias to build the Gate of the Middle Temple.

His Rise was his quick and prudent dispatch of a message to Paris for Henry 8.

He had a most magnificent spirit.

He was a great Builder, as appeares by White-hall, Hampton-Court. Eshur, in Surrey, a noble house, built of the best burn't brick (perhaps) that ever I sawe; sattely gate-house and hall. This stately house (a fitt Pallace for a Prince) was bought about 1666 by a Vintner of London, who is since broke, and the house is sold, and pulled downe to the ground, about 1678. He built the stately tower at Magdalen Colledge in Oxford, and that stately Palace at Winchester (where he was Bishop) called Wolsey-house; I remember it pretty well, standing 1647. Now, I thinke, it is most pulled downe.

His noble foundation of his Colledge of Christ-church in Oxford, where the stately hall was only perfected by him. There were designed (as yet may appeare by the building) most magnificent Cloysters (the brave designe wherof Dr John Fell hath deteriorated with his new device) to an extraordinary spacious Quadrangle, to the entrance whereof was carrying up a Tower (a Gate-house) of extraordinary rich and noble Gothique building. When the present Great-Duke of Tuscany was at Oxford, he was more taken with that, then all the rest of the Buildings he sawe there, and tooke a second viewe of it.

It should not be forgotten what a noble foundation there was for the Chapell, which did runne from the Colledge, along the street as far as the Blew-boare Inne; which was about 7 foot or more high, and adorned with a very rich Gothique Water-table. It was pulled downe by Dr John Fell (the Deane) about 1670, to use the stones about the Colledge.

William Fenshaw Esq told me, that he had seen a letter writt by Cardinal Wolsey to this purpose viz: My Lord, I understand that there is a Reformation in Religion intended by the Parliament; and I wish that severall things were reformed; but let me tell you that when you have reformed, that others will come, and refine upon you, and others again upon them; *et sic deinceps* [and so proceeding], that at last there will be no Religion left, but Atheisme will spring up. The Mysteries of Religion are to be let alone; they will not beare an examination.

The Silver Cross that was wont to be carried before Cardinal Wolsey, fell out of its Socket, and was like to have knock'd one of the Bishops' Servants' Brains out. A very little while after, came in a Messenger, and arrested the Cardinal, before he could get out of the House.

Returning to London from Yorke, he died at Leicester, where he lies buried (to the shame of Christ-church men) yet without any monument.

And though, from his owne store, Wolsey might have
A Palace or a Colledge for his Grave,
Yet here he lies interr'd, as if that all
Of him to be remembred were his Fall.
If thou art thus neglected, what shall wee
Hope after Death that are but Shreds of thee?

Index

The spelling of the names in this Index is not always identical with that in the text; the nearest approximation to Aubrey's many variations has been given.

The page numbers in italics refer to the Lives proper.

Aubrey's habit of numbering peers by their Christian names has been corrected. For instance, Philip (2nd), Earl of Pembroke, was the second Philip to be Earl of Pembroke, not the second Earl of Pembroke.

Bishops are listed under their surnames, Peers under their titles, and Queens under their Christian names. Unless wives are specifically mentioned by name, they are not listed separately from their husbands. Books are included under their authors. Biblical and mythical characters are not included in this Index; nor are the publishers of Aubrey's works.

Old Man on a Bike

SIMON GANDOLFI

The Friday Project
An imprint of HarperCollins Publishers
77–85 Fulham Palace Road
Hammersmith, London W6 8JB
www.thefridayproject.co.uk
www.harpercollins.co.uk

First published by The Friday Project in 2008

2

Simon Gandolfi asserts the moral right to be identified
as the author of this work

A catalogue record for this book is available from the British Library

ISBN 978-1-90-632166-6

Internal design and typesetting by Maggie Dana
Graphics by Carrie Kabak
Printed and bound in Great Britain by Clays Ltd, St Ives plc

For Bernadette, my love, my strength, my wife – and for Wei-Ming Ang, best of companions on the road.

Simon Gandolfi was born in England in 1933. He was dispatched to Catholic boarding school aged six and to South Africa a year later as a war-time refugee. Escaping formal education at 16, he sought jobs that were once the essentials of a writer's experience: ranching, army, trading schooner, crocodile hunter, yacht skipper ...

An inveterate traveller, he lived in Ibiza throughout the 60s and in Cuba during the 90s, criss-crossed the Somali and Ogaden deserts for the UN, rode with Mujahadeen through Afghanistan during the Soviet occupation – experiences that are the foundations of his novels.

Now a mature citizen, he has returned to his roots at the foot of the Malvern Hills, where he shares a cottage with his wife and partner of thirty years, a teenage son dedicated to extreme sports and an equally manic Border Terrier.

Acknowledgements

I have been helped and encouraged and cosseted by so many people on this journey. Let me name a few: Abby and Jed Sheckley in Providence; my daughter Anya in Duchess County, New York; the Weempes in Dallas; Eugenio and Monica Gabatto on the Rio Dulce; in Flores, Santiago Billy and his *brujas*; Marcio and Ashley in Cobán; Joe Brown and Gillian in Granada; in Nazca, Juan Carlos and the staff at the Hostal Via Morburg; wondrous Graciela of the Hotel Argentina, Rio Grande; Luca in Ushuaia; in Buenos Aires, Juan José Rodriguez Lopez at the Internet café who gave so generously of his time and expertise; and the many Honda Agencies that serviced the bike – few charged more than a few dollars and the bike never faltered.

Prologue

Why would a reasonably sane man in his seventies ride the length of Hispanic America on a small motorcycle – a man who is overweight, suffered two minor heart attacks and has a bad back? Stupidity comes to mind ... And flippancy is easy camouflage ...

Age has much to do with it. My wife is younger by almost thirty years. I feel old. I suspect that our teenage sons find me an embarrassment; their friends mistake me for their granddad – or an old tramp.

So, yes, age.

And anger.

Though I have lived abroad much of my life, I am very English, probably something of a Blimp. I believed that honour was intrinsic to being English; in public service, we behaved better.

Then came the Iraq War, the disclosure of Abu Ghraib.

None of my honourable English compatriots resigned, not a Minister of the Armed Forces, not our Ambassador in Baghdad, not a senior officer serving in Baghdad, not the Head of Military Intelligence nor any of his senior colleagues.

They were complicit in Abu Ghraib. So am I. That is the strength of Democracy: the Government is ours; each one of us is responsible for our Government's actions; each one of us is equally sullied.

The alliance to which we are committed is intent on nation building in Iraq ... and Afghanistan. The US has been nation building in Hispanic America since President Quincy Adams's declaration of the Monroe Doctrine (1801). In travelling, I may discover how successful the US has been and discover what opinions the people of Hispanic America have of their neighbours in the North.

US citizens possess an absolute certitude in their superiority. Canadians are poor cousins. Those south of the border are wetbacks, greasers, Latinos – inferior beings. Good ones make good house pets.

Surely we Brits know better?

I visited three high schools in my native Herefordshire. I asked fifteen-year-olds for their image of a Mexican. All gave the same answer: fat, sweating, big hat, drooping moustache, comic accent.

And those from further south? Central and South America?

Drug dealers or crooked cops, corrupt officials.

Such is cultural colonialism – so much is absorbed from Hollywood.

I wondered, as I listened, what those South of the border, the Spicks and greasers, thought of us Brits? Do they imagine that we wear bowler hats, carry umbrellas and drink endless cups of tea? Or that England is a land peopled by football hooligans?

Do they differentiate between Britain and the US?

My wife said, 'Find out. Ride a motorbike. It's something you've talked of doing as long as I've known you.'

'I'm too old,' I said.

'So? Get young again. Get out from behind your desk. Show that an old man can make it. And don't dare write a polemic.'

Polemic is wifely code for obsessive and boring - our sons are more forthright.

And my wife is correct: I have been behind my desk for too long. Writing fiction, I have been seeing through my protagonists' eyes, living their traumas. Time has come to raise and risk again my own head above the parapet, see with my own eyes, experience my own adventure. Latin America is tempting. I am obsessed by its history.

I wrote the best part of two novels in Santo Domingo, capital of the Dominican Republic. Two 16th century mansions form the Hostal San Nicolas de Ovando. The manager set a trestle table in the tower. The river lay below. I would imagine those first tiny Spanish ships lying at anchor. I would imagine sunlight flashing on breast plates and helmets, the strike of steel-shod boots. They were small men, the Conquistadors.

Most had little education. They were filled with superstitions. How could such men in such small numbers capture vast Empires? I have read modern historians. I find them wanting in explanations. Though what do I know? I'm a high school drop-out. And I admit to prejudice. My great grandfather was a famous Spanish terrorist – El Tigre del Maestrazgo. His mother was executed by firing squad. He conquered much of Spain.

Cortés set out from Veracruz and conquered Mexico. I intend to travel all the way south from Veracruz to Ushuaia in Tierra del Fuego. Cortés rode a horse. A Honda 125 will do me fine. All I wish to conquer are my fears. I have faith in the bike. I am less sure of my heart. Will it cope with the rigours of the Altiplano?

More positively, I may lose weight.

The Boys on Bikes

***1906:* My father sits beneath** a thorn tree in northern Kenya. He and his business partner Jack Riddle have been in Ethiopia buying horses. They travel with sixty porters and livestock. Jack is scouting ahead for water. My father writes in his diary a reminder to order a new dressing case from Asprey, a Bond Street purveyor of luxury goods – hairbrushes, clothes brush, beaver-hair shaving brush, cut-throat razors, all with ivory handles. My father will supply the ivory.

***2006:* I buy a used green shirt** and Clancy Brothers sweater at the Age Concern shop in Hereford. My wife asks whether I plan auditioning for a job as a garden gnome. I retort that I am flying to Boston with Aer Lingus and hope for an upgrade.

I fail with the upgrade. However, the immigration officer at Boston's airport is Irish American and appreciates the sweater. He asks what I plan doing in the US. I plan travelling by train to Dallas, crossing into Mexico by bus, buying a motorcycle in Veracruz, Mexico, and riding to Tierra del Fuego. The immigration officer is two years short of retirement. He checks my date of birth.

'You're seventy-three.'

'So?' I say.

'What type of bike?' he asks.

'A Honda 125.'

'For real? A 125?' He grins. 'That's a pizza delivery bike. You think you'll make it?'

I have doubts but what else should I do with the last years of my life? Sit at home and watch TV?

The immigration officer stamps my passport. 'What does your wife think?'

'She's pleased to have me out from underfoot.'

My ex is more concerned. We have been separated for twenty-five years. She collects me from the airport and drives me to her home in Providence, Rhode Island. In the car, she says, 'This thing you're planning is really dumb. I've been talking with people. They all say it's dumb. I mean, going through Colombia and places. And the roads, the way those people drive. You'll get yourself killed.'

I take the bus next day to my adopted daughter's home in Duchess County, New York. Anya reiterates the imagined dangers. I have a history of heart attacks. Why deliberately put myself at risk?

'It's a man thing,' I explain.

And why take a train south to Dallas? No one takes trains.

I am about to write about the Americas. I need to see the US rather than fly over it at comfortable bombing height.

Dallas, Friday 28 April

My forty-eight-hour train journey from New York ends late afternoon in Dallas, Texas. I have slept in a chair the past two nights. Don Weempe collects me at the Amtrak station. Don and Jane and their daughter, Elspeth, are old friends who visit England regularly. I haven't visited Dallas in eight years. Dallas is a great city and the Weempes are generous and considerate hosts. So why does Don plot my death?

Don is a heavy-built six-foot-four-inch good ol' boy, third-generation Dallas, a graduate of Texas A&M University. He makes his money spreading concrete over Texas. He and three friends plan leaving tomorrow at five in the morning on a bike trip. Texas is big and Texans ride big bikes – too big for an old Brit, even a Brit preparing to ride from Veracruz, Mexico, to Tierra del Fuego. In Texas, a Honda 125 doesn't rate as a bike.

I am to follow the weekend bikers in Don's Hummer with their gear.

The Hummer is in Don's front drive. It looks huge. It *is* huge. Back home I drive a fourteen-year-old Honda Accord. My sons are ashamed to be seen by their friends in what they describe as a 'Granny car'. They tilt the seat flat and pretend to be reading a newspaper. Now I lie awake worrying that I won't be able to handle something as big as the Hummer. I worry that I won't be able to keep up with the bikes. I know that Don has a Harley, leather seats and studs. I'll meet the other three riders in the morning.

Texas everywhere, Saturday 29 April

Five in the morning and Don reverses the Hummer out of the drive. I climb in behind the wheel. Big! Wide! Scary!

Home in England, my sons tease me endlessly for driving slowly and holding up the traffic. Now I must follow Don on a Harley and Jack, an airline pilot, on a BMW GS 650.

Rain falls steadily. I hope it will slow the bikers down.

It doesn't.

I follow their tail lights onto the freeway. We speed through Fort Worth and halt for breakfast around seven. Paul joins us, a lawyer on a vast Honda cruiser with a seat the size of a sofa. The bike is a recent purchase. Paul has all the kit: suit with armour plate, million-dollar boots. Unfortunately his boots have filled with water.

We turn off the freeway onto country roads wide enough to be motorways back home. No cops, and the speed edges up. The bikes out-accelerate and out-corner the Hummer. I lose a hundred yards or more on each bend and have to work at catching up. The speedometer touches eighty, eighty-five, ninety miles an hour. My sons won't believe me. Fifty years at the wheel and I was hit with my first-ever speeding ticket the month before leaving England: thirty-three and a half miles an hour in a thirty zone.

A couple of hours at the wheel and I am almost confident. The Hummer is rock steady. I am familiar with the controls. The rain has ceased, the sun is bright and the satellite radio is tuned to Nashville. I risk taking my eyes off the road. Cattle graze vast paddocks. A brace of wild turkeys scurry off the verge and hide in the mesquite.

I follow the boys on bikes into the town of Turkey in mid afternoon. 'Town' in west Texas is fifteen houses and a store that closed in the sixties. We are in Turkey for the annual Bob Wills memorial concert. Bob Wills was a country and western singer. He and his band, The Texas Playboys, topped the charts back in the forties.

The memorial concert is in a dirt field beside Turkey's disused red-brick high school building. Tents and RVs and trailers are parked among the standard farm mishmash of new and disused agricultural machinery – abandoned pickups and rusted metal stuff that even the manufacturer wouldn't recognise. Texas machinery is big. The driver climbs a ladder to reach the controls – no place here for a man with vertigo.

The Bob Wills memorial concert is true west Texas. Three plank-and-scaffolding stands face a stage that is as permanent as anything is permanent in west Texas. Swallows or house martins have nested in the ceiling. The Texas Playboys are up there doing their stuff – those that are still alive, that is. Practised? They could play in their sleep.

Three or four generations of the same family lounge in folding chairs between stands and stage. Stetsons, blue jeans and boots are obligatory for the over-twos. The MC is a local doctor. He knows half the audience by name and knows at whom to direct his quips. Local girls collect dollars for the museum's upkeep. Jack buys a Bob Wills memorial hat while I write my name in the visitors' book and that I come from England. If there is another tourist, he got lost.

I remark on the quantity of old people's transport: electric invalid chairs and golf carts. I am driving a Hummer! This is fun. My mistake is not buying a Bob Wills memorial hat. A Bob Wills hat would have protected me all the way south to Tierra del Fuego – or at least to the ranch down in Argentina where Butch Cassidy and the Sundance Kid hid out for a few years.

I have sinned. I have been overconfident. Pride comes before a fall. I am about to plummet from fearless driver of the Hummer to trembling Brit on the sidewalk. Disaster hits on the freeway into Amarillo. The boys on the bikes thread the traffic. One minute I am tapping along to Garth Brooks on the radio. Next minute I am in panic. The boys on the bikes have gone.

I drive a further ten miles with my gut in a knot. Too late, I spot a biker pulled in at an exit. Is he one of my bikers? Has he seen me?

I take the next exit. A biker races by on the freeway.

What should I do?

Help!

I don't know who to pray to. Saint Anthony is good for finding car keys. I need to find three bikers. Bikers are bigger than keys. My address book is back in Dallas. I don't have a mobile telephone. I don't have a number to call Don. I am a Brit with a Brit's driving licence. I am in a Hummer without car papers. I imagine bad-ass Texas cops ramming guns to my skull, hacking my feet apart. One wrong word and I'm dead.

I pull in at the parking lot of the Bourbon Street Café (live music Saturday night and all the shrimp you can eat for just over ten dollars). Two young women in long dresses sweep in through the entrance. I follow timidly. The restaurant lobby is dark and romantic. I have been outside in late sunlight and am momentarily blind. A friendly female voice enquires whether I have a reservation. I blink a few times and an attractive young lady materialises out of the gloom. She is Texas straw blonde, wears an off-the-shoulder evening dress and stands behind a wooden lectern that supports her table list.

I am probably sweating. I fidget my hands. And I am immensely British. 'I am so sorry to bother you,' I say. 'I'm in a real mess.'

Why does she listen? Why doesn't she call security?

'I'm lost,' I say. 'I was following three bikers. Friends. I lost them. I'm really stupid.'

The lady is curious as to what I am and listens patiently.

I confess that I don't have Don's telephone number and that I don't have the name of the hotel we're booked into. Meanwhile I am blocking guests waiting to be assigned tables (smoking or non-smoking?).

I apologise for being a nuisance and, being a Brit, repeat my apologies again and again. If I could call directory enquiries? Except that I don't have a phone. Nor, if I did have a phone, would I know how to call directory enquiries.

The lady calls on her mobile and obtains Don's home number. She gives me the number and hands me her mobile. I explain that I am unfamiliar with mobile phones. Added to which, I am old and more than a little deaf.

She calls Don for me and we get an answering machine. I leave a message. Minutes pass while I wonder what to do next and while the lady wonders what she can do next (other than assign tables).

Her telephone rings. Don's daughter, Elspeth, is on the line. I try not to sound panicky while Elspeth's response is that of a calm mature woman aged eleven going on thirty. She consoles me. She gives me Don's mobile number.

The lady calls Don, who is surprised at a woman calling. I am saved. And I am deeply, deeply grateful to the Angel of the Bourbon Street Café. I try to imagine the same scene in England at a popular restaurant on a Saturday evening.

I'd still be there, out on the pavement, lost ...

Don leads me to the hotel. We shower, change and head for dinner at the ultimate Texas tourist restaurant. Call for a reservation and the restaurant dispatches a white courtesy car with cattle longhorns bolted to the bonnet. The building is a fake barn with dead deer heads mounted high on the walls. Right by the door there's a steak on display the size of a pair of bricks. Eat the steak and they feed you free for a year. (Eat the steak and you wouldn't *want* to eat for a year.) We are shown to a table beside a dais on which sits a competitor for Cholesterol Man of the Year. He already has a serious weight problem. He is midway through the two-brick steak. He is sweating and wears the defeated look of a foot soldier on the fourth day of the retreat from Moscow (take your choice – German or Napoleonic).

The maître d' shows us to a table right beside the glutton dais.

Don says, 'Great, so we have to look at that while we eat.'

We eat mini-steaks the size of quarter-bricks.

Don and I share a hotel room furnished with twin king-size beds. Midnight and a fourth biker joins the party – Eric, a forty-plus photographer who chews tobacco and rides the same model BMW GS as Jack. Eric bought his bike in the past few weeks. Jack bought his bike in the past few weeks. I guess that these two are competitors in some type of interpersonal rivalry as to who can be the hottest forty-year-old teenager on the block.

Eric unrolls a sleeping bag. I warn him to spread it the far end of the room because old men have to get up in the night and I don't want to fall on him.

The king-size bed is comfortable. We have travelled 600 miles. I have driven a Hummer at ninety miles an hour without fear and am feeling confident as to the morrow.

Sunday is the day of rest. We have miles to cover and are up at seven. First stop is a farm twenty miles out of town. The farm grows Cadillacs. The Cadillacs are planted in a straight line out in the middle of a vast field that may stop at the horizon but probably doesn't. The field is as flat as a skating rink. The Cadillacs are buried nose down up to their windscreens in the earth. Most visitors bring cans of spray paint. The graffiti is interesting. This is a sculpture both impressive and delightfully weird.

Our next halt is in nowhere. This is the Texas panhandle and Galileo was talking nonsense when he said the world was round. The world is flat, believe me. The road runs straight for thirty miles: not a house in sight, no animals, not even a tree. Telephone and power cables that have nowhere to go weave pointless patterns across this vast expanse of nothing. The boys on the bikes ride in a bunch. Travelling a British country lane the boys and I would be *big*. We would fill the road. Children and old ladies walking their dogs would find us threatening. In the panhandle we are minute pieces in a board game. The sun sparkling on bike helmets is the controlling ray operated by whoever plays the game. Reach the end of the board and we fall off.

Mid-morning we enter the Palo Duro State Park. Palo Duro is Spanish for 'tough stick' and the player of the board game has gouged a stick viciously across the board. The result is ripped red canyon country out of a Hollywood Western.

We stop. I take pictures while Eric and Jack strike attitudes at each other and exchange bike seats. Jack's is a custom seat three inches lower than the standard model. Jack has long legs that have been cramping over the past day. I have watched from the Hummer as he wriggles from side to side and stands on the footrests or stretches out his legs beyond the engine.

Eric has the standard seat and has shorter legs. He claims to be comfortable with Jack's seat. I suspect Eric would claim to be comfortable sitting on six-inch nails.

The road we follow from Palo Duro back to Turkey has humps and corners and views forever. Eric and Jack lean into the corners and are gone, chasing each other round the school yard, speedometers registering 120 miles an hour. Don sits on his Harley, solid and sensible as a granite Texas rock. The Harley thunders and competes in vibration with a pneumatic road drill. Only a rock could survive.

Meanwhile, Paul, the lawyer, cruises to the rear cradled in the leather upholstered luxury and law-office silence of his Honda Monster. And I bask in the massive comfort of the Hummer.

Saturday was country and western. Sunday started with *Swan Lake* turned up high and crystal clear on the satellite radio as I swooped across the void. Now I have Beethoven's *Eroica* ramming me through the curves and over the low hills.

My sons would be listening to the Red Hot Chilli Peppers. But a big Hummer? And the Texas panhandle? Believe me, whatever the music, this is serious bliss.

Midday and we have circled back to Turkey and are filling our tanks. This is the third time the Hummer has required gas. The tank takes thirty-five gallons and filling the tank takes a while. We are in a dry county. The help at the gas station reports that we must drive sixty-five miles in one direction or thirty-five in the other to refill the beer cooler.

The Sporting Club is across the street from the gas station. Complete a membership form at the club and you can order a beer. The big square dining room with its high ceiling is delightfully cool. The decor is dead heads on the walls together with framed photographs from the good ol' days of old-timers crouching over dead meat on the hoof (even here, in west Texas, dead Indians are out of fashion – although a dead Mexican might pass muster).

A buffet is set up in the next room: a dozen different salads; fried chicken, grilled pork, broiled silverside, all the vegetables; custard and apple pie. I have the beef. Delicious. The service is typically Texas friendly, full of smiles and goodwill how-are-yous.

A party of freshly barbered weekend Harley riders occupies the next table. They ride top-money bikes with all the fixings: matching luggage, satellite radio, central heating, shoe polish and gold-tap toilets. They travel in company with a Harley support team hauling a Harley trailer behind a three-quarter-ton Ford truck.

Our route onward is a zigzag in search of corners to excite the kids. Paul, the lawyer, tends to hold back a little on the curves. He has ample power and acceleration to catch the pack. Keeping pace in the Hummer is less easy. Hummers aren't designed for road racing. Beer is legal at our next gas stop, although drinking on the premises is forbidden. Eric finds a patch of grass to sprawl on the other side of a telephone post that marks the forecourt boundary.

Next stop is a 500-acre play ranch that Paul and Don have bought. The ranch is off a dirt county road. The BMWs gambol in the dirt. The Harley irons the dirt flat. The Honda is a little skittish and Paul is a little anxious. I drive the Hummer with the windows down and blast Texas with opera.

Texans like to hunt. Don is a leading member of the Dallas Safari Club. He has shot game in about every country where there is game to shoot: Alaska for bear, Argentina for dove, England for pheasant, South Africa for whatever has big teeth, and all the way to New Zealand for a mountain something-or-other. He and Paul purchased the ranch a few months back as a hunting reserve. They will install a weekend trailer home next month.

Don and Paul transfer to the Hummer for the drive to the trailer site while Eric and Jack scatter dirt competitively with their rear tyres. The site is on the crest of a bluff and has views for miles over what, in Africa, would be called 'bush'. Texas bush is mostly dwarf cedar and mesquite. The bluff forms a hook and falls away steeply, right below the site to a fifty-acre patch centred on a spring-fed pond. Thin the mesquite and scrub cedar and you could watch the game come to the water – a Texan version of Kenya's Tree Tops Hotel.

Paul isn't a hunter. He wishes to sit out on the deck of an evening, sip a cold beer with friends and watch the animals.

Jack imagines mounting a twin-barrel heavy machine gun on the deck so he can blast anything that moves.

We drink beer while Don drives us round the property on the ring road they've cleared and down a track that twists between the trees to a second pond. Jack is searching the track for hog tracks. Hogs are domestic pigs gone wild, some twenty or thirty generations back. Jack has a hog obsession. He guns down a hog. He imagines he's *wasting* an al-Qaida bomber. Wasting is Jack's solution to most problems and he enjoys a fine turn of phrase.

We leave the ranch around five p.m. and are faced with a four-hour drive home. We are 200 miles short of Dallas on a stretch of road under repair when Don hits a hole and bottoms his oil pan on a rock.

So now there are three bikes and Don drives the Hummer. I shift to the passenger seat, watch the country fly by and pester Don with endless questions. We have travelled 1200 miles of Texas in two days. We have enjoyed ourselves the way boys do. I have met extraordinary courtesy, kindness, generosity and good humour in every place we stopped. We have burnt enough gas to raise the planetary temperature a couple of degrees. And I have been saved from disaster by an angel: she of the Bourbon Street Café.

Goodbye Dallas

To Mexico, Tuesday 9 May

I leave tonight by bus for the Gulf of Mexico port of Veracruz. I have done in Dallas what a visitor should: watched a baseball match (my first), admired the play of light on the glass facades of Pei's magnificent tower, and glutted on Tex-Mex and barbecue ribs. Today I am invited to an executive breakfast club on the twenty-seventh floor of a downtown office building. The hundred or so members are white and male. Latino waiters serve a vast buffet. When introduced, I mumble a few words of gratitude for Dallas hospitality.

The day's guest speaker has published the history of the United States flag in verse. Each verse faces a full-page illustration of an American family: Mom, Pop and two kids – white, of course. General Tommy Franks has penned an introduction.

Only the army and the Church stand between America and chaos. The flag is their symbol and the speaker is campaigning to have his history distributed to every primary school. He warns us of the 1.2 billion Muslims in the world, every one of whom is taught from birth to hate and kill Americans. Hindus, Buddhists, Asiatics, Africans and Arabs are equally dangerous. A passing joke at the cowardly French raises a titter.

A member whispers to me in Spanish that not everyone present would agree with the speaker.

My bags are in the Hummer. Don drives from construction site to construction site. His workers are Mexican. I listen to the radio and watch the construction of a freeway overpass. Thirty or more huge trailer trucks queue to unload enormous concrete girders. Three cranes swing the girders into place. Trucks feed a concrete mixer the size of a European factory. We pass by the gun shop and eat steak.

Late afternoon we visit a friend of Don's who leases mobile road barriers, traffic cones and road signs. He and his father share a 7000-acre hobby ranch in Oklahoma. The ranch is ringed with deer fencing and they've sunk a million dollars into damming a creek. If they were British, they would have bought a holiday apartment on the Costa Brava.

Don and his friend drive me to the bus terminal. They make jokes at my bravery in travelling by Mexican bus. Mexican buses fall over cliffs. This is Texas. What cliffs? The road is straight. The land is flat. Nightlife is sticky doughnuts at an arc-lit service station. Lights glimmer dimly in trailer homes and in homes indistinguishable from trailers. I have a double seat to myself directly behind the driver. He drives with one hand while eating a half-pint tub of caramel ice-cream.

Entering the US is tough. Leaving is easy. The bus cruises through customs and immigration. I have a moment in which to note a queue several hundred metres long of aspiring Mexican immigrants. Then we are at the Mexican border. I still have my US entry card. I have no exit stamp in my passport. I have left the US illegally.

The Mexican immigration officer asks how long I will be in Mexico. I explain my trip and make a guess at four weeks. He examines me with interest and issues a visa valid for three months.

Dallas is twelve hours and forty-six dollars away from Monterey. The border region is as dry as Texas. The only hills are of dead cars heaped in junkyards. Finally, real hills appear. The highway dips into a narrow valley and Monterey surfaces from within a pale haze of exhaust fumes. The driver pulls into the depot and rushes me across to the bus company that makes the run to Tampico. A morning bus leaves at ten. This bus is new: seats tip all the way back; seatbelts are easy on the shoulders; Kung Fu movies play on the video screen.

I doze on the road to Tampico and wake to my first palm tree of the journey, sisal fields, jacarandas in flower, a flame tree. We pull into the Tampico bus depot at four p.m. Buses leave for Veracruz every hour. I find a trucker's restaurant and eat steak ranchero with fresh corn tortillas and red and green chilli sauce.

I call the Ampara Hotel in Veracruz and book a room. This bus is the most comfortable yet. Again I sit directly behind the driver and watch the speedo. Night falls and we crawl through hill country on a double-lane highway behind a convoy of tanker trucks. Mexico is the US's largest source of oil. Gas torches flame beside collector tanks.

The bus pulls into Veracruz terminal at five the following morning. I have travelled 1214 kilometres at a cost of 115 dollars. Veracruz is hot. The Amparo Hotel is a block from the central square. I have a room with a shower and a ceiling fan. The hotel is clean. My room is quiet. Two windows open on to the central well.

Moto Diaz is the main Honda agent in Veracruz. I had emailed Honda Mexico from the UK. My bike is waiting – a white Honda 125 Cargo. Honda advertises the model as a workhorse. In truth, it is a pizza delivery bike. It has a one-person seat and a large rack for the pizza box. A serious grey-haired mechanic is preparing the bike for my journey. The mechanic assures me that the bike will carry me to Tierra del Fuego *sin problemas*. No problems. I buy a removable rack box and the Honda agent presents me with a smart helmet. Tomorrow I queue for registration plates. I am warned that this may take all day. This evening I celebrate my purchase with a dish of devilled prawns and a bottle of Mexican lager.

I discover a small square around the corner from the hotel, where the middle-aged and elderly play chess at a pavement café. I sip a beer and watch the games and am drawn slowly into conversation.

Veracruz, Friday 12 May

Just before seven I am the first to queue outside the vehicle registration office – a privilege I relinquish to a woman who arrives a minute later, thus I have someone to follow. Doors open at eight. First disaster: all vehicles must be registered at a domicile. A hotel is not a domicile. Although motherly, the counter assistant is insistent. I am instructed to consult the department's director. The director is both patient and sympathetic. He will accept an electricity bill as proof of domicile. He instructs me to find an address, any address. Surely I have a friend in Veracruz? In Veracruz everyone has a friend.

He produces his own electricity bill as an example of the proof he requires, lays the bill on his desk and transfers his attention to an assistant. An hour later the bike is registered and the plates are on the Honda. Mechanics and sales assistants watch as I mount and wobble tentatively round the parking lot. I will take the bike out properly tomorrow, Saturday, when (I hope) there will be less traffic.

Veracruz is tidy for a Mexican city. Trees shade street after street of small shops (how do the proprietors earn a living?). Small restaurants are common, as are ice-cream parlours and mini-cafés that serve a table or two on the pavement. Street vendors don't nag, are happy to give directions and welcome conversation.

In search of riding goggles, I navigate, on foot, the narrow lanes of the market district. Dallas was foreign territory. Here I feel at home. The pace is Mediterranean. So are the chatter and leisurely human interplay. I ask directions and walk pavements striped with sun and shade. My goal is a row of kiosks where bike tyres and inner tubes hang on wooden shutters. I peer into gloom at shelves packed with spares. Most storekeepers are women – or instinct steers me to stores run by women. One advises me that goggles with glass lenses are too expensive – more sensible to buy plastic safety glasses at a hardware store.

I read in a guidebook that Veracruz has a strong black influence. I haven't seen a single black person. The standard skin colour is a rich pale golden mocha – imagine a good sun tan without the red. People are good-looking, particularly the younger generation. For men, long trousers are obligatory. Young women show their tummies. Given the heat, this seems an unfair advantage (not that I wish to display my own gross wobble).

I have taken three cabs. The first driver opined that Veracruz is a disaster. Politicians have stolen everything. Working people can't afford to eat.

The second driver was a sybarite. He boasted of Veracruz cuisine and instructed me to eat at any one of the small restaurants upstairs in the fish market.

The third was elderly and teaches English to his granddaughters. His own English is pedantic and he is contemptuous of North American English. He said that in Veracruz I can walk at night in safety, but in Mexico City I would be murdered.

I am less panicked now that the bike is registered. A cool evening breeze blows inshore. I stroll the streets and actually see the city for the first time (you can walk for miles without actually seeing anything).

So what have I seen now that my eyes are open? A castle built in 1660 and so small it could be a giant's toy – every boy's desire. A ramp leads to a drawbridge and a gate in fierce walls mellowed by age; a look-out post that resembles a pepper pot surmounts a square keep, and a further pepper pot crowns the far corner; cannon defend the battlements. The whole is the perfect size for a TV makeover programme. Imagine the dialogue between the two presenter-designers.

The central square, Plaza de Armas, is pleasant rather than great. The cathedral occupies one side. It has a simple interior lit by chandeliers and is small enough to feel intimate rather than overbearing. The cloister of the city hall runs at right angles to the cathedral; there is a plush hotel opposite. Palm trees shade pavement cafés. Almond trees surround a central stage and bandstand.

I sit in the Plaza de Armas and order a cold beer. Up on the stage, folk dancers stamp their heels. The women wear full floor-length dresses of white cotton gauze; the men white shirts, white cotton pants, high-heeled boots and those hats worn by scouts and the Royal Canadian Mounted Police. The dance is a Mexican version of flamenco, equally haughty and yet less fierce than the gypsy original. (I recall Cuban flamenco dancers being too soft and pliable.)

In the final dance the women carry trays of lit oil lamps on their heads. They glide and spin across the small stage with the charm and grace of women from a bygone era. A near-full moon, its light softened by humidity, floats above a palm tree at the corner of the city hall.

Lamps on tall, elegant lamp posts illuminate the cathedral's facade. The temperature is perfect. The beer is cold. This is bliss.

The folk dancing ends and I stroll to the small square by the hotel for a final coffee – prices are lower here than in the Plaza de Armas. A chess player beckons me to a vacant seat.

Veracruz, Saturday 13 May

I wake in the night and lie in bed unable to sleep. I must ride the bike today. My fears surface. I am crazy to attempt this journey. I should be safe at home weeding a flowerbed and preparing for the hereafter. Or cooking a lasagne for my wife Bernadette and our two sons Josh and Jed. I miss them. I miss my one-month-old grandchild, the divine Boo.

I am not superstitious.

That today is the thirteenth seems unfair.

Unable to sleep, I sort my possessions. How much space do I have in the bike box? Barely enough for my laptop and reference books. I can buy clothes. Books are irreplaceable.

Moto Diez is five kilometres from the city centre on a six-lane highway. I am nervous. I mount the Honda and practise turns in the car park. Mechanics watch. They wonder why I don't ride out onto the road. Fear stops me from riding out onto the road: fear of falling off, fear of panic, fear of being hit by a truck. And there is a further and greater and growing fear: the fear that the mechanics will suspect me of cowardice.

This is the fear that forces me to the car park slipway. Trucks and buses thunder through a fog of blue exhaust fumes. I edge out gingerly onto the highway and stall the motor. I remain astride the bike, kick the starter and almost overbalance. The mechanics have come out of the yard to watch. My palms are slippery and sweat stings my eyes. I dismount at the curb, find neutral and kick the starter again. The engine fires. I mount, open the throttle and engage bottom gear. The bike bucks. I close the throttle. The engine stalls. I long to hide my face in my arms and weep. A small crowd has collected. My ears burn with shame. I dismount again, kick the starter and ease forward along the curb. I keep in bottom gear for the first hundred metres and then move into second. I am still in second when the bike stops. I have ridden 300 metres.

The temperature is in the mid-thirties Celsius. Pushing the bike back to Moto Diez would kill me. I park the bike outside a store that sells plastic pipe. My reappearance at Moto Diez is met with consternation. Have I crashed?

No. I've run out of gas.

The mechanic apologises and rides me back on a scooter with a gas can. He tips the gas into the tank and we repeat our goodbyes. Off he goes. I kick the starter. The engine won't fire. Kick, kick, kick ...

This entire project is insane. I can't cope. I contemplate suicide. The storekeeper (a woman, naturally) suggests I try turning the ignition key. Dumb, dumb, dumb ...

I am facing out of town on a very busy six-lane highway. I don't have the courage to pull into the outside lane to make a U-turn. I ride (crawl) a while behind buses that halt on every block. I take a right down a minor road, then left and left again to an intersection on the highway controlled by traffic lights. I take a left at the lights and am heading back into town. Is this comprehensible?

A six-lane highway is not the best learning terrain.

I stall a couple of times. Manic cab drivers and bus drivers thump their klaxons. I miss a red light. Bikers hurtle past in search of death (memories of the Dallas BMW boys). I crawl. I make third gear. I make fourth. For a short stretch – five metres – I make fifth. I've been riding bikes for years. I've ridden bikes in seriously weird places. So I was younger. What has changed? Modern bikes are easier to ride; brakes function; cubic capacity is harnessed more effectively.

I ride into the city centre. I ride around the city and all over the city. I even have to warn myself against overconfidence. I am in search of a solution to my baggage. I ride from bike shop to bike shop. I examine plastic panniers and leather panniers and leather bags coated with studs. All are both too big for the Honda and too expensive.

I park the bike in the hotel garage and walk two blocks to the fish market for a very late lunch. The market is on the harbour front. Stalls on the ground floor sell fruit, vegetables, fish and crustaceans. The restaurants are upstairs, with concrete worktops, gas rings, and plain plastic tables and chairs. Choose a dish from the menu and the cook screeches at a boy to run below and find the freshest relevant fish.

I order devilled prawns (I always order devilled prawns) and orange juice. The prawns are perfect. So is the fresh juice. I am overweight and this is my one meal of the day. I have cut down to fruit for breakfast and in the evening. But what fruit!

I walk a while, checking out luggage stores. I am looking for two small waterproof school satchels. Cheap is important. Later in the evening I visit the chess players. A four-piece band plays in the square: a singer taps a gourd with an ebony stick, and there are two guitarists and a drummer. United by years of practice, portly couples in late middle-age glide joyfully and with rhythm. A show-off forties accustomed to wealthier territory calls to the musicians and holds centre piste with a late-twenties blonde from the US. He wears a wedding band. She doesn't. They argue between dances, she giving him a hard time. Summoned by his mobile, he takes the call around the corner away from the sound of music. His wife?

Plastic tables and chairs belong to the two cafés each side of the plaza. A row of wrought-iron benches on the pavement are city property. A young courting couple, dressed neatly, share a bottle of water on one of the benches. They dance on the pavement, shy with each other but gaining confidence. The girl's high heels are new or nearly new. Seated again, she surreptitiously scratches her ankle. That is the staple of the tropics: there is always one mosquito.

Four young male Brits dressed in grubby shorts, T-shirts and designer stubble stumble down the pavement to a vacant table. Already a little drunk, they slouch in their chairs, legs spread, and order litre bottles of beer. They talk loudly among themselves and drink directly from the bottle. They aren't pretty.

Veracruz, Sunday 14 May

Every bike has its foibles. There is a knack to starting a bike first thing in the morning. Think waking a teenager on a school day. I fail with the Honda and am helped by a young man down from the capital who has the same model of bike back home. I head out of the city on the freeway. This is easy. Confidence grows. I am on the inside lane. Weekend divers hurtle by. A deep hole gapes dead ahead. Swerve or emergency brake? I go for the swerve. A klaxon nearly blasts me off the road. I pull into the curb and calm myself.

The freeway leads through a rolling countryside of paddocks and clumps of big trees. I turn off the freeway towards Antigua – the site of the original Veracruz founded by Cortés. This is a toll road and bikes and cars pay the same charge: three and a half dollars seems exorbitant for twenty kilometres. Sunday drivers hurtle past. Nervous, I grip the throttle tightly. My hand cramps and I prise my thumb back. Both hands are cramping by the time I reach Antigua. I have ridden thirty kilometres. My backside hurts and my thighs ache. An entire continent separates me from Tierra del Fuego. I am too old. Failure seems certain.

Antigua lies a few kilometres inland on the banks of a muddy river. It is a village of cobbled streets, tall trees, a few ruins and a few houses destined for ruin. The roofless ruin of Cortés' first house occupies one corner of the church square. Banyan roots throttle the walls; an unlikely cannon guards what was the entrance. Children gambol in the square on swings and a slide. The church is charming from the outside. The inside is wrecked by pallid statues of saints in coarse horsehair wigs. One saint lies on his back in a glass case. The sculptor has given him a huge beak of a nose and fake eyebrows. Moths or mice have chewed bits of his hair and his face is chipped and discoloured. A normal child would think *vampire* rather than spirituality. The final awfulness is the vases of dusty plastic flowers within spitting distance of flamboyant trees and frangipani.

Launches take Sunday trippers downriver to the beach. A fisherman lands his catch and I follow him to a restaurant on the riverbank. Twenty or so tables are arranged on a concrete floor beneath a thatched roof. The kitchen is indoors on the other side of a dirt road. I celebrate my mobility with a shrimp cocktail and one of the fisherman's catch fried in crisp, wafer-thin cornflour batter and bathed in a green chilli sauce (à la Antigua). Add two large glasses of fresh orange juice and, at ten dollars, this is my most expensive meal since leaving Dallas. A three-piece marimba band sets up: two men play guitar, and a schoolboy plays drums and a gourd. One musician is probably a minor official in real life – blue shirt, pressed jeans, spectacles. The other has a girth problem undisguised by a flowered shirt. People in the US get fat all over. Mexicans appear to restrict fat to the belly. Why?

I am in Antigua because I intend following the route Cortés took in conquering Mexico. My bible is Hugh Thomas' history of the conquest. Cortés led his army across the Cordillera. The head of the pass is 3200 metres above sea level. From the crest, the Spaniards looked down in amazement at a city far larger than any in Europe. I open the book on the table and try once again to marry the indigenous names on the map of the conquest to a present-day road map. The names have changed.

I glance up at the musicians. The boy on drums has a Tintin quiff and seems embarrassed to be here – replacement for an uncle who got drunk last night? The belly musician is a latent anarchist. Every few tunes he make a run for freedom, breaking out of the routine dadedaddada with a fast riff and intricate flourishes, before surrendering to the reality of a hot midday Sunday on a riverbank with an audience of six, only one of whom is listening – me.

I feel on familiar territory. I recognise the trees and the humidity and the scents and the people taking their time at doing whatever they are doing. I've never enjoyed cities much. In London, we lived out in Kew, which has a village atmosphere. In Cuba, we lived fifteen kilometres out from central Havana in Santa Fe. And our home in England now is the perfect village setting, with the garden backing on to two cricket fields and not a house visible beyond.

Veracruz is famous for the friendliness of it people. The musicians join my table between sets. I discover that the gourd the kid scratches and taps is called a *guiro*. The musicians study the place names on the old map and confess their ignorance.

I return reluctantly to the city. Keeping my grip loose stops my hands cramping. Sixty to seventy kilometres an hour is a comfortable cruising speed. I will need to stop every three-quarters of an hour to avoid cramps in my thighs. I can't envisage riding much more than 200 kilometres in a day, maybe 250. How far is Tierra del Fuego?

Central Veracruz is thronged with happy people in shorts and short skirts back from the beach. I fall into conversation with a Mexican businessman in his late forties. He has visited Europe a few times and is amused at the envy for other people's lives that tempts so many northern Europeans to move to Mediterranean countries. He loathes the term 'Latin America', preferring 'Iberian America'. He is contemptuous of Hugh Thomas' history of the Conquest – he read a couple of chapters and chucked it in the bin. I suspect that he was incensed by a Welshman daring to interpret a Spaniard. His jaundiced view of the US is typical of most Mexicans with whom I talk.

I quote my friend Don to him: 'Everyone is trying to get here ...'

'No one with any choice,' the Mexican retorts. As to his own people, 'The only pure bloods are horses. Everyone of us is a mixture: Indian, black, Spanish. We are all *mestizos*.'

I have been told that Sunday evening at the Café de la Parroquia is a tradition among the bourgeoisie of Veracruz. I hope for an ancient building on the harbour front. I discover a modern caféteria. Fortunately the ambience is excellent for people-watching. A few tables are occupied by elderly Spanish émigrés. The women are anaemically pale and have thin lips, thin hair and narrow chests. They sit somehow folded in on themselves as if nervous of being contaminated by the touch of a sexual deviant. For 'deviant', read 'voluptuous native'. Watching them, I am reminded of the leftover French colonials at a café in Tangier where I interviewed Paul Bowles years and years ago. In Tangier we ordered chocolate cake. The Café de la Parroquia is so clean that I risk a lettuce and tomato salad.

Later, I watch a charming programme of 1930s dancing in the Plaza de Armas and then attend a sung mass at the cathedral. Lit by chandeliers, the cathedral enjoys a tranquil beauty. The congregation is a mixture of holidaymakers and the resident sedate. Men and women are in equal numbers. Many are young. Communicants worldwide wear the same gentleness of expression.

Veracruz, Monday 15 May

Baggage Day: I've bought a small backpack and two satchels at a luggage store. Admittedly, one satchel is dark green, and the other dark blue: they were on special offer. I require a metal sheet to be cut and bent to keep the satchels off the chain and rear wheel. I have directions to an alley of metalworkers. A ragged awning shelters the narrow entrance and I miss it a couple of times. I wheel the bike over the pavement and have the choice of twenty or so small, open-fronted workshops. Artisans in whatever country always know best. They don't listen. I am a foreigner; foreigners, by definition, are short on sense. Work ceases in the alley while the metalworkers argue between themselves as to what I need. I know what I need and what I want. I have drawings. I am surplus to the discussions. Finally one of the artisans confronts me with a drawing. It differs from my drawing by half a centimetre here or there.

A few workers return to their own shops. Most remain as onlookers, all voicing opinions of the work and of my proposed journey and why I should or shouldn't take a particular road.

Cost of the metalwork plus satchels and backpack is fifty-seven dollars. Any solution from a bike shop would have been double. I am well pleased. I shall miss the unfailing friendliness of the Veracruz people – and the food. Veracruz University is my sole disappointment. A history department existed in ancient times. History has been replaced by computer sciences.

Veracruz shuts down for luncheon and siesta. Only the cops stay open. The federal police are equivalent to Spain's Guardia Civil and the most feared of Mexican police forces. Few people voluntarily visit the Federales. The Veracruz HQ is a modern building at an intersection on the fringes of the city. My arrival is a surprise.

Mexican police in Hollywood movies are invariably criminal types, small, swarthy and scruffy. The duty officer is six foot two and blond. His uniform shirt is starched. He wears riding breeches and his boots gleam.

I have with me Hugh Thomas' history and a road map. Surely a federal policeman would recognise the ancient place names? The Fed stands and spreads the map on the desk. Only then do I fully realise his height – big and a cop, the very essence of authority. I feel reduced to the status of a small schoolboy – a curious feeling for a man in his seventies.

The Fed studies the place names on Cortés' route and points to their equivalent on the modern map. He examines me with interest. 'You wish to take this route? On a motorcycle? Tell me, when did you last ride a bike?'

'I don't know.'

'Yes, you do.'

'A while ago.'

'How much of a while ago?'

'Well, I rode a scooter in Havana. That was in the nineties.'

'Not a scooter. A bike.'

'Something like thirty or forty years.'

'Which?'

'I'm not certain.'

'Yes, you are.'

'Well, forty ... more or less.'

The Fed is satisfied: 'Forty. And why do you wish to ride this particular route?'

'When Cortés reached the top of the pass, he looked down on what is now Mexico City. He went on to conquer Mexico. I thought that if I could reach the top, I could go on to reach Tierra del Fuego.'

'The south of Argentina?'

'Yes.'

'All the way on your small motorcycle?' The Fed studies my passport. 'Cortés commenced by marching north. Aged seventy-three, is it sensible to commence such a journey by riding in the opposite direction to your destination?'

The Fed traces the route up the pass on the modern map: 'Much of this is a dirt track. It is probable that I could find fanatic bikers among the transit police to accompany you at a weekend. In all probability you would fall off – many times. Were you to reach the summit, you would see nothing of the capital. The capital is hidden by pollution.'

The Fed traces an alternative route south along the coast. 'This is a good straight road with little traffic.'

The following day I should turn inland. I will encounter little traffic in the morning. Only later will I be on a trunk road. On the third day I will climb a pass. I will cross the mountains at the same height as the pass that Cortés crossed. I will do so on a good surface and meet with few trucks or cars. Rather than north, I will be travelling south towards my eventual destination.

'In the evening you will reach Oaxaca, a beautiful city – a city that is not dangerous.' The Fed folds the road map, hands it to me and shakes my hand: 'Please, in Oaxaca telephone that you have arrived.'

I thank the Fed for his counsel and speed back into town. This is my final day in Veracruz: one more dish of devilled prawns at the fish market. In the evening I enjoy the company of two Mexican businessmen and a recent Cuban émigré. One of the Mexicans, small, intense and with a habit of leaning into you when he talks, is determined to discuss the Falklands/Malvinas war. How could I defend Britain's colonial seizure of Argentine territory on the far side of the world?

I ask how he can defend permitting a bunch of particularly unpleasant fascist generals a military success that would have kept them in power for a further ten years. Would that have been preferable for Argentinians?

The Cuban is vague as to the location of the Malvinas. He dreams of being reborn English or German (a citizen of the United States is third by a distance). The Cuban gives as his reason for wishing to live in England or Germany his desire to live where everyone is white-skinned and has blue eyes and blond hair. Imagine his surprise were he to visit London or Hamburg.

The second Mexican prefers discussing food. So do I. I have no desire to be the spokesman for British foreign policy. The Iraq war is universally unpopular here. Oil is believed to be the reason for the war. Britain is denounced as subservient and obedient to the wishes of the

United States (in return, the US helps Britain in big brother/little brother fashion – just think of the Falklands).

Enough of politics. I bid my farewells and sip a final coffee at the chess players' café.

The Road to Oaxaca

Veracruz, Tuesday 16 May

I have travelled much of my life. A day or two in any one place and I begin to nest, even in a third-rate room in a third-rate hotel. I set photographs of my family on the bedside table, arrange books and papers beside the laptop, buy flowers. Walking the streets, I imagine how my life would be, which part of town would I prefer, what house or apartment building. Un-nesting is a wrench, particularly today. Veracruz has become familiar. I have my routine: fruit salad for breakfast at the restaurant across from the hotel, late luncheon above the fish market, evening beer in the Plaza de Armas, last coffee at the chess club café. Such habits are comforting. I feel safe. Meanwhile Mexicans have competed with my Dallas friends in warnings of the dangers ahead, of precipices and bandits and insane drivers. My own fears and doubts concern my physical capacity.

I make a bed of rolled chinos and long underwear in the base of the rack box to cushion the laptop. Next comes the leather folder of family photographs and waterproof plastic envelope containing bike documents, health insurance certificate and medication prescriptions – heart, cholesterol, blood pressure, water tablets. My green-cord long-sleeved shirt and a short-sleeved jumper go on top. Map, guidebook, small towel, washbag and rain slicker go in the backpack. Further books and clothes fill the satchels. I present the hotel staff with two small wheelie suitcases, tartan flannel pyjama trousers and the bulky Clancy Brothers jumper.

As a departure gift, I treat myself to an early breakfast at the swish air-con café on the Plaza de Armas frequented by the business elite. A tall man enters: early fifties, perfectly groomed and beaming an all-encompassing smile of good will to all men. He is a pleasure to watch as he circles the tables, a soft squeeze of the shoulders for those he knows, a word here, a word there, each greeting gilded with such absolute sincerity. I have seen Tony Blair perform in exactly this way – although Blair has never managed to appear elegant. Blair's suits are never quite right and his walk spoils his performance. You know – the Australian dive master's walk, elbows spread as if by a massively muscled chest: *Hey, I'm a real man's man*. George W. Bush has the same walk. Watch them stroll together across the White House lawn or at Camp David.

I imagine, as I watch this gentleman in the café, that his sincerity is too slippery to remain in place; a moment's inattention and it will slide down his perfectly creased trousers to form a little puddle round his immaculately polished shoes.

Mexican elections are on 2 June. A truck with a speaker system brakes alongside me at a traffic light on the way out of town. The speakers blare a chant of 'Vote for ... Vote for ... Vote for ...' to a sell-soap-powder jingle. The side of the truck displays a poster of the candidate: the gentleman in the café. Delightful to have judged correctly.

I am escaping from Veracruz in rush hour. Drivers of short-haul buses are either paid by the kilometre or are holidaying race drivers. Most of them trained on fairground bumper cars. I ride timidly. I stall a couple of times at traffic lights and suffer the screamed insults and klaxons of those behind.

The road runs along the coast. A chill blustery wind blows off the sea – riding a light bike is interesting. The engine has settled or I am more confident; we cruise at eighty kilometres an hour on the flat. My grip is relaxed, no cramps in my hands. My only suffering is a numb bum. At first the road crosses flat ranch land. Cowboys herd cattle into a corral. Further south the road swoops and climbs over what were once the dividing dunes between sea and a vast lagoon. The dunes are cloaked now with tall tufts of dry wispy grass. I follow a truck up a blind hill marked with double yellow lines. A speeding white Chevy Suburban overtakes.

Federales wave to slow us on the next down-slope. Tipped by the wind, a lorry piled high with sugarcane lies on its side and almost blocks the road. The driver of the Chevy Suburban must have wet his pants.

Occasional tyre tracks lead down to the beach and a parked jeep or pickup. I take a break and munch an apple. The sea is grey beneath low cloud. I watch two fishermen bundled in parkas struggle to cast bait against the wind.

Early afternoon and the road dips down towards a river. Armed with rifles, soldiers or police officers guard each end of the bridge. I stop at a restaurant (tin roof, twenty tables on a dirt floor) to the right of the road and order black-bean soup and bottled water. Three six-seater 4×4s pull in, election posters on the doors: a local senator and his entourage. The senator wears a pale grey safari suit, silk socks, lizard-skin loafers, fat gold wedding band and a slim gold watch on a gold wristband. Why do I notice the socks?

The senator's local representative takes the lead, ordering beer, glad-handing the restaurant's owner. The owner, a plump, dark-skinned woman, mid-forties, is unimpressed. The local rep invites me to join them in a beer. I am a real live tourist, proof of something or other that could be beneficial to the senator. The rep wants a threesome photograph: senator, restaurateur, elderly Brit. The restaurateur retorts that she has no interest in photographs – better they pay for the beers.

The senator and his party leave. The woman brings coffee and sits at my table. 'It's the only time we ever see them,' she says of the politicos, 'when there's an election.' She is an incomer. Her husband is local and well respected: hence the senator's desire for a photograph for the local newspaper. She and her husband have two children. 'They've been promising to build a new school for the past ten years.'

Infrastructure alone won't cure the ills of the system. I tell her of our local high school in Ledbury, Herefordshire: the new sixth-form wing, the splendid new sports hall and all-weather football pitches. Unfortunately some of the teachers are abysmal.

Yes, teachers are often incompetent, agrees the woman – incompetent or uninterested.

If only parents and students had the authority to grade those who teach. However, that is a different obsession.

The road climbs beyond the river into hill country that guidebooks refer to as the 'Switzerland of Mexico'. The hills are steep and green; fat dairy cattle graze paddocks studded with huge shade trees. Two hundred kilometres is far enough for my first day and I ride into San Andres de Los Tuxtlas in mid-afternoon.

San Andres is mostly modern and pleasant enough, although not worth a detour. I find a hotel that could be charming with a minimum of thought and effort. I park the bike in the courtyard and a young man shows me a room on the first floor with a view over tiled roofs. A kinder person would have helped carry my bags upstairs. I manage the rack box and the backpack and then return for the two satchels. I shower and change into clean chinos and a clean sports shirt. A bootblack on the square polishes my shoes. I have only the one pair: Church's good brown English leather.

I find a unisex barber upstairs in a mini-mall. One of the two chairs is occupied by a young woman having the lights in her hair brightened. Her friend, an older woman, shares a sofa with two men. One of the men is advising the other on debt-collection strategy:

'Go when you know he's not there. His mother-in-law is always home. Give her the impression that whatever is between you and her son-in-law is a secret. Say you'll come back the following evening. She'll have a whole night to get out of him what you want. You know what she's like – a real demon. She'll make life hellish for him. He'll be happy to pay.'

A second barber trims my beard while the others discuss provincial cuisine. The barber and the debt adviser boast of a local fish stew. They accompany me to a street-front open booth staffed by a round-bodied grandma. Walls and floor are tiled in white. There are three gas burners, a fridge, four sets of plastic tables and chairs. The stew is a deliciously rich mix of spicy shrimp, prawns, crab and octopus. We split a couple of beers and pay four dollars each.

Later I find an internet café close by the hotel. One side of the café is divided into private cabins occupied by shrieking teenagers, mostly female. I can't post pictures – the connection is too slow.

Catemaco, Wednesday 17 May

I get up at six. I ride south over beautiful green hills to a magnificent lake set against a backdrop of mountains. The movie *Medicine Man* with Sean Connery was filmed in the nearby eco-reserve. I eat breakfast on a lakeside terrace among old friends from the flower and bird kingdoms. Bougainvillea shades the terrace; there are orchids and bromeliads, egrets, herons, cormorants, a bad-tempered roadrunner up a palm tree. One bird insistently calls *weeah-weeah-weeah*; another, *peepee-peepee*; a third imitates a cat's meow.

Out on the lake men dive from row boats for *tegogolos*, a type of freshwater crab. Sun breaks over the water. The mountains are a smoky blue. A cool breeze blows off the water. Total joy. Except for the tasteless coffee.

I ride back through San Andres to San Salvador Tuxlas. San Salvador is a small, clean, pretty town of low single-storey buildings set on a river. The largest known carved stone head from the Olmac period sits in a small temple in the middle of the central square. The massive sculpture depicts a deeply depressed gentleman – perhaps he received his tax bill in the morning post. A small museum on the square displays superb ceramics. I sign the visitors' book.

The curator notes my nationality: 'The English invented football.'

'No,' I reply. 'The English invented rules.'

Out in the square, an early-thirties Mexican rides by on a gleaming quarter-horse. Bridle and saddle are true Mexican finery. So are his riding chaps – carved leather. Turquoise studs the silver band on his Stetson and the silver circlet on his string tie. He sits upright as a bronze statue, raised right hand drooping the reins loose. This is his town. He knows how good he looks: the equestrian equivalent of a pimp in his pimpmobile.

The horse is gorgeous.

I pass nothing but fat horses and fat dairy cows for the next eighty kilometres. The road follows the river through rolling hills. The land flattens and farms change from grass paddocks and clumps of woodland to fields of pineapple. Hitting federal highway 175, I turn north to Tuxtepeca. I flinch and the bike trembles as convoys of big trailer trucks thunder past. Drivers are kindly and allow me ample space. The country is flat and drier. Vast fields of pineapple seem sucked into the distant heat haze. Huge trees shade patches of water.

I rest at a fruit-juice stand run by a plump, good-looking woman in her early thirties. She drops a whole pineapple into a press operated by a long handle of galvanised pipe on which she thrusts her full weight. She asks what country I come from. I drink juice to the Beatles ('Lucy in the Sky with Diamonds') played loud on a small CD player.

The woman is single. She tells me that Mexican men are too *machisto*. She dreams of living in Canada and marrying a man who treats her as an equal. She plays 'Yellow Submarine' as I remount. Two more hours to Tuxtepeca.

Tuxtepeca is a modern agro-industrial city of no great interest. However, I find a good folding knife for a few dollars, a spoon and a small plastic bowl to make my own fruit salad of enormous grapes, mango and crisp apple. I have completed 470 kilometres since Veracruz on thirteen litres of gas, or roughly a hundred miles to the gallon. More important is the freedom of being on a bike, taking whatever road I wish, stopping where I want and for as long as I want. Tomorrow is the big one.

Tuxtepeca, Thursday 18 May

Cortés first saw what is now Mexico City from the head of a mountain pass at 3000 metres. Ahead of me lies a pass of 2900 metres. Cortés rode a horse. I ride a 125 cc Honda. Cortés was the boss and could commandeer a fresh horse from his companions. I can't change bikes. Cortés went on to conquer Mexico. Reach the top and I will have conquered much of my fear of this trip and may go on to reach Tierra del Fuego. This is not so grand an ambition, but I am not a great man. I am merely a writer of moderately mediocre novels.

Tuxtepeca is sixty metres above sea level. I leave at six in the morning. For the first sixty kilometres the road follows a wide river valley between fields of sugarcane. The mountains ahead are hidden in cloud. The valley narrows. I top up the gas tank and add my long-sleeved cord shirt over a sports shirt and thermal vest.

Up, up, up. The road is carved out of the mountainside. Rainforest blankets the almost vertical mountain face. The road twists and turns and twists. Many bends turn the road back on itself. Cloud and mountain hide the sun. I shiver in the chill morning mountain air and stop to add a second thermal vest and a second sports shirt beneath the long-sleeved shirt.

Up. The climb is endless. I overtake a bus. I pass an abandoned pickup. I am in second gear, sometimes first. Fear for the bike, for the engine, is paramount.

Up. The pain in the right side of my chest could be a muscle twinge. It could be my heart. I recall being felled by pain in my chest and arm and crawling across the floor in my hotel room and begging for a doctor. That was fifteen years ago in the mountains of Guatemala. It is extremely foolish of an old Brit on heart medication to be on a tiny bike on a Mexican mountain pass. I am scared that I won't make it. I take deep chill drags into my lungs, testing the air for oxygen. My fingers are numb (cold or tension?). I stop and wave my arms around to restore the circulation and put on a third sports shirt and my short-sleeved jumper. A gap in the undergrowth shows the clouds way below. I take photographs. I remount the bike. My legs feel weak. Turning downhill, I jump-start the engine before continuing the climb.

Up. A lone pine appears among the broadleaf canopy. A further five kilometres and the pines have the victory, the road twisting up through an open forest carpeted with small feathery ferns. The clouds are way down where they should be when you look down from an aeroplane. From an aeroplane, clouds look soft and fluffy and beautiful. From way up here on the mountain road, they are a frightening reminder of how far you will fall if you make a mistake.

Up. The cramp in my left side is fractionally more intense – or is this pain the product of a fiction writer's over-vivid imagination?

I have neither passed nor been passed by a vehicle in thirty minutes. I am alone, totally alone.

Up. The sun hits the pines and I inhale the familiar tar scent of childhood Scottish summers. The trees thin. The summit must be close. The road follows the crest of a ridge. For the first time on the climb I see down to both my left and my right. I stop in the sun to take a photograph. I don't dismount and I keep the motor running. The bus that I had overtaken earlier creeps by and stops. The driver and another man jump down to ask whether I need help.

I long to know how far we are from the summit of the pass. Instead, I play British and say that I am just fine.

Up the last few hundred metres, and then over the brow and halt at a café on the right side of the road. My legs tremble as I dismount. The driver and passengers from the bus gather round. One of them asks, 'Hey, grandfather, how old are you?'

I tell him and another asks where I am going.

'Argentina,' I say. 'Patagonia, Tierra del Fuego ...' For the first time, I truly believe that I can make it.

The woman of the café brings coffee and sets a chair against the wall in the sun. I sit and absorb the warmth while the bus passengers ask questions as to my true intention and where I come from and does my wife approve of my absence and how many children do I have and what do they think of my travels?

I answer with what has become my standard reply: 'What should I do with the last years of my life? Sit in front of the TV?'

'No,' They all agree. 'It is a good thing to travel, to meet different people.'

The woman of the café shouts at her daughter to check the hens for fresh eggs. I eat the eggs scrambled with spicy chorizo, a side serving of refried beans and warm tortillas. The fresh orange juice is perfect. Unfortunately, the coffee is watery and tastes of mud. For once I don't give a damn. I have climbed 2900 metres. The sun is warm. Ahead lies that queen of Mexican cities, Oaxaca, and then country after country, pathways to the romance of exploration and experience.

The road down is equally steep and serpentine. I have to remind myself continually to sit back and not put all my weight on my hands, otherwise my fingers cramp. The valley into which the road descends is dry and dusty, the trees scrappy, the greens of the vegetation lacking the voluptuousness of the northern face. Road signs are immaculate, black curves hand-painted on a yellow background. Each sign is an attempt to portray the road ahead. Common is a broad squiggle rising to a strong arrowhead. There is the tight bend and the right-angled bend and sometimes a double right-angled bend. Most serious is the written warning of a dangerous curve – a curve tighter than a right-angle, that turns back on itself. The boys on bikes would have a ball.

I rest halfway down at a café opposite a primary school and drink fresh orange juice. I chat with the café owners. They have a son in El Norte – the North, the United States. A US flag hangs on the wall. The road climbs again through dry, dusty mountains. The pass is lower than the first. I am more confident.

Finally I arrive in Oaxaca. I have ridden 230 kilometres. Apart from the first short stretch and the immediate approach to the city, I have encountered no more than two straight stretches of road of 200 metres or so.

My intended hotel has disappeared since the publication of my guidebook. I find another, shower and hunt a shoemaker to replace the leather soles on my only shoes. I sit in the shop and chat to the woman owner for an hour and a half. I then stroll in re-shod splendour to the zócalo, the central square, in front of the cathedral. On the way I spot the Hotel Central on Independencia, possessor of a charming patio, and book a room for the following night. In the zócalo, I sit at a café, order a cold beer and chat to my neighbours at the next table. Rain spatters the square and I delay leaving. The rain only strengthens. Suddenly very tired, I walk the few blocks in the rain to my hotel. It isn't there. Stores are closing. Everything looks different in the dim light of the few street lamps. I walk and circle and retrace my steps and begin again.

The rain has become a torrent. I can't see through my spectacles. My feet hurt. Everything hurts. I spot, through an open doorway, an obvious foreigner, a young blonde woman, writing emails at a computer. I circle the block once more, the rain ever heavier. I return to the young woman, an American, explain my idiocy – that I can't find my hotel and don't recall its name – and ask whether she has a guidebook. She has the Lonely Planet. My hotel isn't listed. I try one last time to find it and then return to the Hotel Central. I feel immensely foolish as I explain my predicament and lack of luggage and ask for a room. I drop my soaked clothes on the floor and crawl into bed.

Oaxaca

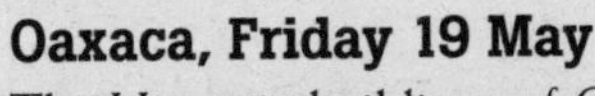

Oaxaca, Friday 19 May

The Hispanic buildings of Oaxaca glow a soft rose in the morning sun. The Hotel Central is a resurrected Spanish colonial townhouse two blocks from the zócalo. My room is furnished with period copies: bed and bedside cupboard, wardrobe, table and an upright chair. A simple cloister surrounds three sides of a flag-stoned patio where a neighbouring restaurant serves breakfast and light meals. Comfortable benches stand against the cloister wall; there are tubs of red hibiscus and jasmine.

This morning I dress in wet clothes and go in search of my bike and luggage. I find the hotel immediately. It is where I knew it was. I searched this street in the rain again and again last night. Fatigue must have left me confused. I need to be more careful. Hence my decision to enjoy a day of rest – although first I will leave the bike at the local Honda agent for its first service.

Mid-afternoon and I work at an internet café without the coffee and a connection that takes forever. In San Andres Tuxlas, I spent an hour trying to post photographs. No hope. Oaxaca is as bad and the mouse has a habit of sticking.

In the evening I sit on the steps in the zócalo and watch a poorly attended political rally. The speakers are drowned by a twenty-piece dance band playing outside the cathedral. A schoolteacher tells me that there will be a strike tomorrow. He asks whether I am an American. I answer that I am English and he sits beside me: 'That ignorant Bush. All the hypocrisy of celebrating the fall of the Berlin wall. Now he's building a wall to keep us out. For us the border is meaningless; we all have relations on both sides.'

Oaxaca, Saturday 20 May

Oaxaca, city of churches. The exteriors are uniformly simple and beautiful. As to the interiors, my prejudices are in good shape. I find the interior of the cathedral abysmal; railings enclose the central aisle and great iron gates forbid entrance to the side chapels. Sinful to chop such magnificent space into tiny pens.

In San Felipe Neri, the vast altarpiece reminds me of the worst excesses of Ukraine's Orthodox decor.

And yet, professing to love simplicity, why am I overwhelmed by the beauty of Santo Domingo's interior with its voluptuous basting of gold leaf? To see this one great church is worth the trip to Mexico.

Most touching to me is the Church of the Society of Jesus. A side chapel is dedicated to the Society's martyrs. I read their names and dates written on the walls and am welcomed by familiars of my Catholic childhood: Edmund Campion, Hugh Walpole, Edmund Arrowsmith. Such English names. I sit in the peace and quiet of the chapel as if among old friends. High above the arched entrance to the chapel is an inscription: *Compañeros de Jesus, amigos en el Señor*. In the chapel dedicated to the Virgin Mary is written in thirteen indigenous Mexican languages and in both Spanish and English: 'Am I not here for I am your mother ...'

The Catholic Church in the USA, Ireland and England may be disgraced for its shielding of sexual predators, but in Mexico the Church is very much alive. These churches are the temples of today's Mexico. Services are full. At any hour you find a scattering of people at private prayer. Watch people cross themselves as they pass on the pavement. The one danger to the Church in Latin America is that a reactionary pope will enforce its withdrawal from the active struggle for social justice.

A day of sightseeing and I retire in the evening to a café on the zócalo, order a bowl of soup and people-watch. Mexicans of all classes dress smartly for Saturday evening in the city. A group of US students stride at speed diagonally across the square. Unbrushed hair, shorts and T-shirts, sandals, sleeveless tops: these young seem to me so untidy and disrespectful of local mores.

Disrespectful or uncaring? Theirs is the ascendant culture.

Oaxaca, Sunday 21 May

I attend Mass at the first church built in Oaxaca – San Juan de Dios: simple in decor, white altarpiece decorated with eight big vases of white dahlias. My travels are solitary and I recharge my human contact batteries by shaking hands at the end of the service with neighbours in the congregation.

Later I visit a small orphanage run by two nuns, one Mexican and the other from Chile. My companions are a paediatrician who gives his free time to the orphanage, his architect wife and their few-months-old daughter. Our arrival coincides with the children's midday meal. The children range from six to eighteen years. Not all of them are true orphans; some have only one deceased parent. However, all come from a background of crippling poverty. Some have suffered permanent brain damage inflicted by long-term protein deficiency. Others are openly intelligent.

I congratulate the Chilean nun, a woman in her early sixties, on the extraordinary peace that reigns in the refractory. '*La lucha*,' she replies. '*La lucha*.' A daily struggle.

So comment Cubans on life under Castro, El Commandante en Jefe.

A six-year-old holds out her arms to me to be lifted, then buries her face in my shoulder. Later, a small boy installs himself on my lap as I chat with fourteen-year-old Theodora who has ambitions to be a secretary and, as she admits shyly, a writer.

Boys, four to a room, sleep on the ground floor; girls are upstairs. The older girls share with the younger ones, as mother substitutes. Toy rubber and plastic animals stand on the dividing walls between the girls' showers. This is a gentle place for kids to grow, gentle and filled with love – so unlike those erstwhile Irish orphanages in which generations of children suffered abuse.

I am told few foreigners frequent or know of the restaurant where we lunch. We eat at a table in the garden. I blanch as the paediatrician orders cockroaches. Thank God 'cockroach' is the local slang for crayfish tails grilled on charcoal. And thank God (or the generosity of the paediatrician) that I never see the bill – I suspect that it would have been more than I usually pay for my food in a week.

Conversation turns to politics. Mexico was ruled for decades with enforced corruption by the Party of the Institutionalised Revolution (a splendidly Orwellian name). In the present election, presidential candidates from the ruling conservative PAN and the socialists are abreast in the opinion polls. The paediatrician expects and hopes for a socialist victory. He is dark-skinned, from a peasant family and worked his way through medical school. He was expected to practise as a state-employed GP out in the country. In studying to become a specialist, he was handicapped by racism among senior doctors in the hospital. Nurses were instructed to report him as drunk if he came to the hospital at night to visit patients. He talks of the countryside and a system of land tenure instituted by the revolution, which condemns the peasantry to poverty. Often they are better off selling their land to big landowners and working for wages. They are victims either way. Many leave to find work in the city. There is no work. Few Mexican manufacturers can survive competition from China and its cripplingly low labour rates.

Oaxaca, Monday 22 May

A day of expectations: I am due to talk to students at two public high schools. I rise early, brush, shower and shave. Clean shirt, clean trousers. My shoes were polished yesterday evening. I breakfast on the patio with two Chilean diplomats and watch a hummingbird poke his beak in the red hibiscus. I wheel the bike out to the road. Teachers within the Oaxaca state system have come out on strike. The teachers are heading for the city.

I visit the most prestigious of Oaxaca's private schools, Blaise Pascal. While waiting to be interviewed by the headmistress, I sit in the shade of a jacaranda tree outside the school caféteria. Mid-morning break heralds the any-school-in-the-world charge. In Herefordshire, students demand bacon butties. Here, the favourite is stuffed tortillas. Dress is less formal: jeans, trainers, school sweatshirts.

The paediatrician asked yesterday whether I found Mexico racist. I replied that it was difficult for a foreigner to be sure, that I believed it was less so among the younger generation. Now I watch the younger generation in their break. At my age, so much is a reminder of the past. I spot one splendidly sulky, heavy-jowled Catalan matron of fifty going on seventeen. A group at a table are identical in gesture and in the way they laugh to my son Josh and his friends. I see no demarcation by colour. Do I know how to look?

Two teachers have called in sick (the strike?). The head of the English department, an Englishman, is delighted to inflict me on his students. A young Mexican American is in charge of my first class. This is her first day teaching at the school. Classes are conducted in English and she asks me to speak to the students in English. Most of the students are sixteen. I relate a little of my background as a writer and the purposes of my journey. I search faces for irritation, boredom, contempt.

I ask in Spanish whether they understand, more or less.

These are teenagers. Naturally they respond with silence.

'More?' I ask.

More silence.

'Or less?'

This raises a shy laugh.

I ask for questions. From teenagers? Stand out from the group? Am I crazy? They will keep their questions for each other out of class.

So I ask the questions. How many have relatives in the north – the US? Four raise their hands. What do they think of Bush planning to build a wall?

'Stupid,' a girl says, and the class nods.

They know of Condoleezza Rice?

Yes.

She made a speech in Europe stating that Americans never torture. Do they agree?

Nobody moves.

Have they understood? I rephrase the question. 'How many of you believe that the American government condones torture?'

Serious stuff is embarrassing. They whisper to each other. One raises his hand, then another, then all together – although no more than shoulder height.

I ask what differences exist between their parents' generation and their own.

'The way we think,' a girl answers to general agreement.

'Think in what way?' I ask.

'You know,' accompanied by a teenage shrug that I recognise from home as a definite end to the conversation.

I try a different tack. 'I have sons. Jed is sixteen, Josh twenty. If I asked them the same question, they would say that I wouldn't understand. That's what you tell your parents, right?'

Laughter.

A boy asks, 'What do you think the differences are?'

This seems of general interest – or it gets them off the hook of being required to supply answers themselves.

I say that that I made my first trip through Mexico in the early eighties. I don't recall ever seeing young people kiss on the street. Now it is moderately commonplace.

'What else?' a girl asks.

I think, what the hell? Go for it. I tell them of the paediatrician's accusations of racism – that I had been watching them at the canteen.

They wait.

I say, 'I'm a foreigner. I can't tell. I don't know how to look – although it seems to me that, if racism does exist, it is less common among your generation.'

These kids are from wealthy families, pale to bronzed. Many glance involuntarily at a dark girl in the front row. What would she say? And will they discuss the subject among themselves after class? Or will they dismiss me as a silly old foreign fool?

I take two more classes of the same age group, the last on the approach to midday break. Students are keen to get out of class. I stand by the door and slow them by relating, as a lone traveller, the warmth of companionship I feel when shaking hands after Mass. The students shuffle into line. Although embarrassed, they are generous of nature and smile as they clasp my hand. A few even mumble one of those monosyllables that pass among teenagers as conversation.

I have one more class for a full fifty minutes in the afternoon. These are final-year students. Three of the male students make it clear that I am a nobody and talk instead to their girlfriends. One of the girls asks permission to visit the bathroom. I say that I am not a teacher – that whether she goes to the bathroom or not is her decision. A second girl asks and I give her the same answer.

Three girls in the front ask me about writing and what books I read and what I know of Latin American writers. Great. We form a foursome and leave the other students to their own devices. I am delighted that they discuss only Hispanic American writers. Having just read *Like Water for Chocolate* earns me a little street cred. Two of them are admirers of the Márquez/Allende brand of fantasy/mysticism. I suggest Salman Rushdie as Márquez' equal and more directly political. The third girl is more taken by reality and politics.

I end by telling all those that remain in the classroom, the conversationalists who have ignored me (those that haven't gone to the bathroom and stayed there or wherever they stayed), that I had been asked by the first class what changes I saw between theirs and their parents' generation. I had seen four male students enter the headmistress's office wearing baseball caps. None of their parents would have been so ill-mannered.

Striking teachers have been arriving in Oaxaca all day. They stretch tarpaulins across streets in the city centre, and make beds of flattened cardboard boxes on the pavement. Hundreds sleep on footpaths and in the centre of the street. They lie curled on their sides and they lie on their backs. Some, accustomed to good mattresses, can't sleep. Tourists duck under the tarpaulins as they wend their way to and from the cafés on the zócalo. On each street and square, small groups of union officials gather in conclave.

The Chilean diplomats and I talk until late on the hotel patio. Chile has a new president, Michelle Bachelet, a socialist and a single mother. Her father was arrested for opposing the US-backed anti-Allende coup and died in prison. Both the new president and her mother were arrested and tortured.

Richard Helms was the CIA director.

Henry Kissinger was US secretary of state.

Richard Milhous Nixon was US president.

Helms and Nixon are dead. Kissinger is revered as an elder statesman.

The Chilean diplomats find it ironic that so many socialist governments have been elected in Latin America during George W. Bush's neo-con administration. Add the disasters of Iraq and Afghanistan, and Bush, by his own conservative standards, is the most unsuccessful president in US history.

As to Britain, the Chileans are disgusted that Tony Blair, a professed socialist and leader of a Labour government, should have enslaved himself to US neo-cons.

Road to Tehuantepec, Tuesday 23 May

Seven in the morning and the ten central city blocks of Oaxaca resemble a refugee camp and already stink of human urine and faeces. Imagine if the strike continues for a week, or even a month – as it has in the past.

This strike is an annual affair and coincides with the run-up to final exams. The exams are cancelled, with all students given a fictitious pass grade into university. Universities then have no idea as to the true achievements of their entry students. Meanwhile hotels and small shopkeepers despair at the loss of tourist income.

How will the strike affect the presidential election on 2 June? Mexico's TV commentators are invariably white and right. In the past week, a vituperative press and TV campaign (financed by the oligarchy) has put the PAN (Conservative) candidate marginally ahead of the centre left.

Oaxaca has been good to me. The Hotel Central, its staff and its lovely patio provided a home from home. The owners were immensely kind and hospitable, and both informative and intellectually provocative. All but four of the students at Blaise Pascal were courteous and patient. The kids at the orphanage were loving and deserve to be much loved. The church congregation blessed me with their companionship. Now back on the bike.

I take the road to Mitla. The ruins at Mitla are ancient. I try to find them interesting. My imagination won't function. My guidebooks ignore the road northeast from Mitla towards Zapotec so I take it out of cussedness. The road climbs for eighty kilometres. The ascent is more gradual than the ascent from Tuxtepeca. I feel fine. However, I am growing familiar with the Honda's performance and I know that we are well above 2000 metres. This is a dry country of thin soil and dust and rock. The mountains seem endless. Cactus forest gives way to conifers. Branches are tipped with flared bunches of bright green needles, looking like something between a bright-green lavatory brush and the grass skirt of a whirling ballet dancer.

For the traveller, the views are magnificent. However, real people inhabit the scattering of villages that cling to the mountain, with lives of a terrifying harshness.

I pass through a small town. Election time and an obvious politician (white, naturally) waves and wastes on me a dentifrice smile as I bump over a sleeping policeman. He is playing at being one of the boys for the day. He stands beside a gleaming double-cab pearl-grey pickup. I buy a bottle of water at an open-fronted stall and watch a while as he glad-hands the townsfolk.

A vast building is under construction above the town. On flat land you would presume it was an aircraft hanger. I ask a middle-aged male passer-by and he tells me it is a conference centre. Here? Up a mountain? The entire population of these barren mountains might fill half of it.

The man grins and says, '*Algo politico*'. Something political – magnificently visible proof of a politician's interest in his electorate – what North Americans refer to as 'pork-barrel politics'.

I ask how people survive.

Every family has members in *El Norte*.

'*Ilegales*?'

'*Claro*.' Clearly.

Near the top of the pass, the road surface changes from tar to dirt. A road sign at an intersection names places that I don't find on the map. I haven't seen a car or a truck in the past half-hour. Vultures and buzzards float far overhead. I'm a little nervous. Nervous? Frightened? Yes, a little frightened. The space is overwhelming. Such emptiness.

An ancient pickup pulls alongside. The radiator belches steam. Both the driver and his companion are darkly featured. Raggedy parkas puff them up so that they seem square – memories of the dwarfs in Snow White. Neither man has shaved in a while. The driver has long hair. I don't have much confidence.

I ask which road leads to Zapotec and how far.

'Very far.'

'Is the road dirt all the way?'

'Yes, dirt all the way.'

'Good dirt?'

The driver shrugs. 'Some good, some bad.'

'Very bad,' confirms his companion.

The driver rams the pickup into gear and lets out the clutch.

Would retracing my route be wise or cowardly? Fear of seeming cowardly has dumped me in many a catastrophe over the years. I am older and wiser – or older and more cowardly. Either way, I turn and swoop back down the mountains and take the Pacific Highway to Tehuantepec. The highway follows a river, the river escapes, the road recaptures it. The road surface is excellent. I make good time. The coastal heat beckons. Vast trucks creep upwards or race past on their descent to the port at Salina del Cruz. Coaches gleam in their livery.

I stop for a juice at a roadside shack. The woman owner is thrilled that I am a Brit. Her daughter, Patti, is learning English at high school. Patti is shouted for. Patti has fled. She is captured and returned to a table in the shade at the side of the shack. She is a shy girl with a sweet smile and a few last remnants of puppy fat.

The mother waits expectantly for her daughter to speak English.

Patti looks glum. I imagine doing the same with Jed if a Spaniard passed by. Jed would kill both me and the Spaniard. Patti, thank God, is a pacifist.

A car stops and Mum leaves to serve the driver and passengers. Patti and I speak in Spanish. Patti says that she has learnt a few English words and can write a little but has no practice in speaking.

Jed and his friends would say the same of school French – although, as with Patti, they would probably succeed in conversing if left alone with someone of their own age.

Mum returns and I assure her that we have been speaking English.

Mum beams.

Patti looks grateful. I give her one of my visiting cards: *El Viejo y Su Moto*. The old man and his bike.

A further fifty kilometres to the coastal plain: the Honda kicks up its heels. We speed at ninety kilometres an hour. Ha! to Jed and his friends who mock that I even delay other oldies when driving our ancient Honda Accord back home.

Tehuantepec is a small town, peaceful after Oaxaca. Most houses are single-storey. Good signposting leads me directly to the central square. A heavily built townsman is parking a big Nissan. I ask directions to an economical hotel and find myself a block away at the Doraji. The hotel has a welcoming central patio and a large café. I take a spotless single room with fan and functional bathroom on the top floor.

It is late and most restaurants are closed. Fortunately the café around the corner at the Hotel Oasis is open. I eat devilled prawns (yes, once again). And so to bed.

Tehuantepec, Wednesday 24 May

Tehuantepec is home to a tribe of Boadiceas. For the ignorant, Boadicea was a Brit queen reputed to have minced invading Roman soldiers beneath scythes attached to the wheels of her chariot. Tehuantepec's Boadiceas stand in the back of *moto-caros* – small three-wheeled trucks based on a motorcycle and always driven by men. I haven't seen these elsewhere in Mexico. The women wear long dresses and appear imposingly fierce. I avoid being minced and discover the Caféteria Pearl on the street opposite the Hotel Oasis: excellent breakfast – eggs, ham, juice.

I return to the hotel and brush my false teeth. Idiot! I drop them on the tiled floor. The upper plate snaps in three places.

The concierge at the Doraji directs me across the church square to an orthodontist. The orthodontist, Fernando, is dark-skinned and medium rotund. He has ambitions to be a writer. I sit at his desk and read a polemic. Here is deep anger at the PAN (Conservatives), the oligarchy and their servants in the media. Fernando has no expectations that the candidate of the PRD (centre left), Obrador, can cure the ills of Mexico. But at least Obrador would try.

So much for politics. We progress to Fernando's first novel, almost complete. We discuss personal loves. Fernando recommends the Mexican realists (Jose Emilio Pacheco: *Las Batallas en el Desierto*).

My teeth are fixed. Fernando drives me to his home. We drink beer. Fernando's wife Elena serves us enough nibbles to feed an army. Their sons arrive: Juan Pablo, eighteen, and young Fernando, almost sixteen. The boys have a band. They won a national youth competition with their rendition of 'Californication' by the Red Hot Chilli Peppers – my son Josh's favourite group. Josh has seen them live twice.

The sitting room is uninhabitable, every chair and sofa covered with assembled and disassembled and partially assembled pieces of sound and recording equipment. We sit in the dining room. Out come electric guitars. Juan Pablo sings Pink Floyd – Josh's other favourite. We drink more beer. Elena places more food on the table. Young Fernando fails to connect to my website: while downloading music, they have infected their computer with a splendid array of viruses. Their father keeps his laptop locked in his office. The sons protest that they need a new computer. This computer is six months old and already an antique. Where have I heard this conversation? Guess. We are in Old Home Week!

Fernando insists that I must see a side to Tehuantepec no foreigner visits. Juan Pablo accompanies us. Young Fernando has school in the afternoon. Elena owns a mobile phone store and must attend to business.

I should have guessed from Fernando's girth that he wishes to show me a restaurant. The restaurant is on the banks of a canal ten kilometres out of town. The family swim in the canal on Sundays before and after eating. Today Fernando orders monster shellfish cocktails of shrimp, baby octopus, oysters and crab in a hot sauce. A dish of grilled crayfish follows. And we talk.

Young Juan Fernando is off to university in Mexico City this year to read history and intends to be a research historian. We discuss Bush and Blair and an ignorance of history that has led them into the Iraq war. We discuss the border that is not a border. They refer, as do most Mexicans, to '*El Norte*' rather than 'the United States'.

Fernando has brought a bottle of Terry brandy. We discuss the European Union. Then racism.

My doctor friend from Oaxaca suffered from racism at medical school and while working as an intern. So has Fernando. Fernando wonders at the Islamic ghettos created in English cities. He asks how he would be treated in an English *taverna* – a pub. Would he be mistaken for a Muslim and be in danger?

More probably a West Indian, I answer, and no, he wouldn't be in danger.

I am seated across the table from Fernando and his son. Beyond them are the canal and a line of great trees shading the water. This is one of the most pleasurable meals of my life, both in food and in conversation. I am incredibly fortunate and deeply grateful.

Back in town I duck into Elena's shop to offer thanks for such hospitality. Elena gives me a medal of the Virgin of Guadalupe to watch over my travels. I leave her store. The steel security shutter isn't fully raised. My forehead crashes into its edge. Blood flows down my face. Rather than display the Virgin's failure, I stride off across the square. Elena must think me exceedingly rude for not turning back to wave goodbye.

The concierge at the hotel finds disinfectant and a plaster. She and a maid and I sit in the lobby and watch a Mexican TV soap. All the characters are white or whitish. Certainly none is indigenous. The maid and the concierge are medium dark. Wine and Terry brandy have made me mischievous. I ask the concierge whether the soap is Mexican.

The maid giggles at my stupidity. 'Of course it is Mexican.'

'But the characters: are they Mexican?'

'Of course they are Mexican.'

I admit to being confused. 'From which part of Mexico do they come? Is there a province where all Mexicans are white?'

How could I believe such nonsense?

'But look at the soap,' I say. 'Even the servants are white. Everyone I see on television is white – except on the news programmes. Although the presenters are always white.'

The concierge says, 'It's true.' And to the maid, 'Yes, it's true.'

They were content watching the soap. I have made them uncomfortable. The job of a writer is to provoke thought – particularly uncomfortable thought. I wish that I were a better writer. What is worthy in a good writer is merely arrogance in the mediocre.

The Monk and Mister Big

An idyllic beach, Thursday 25 May

Be patient. This chapter concerns a small Mexican village on the Pacific coast, a community in which the villagers take turns collecting garbage, being police officer or whatever requires doing. The community is under threat.

I heard of the village from a delightful young Irish traveller in Oaxaca, Eoin Hennessy. Eoin was flying home from Mexico City after exploring much of South and Central America. Eoin was the first person with whom I had talked in English since boarding the bus in Dallas. He suffered my verbal diarrhoea patiently, learnt of my interest in students and told me of a Korean American teaching at a school in a village on the Pacific coast: surely a curious and unique combination? The village is 145 kilometres north. I should head south to Guatemala but the temptation to investigate is too strong.

What a morning! A heavy rain fell in the night and you can taste a sharp fresh cleanliness to the air. An excellent highway unwinds through hills speckled with the white blossom of frangipani trees and trees that resembles wild figs. There are sudden patches of deep-rose creeper and startling blue. Vultures and buzzards hang overhead on dawn patrol for whatever has been squashed by the night's traffic. Between the hills, I catch glimpses of the sea and miles of deserted beach. I rested yesterday. My bum has un-numbed. This is biking at its best.

A short stretch of newly laid concrete track leads off the coastal highway. The concrete ends at the crest of a ridge. I ride cautiously downhill on powdery dirt to the village. I park at a home on the square opposite an obviously official building and enquire of a man seated in one of those bought-on-sale white plastic chairs whether the building is the school. He asks why and I relate my search for a Korean American teacher.

'Sit a little,' he invites and introduces himself as Eduardo. The Korean (no villager refers to him as 'the American', not even 'the Korean American') doesn't teach at the school. He gives private lessons. He lives in a house nearer the beach. At this early hour he will be watching the surf through binoculars.

Eduardo will lead me to the Korean's home. In a short while Eduardo will collect the village garbage in the black Ford pickup that he has driven home from *El Norte*. Collecting the garbage is the time for Eduardo to show me the house that the Korean occupies. Meanwhile I must give an account of myself and why I wish to meet with the Korean.

Children surround us, a small tribe, the elders perhaps listening while the young giggle and shove each other. Eduardo is in no hurry. I must adjust to the slow tempo of his investigation.

I recount my journey and that I am a writer, an *Ingles*.

'*Inglaterra?* Is that close to *El Norte?*'

'Not close,' I say. 'In Europe. In the north of Europe.'

Perhaps satisfied, Eduardo relates a little of his own life, of the three years in Taos where he worked as a roofer for a gringo, a good employer who insured his workers, even the *ilegales* – fortunate, as Eduardo injured two fingers while on a roof.

In turn, I speak of my father-in-law, a fine, dearly beloved Irishman. He came to England in search of work as a labourer and his arm was trapped in a cement mixer while he worked alone on the roof of a tall apartment building.

My father-in-law and two of his brothers came to England on the false promise of well-paid work. Eduardo paid a smuggler 1500 dollars to lead him across the frontier. Later Eduardo saved the same amount to have his wife brought across. A daughter was born in *El Norte* and has papers.

Eduardo intended returning to Taos in June. He is a good worker. His gringo employer keeps a job open for him. Now there are new laws in the north, and greater difficulties and dangers in crossing the frontier. Eduardo is unsure whether crossing is possible.

The economy of his family depends on his going. These are anxious times.

'Do many villagers go to the north?'

'Many,' Eduardo says. 'To Taos, alone, more than one hundred.'

'Do they return?'

My question is stupid. Naturally people return. This is their village. Although now, those that are away will be afraid to return home. The new conditions will force them to stay in the north to be sure of sending money home. How could families survive without money? Here in the village there is no work.

Then, almost casually, Eduardo mentions the *torneo*.

In June an international surfing tournament will be held on the village beach. Outsiders are organisers of the tournament. The tournament will be shown on television and reported with photographs in magazines and newspapers. The village will be famous. Many people will visit.

'More money will come,' I suggest.

Eduardo agrees, although he seems uncertain, hesitant.

'The value of property will rise.'

'Yes,' Eduardo says. 'Yes, many people will wish to buy lots.'

I tell him of the early days in Ibiza, the fifties, and that all the young men were friends. We, the few foreigners, together with the Ibicencos, partied together. We went to the beach together, went fishing. Twenty years later my first wife, Cate, and I returned to Ibiza and dined at the Olive Tree in San Antonio. The owner was one of those young men.

'How is Paco Tuels?' we asked. 'How is Juan Jesus? And Antonio of the Ferry?'

The restaurateur's replies were non-committal. Later, when the rush had cleared, he sat at our table and we drank brandy together and he told us, sadly: 'In the days you remember, we were all friends. Now we are business competitors.'

I follow Eduardo through the village and wait while he loads garbage from other families. Many of the homes are in that curious and very Mexican condition of waiting for more funds to be extended or finished or painted. It is a small village, at most a hundred houses, and easily swallowed – a small mouthful to a rich, powerful investor with the right political links. This was the story of Ibiza.

The road to the beach is gated. The village commune charges visitors an admission of ten pesos. Eduardo enquires for the Korean. The surf is good. He went to the beach an hour or more ago.

Eduardo stops my hunt for change. For me, entry to the beach is free. Thus I am placed under an obligation of friendship to the village. This seems to me to be quite deliberate. I am, of course, a writer, and possess a writer's imagination.

The dirt track to the beach has been graded. A rich irrigated vegetable garden – *huerto* – of papaya and citrus lies below the track to the left. The *huerto* ends in a lagoon that fills at high tide and is flooded with fresh water when there is heavy rain. The track leads to a sand parking lot shaded by a few small trees. A concrete hut houses clean lavatories and showers – his and hers. A big palm-thatched hut, a *palapa*, shades a bar and kitchen and a score of standard white plastic tables and chairs. A few hammocks swing in the shade of an adjoining *palapa*. A steep hill hooks round the right end of a gently curving mile of perfect sand. The hill jabs a point of massive boulders into the sea. Waves break at the point. The surf is vertical and forms a perfect barrel again and again and again ... and again.

The *palapas* belong to the community. Two young women tend the bar. One is remarkably pretty. An older woman is the cook. She should be described as the chef. The snapper she grills for me is perfect, skin crisp, flesh moist, a touch of garlic. But I get ahead of my story ...

I ride into the parking lot and spot the Korean crossing from the *palapa* towards a 4×4. He is unmistakable. He possesses the perfect body of a movie Kung Fu warrior. He wears a towel draped over his head as if he were a monk striving to concentrate on his breviary or merely exclude the distractions of the outside world. The villagers call him 'the Korean'. I prefer 'the Monk' – although I doubt that he is celibate.

I said, 'I think I've come to see you.'

Even monks can be surprised.

I explain my mission – that a young Irishman had told me of him and that he teaches English at the village high school: that I have already learnt that this is incorrect, that he gives private lessons.

Much is happening in the village and the Monk is suspicious of my sudden appearance. He asks where I learnt of Eoin's mistake and how I knew where to find him. I reply that Eduardo of the garbage informed me and add that this is a small village and that most villagers must know the Monk's movements – certainly those who are interested.

The Monk admits this truth. However, he remains suspicious and excuses himself. He has students in the afternoon and must prepare.

'Perhaps later,' I suggest.

Yes, perhaps later – although he is unenthusiastic.

I order a beer in the *palapa* and watch the surfers out at the point. Later, I notice the Monk in conversation with a tall young blonde woman under the second *palapa* that shades the hammocks. The towel is up, protecting the Monk's privacy.

A loud confident voice heralds the arrival of four men and a young, tall, good-looking woman, perhaps a gringa. The voice is a big burly man overaccustomed to dining people on a corporate expense account: black hair streaked with silver, clipped moustache, fleshy sensual ears. Confident of his power, he wears shorts and a T-shirt; the other three men are uncomfortably warm in slacks. One wears a long-sleeved shirt and round-lens spectacles and carries a briefcase. The gofer, I calculate, as he crosses to the bar to order. I catch his attention. We find that we share Cuba as an experience, he having studied tourism in Havana for two years. Now he is an official at the Department of Tourism.

'The *torneo*,' I presume – as if fluent in village happenings.

'Yes, the *torneo*.'

Mister Big represents the money, the sponsors. He lays plans and papers on a table and does all the talking. I am at the far end of a double table and am unable to overhear. Frustrated, I order the grilled snapper at the bar and then return to the end of my table closest to the money group and can hear much of Mister Big's discourse. The plans for the *torneo* show where marquees must be sited, new *palapas*, judges' stands.

The gofer is a non-contributor – at most he holds a watching brief. Of the remaining two men, one is quiet and yet clearly necessary and in need of persuasion. Later I discover that he is the president of the community. The other man is also of the community. I will call him Mister Keen. He wears a shirt with no sleeves and a baseball cap and, in eagerness, leans across the table to hungrily inhale the big city power emanating from Mister Big. The woman interjects the occasional remark and orders watermelon from the bar. (Is she with Mister Big? Related to the sponsors? Or a TV company?)

Listening, I wonder what Mister Big really wants. Unbelievable that those behind him would fund, out of the goodness of their hearts, an international surf *torneo* on an unknown beach that possesses no infrastructure. I look down the perfect beach with the perfect surf and imagine the apartment blocks and the hotels and the swanky surf club at which the villagers will be servants. It strikes me as intolerably sad. Yet this is the perfect moment for the money men to make their move. The villagers fear a future in which passage to the north is closed. How many will reject alternative blandishments? How many can afford to resist?

I imagine that Mister Keen is already mounting the yes campaign.

And the president of the community? He seems bewildered, and as much by the physical force of Mister Big as by Mister Big's fluent exercise of the language of persuasion.

The discussion ends. Mister Big rolls his plans and passes my table. He is professional in his attention to detail and has noticed my conversation with the gofer. Could I be influential in even the smallest way?

Am I being cruel, vindictive? Am I demeaning a decent man, a man who is naturally friendly (although friendliness is also his stock-in-trade)?

He delights with the open warmth and charm of his greeting.

'How's it going?' I ask with equal warmth.

'Difficult, although we're giving them everything they ask for,' he says – then dismisses the weight of difficulties with a lift of those powerful shoulders. 'I've had easier tasks in the capital on major projects.'

'In the capital you know who to pay,' I say.

'Precisely.'

My understanding is proof that we are on the same side – whatever the side is. He is employed by a company of lobbyists, men who know the right people, the movers and shakers who can make things happen. He writes his address and his email in my notebook. We shake hands and I watch him lead his group back to his outsized 4×4. He has a powerful walk and meets the world square on. Be crushed or move out of the way. And I muse sadly that the teeth are already here, the teeth of the mouth that will devour a community.

The staff of the *palapa* have observed Mister Big stop at my table and our conversation. Now they watch me, perhaps waiting. I worry that I am arrogant in judging the best interests of a community of which I know so little. What is now a simple surfer's paradise is possibly a purgatory of penury for the villagers. And yet ...

I order a fresh beer and sit at the table closest to the bar with my back to the sea and address the women. The *torneo* – what do they think?

They answer with small shrugs of uncertainty.

'We will see,' the pretty one says, and the others nod. Yes, they will see.

Yet it seems to me obvious that they have no concept of what they might see. I recall for them my first visit to Flores, a small town on a lake near the wondrous Maya site of Tikal in Guatemala. Thirty or more years ago the women of the town met at a different house each night to arrange the flowers and decorate the church. A mere ten years later, television had reached the town. I found only three women arranging the flowers. The rest were at home watching TV. The companionship of those evenings had been killed. The rich sense of community was dead. Nothing remained that would tempt their children to return.

The older woman, the chef, is the first to nod. I ask where I can sleep and the women direct me to a row of small wood-walled *palapas* by the entry gate. The owner was the first of the village to reach Taos. In Taos, he was legal and had his own business. He has returned for good. What does he think of the *torneo*?

'We will see.'

I unload the bike, shower, change into shorts and return to the beach. The Monk is reading at the centre table beneath the *palapa*. The towel protects him.

Brave, I approach. I ask whether he is free. Might I sit with him? So we begin what quickly becomes a friendship to be treasured.

The Monk went to the US when he was eleven years old. He recounts his schooling in the US: of scholarships to private school in California, Berkeley and grad school at Harvard. He interspersed his later studies with spells in the world of banking. He was respectable. He did the right thing. He wore the right suit and the right shoes and the right tie. And sometimes he surfed.

Harvard Business School undid him. He was studying finance with grad students from similar money-management backgrounds. He discovered something missing in them. They had no fixed beliefs. Their judgement of right and wrong depended on the situation. These were the future leaders of corporate America. The Monk envisaged an endless parade of Enrons, of small investors bankrupted or robbed of their pensions. At first he was merely uncomfortable in their company. Perhaps he became nervous of infection. Perhaps he became nervous of his father's judgement (his father is a famously crusading and respected newspaper editor back in Korea, a poet, a writer of important books). So the Monk loaded his surfboards on his truck and drove south and discovered a beach with the perfect wave.

Only later, and little by little, did he discover a community that was self-protecting and to which each member contributed. Teaching English is the Monk's contribution. He teaches both children and adults. This seemed to him sufficient contribution until the *torneo* surfaced. He finds it remarkable that I understand the threat and that we share a near-apocalyptic vision. He suspects that I am an investigative journalist. He hopes that I am an investigative journalist.

I confess to being merely a mediocre novelist.

But I will write of this?

Certainly.

Will I write that Mister Big and his backers are paying the community 450 dollars for the use of the beach – that the community is to volunteer an unpaid workforce of 200 men to complement the 300 that Mister Big will import?

That the community has accepted so small a fee confirms the menace.

Mister Big must be licking his lips at such innocence.

For the moment, no land can be sold to an outsider without the community's agreement. That could change. For the right people, political pressure is easily acquired – such is Mexico's history. A major tourist development must be to the nation's benefit (the developers' benefit being synonymous with that of the nation).

The Monk's nightmare is not the destruction of his perfect beach. It is that these people with little experience or understanding of the outside world, people who have welcomed him warmly, will lose the very special dignity that accompanies their independence; that they will be dispossessed and become servants in their own homes.

Already Mister Keen is working on their fears and tempting them with profit. Others have approached the Monk for advice. The Monk was a banker. He understands the worth of holding a *torneo*. So he advised them and was summoned by the representative of those with power and warned that, in interfering, he endangered himself.

Threatening the Monk is an error. He is his father's son. He marshals his forces.

We share a simple dinner in the evening on the terrace of the local store. Light is by Coleman lantern. We drink cold Corona beer and listen to the quiet anger of the storekeeper: 450 dollars – so many children in the community and no health centre. A health centre should be the first of their demands.

The Monk and I are careful not to peer into the surrounding darkness. We sense the presence of other villagers listening, men and women hidden by the night.

I pay the vast sum of three dollars for six beers and a plate of meat-stuffed tacos.

And I ignore, with good humour, the belittling of my Honda by a chemically recalibrated surf addict mislaid by California who has joined us. The surf addict insists that 200 kilometres is the furthest I could ride the Honda in a day and that so small a bike is incapable of crossing the Altiplano.

The surfer has lived between Mexico and Central America for years and has been enlightened by the herbs and mushrooms of the region. He states as fact that corpses of seven-foot-tall aliens have been discovered in stone sarcophagi unearthed from the burial chambers beneath Central America's pyramids. A friend of his witnessed the opening of a sarcophagus.

Later, in bed, I consider the senators and members of Congress in Washington – the decisions they make concerning the frontier that is not a frontier and of how little interest or understanding they have in the destructiveness of their decisions. Their one desire is to keep their snouts in the pork barrel. What value has a small community in Mexico? Let it die in the name of progress.

Pan-Americano, Friday 26 May

I am tempted to stay in this small village, to record the happenings. But I am committed to writing a different book, the book of my journey. This village is only a chapter. Let this be clear: I am totally unmoved at the mockery of my Honda and of my own stamina as a rider. The reader would be ridiculous in suspecting that I would be so adolescent (in my dotage) as to rise to the challenge of a hallucinating near-fifty (yes, all of that) surf addict. Never. Yet I find myself on the road at seven this morning and determined to reach Tapachula – 500 kilometres.

The coast road is glorious. Trees are in blossom and the Honda slices through fresh perfume. A freeway bypasses Salina del Cruz and Tehuantepec. I stop for breakfast at a roadside *palapa*. At the state border an official welcomes me to Chiapas.

'To Argentina? Patagonia? Bravo!' He shakes my hand and claps me on the back.

The Chiapas littoral is mile after mile of magnificent green paddocks. Cows and horses graze in the shade of trees that would dwarf the tallest oak in an English park. Cloud blankets the forested mountains that rise directly behind the ranches.

So my bum is numb – this is a countryman's visual heaven.

I pause for cold water and a packet of nuts at a tiny roadside shack with two white tables and six chairs. A man in uniform is the only customer. The earth crumbles beneath the Honda's stand and the bike tumbles sideways. The man in uniform attempts to save the bike and burns his palm on the exhaust. He holds ice in his hand and boasts of the beauty of Chiapas and enquires of my journey and what I will write of Mexico.

The owner of the shack and her daughter listen, as does an old white man with pale blue eyes and a grey bristle-beard who has shuffled across the highway from a five-hut village.

'That Mexico is an immensely rich and beautiful country with many poor people,' I answer.

My listeners murmur their assent. Despite my protests, the man in uniform and with the painfully burnt hand insists on paying for my water and the packet of nuts. Mexican generosity is inescapable. There is a moment in which I consider turning back to the village on the beach and writing the book of the Monk and Mister Big. Instead I ride on into the evening and Tapachula and am caught in a deluge as I attempt to decipher the guidebook's directions to a hotel.

Who writes this stuff? *One block from the central square?* A square has four sides and is more than one block long and all streets are part of an incomprehensible one-way system.

A kind young man wearing jewellery suggests two hotels. He assures me that both are clean, cheap and comfortable. His directions are precise. I find without difficulty the Hotel Cavatina. Saintly staff hike the Honda over the high curb and wheel it to the far end of an entrance lobby that runs the full depth of the hotel. I take a room on the top floor, with a double bed, fan, bathroom and the best, biggest, thickest bath towel I have yet experienced.

I work an hour at a pleasant internet café peopled by a bunch of students with whom I chat before being directed to an old-fashioned café, dark wood panelling and wood-bladed ceiling fans. I drink cold beer and eat liver and onions with chilli and a flan.

Writers write. They also suffer painful cramps in their thighs at night if they are old and dumb and feel challenged and ride a small motorcycle 500 kilometres across Oaxaca and the Chiapas littoral in one day. The Honda was mocked, not the man. The Honda remains victorious.

And there are no seven-foot-tall aliens in Central America, in or out of sarcophagi.

Tapachula, Saturday 27 May

I breakfast outdoors on the central square. The electricity supply has been cut at the internet café that I used last night. I find an alternative that is more comfortable and run by equally pleasant people. Bringing my writing up to date takes ten hours, with only a break to fetch my laundry and eat a fruit salad. In the evening I people-watch on the central square, drink a beer and eat a steak. My last meal in Mexico.

To Antigua

Talisman, Sunday 28 May

Today I cross the first frontier of my bike journey. Guidebooks recommend Talisman as the least difficult crossing for motorists. However, writers warn of delays, illegal charges, swindling money changers, robbery in the public lavatories – and the necessity of an international driving permit. I don't have an international permit. Mine is the standard piece of plastic issued in the UK.

I am anxious and sleep badly. Rising early, I ride through empty streets. The sun rises as I leave town. The first rays pierce the trees and the wet tar glistens. Frontiers make for profit and I pass big houses set back from the road. I brake at the border behind a pickup. A stocky fifties wearing a white Stetson thrusts a wad of grubby banknotes in my face. 'Change. Change money.'

I take the excess Mexican pesos from my shirt pocket. The Stetson whips the bills from my hand. Shove and I'll tumble sideways. The bike will pin my leg. I picture the Stetson disappearing into the jungle.

The Stetson taps numbers into an adding machine. The figures are less intelligible than a Thai movie. 'Good journey,' he says, hands me a few Guatemalan banknotes – quetzales – and transfers his attention to an approaching bus.

Trees drip on a huddle of low, tin-roofed timber buildings. The buildings need a paint job. The national flags are wet and droop dispiritedly. A Mexican cop says, 'Hey, old man, where are you going?'

'To the south.'

'Where in the south?'

'Argentina.'

'On that small bike? Never.'

A Mexican immigration officer and two customs officials come out to investigate. They are small men of mixed race, neat in their uniforms. They ask whether it is true that I intend riding to Argentina.

'On this bike, all the way? For how many days will you travel? What opinion has your wife of your travels?'

Had I enjoyed Mexico? What did I enjoy most?

They laugh when I answer, '*Camarones a el diablo*'. Devilled prawns.

A customs official prods a saddlebag. 'Where are the locks? You must have locks. The south is peopled by thieves and bandits.'

'Even Guatemala. Guatemala is dangerous. Ride only in daylight.'

I have armed myself with photocopies of the bike's registration, purchase receipt, passport, driving permit. I stop a couple of minutes at the Guatemalan sanitation post – mostly we joke. To the Guatemalan customs officer, I apologise for an obvious incompetence in the completion of forms. He tells me not to preoccupy myself and completes the paperwork himself. In all, I am thirty minutes at immigration and customs. The three customs officers come out of the office to wave me on my way.

I seem to have developed an addiction for mountains. From the border I head towards Quetzaltenango. The easier route keeps to the Pacific littoral. I branch left on the RN1. A little beyond the intersection, an extraordinary building has been under construction for the past twenty years. I am told that it is a private house; it is the size of a hotel. It stands on the side of a hill behind iron gates decorated with lions rampant. It is part eighteenth-century French chateau and part Moghul palace. Those whom I ask are either ignorant or reluctant to tell me anything of the owner – although I gather from the interplay between my informants that they believe him more than eccentric, a little crazy.

I pause for an excellent breakfast at the entrance to San Paulo at the Rancho de los Sora. I count the quetzales given me at the border and scribble sums in my notebook. The Stetson was honest.

RN1 climbs over the flank of Ajumulco, 4220 metres, the tallest volcano in Guatemala. Coffee plantations cling to the slopes. The views are superb until I hit the first cloud strata. The road climbs through the cloud into a thin layer of clear air before entering higher strata of cloud. The upper clouds are wet. I freeze and drip and am totally miserable. I picture myself in the eyes of a sensible hotelkeeper – an aged tramp on a small bike. No, not a good prospect.

Quetzaltenango has cobbled streets and a one-way system that is bewildering seen through drenched spectacles. Wet cobbles are as slippery as ice. I slither downhill into the Parque Central, with a cathedral across the square, take a right to escape the traffic and spot Hotel Kiktem-Ja. The hotel is on a one-way street. Continue half a block beyond the square and the hotel is on the right. Drive into the courtyard: a good bed, plenty of blankets, excellent hot water in the bathroom. The hotel would be more welcoming if the owners repainted the floors and ceilings – black is not a lively colour. But at least geraniums cascade from the gallery surrounding the upper floor. The room costs more than I need to pay, but I am tired, wet and cold and the receptionist doesn't quake at my appearance.

I work at an internet café until nine and catch up with correspondence. The owner of the café is a biker. His big BMW dwarfs my Honda. Mario directs me to a waiter-serviced caféteria. I eat a thick, tough, overcooked steak with guacamole and refried beans. Tomorrow I'll try the stew.

Quetzaltenango, Monday 29 May

Before leaving England, I discussed my trip with students at two local high schools. The British Council runs teacher and student exchange programmes. 'Runs' is a misnomer. The Council has brochures and a website advertising the programmes but little finance to implement them. I had a meeting in London with Dominic Register, an official at the British Council. Dominic suggested I publicise the programmes on my travels. I did so in Oaxaca. Now for Quetzaltenango.

I dress as smartly as my limited wardrobe permits and have my shoes polished by a bootblack in the Parque Central.

Students at my first port of call, a private school, are occupied with exams. My second visit is a sixth-form technical college. The students are too old: I wish to make a comparison with the students of a certain age who I interviewed in England. The principal warns against my visiting state schools where teachers are underqualified and English is taught from a dictionary. She suggests I try a second private school that employs teachers from the United States. To reach the school, I navigate a series of empty lots strewn with builders' rubble. An armed guard opens solid iron gates set in a high wall. Statues of the Virgin and of Christ dominate a patch of neat lawn to the right of the gate. Walls and gates are the norm in Guatemala. Foreign-run schools in Guatemala are always financed by a church. No statues and this would be evangelist territory – unsafe for a Catholic, even a lapsed Catholic. The Virgin of Guadalupe pin gleams in the collar of my green-cord shirt – green for Ireland, Ireland for Catholicism. I am shown into an office. A young lady sits behind an imposing desk. Her card states that she is a *licenciada*. Licensed in law or philosophy? I outline my purpose and hope to be offered a whisky mac by a priest from County Mayo.

The *licenciada* is a daughter of Guatemala's vicious clandestine war. Murder, execution, assassination or fatal accident were the rewards for harbouring the wrong political thoughts.

The manner in which she fingers my card saps my confidence. She asks what questions I intend to ask the students. She will peruse my website before discussing the possibility with the principal. Will I call her in the morning?

'With pleasure,' I say, while mentally reviewing my site. The one piece of fiction is moral. It is humane. Would the *licenciada* be shocked at discovering that sexuality is its subject?

Should I cut the piece? Can I reach an internet café before the *licenciada* reads it? Why am I even thinking of cutting it? It is what I do best – or believe that I do best: portray characters in moments of intimacy.

The piece remains on the Web. I call the *licenciada* in the morning, only to be informed that the principal wishes to examine my work before reaching a decision the following morning.

What can I say, other than wonder weakly whether an elderly

English writer could corrupt students of a good school in a mere thirty minutes? I thank her kindly and excuse myself. I have an appointment on Lake Atitlan.

I take the road down to the Pacific littoral. Recent torrential rains have swept bridges away. A truck and trailer have slipped off a corner on one of the dirt-surfaced diversions. Retalhuleu is well worth an uninteresting cup of coffee. The mountains are cloaked in coffee. Coffee is Guatemala's biggest export. Why does the coffee served in cafés taste of mud?

From the coast I take the main highway towards Guatemala City (very busy), and then turn off towards Lake Atitlan on a narrow paved road that first crosses fields of sugar before climbing though cattle ranches and rubber plantations to coffee plantations and on into clouds in which Friesian dairy cows are barely visible in mountain paddocks.

I drove this area in the final years of the clandestine war in a borrowed car saved from the scrapheap. I recall mist and visibility down to a few metres and the pop of the rear tyre bursting. I got out of the car and walked round the back and looked at the tyre. I recall that I was on a ridge with pine forest on the left of the road. Four men appeared out of the forest. I write 'appeared' because they made no noise. They wore woollen ponchos and felts hats pulled low to hide their eyes and they carried machetes. They looked at me and they looked at the burst tyre.

One said, 'The tyre has burst.'

I said, 'Yes,' and the others nodded in agreement.

One said, 'Do you have a jack and a spanner?'

'I'm not sure,' I said.

'Then we should look.'

I fetched the keys from the ignition. One of the men took the keys and opened the boot. He passed the jack to one man and the wheel brace to another and lugged out the spare tyre.

The men changed the wheel in absolute silence. They replaced the tools and the punctured tyre in the trunk, closed the trunk and handed me the keys. Then they vanished with equal silence back into the forest.

I remember sitting in the car for a while, shivering and semi-paralysed while the mist condensed and formed rivulets on the windscreen.

The cloud is as thick today and turns wet as I cross the shoulder of the volcano. I shiver and freeze in light rain on the descent towards Panajachel on Lake Atitlan. I ride down the main street and turn right at the pink-walled bakery to a small hotel within gates. I bargain a good room with an excellent hot-water shower down from one hundred to seventy-five quetzales. I walk towards the lake and the Hotel Dos Mundos. The Dos Mundos is beyond my present budget. Palm trees surrounding the pool have grown in the past ten years. I find room 12 and sit on the steps. Here I suffered my heart attacks. Ten years ago I crawled in agony out of this room and begged for a doctor. The doctor arrived on a trial bike and jammed a needle in my butt. I don't know what else he did. I blacked out. The doctor worked at the state health centre up the street. He was training to be a heart specialist. So I survive. Back home in Havana none of my medical friends believed that free medicine and state-employed doctors existed outside Cuba – particularly in Guatemala.

I ask at the health centre and am told that doctors usually stay only a year. Nor can they put a name to my saviour – sad, as I am in Panajachel specifically to thank him.

Stalls selling clothes and rugs and blankets woven in brilliant colours by upland artisans are interspersed with mini-restaurants on the main shopping street. The street is narrow. On my first visit it was little more than a dirt track. Now it is tarred. Rain buckets down and the street becomes a river. Unable to escape, I order vegetable soup at a tiny six-table restaurant. The soup is good and freshly prepared. I know because I wait half an hour to be served. Trapped by the rain, I read the newspaper. The front-page photograph shows a car pockmarked with bullet holes: driver, wife and three children are dead. A leading article quotes a police report of 1200 armed attacks on buses in Guatemala City over the past five months.

Thunder explodes through much of the night. Meanwhile an equally noisy French group in the next room sort and pack their market plunder in preparation for an early bus.

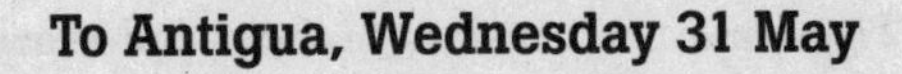

To Antigua, Wednesday 31 May

I leave Pana at nine o'clock on the steep climb towards Guatemala City and am rewarded for the misery of yesterday's descent with wonderful views of the lake and of the volcanoes rising beyond the far shore. The volcanoes wear raggedy miniskirts of pearl-grey cloud. I halt near the crest and watch a launch, made tiny by distance, drag white vees across the water. The vees seem tired and soon collapse to leave the lake calm and unmarked. The weather stays dry and I enjoy a fine run across the crest, with splendid views of forest way below. The great cone of Ajumulco dominates the horizon.

The road crosses an upland plateau of small farms. Curls of colour in the fields are Maya women stooped to harvest cash crops of salads, garlic and spring onions. Ancient pickups with bent chassis crawl crab-like past heavily laden donkeys.

When riding, I smile at everyone. In Mexico I became accustomed to smiles in immediate reply – cops included. Guatemalans are slower to respond or more cautious in responding. Perhaps these Maya peasants of the uplands have less to smile about or are unused to people smiling at them. Or do the scars of the clandestine war hamper their response – a war in which some 150 000 indigenous Guatemalans were butchered?

I ride into Antigua in early afternoon. I had expected this jewel of Spanish colonial architecture to cast its usual magic. Much has changed in ten years. I recall shops and cafés and guesthouses sprinkled among private homes. Now there is only commerce. Magnificent sixteenth-century doorways and passages to inner patios have been desecrated with kiosks in the scrabble for each extra dollar. The central square is backpacker territory. Maya women seem interlopers. Humble, they crouch as the backpackers hunt for bargains among the bundles of hand-woven clothes and blankets.

I search for a room within my budget and am shown a series of windowless cupboards attached to dank horrors that I am assured are bathrooms. Finally I strike lucky, both in hotel and in owners, who drop the room rate for an old man.

Charming young English honeymooners are fellow guests. The honeymooners have four months of travel in which to decide what to do with their lives. They find Guatemalans friendly and eager to talk. However, their smattering of Spanish limits conversation to the likes of 'Have a good day'.

I miss the openness of Mexicans. With the election imminent, every Mexican, peasant or plutocrat, discusses politics. Guatemalans are cautious.

I find an internet café and call my friend, Eugenio, by telephone. Guatemalan Eugenio owns a teak and rubber plantation and a small resort and marina down on the Rio Dulce. He forbids me to ride through Guatemala City and is driving up to Antigua in his double-cab Ford pickup. I had thought, when planning this journey, of Eugenio's home as an oasis. Now I am nervous. I am twenty-five years older than Eugenio. He has married and has a baby son, Andresito. Will his young wife think of me as an intrusion, an aged ghost emanating from Eugenio's bachelor past? Or simply a boring old Brit?

In the evening I visit the home of an acquaintance, an elderly Guatemalan. A wealthy businessman, he lives in a gated community on the outskirts of town. Antigua, City of Eternal Spring, is 1500 metres above sea level. Days are warm while evenings are chill for thin blood and old bones. We enjoy our wine in front of a wood fire. My host talks of Bush and company and his loathing of their ignorance of history and of the wider world. He recounts that his younger brother, an architect in the northern US, begs him to be circumspect when telephoning, as all calls from abroad are monitored. The harnessing of fear to impose draconian laws heralds a rebirth of fascism: the conqueror wears the clothes of the conquered. As it was under Mussolini and in Nazi Germany, so it is becoming in the United States.

I report the views of two elderly respectable conservative brothers. The wine is good. I listen to my host without comment, enjoy the warmth of the fire and relish the change from bike seat to well-upholstered sofa – and, yes, the familiarity of fine European furniture and paintings and Persian rugs. Ease is easy. So is silence. My silence at the Dallas breakfast club has left me uneasy, ashamed. There too I was a guest.

I ride back to town in moonlight. The three volcanoes that overhang

Antigua are massive monuments against the night sky. Jasmine scents the air. Antigua remains full of beautiful buildings. I ride with care on the cobbles and ask of myself, as always, who were the architects? Did the Conquistadors number camouflaged Muslims among their numbers? We know of three *recursos* (Jewish 'converts' to Christianity) among Cortés' followers. Cortés' neighbours back home in the Extremadura of his childhood were Islamic owners of a vineyard. I imagine myself a bright Islamic kid of the period. Banned from Spanish universities, where would I have studied? Perhaps at that great centre of learning, Baghdad. Returning home to Spain, I would have been faced with the bigotry and zeal of Christendom. What then? Surely I would have been tempted to change my name to José Jesus and venture a future in a New World.

Antigua, Thursday 1 June

Ten years have passed since my last visit to Antigua. Of my friends, all but a Guatemalan painter and her Frenchman have abandoned the city to commercialism and moved to gated communities on the outskirts. I recall eating dinner in this house on my last night in Guatemala. We sat in front of a wood fire and drank rum and discussed a future of hope that accompanied the peace process.

Today, the artist, a liberal educated at university in Europe, talks of the nihilism that drives the country's urban youth to kill for a few quetzales and ape the most extreme details of the sexual act as they dance the *raegeton*.

The artist's son was twelve or thirteen when I last visited. Now he is a six-foot-six Adonis back from college in Colorado. He guides tourists up volcanoes and teaches rock climbing. He is exceptional in having returned. The majority of his generation, the offspring of my Guatemalan friends, are in Spain, Canada, *El Norte*, even England. Do they sense, if only subconsciously, that they have no future in Guatemala? Or that Guatemala has no future?

Eugenio arrives to collect me in his pickup and I meet his wife, Monica, for the first time. She is young and dark and classically beautiful. Their son, Andresito, aged twelve months, is a darker replica of

Eugenio. The Honda is loaded onto Eugenio's pickup. We drive down from Antigua into the capital and lunch on a delicious lasagne at the apartment of Eguenio's mother. Parents and grandmother play with Andresito while I make notes in my journal of a conversation earlier in the morning.

The speaker was a woman, a Guatemalan. She talked of massacres during the clandestine war, and of a country in which, for thirty years, governments placed no value on life. She talked of Big Brother up north, who places no value on the lives of Latin Americans, of Arabs, of Asians. Bomb anyone you don't like (the enemy). Why care if there are civilian casualties? Why be surprised when gangs of city kids in Guatemala have as little care for life? The gangs are an import from the US. Many of the kids were raised in the US by parents who were illegal workers caught by US immigration and expelled.

'They see the corruption in government. We used to think it was only us. We thought that countries outside, in Europe, were different – countries like England. Now we learn that all governments are the same. Look at your Tony Blair. He is a liar like the rest. What hope is there? Why should the kids have hope?'

Grim.

Rio Dulce, Friday 2 June

Guatemalan drivers believe in God rather than in brakes and the rules of the road. The highway from Guatemala City plunges through dry mountains and sparse pine forest. Each corner is a lottery in which survival is the prize. The air turns humid on the plains of the littoral. This is banana country. The Rio Dulce flows into the Caribbean. Only one bridge crosses the river. A truck-stop at the northern end of the bridge has blossomed into a small town. The bridge is the frontier into the little-explored and scantily populated province of Peten and the town is named Fronteras.

I first visited Fronteras some twenty years back. In those days Fronteras was a dump. It remains a dump, but a very likeable dump. I have a soft spot for dumps. On my first visit farmers on horseback rode the only street. Now long-legged young women in short skirts weave through the truck traffic on motor scooters. A few new buildings exist; banks have opened branch offices; tin shacks have grown concrete walls; some are freshly painted – as are the whores who advertise their charms as they take the sun outside the brothel. The whores seem to me a little younger. I may be mistaken. I have reached an age when I mistake police officers for school kids in fancy dress.

Above the bridge, a short stretch of river ends at the narrow entrance to Lago Izabal. At over fifty kilometres in length, Izabal is the largest lake in Guatemala and was the road of conquest into the interior for the Spaniards, who built a fort to protect the approach to the lake from English pirates.

The river expands below the bridge into a twenty-kilometre lake dotted with mangrove islands and indented with creeks and side rivers and streams that are swallowed by jungle. Below the lake, the river is squeezed for the final fifteen kilometres into a narrow gorge. Vertical cliffs tower a hundred metres above the water and are cloaked in trees and ferns and creepers. The gorge ends at the sea and at the small Caribbean port of Livingston. No roads lead to Livingston. There is only the river and the sea.

Eugenio's resort at Hacienda Tijax is on the river. Eugenio's land slopes from the shore up to a ridge from which there are views through 360 degrees to mountains in the distance and both down the Rio Dulce and up towards the Spanish fortress of San Felipe.

I had expected Eugenio to site his house on the ridge. He has chosen to build further down the hill. The house is on two floors. French windows open from each room onto shaded verandas. The house faces down a valley of cattle paddocks to a fringe of forest that hides the water. The distant mountains are the least imposing of those that are visible from the ridge. It is a restful view. It is undemanding. You may look or not look. You can read a book in peace.

I understand Eugenio's choice of site. He has enough demands put on him each day with his resort and his small marina and the restaurant and the rubber plantation and cattle rustling and the fear of forest fires that could destroy the teak plantation. I understand the armed guard who patrols the hacienda and I understand the dogs and the gate and the high wire fence fixed to white ceramic insulators that surrounds the garden.

Eugenio is never short of courage. If anything, he seeks challenges. He survived the clandestine war. He directed aid for the Ministry of Finance in the aftermath of the 1976 earthquake, worked with the Maya and lived in their villages. He sails his sailboat single-handed. In this house, while still a bachelor, he was robbed at gunpoint by three men. Now he has a young and beautiful wife and a small son to protect.

I wrote, ten years ago, much of the Guatemalan section of a novel, *Aftermath*, in the restaurant at Hacienda Tijax. The marina is bigger now. Eugenio has added a swimming pool and an open-air jacuzzi; the guest cabins are made of wood and are mosquito-proof. Ten years ago, Eugenio and I lived in open-walled *palapas* and I defended myself against mosquitoes with an electric fan. Oh, and Charlie, Eugenio's dog of very mixed parentage, ate one of my brown Church's shoes. I wear brown shoes by Church's on this journey. They are comfortable and, under normal conditions (riding motorcycles, climbing mountains, crossing forests, fording rivers) are indestructible. They are made of high-quality leather. Flexible leather. To a Guatemalan dog, they appear delectable. Eugenio has a pack of dogs. One is a puppy, a spotted Brazilian mastiff with feet as broad as snowshoes. The puppy will be truly massive if he grows into his feet. For the moment he believes he is very small. I write on the veranda. He tries to climb on my lap. I reject him. He droops his head, eyes so mournful that I expect tears. Off-guard, I concentrate on my journal. He lays his head on my Church's-shod feet and drools a little. The drooling betrays him. And every now and again he has a little lick at the leather – just a taster.

Rio Dulce, Saturday 3 June

Morales is forty kilometres from Fronteras and is the Province of Izabal's administrative centre. It was founded as a company town in the early 1900s and, for half a century, was the capital of United Fruit Company's Central American empire. In 1951 Guatemalans elected Jacobo Arbenz as president in free elections. The Arbenz government passed a law to purchase uncultivated land from large landowners for redistribution to landless peasants. United Fruit owned tens of thousands of hectares; much was uncultivated. In 1954, the CIA protected United Fruit by mounting a successful coup.

Allen Dulles was the head of the CIA. He had served on the board of United Fruit.

John Foster Dulles was Eisenhower's secretary of state. Dulles' law firm represented United Fruit.

President Dwight D. Eisenhower's private secretary, Ann Whitan, was married to United Fruit's head of public relations.

The coup was the catalyst that sacrificed Guatemala to thirty-six years of torture and assassination and massacre – the clandestine war.

I was researching *Aftermath* when I last visited Eugenio. Josh, Jed and I had our home in Cuba while Bernadette ran her business in England and visited us every six weeks. In those days Eugenio did his banking and his chores in Morales. He would drop me off on Main Street. He knew where to find me. I would be in one of the Chinese stores, mouth open, gaping at the multiple choice: three different makes and sizes of refrigerator, same for TVs, bikes, scooters; any quantity of trainers. For Eugenio this was a corner shop. For a resident of Castro's Cuba, such shops offered the combined joys of Harrods and a Wal-Mart.

On the way back from Morales we would stop off at a carwash, where the owner served good chicken soup in the shade of a *palapa*. I drew on the carwash for some of the action and the main relationships in *Aftermath*. In those days, the carwash had a dangerous reputation. The proprietor's husband had been gunned down. So had other men in fire fights. The widow had been left with three small children to support. The children were timid in the presence of strangers and I remember the widow as a warm, kindly woman. She is not the woman in my novel.

Eugenio hasn't stopped at the carwash in a while and it has changed hands. The new owner worked legally some years in *El Norte* as a mechanic and has a green card. He bought the carwash with his savings. He has no previous experience of restaurants and the chicken soup is a disappointment. I doze in a hammock beneath the *palapa* while Eugenio gives him advice.

Eugenio has built a tower on the crest of the ridge overlooking the Rio Dulce. 'The road is rough,' Eugenio warns. 'Don't try riding your bike. I'll run you up in the pickup once I've finished down at the hotel.'

Monica has taken Andresito into town. I wait a while, reading. Then I recall Ibiza in the sixties.

I recall riding my red Bultaco Matador 350 trial bike.

I picture myself as I pictured myself then: chest thrust out as I gripped the wide-spread controls, white canvas trousers over Frye boots, grandad T-shirt, sun-bleached locks in a coronet of Moroccan beads. Wow, was I something. Every girl's dream (in my dreams).

So what has changed? Nothing, I decide, and kick the Honda alive. The track is hard dirt for the first fifty metres. It turns uphill. The front wheel slides into a deep rut. My ancient legs don't have sufficient strength to hold the bike upright. I sprawl with my left leg trapped under the bike and my right calf on the exhaust. In struggling free, I kneel on the exhaust.

As Monica, Eugenio's young and intelligent wife, remarks as she drives me to the pharmacy: 'Hey Simon, remember: you are an old man. You need to be careful. And you should never wear shorts on a bike.'

Careful and I wouldn't be attempting this dumb ride to Tierra del Fuego.

The ointment on my burns resembles mayonnaise. Saturday evening I sit by the pool at the resort and chat with an ex-cop from Israel. The Israeli served in the anti-terrorist squad back home. He remarks that Israel is more or less at peace now that the wall is built. The US is about to build a wall along the dividing line between *El Norte* and *El Sud*. Such walls are statements of despair and of defeat. The Great Wall of China failed to keep out the Tartars. Hadrian's Wall signalled the beginning of the end of the Roman Empire. Hitler's army drove round the corner of that great wall of interconnected fortresses and bunkers, the Maginot Line. The Berlin Wall was pulled down by joyful citizens.

However, let us be generous and consider the financial needs of those morally righteous members of the US contracting fraternity, those who loyally contribute to the Republican Party's war chest. Think

Cheney, think Rumsfeld, think Halliburton. They are always in need of a little extra cash and the Iraq war can't last forever. And a word of encouragement for the upper middle classes in the United States: Don't fret. Your Mexican servants will find a way through the wall or over the wall or round the wall.

Rio Dulce, Sunday 4 June

My leg hurts. I sleep badly and am awakened shortly after first light by horses out on the farm road. The horses have escaped from a paddock. I doubt whether there is much I can achieve – maybe stand in the road and wave my arms while one of Eugenio's farm workers corrals the beasts. I tiptoe barefoot downstairs and out onto the veranda. The mastiff puppy sleeps on the veranda. He wakes. He spots the open door. He thinks 'Kitchen!' and charges.

I shut the door on his muzzle.

The keys are upstairs on my dressing table.

Monica and Eugenio sleep in on Sunday mornings (with Andresito's permission). I sit on the lawn. I am not doing well: burnt leg, locked door. Add a further confession: I left my new digital camera in the cafeteria in Grand Central Station, New York. I am only in the early stages of my trip. I am not doing well.

A hummingbird distracts me. The view is tranquil. The mastiff puppy forgives me. True, my bare feet are a disappointment: he prefers leather. He rests his head on my lap and glances up with mournful sympathy. Little by little I relent in self-criticism.

Yes, I admit that burning my leg was the product of adolescent stupidity. However, I recall wrecking my leg on my Bultaco Matador in the distant past, laying the bike over and sliding into an unexpected traffic island on the road to Ibiza town from our home in San José. This was a main road that I rode every day. True, it was after midnight and what mind I had had drifted far off course. I am forty years older now and should permit myself a little slack.

Nor should I fear the onset of senility merely because I left the camera at Grand Central.

My sons continually lose their clothes and books and mobile phones. They leave them on the bus and on trains and in sports halls and on park benches and in friends' homes.

I have been sitting on the lawn for a couple of hours and have reached this stage of near self-congratulation when Monica appears. She carries Andresito on her hip. I am startled by her extraordinary beauty. Monica is somewhat startled at finding me on the lawn. She asks what I am doing.

'Thinking,' seems a suitable reply.

Rio Dulce

Rio Dulce, Sunday 4 June

We are on a Sunday family outing. Eugenio, man of the house, drives. Grandad – that's me – sits up front beside the driver. The little woman and the baby sit in back. Eugenio is taking us down river to Livingston in his outboard-powered speedboat. I've draped a nappy over my burns and wear Eugenio's straw work hat at a rakish angle. I fancy myself.

Monica says that I resemble an old wreck.

Tall trees intermingle with mangrove along the lakefront. There is no road down the river, no route for kidnappers. Children are safe and the river is the playground of wealthy Guatemalans of Eugenio's generation. The cost of transporting heavy building materials would be prohibitive; their holiday mansions are constructed of wood and thatched with palm fronds and blend into the vegetation. Thatched boathouses shade their motor yachts and speedboats and their kiddies' jet-skis.

We slam across the wakes of shrimp boats chugging upstream and taxi launches and the occasional yacht. Our first destination is a school close to the entry to the gorge. The school recruits bright kids of both sexes from Maya villages and educates them to be leaders in their communities. The school is the brainchild of a US citizen.

Eugenio makes fast to the school jetty. The buildings are wood and thatch. I meet with a couple of Maya late teenagers in reception. These are bright kids. They communicate among themselves in quick glances. Their smiles are almost too welcoming. The founder is downriver at the restaurant the school runs in Livingston. I should meet with the founder and with the students accompanying him.

The gorge does something to me. Eugenio claims I suffer an epiphany. Perhaps it springs from my Spanish heritage. I identify emotionally with those first Spaniards sailing their small coracles up this gorge. The Spaniards were small men of little education and many superstitions. Their ships must have felt minute and fragile in the shadows of the great cliffs. They knew nothing of what or who lay ahead. At any moment they could be crushed by boulders hurled from on high. I imagine that they prayed silently. The gorge opened. They sailed into sunlight. Ahead lay kilometres of fresh, open water, fields of water lilies. Streams cut into the limestone. Hot springs bubbled. Islands were white with ibis. Away in the distance lay a ring of purple mountains. The beauty must have blown their minds. They must have imagined that they had discovered Paradise.

Today sunlight cuts a line of brilliance midway up the southern face of the gorge. Long streamers of frangipani twist between the undergrowth and lay swathes of cloying temple perfume across the river. The river is dark. The water has a strong earthy scent. An indigenous child fishes from a tiny canoe beneath the overhang of a vast tree. Eugenio slows to avoid swamping a dugout overloaded with two trussed pigs and a family of ten.

Livingston announces itself with reggae blaring from competitive boom boxes. The town has the feel of an island. The majority of the inhabitants are Afro-Caribbean. The school's restaurant is on the riverfront. Tables are arranged on a big deck shaded by a tin roof. The school's founder is in his forties, a tall fair-haired man, thin and quiet and confident. He has become acknowledged in the aid industry as an expert on indigenous development and travels widely to conferences concerned with aid to the developing world. The restaurant is a new venture and caters for passengers off cruise ships.

The founder seats me at a table with four final-year students. Ask a question and one of three answers at length. Their purpose is community development. Development is instigating programmes that will improve health and earn money for their home villages without disturbing the traditional culture. Each of them intends a career in eco-tourism.

The school graduates thirty students a year: ten years and that's a lot of eco-tourism guides and a great many pristine Maya villages with pristine handicraft markets and, of course, a wise shaman preparing herbal medicines blessed by a few traditional Maya magic spells.

I ask whether the students have considered entering politics.

No, they have no interest in politics. They are too young.

Young? At eighteen and nineteen?

The fourth student is the dilemma. Each of the other three is fluent in the spiel (I am sufficiently old and experienced to recognise a spiel). This fourth student doesn't bother. I keep catching his eye and he is ready each time with this eye-to-eye twinkle.

It is a real bad-ass twinkle that says as directly as any words: 'Hey, old man, you don't believe the spiel. I know you don't believe the spiel. You know that I know that you don't – so now what? You and I? Do we keep playing the game?'

He continues twinkling.

I keep playing the game. It has become more than a game, a challenge.

I ask what the students think of Chavez and his ideas.

They have never heard of Chavez.

What do they think of Morales?

They have never heard of Morales.

Graduates of a school for indigenous community leaders, and they are ignorant of the first indigenous president of Venezuela and of the first indigenous president of Bolivia.

The silent student twinkles as brightly as a Roman candle.

Monica and Eugenio return to collect me. The school's founder joins us. I ask whether he boards the cruise ships. Of course he does – and he describes to the passengers the good that the school does for the Maya and collects subscriptions to finance the school and ships the passengers ashore to the school's restaurant, where they eat lobster as an act of atonement for their wealth.

Meanwhile, the restaurants owned by native Afro-Caribbean Livingstonians have lost the cruise-ship custom.

I have taken a couple of painkillers and am slightly dizzy. Eugenio steadies me as I climb down the ladder to the speedboat. We pull away from the dock and turn upriver. I look back. The school's founder waves. And I wish that I didn't see flames and sharpened machetes.

Café Conversation

Rio Dulce, Monday 5 June

Ex-cop: In Guatemala it is a circle. We change one president for the next, one government for the next. They all steal. Sometimes I think we should get a good man from outside, a foreigner.

Businessman: Hand over the running of the customs to the Swiss? Why not the economy to a team of Swiss bankers?

Café owner: It is no better in Cuba.

Ex-cop: I want my little bit of freedom to choose my own mistakes. Dream that things can be a little better for my children. We can all eat in this country. Not all people can afford meat, but everyone can buy vegetables and fruit. We are healthy.

Businessman: The only foreign aid is food aid. Even the rich in the government can only eat so much. Anything else they will steal and sell.

Café owner: Even our own people. The delegation we elected here to negotiate with the mining company has sold us out.

Flores to Copan

El Petén, Tuesday 6 June

Eugenio has taken a few days' holiday to ride with me north through the Peten. Yesterday we visited Morales, where I bought a horseman's leather gaiter to protect my right leg. Both Eugenio and the storekeeper advised that I would look peculiar wearing only one gaiter. A fat old man with a white beard riding a small bike across the Americas *is* peculiar. A gaiter won't improve my image.

I chose to travel in the rainy season. I have been blessed with greenery even in the wastelands of the Texas panhandle. Now Eugenio and I are staying with an eccentric French conservationist, Santiago Billy, on the eastern littoral of Lake Petén Itzá. Clouds rise from thick forest on the far shore in layers of greys that range from almost white to almost black. The waters reflect the layers and we watch, from the small *palapa* at the end of Santiago's jetty, rain squalls chase each other across the forest before joining forces in a solid curtain that shatters the calm of the lake and thrashes the surface into silver foam. You can keep your days of endless sun. This is glory.

Flores is the capital of the Peten and occupies a small island at the south end of the lake. Some twenty-five years have passed since my last visit. I stayed at the one hotel in town. I was directed to the one restaurant, where I ate a lake fish grilled over coals. The fish was sprinkled with finely chopped garlic and served on a bed of rice. It was delicious.

The lake rises and falls. No one knows why. When I was first here, the level was some six feet higher than it is now. The two roads that connected the Peten with the rest of Guatemala would have been rough-going for a Centurion tank. I saw no other foreigners in the two nights I stayed and explored the narrow streets after a day among the Maya pyramids and temples of Tikal.

Now the roads are smooth tarmac. Foreigners and *forasteros* (Guatemalan people from outside the Petén) have transformed the semi-abandoned town of my memories. This new Flores reminds me of the newly discovered Ibiza of the mid-sixties, with boutiques and restaurants and cafés and small hotels on every block. The single-storey buildings are freshly painted in a pleasing medley of pastel colours; the cobbled streets are newly patched and alive with visitors and NGOs.

Rather than staying in Flores, Eugenio and I are visiting with a friend, Santiago, at the far end of the lake at El Romate.

Santiago's hotel, Mon Ami, is more suitable for the young and for those who speak French or Spanish and are interested by the region's nature and ecology. Swimming in the lake is a delight denied me by the leg. However, to sit at the end of Santiago's jetty and admire the sunsets, drink a cold beer or piña colada, and eat one of those admirable fish for dinner is sufficient pleasure.

Today's politics fascinate me as much as the history of Guatemala – not the history of history books but scraps to be sewn together. I suspect that these are the interests of most mature travellers. We tend to be more curious than many young travellers. We have little desire to sprawl on the beach. We are too old to surf or clamber over glaciers. We walk a while but not too far. Then we want to sit in the shade and listen to the peoples of the countries through which we pass and learn of their lives.

Lago Petén Itzá, Wednesday 7 June

Today Santiago attends a breakfast meeting in Flores with the minister of agriculture. My burns look ugly and Santiago insists that I accompany him to a clinic. The doctor orders me to return in three days. Meanwhile I am to rest: no alcohol, no dancing, no sex. I quote Santiago. I am not listening. I am hypnotised by a huge hypodermic and an immense bottle of antibiotics, together with pills and dressings and creams with which I must medicate and anoint myself.

The injection of antibiotics leaves me with a large throbbing bump in the butt. Sitting is a pain. Meanwhile Anita and Nora, Santiago's staff, search the forest and return with baskets of leaves and roots. They infuse their finds in hot water and insist I bathe the burns. They are small commanding women. They cook, clean and do the laundry. Disobedience would be foolish. I do jungle by day and pharma at night.

Eugenio and I had intended to ride a huge loop. My wretched leg has frustrated us and Eugenio returns to the Rio Dulce.

Lago Petén Itzá, Thursday 8 June

For the past few days I have been pursued by a middle-aged hen. Today the hen slinks into my room while Nora collects my laundry. I discover the hen on my bed. She has laid an egg.

Meanwhile the war between pharma and *brujería* – witchcraft – continues.

Lago Petén Itzá, Friday 9 June

Yesterday it rained hard all day and through the night. The lake has risen fifteen centimetres. The lake is approximately fifty kilometres long by four kilometres wide. At breakfast, I ask Santiago, a graduate of one of France's prestigious *Grandes Ecoles*, how many tons the rise represents.

I await an answer.

We drive around the lake in Santiago's pickup. The road cuts off a narrow inlet near the far end of the lake. The inlet is some four hundred metres long and is dammed by the road, beneath which runs a single conduit. With less room to expand, the inlet has risen one and a half metres above the main body of the lake. A giant whirlpool swirls above the entry to the conduit. Foam gushes thirty metres from the exit of the conduit. All that unharnessed energy – what is the pressure?

Such questions interest an old man.

Lago Petén Itzá, Sunday 11 June

Both Nora and Anita, Santiago's resident herbalists, have Sundays free. They are replaced by Maria, five foot one when stretched and aged sixty-five. A fine bone structure suggests a youthful beauty confirmed by a niece who drops by to assist in preparing breakfast. Maria is no slouch in the war against modern medicine. One glance at my leg and she is off to the jungle. First comes aloe slime, followed by a poultice of a long leaf that I don't recognise (does it grow only in shadow and on the tombs of deceased witches?). Horror of horrors, my leg turns blue. I must visit the doctor tomorrow. How to hide this indelible evidence of witchcraft competition?

Santiago is the *brujas'* accomplice.

I hope he will be caught and burnt at the stake.

Meanwhile he and I (and my blue leg) take the truck and go hunting for a pig.

This is a bloody tale. Vegetarians should read no further. The idea was mine. Tonight is full moon. The sky is clear. This is no time for skulking in a hammock. *Avante!*

Santiago is not only Guatemala's pre-eminent conservationist. He is also famous as the discoverer of the most important Maya site in the Peten jungle since the uncovering of Tikal. Today our prey is a young pig.

I am an expert on the Hispanic American variety. I once spent an entire Christmas Eve in Cuba hunting down an illegal pig. Nervous of authority, the illegal pig was on the move. We finally ran it to earth at six in the evening. We were in a Moskvich. A close friend, Carlito, was my companion. Rum was the fuel of our investigation.

Santiago doesn't drink.

A *lechón* – a piglet – would be perfect. We intend barbecuing it whole over charcoal. Santiago, confident, telephones a dinner invitation to the director of the Peten's protected areas and his family.

First we explore El Remate, where we are offered the runt of a litter reared on a refuse heap that is ninety per cent plastic bottle. Two further pigs are too big. We return on the lake road and meet with a farmer dressed for Sunday in a spotless white straw Stetson, polished boots, clean jeans and a flowered shirt. His wife owns two pigs. Santiago and he discuss neighbours and what effect the full moon will have on the weather. We then follow the gentleman up a jungle path. His wife appears, driving two pigs. One is russet, the other more a rose pink. They possess fine straight backs and rounded rear ends. I am the expert. I select the russet and am quoted twenty-five dollars.

I am about to negotiate.

Santiago murmurs, 'The man shot two neighbours last year over a boundary dispute.'

End of negotiation. And I pay a further three dollars to the wife for slaughtering and stripping the pig of its bristle.

We have soy sauce, honey, unlimited garlic, chilli, concentrate of tomato, both limes and lemons. We search the village *tiendas* for fresh ginger. A gullible young French couple watches as we light the charcoal in a half-drum. The French are concerned primarily by the price and availability of marijuana. They display no interest in nature or in the great Maya ruins. However, the pig fascinates them. From where did we get it?

From the road, Santiago answers: 'In Guatemala, any animal straying onto the road becomes public property.'

I contribute the important detail that Sunday is a good day for catching pigs in the road as the owners are in church.

Further details develop: that Santiago chased and caught the pig and that I hit it over the head with a rock.

The French girl asks what sort of rock.

I am stumped as to why this should be important.

'A round rock,' Santiago explains. 'A pointed rock would have made the pig bleed and mess up the back of the truck.'

Later we overhear the couple discuss our hunt over their smoke. They seem impressed at our expertise rather than doubtful of either our morality or our veracity.

The young woman asks Anita for further details. Anita accuses me of boasting: yes, I had hit the pig on the head with a rock, but I had only stunned it. Santiago, schooled in the ways of the jungle, had done the actual killing with his machete.

Earlier in the week Santiago had told them of my family's four-generation commitment to the manufacture of plastic boots. The Frenchman asks me the mark of boot. I explain that my family are merely manufacturers and imprint the boots (an advantage of plastic) with the mark of the importers. Later the Frenchman overhears me speak of a past visit to Guatemala and asks whether I was here on business. I admit my family's contract to supply plastic boots to the Guatemalan army.

The French are headed north to Mexico. I am tempted to point them in the direction of the smoker-surfer, he with proof of seven-foot green aliens buried beneath Central America's pyramids. I could add that the aliens were discovered wearing plastic boots. This is a time of Franco-American strife. Guiding the young French couple into a spiritual alliance with a North American would be a good deed.

The pig is delicious. Judgement is in the eating. Our guests eat three servings each. I sit at the table, content, and enjoy the conversation.

What have I learnt over the past few days in which my leg has been a battle ground for the forces of modern medicine and the *selva*, the jungle?

I have talked with men and women at small restaurants and at internet cafés and at water-stops on the road to Flores and in Flores. Violence is their one concern. No wonder. The newspaper today gives police statistics for Guatemala City: 1200 armed assaults on city buses between January and 1 June – twenty drivers killed.

People talk of the need for a strong man to combat endemic violence.

General Molina is mentioned (I note in today's paper that he has resigned his present position – the better to campaign for the presidency). Others warn that generals have little respect for human rights, that their attitude to human eradication is also general. I consider that shudderingly explicit expression used in the United States, 'wasting' – not as in wasting human resources but in laying waste.

I have learnt that mountain and forest make difficult the tracking by radar of small aircraft and that airstrips on haciendas in the Petén are the refuelling stops for drug flights to the US. Permission is necessary for raids on private property. Applying for permission for a raid outpaces email in warning the narco-traffickers.

I have been told that small farmers are reluctant to improve their farms for fear that a narco-trafficker will make an offer that would be suicidal to refuse ... and that, in earlier times, in the years of the clandestine war, army officers made the offers that could not be refused. Some of those officers are now the narco-traffickers.

I am told that narco-traffickers will pay the commander of a military airstrip half a million dollars for its use – the alternative is the killing of the commander's family. The wife of my informant argues that there is a third, and more common, alternative: that the commander negotiates a higher price. In Guatemala, everything is open to negotiation.

Lago Petén Itzá, Monday 12 June

I have attempted to scrub the blue evidence of *brujería* from my wounds. I recall a somewhat similar situation in the Ogaden desert in my youth. My leg swelled. It became a liquid-stuffed balloon. A North American Seventh Day Adventist manning a medical mission was the nearest doctor, 500 miles south on the banks of the Wabe Shebelle river. I reported my predicament and my destination over the radio to my department. I drove across a desert of red dust. The doctor was on patrol. He would return the following afternoon. A young blonde Seventh Day Adventist nurse examined my leg. She prayed for my soul at the dinner table and proffered cold root beer from an immense refrigerator.

My men had pitched camp across the river from the mission. I awoke to find the leg back to normal. Doubts had been cast over the radio as to the seriousness of my infirmity. I was suspected of driving 500 miles merely to an assignation. Now the nurse risked damnation in the eyes of her fellow missionaries.

The nurse and I spent the forenoon beating the leg with wet knotted towels. We achieved a slight swelling round the knee.

These are my memories as Santiago drops me at the clinic.

Blue is unpopular.

The doctor growls.

A tough, square, sadistic nurse, she who wielded the hypodermic, scrubs the scabs from my burns with sulphuric acid (judged by the pain). Bandages are applied, not to cure but to ward off further interference. I am told that I can travel – fast, is the implication, fast out of reach of the jungle witches.

The leg is clean.

It is healing.

Your guess is as good as mine as to which treatment has been most efficacious.

Across the Petén, Tuesday 13 June

Santiago has insisted on accompanying me. His monster Honda trail bike would be insulted by association with my 125. Santiago will ride his sixteen-year-old daughter's Suzuki 125.

I summon Santiago at a quarter past seven from the virginal purity of his brand-new king-size bed and inner-sprung mattress (purchased yesterday). Santiago appears at half past. Facially he resembles Jack Nicholson. This morning he resembles Jack Nicholson on a bad day playing Jack Nicholson on a very bad day. To look this ravaged is an achievement given that Santiago hasn't had a drink in two years.

We leave at half past eight.

Santiago looks better under a full-face helmet.

We head for Santa Anna and San Francisco, where Santiago circles the square before halting at a charming thatched cottage set in a large garden (what North Americans call a 'yard'). The owner is a nurse. She is the mother of six daughters, each more beautiful than the last (so attests Santiago, who yearns after them). The mother serves coffee and cookies and recounts that two daughters have married Canadian missionaries. The fourth or fifth appears from town. She is beautiful – although less beautiful than the mother at the same age. This is my judgement on being shown a framed photograph of the mother's wedding. The mother purrs and exchanges Bible quotations with her daughter, who sits on the arm of her mother's armchair and threads her mother's curls between slender fingers. Yearn on, Santiago. Your loves (even if you could concentrate on a single daughter or remember how many daughters there are or which daughter is which) will remain unrequited.

Courtship in this family is done with the Bible.

However, we do see a jaguar cross the road. Not the full-size version: an onza – *Felis yagouaroundi*.

In Santiago's company, I have seen a mountain fox and squirrels, watched and listened to howler monkeys, and spotted a vast variety of birds. Now we speed towards the river that marks the Petén's southern boundary.

The rains have been fierce over the past weeks. We hit diversions where the tarmac road has been swept away or eroded. At Sayaxche the river is in flood. The ferry is on the far side. The crew are eating breakfast or lunch or a mid-morning snack. An impatient truck driver pointlessly beats a tattoo on his klaxon.

Santiago and I park outside a thatched-roofed *comedor*. Paul Theroux writes that he hates the use of foreign words in travel writing. I know of no English word for *comedor*. A *comedor* is not grand enough to be a restaurant; nor is it a café. It is a place where you eat. This *comedor* is typical. Plank walls are waist-high, leaving a gap below the low eaves for light to enter. It has a rough unpainted concrete floor, plastic chairs, tables with plastic tops, an upright cold cupboard and a kitchen in the back that would give a health inspector a heart attack.

We drink good coffee. I eat eggs and refried black beans topped with cheese and chilli sauce. Santiago orders steak.

The ferry is a flat-topped barge pushed by an outboard-powered launch lashed alongside. Three trucks, a car and six bikes make a full load. The water is thick with earth washed down from hillsides denuded of their forest cover. We watch a little anxiously as the current sweeps the ferry broadside.

Beyond the river we cross rich ranch land. One vast spread is the property of a narco-trafficker; fences are neat, farm roads in good repair, cattle in prime condition.

Chiec is little more than a truck-stop with a service station and a new hotel. We are off the tourist track and pay less than ten dollars each for clean air-conditioned rooms with bath. The rooms open to a first-floor veranda overlooking the car park. Giant concrete mushrooms and real palm trees and acacias and an immense cedar tree shade a swimming pool. A waterslide plummets through hollow concrete tree trunks.

Chicken noodle soup is out of a packet. Santiago gnaws the better end of a bad steak. The bill is three dollars. We remount and head back twenty kilometres to the cavern system of Candelaria.

Entrance to the caverns is on the right of the road when heading towards the Petén. Santiago met this morning on the road with a Frenchman, Daniel Dreux. Daniel is a member of the group that first explored the caves some thirty years ago. The caves were known to the local Maya – thus explored rather than discovered.

Daniel has built a hotel at the caverns. A large concrete road sign promotes the caves as being a community project financed by USAID, a gift from the people of the United States of America. Small symbols advertise the facilities: toy car, knife and fork, bed.

Santiago leads down a narrow gravel road. The road twists and turns for a kilometre. The gravel ends and we slither on rutted mud. Finally we face a near-vertical ascent. Santiago roars to the top. I fail halfway. Santiago scrambles down what is a mud slide rather than a road and helps me turn the bike across the slope and hitch it onto its stand. I am irritated – and a little frightened.

We climb the slide. A narrow serpentine path leads down the mountain. Much of it is stone steps. My leg hurts. I curse whatever lying son-of-a-bitch marked the road sign with a toy car. A mule would find the track tough.

Santiago cheers me with a promise of cold beer. A French hotel must have cold beer.

The path debouches onto a lawn that hasn't been cut in a month. A few huts promise discomfort. A Maya woman conducts us to a visitors' centre.

Posters describe the caverns as the site of Maya rituals. The posters carry the insignia of USAID.

There are no French.

The woman has never heard of the French.

There is no cold beer.

Santiago wishes to visit the caverns. I wish to climb slowly back up the mountain, retrieve the Honda and ride carefully back to the main road. I want to reach the highway before nightfall and before rain turns the track into a quagmire. I know my capabilities. Crawling around caves in the dark while being devoured by mosquitoes is a negative.

I pause for breath twice on the climb. I traverse the slope on the Honda with the timidity of a novice skier on ice. I ride with care and regain the highway. Santiago will be at least an hour. I ride down the road and discover a second concrete sign promoting the caverns. This sign is emblazoned with the logo of the European Union. The symbols are identical to those on the USAID sign: toy car, knife and fork, bed. At least the US financed a track. Here there is only a grass path.

An elderly man tells me that Don Daniel is at the hotel. The hotel is through the trees. 'Park at the farm,' the old man instructs and points to a house on a small hill. I ride up the drive and find a Guatemalan woman feeding chickens.

'Yes, indeed,' she tells me. 'Don Daniel is at the hotel. You may leave your motor bicycle here. Parking is five quetzales.'

I ride back to the USAID sign. A minibus unloads a man in his thirties, clean jeans and boots, a clean shirt, briefcase. He is of the community and asks whether I have visited the caverns. I reply that the road defeated me, that the car symbol on the sign is deceitful.

'It is for parking,' he says.

I retort that the only parking is on a mud slope. 'The caverns belong to the community?' I ask.

'Yes,' he says.

'Then why does the sign bare the symbol of USAID rather than the flag of Guatemala?'

'The United States paid for the development,' he says.

'A gift to the community?'

'Yes, a gift.'

'Should givers of gifts boast of their generosity?'

He looks up at the sign.

'Or is the development an advertisement for the United States?'

He is uncomfortable. He thinks a while. 'It is publicity for the Americans.'

'And the posters in the visitors' centre. That's a great deal of publicity. At least they should have finished the road.'

'We would have more visitors if the road was finished.'

I agree. 'Were many of the community killed during the clandestine war?'

My change of direction confuses him. 'Yes,' he says. 'Yes, many were killed.'

'By the army?'

'Yes, by the army and by the police.'

'The guns and ammunition – were they marked as gifts of the people of the United States of America?'

Before he can answer, Santiago roars up the track.

Santiago introduces himself. He and the man discuss the cavern system. There are two entrances. Don Daniel has a hotel at the second entrance. The caves are on the community's land. Don Daniel has stolen their land.

Santiago attempts to play the peacemaker. 'The quarrel must damage tourism.' And to me: 'We are in a war zone.'

We ride down the road to visit the opposing army.

We park at the farmhouse, cross the road and slither down a grass slope to a path. Within the jungle, the verges of the path are planted with medicinal plants. We reach a bridge and a wooden bower with seats and a notice requesting that visitors remove their footwear. We follow a wooden walkway to thatched buildings. There is a restaurant. The cook is an indigenous woman in traditional dress and blouse. Her hair is bound in a pigtail.

A slim French youth serves cold beer.

Two Frenchmen join us. Don Daniel is in his mid-sixties, tall, heavily built. Jacques is lighter, younger, curly hair turning grey.

Daniel tells us that a syndicate from the US wanted to buy the hotel. Daniel refused. A few months passed and USAID began financing the rival project. The community had no previous interest in the caverns. It is an American conspiracy.

Santiago mentions land titles. Daniel storms off down the wood walkway.

Jacques leads us to a river that springs from a cave. The water runs for perhaps thirty metres before disappearing into the mouth of another cavern. A boat can follow the river through caverns for thirty kilometres.

Jacques shows us the rooms and bungalows. Taste is impeccable. The jungle is beautiful. And yet ...

None of the rooms has a private bathroom. To pee, you have to walk down a path. At night? Losing your slippers, stubbing your toes ... snakes, scorpions. No, not for the elderly. However, this is only the beginning.

There is a dark and heavy feel to the place. The atmosphere is French colonial: Indochina circa 1930: a turgid drama of overcomplicated loves and deceits shot in dark sepia.

Most disturbing is a small school for Maya children.

To Cobán, Wednesday 14 June

Santiago is a good friend and has been a great host. He must return to his hotel, Mon Ami. I head towards Cobán. Dawn, and mist clings to magnificent trees. I am at one with the Honda. I marvel at the precise positioning of the seat to suit a man of my exact proportions. I revel in rediscovering the joyous enthusiasm of my youth. I swoop into curves. The motor responds instantly.

I pull into a tiny *comedor* to wait out a rain storm. A seven-year-old beauty serves a bowl of coriander-flavoured chicken soup. She is the only member of her family comfortable in Spanish. I ask why she isn't at school.

Because boys attend her school in the mornings, and girls in the afternoon.

Being a pompous old man, I warn her of the importance of education. Only education will free her from service to a man.

I play lion games with her younger siblings: big roar and they flee giggling, only to creep back for a repeat performance.

I played the same game with my own children.

My younger sons enjoy the same music and wear the same clothes as the sons of my Hispanic friends. Our sons have similar concerns and anxieties and preoccupations. We, their parents, have similar concerns and anxieties and preoccupations.

Although travelling, I am on familiar territory.

We are always on familiar territory, all of us. Yet we divide ourselves from this reality by erecting fake barriers and boundaries of nationality and race and religion.

Cobán, Thursday 15 June

I am evilly treated with divine comfort. I am staying with friends on their *finca* some kilometres outside Cobán. I awake to a sunrise of blushed gold filtered through white curtains. I hobble to my bathroom. The bath was rescued from an old house. It is vast and softly curved. It sits in a bow window. The taps are solid brass. Water gushes hot from the hot tap and cold from the cold tap. A brick path passes beneath the window. Above the path rises a vertical bank of red soil fringed at the crest with grass. Dew on the grass reflects the early rays of the sun. The grass appears to be licked by flames that dance rose and gold on the cliff edge.

My spectacles lie on the edge of the bath. I reach for my book. *Tap-tap. Tap-tap.*

I peek over my book and am confronted by a small bird with a yellow breast. The bird pecks at the window. Its wings whirr as it climbs the glass. Its strength saps and it slithers down to the window ledge. *Please*, I whisper, *please don't harm yourself*. But the damage is done. Guilt invades me. I am responsible for the bird's desire for self-destruction.

The bird perches on the thick shoot of a bromeliad and peers in at me (or at its reflection). *Depart*, I plead. The glass is too thick or my powers of thought transference are dysfunctional this early in the morning. Or the bird is really dumb. Or sadistic. It is deliberately fracturing the basking bliss of this, my first hot bath in two months of travel. I hate the bird.

And I hate my hosts for steeping me in such wonderful comfort.

They know I must move on and that I am moving on into the unknown and that quitting such safety and such beauty and such friendship will be tearful.

Cobán, Friday 16 June

Guatemala is inundated with missionaries, mostly from the US. My favourite is the Church of God. Other churches are the church of whom? The Devil? Or perhaps the Federal Reserve? We have Baptists and Anabaptists, Evangelicals, Seventh Day Adventists ... and then, of course, those pale-faced Mormon lads in their tasteless ties. Today the feast of San Juan is celebrated in the village above which my hosts have their farm. Marcio and Ashley are vague as to which San Juan. Not that it matters. There is a big parade, men and women dressed in their best – men mostly in white shirts and dark trousers, women in long woven skirts and white blouses. Food stalls line the main street and a Ferris wheel turns slowly. We eat at a table in a front garden. The stall is in aid of damaged local children. The food is the traditional feast-day food of the area – rich turkey broth with a turkey leg or thigh and a chunk of smoked beef.

The Mormons sneak in.

Mormons are always white and are always pale. Are they scared of the sun? Or scared of being mistaken for the people they have come to save? And why always two of them? One is more than sufficient. Are they scared? Or do they need to watch each other so neither does a runner with the collection box?

I watch as they approach the elderly lady collecting the dinner money. They sidle. Maybe that comes with unlimited rejections. The lady sends them packing. They slink back, sneak-thieves on the prowl for a victim. Table to table. None of these people, indigenous or near-indigenous, is wealthy. They spend their spare cash on their own sick. These pink rats' attempts at nibbling are obscene.

However, Guatemalans are polite.

Back home, Native Americans, those whose great-grandparents survived slaughter by these Mormons' great-granddaddies, might shoot an arrow up their butts. And the inner-city slums of the US are too dangerous for sweet white kids in ties.

Cobán, Saturday 17 June

Over these past days I have been cherished by my hosts, Ashley and Marcio: hot baths, breakfast, being driven into town where I spend the day at an internet café run by two kindly sisters. The sisters allow me to set up my laptop at a vacant desk where it stays throughout my visit to Cobán. They remain patient when I miss the step down into their bathroom, slam the handbasin off the wall and end with my head in the lavatory bowl.

More important than the cherishing has been the conversation. Way back, Marcio's family were Spanish. They had been Guatemalan for a couple of hundred years before the United States annexed California. By training, Marcio is a plant pathologist, and he has a fine collection of orchids out at the farm. However, as with many men brought up in what people call 'the third world', he has many accomplishments. During the clandestine war he sold everything in twenty-four hours to ransom his wife and children from *guerrilleros*.

Taking shelter in the United States, he earned a good living as a carpenter while attending night classes in business administration. Now he grows macadamia trees, several thousand, and Dobermans patrol within a tall fence that surrounds the house and garden. Apart from the farming, he and Ash run a hotel in Cobán, Casa d'Acuna.

The hotel is a resurrected colonial townhouse. The resurrection has been done with the same attention to detail that they have lavished on their own home. I made notes on my first visit: china doorknobs, spotless bathrooms with real hot water, fresh flowers on the tables, orchids on the patio and syrup feeders for the hummingbirds. The hotel is a partnership with staff, and the staff's pride in their work is obvious. Rooms are reasonably priced and travellers find it an excellent base.

Marcio, Ash and I eat dinner at the hotel tonight. We are a little solemn, a little sad. Travelling is a series of goodbyes, and I leave tomorrow.

Sadness overwhelms me as I lie in bed. I think of those I will leave behind. Eugenio is a brother to me: a younger brother when we first met; now, as I enter my second childhood, an elder brother. And of course there is Santiago, fierce hunter of pigs, my present hosts Marcio and Ash, and Juan Fernando, Lucia and Eric up in Antigua.

Unable to sleep, I read Paul Theroux's *The Old Patagonian Express*. I have reached page 150. Theroux is in Costa Rica and hasn't yet met anyone he likes. Nor has he met anyone to whom he doesn't condescend. This is a malady of travel writers. I read a dozen travel books on Latin America before departing on this journey.

However charming and amusing and well written the books, the writers seldom encounter anyone of greater education or social or financial standing. Apparently it is possible to travel through Patagonia without being aware of a city of a million inhabitants, of factories and schools and a university, of office buildings and apartment blocks serviced by elevators. No wonder those school students I talked with back in England pictured Mexicans as sweaty fat men wearing sombreros and speaking with funny accents.

Goodbye Cobán, Sunday 18 June

Breakfast is a real Sunday breakfast: fresh orange juice and fresh fruit for health; bacon, chorizo and French toast with real maple syrup from Canada for cholesterol; great coffee. I load the bike and Ash photographs Marcio and me beside the bike.

Marcio advises me of a shortcut to the tar road. I ride on good dirt for twenty kilometres. I ride slowly and smile at people and call greetings. I am rewarded with smiles and 'good mornings' – so different from the highlands of my first two days in Guatemala. The first fifty kilometres are coffee *fincas* or dairy farms. Occasionally there is a splash of colour where bougainvillea spills over a fence.

The paved highway drops in smooth curves to El Rancho, a distance of 150 kilometres. I am in tune to the road's rhythm and am reminded, as I lean into the bends, of skiing in spring snow. This is glorious biking.

I sweep though pine forest and inhale the scent of pine tar. The road drops from cool mountain air to coastal heat. At El Rancho I gas up beside two massive BMWs. The BMWs are fitted with all the kit; so are the riders (shades of Dallas, although these two are Guatemaltecos). The fitted luggage cost more than my Honda. We laugh together and shake hands and ride off in different directions – they back to their offices in the capital, me to turn south at Rio Honda towards the Honduran frontier.

Riding gives ample time for thought. I muse on the cowardice of the novelist – or my cowardice. As a novelist, I choose safety. When confronted, I have been ready always with the novelist's excuse. 'That was a character speaking. That wasn't me. It's a novel.'

Now I write fact as I perceive it; I place my own opinions before the reader; I do so from a country in which horrific violence is commonplace and where fear is as normal as eating breakfast. This is a country where the people suffered thirty-six years of a hell that historians now refer to as 'the clandestine war'. Approximately 160 000 indigenous Guatemalans were slaughtered with the aid of US military advisers and by Guatemalan military trained at the School of the Americas in Georgia. The war was the fruit of the United Fruit Company. It was instigated by the CIA and financed by the generosity of the people of the United States of America. USAID signs are obscene. So is the moral posturing of those who financed the *guerrilleros*.

Honduras

To Copán, Sunday 18 June

I have been fortunate in choosing the right months for travel. The road through Zacapa to the Honduran frontier crosses country that Paul Theroux writes of as dusty desert. Now vivid green hillsides quiver beneath a breeze that flutters emerald growth on the trees. The river flows full between irrigated patches of field. Storms have torn boulders from the slopes. I ride with extra care on a road that twists through narrow valleys.

Guatemalan and Honduran immigration officials share a low building. The Honda and I and our eventual goal of Tierra del Fuego are a great source of shared laughter. I negotiate the exchange rate up a few points with a money man in a white Stetson. The money man photographs me with the Honduran and Guatemalan immigration officials.

Documentation at Honduran customs takes less than ten minutes. However, the customs chief has the football World Cup on his office TV and insists I join him for a cold beer. France are playing Korea and I am delayed an hour.

I ride into Copán in late afternoon. A truck pulls alongside. The driver hands me a card. He owns a hotel. The room is fine.

The Maya ruins have made Copán affluent. It is a small, pretty town of perhaps fifty blocks divided by cobbled streets. Domestic architecture is mostly single-storey Spanish colonial, freshly painted and in fine repair. I draw cash on my debit card from an ATM at one of the banks on the central square and find an internet café. The manager, Isabelle, plies me with coffee while I read and write my mail. Dinner is beer and a steak with the normal trimmings: tomatoes, fried bananas, black beans, avocado, green salad.

Copán, Monday 19 June

I intend to catch up on my writing and am up early, walking down to breakfast at the restaurant where I ate last night. Quarter past seven, and I order orange juice and coffee with eggs. This is Central America: the eggs come with refried beans, fried bananas, avocado. The coffee is good. Have I finally reached coffee heaven? Or is this glory particular to Copán? Breakfast is served on a terrace that gives onto a jungly garden.

Replete, I wait, sitting on the curb, for the internet café to open. This is a town of hope, wonderfully refreshing after Guatemala. Householders and shopkeepers are out sweeping the pavement and watering the cobbles to lay the dust. Passers-by greet me. A new Hyundai pickup delivers five-gallon water bottles. Three-wheeler suicide scooter-cabs gleam. The Isuzu refuse truck is new and polished.

The women of Copán celebrate their wealth. Plump-voluptuous is the figure, T-shirts stretched at breast and belly. I greet a woman, mid-twenties, wearing a gold belt wide as a cummerbund. A roll of silky brown belly breaks free of a short tight black top and spills over the belt. She strolls with swagger, proud of her girth. No place here for Kate Moss. The generous townsfolk would think her starving and pursue her down the street with stuffed tortillas.

I ride my bike the mile to the Maya ruins. Guatemalan cops remain expressionless as they stare. Here a cop armed with a rifle waves at me from the roadside. The entrance fee to the ruins and the museum is fifteen dollars. I prefer sightseeing at my own pace and buy a guidebook rather than join a tour group. Big parrots greet me. I take their photographs. Delighted, the parrots nod and squawk.

The ruins are great as ruins go. The setting is magnificent, the surrounding bowl of mountains green this time of year, as are the huge trees and cropped grass between the pyramids and ball courts and acropolis.

I sit in the shade on the lower steps of a pyramid and face the sloping side of a pyramid some thirty metres high. A pale young blonde woman slips on the descent behind me and twists her ankle. She is a missionary, wouldn't you know? From Minnesota. She and an older male of the species are in company with a Guatemalan doctor, female, and two others who translate for the missionaries the word of God. The doctor requests a bandage to wrap the ankle. God is off duty. I provide the bandage I wear on my right leg when biking.

The missionary's mishap has destroyed my ability to concentrate on or be impressed by the Maya gods. My guidebook recounts that succeeding Maya kings destroyed many of their predecessors' monuments and rebuilt on the same sites – each succeeding pyramid taller and more impressive.

The kings *built*?

Kings don't build. Their subjects build.

I know the system well from having lived in Cuba: The following will volunteer ...

Imagine cutting those thousands of stone blocks in the quarries, cutting them without steel. Imagine transporting the blocks without the benefit of the wheel. Imagine the thousands of bent backs and broken limbs and crushed fingers.

I walk a little, sit a little, admire the grey of the stone so well presented against the brilliant green of the rainy season. I talk with an English woman and her father: she is teaching at an English private school in El Salvador. Later I notice what I mistake for leaf insects beside a path. I look closer and discover a column of ants carrying freshly cut leaves on their backs. Leaves are lighter than stones and easier to cut.

I fall in with a Puerto Rican and his girlfriend. She is small and the steps up the pyramids are steep and high. We decide the height of the steps was designed to so exhaust the sacrificial victims that they would find relief in having their hearts gouged out with an obsidian knife. We listen to a guide joke about human sacrifices as he explains the ball game to a noisy troop of North American students.

My guidebook is Honduran and doesn't mention human sacrifice.

One of the North American students is unaware that he has dropped his camera in the long grass. A Guatemalan with the Minnesota missionaries calls to the student. The student turns back, picks up his camera and walks on. The Guatemalan's spirituality takes a knock. Turning to her companions, she says, 'Nice of him to say thank you.'

A group of Guatemalan daytrippers gather at the entrance to the ball court. One asks where I am from. He and his companions are members of a small manufacturing cooperative in Zacapa. The co-op is being bankrupted by Chinese imports. They need to retool but nobody is willing to invest. Investors have lost faith in the future and fear the violence.

His companions agree that the Chinese are the great threat, the Chinese and the violence. The violence in Guatemala City is very bad. Even out in the small towns. One man claims that the violence is deliberately fostered by the government to destabilise democracy. The rich want another general.

The Guatemalans depart and I sit a while, flipping back through my guidebook. Why was each of the great Maya sites abandoned? I think of the ants – and of bees swarming and moving on. I imagine the work entailed in endlessly building bigger and bigger pyramids. Perhaps sovereigns demanded too much of their subjects and self-glorified their kingdoms out of existence.

In the site museum, I am entranced by a collection of small heads sculpted in clay. Maya art is stylised, and yet sculptors have sneaked in a smile, glance or grimace totally familiar to me from my own social existence. Dominating the display is a replica of a temple in its original colours. I imagine myself a Mayan peasant. The vastness of the pyramid would stun me. I would tremble at sight of the grimacing god with his ghastly fangs. Centuries of rain have cleansed the stones of their rivulets of human blood. Age has mellowed the sculpture. However, we should remember, we tourists, as we wander the clipped lawns, that the original purpose was to terrorise.

Many travel books relate ordeals: breakdowns, fevers, bandits, ghastly food, horrid people. Good days are boring. So, yes, I enjoy my day in Copán. However, permit me my grump: I am writing in the internet café this evening. A group of students from the US charge in, yakking at each other, shouting the length of the café. We, the staff and those already seated at a terminal, are made to feel as if we are non-people. The Hondurans in the café judge the students as typically arrogant gringos.

Tomorrow I will be off early. Maybe I will find a TV somewhere along the road on which to watch the England–Sweden World Cup match. I could, of course, return to the Honduran frontier post and share a cold beer with the head of customs.

Wrong road to Macao, Tuesday 20 June

I ride out of Copán early and stop at Santa Rosa for an excellent breakfast. Santa Rosa is as clean and pretty as Copán, low Hispanic houses neatly painted. Breakfast is slices of beef skirt with eggs, beans and cheese, a huge glass of papaya juice and excellent coffee.

I have been riding through lush ranch land. Poverty is less obvious than in Guatemala. There are fewer mud hovels. The main highway is decorated with banners warning of banditry and that silence is the bandits' friend. The gas station has guards, one armed with an automatic rifle; a second sports a .45 revolver, bullets massive in his belt. 'Yes,' he says, 'there are many robbers.'

I reach Gracias at noon. Gracias has little to be grateful for. A side road leads off the main highway towards Esperanza. The road cuts through mountain country. The tar ends. I hope this is only for a few kilometres. Wrong. It is rough dirt all the way, deep potholes and ravines gouged by the rains. Strange that a bum can be both numb and hurt.

My guess is that Esperanza is so-called because the founders hoped that it would improve with time. It hasn't. The stores on Main Street sell third-hand clothes. All the stores. The stores on side streets sell fourth-hand clothes. Half the trucks in town appear to have broken down –

hardly surprising given the state of the road. My Honda rates as a Rolls Royce. I stop at an air-conditioned Chinese restaurant on Main Street to watch the England–Sweden match. I have a cold beer and delicious Chinese barbecued beef. The match is a disastrous draw. Enraged, I ride on into a massive thunderstorm and sulk for an hour beneath the inadequate shelter of a pine tree. Sun breaks through and I dry as I ride.

The dirt road is tricky, not only because of the wet; some stretches are bare rock, others no better than a riverbed. I ride much of the way in second and even first gear. Glorious vistas of pine-cloaked mountains compensate for the discomfort. The river valleys in this area supply much of the nation's vegetables and there are few signs of poverty. Houses are square with peaked pan-tiled roofs. The centre section is an open space without doors, front or back, and channels the breeze. Sometimes the space is furnished. More often it houses that most important member of a Central American family: the double-cab pickup truck.

Horses graze small patches of greenery. I catch glimpses of horsemen between the trees and pass them on the road. My brother and my adopted daughter are horse-mad and my thoughts are with them much of the day. I rode on horseback across chunks of Afghanistan both before the Russian occupation and during it. In those days I dreamt of riding with my brother north through Chitral in the tribal areas of Pakistan. Such rides were possible. We would have met kindness and hospitality. No longer. That world is closed to us.

Macao is a larger version of Esperanza. A small river divides the town. The folk of Macao are attempting to dam the river with refuse. Two heifers stand in the water beneath the bridge on Main Street and graze the grassy bank. I ride around town a couple of times in search of a hotel. Available are roach- and rat-infested hellholes that Dante would have imagined as stopovers on the descent to the Inferno. I pass through a pleasant square on the outskirts of town where a kindly policeman directs me to a modern hotel hiding in a big garden courtyard. The Medina has comfortable rooms for ten dollars – a reduction of two dollars for a pensioner. Creepers clamber over the walls. I look forward to hot water. An electric storm hit earlier in the day and the electricity is off. I take the manager's advice to walk around town while they fix the power.

I stroll the streets, get caught in a deluge and am holed up in a pool saloon for an hour. Drunken Honduran pool players are unnerving. I chat with a sheltering schoolteacher whose niece works in Spain. The niece has been to Frankfurt for a week's holiday. Was that near Barcelona?

'Not very,' I say.

Meanwhile thunder crashes and lightning flashes on streets transformed into rivers in spate and drunken Hondurans yell at each other across the pool tables dimly lit by paraffin lamps.

Will this do as a proper adventure?

The rain thins and I make a dash for a Chinese restaurant on the same block as the Hotel Medina. A few candles supply the light. I face a table of four – three men and a woman with a dipping neckline who keeps her mouth shut. One of the men dominates the table. He is big, shorn scalp, gold necklace, gold bracelet. He possesses a big voice and has charge of the controller for the TV – as I discover when electricity returns. Is he a local gangster or a short-order cook back on holiday from Nueve Yorke and determined to impress?

Massacre tourism, Wednesday 21 June

Three travellers over the past weeks have stressed the pleasures of Perquín in northern El Salvador. 'Hey, it's really great. It's a must. You'll love it. They've got this great museum with photographs and stuff. You know, like the war that went on?'

Except ...

Do I want to visit the sites of massacres?

Do I want to admire photographs of the victims?

Am I gripped by smashed US helicopters as sculptural art?

Is massacre tourism my *thing*?

Not really.

I've seen too much death up close. I've ridden on horseback through countries where every village has been bombed, where seventy percent of the population has fled over the borders to vile camps. I've lain behind a rock beneath a pile of Afghans while a Russian gunship pops at us.

I've driven through countries suffering total drought: where survival of the breeding stock of the nomadic tribe is the one essential: where old folk and infants are abandoned.

Worse, I have used my imagination to describe a horrendous massacre in *Aftermath*, only to read in the Peace Commission's report of a similar massacre perpetrated by the Guatemalan army.

So, no, I think I'll give Perquín a miss.

Paz sounds a better destination – then on to the Honduran capital, Tegucigalpa. I enjoy typing 'Tegucigalpa'. It has a ring to it. I am dyslexic. Correctly spelling such a difficult name is satisfying.

Four police in a jeep wave me down as I pass a stand selling watermelons. They ask which road I took and wasn't I aware of bandits? I admit that I have read warning notices. However, all Hondurans I have met on the road have been kind. The sergeant says that I have been lucky, gives me a slice of melon and warns that I must be careful in Tegucigalpa. 'There are many thieves in Tegucigalpa.'

Tegucigalpa faces a decision: will it fall down today or wait a little? The city is not sited on a geological fault, nor has it been bombed. It merely looks that way. And some of the people I pass on the outskirts are reminders of refugees from a war zone or an earthquake. A woman, barefoot, her dress raggedy, carries a baby in her arms. An older infant lolls in a grubby cloth tied across her back. A third child follows, hair tangled, barefoot. They have nothing. Nothing.

What will they eat tonight?

Where will they sleep tonight?

Will they survive the night?

I ride into the city centre and find the best hotel room of my journey so far at Hotel Boston. The room is five metres by five, high ceiling with old-fashioned ceiling fan, tiled floor, large bathroom with hot water, window and doors onto a balcony. No matter that the street is noisy in the early morning. I rise and enjoy watching the city wake.

There is an excellent Chinese restaurant on my left. Upstairs is good for people-watching. I order a chop suey for five dollars. The waiter doesn't warn me that dishes on the main menu are for four people. I am served a chop-suey mountain.

I meet with three medium-level government administrators in from the provinces for a conference. The conversation soon turns to the main news of the week. The Honduran president has met with President Chavez of Venezuela to discuss Honduran oil requirements. The Honduran president is presumed to have been trying to make an advantageous deal – odd behaviour for a president. The US ambassador to Honduras has reacted by cancelling all Honduran applications for US visas. This is a serious threat to the country's economy – Hondurans abroad remit in excess of one billion dollars a year.

The three administrators are enraged. 'As if we are children to be punished,' one protests.

Another points out that the US imports oil from Venezuela.

Let me paraphrase the rest of the conversation:

For years the US used Honduras as a base for the wars it sponsored in the region: to unseat the Sandinista government in Nicaragua and fight the left-wing guerrillas in El Salvador and Guatemala. Successive US administrations have treated Honduras as a colony, influenced the choice of government, been accustomed to obedience. Now the US has no further use for Honduras. Honduras can sink in the muck largely created by the US.

One of the administrators insists that the US is responsible for the epidemic of violence in Honduras. The US gave so many arms to the Nicaraguan Contras. The Contras sold them once the war was over. An AK47 or M16 sells for thirty dollars. And the US Immigration Department has expelled so many young men, Honduran by parentage but kids who have never been in Honduras, kids infected with the American gang culture.

These three Hondurans are conservative rather than rabble rousers of an anti-American left. I merely relay their arguments and anger. Their judgement is that of the loyal servant or mistress discarded by an ungrateful and thoughtless master.

Onward to Danlí, Thursday 22 June

A minivan driver kindly leads me from the centre of Tegucigalpa to the Danlí road. The road seems the same as the road in from the west. Pine forest is pine forest, mountains are mountains, a tar road sown with mantraps is much the same as any other tar road sown with mantraps. Honduran mantraps are potholes fit to swallow a Mack truck. In sunshine, the potholes show as dark pools of shadow. Today is a grey day and the potholes appear at the last moment.

The mountains end. The road crosses a flat valley with further mountains in the distance. A miracle appears on the right: disciplined acres in the midst of standard Central American chaos. I am travelling at eighty kilometres an hour. I glimpse cropped lawns, neat single-storey buildings arranged with obvious logic, avenues of palm trees. I must stop. Ahead lie storm clouds. This is the rainy season. A storm in the late afternoon is standard. I want to reach Danlí before the rain. But I am a writer. I ride a further two kilometres before making a U-turn and backtracking. I have discovered Zamorano, the US-funded Agricultural University of the Americas.

To be brief, Zamorano was founded in 1942 as the brainchild of a retired director of United Fruit. The project was funded initially by the United Fruit Company. Now it is funded by the US taxpayer and has an independent board of trustees. Students come from all parts of Latin America and the Caribbean.

Endless conversations between confused gate guards and equally confused administrators gain me entrance to the English language department and an interview with a well-meaning young teacher from small-town USA.

What should a writer publish? Everything – or should he edit himself? I talk for an hour with the teacher. He has taught at Zamorano for two years. He is homesick. He misses those small-town family celebrations of Thanksgiving, Halloween and Christmas. Although married to a Honduran, he seems a little lost.

Is he made nervous by my probing? Is he defensive in his replies? Perhaps.

I enquire as to the feeling of the students towards the United States.

He replies that he hears some criticism from South Americans, but that Central Americans in general hold a positive view of the US.

I mention his opinions to a senior member of staff, a Latin American. He raises his eyebrows in despair. 'When will they ever learn?'

He has lived in the US. He recalls any attempt at discussion of US foreign policy as seen as criticism and that he always received the same retort: 'You don't like it, why don't you leave?'

He is proud of Zamorano's achievements. It is of great importance to Latin American agriculture. And yet one moment of stupid bullying, as with the present cancellation of US visas for Hondurans, destroys all the goodwill the university has earned the US.

I pay for my visit to Zamorano with a drenching and arrive in Danlí exhausted and resembling a river rat. The Grand Hotel is at the entrance to town. The hotel's swimming pool is no longer in use and the hotel food is disastrous. However, the room and bathroom are fine, the water is hot, and I have a fan and cable TV. I am feeling my years and am in desperate need of the bed.

Danlí, Friday 23 June

Hondurans have been kind to me. Danlí has a great feel. This is a personal opinion and based on little evidence. Danlí may be the centre for all sorts of viciousness. It is a small, sleepy town with a good church and an excellent market. Outsiders might judge it a dump. It is a dump, but the people are warm and open. The chain on the Honda requires adjustment and the bike needs a check-up. Carlo the Kikuyu is recommended. I expect a Kenyan, or at least a man who looks like an African from Kenya. Carlos the Kikuyu is a standard *mestizo*. His shop is a tin shed by the market. We chat while he works. He refuses payment, insisting that contributing to my adventure is sufficient reward.

I take my shoes to be mended in the covered market and find a laundry – all my clothes are either wet or dirty. I abandon a hopelessly slow internet connection on the church square and discover a great internet café, Technochat, midway down the street to the Grand Hotel.

I fall into conversation for more than an hour with a woman, the owner of a store selling stationery and natural medicines. An odd combination?

She had wanted an education. Her father owned a tiny store up in the mountains and was too poor. Married at seventeen, she bore her first child the same year and remained married for fifteen years before divorce. Her husband had gone to work in the US.

'Men return from the US changed,' she explains. 'They are rude and all they do is drink and go with women.'

She believes that people in the US, white people, have contempt for Latinos. 'How can they not?' she asks. 'They only meet those of us who have no education. Those are the only Latinos who go north.'

In Danlí parents are unable to support their families. Her son-in-law is a barber. Some days he is without a single customer. Weekends are better. Some weekends he makes as much as twenty dollars. Labourers earn five dollars a day – not enough to feed a family. So the parents leave. Many of the fathers leave for the US with good intentions. At first they send money. Then they find a new woman, have other children. The money ceases. And now there are the gangs – the sons of those who have gone to the US. The sons are sent back by the Americans. The sons are evil. They think nothing of shooting people for a few dollars.

She is equally critical of Spain: Spaniards are even more racist than white people in the US. She has heard this from her friends who have gone to work in Spain. Many women from Danlí go to Spain, the men to the US.

As for herself, she is blessed in belonging to a church that sends medicines from the US for its members. She was ill and would have died but for the church. I refrain from asking whether the church members who send the medicines are white North Americans – or whether the natural medicines in her store are ineffective.

Many customers enter the store during our conversation. Her daughter serves them. She is training her daughter to take over the store. Then she will go to Spain and work until she has saved sufficient money to buy a new pickup and build a second house that she can rent out for her old age.

I report what I hear. I neither edit nor provoke.

Tomorrow I leave for Nicaragua.

Nicaragua

El Paraiso, Saturday 24 June

Crossing from Honduras into Nicaragua takes thirty minutes. I am pestered by a boy who ought to be in school. In exchange for a tip, he wants to help with my documentation. I don't need help. He does need money. I give him my documents and he pushes them through the window at which I am already standing – much to the amusement of the officials. I ask the Honduran customs officers (two women) for a goodbye kiss. They chase me from their office amidst hoots of laughter. In Nicaragua, third party vehicle insurance is obligatory. Add small fees for an import permit and a temporary permit and various stamps in my passport and the total amounts to twenty-five dollars. This is the first border at which I have been charged anything.

León and Granada compete in Hispanic colonial charm. The Spanish founded both cities in 1524. León was the nation's capital until the mid-nineteenth century and is my present destination.

Poverty is obvious close to the border. The highway crosses a dry area of rain shadow. The nearer I get to León, the more affluent the farms and houses become in countryside of spiky hills scattered with trees and rich fields. The truck of a very fat Nicaraguan driver parks opposite a *comedor* on the left side of the road. The driver's girth is recommendation enough; I pull in for breakfast. A pretty waitress in her mid-teens serves me the standard fare of eggs, beans, avocado and fried bananas, with a big tin mug of fresh orange juice. Coffee comes in a big cup. It is strong, unsweetened and delicious. The fat driver is telling stories at a nearby table. Here is a snap judgement: Nicaraguans are noisy.

The highway is in excellent condition. The sun comes out. I feel great. I speed. I overtake a couple of trucks on a hill. I am pulled over by five cops in a pickup. Three hundred cordobas is the statutory fine for crossing a solid yellow line while overtaking a crawling truck on a hill. A cop shows me the paragraph in a pamphlet on road safety. The fine must be paid at a bank. I plead my age. I plead poverty. The cops settle for one hundred paid in cash – approximately six and a half dollars.

The highway from Honduras to Managua, capital of Nicaragua, is good, as is the highway from Managua to León. I turn right at San Isidro to cut the corner. The road must have been good once. Now the tar is crumbling. Short stretches are dust and gravel. In other places I weave between elephant traps. At a guess this is a land of big ranches and poor villagers, a land where the landowner's horses are better fed than his workers. That is how it appears. To the left rises a chain of volcanoes. One is a perfect cone. Made of rubber and miniaturised, it would serve as a golf tee.

I park in the city centre and walk five blocks west, five blocks east, five north, five south. The architecture is Spanish colonial: single-storey houses built around a central patio, high ceilings, pan-tiled roofs. Some are grand. Some have been restored. A convent has been transformed into a hotel, of which the central garden is perfectly groomed. No guests are visible. Perhaps they are young lovers indulging in bedroom frolics.

I discover a peculiar hotel. The building is early colonial and at one time must have been splendid. In its present condition I wouldn't recommend it to a dead dog – although live dogs would enjoy the rats and overgrown patios. To be in character, the woman owner should drink gin out of a Tennessee Williams teacup with a broken handle. I stay for the opportunity to talk with two young Nicaraguan university students. One studies computer sciences. When he qualifies, only those with good eyesight will catch the flash of his departure – his degree will be his passport out of Nicaragua. The other is the youngest of six. His older siblings have marketable qualifications and have already emigrated. His mother insisted that he study law. Nicaraguan law is moderately useless inside Nicaragua. Outside Nicaragua, it is totally useless. He will have to stay home. Clever Mum.

León is a bigger version of Antigua, Guatemala, except that it is short on maintenance and there are few tourists.

No tourists equals no shops – working-class Nicaraguans don't earn shopping money.

The government has sold Nicaraguan labour cheap to Japanese and US multinationals. The multinationals operate factories within tax-free zones. Seven such zones are the government's pride. Multinationals repatriate all profit; Nicaragua gains nothing. I am told this by a woman who was administrative secretary to one of the leaders of the Sandinistas. She assures me that she will always be a Sandinista in her heart. She no longer votes Sandinista – the speed with which power corrupted destroyed her faith.

She tells me that workers in the tax-free zones earn a dollar a day. I must check her statistics.

Certainly León suffers from cash shortage. This is Saturday evening. The one café across from the splendid cathedral in the central square is almost empty. The prices are reasonable. Sunday morning I drink juice after attending Mass. Two couples and a single man are the other café customers. The square is superb. Were this Mexico, customers would queue for a table.

BUSH GENOSIDA is written in huge letters on a wall facing the cathedral. Bush is not guilty of genocide. Mostly what he does is make mistakes. We all make mistakes. Being president of the most powerful nation in the world, Bush's mistakes are on a large scale. Both Bush and Blair distorted intelligence. They lied to their own nations. Colin Powell deceived the United Nations. This is proven fact.

Deception is not genocide.

Although inaccurate, at least the scrawled message is specific in whom it accuses. It doesn't accuse US citizens or even the United States. Bush is the target.

My personal hate is Halliburton and those in the present US administration who continually award Halliburton contracts that are licences to print money. However, those employed by Halliburton must be average Americans and I have as many close American friends as I have British friends.

I have an American adopted daughter whom I adore and an American ex to whom I am close and who is always generous and supportive. I believe I connect with my daughter's brother – certainly I had a great time in his company when I was last in Providence. These are a type of American I have heard referred to in the southern states as 'those Jewish people' – as is my American agent in California, a kind, gentle, cultured man of absolute integrity.

My friend in Dallas, Don, is perhaps more the image foreigners have of an American. But a day spent driving round his construction sites is both instructive and a delight. He has wisdom and a slow dry sense of humour. He knows his clients and he knows his work. He is wealthy because his workers like and respect and trust him and don't let him down. His workers are Mexican.

I write this lest readers believe my own views mirror those I report. This is a journey of discovery. I am not in the judgement game. I have insisted to Central Americans again and again the importance of avoiding generalisations, of not labelling people.

I ate a red snapper, fresh and perfectly fried, last night at a fish restaurant to which I was recommended by a portly lady. I was one of three customers. León claims to be a city of intellectuals. It has never been wealthy. Meanwhile, I see from the newspaper that León's rival city, Granada, is suffering from a glut of tourism. My ex-Sandinista informant of last night claims to prefer penury to being overwhelmed with foreigners.

León, Monday 26 June

I take coffee this morning with an elderly maker of grandfather clocks. He is a fan of big band music. Heavy rain fell all last night. Trapped in my ghastly hotel, I was in bed by seven and reading a history of the Catholic kings. In Guatemala or Honduras, the electricity would have failed at the first clap of thunder. I waited for my fan to stop whirring. I foresaw sweltering through the night and being devoured by mosquitoes. To the contrary, I required a vest and pyjama trousers against the chill.

Today we enjoy a fine sunny morning. The clockmaker and I sip coffee on his patio and listen to a Glen Miller recording. The electricity fails.

Later in the morning I am interviewed for Nicaraguan TV astride my bike outside the cathedral. Directly above me stands a large stone lion. The photographer gestures that I should pull in my belly. I retort that I *am* pulling in my belly. We finish the shoot and I pump the journalist for facts.

My female informant, the ex-secretary to the Sandinista leader, claimed that workers in the tax-free zones earn a dollar a day. In fact the average wage is 120 dollars a month, sufficiently low not to require exaggeration. All employers pay health insurance and pension contributions. Some supply free housing.

I thank the journalist for having confirmed one of my favourite adages: that the politically committed are seldom committed to accuracy.

Meanwhile I have uncovered a crime committed by the United Nations. UNESCO, a UN agency, funds restoration of World Heritage sites. León competes with Granada and with Antigua, Guatemala and San Miguel de Allende, Mexico, in Spanish colonial architecture. I am delighted to find UN offices in a restored colonial building.

I enter and recoil with horror. The pillars supporting the patio terrace have been sculpted with cement to resemble the trunks of palm trees. The pillars are painted shit-brown and varnished. A kidney-shaped plunge pool is painted pale shiny chemical blue. The walls of the pool rise nearly a metre above the floor of the patio, thus destroying all sense of space. The conference area to the left is separated from the patio by moulded concrete blocks patterned with holes. The blocks are painted gloss white.

I could continue.

This evening I am trapped by a storm while sipping juice and talking with a Spanish volunteer. The fashion for volunteering commenced in Nicaragua during the romantic period immediately following the fall of the Somoza dictatorship. It continues: mostly young people from Europe helping in schools.

I have a dinner date at the home of an elderly Nicaraguan teacher whom I met in the cathedral square. I dash through the rain, only to discover that the other guests have sent their apologies and the dinner is cancelled. My host is a conservative. The storm intensifies. Rain drums on the tin roof. The teacher seats me in a rocking chair. Imprisoned by the downpour and good manners, I listen to a stream of conservative platitudes.

I have suffered such evenings in the past. Most effective is to refrain from interjecting so much as a cough lest you prolong the lecture. My host takes my silence as evidence of my opposition. No food arrives, not even a nut. I have brought a bottle of rum. The rum stands unopened on a tray. I have brought fresh limes, fresh mint. The tray is within my peripheral vision. Such cruelty.

Las Penitas and on to Granada, Tuesday 27 June

I packed last night. I was eager to leave. I wash one last time in a shower ingrained with grime, leap the pools leaking from beneath the lavatory bowl, slip into sandals to keep my feet dry of the sewage seepage. Did I describe the ceiling of moulting hardboard? The bugs? The odour of wet rot? The terrifying electrical fittings?

The information I gained from the two university students was priceless. Six and a half dollars a night for the room was outrageous overcharging. I deserve a medal for staying the course.

Breakfast at Las Penitas beach will serve as my reward.

I am out of the hellhole just after six and at the beach by seven. The sky is overcast. Beach resorts need people. They require smiling faces and an amplitude of tanned naked flesh. This is midweek, out of season, and rain has been falling much of the night. The dirt road and the beach have been dyed brown by the rain. The broad, rain-weighted leaves of the sea grape trees droop with depression. I turn right and ride one street in from the beach. The uncertainties that typify a Nicaraguan existence are evident in the quantity of buildings abandoned mid-construction. A couple of fibreglass fishing boats are hauled up the creek at the far end of the beach where palm thatch *palapas* drip.

I meet with a young British couple loading packs onto a bus outside a backpackers' haven. The kitchen is shut. Everything is shut. I ride in the opposite direction. I have a nose for the French. I believe that I could find a lone Frenchman in the Sahara. Patrick, owner of the Oasis, is easy quarry. He is dozing in a hammock. He prepares coffee that tastes of coffee. The clouds clear while we exchange life experiences. Patrick's cook produces scrambled eggs and fresh orange juice. The beach dries. Sand is transformed from brown to rich gold. Trees perk up. Abandoned plastic bottles gleam.

The rooms at the Oasis are large. You can ride a wheelchair into the bathrooms. Two bungalows are for rent. Everything is clean and orderly and practical. Surf breaks a hundred metres out from the beach. I take photographs to arouse the jealousy of my sons back home in the English rain.

I slalom potholes on the road back to León. Wet vegetation is brilliant in the sunlight. A bridge divides a small lagoon. Two men fish with a net; two others swim and splash in the muddy water, maybe driving prey. The men are laughing. They wave as I pass. I stop to ask whether they are fishing for fish or prawns.

'Prawns. Big ones,' one of the men shouts, spreading his hands.

The men are having a ball.

So am I.

A chain of volcanoes runs the length of Nicaragua. Volcanoes explode. Earthquakes are frequent. You would expect Nicaraguans to be jumpy. They seem very much at ease. Two good roads lead from León to the capital, Managua. The northern road runs beside the smaller of the country's two vast lakes and is less busy. Wood-fired brick kilns worked by soot-blackened men are as sixteenth-century as the early churches of León – although less beautiful.

I avoid capitals. They are noisy, polluted and often dangerous. Helpful drivers point me onto the road through to Granada. Granada has a reputation as a party town for travellers. The city is perfectly sited on the shores of the largest lake in Central America. The architecture charms aficionados of Hispanic colonial architecture and many foreigners are buying property. The central square is magnificent. So is the cathedral. I book into a hotel recommended by Frenchman Patrick. I have a double room with a fan and a good-sized bathroom. The electricity is off in this segment of town. It is on in the centre. Parking in the cathedral square, I find an air-conditioned internet café. A tornado hits the square while I write. Tiles off a hotel roof lie scattered in the gutter and on the roofs of parked cars. The Honda is blown over but is unharmed.

Electricity is back on at the hotel. I shower and chat with the German owner before riding down to the lake, where the hotels are in darkness along the waterfront. Later I find a *comedor* near the hotel. I have a beer, steak, white rice and black beans, fried bananas, cabbage salad and banana chips. The food is good. Lights go out while I eat, bringing back memories of Cuba. Back at the hotel I chat more with the owner until the electricity returns. This is a daily occurrence – a great boost for tourism – although many of the North American residents are too old and spaced out to know whether the lights are on or off. A front-page scare story in the local English-language newspaper warns: SEX TOURISM IN GRANADA. Even a sexual thought would put these oldies in an ambulance.

I lie in bed and watch a rerun of the France–Spain match. One goal each is the score when I switch off the TV. I learn later that the match ended with two great goals by the French. That's the way life goes.

Granada, Wednesday 28 June

Granada is a mad house. An elderly North American beckons me onto the terrace of his small house for coffee. He has forgotten to fit his false teeth and is difficult to understand. He is one of twins, so he recounts. His mother and twin brother died in childbirth through the incompetence of his grandfather, a doctor with cataracts.

The American rediscovered his mother on a coffee *finca* in Costa Rica six years back. She has been reborn as a coffee picker. He shows photographs and relates a series of dates that prove that one of his reincarnated mother's children is his reincarnated twin brother. The dates and maths confuse me. The American seems confused as to which of two smouldering cigarettes he should smoke. He holds one in each hand and waves them in emphasis of the crucial proofs in his family history. One cigarette is tobacco; the other is herbal.

I escape and sit at a pavement café off the square and sip papaya juice. A threesome occupies the next table: two European women in early middle-age are dressed in expensive casuals; their companion is a handsome Nicaraguan some years younger. One of the women has bought an island. She complains at having overrun her budget in building a house on the island. She is off to London and Sydney to buy two further properties. The property market in London is already high and she has little expectation of a profit. She has high hopes of the Australian investment.

An old lady with badly bowed legs hobbles by and asks for alms. The handsome Nicaraguan man tells the old woman that they have no money. The old woman shuffles on.

I apologise for interrupting. Curiosity impels me to enquire what sort of island the woman owns: eight acres with palms and perfect beaches off Nicaragua's Caribbean coast.

Granada, Thursday 29 June

School students attend a sung High Mass today at the cathedral. The girls parade after Mass, marching back to school to the beat of drums. Stick whirlers lead the parade. Next come marching girls waving red plastic pompoms. The stick whirlers wear gold miniskirts; the pompom girls wear red. A conservative pope reigns in the Vatican. I wonder what his views are regarding miniskirts.

My own views are practical: condoms are a sound investment.

I chat at a pavement café with a Texan my age who lives in Granada. He invites me to his home. The invitation is for tea or perhaps a drink. I have been on the road two months. I need sprucing. A corner beauty parlour displays an impressive pyramid of diplomas. With luck, one of the diplomas is for returning youth to old faces.

The Texan and his British wife have resurrected a dream house near the cathedral, Spanish colonial and two patios deep. They have built a second floor above the centre section that separates the two patios. The raised floor is not visible from the street; nor does it overlook the neighbours. It is supported on earthquake-proof pillars to protect the original adobe walls of the ground floor. One side is open. The view is perfect across ancient pan-tiled roofs to the massive cloud-wrapped volcano that dominates Granada. A vast unglazed window faces the opposite way and collects the breeze in proof that a well-designed space has need for neither air-conditioning nor fans. A pool fills the rear patio; the front patio is jungle garden. The floors are baked clay. Furniture is sparse and simple. Conversation is warm, beer is cold. We dine on a delicious stir-fry. Perfection.

I discover that my host began his adult life as a respectable and successful Texan businessman. A romantic failing made him buy his siblings' shares of the family ranch. Worse was to come. Aged fifty, he discovered hot-air ballooning. He learnt to pilot balloons, gained a licence, sold up his business and spent ten years living and flying professionally in the heart of Kenya's Masai reserve. Recently he paddled a canoe down the San Juan River from Lake Nicaragua to the Caribbean.

His property taxes back in Texas have quadrupled. The greatest increase is in schooling for children of illegal Latino immigrants. My host's objection is to the woeful education rather than the taxes. Educate children successfully and they will be a credit to their communities and to the USA. Educating them badly is both immoral and a sure route to future social problems.

As for politics, he has a deep contempt for the entire Bush family. He has known them all his life.

Granada, Friday 30 June

You have met the toothless American with two cigarettes and a reincarnated mother. Meet another of Granada's happy hunters. This one I invited out for dinner. Serial killers are hot news on the media. This is a serial non-killer. She has attempted to commit suicide on three occasions and twice tried to murder her lover.

One failure in self-killing, OK. Next try, you climb a few extra floors before jumping out the window or find a taller building. As to murdering her lover, how difficult can that be? They shared a bed. Didn't she store a baseball bat in the umbrella stand? I would understand if she were a vegetarian and shocked by blood. However, she wolfs down half a barbecued chicken while relating that she has been saved by meditation, alternative medicine and studying the works of Carlos Castenedes.

Carlos Castenedes is the macrobiotic brown-rice sixties, marijuana, peyote, mescaline, LSD and spiritual enlightenment through reading *Zen and the Art of Motorcycle Maintenance* (I have the Honda serviced at Honda agencies).

As to meditation, she is messing up on the dose. She is fine and calm and interesting through the chicken course. Then she insists that we walk a few blocks in search of carrot cake. The meditation medication runs low on the walk. She suffers a metamorphosis from church mouse to F this and F that to the accompaniment of a shrill giggle.

Pray God she doesn't have a baseball bat handy.

Not that I have any intention or desire to share her bed – but we are guests at the same hotel.

Sticking with crazies, did I mention having dinner in a Granada *comedor* with an Australian tax lawyer, mid-forties? Free biking is his insanity, riding down mountains and over mini-precipices. My youngest son, Jed, would understand. Maybe it's a cure for boredom. If so, it is a little extreme.

Granada and onward, Saturday 1 July

Saturday morning, I watch the England–Portugal football match at a corner bar with a big-screen TV. The bar is the local hangout for US citizens resident in Nicaragua to drink cheaply and get laid. I sit at the bar. A girl with silver nails and vaguely bleached hair sits at a table beside a North American in his fifties. She looks fifteen. The man comes to the bar. The girl is his trophy and he shows the girl's ID to the man sitting beside me. The ID records that she is nineteen. The ID may be the girl's and it may be authentic. He sits back down beside her. She leans a little away from him as he strokes her arm. Later he returns to the bar for a fresh beer. Midday and his eyes are already marginally out of focus. The girl looks around. Anyone can read her thoughts: 'I'll be in bed with that drunk soon. Yuk!'

This is one couple. There are others much the same, together with the standard solitary drunks who have failed at AA. North Americans yell for England. The few Latinos identify with Portugal; most are uncertain as to exactly where Portugal is.

A ride along the lake across rich green ranch land studded with big trees is a fine way to clear your head. The turn to San Juan is thirty kilometres short of the Costa Rica frontier on the Pan-American Highway. The approach to the beach town is through country spread with giant green molehills tufted with small trees. Hills ring a small wooden stadium. People stream in off the road. A cop tells me that the town is holding a rodeo. I pay for a shade seat on the upper terrace. A brass-and-drum band blasts a Latin American version of circus yah-yah music. Hawkers shout their wares: ice-cream, sodas, cashews, banana chips, chitterlings, barbecue meat.

A brass-band clarion heralds the launch from a chute of a bull calf with rider. The calf bucks a few times, becomes bored. Granada was an aberration. I am back where I want to be, back in Central America.

I sit in San Juan at an open-air waterfront bar with a retired dealer in truck parts from Pittsburgh. The bar is the least pretentious on the bay. The owner, a woman in her sixties, owned half the hill that forms the right hook of the bay. She and her family sold the hill for a ridiculously small sum some years back. They had no concept of its worth. Now big houses dot the hill.

The American is angered that developers took advantage of a nice woman and her family. He has invested in a couple of fishing launches that her sons run. Fishing has been poor the past weeks. The American is considering opening a furniture store in partnership with the woman. They are not in a relationship. The woman is merely someone the American likes and admires. He is bored being idle and enjoys being part of a community. He drinks Bacardi Breezers; I drink a beer; we eat prawns in chilli. Breeze blows off the sea. The moon does its thing, as do the stars. Nothing special happens – a pleasant evening and so to bed.

I have found an air-conditioned room mid-block back from the beach in an old hotel built of wood and with a tin roof. The room opens off the first-floor terrace. The bathroom works. Sheets are clean. The mattress merely sags a little. I have been away from such places a while and have forgotten coconut rats. San Juan rats are in training for the relay races at the rat Olympics. Morning training commences shortly before five. First the athlete rats sprint up and down the ceiling. Soon the rat coaches get in on the act with their shrieks and chittering.

Better get out of bed, shower and head for Costa Rica.

Costa Rica

To the Nicoya Peninsula, Sunday 2 July

The frontier posts on the Pan-American Highway are big and busy. Leaving Nicaragua is slow rather than difficult. Costa Rica is good-natured, although definitely slow. I carry photocopies of everything from the size of my belly button to the circumference of my ears. I meet a young Argentinian driving a white Dodge semi-sports car home. The Argentinian is less experienced. He knows neither the registration number of the Dodge engine nor where to find it. I enter customs behind him. He overtakes me on the highway some three-quarters of an hour later. Perhaps we will meet again, possibly in Panama.

I see no hovels as I speed down the Pan-American Highway. I note less refuse on the verge than in other Central American countries. The land is more cared for, big trees are left standing to protect the soil. And, yes, there is a feel more of organisation than of chaos. I turn south at Liberia towards the international airport. Miles of US-type hoardings advertise car hire and real estate. What is unreal estate?

A hardtop road leads to Samana – according to my four-year-old guidebook, a quaint little village on a safe beach. The village has become a resort and is crowded with Sunday coach trippers. More signs for real estate, for condominiums. The signs are in English. I take the coastal road down the Nicoya Peninsula. The road is dirt but good dirt. This is hill country, green and beautiful. White Brahmin cows graze paddocks. White walls and white entrance gates wall off the coast. Apparently condos in Costa Rica are vast gated communities as opposed to apartment blocks.

The dirt road twists between steep hills. Sunday afternoon and each village is in mid-football match. Beer is drunk in vast quantities. I stop for water and the barman insists on buying me cola. The cola has a strong taste of rum. A man chants rapidly into a mike round the back of the bar. His accent is strong. I catch a few numbers. Psalms? Verses from the Bible? And threats that this is the audience's last chance, absolutely the last chance! That much I understand. Then more numbers.

I presume an evangelist preacher is denouncing the twin evils of football and inebriation.

I ride round the corner into a cattle auction.

The sun is setting. I have been riding for twelve hours and have reached that point of fatigue where making decisions becomes almost impossible. I spot a boutique hotel (so advertised) at an intersection. Boutique hotels make my wallet flinch.

I take the other road. It leads downhill. A second road bears a sign to a beach. I hear a bike behind me. I brake and turn to ask the driver's advice on where I can find a comfortable and affordable bed. In that one moment of inattention the Honda slips. I lie beneath the Honda. The leather gaiter saves my leg from frying. One mirror is smashed.

Two men on the following bike lift the Honda free. A shard of mirror has sliced my right hand.

The bike riders insist I return to the boutique hotel for first-aid. One rides my bike; I sit pillion behind the other. The wound is washed. Blood spurts. A Costa Rican family in a Land Rover are newly arrived guests. The husband, an investment banker, drives me to the village of San Francisco Coyote. The owner of a local restaurant telephones the doctor. I wait in the restaurant and watch Al Pacino on TV in a gangster movie. Doctor and wife arrive. The wife wears a mini-miniskirt. Owners, staff and clientele of the restaurant watch while I am injected, scrubbed and sewn. I bleed more copiously than the actors in the movie. The audience is mine.

The doctor scrubs my wounds with the energy of a cleaning woman scrubbing a dirty bath.

I don't like to watch.

Where else to look?

Look up and I confront an audience as eager for gore as aficionados at a bullfight.

Look down and I confront the delightful thighs of the doctor's wife. The doctor may be enraged.

Such are the dilemmas of the walking wounded.

I have eleven stitches in my hand. I have lost blood. I need a comfortable bed. And I must grab the opportunity to talk with a Costa Rican in the upper echelons of the country's professional classes. The bikers have brought my bike to the village and parked it behind the general store. A villager gives me a lift in his pickup to the boutique hotel. The banker family are the only guests. Orchids abound. Quiet is an understatement. Imagine a non-denominational chapel in an upmarket funeral parlour.

The manageress is from the Philippines. Her accent is familiar to me from past travels in Asia, as is the gentleness in her voice and the soft uh-huh of agreement with which she answers my arguments. I negotiate the room rate down from 120 dollars to eighty. Breakfast is included. So is an acre of stone floor, an emperor-sized bed and a bathroom for sybarites.

I don't eat dinner. The banker and his wife join me in the lounge once their children are in bed. They have worked in London, which they loved (or they are polite), and in Miami, which they hated for the domination of the new-rich Cubans whom they found ostentatious and vulgar. The banker visits Cuba regularly on business – bearable, he says, for three or four days. He can pretend he is a tourist and ignore the reality that Cubans suffer: poverty, lack of freedom.

The rash of condominiums on the peninsula is another hate. Prices will double once the coast road is tarred (paid for by the Costa Rican taxpayer). Already Costa Ricans, even of their financial bracket, are priced out of the market in their own country. They have been forced to reassess their view of themselves. Costa Ricans had considered themselves different from other Latin Americans, more advanced, more cultured, more organised, more on a par with the United States with whom they were natural allies.

Only a few years ago they would have identified with the US team in the World Cup, and yet now the banker's friends celebrated when the US was eliminated.

The Iraq war has changed their perceptions of the United States (I quote the banker). Access to satellite TV has forced open their eyes. They watch bombs and shells fall. They watch American soldiers abusing Arabs. The US did the same in Panama, killed hundreds in the desire to grab one man. The lives of Arabs and Latin Americans are of no importance.

What I write will be offensive and hurtful to my daughter and to my American friends. Should I act as censor or write what I am told?

Or am I goaded by guilt at having remained silent at the Dallas breakfast?

Thunder smashes me awake. Disoriented, I lie shivering with cold. Lightning shows a picture window, terrace, trees bent under a silver downpour. The cold is air-conditioning. I stagger to the windows and out to the room's private terrace. I arrived after nightfall and am unprepared for my surroundings. The hotel is on a ridge. Lightning displays black waters of a river below the terrace. An animal shrieks. Thunder shakes the terrace. Trees quake beneath a squall. Fresh sheets of lightning appear to dazzle, and I see, through the rain, surf break across the mouth of the river. This is a Conrad vision. I creep back to bed and curl into a foetal ball beneath the goose-down duvet.

San Francisco Coyote, Monday 3 July

The curtains are open to the terrace. I wake at dawn. My watch broke in yesterday's fall. No matter, this is too beautiful a time and place for bed. I tiptoe out to the pool terrace and see the river clearly for the first time, waters brown in spate. Two curls of chocolate sand mark the corners of its mouth. Palm trees hide the beach. I sit alone by the pool and watch surf break, three white lines. A howler monkey hollers back in the trees. Birds chatter noisily. The tide shifts a flock of pelicans off the sand. Clumsy on the ground, they are wonderfully graceful as they glide upriver into the trees. I watch a pale-yellow butterfly. Workers arrive to mend storm damage, to collect broken branches. They work in silence. The Filipina manager presents me with a steaming mug of black coffee. I have been up an hour. It is six o'clock.

The hotel and the doctor have absorbed my cash. I don't carry credit cards. I require a bank and an ATM.

The hotel is on a vast ranch owned by an American billionaire. He has owned the ranch for thirty years. He flies in from his home in Hawaii on his private jet each month for a few days. The hotel is a recent hobby (its losses are tax-deductible).

The river is high after the storm. The farm manager drives me by pickup to the river ford. I cross the footbridge and walk two kilometres to the village of San Francisco Coyote. I find a mechanic to overhaul the bike. He directs me to a parts shop, where I find replacement mirrors – genuine Honda parts in a community served by two general stores and a kiosk selling cheap jeans and T-shirts.

The nearest bank is in the town of Jicaral, thirty-three kilometres down a dirt road. The bus journey takes two hours.

The doctor instructed me to rest my hand for three days – no riding the bike. I am settled into a cabin behind one of the two general stores in the village of San Francisco Coyote. I have a bathroom and a fan. The shower works. The bed is comfortable.

Two Costa Rican businessmen and their families occupy the remaining three cabins for the night. The men are brothers. They are accustomed to greater luxury. They complain that they were double-booked into a rental home in one of the condominiums for the first night of the school vacation.

A Dutchman with a development on a hillside beyond the boutique hotel has ridden my bags over from the hotel on his quad-bike. Bush telegraph alerted him to my accident and he drops by the general store to check who I am and whether I am OK.

I eat an early dinner after the near three-hour ride back from visiting the bank in Jicaral town in a retired US school bus. I order steak and am faced with two thick chunks of meat each the size of my shoe soles: salad, fries, fried bananas, two beers. Four dollars is not excessive. The restaurant belongs to the storekeeper.

A terrace at the front of the store shades a bar and four teak tables and benches. I sit after dinner with the storekeeper and a twenty-something university graduate. The storekeeper talks philosophy. What is the route to happiness? Do I believe in a god, an afterlife? Would I prefer coffee or another beer?

'Black coffee would be just fine,' I say.

I also say that I would prefer a night in his cabins than a week preparing for death in the funeral parlour atmosphere of the boutique hotel.

I talk with the two brothers of the holidaying family over breakfast. The elder brother complains of foreigners owning all the best land in Costa Rica. Neither brother cares much for foreigners. Foreigners corrupt Costa Rican society. They breed prostitution and spread their drug culture. The elder brother is a fan of the Somoza years.

'There was no crime,' he tells me (not mentioning that the Somozas and their cronies stole the entire country and murdered anyone who argued). 'The roads were properly maintained,' he states. 'Under Somoza, we had thousands of road workers. There was work for everyone.'

He is also a fan of Castro. 'There's no crime in Cuba.'

Unless depriving a people of their freedom is a crime.

Clearly his father was of the privileged class in the years of the dictatorship.

I am here to report, not to argue. I nod politely.

Village life is fun (for me). I watch the comings and goings from a bench outside the store. The under-forties are on wheels, two or four, and mostly motorised. The elders are on horseback. A reasonable horse costs eighty dollars. Add saddle and bridle and you are mobile for 150 dollars. Fuel grows on the roadside.

Most have heard of my accident. I field a stream of enquiries as to how I am and whether it is true that I intend riding to Argentina. A trio from a turtle-protection group drop by to chat. One is from Mexico.

They collect eggs and take them to a hatchery. They launch the baby turtles into the sea. Shrimp boats work a mile offshore. Shrimping is the preserve of the Taiwanese. The shrimp nets sweep up the baby turtles along with the shrimps and about everything else.

A public telephone is attached to a post at the intersection outside the general store. The female half of a pair of young blond foreign lovers talks at length. The male half hovers. She retreats to the tree that shades the post – seeking a privacy of which he is nervous.

Two tin placards are nailed to the fence posts. The notice on the left advertises LA NACIÓN SE VENDE AQUI – *The Nation* (a newspaper) for sale here. The second placard advertises Coca-Cola. The coincidence of the juxtaposition amuses me.

A plump young woman in tight short shorts and a stretched pink top that almost covers the bits she wants covered is a pinball addict. She rides up every half-hour or so on a pushbike to play the left-hand machine of the two in the bar area of the store.

The Dutchman arrives on his quad bike. The storekeeper's wife invites us to lunch in the kitchen – delicious vegetables of which I recognise baby okra and green beans.

The Dutchman drives me over to see his property. The land stretches up a hillside. The top section is reserved for wildlife. The lower slope is divided into one-hectare lots. Most of those he and his partners wish to sell are already sold. The rate around here is eight dollars a square metre and you can have a good three-bed, two-bath house built for 50 000 dollars.

The houses are set well back among trees on the Dutchman's land and are invisible from the road. The Dutchman has lived here for the past fifteen years and tends the houses and oversees new construction. We drive down to his neighbourhood restaurant a hundred metres up the road from Coyote beach. The beach is four kilometres long and is divided by the river. At low tide, you can wade across the mouth of the river. There are no buildings on the beach.

We each eat a fried snapper caught that day and drink a few beers. Six to be exact.

The benches outside the store are a fine place for chat. My companion this evening is an economics student in his final semester. He is a fan of the Red Hot Chilli Peppers. He and his sister are students at the country's premier state university. Away from home, they rent an apartment for 200 dollars a month. Their parents are comfortable financially. Poorer kids share a room or a cupboard. Even this sacrifice is well beyond most budgets.

The student is responsible for his younger sister – difficult on occasion. He and his friends take little interest in politics. National politics are too corrupt. Two ex-presidents are in jail. He is angered by the sale of Costa Rica's coasts to foreigners. As for foreign affairs, Costa Rica is little more than a US colony. The US does what it likes in Central America. Look what it did in Panama. And what it is doing in Iraq. The US invasions of Iraq and of Panama are the same, except in scale.

On to San José, Wednesday 5 July

Guidebooks warn of the usual dangers to be encountered in San José, capital of Costa Rica: robbery, rape, pillage. San Francisco Coyote was a pleasure. I leave with regret. We had heavy rain in the night. The dirt road across the Nicoya Peninsula is slippery. I wear leather work gloves bought at the hardware store in Jicaral and I pay great attention to the road. The final few kilometres along the coast to the ferry are cratered hardtop. I stop at a café on the hill down to the ferry terminal. I rest my butt on a comfortable chair and prepare for a peaceful breakfast and a cup of good coffee. All hell breaks loose. Hells Angels! Or a wild bunch of late-thirties reliving their adolescence. They come armed with trail bikes. They work the throttles, *brrrrm, brrrrm* ...

They are connected through college or work or accident. Most are from the States, although one is a Brit, one from Peru and one a Nicaraguan with whom I talk on the ninety-minute ferry crossing.

The Nicaraguan's field is telecommunications. He was based for twelve years in the US and travelled widely for his employers – Africa, Latin America, Europe. Marriage and two small children persuaded him to give up the travelling. Back home in Nicaragua he has his own business in telecommunications. He is a pro and doing well. He is nervous of the coming elections. Political memory has a ten-year lifespan. The electorate have forgotten the misery they suffered under the Sandinistas. They will forget or forgive the thievery and corruption of Ortega. Many will vote for the anti-American Ortega as a snub to the despised Bush. Others will believe the socialist dream. Nicaragua will suffer a new period of chaos and economic ruin.

He talks bitterly of Europeans falling for the romantic image of the Sandinistas, of deliberately ignoring the truth.

In reporting his beliefs, I will earn the ire of many broadly to the left of the political divide. My reports of those critical of the US will have earned the ire of those on the right. All in all, I am doing well ...

I ride up over mountains to San José through coffee plantations and past suburban mansions with trim lawns and big gates. The gates of the wealthy are less guarded than in other Central American countries.

I am nervous of riding in capital cities and seek a hotel on the outskirts. I have been warned by ex-pats in Nicaragua that San José is unsafe. I stop at the roadside to enquire of locals. They tell me 'Nonsense!' and advise that hotels in the city centre are cheaper and there is more choice.

I consult my guidebook and decide that, for once, I should experience a backpackers' hangout. The city is easy to navigate. The hostel is on Avenida 6. I request directions only twice. A tiny room with a fan and a window to a corridor sets me back twenty-two dollars. This is an English-speaking haven – even the few French are attempting English. I sit in the caféteria with a young English woman, arrived this evening from the UK. She is a conservationist and will work for six weeks on the Caribbean coast as a volunteer before flying to Peru to join a tour of the Inca Trail and so on down across the salt lakes of Bolivia, Chile and the Argentine, to where?

Where would any sensible English woman head?

Tierra del Fuego!

We check our emails and head to our respective beds.

A birthday party is under way at the small swimming pool in the central patio. Most of the celebrants are Brits. Latins, and we would hear music, a few good voices. With these Brits, simply being noisy appears a high priority.

To the Caribbean, Thursday 6 July

I rise at dawn and discover girls curled in armchairs and on benches. I write that they are girls because they seem too young to be described as women and I worry that 'lasses' is too old-fashioned a word even for this old fogey.

The noise has gone out of them, the group spirit has evaporated. Isolated one from another, they appear very young and pale and vulnerable and waif-like. A boy and a girl are in the pool fishing for pieces of a smashed wine glass. The boy has found a mug broken in two. A wet packet of cigarettes lies on a table. Two of the cigarettes have rolled onto the wet tiles.

I overhear the girl say, 'It was probably my fucking fault.'

The word seems particularly ugly at this hour, almost desperate, and I wish that comforting her was possible.

They leave the pool while I surrender my key and retrieve my deposit. I pass the pool on my way to pack the Honda in the rear courtyard. The kids have left the two cigarettes on the tiles. I pick them up. They melt in my palm while I seek a bin.

I wear two shirts and my windcheater for the ride up over the mountains this morning. Slopes are swathed in netting. Something called *belecho* grows beneath the netting – a new word.

I stop for breakfast at a proper roadhouse with a spectacular view. I have time to drink one mug of coffee before the Christians arrive. They refer to themselves as a family and travel in three Toyota Coasters. They belong to a church in Detroit and have been on a mission trip here in Costa Rica and now are enjoying well-earned R&R. Most are in their late teens. They are accompanied by an interpreter and I learn that *belecho* is a fern – exports to garden centres.

An adult woman and two teens join me at a window table. I recount discovering the English martyrs, familiars of my childhood, memorialised on the chapel wall in Oaxaca. The teen daughter asks what I write. I reply that I write about people acting under pressure. I suggest that church education prepares us to resist pressure (I am doing well).

I mention a simile I care for: that we are born on the platform of a child's slide; once we put our foot on the slide, how far we slip is a matter of chance (I am still doing well); there is no fundamental difference between Eichmann and the person who merely makes anti-Semitic remarks (not so good – not good at all).

I am unfamiliar with the religious sects of the United States. I forget that many hold curious and, to Europeans, unpleasant views on those they refer to as 'those Jewish people'.

The lady excuses herself. She has matters to attend to. Her children follow. To my left, a volcano wears a cap and shawl.

The highway twists down through the mountains towards the Caribbean. Roadwork backs up the traffic for a couple of kilometres. I creep past the queue. A worker holding a red flag asks where I am going. I tell him. He waves me through and tells me, 'Good luck, old man, and take care.'

So many people have wished me luck, people imprisoned by lives of constant struggle; people who have never sampled liberty of choice in what they do: *La lucha, la lucha*. Along comes a fat old man on a small bike and they dream for a moment. If the old man can, then maybe, maybe some day, just maybe ...

And I, as I ride on, am immensely grateful and proud – proud that I am, if only for a moment, part of a dream. Failure would be to betray all those well-wishers.

I reach the littoral. Central America is coffee, sugar and bananas. This is banana country, warm and humid. A straight road with broad grass verges trimmed and planted with bougainvillea divides endless rows of banana trees. A pale-blue plastic sack protects each bunch of bananas. An image arises of movie cold stores where Mafia hoodlums hang corpses among the beef carcasses.

I stop for coffee and a bottle of cold water at a roadside stall and pack away the two shirts and windcheater. The next turn on the left leads to the offices of the second-biggest independent banana plantation. Dole (US) is the biggest independent. So much I learn after an hour's wait to meet with the plantation manager. He manages 4000 hectares. Count the packing sheds, maintenance workshops, drivers and office staff, and the plantation employs over 300 people.

The offices are neat and freshly painted, clipped hedges border the drive. Obsessive, I notice a loose light fitting.

A further forty kilometres brings me to Puerto Limón. I treat myself to a fine room on the second floor at the Hotel Miami: air-con, hot water, cable TV. The internet café round the corner has air-con; connecting the laptop is easy and I download a week's photographs from my camera. Work done, I walk the streets.

I am trespassing on the grave of the United Fruit Company. Puerto Limón was once a Company town. At the Hotel Miami, a photograph (circa 1902) of United Fruit's weatherboard headquarters shares wall space with two photographs of banana boats of the same period loading alongside United Fruit's wharf.

In those days, Limón had the same by-laws as Morales in Guatemala. Native locals were obliged to step off the pavement when encountering a white Company official.

Limón's waterfront is a relic of regal glory. I stroll at night along the pavement below the seawall. Loving couples share the wall with family groups. I pass a clump of oldies trying to recall their recollections. Five kids kicking a ball give me a 'Hi!' and a grin. Five elderly men are recording a local radio programme at a table in the town's smartest hotel. I sit at the bar, drink a beer, chat with the manageress. A designer enters to show the manageress the logo for this year's October carnival – a mundane young gnome. I dine at a Chinese restaurant on wonton soup.

Limón, Friday 7 July

Today is a day of rest. I sleep late and rise to a view from my window of the Caribbean – not the Caribbean Sea, but a Caribbean population. In riding south through Central America, I haven't been aware of race. People were Honduran or Nicaraguan or Costa Rican. Although some were a little darker or a little paler of skin, there was no discernible division. Now I dress and cross the street for breakfast at a Latino-owned *comedor*. The two women who take my dirty laundry under a steel grill are palely Caucasian. I have run out of business cards; the printers are Afro-Caribbean women. An Afro-Caribbean bootblack polishes my shoes. I note that truck drivers are mostly Latino. Latinos run small stores, small businesses and restaurants. Owners of the few big stores and businesses are Chinese, Lebanese or Syrian. Street sweepers are black, as are the drivers of the swankiest cars.

To Almirante

The littoral, Saturday 8 July

At first the road to Panama follows the coast. Even the shanty towns of Costa Rica's capital looked cared for. Here, on the Caribbean littoral, wooden houses rot unpainted among the palm trees: evidence of poverty or of neglect?

The road swings inland. Puffs of smoky cloud spill from pockets in the mountains bordering the banana plantations. A river divides Costa Rica from Panama. Waiting in line at Costa Rican immigration takes a few minutes. I am alone at customs. Panama is the far end of a Chiquita Banana Company railway bridge. Loose and uneven planks lie end to end across the sleepers each side of the rails. Rain has been spitting and the planks are as slippery as a greased pole. I edge across in first gear, one foot on the rail, one on the planks.

Two truck drivers wait at the customs window in Panama. I tell them of my fear. They warn me of a second bridge on the road to Almirante; the second bridge is in worse condition and three times as long. Cars have crashed. For bikes it is very dangerous. Many people have fallen. Recently an American broke his arm. A German broke a leg.

Jungle cloaks the mountains. Rain spits from a charcoal sky. The river is in flood. The Bridge of the Americas scares me. It is a railway bridge approximately 200 metres long. The flat base is supported by concrete piles and runs within a tunnel of box girders. Road transport drives on loose planks laid either side of the train rails. The planks are uneven and slippery. Many are missing. Twisted guardrails warn of past misadventures, and much of the safety netting has been ripped away. A bigger bike than the Honda would slide through the gaps. The fall? Fifty feet.

The traffic lights show red. I wait astride the Honda and cringe as the planks lift and clatter beneath approaching trucks. My spectacles fog and my nose drips. The lights change to green. An impatient driver honks his klaxon. Walking the bike would delay him – and he would suppose me a coward. I ride twenty yards before the front tyre slips in a gap between two planks. Desperate to save the Honda, I tip inwards across the rails and sprawl beneath the bike. I look down between the railway sleepers at muddy foam. Drivers pound down the track and heave the Honda off my leg. They warn me that the bridge is dangerous – as if I require warning. They lift me on to my feet and the bike into the back of a truck. I sit up front in the truck with a young driver.

Almirante is a further fifteen kilometres. The sky clears. A good tarred road twists between forested hills. The sky has cleared and sunlight streaks the canopy. The mountains of the great divide tower above the hills. Beyond lies the Pacific Ocean. The driver warns that the mountain road is dangerous, that my small Honda lacks power for the ascent. He warns of hairpin bends and of precipices and of the many truck drivers who delight in squeezing a biker off the road. He warns of thieves in the mountains and that there are no farms or houses. I can expect no help if I fall.

I catch glimpses, between the hills, of the Gulf of Bocas del Toro. The waters are deep blue and spread with islands, some lightened with pale crescents of sand. The truck is new and the seat is as comfortable as the armchair back home in my study. The stitches in my right hand itch. My left shoulder, thigh and knee ache from the tumble. I imagine how pleasant it would be to end this idiotic journey and sit on a beach drinking piña coladas. A reality check reminds me that I find beaches boring and piña coladas sickly sweet. So much for fantasy.

The driver tells me that Almirante has seen better days. Once it was the capital of the United Fruit Company's empire. Railway lines to the docks carve the town in two. Main Street is mud and ruts. Paint peels and flakes from the weatherboard buildings. Tin roofs crumble with rust.

The driver warns that few tourists stay in Almirante. Tourists take the ferry directly to the Gulf island resorts of Bocas del Toro. The driver knows of only one hotel. My heart sinks as we approach the Pension del Station. The first-floor balcony droops. The walls sag. A guest sneezes and the entire hotel will collapse.

My saviour has a delivery to make to the biggest store in town. The storeowner recommends a new hotel across the road run by a friendly mother–daughter partnership, the Hotel Puerto del Almirante. Rooms are on the first floor above the storekeeper's warehouse: twenty-five dollars with bath, TV and air-con. I protest to the daughter that I am a pensioner. She halves the rate. The room is large, the double bed is comfortable, the bathroom functions, the air-con is silent perfection. An added comfort is the pedestal fan aimed at the bed to keep intruding mosquitoes at bay. The daughter apologises: the TV isn't cable.

I dump my gear and buy a couple of cold sodas to share with the truck driver. His home is in Panama City. He and his wife have three children. The eldest, a boy, is six. The driver earns 420 dollars a month and works a seventy-hour week.

How to reward a Good Samaritan without giving offence? I finger my billfold, slip out a twenty-dollar note.

The driver understands my embarrassment. He says, 'Please, old man, there is no need. You are a guest. We are friends.'

A second trucker, witness of my fall, drops by. We sit on a garden wall in the shade and chat of family and the days the drivers are away from home and why an old man chooses to ride from Mexico to Tierra del Fuego. Both drivers warn me of Colombia. Colombia is truly dangerous. For certain, I will be kidnapped – or shot by bandits. Colombian bandits murder travellers for a few dollars.

Neither driver has visited Colombia.

The mother of the hotel partnership directs me to a restaurant round the corner. The restaurant is closed. I find a Chinese alternative on the next block. A dozen Filipinos off a banana boat screech encouragement as they watch a TV championship fight between a Filipino boxer and a North American. Half a dozen local girls at the same table fight for the sailors' attention. I choose the corner table furthest from the TV and sit with my back to the wall. A skinny Chinese cook takes my order of shrimp-fried rice and a cold beer. A permanent scowl suggests that the cook hates mankind and probably spits in the food. The beer comes with a grease-smudged tumbler. I drink from the bottle.

The Polish chief engineer off the banana boat invites himself to join me. He is a six-foot-two time-bomb with a short fuse, red face, grey-blue eyes, grey hair en brosse. A pot belly bursts a short-sleeved Hawaiian shirt; baggy blue shorts have been through the wash a few hundred times; a strap is missing from his right sandal. He is drunk and mistakes shouting at me for conversation. Much of his shouting concerns deck officers: all deck officers are idiots. A second subject is racism. Foreigners (non-Polish) believe all Polish people are racists and idiots.

'Not so,' the chief insists.

As proof that he is not a racist, the chief cites his recent promotion of a Filipino to assistant chief engineer.

'They love me,' insists the Polish engineer of the Filipinos and shouts for more beer. 'I am their king. Of course they love me.'

I keep silent. Silence is advisable when closeted with a bomb. Even indicating agreement with a weak smile could be dangerous.

The chief bellows for the newly promoted Filipino engineer to come pay homage – which he does, a quiet man, well-mannered, wearing round, wire-rimmed spectacles, chinos, a crisply ironed white shirt. The chief parades him as he would a prize dog, then dismisses him and returns to his criticism of deck officers.

'Tomorrow, I show you ship. You see I speak true. All deck officers fucking idiots.'

I swear to visit the ship. The skinny Chinese people-hater shoves a bowl of rice and what might be shrimp on the table. I wonder whether the small black objects in the rice are seeds or rat droppings.

Retreat might be possible. 'Forgive me,' I murmur. 'I don't feel too well.'

A pale street lamp lights a male group seated on a low wall outside a general store. Most are Afro-Caribbean, smokers and sucking on beer bottles. Conversation dies as I enter the store. Antipathy for a stranger? I buy a pack of biscuits and retire to the hotel.

The hotel floors are polished wood. I carry my shoes up the stairs to the first-floor balcony. Arc lights at the docks glow beyond the roofs of the bungalows. The Polish engineer's ship is loading and an incessant whine of winches comes from the banana wharf. A truck rattles as it crosses the railway lines. Moonlight glistens on the bay. Fishermen's lanterns speckle the sea. So to bed between fresh clean sheets. Panama marks the end of Central America. I have survived. I feel moderately proud and good about myself.

Almirante, Sunday 9 July

Yesterday, on the road from Limón, I bought new batteries for my camera at a small roadside store. The batteries must have been old or stale (if batteries go stale). They were flat when I reached that awful bridge. I am out of bed by half past five this morning and bike back with fresh batteries loaded. I photograph the bridge, and then stop for breakfast at a truckers' café midway between the bridge and Almirante. The café is built on a ridge overlooking the highway. It is not much of a place. The floor is cement, as is the kitchen counter. Wooden posts support a thatch roof. A couple of hammocks hang from hooks. The upright chairs are old and have carved leather backs. Sit at one of the four tables and you look down over rich jungle to the island-spotted gulf of Bocas del Toro.

A girl, eight years old, sweeps the floor. Her brother, four years older, is outside lighting a fire laid in a half-drum. The mother fetches me a cup of freshly made coffee.

I question the daughter on her school and whether she enjoys books and reading. Being a pompous old man, I tell her that education is the only road to freedom.

The mother agrees. 'There is so much competition now.'

A white butterfly in a hurry flies directly across my view. Most butterflies appear aimless. Is this one aware that life is short? I note other butterflies, red, yellow, copper-coloured. Birds work up a racket while I eat puffed pancakes with chopped steak in a tomato sauce. The sun shines. We are a thousand feet above sea level and the air is cool. The family house is a further fifty metres up the ridge and nestles against the trees. This must be the most perfect truck-stop in the world. Riding back to Almirante, I realise what an idiot I am in talking freedom to the young girl. What do I know? Maybe she is already living close to Paradise. Equally, she may feel condemned to jail by birth.

Almirante was United Fruit. Now the name is Chiquita Banana. Chiquita's air-conditioned HQ is in the port area. Entry is via guarded security gates. Two of Chiquita's fleet lie alongside a concrete wharf. The wharf belongs to Chiquita. To board a ship, I require clearance from the Big Men. The Big Men are Panamanians of Afro-Caribbean heritage. Although bilingual, English is their home language. They are well fed and well barbered. They are obviously superior and bask in their superiority. Their open-plan office is on the first floor. Windows overlook the port. I explain my presence. Much telephoning ensues before I am issued with a visitor's badge and a green hard hat.

The Polish chief engineer greets me at the top of the gangplank. He wears the previous evening's baggy shorts and Hawaiian shirt. Perhaps he slept in them. The ship sails in an hour and he conducts me on a whirlwind tour of the engine department. The control room is screens and switches. A steel door leads to a bank of computers that control both ship and cargo. The chief demonstrates opening and closing one of the many valves that balance the fuel load. Next we visit the engine, which seems small for such a big task. Down a deck level, I realise the massive depth of the cylinders. We visit pump rooms and more pump rooms, filter rooms and more filter rooms, heating units for the fuel oil, cooling units for the cargo, climate control for the cargo, generators, spare generators, more generators. The tour is designed to impress. I am impressed.

We return to the control room. 'I am university engineer, educated man. Harrison Ford, bullshit,' announces the chief as he imitates the actor spinning imaginary control wheels. 'Open this valve, open that valve. Big captain in white uniform save everyone. All bullshit.' The chief jabs a finger at a flashing red light. 'Captain, idiot. You think he know what is? Bulb break in cabin, he call me how to fix. Deck officers all idiots.'

What else did I learn? Bananas are picked green and put to sleep while travelling. Reaching their destination, the bananas are given a whiff of gas, awaken and turn yellow. I know what gas and the climate control that puts them to sleep. And I know that Chiquita has sold off the trucks and trailer-tractors that transport the containers from the banana plantations to the wharf. The new truckers borrowed from the banks to buy the tractors. Debt keeps them vulnerable. They can't argue prices with Chiquita and they can't strike.

Joni runs the best breakfast and luncheon place in town. I have chopped steak in pepper sauce served with salad, coffee, and the round, flat, fluffy pancakes that, in Panama, serve for bread. I decide to stay in Almirante for two more nights.

Early-fifties Joni is an ample matron, part Irish from three generations back; the rest is Afro-Caribbean. Joni's grandad came to Almirante from Jamaica to work for United Fruit. Joni recalls Almirante under Company rule. The town was clean and ordered. Infrastructure functioned. Trains ran on time. The same is said by the old folk of Mussolini's Italy and Nazi Germany and the Indian subcontinent under British rule.

An old man enters with packets of pancake dough.

'Just the one today, Pappi,' says Joni.

'As you wish, my love.'

We return to comparing United Fruit with Chiquita Banana. 'Chiquita is all measurements,' says Joni. 'All Chiquita care is measurements. They measure everything.'

Later I chat with a successful local businessman at his office behind his warehouse. He is Jewish. His father emigrated from Palestine as a young man and he has inherited from his father memories of a gentler Middle East, memories that predate the Second World War, of communities that were fuzzy-edged and seeped into each other, Copt and Druse, Jew and Muslim, Armenian, Catholic and Orthodox. Both his wife and his mother are Panamanian Catholics and he abhors the modern simplification and stark lines of demarcation: Them and Us.

'In Panama we do business together, Jew and Muslim. Most of us are *in* business together. We think similarly and are comfortable in each other's company.'

The businessman fields telephone calls before switching our conversation to Almirante. 'United Fruit was king, paternalistic. Chiquita is accountants. Kings give gifts. Accountants respond only to financial logic.'

In its heyday, United Fruit made the market price. Now competition among growers and overproduction has switched power to supermarkets. Supermarkets respond to the demand in rich countries for cheap food.

The businessman judges that United Fruit was both good and bad. Employees were moved from plantation to plantation, from Company town to Company town, and housed according to rank. Houses were maintained by United Fruit; United Fruit cared for employees' health, their pensions, educated their children, decided what stock was available in the Company store. In return, employees were loyal to United Fruit rather than to Panama, Costa Rica or Guatemala; their roots were in United Fruit rather than in Almirante. Now townspeople feel both abandoned and betrayed. Self-direction and maintenance are foreign to them. Houses crumble. Rubbish collection is sporadic, power failures frequent.

The businessman asks whether I have been to Bocas.

I will take the early ferry tomorrow.

'That is where all new investment is,' he tells me. Tourism is vital to the nation's economy. Tourism depends on Panama's unique flora and fauna. He fears a powerful investor moving in, a financial entity with no care for the environment. He asks me to tell my readers to support Greenpeace.

Readers, support Greenpeace.

Bocas, Monday 10 July

Fast twenty-seat passenger launches leave for Bocas from Almirante when they have a full load, say every half-hour between six in the morning and six-thirty in the evening. The crossing takes twenty minutes; the fare is three dollars and subsidised by central government.

I want to explore the island by bike. The car ferry is an almost square flat barge surmounted by a bridge and a café. The ferry has a maximum speed of six knots. The fare is ten dollars each way for rider and bike. The first morning sailing is at six. The ferry is often full and I have been warned to arrive early. I leave the hotel in the dark.

A car loads first.

The stevedore directing the loading calls, 'Simon, bring your bike.'

I have been travelling three months. Hearing my name called in a strange land at half past five in the morning is oddly cheering. So is chatting with a couple of truck drivers. Six Mack trucks are carrying sand and gravel for one of the islands where a gringo (the driver's term) is constructing a housing development for billionaires. One of the billionaires is a famous US basketball player. The drivers recount that the player's house will cost two million dollars (they learnt this on TV).

First light shows a thin mist clinging to the trees along the mountainside. Red lights flash on the Cable & Wireless radio masts. The floodlights along Chiquita's pontoon are exactly spaced. Thick black cloud lies over the sea to our left. The water is almost black. An inbound passenger launch leaves a white trail. The smell of frying chicken drifts from the open window behind us and a tin spoon clatters against a cooking pot.

I breakfast on pancakes with sausage and miserable coffee. Meanwhile the conversation has turned to bikes. A truck driver owns a broken Yamaha. A second driver claims to be a bike mechanic. 'Buy the parts,' he says. 'We'll put it together on a Sunday. Start at six.' He acts assembling the engine. '*Ping-pam, ping-pam, ping-pam*, finished by four.'

This same truck driver was in the army at the time of the US invasion of Panama. 'Twenty-three dead,' he says of US soldiers. 'It's a big lie, Pappi. We shot them in the sky. *Pom*,' he goes, aiming an imaginary rifle. '*Pom, pam, pom, pam*. I tell you, Pappi, twenty-three is a big lie. And how many they kill? Thousands.'

All these dead to arrest one man: the US could have grabbed Noriega any time, claims the driver. The invasion was on 20 December.

On 18 December, Noriega visited a US base (I have no idea whether this is true – nor can I recall the year and I am embarrassed by my ignorance). The driver believes that the invasion of Panama was a practice run for the invasion of Iraq. He accuses Americans of believing they can do anything they wish. The other two truck drivers nod their agreement. Perhaps they agree from fellowship for a fellow trucker. I keep silent.

I am becoming obsessive (or I now recognise my obsession) in my demand for detail. I am interested in the cost of a used Mack truck. One driver's Mack is twenty years old. Value in Panama – 5000 dollars. This driver used to drive mules (the motive part of a trailer truck) until Chiquita forced down the freight rate. Four hundred and fifty dollars is the freight on a load of gravel out to the island. The crossing takes two and a half hours. The driver makes two trips most days, six days a week. He leaves home at four-thirty in the morning and returns home at eleven at night. The truck owner pays by the trip. The driver earns nothing while the truck is in for repair or service. A good month, a month without breakdowns, he earns 500 dollars. His brother is a labourer on a banana cooperative. Chiquita has cut the price of bananas and the workers are on strike. The brother telephoned in the night: his family has no food.

Bocas is a beautiful tranquil island of wooded hills and beaches. A small island, but it is on the world map. It has arrived. It is a non-tourist tourist destination. The architecture is wood-shuttering Cape Cod-Caribbean in pastel shades. Every building on Main Street sells something: food, booze, tours, real estate.

Two weeks on the island and tourists enjoy the delusion of belonging. They become prey for male middle-aged ex-trendies with tans and ponytails who hustle real estate. Hustlers and marks sit in conference in bars and restaurants. On sale is the dream of owning some easy business, life without stress, yearly holiday of 365 days, sun, sand and sex.

The scene is familiar: Ibiza, Block Island, Hydra, Mykonos ...

I need a hospital. Eight days have passed since I sliced my hand. The stitches are due out.

Bocas hospital has an emergency unit with air-con. An indigenous child with an infected foot is the only other patient. A nurse sits me on a chair and sets to work with tweezers and blade. The removal is painless. The nurse dreams of being a writer. She doesn't read. Read two pages and she has a headache. The headaches began soon after she left university. She has medical training: suggesting an eye test seems presumptuous. She despatches me around the block to pay. I pass an open window and see a skeletal old man curled up on a bed. He groans as he attempts to roll over. I glimpse my own reflection in the glass. I hunt down the cashier's counter and pay five dollars.

Light rain falls as I ride the few kilometres across the island. The road rises through low hills. A patch of bamboo forest caps the crest. Weighted by rain, the bamboos arch over the road. Cattle graze shaded paddocks between the woods. Lots are advertised for sale. A development of cheap tasteless wooden holiday homes would benefit from a can of gasoline and a match. The bay at the far end of the island opens to the sea. Turn left and a sand track leads to the Institute for Tropical Ecology and Conservation. The teachers are North American. So are the students. Some are from Canada, most are from the US. I read the literature: ITEC is a not-for-profit organisation based in Gainesville, Florida.

The school is on a sand beach protected by a reef. A further reef projects from the next island. Students eat at a next-door restaurant. The restaurant has a small orchard: breadfruit, guava, a calabash tree. I order coffee and watch, between the palm trees, waves break on the reefs. A lone pelican sits on a marker post fifty metres out. Two parrots nibble my ankles beneath the table.

The parents of a student I chat with have paid 2500 dollars for his five-week course. He is from New England, a great kid, a quarter Indian (as in Asian). Once he has his master's, he intends entering business. Business is exciting. He is having a great day. So am I. He believes that the Iraq war is the right war. I resist relating the opinions voiced by the driver of the Mack truck.

I stop at the Smithsonian Institute on the way back to town. Staff are out on the reef. The administrative secretary gives me a beautifully produced catalogue of the Institute's work in Panama. I will send the catalogue to Mark, the younger son of my first marriage – he is a marine biologist.

Back in town I sit at the end of a small quay and munch a sandwich while watching the traffic. Bocas cabs are small outboard launches. A tourist group arrives by launch from Almirante. They pile upmarket luggage on the quay. They require a boat to take them fifty metres to a plush new hotel on the waterfront – a confectionery of white-painted weatherboard that has cost (I am told and believe) a million dollars. An indigenous local boatman poles his boat over to the quay and is scorned by the hotel's white greeter who spots half an inch of water in the bilges. The greeter instructs the tourists to wait while he fetches a better boat. He ignores the boatman.

The boatman sponges the offending water out of the bilges. He is a patient man, perhaps a little closed. I ride with him over to a neighbouring island. A steep wooded ridge runs the length of the island. A strip of small raggedy wooden houses cling to the shore and are served by a seemingly haphazard rash of plank-on-post docks. The boatman patrols a while, collecting passengers one by one. A young health worker has a date at a shoreside bar. A young Israeli woman (resident here for three years) works at the plush waterfront hotel back on Bocas. The boatman drops her at the hotel's dock. The boatman and I laugh together. The trip has been fun.

The ferry from Almirante is on its second run. It unloads a couple of 4×4s and a freezer truck at Bocas. The Mack trucks are on board. I park the Honda and sit with the drivers outside the ferry's café. A truck driver points to the first of the million-dollar homes in the Bocas archipelago. The house sits on the point of a wooded island. A second house is a further kilometre down the same island and we spot a third before the ferry heads in through mangrove thickets to the private dock on Frefor Island.

Frefor is an island without a village. It is an island without Panamanians. The developer and his staff are from the US. They speak English. Most of the workers are of West Indian background. Shifts are delivered by launch. The workers are big muscular men dressed in American work clothes. They appear well fed and carry themselves with a certain arrogance. It is an arrogance often evident in those employed by the very rich.

The sun breaks through the clouds and the sea gleams between patches of mangrove. Frefor is a long jungle-cloaked ridge. The million-dollar homes are on the far side facing the open sea. The ferry turns in to the private dock. I watch the Mack trucks dump their gravel a hundred yards uphill. I hope that a sufficiency of billionaires will enable the drivers to buy their own trucks.

The ferry is slow. We load trucks and cars in Bocas and head back to Almirante. A young mulatto woman enquires whether I have a girlfriend, a *novia*. I answer that my wife is my *novia*. She tells me that many gringos on Bocas have *novias*. I believe her. She has failed in seeking a gringo – partly, perhaps, because she gnaws her nails. She is also awkward in her movements, consumptively thin and divorced of charm. She has no money and hasn't eaten. Fish and pancakes cost a dollar fifty. She doesn't thank me. One of the truck drivers and I quiz the cook. She earns 250 dollars a month. She is a competent cook of simple food. Billionaire owners of houses on Frefor earn 250 dollars a minute and enjoy more sophisticated tastes.

The great divide, Tuesday 11 July

Today I will cross the isthmus from Atlantic Ocean to Pacific. The Cordillera Central is the spine of the isthmus. The mountains peak at nearly 3500 metres. I have become accustomed to climbs and have faith in the Honda. A storm battered the coast during the night and I awake to rain beating on the roof. I pack only to be warned that fallen trees have blocked the mountain road. Borrowing an umbrella, I walk to Joni's and enjoy a leisurely breakfast.

The rain eases and Joni dispatches me with a kiss. Hills ring the gulf of Bocas del Toro and the road swoops and climbs as it follows the coast. Massive trees blanket the slopes. I ride slowly and swerve round great limbs that have been ripped down by the storm. Much of the cloud has cleared. Light and shade patchwork the tarmac and sunlight streaks a sea spread with mangrove islets. The coast hooks to the south and mountains rise sheer from the shore. The views are of a hardly credible beauty.

I park on the verge and take photographs. A further fifty yards and I stop again. So it continues, view to view, photograph to photograph. I have fallen into the trap that, years ago, in past journeys, made me give up photography: the temptation to be caught behind the camera, pit view against view. Which makes the best picture?

The cure is simple: stuff the camera back in its bag and revel in the ride.

The Atlantic coast was hot and humid and jungly. Now the road winds inland up steep narrow valleys. Tropical forest gives way to pinewoods. Wispy clouds shade the sun. The pines thin. The road breaks clear into a harsh dry landscape of rock and scrub. A vast reservoir lies to the left of the road and the temperature plummets. I stop to pull on a second pair of chinos, a second undershirt, long-sleeved shirt and jumper.

Yesterday, from the ferry, I counted four lines of mountains rise one above the other. The fourth is the divide. I creep towards the summit. Only the curvature of the earth separates me from Africa to the east and, to the west, Asia and Australasia.

The truck drivers on the ferry warned of the wind that rips across the peaks of the Cordillera. They never mentioned the sudden fear that strikes as the wind hits, the vulnerability, a sense of being less than the smallest pinhead. I am alone and on a small bike. This is no place to linger.

Cross the divide and you are in steep uplands. Dairy farms with Swiss names cling to the high slopes. Descend towards the Pacific and you cross the rolling grasslands of wealthy ranchers. The openness of the countryside brings a sense of freedom. The temperature is ideal. I pack away the extra clothes and speed in shirtsleeves on a tarred lane between small shade trees. The sea sparkles way in the distance. Racehorses graze neatly fenced paddocks. I zip past a lone tractor pulling a trailer – no further traffic on the road. My writer's mind takes control. Ideas and insights tumble one over the other.

Glorying in my genius, I miss a road sign.

I shoot straight across a right-angled T-junction. The front wheel bucks as it hits the verge. Long grass ends at a barbed wire fence. The headlight strikes a fence post. I sprawl beneath the bike. Bloody hell, what have I smashed? Is this where it ends?

I imagine broken bones.

Moving could be harmful.

A car crunches on the verge. Doors open, followed by hurried footsteps. A man asks, 'Are you hurt?'

My head is buried in long grass. I say, 'I'm not sure.'

The bike is dragged upright. I move gingerly, checking my limbs for fractures. A woman tells me to be careful. I am being careful. I sit up and face my rescuers: father, mother, son and daughter in early teens. All four wear expensively casual haircuts, tailored jeans and those sports shirts logoed with a curly-tailed crocodile. For jewellery they share a gleaming two-tone Toyota Landcruiser.

The mother's expression suggests concern. The father holds the Honda upright and is irritated at the delay. 'Your arm's bleeding,' the girl observes with that teenage tonal amalgam of contempt for and delight at misadventure. 'You've trodden in dog poo' is a favourite.

I am aware, of course, that I don't look my best. I see myself through their eyes: an old Brit seated in long grass, plump, bearded and somewhat bemused.

'Didn't you see the road sign?' asks the father.

'No,' I say.

'You should be more careful.'

'Yes,' I say.

I should appear grateful. I probably look sulky. I wish that the boy and his sister and their parents would return to their vehicle. I clamber to my feet and help the father wheel the bike to the road.

The boy says, 'The headlight's broken.'

The light is buckled, glass shattered, the left-side footrest bent – no further damage visible. I know from previous falls that the engine will be flooded and won't fire.

I prop the bike on its side rest and say, 'Thank you for your assistance. I'll just sit here a while and get my breath back.'

The father can't resist reminding me to be more careful. The son sneers. The daughter offers me a tissue. The mother says, 'Well, if you're quite sure.'

The family board their Landcruiser. Mother and daughter wave. I attend to a small hole gouged by the barbed wire in my right upper-arm. Then I walk a short way, testing my legs. I wheel the Honda to the top of a slope, mount, gain speed and release the clutch. The engine splutters and fires. Both the bike and I are a little battered but we are back in business. And I have a goal.

The small towns of Bloquet and Volcán nestle on the lower slopes of the Cordillera. Bloquet is sick with an infestation of weekend and holiday housing developments. Why must the houses be so utterly without charm? However, the altitude produces a climate perfect for temperate-climate fruits and vegetables. A sign on the roadside on the outskirts to Bloquet signals a side road to my destination: Fresas Marie.

I have discovered similar summer cafés down lanes in Devon, England, in Austria and Switzerland, in Providence and Upstate New York. The cafés are invariably owned by single women on the plump side, widowed or divorced and blessed with gorgeous smiles. The cafés are small, the ceilings low. The decor is a little too designer quaint and overdecorated with china statuettes and painted plates. Bunny rabbits cast in cement struggle with garden gnomes for supremacy among flowerbeds. Who could give a damn? I am here for the fruit. I sit in the sun and glut myself on fresh-picked strawberries blanketed with whipped double double cream – surely a luxury equal to munching a freshly picked peach in the Antarctic.

And Marie of the lovely smile is too polite to enquire as to what damaged the Honda's headlight. Bliss.

David to Panama City

David, Tuesday 11 July

David is a modern city of reasonable size. The streets are clean; the city feels safe. I book into the Hotel Iris on the cathedral square: a good clean room with air-con and hot water in the evening, but not in the morning. I need a new headlamp. I draw a blank at the local Honda agent and ride sixty kilometres to the Costa Rican border. This stretch of the Pan-American Highway is four lanes with a centre division. Imagine the frontier town of Paso Canoas as one big shabby shopping mall. I find a lamp and two replacement mirrors. Back in David I photograph my bike among a dozen of its twins outside a Domino Pizza Parlour and then dine for three dollars at a good Chinese restaurant.

To Panama City, Wednesday 12 July

David to Panama City is 450 kilometres on the Pan-American Highway. The highway is mostly two lanes across cattle country of rolling hills and big shady trees. Crests of hills add interest for Panamanian drivers of flash 4×4s. Why wait to overtake a truck when you can have yourself an instant adrenalin fix from a near-death experience?

A downpour threatens. I park under the tin eaves of a warehouse pretending to be a dance hall. A mechanic is dropping the gearbox out of an old truck parked on the curb. The driver or owner watches. The rain hits and they sit with me at the bar in the empty dance hall. A woman of immense curves serves us cold sodas. She wears a black leather skirt that almost covers her rump. We three men could shelter comfortably in her cleavage. The mechanic jokes with her. The owner or driver of the truck doesn't joke. His livelihood depends on repairing the gearbox and whether he can afford the parts. His three children are at primary school. His father died in a road accident and he supports his mother and grandparents.

Guidebooks warn that Panama City is dangerous – even by daylight. My destination is the Hotel Caribe on Central Avenue, a big American-style high-rise that is easy to find and has a garage for the Honda. The elevator takes forever. A Panamanian family with two children wait. They are joined in the elevator by a black pimp dripping gold, the pimp's late-sixties American client and an overpainted retirement-age street whore.

The night manager is a young fair Spanish immigrant. The Spaniard complains that Panamanians can't run anything. They need foreigners. I could call him racist. I prefer to bargain the room rate down from thirty to twenty-five dollars. The bed is great. The TV controller doesn't work. Nor does the light in the bathroom. I am too tired to complain and I am mad in the morning at finding the Honda moved and punctured.

I can read the watchman's thoughts: *Hey, the old fool is going to have to pay to have it fixed.*

Yeah, but I'm not paying you.

I push the bike up the ramp and around two blocks to a puncture-repair shop. We remove wheel and tyre in time for an electricity cut. Result: I waste the morning – if wasting is being directed to a street stall that serves a great breakfast with two cups of coffee for eighty cents and finding a perfect hotel with a hot-water power shower, air-con, cable TV and a good restaurant for sixteen dollars.

First impressions of Panama City? Cabs stop so you can cross the road. And I haven't been mugged.

Panama City, Thursday 13 July

The old part of Panama City dates back to the 1670s. Rather than Old Panama, it is called Casco Viejo, 'the Old Compound'.

Old Panama exists. It is a collection of overgrown ruins out of town towards the airport.

The buildings were beautiful before they were torched by that great English hero Henry Morgan.

The buildings were beautiful before they were torched by that vicious murderous English pirate Henry Morgan.

My paternal family are English, Italian and Hispanic. My great-grandfather, Ramon Cabrera, was a Spanish terrorist. He built his terrorist band into an army, won battles and became the Marques del Ter, Conde de Morella. I must make a speech in Morella on 6 December in celebration of his two-hundredth anniversary. Doing so, I will glorify a terrorist and become a criminal according to the inane laws proposed by the present British government and passed by Parliament. The British government is sadly short of historians. Most are lawyers. Historians would have known better than commit British troops to Iraq and Afghanistan.

Casco Viejo is a slum undergoing gentrification under government guidance. Streets have been paved. Official buildings gleam. Buildings awaiting resurrection have been given a coat of pastel paint. Brass bell-buttons sparkle beside new doors on buildings already resurrected. The doors are lined with steel. Police patrol – some on pushbikes and wearing shorts and biker helmets. The first upmarket restaurants have opened behind closed doors (to protect the electrically cooled air). The poor sit on doorsteps.

I enter a store in search of a ballpoint. The goods on sale are in one half of the room: a few Panama hats, black waistcoats embroidered with golden animals. A grey-haired lady has collapsed on a sofa beside a cutting table in the remaining part of the store. Her husband sits at a worktable trimming silk lining for a pair of evening slippers. The lady is overweight and has difficulty in rising. I apologise for disturbing her.

'It is the heat,' she says, and wipes her forehead on her forearm. The heat and she has a headache.

I have been walking an hour. My feet ache and I agree as to the heat.

She pours me a glass of water from a plastic jug.

I would be rude in not drinking – possibly unwise in drinking. Travel is full of such quandaries. I drink and sit in a wicker chair beside the worktable and write up these notes.

Casco Viejo, Friday 14 July

I return to Casco Viejo district late this morning. Yesterday I discovered a *comedor* that sells fresh, unsweetened pear juice. Today I drink two glasses. Later I sit with two women on a bench in the cathedral square. The women are schoolteachers. They ask whether I enjoy their country and what I enjoy.

I speak truthfully of the friendly openness I encounter and of the beauty of the countryside. Pleased, they ask whether I have visited the church with the golden altar. The altar is a survivor of Henry Morgan's vandalism/heroism.

I reply that I have and that I have walked the streets and squares and that Casco Viejo will be very beautiful once it is all restored.

'It will be for tourists,' the younger of my companions says. 'That is what the government plans. It will be too costly for ordinary people, for the poor.'

This teacher is in her fifties, a thin, somewhat severe woman, black, her hair dragged back in a tight tuft.

Mention of the poor starts the elder teacher talking of the US invasion of Panama in 1989. She is a plump, white, motherly woman in her sixties, hair dyed a golden brown and set in youthful curls. She cradles a transparent plastic portfolio on her lap. Her fingers are chubby; she wears a gold wedding band together with an engagement ring set with a fragment of green stone.

We sit facing the cathedral. The two white towers gleam in the sun. The plump, motherly schoolteacher is reluctant to talk of people. She talks of the apartment buildings in the district that were destroyed in the invasion: although not luxurious, the buildings were an improvement; the district possessed a true feeling of community.

She repeats the accusation levelled by the Bocas truck driver: that Noriega was easy to arrest. There were many opportunities. He travelled out in the country, walked in the streets.

'So many people died.'

She speaks of her neighbours, an entire family. All were killed. The grandmother was seventy-three (my age). The youngest child was only six, a girl. The teacher says that none of the houses of the rich were damaged, none of the rich were killed, none of the captains.

The younger teacher nods agreement. 'The captains knew,' she says. Her husband was second-in-command in Colón (a cop?). On the eve of the invasion, he sent one of his men with food and instructions that she wasn't to leave the house.

'It was against the poor,' the motherly teacher insists. Poor people weren't important. Artisans died and poor people who sold fried fish on the street corner and on the beach at weekend. 'Very flavoursome,' she assures me, 'Fried with chilli and with garlic.'

Memory of the fish is a trigger. She weeps, and yet her tone of voice remains calm, almost wondrous, as she talks of her sister who had lived on the top floor of a building. 'They shouted that everyone must come out into the street or they would be killed. There was so much blood in the elevator and bits of bodies, hands, legs, a head.'

Her sister died two days after the invasion. 'It was the shock.'

Her friend, the thin teacher, passes her a handkerchief and she wipes her eyes.

'They lied,' she says. 'They killed more than 5000 people. They buried them with tractors. They are hidden there deep down in the area that is called Arenal. It was Henry Ford and Arias Calderón. They wanted to do it.'

In the evening I talk with a successful Panamanian businessman in his fifties, a computer expert. 'Yes,' he says, 'There were thousands killed.' And, yes, it would have been easy to capture Noriega. The invasion was unnecessary.

He cites the booming Panamanian economy as the reason for the invasion. The canal was due to be handed over to Panama in ten years. The US was losing control. The invasion was a warning to Panamanians of their inferior status.

The Pentagon named the invasion 'Operation Just Cause'.

I have not met a Panamanian who agrees.

Miaflores, Saturday 15 July

The Panama Canal is what the US did best. The project demanded absolute support of a government ruthless in pursuit of a benefit to the US. It demanded great vision and determination, brilliant planning and design, a massive workforce and vast finance.

Miaflores dock is a short run from Panama city. Entrance is eight dollars for an adult, half price for pensioners. The museum is fascinating: clear explanations, great models, aquarium tanks, cabinets of insects.

I sleep through much of the promotional film in the theatre. My spectacles fog each time I leave the air-conditioned building.

Something nags – I don't know what.

Realisation takes a couple of hours. The canal is the only garbage-free zone in Central America. Grass is mown between the roadways and rails. Windows shine. Workers are professional. They know their jobs and have no need to shout.

The restaurant is good. Prices range from reasonable to luxury: eight or nine dollars for hamburger or chicken with rice, fourteen dollars for Thai sea bass steamed in banana leaves, thirty-five dollars for San Blas crab.

I buy bottled water and a pack of peanuts at the ground-floor cafétería and watch the ships go by.

Most people watch from the fourth-floor deck. Don't. Looking up at the ships from ground level gives you their true immensity. I witness the highest-price transit ever to pass through the canal. The ship, MSC Fabrienne, was built to the maximum permitted size. She carries 4500 containers for a transit fee of 246 666 dollars.

From ground level, the hard hats at the forward bulwarks resemble a scattering of M&Ms. A lone pelican sits on the lock gates. Frigate birds float overhead. Low cloud closes in and rain hides the conical hills.

Panama City, Monday 17 July

Panama City is splendid at providing contrasts. The old quarter of Casco Viejo commands the western end of the shore; the ruins of Panama Viejo mark the east. I entered the city through a hinterland of slum tenements as grim as those on the outskirts of Havana. My hotel is in a mid-market district for both foreign tourists and Panamanians visiting from the provinces. Internet cafés abound, restaurants are reasonably priced and streetwalkers appear at night.

Turn left up a block and you find traffic-congested streets of pavement stalls and supersaver stores. I buy three lightweight short-sleeved shirts at one and a pair of chinos.

Turn right and you head into a land of pristine high-rise cathedrals. Money is god in this BMW banker territory of dark suits, polished shoes and respectable ties. Cops are the streetwalkers. They linger at every entrance and on most intersections. Pavements are swept, shrubs are barbered, grass dividers shaved and watered. Even the poor are neatly dressed – money, however dirty, demands clean servants. Panama is a laundry for dirty money.

I meet with a retired police captain in Casco Viejo. He was born in Casco Viejo and lives there now in a house that belonged to his father. He was a lieutenant of police at the time of the invasion. The US army arrested him and held him in jail without charge for five months. The US army arrested all the officers of the police force and of the defence force. The city was undefended and was ransacked. Is this a familiar scenario?

Panama City, Tuesday 18 July

The Darien Gap divides Panama from Colombia. No roads cross the Darien. Thick jungle and mountains are the territory of indigenous people who object to strangers, narco-traffickers, Colombian *guerrilleros* (narco-traffickers) and Colombian paramilitaries (narco-traffickers) fighting the *guerrilleros* for control of the drug trade. The standard route is by sea through the San Blas Islands to Cartagena. Or you can fly.

I decide to try the Pacific coast. Why? To be different.

Perhaps I should ask myself why people avoid the Pacific route. Instead, I study maps, read a couple of guidebooks and talk to a few fishermen down at the fish market.

Boats leave the Fiscal wharf near the fish market for Jaque, eighteen hours south down the coast. From Jaque canoes run down the coast to Jurado in Colombia, four to five hours of unsheltered sea passage. Jaque has an immigration post so I can book out of Panama. Jurado has nothing. Certainly not a road. So I need a second canoe or launch from Jurado to Bahia Solano, where I can book into Colombia.

How big are the canoes?

I ride to the Fiscal wharf this morning. The wharf is roofed to protect cargo. It is a slum and it stinks. Oswald is a big black immigration official with a big kind heart. He has elected himself my transport counsel. We walk down the wharf. The boat that can take me to Jaque lies alongside. It is forty feet long. The hull is of rough planks. The deck planks are rougher. Dockers manhandle sections of mahogany tree trunk from a small hold. A wheelhouse or cabin sits on the after deck. A can of paint passed the boat some years ago and forgot to stop. Even a casual inspection gives pause for doubt: What keeps it afloat?

I enquire of Oswald whether there is another boat.

'Next month, maybe,' Oswald says.

I say, 'Oh.'

I repeat the 'oh'. Then, 'This maybe-boat: how is it?'

'The same,' says Oswald, in whom I sense compassion.

'Oh,' I say.

The captain of the hulk inspects the Honda and quotes the fare.

Oswald expects me to negotiate. Negotiating is tough when the alternative is a maybe. I agree the fare. I have betrayed Oswald.

Oswald, a football fan, watched the pathetic effort of the English in the penalty shootout against Portugal in the World Cup. He condemns English footballers for lacking courage.

Not negotiating places me in the same category.

I am not doing well.

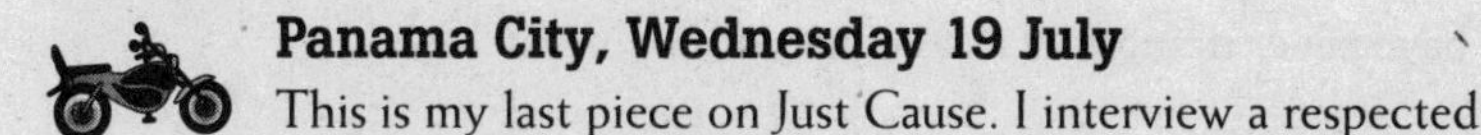

Panama City, Wednesday 19 July

This is my last piece on Just Cause. I interview a respected journalist at the offices of the leading Panamanian newspaper. This is his account: Have no doubts – Noriega is a vile man. A group of defence force officers arrested him on 3 October 1989. The officers telephoned the US embassy. The embassy refused support. The officers were at a loss as to how to act. A majority of the group fled to the Canal Zone. Noriega persuaded the remainder to release him. Noriega had nine of this group shot the following day. The US invaded Panama on 20 December 1989. The 'Just Cause' was to arrest Noriega. A minimum of 1000 Panamanian civilians were killed in the invasion. The city was ransacked.

The journalist describes the US soldiers as country boys, young, ill-educated and inexperienced. They often fired from panic. The blame for the killing of civilians and for ransacking the luxury stores at the airport by US soldiers lay with incompetent officers.

For Panamanians, the invasion remains an essential ingredient in Panamanian–US relations. I suspect it is considered of very little importance in the US and that few North Americans recall or ever knew or bothered to learn the details.

'Just Because' was the Pentagon joke name for Operation Just Cause. George H.W. Bush was the US president. The US army estimated Panamanian deaths at 516, while an army internal memo put the figure at over 1000. An independent commission of inquiry (US) put the figure at between 1000 and 4000. Some 15 000 civilians were displaced – most were working-class. Widespread looting bankrupted many businesses – insurance companies refused to pay, naming the invasion an act of war. A great museum was ransacked. This was to arrest one man. Shades of Iraq.

Hugh Thomas (although a Protestant, a good historian) writes of Cortés' conquest of Mexico: To a good general, history is as important as geography.

US generals and the Bush family either disagree or are too lazy to do their homework.

Let me give the last word to the Panamanian journalist: The gringos have never thought of us as equals or important.

Panama City, Thursday 20 July

I visit the boat and captain at the Fiscal wharf. The captain has the charm of a tent-peg mallet. I wait ten minutes before he acknowledges my existence. Meanwhile I talk with a Coona woman shipping yams. Coona are the indigenous people of the Darien. She has returned recently from both Jaque and Bahía Solano. She assures me that both places are pleasant and safe (most places I visit, safety is a given). She provides the name of a Jaque boatman for the trip to Bahía Solano. He sails on Tuesdays or Wednesdays so I will be stuck in Jaque for five days. The Coona woman paid seventy dollars from Jaque to Bahía Solano. I suspect she is a tough negotiator while I have proved a walkover and I own a bike. Bike fare always exceeds people fare.

She tells me that there is no road out of Bahía Solano: if there were a road, only a suicide would travel it.

'You said Bahía Solano is safe.'

'The town is,' she says.

So I require a boat south from Bahía Solano to Buenaventura, three days, if and when there is a boat. I do some basic maths and dislike the result. I also dislike placing myself and my negotiating ability at the mercy of boatmen in Jaque or Bahía Solano.

I park in Plaza Herera. The pear lady has fresh pear juice in the icebox. I sit at a computer and email a query to Kelvin at the Black Sheep hostel in Medellín: can I fly the Honda up from Bahía Solano?

I pour myself a second glass of pear juice. The pear juice woman reminds me of a Cuban, the owner of the longest-surviving private restaurant in Santa Fe. Both women are short and square; they dress identically: baggy grey T-shirts, baggy jeans cut off at mid-knee; they wear their hair short-short and they walk with their elbows out (not, as with Blair and Bush, to appear manly but to bypass ample bosoms and ample hips). I tell her the problems of Bahía Solano.

She warns me that Colombia is dangerous.

'Not Bahía Solano,' I reply.

'All Colombia,' she insists.

I drink my pear juice and check the BBC website for new destruction meted to the Lebanese by Israel. I recall Lebanon as more beautiful and less crowded than the South of France. I recall the warm company of kids my own age, of laughter and great food and dancing through the night at cafés up in the cool mountain air, the lights of Beirut spread below and the arc of the seafront. My recollections of Lebanon are ancient, over half a century old.

Kelvin brings my knowledge of Colombia up to date. I cannot fly the bike from Bahía Solano to Medellin. I am committed to a three-day boat trip from Bahía Solano to Buenaventura. How often do the boats sail?

My mind is jelly. I must think. I write a letter to my grandson Charlie Boo. Charlie Boo is four months old, a good age for a sage. I explain that the trip is in four stages and that the first three destinations have no road communication with the outside world. I describe the disaster of a boat and the unfriendly captain charged with my wellbeing on the initial stage to Jaque. Then I search for a rationale understandable to a four-month-old sage.

What is my purpose?

To travel through Colombia.

Buenaventura is in the south of Colombia. I will have to ride a vast northerly loop to see anything of the country.

I want to sail. Why did I buy a bike?

Because I am afraid of seeming afraid if I chicken out.

Hardly a sensible rationale.

Nor am I a competitive traveller. I don't give a damn whether I am the first outsider to visit a place or the five-billionth. I travel because I enjoy travelling. I visit places that I expect to enjoy. I desire the travelling to be enjoyable. Leapfrogging down the Pacific coast in a series of doubtful boats and canoes at an unknown price conforms to none of these parameters. Call it off. Switch to the Atlantic coast. Ship self and the bike to Cartagena.

Late evening and I sit outdoors at a café in the company of a young American botanist who works out of Jaque. He says that Jaque is safe but not that safe. He keeps a low profile and keeps each visit down to an absolute maximum of two months. Longer and he could become too tempting a target for kidnappers. Only a lunatic would attempt travelling in Colombia's Choco Province, of which only Bahía Solano and Buenaventura are safe for a short visit. Bahía Solano is bearable if you have a reason to be there. Buenaventura is a dump.

I feel good at having made a sensible decision. I head back to the hotel. While preparing for bed, I drop my top teeth in the sink. The plate was repaired in Mexico. It snaps in three pieces. One piece disappears down the drain. I sit on the bed with the two remaining pieces cupped in my hands. I am a writer and I turn for consolation to my laptop. The battery is flat. I plug in the charger. Nothing happens. I feel old and stupid and very alone. I want to go home. Help.

Resolute, Friday 21 July

I have been drifting. I need to take control. First I must find an orthodontist. I am up at seven and consult the receptionist. The receptionist gets the giggles over my teeth. She consults the hotel owner while I gum a plate of scrambled eggs. At half past eight I sprawl in a luxurious dental chair at the Clínica Rojas Pardini. My mouth is full of gel.

Travellers (and particularly their families) from England and the US doubt the quality of Latin American medical practice.

The heart specialist I consulted in Guatemala years ago was Johns Hopkins plus standard extras.

The orthodontist overseeing the mechanic taking an impression of my mouth is Boston plus standard extras.

At half past nine I am equipped with a fully re-seated set of top teeth. The dentist is kind to pensioners – or enjoys the concept of my trip. He tells me to pay the dental technician fifty dollars.

I feel back in control.

I leave the bike for a total overhaul at the Honda agent, Promotos.

I cab across town to Electronico Chino, where a Chinese genius repairs the charger for my laptop.

I hit the internet and discover a German sailing association that owns a schooner, *Stahlratte*, that makes the run through the San Blas Islands to Cartagena and back.

Perfect. I call their mobile. They take bikes. They have a Japanese biker booked on this coming trip. The fare is 500 dollars, to include food, wine and the bike. The yacht is at Porto Vinir in the San Blas Islands. They sail Monday for Cartagena. A Coona launch leaves Mirimar at midday, Saturday, for Porto Vinir – fifty dollars for a bike and rider. Mirimar is eighty-five kilometres east of the Colón highway. No problem. I head to the nearest bank and stick my plastic in the ATM.

Stick plastic in an ATM and you get money. Or you get a message. I get a message to call my bank. I try two other banks and the ATM in a casino before calling the UK. A woman with a young voice answers. I tell her my card is blocked.

She consults whatever requires consulting and says, 'No, it isn't.'

'It is,' I say. 'I've tried it in three machines at three separate banks and at a casino.'

'Well, it's not blocked,' she says.

'Why can't I get any money?' I ask.

'Possibly the system is being updated,' she suggests.

I try to sound neither desperate nor infuriated. 'How long does that take?'

'Not too long,' she says. 'You can try the ATM again in the morning.'

'I have to pay for a boat ride in the morning.'

She says, 'Well, that's all I can suggest.' It is a Saturday summer morning home in England. She will finish work soon and sit with a boyfriend in the sun outside a country pub.

I will worry through the night.

My best option is to ride down to Colón early. I will be closer to Mirimar. If the ATM refuses my card, I can talk with the local bank.

Colón and Portobelo

Colón, Saturday 22 July

Guidebooks claim that Panama City is dangerous. I have ridden through the city over the past week. A barrio has a look of danger; I find a different route. I have been careful and have never felt threatened and have been assisted with courtesy when asking for directions. I have had a great time.

Colón is different.

Colón is dangerous.

Development has passed it by.

No skyscrapers, no flash banks.

Not even a decent downtown hotel. No sensible visitor would want to stay downtown.

I stop by a couple of cops patrolling the pavement on the central avenue. They direct me to a bank and call a motorbike team to escort me. The two cops who escort me ride a trail bike and wear dark-glass space helmets and flak jackets over combat camouflage. They carry machine pistols and automatics and clubs. I follow them to the bank. The bank has three guards. It is a small bank – no bigger than a branch bank in a small English market town.

I carry a debit card in preference to a credit card, because I reason that debit cards are of less use to a thief. Debit cards are also of little use to the Colón bank. A kind teller presumes I have misused the ATM. She tries the card and gets the same message: Call my bank. Saturday afternoon in England and my bank is closed for the weekend.

We are plastic-dependent. Even more so when travelling. I am stuck. I am in jail. Plastic is my jailer. Will plastic release me on Monday? Meanwhile what to do?

Maybe the Germans from the *Stahlratte* will be at Mirimar. I can explain my predicament. Mirimar is eighty-five kilometres east along the coast from the Panama–Colón highway. This is a weekender coast. Schools are out on summer vacation and the wealthy are down from Panama City. Flash family 4×4s come loaded with surfboards and ice chests.

The road is good for the first thirty-five kilometres to Portobelo. Beyond Portobelo I weave between potholes. The road is hard dirt for the final stretch. Rain falls as I walk the bike across one of those plank-on-plank bridges. To me, this is a different country. It is not Latin America. It is Caribbean. The sea is ever present, palm trees, almonds, sea-grape trees. Most faces are black. Men favour sleeveless undershirts. Small girls wear their hair braided. Big girls and women have the curls ironed out. Each village carries the scent of fried fish and the music volume is on high.

No Germans are in Mirimar. How do I know? Mirimar is too small to hide a chicken. The dirt street is wet; the trees drip. Small thatched and tin-roof houses sit miserably among the puddles. A Yamaha low-rider loaded with packs is parked outside a shack. The Japanese biker and his girlfriend eat fried fish on the small terrace. His hair is cut shoulder length; he wears string and leather bracelets and amulets round his neck. She has studs in her tongue. They both speak some English. She has been living in Mexico and speaks better Spanish. I relate my plastic jailer. We share biker experiences. They find 300 kilometres a full day's ride. Further and their hips hurt. I guess the pain is caused by the angle at which they sit on the low-rider. The low-rider looks cooler than my Honda pizza-delivery bike. However, I sit upright on the Honda. All I suffer is a numb butt.

We walk to the dock. A big dugout canoe lies alongside. I would guess it is thirty feet in length. It is narrow of beam and powered by an outboard. The bulwarks have been heightened with planks and it carries a cargo that is mostly Coca-Cola. The captain, a Coona, has his crew shift the Coca-Cola aft to make room for the Yamaha. The canoe is five feet below the dock. They tie a strip of canvas to the bike and lower away. I would be scared for the bike. So are the Japanese. Up there in the bows, the bike is going to get wet in anything other than a glass-flat sea. Islands of mangrove protect the shore and we can't see the height of the waves. We say our goodbyes and our good lucks. I watch the canoe slide out from the dock and head out between the mangrove. Maybe the plastic jailer did me a favour. I return to the terrace where we met and eat fried snapper.

Portobelo, Sunday 23 July

I have found a room in Portobelo, base for the annual Spanish treasure fleets for 150 years. In truth, the town is no more than a village. It guards a lovely bay. It boasts three small ruined Spanish forts, a Spanish customs house that now houses a museum, a small walled Spanish cemetery and three churches. One of the churches displays a famous statue: a black Jesus.

Columbus visited in 1502. The road to the Pacific, the Camino Real, started here. What more could a tourist town desire?

Portobelo should be beautiful. It should have charm. It has litter. It is strewn with the detritus of the fast-food era. It is polystyrene paradise, a visual symphony to cellophane, a sepulchre for discarded Styrofoam cups.

The restaurants serve genuine Caribbean food, fried, fried, fried.

Drake's is the gringo yachtie haven. The owners are a Canadian and his Fijian-born wife. Presumably neither of them is a historian: Drake torched Portobelo. I leave a message for any yacht sailing for Cartagena.

I ride thirty-five kilometres from Portobelo to Sabanitas, junction of the coast road and the Panama City–Colón highway. I work at an internet outlet for a couple of hours. Then, for the hell of it, I cross the highway to the town's only bank. I stick the plastic in the slot and ask for 200 dollars. The ATM spits out the cash. Too late to catch the Germans.

Portobelo, Monday 24 July

Dawn and Portobelo lies under a tablecloth of charcoal cloud. The cloth has a paler fringe at the horizon. The one window in my room at the Hospedaje d'Aduana overlooks the bay. Rain falls steadily. The yachts lying to anchor are almost hidden. Closer to shore a line of pelicans rises to a barely noticeable swell.

This coast may be a holiday paradise for the wealthy young of Panama City. Perhaps they don't notice the trash. The trash and the attitude. The attitude is unavoidable. This is the first area in 6500 kilometres of journey in which people have tried to scare me as I ride by, shouting suddenly or pretending to throw a stone. Not often, but it happens. Kids, mostly, teenagers.

The cops stop me at a checkpoint. They tell me to check out the Coco Solo wharf in Colón for a trading vessel sailing for Cartagena. Coco Solo lies to the east of the highway. I don't have to ride into the city. A Latino *mestizo* at a bus stop gives me directions. I ask whether it is safe.

'Be careful,' he answers.

Great.

I ride a kilometre and enquire again of a guard at the entrance to a container wharf.

'Keep going,' he tells me. 'And be careful.'

I pass the flooded entrance to a row of tenements waiting to be cast in a horror movie. Beyond the tenements lies an opencast litter mine. Rain falls. The road narrows between walls of sugarcane. I ask directions of a black woman walking with a cute daughter beneath a pink umbrella. The woman tells me I should have taken the flooded entrance. I turn back. I want to keep going right on back to the highway.

I have already chickened out of sailing to Jaque.

I take the turn at the tenement buildings and ride gingerly through the flood. The docks and ships lie ahead behind a twelve-foot security fence. The road is flooded to the fence. Half a dozen men in semi-rags are picking through the litter dumped to the right of the flooded road.

I imagine myself through their eyes: a fat juicy pigeon. Hitting a pothole hidden beneath the floodwater will put me in serious trouble.

A medium-dark middle-aged man in cap and dungarees picks his way along the edge of the road from the dock. He tells me that there are no boats in for Cartagena. I should try the wharf on Fifth Street, Colón.

I ask whether Fifth Street is dangerous.

'Dangerous, yes. But not as dangerous as where you are now.'

I turn the bike very, very carefully and ride back through the flood and out of Coco Solo.

The main avenue in Colón is a dual carriageway. Trees shade the avenue. If it were safe, it would be a pleasant place for a stroll and a little window-shopping. I stop on the avenue to ask a woman directing traffic for directions to Fifth Street. She advises me to enquire of a proper cop. I follow her directions to a cop shop and find myself at the entrance to a slum street of crumbling tenements. This is a street that I wouldn't enter in an army tank. I do a quick U-turn back to the avenue. A fellow biker, a clerk type with a briefcase, pulls alongside. I ask for directions. He tells me to follow. We cross the avenue and he halts at a couple of cops (checking out the war zone?).

The cops signal us on and we make it to the Fifth Street dock.

Guards direct me to the captain of a small trading vessel. The captain tells me of a vessel due on Thursday and expected to sail Saturday for Cartagena. The captain tells me of another biker seeking passage, a Chino. 'Chino' encompasses anyone with almond eyes.

Enough for one day. Enough of Colón. I am in need of a cold beer.

Portobelo, Tuesday 25 July

I am stuck in Portobelo. I have a room with a bathroom. The bed has two foam mattresses and tissue-thin nylon fitted sheets that slip off the mattress corners if I sneeze. The bathroom has cold water, bearable after the first strike. The cotton towel wouldn't dry a damp mouse. I could do with a shelf above the sink. Instead, I balance the tubes and cups and soaps of old age along the back of the sink from where they fall whenever I move. I breakfast on scrambled eggs and great coffee at a thatch-roofed restaurant across the road. A bright, pretty girl of seven has adopted me as an auxiliary grandfather. She is very dark with naturally straight hair and an unnaturally wicked smile. I believe that she is the cook's daughter. I could be wrong – Caribbean relationships are complicated. She has shown me how to use the washing machines at the launderette and walked me to the health clinic to have a stitch removed from my finger – a stitch the nurse in Bocas had overlooked.

A black man I believe to be my temporary granddaughter's true grandfather has a habit of discussing politics and social issues while I drink my second cup of coffee of a morning. He tells me there is no work to be had in Portobelo. He tells me that none of the black people own farms. The Latinos own all the land. The Latinos bought the land from the black people for next to nothing. He tells me that modern youth is utterly corrupted. Thirty years ago you could walk through Colón counting hundred-dollar bills and be as safe as in a bank safe. Now kids kill you for a five-dollar watch.

Portobelo, Wednesday 26 July

I ride down the coast and take a side road through palm trees that leads to a small village. A boy-man tells me of a foreigner who owns a bar the other side of a hill. I ride a dirt road over the hill and down to a collection of huts and a couple of houses on the shore. The foreigner caretakes yachts that lie at anchor inshore from clumps of mangrove protected by a reef.

I ride down a path between trees and over two narrow concrete footbridges. The foreigner's house is whitewashed concrete block with a tin roof. A big covered deck leads to a concrete dock supported on concrete-filled oil drums. A small black dog on a chain snarls and lunges at my ankles. A toucan watches me from a large cage. A shy immature mulatto girl, fourteen or fifteen at most, appears in a loose cotton dress. The foreigner is away in Colón. The girl brings me a tin mug of iced water.

I ride back down the path and across the footbridges. The littoral is rolling hills and valleys. I ride a kilometre down a farm track. The farm-

Emperor of Hacienda Tijax

Pork roast – lago Peten Itza (Guatemala)

San Blas Islands

Morris Minor (Honduras)

Tegucigalpa – art deco barber (Honduras)

Perfect volcano (Nicaragua)

San Juan rodeo (Nicaragua)

Catholic pompom girls, Granada Cathedral (Nicaragua)

Body bags (Costa Rica)

San Francisco Coyote (Costa Rica)

Costa Condominium (Costa Rica)

Piggy in the middle (Costa Rica)

World domination (Panama)

Almirante – biker hotel (Panama)

Bocas – tourist hotel (Panama)

A bridge too much (Panama)

Ship from Hades (Panama)

Perfect truck stop (Panama)

Cadillac Farm (Texas)

Girón story teller (Colombia)

Cartagena office block (Colombia)

Road to Puno (Peru)

Nazca gold miner (Peru)

Nazca school fête (Peru)

Reality (Peru)

Cochabamba Classic Bike Club (Bolivia)

Lake Titicaca – San Pablo ferry (Bolivia)

Miners' picket (Bolivia)

LaLa Land (Argentine)

Patagonia – on and on and on (Argentine)

Caleta – Soviet art (Argentine)

Tierra del Fuego – destruction (Argentine)

house stands on the tip of a promontory. The farmer and his wife are Latinos. They run a small dairy herd on 300 hectares. Their two sons don't care for the land and work in Panama City.

Portobelo, Thursday 27 July

Portobelo awakes to a second day of incessant rain. The Spanish treasure fleet gathered annually in Portobelo Bay. Now the few yachts anchored offshore look miserable and unromantic. None is sailing to Cartagena. I sprint across the road to breakfast. The Spanish bridge is diagonally across the street. The bridge once carried the treasure of the Americas to the customs house in Portobelo – the town was sacked repeatedly by the Brits. Drake was first – he died here and is buried offshore. The list contains all the great names of pillage: Parker, Morgan, Vernon, Kinghills – all put Portobelo to the torch. Presumably they attacked in the dry season. Today you would require a loaded petroleum tanker.

Portobelo has been declared a World Heritage Site. The Spanish bridge is being strengthened and the cobbles are being replaced. This cobbling is the only work in town. Six men are unoccupied with the cobbling. They have rigged awnings against sun and rain and sit on the balustrade and chat among themselves.

A black woman wearing a pinstripe business suit sips black coffee at the next table. I watch her watching a couple of black men at the far end of the restaurant veranda. The men's speech is loud and comes in brief rapid bursts. They are wired. The one man is unable to keep still. His movements are as jerky as his speech. The cook has brought his breakfast. He forks a mouthful of sausage, only to be distracted. Up he jumps and crosses the street to the Chinese supermarket for a quick talk with a man in a pale grey hoody. He returns and actually eats the first forkful of sausage. Then he is back to the Chinese, then down the street. He returns with a cardboard container of orange juice. He picks at his food a moment and then is off to speak with the six men sitting under awnings at the Spanish bridge.

I continue watching the pinstripe woman. Read her face and you know that she is thinking: 'Lord, am I really part of this?'

She finishes her coffee, checks that all four doors of her dark-grey Nissan car are securely locked and boards a white Health Department 4×4. Four vultures sit on the roof of the Chinese supermarket. I eat my eggs.

In Colón workmen have closed Fifth Street midway between Central Avenue and the wharf. I backtrack down Central Avenue. How can I tell which street is safe? I take a right, ride to the end, take a second right and am at the gates to the wharf. The boat for Cartagena has not arrived. It should be in tomorrow. My informant is the skipper of a boat heading through the San Blas Islands to Cartagena. I am tempted. However, the voyage will take three weeks. Waiting in Panama has already put me behind schedule. I don't have three weeks.

The guard at the gate warns me to take a left outside the gates to return to Central Avenue. Turning right would take me into dangerous territory. Right is the way I came. Ouch.

The guard also tells me of a second biker seeking passage: the biker is a Chino.

The relationship between men and women in Portobelo confuses me. The sexes seem separate species, and communication between the two is clearly difficult. Mostly it consists of women shouting at men. Whatever the message, it seldom gets through. I remark on this to the cook while eating breakfast this morning. She replies that the men here are cold. She asks where we live and in what type of house. I describe our cottage and the garden and that Bernadette told me yesterday on the telephone that she had saved a failing rose bush. For medicine she had used horse manure from the dung heap behind my brother's stables.

The cook complains that no man has ever given her a rose.

Riding back from Colón, I stop at the big supermarket. I buy fruit salad and a packet of cured pork loin for my dinner and a bunch of pink roses for the cook. The cook says that I am a good man and gives me a hug and a kiss. My temporary granddaughter giggles. I drink coffee and watch the traffic pass through town. Public transport is old school buses imported from the US. The buses have names: Doña Lola, Conquistador, Niña Jenny. The sides are painted in stripes and often bear cartoon characters. The back is the real canvas. Some subjects are religious: the Resurrection, the Angel Gabriel. Others have pictures of the jungle, rivers, a puma. I spotted a Swiss mountain scene. On others, scenes are drawn from fantasy movies.

Cherished buses have their exhausts extended with chrome pipes rising vertically up the back and all buses have messages painted across the windscreen. IN GOD WE TRUST is a favourite. Bikers are vulnerable. I would prefer the driver to trust less in God and have better visibility.

Colón, Saturday 29 July

I ride to the Fifth Street wharf at noon. The boat for Cartagena is in. The skipper will take me. The bike is a problem. Why? I don't know. The skipper will tell me midday on Monday whether he can take us both. He will give me the fare at midday on Monday. I shall spend the weekend chewing my nails.

As insurance, I ride out to the Shelter Bay yacht marina. The road crosses the canal. The bridge is a steel grid on top of the lower lock gates. Water boils out of the sluices on one side while the bows of a massive ship tower above on the other.

Beyond the canal, the road leads to the marina through the rich forest of a national park. I speak with the director, a grey-haired, grey-bearded, big-bellied American eating lunch in the clubhouse with his decorative female Panamanian assistant, probably thirty years his junior. The assistant shows interest in my journey. The director sends me outside to talk with the janitor, a Coona Indian.

The Coona is fishing off a dock with a weighted line and crab for bait. He pulls in a couple of fish while lecturing me on what is good food and what is bad food. Bad food is what people eat at Chinese restaurants. The Chinese cook rats and cats and dogs – again, I quote. Meat in fried rice is rat.

The Coona is fifty-nine years old. He was out of work for a year. He visited all the factories in the Free Zone. He was told either that he was too old or that they would be in touch. They never were in touch. He has four children and three grandchildren to feed. He went hungry often. His mother-in-law does sewing and embroidery work to sell to tourists. The mother-in-law was hard on him, nagging and demanding why he didn't work and why he was reading all the time. The Coona was reading the Bible. He reads the Bible every day. God answered his prayers with the janitor's job. Solving difficulties is all a matter of praying and waiting. God will answer prayers in his own good time.

The Coona is close to tears while relating his trials. Although a sweet man, he is of little help to an aged Englishman with a bike in need of a boat. The marina director and his assistant are in the warehouses. The assistant asks how I progressed with the Coona. I tell her of his mother-in-law and she giggles. The director is irritated so I leave and ride to the shopping mall outside Colón on the Panama City highway.

I have lost the knife I bought in Mexico. I try a big hardware store. The security guard is an off-duty cop – a sergeant, no less, and a fanatic biker. What sex (the cop not the bikes)? Female, mother of four, and a widow. Her left leg twists through 200 degrees – that was the Harley wreck. The weird elbow was a BMW. A Yamaha 750 did for her right knee. She is impressed by my leather leg gauntlet; her right leg has burn scars up to mid-thigh. She is wearing uniform biker's breeches; we can't compare scars.

Her sergeant's pay is 600 dollars a month. She has two kids at school and two in further education and supports her mum. Do the sums and you understand the need for extra income. We chat for half an hour out on the pavement. A lovely woman.

Colón, Monday 31 July

I have met with three Americans over the past few days. The first is ex-military on a disability pension. A staff-sergeant, he lost his left forearm in a parachute accident while serving a second tour of duty in the Canal Zone. He has bought a house in the Canal Zone from the Panamanian government and lives here with his second wife, Panamanian, and their baby girl. He is a Puerto Rican, Spanish-speaking, a small, thin man, grey-haired. He talks indignantly of America's surrender of the canal. In the old days Panamanians working in the Zone were paid American wages, as were the many employees of the American Zoners. The Panamanian government boasted of taking over the canal for the benefit of the Panamanian people.

So now who lives in the Zone?

Foreigners employed in the Free Trade Zone. Their Panamanian employees are paid the minimum wage: approximately 280 dollars a month.

Ernesto finds this ironic and is bitter at the treatment of the working class. As to the Iraq war, he believes that the US had to do something after the attack on the twin towers.

He is a keen angler, fishing from a dugout canoe. He holds the line in his right hand and loops the slack round his left stump. He catches good-sized fish and red friction burns from the line ring his stump. He suggests that I am courageous in riding a bike through Latin America. He asks how I feel on the bad days. I am ashamed to have bad days. This man is an expert on bad. He is an everyday hero.

The second of the three Americans is a teacher of history at the American school in Honduras. He is from New England. He is in his early thirties, a tall, quiet, thoughtful man. We discuss history and Central America and the war in Iraq. His father, a middle-of-the-road Republican, is against the war and believes that the US should withdraw immediately; the teacher votes Democrat and is also against. However, he believes that he would have enjoyed the army, the comradeship and being part of a team. He sent me an email yesterday. I thank him.

I met the third American in Portobelo – a yachtsman. He is one of a threesome at the restaurant where I eat dinner. His companions are a couple. The man is a Polish software engineer, also with a yacht. His girlfriend is English.

The American is a small man, pugnacious and opinionated – not much of a listener. He has read Tad Szulc's biography of Fidel Castro and spent a week in the Havana marina with his son and his son's friend. The son speaks Spanish. The yachtie doesn't. Yet he is an expert on Cuba. He suffered a painful (to him) divorce, which he blames on the confrontational system of justice the US inherited from the Brits. He blames the same confrontational system for most of the world's woes. He is obsessive on the subject. He harbours a hatred for authority of any kind. He warns me of Colombia, that the immigration and customs officers will let me in only for the cops to shake me down.

Were I Colombian cop, I would shake him to death. Half an hour of his company and I want to scream. I have sympathy for the engineer, an intelligent man, and for his bright, funny, English girlfriend. The freedom of the seas imprisons yachtsmen in odd company.

Colón, Wednesday 2 August

My passage is confirmed. The boat, *Don Sebas*, is a small trading vessel, twenty metres long. It sails from the Fifth Street Wharf for Cartagena. When? Today, tomorrow, the day after ...

How much? Two hundred dollars. There will be another biker: 'the Chino'. I ask the Chino's nationality. The captain shrugs. How should he know? A Chino is a Chino.

The captain buys copra in the San Blas Islands and the voyage takes around five days. Food is included – fried fish. Maybe a lobster.

Flying me and the bike to Medellín would cost 800 dollars.

Shipping the bike to Cartagena by container is 350 dollars. Add my airfare.

The German yacht was 500 dollars plus fifty for a dugout canoe out to Porto Vinir in the San Blas Islands.

Two hundred dollars is a bargain.

I move base from Portobelo to Colón. I have discovered a hotel out in what was the US Canal Zone. The Harbor Inn is close by the luxurious Melia. I pay for a big room with bath, a great bed, hot water, aircon. Staff are friendly, I have internet connection and the area is safe.

I ride to the canal and watch pilot vessels whiz across the lake to huge ships and watch the ships ease through the lake to the locks. Locals are used to the sight. I never tire of watching. Construction of the canal was the US at its best. Now Panamanians run the canal. They run it equally well.

I have a few beers with a retired governor of Colón province – he drinks Margaritas for the first hour. He believes that termination of the criminals is the only solution to crime in Colón. He gives The Black Hand in Brazil as an example. I am a liberal. I am against popping people without trial. I might feel differently if forced to live in Colón. Riding through on my bike is sufficiently scary.

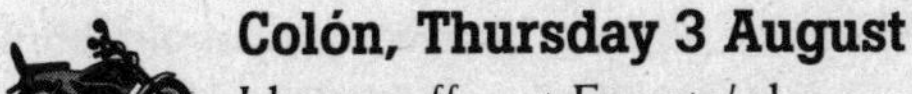

Colón, Thursday 3 August

I have coffee at Ernesto's house. Ernesto is the one-armed Puerto Rican ex-military. Ernesto is ambivalent as to the governor's belief. Shooting the mini-gangsters wouldn't solve the problem in the long term. Neither would employment or better education. Essential is personal responsibility.

'About every man I know here has a wife and three women on the side, all with kids. The men sit around in new shirts and pants and trainers. The kids go hungry.'

And not only the men are to blame: the women get pregnant in the hope of getting something out of the man. Three kids by three different men is common.

The kids have inadequate and irresponsible fathers as role models and worse role models in the music industry. Panamanian rap shocks and offends Ernesto. Rap has become less brutal in the US while, in Panama, it has become more vicious. Role models rap vile sexual obscenities and glorify violence.

Ernesto drops me off at the Zona Libre, the Free Zone. Free is freedom from import tax. The Zona Libre is as big as Colón. A wall surrounds it, guards at every gate. Within the walls is street after street of back-to-back shops and warehouses. What do you need? Five dozen pairs of trousers in assorted sizes and colours? Two dozen Dior sports shirts? A 5000-dollar Longines watch? Cooking pots, table china, tools, outboard motors – what ever is manufactured can be found right here in the Zona Libre ready for onward shipping to wherever.

Much of it is manufactured in China by workers on near-slave wages.

China's low wages guarantee unemployment for workforces in other developing economies (socialist togetherness). Forget multinationals as the big-beast criminals of the liberal establishment. Chinese wages are the monster. We must forbid imports from any nation without a reasonable minimum wage and we must insist that health inspectors check factories.

Why was I in the Zona Libre?

To buy a fishing rod for the voyage through the San Blas Islands on the good ship *Don Sebas*.

I have met the Chino. His name is Ming. He is forty years old, born in Indonesia of Chinese parents and a US citizen. He is an electronics engineer with a doctorate and has been granted a year's sabbatical by Hewlett-Packard in the hope that he will free himself of the travel bug. He rides a 650 Suzuki Endurance trail bike with a nine-gallon gas tank. He finds the 650 way too big and heavy for the trip.

Ming the Merciless has a red line across his throat. Three kids jumped him half a block from his downtown Colón hotel. All three carried knives. One held a knife to Ming's throat. The remaining two emptied Ming's pockets: five dollars.

Is Colón dangerous? Too damn right!

The harbourmaster on the Fifth Street wharf shows me the .38 revolver in his desk drawer. On the street, he carries the revolver tucked in his belt. Today he is wearing black baggy shorts and a gold-on-black Ghana shirt that balloons over his belly. I don't like to ask how he expects to make a quick draw from under his belly. Fact is, he would be dead, buried and gone to wherever such men go before laying a finger on the revolver's butt.

I stop off at the shopping mall and meet the Polish software engineer with a yacht and his giggly Brit. I say 'his' because she is his – not as a possession, but, as one says, 'my love'. They are in love. I notice so many small signs, the touch of a finger, the way their eyes meet, the ease with which they laugh together. They had read on my blog of my boat delay and had been planning to run me down to Cartagena on his twenty-eight-foot sailboat. A Honda 125 would just about fit on the deck.

Meanwhile they are searching for three-dollar shirts for him and a skirt for her. He needs a new shirt. The one he wears has lost its sleeves and advertises a career in boat maintenance: varnish, red lead primer, teak stain. For a top, the giggly Brit wears what might once have been a see-through nightdress now cut off above the belly.

They tell me that the unpleasant little American yachtsman with attitude had been thrown out of every bar on the Rio Dulce, Guatemala. I try to imagine what would get a man thrown out of a bar on the Rio Dulce. Fronteras is the AA capital of Central America. In their day, these AA members were serious drunks, men and women who could start a riot while barely capable of crawling across the floor. They were never thrown out. So I guess the American was thrown out for boring his fellow drinkers half to death.

Colón, Friday 4 August

Ernesto has been driving me round in his 4×4. We visit the Fifth Street wharf. A French biker on an ancient BMW with sidecar has come to inspect our transport. He has been travelling for-ever.

I visit Ernesto's home in the evening. Javier, the son of the owner of the Harbor Inn, has waited up. Javier runs the restaurant and bar. He and I sit at the bar, drink beer and yak until two in the morning. Untrue to write that I will miss Colón. No one could miss Colón. However, I have made good friends, kind and generous, with whom it will be a privilege to keep in touch.

Holiday Cruise

Colón, Friday 4 August

Ming and I and the bikes are on board. What a performance. First come the extras. Twenty dollars to load each bike. Ming is quiet and polite and speaks little Spanish. The boat crew mistake good manners for weakness. Mistake. Ming knows his mind and doesn't shift without considerable thought. We argue twenty dollars each down to fifteen for both. I do the talking.

The big black woman in the big-bellied wharf-master's office tries to hit for an extra ten dollars for customs clearance. I ask to be shown the regulation in the book. She surrenders sulkily. Colón, Colón, why art thou Colón? And why do downtown Colonese behave so shittily?

Not all. The gate guards are friendly and helpful. The extended family who run the bar-café at the gate are always welcoming.

Night-time and a crescent of lamps and palm trees give Colón's waterfront a spurious normalcy. Latino dance music blares from the café. A cool light breeze rises off the sea. I count sixteen ships out in the roads and listen to the throb of a tug's diesel engine. The immigration officer has visited. Much shouting accompanied his discovery of two extra men and a young woman not entered on crew or passenger list. He has departed with the captain and our passports. We were due to sail some time between midnight and two.

The money man is yelling at his cell phone.

I will refer to the money man as 'MM'. He is medium brown,

paunchy, clipped hair, wears spectacles and is forever on a cellular telephone. He shouts at the telephone to make sure his message reaches whoever he is talking with. Shouting has become habitual and he carries it over into general conversation. I fear an argument over payment for unloading the bikes. I attempt to clarify exactly where and when and how we disembark.

MM decides that I am stupid. 'Look,' he says, 'we are *contrabandistas*.' Smugglers. 'We come in to the coast and unload when we receive the all-clear. Three days, five, twenty ...'

'At a wharf.'

'On the beach.'

'Oh,' I say.

I tell Ming.

Ming is a student of Zen Buddhism. He smiles and says, 'We wanted an adventure.'

We sail from Colón at half past four. My fellow male passengers sleep on top of the deck cargo. They resemble a line of sardines. I bought a foam exercise mat in Panama City. I find space on the edge of the cargo below a car seat and a fold-up bicycle. I have to get up in the night. I pee over the rail and then lie awake. Sailing is a relief.

Deck cargo adds to the ship's roll on heavy swells from the north. A pretty pale mulatto in her late teens is the only woman. She is first to throw up. So does a thin black man who smokes both dope and a white powder up on the steel canopy shading the afterdeck – he narrowly avoids my shoes. A young male Latino is a further casualty. Ming speaks of a headache. I sit forward of the wheelhouse on a steel hatch in the early afternoon and watch the coast. Curious as to our progress, I ask MM where we are. We have passed Portobelo. He points to Mirimar and tells me we will sleep the night at one of the San Blas Islands.

We round a point and see the first of the San Blas Islands spread in a vast circle. The islands protect us from the swell. I consider alerting Ming. He lived his first nineteen years in Indonesia. He is familiar with small tropical islands, coconut palms, mosquitoes, beaches infested with sandflies. I let him sleep a further hour.

San Blas Islands, Saturday 5 August

I consult Ming as to whether this vast circle of islands is an atoll. Ming's doctorate is in electronic engineering rather than geography. His intellectual honesty is restful. When questioned on something of which he is ignorant, he says, 'I don't know.' Then he considers the question for a while, turning it this way and that.

We share a broad ignorance of the San Blas Islands. We know that they are Coona territory. The outer islands are seldom more than a hundred yards in length, uninhabited and the most romantic. Low mounds of pale, freshly washed sand, they sprout a single topknot of skinny coconut palms. Foam breaks over rock and coral between some islets. In the lee of the reef lie yachts at anchor in silken waters, where the breeze keeps the mosquitoes and sandflies at bay. The inner islands are larger, often fringed with mangrove and harbour communities, thatched huts packed close.

We approach Tigre Island the day of the Coona intercommunity football tournament. The football field is the only open space on the island. Dusk and we watch the players in the final match pelt helter-skelter in pursuit of a ball that is invisible to us.

Our captain eases the *Don Sebas* towards the end of a crude wooden jetty. Three Coona men sit on the jetty. They ignore the *Don Sebas*. The ship nudges the jetty and a sailor hurls a line. The line falls in the water. Only then does a Coona rise and wait for the next throw. I sense no hostility. Lack of interest is nearer the mark.

Ming and I stroll through the village to the football field. The huts are thatched roofs, stick walls, sand floors and no litter. We are greeted with quiet politeness by all those we pass. They are small people, Tibetan in feature, although dark skinned. The women are noticeably square of shoulder and wear footless stockings of strung beads.

A fence protects the open area surrounding the football field. A notice proclaims a tourist zone. A row of ten small huts is the community's tourist accommodation. A small thatched restaurant faces the huts from across the field. The shaded terrace is in two sections, male and female. Two young blonde German women eat dinner in the female zone. Two teenage Coona maidens sit at a second table with their backs to the football match. Fish, yucca, rice and fried bananas are on the menu. Ming and I order bottled water. The water comes chilled from an old kerosene icebox. The plastic seals on the bottles are torn. Presumably the bottles have been refilled from the village well. The two German women have their backs to us and intend keeping their backs to us. Travel is competitive among many backpackers. These young women were the sole foreigners on Tigre Island. This is their adventure. We are unwelcome.

The crew and passengers from the *Don Sebas* arrive at the field. They are boisterous and out of place.

Ming and I are the foreigners on board the hell ship. Foreigners are stupid by definition. Next are two oldies, one of whom is marked by posture as ex-military. He is a tall man, mahogany-skinned, balding, clipped military moustache and a bush of white sprouting from his ears. Our conversation is limited to his barked greetings in English. These are his only English words. Speaking Spanish to me would show ignorance or weakness on his part so we have no conversation. His companion is a small black man, monosyllabic.

The handsome young Latino and the skinny black man who threw up close by my shoes make a couple. Mostly they sleep. When awake, they clamber on to the canopy and return with glazed eyes.

A tattooed ex-prisoner in his late twenties joins them on occasion. He is heavily muscled and forever exercises his neck as boxers do in the movies. He has been free a while and his jail muscles have grown a layer of fat.

I suspected a small middle-aged Latino man with hooked nose and sunken mouth to have lost his teeth. Not so. He is the most companionable of those on board and sits with me in the bows. He has been working in Panama. He is returning home with a gift for his wife: the carefully wrapped sections of a wooden bed frame, a double bed.

Of the crew, the cook is fifties, balding and underweight – not surprising given the food. He wears shorts and a saffron shirt and squats on deck to scrub his pots at the tap, chop meat, fish, peel yucca, slice onions. MM shouts. The captain and the engineer are brothers. The captain speaks quietly and seldom. The engineer never speaks. The assistant engineer-deckhand is a muscle-bound oaf. He believes that he is a brilliant humorist. All his jokes are gross and illustrated with gross actions. Most involve effeminate males. His number-one friend is the companion of the young girl. The girl appears only when we dock. While at sea, she is prostrate in a small dank airless six-bunk cabin aft of the wheelhouse. The cabin opens on to the galley area. Little wonder that she throws up. Her man is off-black, late twenties, with a good body and ready mouth. He is also an addict of jokes at the expense of the effeminate. He has a loud voice and acts his jokes. I find him vile from day one – a judgement supported when he boasts of his conquests and of putting the girls to work in Cartagena – a pimp.

Ming and I seek peace on the afterdeck canopy. The smokers visit briefly for refills. Midnight and rain forces us back onto the cargo. The discomfort is barely eased by brief interludes of sleep.

Mid-evening, a fullish moon, and Ming and I walk through Tigre Island village. MM is shouting on the telephone at a cabin by the community meeting house. Cable & Wireless is the provider. The connection is by radio. I have twenty minutes left on my Cable & Wireless plastic and could call home. Bernadette has a rough day ahead and might consider being woken at four in the morning as more unfriendly than loving.

Seats in a semicircle face across swept sand beyond the community house to a table on which stand a hi-fi or lo-fi system. A Coona man asks whether we need bread. All Coona appear to speak quietly and I don't at first understand that the bread is merely an excuse. His true wish is to show us a badge on the door of his hut. The badge was given him by a biker stranded on the island for a month while waiting for a boat. It is the badge of the Latin American Biker's Association, Montevideo, Uruguay.

The Coona man recounts the occurrence of the Latin American biker with the same almost childlike simplicity that I recall in the marina janitor persecuted by the irritable mother-in-law. Childish? Simple? Or full of wonder at a world we take for granted and despoil?

San Blas Islands, Sunday 6 August

Mid-afternoon and the skipper creeps through a narrow channel between reefs to shelter in the lee of the only San Blas island with a hill. Next comes much yelling as he runs the *Don Sebas* aground while approaching a concrete wharf where two ships already lie.

I wondered this afternoon whether dislike of sailing by night is a Coona thing. Or is the skipper doubtful of his ability to thread the reefs? I asked to see the chart. There is no chart. Ah. Nor are there any lifebelts. The dinghy is powered by a temperamental outboard and has no oars. I relate this information to Ming the Unperturbed. Ming is unperturbed. Logic protects him. We wanted an adventure. We are having an adventure.

Ming and I are ashore on an island with a hill. We have eaten next to nothing since boarding in Colón. We have slept briefly. We haven't bathed and we haven't defecated – the lavatory is as vile as the crew's humour. A Coona man asks where we come from and where we intend travelling. He is polite, cultured. He owns a thirty-foot dugout canoe and two outboard motors. Women buy in Colón's Free Zone. The Coona runs them into Colombia. He has made two trips this week.

We are not smugglers. We are legal – a strange concept to this Coona.

We long to be put ashore at a regular port in Colombia, a port with immigration officers willing to stamp our passports and customs officers happy to document our bikes.

Very weird.

The Coona ponders: Well maybe, although it is unusual. Perhaps this once.

How much?

Again he ponders. Say, 150 dollars for Ming, self, Suzuki and Honda?

How long?

Depending on the weather, five hours, possibly six.

Ming and I imagine the hellish alternative: darkness, rolling deck, blackmailed over unloading charges, a launch to an unknown beach. A hundred and fifty dollars is cheap.

Can we talk in the morning?

'Certainly,' says the Coona. 'Talk any time.'

The Cable & Wireless office is a thatched hut with stick walls. Connection may be slow and there are four plastic chairs. A stick screen divides the chairs from two cabins. MM is bellowing at the telephone. Will we sail tomorrow? MM doesn't know. Nor does he know our precise destination – or the destination is secret.

Of the two boats alongside the village wharf, one has made two approaches to the Colombian mainland, only to be warned off. Ming and I imagine being arrested, the only legals.

A young Coona sits with us. He introduces himself as David. He speaks competent English. He is nineteen years old and in his last year of high school in Panama City where his dad works as a carpenter. David has a website and intends working in the islands as a tourist guide.

Behind us, the village kids are watching a DVD in a community hut – for the Coona, everything has its place. The kids are very quiet. Ming peeks in. The movie is a Hong Kong kung fu.

Ming and I ask the two women on duty at the community store whether prawns are available.

Certainly – and lobster and fresh fish.

Our juices bubble in anticipation.

But not tonight, say the women. A girl child has been born in the village. Girls are the core of the Coona community. The birth of a girl demands much ceremony. Everyone is tired. Tomorrow we can eat prawns.

With chilli?

Certainly with chilli.

Ming and I love this island. We love the people. We love their good manners and their quietness and their consideration – and we love the thought of escape from the *Don Sebas*. We will spend two days here before shipping the bikes by canoe to Turbo. We will swim from a clean beach. We will eat *camarones a el diablo* – devilled prawns.

The crew summon us to eat on board.

Ming and I would rather starve.

In the morning we will talk with the owner of the canoe.

Colombia, Monday 7 August

Ming and I sleep up on the canopy. Rain drives us in. The revolting deckhand has occupied my nook. I doze in one of the loose car seats. The ex-military man swings in a hammock nearby. His farts would startle a deaf horse. Ming fares little better. We rise with dawn and spot a canoe speeding through the reefs. Our canoe. Our saviour.

We rush to English-speaking David's house. It is not his house. Coona houses belong to women. The man moves in to his wife's house – or, in David's case, his mother-in-law's house. The mother-in-law is baking bread. High-school David's wife sits in a hammock. She and David have one small toddler. A second is on its way. David is picking coconuts on the mountain with his father-in-law and his wife's younger brother.

Mother-in-law is deeply serious, a thinker, and committed to the community.

She had wanted an education for her daughter. Education is important. Throughout the world, women are considered merely part human and part beast of burden. Only education will free women. She is less wondrous than Coona men, more practical. She talks of another daughter in Panama City who has a *mestizo* child and has taken on Latino ways. It happens, she says, although mostly it is the men who leave. The community demands responsibility from each member. Few men are responsible. While she talks, she feeds us delicious bread and fish smoked in a rolled leaf.

We leave to speak with MM. MM is on the telephone.

David arrives from the mountain with a sack of coconuts. The owner of our canoe has crossed to another island to meet the flight from Panama City.

He will return in the early afternoon – if the plane is on time.

The crew hustles us to board. MM has the all-clear. The hell ship is sailing. Our options have run out.

No land in sight and ten-foot rollers all afternoon and into the night as we cross the gulf. Cloud covers the moon and we sail without lights. Tension is thick and heavy as a loaf of wet bread. We peer into the dark. At three o'clock a small light flashes.

A deeper blackness gains shape – rocks and walls rather than trees. Five big outboard launches speed alongside. Two huge men are the first to board. Twenty black stevedores follow. Side tarpaulins are furled. Tarpaulins are yanked clear of the deck cargo. The big men stand on truck tyres to conduct the unloading. Everything is labelled. Stevedores shout the name on a bale or carton. MM shouts the launch number. These are pros. They have done this a hundred times or a thousand times. The speed impresses. MM screams for extra care as two big jet-skis are manhandled into one launch. Two outboard motors follow – high horsepower by the size of the cartons. This is an upmarket launch, side rails, centre wheel. I watch as it speeds off into the night. The skipper warns us to tell immigration and customs that we came by launch from the Panamanian border.

Ming and I and the bikes are last to be loaded off the hell ship. First there comes an argument over payment to the stevedores. We settle at twenty dollars for each bike and find ourselves in an open launch at half past four in a pitch-black morning. The coxswain is an onlooker while three black stevedores lower the bikes. The outboard won't start. The coxswain curses and yanks the starter cord a dozen times. The motor fires. The coxswain engages forward gear. The motor stalls. The coxswain curses and yanks the cord again while the crew of the hell ship watch and bawl advice.

Neither Ming nor I is confident.

Finally we splutter away from the ship. We run at most a quarter of a mile to a beach below rocks and a ruined stone wall. Two of the black men leap into the water and hold the launch steady against the surge. Ming and I prepare to disembark. The coxswain disabuses us. The black men want twenty dollars. We have negotiated the price to be paid on arrival. Apparently this isn't arrival. Rather than argue in the dark, I pay ten and we head back out to sea.

We run parallel to a heavy swell. Cloud covers the moon. The launch rolls, the launch pitches, the motor stutters. This is not good.

True, it is an adventure.

Not all adventures are good.

Twenty anxious minutes pass before a thin scattering of lights in the distance indicates a coast. Clouds clear. The moon is almost full. We discern low buildings, a ramp, a dozen men waiting. The crossing, if it was a crossing, has taken forty-five minutes. The outboard stalls. There are no oars. Waves threaten to fling the launch on the rocks. The coxswain yells at his assistant, who fights the bows straight with a long punt pole.

All the men waiting on shore are black. They are shirtless and wear shorts or pants rolled above the knee. They wade out, grab the launch by the stern and run it up the sand. They lift the Honda first, carrying it clear of the water and up the stone ramp. The Suzuki weighs a ton. The men gasp and complain and yet keep the bike dry. I watch them and feel immense relief. Finally the awful voyage is done with.

Colombia

Illegal immigrants, Tuesday 8 August

The ramp serves a village of low mud shacks. One of the men fetches fresh water and rinses salt from the bikes while we explain the mathematics of the price agreed on the hell ship minus the ten dollars paid to the two men already disembarked. The men are wonderfully good-natured, friendly, curious. They laugh among themselves and at the weak jokes I attempt and they accept the maths.

I long to ask why black people do all the heavy work. Is this an all-black village? Or is Colombia similar to the rest of the world?

The Honda fires first kick. The Suzuki is electric start. We ride down a deserted street of dry rutted mud with first light paling the horizon. An hour later we are in a small town, San Bernardo. We find a police station. A disinterested cop listens to our story and studies our passports in that way officials do when they would rather be doing something else. He imagines filling forms and more forms. Ming's 650 Suzuki Endurance with its nine-gallon gas tank is more interesting.

Where do we intend going?

Cartagena.

Then go to Cartagena.

We need food and drink. Our dollars are useless. The bank won't open for another ninety minutes. We ride to the next and larger town. We eat fresh-baked sweet rolls and drink great coffee on a small square across from a bank. Colombians surround us. They, too, are friendly and curious. After Colón, this is heaven.

The bank opens. They don't change dollars. The four ATMs in town are down.

Our predicament is discussed on the café terrace. A small boy leads me through the market to a hardware store. The elderly owner has a Jewish name and wears a gold crucifix on a gold neck chain. He changes twenty dollars at a punitive rate of exchange. We pay for breakfast and ride towards the coastal resort town, Tolu, midway to Cartagena.

I lead. Ming follows. Cops stop us at a roadblock. They ignore the Honda. They ignore our passports. The Suzuki has their total attention and their total admiration. Are they bikeists or biggists? Your call.

We ride through ranch lands towards Tolu. The ranch houses are of a richer class than those I have seen on this journey. There is greater taste in the use of the land – countryside as art as in much of the United Kingdom. There is less litter.

The Bank of Colombia is in the central plaza in Tolu. A kind ATM spits pesos at us. We head on to Cartagena. We are illegals. We hit a roadblock every twenty or so kilometres. Most times the cops wave and pass us through. Those that do stop us do so to admire Ming's Suzuki. They find us an odd couple and they laugh easily. Perhaps we are odd.

Slender Chinese Ming, the putative Zen Buddhist monk, is ageless and rides a vast bike.

The fat Brit on his pizza delivery Honda is Caucasian and clearly well past his prime. As travelling companions go, definitely odd.

We have enjoyed little sleep over the past three days. We have waded ashore. We have ridden for eight hours. Ming is in shorts and a T-shirt. I wear a long-sleeved red-cotton shirt and chinos that had seen better days when they were new. We are unwashed. We stink. And we are illegals.

We follow the signs to the historic centre of Cartagena. The road swings round the bay and we spot a yacht marina. We need advice and Colombians who deal with yachts deal with customs and immigration. Alirio de Avila Lora is boss of warehousing and imports at Todomar Marina S.A. He listens to our story and despatches us behind a guide to the Office of Immigration.

We explain our case to an official. His boss must decide our fate. We wait nervously on an old sofa in an outer office.

Four female officials occupy the office. One is dealing with two young foreign women, one of whom is bored and reads a book while her friend has her fingerprints entered. Reading strikes me as neither politic nor polite. A middle-aged Italian complains loudly at another desk. His voice is brutal and he jabs fingers at documents he presents and at papers that the woman official peruses. The woman catches my eye and raises her eyebrows in exasperation. I reply with a grin of sympathy.

The exhausted Ming has dozed off and is tilting sideways. I dig him in the ribs. The boss returns. Once more we recount our story, apologise for our appearance, explain that we came directly from the road. He asks how long we intend staying in Colombia.

We say, 'Ten days, possibly two weeks.'

We return to the outer office. I ask one of the women what nationalities she finds most courteous and which are the most arrogant.

She answers without need for thought: all Ecuadorians are courteous. Italians are invariably rude and arrogant.

The boss returns our passports. He has written sixty days on a Cartagena entry stamp. 'Hurry,' he tells us, 'and you will reach the customs offices before they close.'

Our guide has been guarding the bikes. He leads us to the customs. We are directed to a large open-plan office. We relate our adventure to an official, who finds us hilarious. He gathers his fellow officials. They find us hilarious. Ming is the centre of attraction. Ming is a make of cellular telephone imported from China.

What does 'Ming' mean?

'It is my name,' Ming says.

'But it has a meaning?'

'People,' Ming says. 'Ming is people.'

We are part of an ongoing joke between our official and the boss. The boss is a dark tall elegant man. He speaks with Ming in English – not about our bikes or illegal arrival in Colombia but about matters of language and Ming's past. And didn't we consider that travelling with smugglers was dangerous – that they could cut our throats and dump us in the sea?

Meanwhile import papers for our bikes accrue signatures as they circle from desk to desk. A beautiful young woman enters their numbers in a ledger. The boss adds a final signature and we can leave.

I say to the boss that I am reluctant to leave when faced by such beauty. The boss laughs. The woman asks for a translation.

'Be satisfied,' her boss says. 'Satisfied that it was extremely complimentary.'

I kiss her hand and we leave.

We are legal.

I remark to Ming that, were this England, we would have been filling forms for a month.

Ming says, 'Chinese and a weird beard – in the States someone would have shot us on the beach.'

We have rooms at the Hotel San Philipe. The hotel faces across Centenary Square to the Old City. The elevator works. The rooms are large and air-conditioned and have good bathrooms with warm-water showers. We have three beds each – all air-conditioned rooms have three beds. I wish to know what particular Colombian custom this satisfies. The receptionist giggles.

We check email at an internet café and report our safe arrival to family and friends. Ming admits to a band of students that he is a US citizen. The students accuse the US of having stolen Panama from Colombia. To become a US citizen, Ming passed a citizenship exam. The syllabus didn't mention Colombia.

Cartagena, Wednesday 9 August

I, who wake for a pee three or four times a night, sleep the sleep of the just, eight hours straight. Ming does likewise. We breakfast at the hotel (ham and eggs, juice, coffee). We walk the old city. We stroll unafraid for five hours in the morning and a further three hours in the afternoon. We visit museums and churches and peep into private houses and ask permission to visit the shaded patios of official and unofficial buildings.

Cartagena is Spanish colonial at its best, painted in soft pastels of blue, white, red and ochre. The buildings are cared for. There is little litter. Beautiful, beautiful, beautiful. And the people. Students from the university spill off the pavements, sensuous and light of spirit. The gene pool is bewildering.

In the evening we drink cold local beer in a square beneath the city walls before progressing to an open-air restaurant. The owner is so obviously Italian (I ask, and am correct). A tall, handsome man. His walk retains a vestige of youthful swagger. The weariness and anxiety in sunken eyes betray him. A smile that switches off the moment he turns his back; the greying hair long at the back and lifeless after years of late nights and kitchen heat, the necessary cigarette: all these contribute to the portrait of the immigrant in an uncertain political and economic climate.

Ming and I order the dish for which Cartagena cuisine is famous: a fish and shellfish stew. The stew is rich with prawns and baby octopus and clams. We are surrounded by the perfect architecture of the sixteenth century. We have escaped from the hell of the ship and of Colón and find ourselves in heaven. We have shared an adventure that was often stressful, mostly uncomfortable and sometimes dangerous. We have become friends – not in a casual 'Hey, do you know my friend Ming?' sort of friendship but a friendship of true affection and of shared thoughts. Tomorrow we will part. Ming has a friend to meet and I have my work. We plan to meet in Bolivia.

Cartagena, Thursday 10 August

Today I work. I walk and walk: first to the marina to thank those who helped me and Ming with advice when we first arrived. My Mexican bags have holes. I buy new ones in the market and watch a cobbler for a couple of hours while he adds reinforcing. I find a good road map and a book of Spanish verbs at a bookstore in the historic quarter. I bring my writing and correspondence up to date.

Supermarkets sell fat-free yoghurts. I buy two, take them to a juice stall and have the lady spin me a smoothie. In the evening I walk past the second-hand bookstores on the square to the prawn and oyster stalls and dine on a huge prawn cocktail for two dollars. Each stall has a few plastic chairs, good for people-watching. For cabaret I watch teams of speed-bladers circle a banked concrete hippodrome. Finally I head back into the historic quarter for a beer. A genius did the lighting of the cathedral. The three domes for the Trinity and the clock above the main entrance glow a pale soft gold against the midnight blue of the sky. Ming has gone but Ming is here. The calm with which he ponders leaves a comfortable aftertaste.

Tomorrow is a day of rest. I will eat more prawns, enjoy the architecture, admire the people and enjoy myself.

On the road again, Saturday 12 August

I am mobile and South America lies ahead. The sky is blue. The few clouds are charming puffs of white. I have escaped the rain.

Although wet, Central America was easy. The countries are small and crossed in two or three days. South America is vast. Colombia is vast, even that half that has roads.

In heading directly south to Medellín, Ming re-rode our first day's travel. I decide to circle. I head northeast along a coast of beaches and brilliant blue sea to Barranquilla. I spot a Honda agency in Barranquilla. I need a replacement for a mirror broken while unloading from the hell ship. No mirrors – however, the agents (husband and wife) insist on giving the Honda a quick service – free of charge. A young mechanic works while we chat. My travel impresses. I feel a fraud. I have ridden a bike, no big deal. I have enjoyed myself, met interesting people, made new friends, made a few dumb mistakes.

From Barranquilla, I continue along the coast towards Santa Marta. The highway runs between sea and lagoons. Fisher families live either side of the highway. They live in flimsy shacks crammed one against the other on salt flats that frequently flood. The shacks must be damp. The heat on the coast is intense. The air stinks of hot wet salt and last week's fish. Canoes under small square sails slip across the varnished surface of the lagoons. Photograph them and you have beauty. Photograph reality and you come close to hell.

Highway 45 to Bogotá splits from the Santa Marta highway fifty kilometres from Barranquilla. Truck traffic is heavy. Many trucks are empty. I discover later that these are coal trucks returning to the mines. The mines are US-owned. My informant is an ardent supporter of the Venezuelan president, Chavez. He tells me, 'Gringos take everything and leave us with nothing but disease.' Presumably he refers to silicosis.

The empty trucks spit coal fragments. My face stings. My gloves and shirt are black. Traffic is too heavy for enjoyment of the countryside. Soldiers guard the road, seldom a kilometre between posts. Police roadblocks are frequent. Most police wave me through. Those that stop me don't ask for documents. They are merely curious as to how far I have travelled and how far I intend travelling. I answer that I fear wasting my last few years rather than seeking new experiences.

They enquire of my family and what my wife thinks of my travels.

I reply that she would rather have an old dog that hunts and sometimes brings gifts back from the field than one who hardly moves from the hearth.

Navigating the truck-infested highway is exhausting. I stop early at a town that has no reason for existence other than to service trucks and drivers. I find a reasonable room with bath, fan and lock-up parking for six dollars. I sit on the terrace and drink soda with fresh lime. A gang of curious ten-year-olds and a young waitress sit with me. They question me on life in England, bikes and travel. I question the children on family, school and ambitions – and the waitress on boyfriends, wages and her opinions of the town (jail from which she hasn't sufficient schooling to escape).

I drink a beer with a dinner of rich chicken and vegetable soup followed by steak and onions with plain boiled rice. Trucks thunder by. None of the drivers is black – why do I notice such things? Early to bed: I intend reaching Girón tomorrow (420 kilometres): a small Spanish colonial town that is a national monument.

To Girón, Sunday 13 August

Both Ming and I had imagined the Darien gap as impenetrable swamp. Instead we sailed past fold upon fold of jungle-covered mountains. Colombia has an image problem and Hollywood is a lousy PR agent. Hollywood projects images of brave US citizens (Harrison Ford) fighting cocaine barons of Medellín and Cali. The scenery is jungle. The men wear grease in their hair. Tom Clancy is a great promoter of the same image. I am on the road by quarter past six and travel for six hours through a vast parkland of great trees and lush paddocks, clean streams, fat cattle and sleek horses. Everything is cared for and there is almost no litter – but why fences, I wonder? Surely where shrubs grow fast, hedges would be more economical and more decorative. To my left rise mountains and the border with Venezuela – dangerous territory.

Trees line the road and I ride in a green tunnel from which soldiers in camouflage emerge every kilometre or so to wave at the weird old man with a beard on the small white Mexican bike.

I pass plantations of oil palms. Crossing a river, I note that cormorants float low in the water. I recognise but am unable to put a name to a pair of birds, black with thin curved beaks. Neither can I name a small raptor with white patches on tail and wings. Fun to carry a bird book – but I don't have space.

A ride of 420 kilometres: I am beginning to tire, my butt hurts and my hip joints ache. The final section threads through green hill country. Roadside notices advertise campsites and swimming holes in the rivers. I am too tired to enjoy the views.

The side road to Girón forks right off Highway 45A a few kilometres short of Bucaramanga. Girón is a whitewashed Andalusian town transported to a bowl in the Colombian mountains. A small river winds through the town. All roads are cobbled. Most houses are single-storey; all have pantiled roofs and wood shutters. I find a room on the first floor of a beautiful boutique hotel on the Plaza Central. Trees shade the plaza. Sunday and the town is full of daytrippers.

I shower and rest an hour before taking a second shower and venturing out. This is the hour of the Sunday *passeo*. Courting couples hold hands and giggle. Their elders are more taken by the food off street stalls (corn, grilled meat, beef sausages, ice-cream). Bells ring. The religious enter the church for evening Mass or cross themselves.

Girón is bliss. I walk and walk and people smile and greet me. I find two smaller squares. Both are shaded by trees. A small, simple, sixteenth-century church overlooks the first. A storyteller performs in the square to an attentive and appreciative crowd. He relates the fable of a German immigrant family and their Alsatian. The punch line is that there is no point to life without heart.

I watch the kids seated cross-legged on the cobbles. Spellbound is a good description. No wriggling, no 'Mum, fetch me a Coke'.

The Polish yachtsman with the giggly Brit in Portobelo is a software engineer. Ming is an electronics engineer. Tonight I eat dinner on Girón's central square with a chemical engineer. A Bolivian of German and Serbian heritage, he lives in Girón and has established the first bio-diesel plant in Colombia. Palm nuts provide the raw material. Three of his plants have been sold in Bolivia. Although in his sixties, he remains as enthusiastic as a kid (dumb statement – so many kids complain of being permanently bored).

To Villa de Leiva, Monday 14 August

The highway from Bucaramanga follows a green river valley a short way before hitting mountains. The Honda and I are well rested. We face only 300 kilometres to Villa de Leiva. No reason to hurry and I am at one with the bike as we swoop into the curves. We climb and climb. These are dry mountains. Even the air feels brittle. Brilliant sun sparkles on rock. Views are astounding.

A statue to the Virgin Mary blesses the inside of a curve near the head of the ascent. Headlamps rather than flowers are the offerings. Some of the lamps are connected to a power supply. At night, the statue must be a beacon.

I stop at a café at the summit of the pass and ask the woman serving behind the bar why headlamps for the Virgin? Surely this a special cult, a celebration of some extraordinary occurrence, a miracle, a vision?

'Lightbulbs last longer than candles,' she tells me.

Travelling brings such wondrous surprises.

The woman asks where I have come from and where I am going and refuses payment for my coffee.

Turn a corner and I have changed climate and landscape. Here all is green. Dairy cows graze upland paddocks. Silver-grey moss drapes trees shading coffee bushes. Honey is for sale beside the road, and apples and pears. I pass patches of tobacco, the drying barns open-sided. What tobacco grows at this altitude, so different from the humid climate of Cuba to which I am accustomed?

These uplands farms are so different from the industrialised agriculture of the United States. Fields have been created by centuries of back-breaking toil. I think of upstate New York and those small fields of the early settlers now uneconomic and abandoned to woodland.

The highway leads to Bogotá. I take a left fork to Tunja. The road rises to around 2500 metres. I ride through a narrow defile, a stiff chill wind blows in my face and the Honda is a little breathless. Beyond are fell lands that recall the Cheviots and Westmorland, although without the drystone walls. The road drops into Tunja, a university town, and then zigzags upwards and upwards across barren mountains. A final drop takes us into a wide bowl. Villa de Leiva is to the right. All the houses are whitewashed. Most are single-storey. Cobbles are small: the streets of Villa de Leiva are paved with river boulders. The Honda bumps and skitters. I find a pretty room with bathroom at the hotel Villa del Sol and negotiate an out-of-season nightly rate of ten dollars for two days. The hotel is spotless, the shower piping hot.

Villa de Leiva, a chill evening and the vast cobbled plaza is deserted. It is a space that demands movement, cattle, horses, market stalls. Its emptiness threatens my composure. I feel very alone as I walk uphill to a restaurant recommended by the woman of all tasks at the hotel. She is a woman to be admired and trusted, very matter-of-fact. She tells of her daughter, five years old. No, no husband – most men here are irresponsible. Better to remain single than share life with someone for whom you have no respect.

She is a good guide to a good meal. I have fasted all day and order *churrasco* (grilled steak). The steak is vast, tender and full of flavour. I flirt with a young woman, two years old. Her father is French, chief chef at the French embassy in Washington. The mother is Colombian. They met while Bertrand was chef at the embassy in Bogotá. He and I drink coffee together. He talks of his future. He has a reputation in Washington. He would earn top money in a restaurant. The thought of living in the US horrifies him. Everything revolves around money. I hear Ming speak and the Korean monk on the beach in Mexico and the Polish software engineer who deserted a top job in Boston.

Bertrand's wife wants to move home to Colombia. Bertrand would like to try Chile. An opening at the embassy in Santiago would give them an opportunity to sample the life. He has already researched fees at a good private school: 2500 dollars per annum.

Villa de Leiva, Tuesday 15 August

Villa de Leiva is a classic example of early Hispanic urban planning. All streets meet at right-angles. No house is sufficiently tall to block the breeze from its neighbours. The exteriors are simple – display of wealth was both dangerous and vulgar. Peek through doorways and you glimpse greenery and perhaps feel a soft breeze cooled by a fountain or pond. So, yes, Villa de Leiva is very Spanish. It is also very Moorish.

Hundreds of years of Moorish occupation must have left few Spaniards of pure Hispanic blood, whatever that is. I am part Spanish. Thus, almost certainly, I am part Moor – and also Italian, German, Scots and God knows what besides.

That Spanish-Moorish part imagines those settlers in 1570. They were men of small stature, small education and many superstitions. I scan the parched mountains that surround the flat green valley of which the town is kernel. I imagine that the mountains must have made those settlers from across an immense ocean finally feel safe: safe because the mountains enclosed an understandable space, and a space they could defend. I wonder how many (or whether any) closet Moors were of their number. Historians tell us of closet Jews. We remain in ignorance of Muslims. Strange.

I cross the plaza to admire the Carmelite convent. Founded in 1645, the convent remains occupied by nuns of the order. The walls of the houses opposite are recently whitewashed. Spattering of whitewash on the cobbles shoots me back in memory to a rented house in Ibiza Old

Town with my two elder sons, Antony and Mark. I am overcome by a longing to hold them in my arms as they were then, silken-skinned midgets bronzed and bleached by the Mediterranean Sea and sun. In my longing they meld with their half-brothers at the same age. The sense of loss leaves me exhausted and I sit on an oblong marker stone in the plaza. French chef Bertrand and his family pass by and I take their photograph. The pain ebbs. The sun shines. I watch people cross the cobbles.

A group of Spanish-speaking black people are obvious tourists. Few black Colombians live up here in the mountains. Villa de Leiva is Indian, white Hispanic and a mix of the two. Yes, and a sprinkling of incomers drawn by beauty and a low cost of living.

I need Bernadette. I head for an internet café and check email. Bernadette reports that two of my sons, half-brothers, have been discussing universities on the telephone. Melding.

To Tunja, Wednesday 16 August

I eat breakfast at the Hotel Villa del Sol. The owners and staff are in the kitchen. The quietness with which they speak and work reminds me of the San Blas Coona. I expect cold on the pass to Tunja and dress in long-coms, thick chinos, high socks, thermal vest, cord shirt, short-sleeved jumper, windcheater. I was tired on Monday and anxious to reach Villa de Leiva and suffered the mountains merely as a barrier to cross. I am fresh today and glory in the climb.

Centuries of erosion have stripped the mountains bare. The rock has a rose tint that darkens as cloud shadow snakes over the ravines. A few minute vegetable gardens nestle among the rocks. Reach the crest and I am back in Westmorland and the Scottish borders. I stop at a police post to discover the altitude. A cop tells me – close to 4000 metres. He and his partner shake my hand and wish me well on my travels.

A university city, Tunja is full of students. In architecture it is a mix of the historic sublime and mediocre modern. A policeman accompanies me to a car park and instructs the guard to watch over my bike. I am about to pay. The policeman tells me to put my money away and walks with me to visit a church that has been converted into the municipal library. Few books are new. The librarian shrugs dispiritedly: governments have other priorities.

I attended seven o'clock Mass this morning at Villa de Leiva in the parochial church on the plaza (the only time it was open during my visit). The church is big and plain. I like plain. We were a congregation of twelve. I felt nothing. Here, in Tunja, I visit the church of Santo Domingo. Built in the final years of the sixteenth century, the church is small and panelled wall to wall with carved wood, richly gilded. I don't like ornate and yet I am overawed.

Two early colonial mansions remind me of houses I have visited in Morocco and in Santo Domingo, capital of the Dominican Republic. These are homes built in the first half of the sixteenth century. They are simple in construction, unclad wooden beams, polished board floors, plain plaster. One of the homes has a view from the upper gallery of the Carter Bar, except that this is Colombia rather than the borders of Scotland. We are at 2800 metres above sea level. I walk a couple of hours without feeling breathless and buy a smart rain jacket marked down to twenty-eight dollars.

Small, dark cafés abound where students can discuss metaphysics, revolution, rap artists and football. I find a light café and eat fresh strawberries without cream or sugar. Two pretty young women enter. They select a huge pastry filled with berries and cream and topped with ice-cream. I warn them that guilt-free pleasure in such joys is for the young. 'Enjoy while you can.'

Tivasosa is forty-eight kilometres northeast of Tunja. I have been told that it is unique both in colonial architecture and in having a woman mayor and a woman chief of police. The town is small, tidy and clean. The central square is pretty, no more. The mayor is a man; so is the chief of police. So much for my informant! I ride back to Tunja. Friesian cattle graze small fields protected by small woods. The hills are so Westmorland that I expect to meet a friend, Tom Lowther, walking a lurcher. Even the thin drizzle is familiar and I am cold, despite the addition of the new jacket. I am also happy – loneliness has no place in this familiar landscape.

I book into a modern hotel on the outskirts of Tunja and am welcomed into a group seated on couches in the lobby and drinking great coffee. The couches are upholstered in shiny brown fake leather. Two elderly farmers (OK, probably ten years younger than me) are buying a new trailer for what they call here a 'mule' or 'tractor-mule' – the part of a trailer-truck that has the engine and driver's cab. The trailer is an investment. They wear thick grey ponchos all evening. They sit side by side on a couch half listening to the conversation and half watching the TV news. They are accompanied by a younger man, fifties, tall and sort of city, who leafs though a trailer catalogue. A fourth man is from Bogotá and sells cured hams. I undergo the usual inquisition: Where am I going, where did I start out, what are my impressions of Colombia?

I reply that I knew of Colombia only from the movies and books. The Colombia I have ridden through came as a surprise. It seems so normal and so agriculturally rich and developed – so European.

'Americans know Colombia only for cocaine,' the city man says.

'And Europeans,' the ham man adds. 'All foreigners think the same.'

'It's the movies,' I say.

'American movies,' the city guy says. 'Americans finance the drug trade and they blame Colombia. Drugs are an American problem.'

I had heard the same in Guatemala from both a senior police officer and the head of a security company: that ninety per cent of crime in Guatemala was financed by the US.

Through Bogotá, Thursday 17 August

Colombians are extraordinarily kind. This morning the ham salesman takes two small painted amulets of the Virgin and Child from round his neck as a present to protect me on my travels.

I ride away from the hotel at seven. I have added an extra undershirt and a second pair of trousers against the cold. I need a ski suit. Mist shrouds the highway for the first twenty kilometres. Sun breaks through and I find myself in a land of lush green hills that are even more reminiscent of Westmorland and the Scottish Borders than those of yesterday. I funk Bogotá. I am not in the mood for big cities. The traffic terrifies me. The young driver of a new blue GM Corsa draws alongside to ask where I am going and wish me good luck. So do two cops on a big police bike. Try riding a small Honda through Bogotá traffic while sandwiched into a three-way conversation. I yell to the cops that I am trying to find the Pan-Americano. The cops activate their flashing blue light. The cop riding pillion beckons me to follow. The police hurtle across an intersection. My memory of the following ten minutes is blank. I suspect that I rode with my eyes shut.

Beyond Bogotá the road drops, following a river. Each side of the road sprouts weekend homes and hotels and restaurants with pools. Why would people build on the verge of a busy highway? Colombians must enjoy noise.

I stop and peel off a pair of pants, two jackets and a shirt. A great flat hot plain lies ahead. I ride between huge paddy fields, vast fields of cotton and a few fields of tarragon that my informant believes is used in brewing beer. Trees shade much of the road. I pass Giradot and cross a long bridge frighteningly high above a river that flows through a narrow gorge of greenery. Ibaque is next, and then the Quindio Pass – 3350 metres at the crest.

Colombians regard double yellow lines as a challenge. Drivers of huge trucks overtake on blind curves. Add a car on the outside hard shoulder and a couple of bikes whipping through on the nearside hard shoulder and you have the picture. One further detail – the almost sheer drop.

All Colombian drivers drive in the same manner, understand the rules and are miraculously good-natured. The cops wear camouflage and would be invisible but for phosphorescent chest stripes. They stop the occasional bus and check papers. Mostly they are umpires ready to call foul on one or other driver in a collision.

Meanwhile local farmers carry on their trade as if they were farming a flat field rather than a precipice. Lose your footing and you slide a few thousand feet. Terrifying! The men are small and dark and wear hats and boots and ponchos. Vegetables are the product. Posts and wires for tomato vines march up a near-vertical slope. A dozen packhorses carry sacks of potatoes.

Farms give way to pine forest for the final few kilometres. I have both my jackets back on. Cloud closes in. Wind hits at the summit of the pass. Visibility clears. Way below, pale fluffy cloud rolls against the mountain face. Overhead, darker cloud threatens rain. I have underestimated the time needed for the climb and head downhill in a race against nightfall. I have to brake to a halt three times or be crushed by oncoming trucks both overtaking and swinging wide on a curve.

The city of Armenia lies at the foot of the mountains. A young cop stops me in heavy traffic on a bridge into the city. By law, Colombian bikers display their bike plate numbers on their chests and back. I don't. Why don't I? A police sergeant arrives and tells the young cop to stop being stupid. The sergeant then stops a local bus to ask the driver for directions to a hotel.

I have commented previously on the extraordinary helpfulness of Colombians and of their friendliness and the interest they take in my journey. I do so again. They help and they help and they help.

An earthquake in 1999 destroyed much of Armenia. I feel churlish in adding nothing more to my description of the city. I don't have anything to add.

To Popayán, Friday 18 August

Glorious day. I ride towards Cali across what I believe to be a flat open valley. Hedges surround huge mansions built by coffee barons in golden years. Coffee prices are rock bottom. FOR SALE and FOR RENT signs are common. A gorge opens to the right. A gorge opens to the left. What I had believed to be a flat valley is a promontory that narrows and narrows. I ride down onto a vast plain of sugar fields and cotton. A small stream borders a field of cotton. Giant bamboos grow along the stream bank. The cotton is in bud. The surface of the field is white. The feathery fronds of the bamboo are a pale brilliant green.

I stop at Buga.

Here, on the Guadalajara river, Christ appeared to the early Spanish settlers in the years from 1570 to 1575.

A huge redbrick basilica celebrates the visitations. The basilica was completed in the early 1900s. It has been further modernised with lighted red signs marking the bookstore and the office that receives applications for Masses of remembrance.

Inside the basilica, a video of the service is projected on flat screens attached to the pillars. Electronic noticeboards display the time of masses. The arches supporting the main dome are lined with electric Christmas lights. Gold leaf abounds and so do worshippers; the pews each side of the central aisle are three-quarters full for midday Mass. The priest is in mid-sermon when I enter. He is in mid-sermon when I leave. This is religion for the TV age, Catholicism designed to compete with TV evangelists.

I gaze down from the entrance at an avenue of shopping arcades. All the shops sell religious tat. The streets leading left and right of the basilica are similarly lined. The whole forms a cross on which is crucified both religious and artistic taste. A recreation of the tower of the original church stands beside the basilica, the church built by the original settlers. It is small, simple and unadorned.

A right turn off the freeway takes me eighty kilometres through hills to Popayán. A cop on a Yamaha toots a greeting and waves as he speeds by up the first hill. I think of the horrid little American with the yacht at Portobelo. Of Colombia, he said, 'The cops will shake you down.'

The road to Popayán follows the crest of a ridge for part of the way. The sky is almost black directly overhead; to the east a long clerical-grey blanket drapes the peaks of the Cordillera Central. The mountains to the west are further away; pale grey cloud clings to their lower slopes; their spiky summits are brilliantly sunlit. Between lies a hilly land of paddock and woods. Sunlight penetrates gaps in the cloud; hills are a patchwork of light and shade.

On one hill, a Renault, overtaking across double yellow lines, has smashed head on into a truck. The impact has hurled the Renault across the retaining barrier. Cops are measuring skid marks. A parked ambulance presumably contains the dead.

On the next climb, I catch a second ambulance, lights flashing, and follow it into Popayán.

At 1760 metres, Popayán is cool and served the early sugar planters as a hill station. The centre is white Spanish colonial. Dusk and I search for a colonial-type hotel with atmosphere, as recommended by my guidebook. The first no longer exists, the second is full and I can't find the third. I pull up beside a late teenager on a scooter eating a creamy dessert out of a plastic container. She leads me to the third: the hotel is full. She takes me a short way out from the centre to a modern hotel without atmosphere but clean and with parking and hot water.

My guide is a final-year medical student. Her first name: Lady.

Popayán, Saturday 19 August

Popayán is in three sections. The universities have their own barrios, while a modern commercial city has expanded beyond an unspoilt sixteenth-century core that occupies a round-topped hill. All the houses are painted white in the historic zone. The streets run at right-angles. Look down any street and you see greenery at the end, either trees or hills or mountains. The plaza occupies the crest of the dome. The plaza has a cathedral and banks and government buildings. It also has an arboretum. A bronze statue of a martyr of the War of Independence is the kernel. A ring of massive conifers surrounds the statue. Royal palms ring the conifers. The outer ring offers a mixture of different trees, two of which are clothed in pink blossom. Offices, factories and universities are in the modern barrios so the city centre is semi-deserted much of the day and the churches are closed.

In Colombia, churches open for the celebration of the Eucharist or for Mass, weddings or funerals. They are not offered by the priests as tourist attractions. I find myself attending a funeral at the church of San Francisco, a celebration service at half past four in San Francisco, a celebration of the Eucharist in the cathedral, and portions of three Masses at San Augustín, La Encarnación and Santo Domingo. A congregation of only twenty-two is at Mass uphill at the tiny La Ermita. The church has a good feel and the young priest delivers a kind sermon. The priest might notice if I leave before the end of the service. He might imagine himself at fault. And I don't wish to be rude.

A juvenile U2-soundalike performs in one of the other churches – I don't recall which. Would guitars have been standard fare when the churches were built? Apart from which, what can I write? That Popayán has it in spades over any other Spanish colonial city I have visited on this trip. The feel of the city is right. It is a city where you could live. It isn't purely, or even more than minimally, a tourist destination. It is a city where local people work and study and bear families and struggle to survive. It is clean and the architecture in the centre is beautiful. The people are friendly.

I was directed to a great truckers' and farmers' restaurant last night. I was served a steak big enough to give a tiger indigestion.

This evening I discover a café with six pool tables and seven slightly bigger tables without pockets and an advertisement at the door for an anthology of poetry. Tables in the entrance are occupied by elderly gentlemen drinking beer: you can't make a living serving coffee in Colombia; too many places give it away free. Later I mingle with the young at a cultural centre. Tomorrow I head for the border.

To Ipiales, Sunday 20 August

I lie in bed early this morning with a depression for company. I feel old and I am very tired. I want to give up, go home, sleep in my own bed with Bernadette, talk with my four sons, cuddle my grandchild Charlie Boo, drive over the Malvern Hills to see my brother and my sister-in-law, cook for everyone, sit among my own books, mow the lawn, prune the roses, bore everyone to tears.

I can't give up.

I lie in bed and remember testing myself on that first mountain pass in Mexico. I had to prove to myself that I could make it. Pass the test and I could reach Tierra del Fuego.

And riding a bike is far easier than writing a novel.

So I get up and dress in warm clothes, finish packing for the umpteenth time, lug the bags downstairs, strap them on the bike and wheel the bike through the lobby and out to the road. The staff watch as I lift the choke on the carb. The bike fires first kick. I feel more confident. Right, let's do it! Three hundred and seventy kilometres to Ipiales. *Brmmm, brmmm, brmmm*.

The day starts out chill. The road rises a while and then drops fast in a series of swooping curves, dairy farms, coffee, everything green with a few splashes of blossom colour, blues, pinks, vivid bougainvillea. Big mountains, left and right, are harsh as they close in on the road and suddenly I am in near-desert. The temperature is way up in the thirties. The road follows a river with bathing pools advertised, and Sunday people in swimming clothes carrying towels and a couple of small kids wearing inflated animal rings on the main street, or only street, of a gas-station-and-bus-stop sort of town.

The valley narrows to a gorge and up we go again, up and down, weaving through mountains scoured of soil and crumpled in a giant's hand, hairpin after hairpin tracing the sharp folds. I cross a terrifying bridge from which I dare not look down, and then up again on the last long climb. The bike rides oddly. My gut tightens. I ease into the concrete ditch on the side of the road. The rear wheel is punctured. Damn, damn, damn.

On the way up, I had noticed a farm on the left-hand side. I ride back slowly, stop at the gate and walk down a concrete ramp to the farmhouse. The farmer meets me at the door, a square, well-muscled man in his forties – a child's plastic wheelie toy out in the yard, no sign of a wife. Sure, he tells me, of course I can park the bike back of the house. I need anything? A drink? Any help?

'I'm fine,' I reply, although I am nervous. I last took a wheel off a bike somewhere back in the early sixties. I tell myself that mechanics is logic. I lay out the tools and set to work. No problems. The farmer tells me to leave my kit in the house, drives me to the last town to have the tube repaired and insists on waiting, and then drives me back.

Thank you, farmer.

He is a widower with two daughters, the eldest with children of her own (hence the wheelie toy in the yard). He farms onions and pigs. The pig manure keeps the soil rich and he grows two crops a year on the terrace by his house and on a couple of terraces lower down the gorge. He has a good house, modern kitchen, modern bathroom. The floors are tiled, the furniture a little formal. He drives a Mitsubishi jeep, ten years old and immaculately maintained. He is dressed in clean chinos, clean boots and a fresh white T-shirt. He notices that I find his Spanish difficult and speaks carefully. He is about as far from the Hollywood version of a Colombian as you could get. He knows the image outsiders have of Colombia and Colombians and it irritates the hell out of him.

To me he is one more typically kind, generous and thoughtful Colombian. I have met none other on my journey through a country against which everyone warned me.

At nearly 3000 metres in altitude, Ipiales is cold. A thin drizzle doesn't help as I consult the guidebook. I pass a hotel and find that it is recommended by some masochistic lunatic. It is a four-dollar dump. I don't have the energy to search further. I dump the bags on a bed. I don't unpack. I find an internet café, do my mail and eat a piece of rubberised boot leather and cold gooey rice in an icy restaurant where all the locals are wearing ponchos and keep their hats on in case their hair freezes.

Readers may wonder what there is to do in Ipiales on a Sunday evening. I don't have a clue. I am in bed by nine. Thank God there are two beds in my room. I add the blankets from the spare bed to my bed and huddle down.

Good riddance, Ipiales, Monday 21 August

I clamber out from under the weight of blankets at six and shiver as I scratch my four-dollar bedbug bites. I drag the clothes back on that I wore yesterday, take my morning pill and head outdoors. I want the bike serviced – two hours until the Honda concessionaire opens. I search a breakfast place with doors. The citizens of Ipiales – at least the restaurateurs – dislike doors. Maybe doors keep customers out. They might keep the cold out. Perhaps Ipialesians enjoy cold.

I eat scrambled eggs and drink coffee in the most crowded restaurant open at that hour – the more people, the more heat. Not in Ipiales. Ipiales is on a one-city campaign to offset global warming. I wait outside the Honda concessionaire until half past eight before someone tells me the shop is shut for the day – a private fiesta of some kind. So much for Ipiales.

I flee for the border. There, beside the highway, immediately outside town, is that hallmark of Anglo-Italian enterprise: a Forte Travelodge! True, I swear to God.

Ecuador

To Quito, Monday 21 August

The Colombian frontier officials are polite, helpful and humorous. I have been warned of Ecuadorian officialdom. I have been told to expect endless delays and endless tiresomeness. I draw up at the customs post. The tall uniformed customs man who approaches is a travel fantasist. He wants details of my trip. What had I enjoyed most? What were the disappointments, the scares? We chat. A second uniform joins us. The first accompanies me to a window to have the import papers for the bike completed. The inspector shows me where the engine and chassis numbers are on the Honda – something I ought to know.

At immigration I fall in with a group of Ecuadorians heading for a salsa fest in Cali and a young Scottish couple with whom I chat of the similarities we have found between these uplands and the Scottish Borders. This is the first time I have spoken English since Ming left Cartagena.

I had expected a minimum of two hours at the border. I am through in one, much of which is taken up with travel rap and advice. My guidebook warns of a police post outside the next town and that drivers should have their papers ready. I approach the police post. The policeman grins and waves me through. And something has happened. I am feeling insanely pleased. Insane because I am trembling with cold and a steady drizzle stings my cheeks.

The road has climbed from the frontier. Cloud covers the hilltops. Visibility is poor. Why am I feeling pleased? Sure, the hills are familiar. I could show my brother a photograph and he would presume that I had been in the Cheviots. However, there is something new, something really cheering. It takes me a while, maybe a few kilometres. Then suddenly I understand. Ecuador has hedges.

I ride into the capital, Quito, in the evening. I find a big room with an angled view across the square to the church of Santo Domingo. From my bed I can see a massive statue of the Virgin that watches over the city from a hilltop. The water in the shower is hot and the shower has a shower rose. I have internet in the hotel.

Quito enthrals me. I spend two days revelling in tourist things. I walk the historic quarter, visit half a dozen museums and a dozen churches. Highlights? The Chapel of the Rosary in Santo Domingo. Disappointments? The Jesuit temple.

The Chapel of the Rosary is a place of prayer through which tourists tiptoe. The Jesuit temple is a museum in which the rare religious tiptoe among the tourists.

The refectory in the monastery of Santo Domingo is an essential visit. The walls are panelled with portraits of friars in their moments of martyrdom. Roasted, beheaded, stabbed, strangled, stretched – it is all up there on the walls, great decor to admire while eating dinner. My favourite is the monk forced to eat his own eyes.

The carved wood ceiling in the choir loft at the Church of San Francisco is superb. So are the ceramics at the Museo Nacional del Banco Central in the New City. The layout of the exhibits is exceptional – surely one of the great museums of the Americas. Some of the ceramics and the oil painting on alabaster in the Museo de San Francisco possess an amazing luminosity.

Ghastly are the paintings in the 1920s mansion of the heiress Maria Augusta Urrutia. Noted for her charitable works, her weirdest act of charity was in supporting an Ecuadorian artist whose vast paintings are a mix of pre-Raphaelite without talent and worse art nouveau. The architecture is little better, the patios are mean and the house lacks a single comfortable chair.

Moto Andes service the Honda – oil change, brakes, chain tension, etcetera. The chief mechanic shows me how to set the valves and clean the petrol filter. They bill me seventeen dollars.

I forget my backpack in a workman's restaurant. I return to find it stored in safety on top of a cupboard. Ah, those thieving natives!

I enjoy female companionship, an Ecuadorian, a professor of Spanish. She is a woman of my age or older. Dark spectacles protect her eyes and she is neatly dressed in matching woollens and proper shoes. We meet because I hold a church door open for her. Together, we visit two churches and two museums. She asks my nationality and whether I am Catholic. I reply that yes, I am Catholic and that I am English. It is an easy answer.

The truth is far more complex. In the solitude of this journey, riding a bike day after day through strange territory, often feeling my years, I have thought much of what I am and what I have made of myself. I am a writer – that first and foremost. By culture, I am Catholic. I admire that pre-Conquest fusion of Spanish Catholicism and Spanish Islam that reached its architectural summit in the Americas. In my youth this admiration drew me to the Sufi tradition of Islamic mysticism. I am a European with roots deep in the soil of Worcestershire and Herefordshire, and yet I often feel more at ease in the French language. I feel a great affinity with and admiration for the Spain of my Spanish forefathers, the Spain of the Conquest, and I feel at home here in Hispanic America. So there you have it: in every sense, a *mestizo*.

Guidebooks can wreck a trip with their warnings of danger. So can hotel staff. My advice? Ask a cop.

The cops in the historic quarter of Quito mostly come armed with Rottweilers. We were presented with a Rottweiler as protection when living in the Dominican Republic. I warned my son Jed, aged three at the time, that the Rottweiler was not a play dog. Jed mounted astride the poor beast and bashed it over the head with a coconut.

Unsurprisingly, the beast looked stunned.

I recount this tale to a cop. He grins and says, yes, Rottweilers are in truth big softies. As to walking after dark, the cop advises, 'Not alone or late at night' – a warning applicable to most big cities.

I dine in an upmarket restaurant by the cathedral and walk an hour. The food is excellent, a salad of heart of palm, fresh asparagus, avocado and the normal greens and reds. Next comes a fat fillet of fish in caper sauce. The manager passes by and asks whether everything is in order. I look down at my plate wiped clean with garlic bread and we both laugh. As to the great churches and monasteries of the city, they are superb and lit brilliantly, domes and spires pure magic against the night sky.

The United States inherited nothing of equivalent cultural importance from the Founding Fathers. Even the tale of a few witch burnings appears minor when compared with a friar forced to eat his own eyes. Less you suspect me of being anti the USA, the Founding Fathers were Brits – as I have been reminded more than once by Hispanic Americans on this journey. I have also been reminded that every Conquistador married an indigenous woman, while neither the Founding Fathers nor their descendants have ever mixed.

The Route to Baños, Thursday 24 August

Ecuador is on the equator. In my subconscious, I equate the equator with sweat, sunburn and mosquitoes. I am riding towards an erupting volcano spewing white-hot pumice. Definitely warm. I wear a thick shirt, three undershirts and a sweater, long johns and thick chinos, a bright-blue rain suit. Reasonable protection?

Not even halfway to reasonable.

I am riding at seventy kilometres an hour into a head wind. I wear a bright-blue suit bought in Bugo, Colombia, in the hope that it would prove miraculous. My gloves are too short in the wrist to overlap the cuffs of the jacket. The wind races straight up my sleeves. It is a vicious wind. God knows from whence it blows. Probably off some ice-bound mountain of which Ecuador suffers a surfeit. Ah, yes, and another point: I am crossing a fell with the road peaking at 3400 metres. Take the highest mountain in the United Kingdom, triple it and subtract a smidgen. This is the type of idiotic sum I do to stop dwelling on how cold I am.

How cold am I? Freezing.

I am heading for Latacunga, eighty kilometres south of Quito.

Latacunga is down a few metres.

Latacunga is cold. A pair of nice cops tell me to park my bike up against theirs in the no-parking zone on the main square. The garden in the centre of the square is beautiful, complex and immaculately maintained. The interior of the cathedral is austere. The colonial mansion of the Marquises of Miraflores is built of grey volcanic stone. The mansion has been restored and opened to the public. The restorers have done a great job. Imagine a downmarket theme restaurant for the Party elite in the old Soviet Union.

I ride serenely downhill towards the hot springs resort of Baños when a truck driver nearly kills me. The driver is racing another truck. The two trucks race abreast on a road narrowed by a drift of fine volcanic sand bordering the curb. Brake hard in the sand and the bike will slide. The truck misses me by less than a metre. Son of a bitch. May he die a painful and inglorious death.

I am presumptuous in complaining of a solitary near-death experience. The volcano, Tungurahua, has spent the past few months attempting to kill the citizens of Baños. The volcano has done a fine job in killing the resort's economy. This is high season and the town is empty bar a few volcano watchers and the usual dimwits who never watch TV news or read a paper. Of which category am I? Take your pick.

Baños is a small town and sits on a ledge near the bottom of a river gorge. The volcanoes that surround it are up close. Tungurahua is the tallest and the nearest. I pass men clearing pumice and boulders from the road on my descent into town. I have been half-frozen earlier in the day and came close to being killed by an over-testicled truck driver. Now I find myself in a dump. Baños has an ugly church and two nondescript squares with nondescript gardens and a rash of mini-hotels. Most buildings are in the process of gaining a new level or have owners who contemplate a future of further levels. The new levels require vertical steel reinforcing rods. With all this uncloaked reinforcing, you have a metallic porcupine. Most shops are small and sell similar hand-knitted items of indigenous tat. Restaurants are in overabundance, few evidence any taste in decor. Nor am I enthused by whole peeled guinea-pigs cooking on pavement barbecues. Add scores of tour agencies all advertising on scruffy billboards the same hells: white-water rafting, volcano scaling, jungle treks, swami searches, biking, quad biking, enduro-biking, horseback riding and every kind of massage and bath, and you have a picture common to such dumps, a picture I could do without.

I find a hotel owned by a Frenchman. The Frenchman hasn't visited in a while. A charming and very pretty receptionist tells me that the Frenchman is scared of the volcano. She shows me a great room that has a table in a big window. The window gives onto two non-exploding volcanoes. The exploder is to our rear. The room has an ample bathroom. The water is piping hot. I thaw and feel better, more optimistic. I walk the town and am met by a mirage: a sign above a small restaurant announces LA CUISINE DE PROVENCE.

Surely not?

I push open the door. The man sitting at the table in front of the small bar is unmistakably French. He is fair-haired, middle-aged and chubby – as are most chefs (other than the dieting stars of television). Six o'clock in the evening and he has been at the stove since midday. Now is his hour of relaxation before the dinner clientele arrive. He offers me a glass of a good red wine from Chile. I feel at home. We chat.

Marianne's has been open fifteen years. The owners are a local family adopted by Michel. Marianne is the mother figure. The restaurant has twelve tables. Decoration is mostly framed cartoons from the twenties. The menu is simple: salads, two soups, pasta, steak au poivre, *daube*, boeuf à la marocain and three desserts.

I return at eight and order the steak au poivre. Michel has taught a local slaughterer the arts of a French butcher and the steak is the first truly tender cut of beef that I have eaten on this trip.

A Spaniard asks to share my table. A salesman in his late twenties, he is Catalan and from Barcelona. He is at the end of a five-week vacation. He hates Ecuador. The people see a foreigner, they eat him (slang for overcharging). I reply that I must be privileged in being old, that Latin Americans care for the aged.

The Catalan eats crudely a vast plate of spaghetti, drinks bottled water. I ask for a second glass of wine.

The Catalan calls for his bill with neither please nor thankyou. The bill comes and he grimaces. 'Five dollars for a spaghetti.'

I say, 'You can eat at a *comedor*, a dollar fifty.'

'I can't eat that shit.' He stuffs his wallet back in his trouser pocket and departs.

Two local musicians perform music of the Andes. The atmosphere is friendly, the people good-natured. I sip a third glass of wine.

Back on the street, I clean my spectacles. I notice flames way up above the town. Tungurahua is erupting. I replace my spectacles and discover that I am looking in the wrong direction at the wrong volcano. The flames are a crucifix of electric lights. Baños remains a dump – it is a very pleasant dump.

Baños, Friday 25 August

This morning I chat with a woman tour operator two doors up from the hotel. She has two German clients for a half-day of white-water rafting tomorrow. She requires six. She doubts whether there are six tourists in Baños. The town exists on tourism. The town is dying. The Iraq war, the Israeli destruction of Lebanon and the price of oil cause anxiety. Add fear of terrorism. Then comes the final whammy: TV coverage of Tungurahua in eruption and refugees fleeing from their farms on the upper slopes.

A gentle rain from heaven?

Not too unpleasant if you have an umbrella, are holding hands with your sweetheart and expect to be sharing his or her bed soon.

A rain of boulders is different. Boulders aren't romantic. Nor is a great big volcano spewing lava at your hotel bedroom window. You don't want to get in bed. You want to get in your car and get the hell out of wherever all this threatening stuff is happening. As for voluntarily visiting such a place, no thanks.

However, I am in Baños and I have developed a weird loyalty to the dump. Very weird. Although not so weird as to risk my life white-water rafting. This is where being in your seventies is useful. You can refuse such offers without appearing rude.

A young and unreasonably beautiful blonde lady approaches me on Main Street. She asks whether I speak Spanish.

I say, 'More or less.'

She asks how long have I been in Baños and how long do I intend staying and doesn't the volcano frighten me?

'Not a bit,' I boast, playing the masculine hero. What could a little-bitty volcano do to a real man? Or to an unreasonably pretty young blonde lady who is under the protection of such man?

She asks me to repeat all this for Latin American cable TV.

'Sure,' I say. 'Delighted to be of help.' Both to her and to Baños.

I add a few embellishments for the camera: the great restaurants, the mountain walks (across white-hot ashes?), white-water rafting.

I have impressed her. 'You white-water raft? At your age?'

'Absolutely,' I say. 'Going tomorrow. River is in great shape.'

This is the movies. I am on camera. It is not for real. And it is for the unreasonably beautiful young blonde lady. To impress her.

Half the town watches the interview. It is broadcast at midday and on the six o'clock news. The woman tour operator two doors up from the hotel sees it. She expresses her delight at my change of mind. She has two Canadians as well as the two Germans. With me, that makes five. Plus two girls staying in my hotel who still have to confirm.

What can I answer?

I try, 'Is it safe for a man my age? You know, an old man with a heart condition? I don't want to be a nuisance to the others.'

'Do you take medication?' asks the tour operator.

A ray of hope. 'Absolutely. Four pills in the evening and one in the morning.'

'Then that's all right,' says the tour operator. 'That will be thirty dollars. Sign here.'

I eat once more at Marianne's – last dinner for the condemned. I choose the *daube*. Delicious. And I learn more of Michel. His parents owned a vineyard and a small hotel in Burgundy. Michel wished to be a doctor. His father had doubts as to Michel's aptitude. His terms for supporting Michel through his studies were that Michel also study hotel management and spend his vacations working in restaurant kitchens.

Michel qualified but never practised. The father is dead. The hotel is sold. Michel's mother keeps a watchful eye on the vineyard.

Baños, Saturday 26 August

A petard is something upon which you hoist yourself. Am I hoisted – or petarded? I am also suffering from palpitations. I should keep this a secret. Real men don't suffer palpitations. Palpitations are a woman's complaint. Women, being more sensible than men, take heed. They face whatever it is that gives them the palpitations and conclude, no. No, we won't do that.

Were I a woman, I would not go white-water rafting. I am not referring here to any other woman: merely and specifically to the imaginary seventy-three-year-old woman I would be were I a woman. I would be suffering from palpitations and conclude that white-water rafting wasn't my bag.

Uneasy with my own nervousness, I sit down to breakfast up on the hotel terrace and ask the two young women serving whether the volcano scares them.

They answer that they are scared but not very scared.

They might be offended were I to ask whether they suffer from palpitations. Anyway, I don't know the Spanish equivalent and palpitation is difficult to portray in sign language without giving offence.

And of course there is nothing voluntary in their situation. Baños is their home. This is their job. Where would they go? What other work could they find?

While all I need say is: 'Actually I've changed my mind. Keep the thirty dollars.'

I sit on a bumpy sofa at the tour operator's office. Two young physios working in London arrive. Next are a Canadian couple, sociology students. The woman is blonde and wears her hair in ringlets. I recognise her legs. They are of an attractive shape. However, what are recognisable are the bumps and bruises and scars. She is a suicide addict (she would blah on about extreme sports). Introduce her to my youngest son Jed, and they would relate immediately. They would get right into the scar game:

Yeah, that was the zone championship.

The track was wet. I hit this tree.

Some idiot got in my way.

I didn't see the cliff.

They have real cool ambulances.

Meanwhile we wait for the two Germans. Our guide for the day suggests that the Germans are tired; they were mountain biking yesterday and did this swing thing off a bridge. No, not bungee jumping. You wear a harness attached to a rope and dive way out from a bridge so that you swing in huge arcs.

'Over what?' I ask.

'A canyon.'

'With rocks?'

'Of course, with rocks.'

Why would I go white-water rafting with maniacs?

The Germans are male nineteen-year-olds from Leipzig, the old East Germany. The guide is unaware of the teenager-imposed curfew on European teenagers rising before eleven and fetches them from their hotel. Alex will be studying politics at university. His partner in craziness studies football and hopes to be a history teacher – however, he goofed off at gymnasium and doubts whether his grades are acceptable. He has very white legs and has been collecting mosquito bites – the ones that are wet in the middle, yellowish at the edges and give pharmacists a warming scent of imminent profit.

We drive forty-five minutes in an open-sided truck with a rubber boat on the roof. The benches are fixed to cram in the maximum quantity of small indigenous Latin Americans. We are cramped sitting sideways.

I talk with the ringlet Canadian, Kay. She has given up extreme sports and has lost twenty pounds in muscle weight. I have lost sixteen pounds of pure fat. Kay has been taught the politically correct generalities of the Conquest: the Spaniards were evil; they destroyed the indigenous culture.

I remark that the indigenous culture was feudal. A clique of the most senior nobles served the king. Beneath came the senior provincial nobles and a layer of lesser nobles. Nobles didn't work. Non-nobles worked their butts off. Conquistadors came of a feudal system. They came at best from the lower strata of lesser nobles. In America, they married the daughters of the most senior nobles – advancement closed to them back home. No one weeps for the destruction of the feudal system in Europe. Few weep for the fall of Soviet feudalism. The Conquistadors should be criticised for maintaining the feudal culture. Many of those with education (mostly friars) did precisely that.

We head down a dirt track to a wooden bridge. The truck is too big to cross the bridge. The rubber boat is transferred to a pickup. The pickup crosses the bridge and disappears into the jungle. We cross on foot. The three women take the lead. Absolved of responsibility, we men trail along in their tracks and discuss serious matters – mostly football, the World Cup. We walk and we walk – maybe a mile uphill before the pickup catches us. The pickup had turned down a side track through trees immediately on crossing the bridge. Our fearless leader was too dumb to leave one of his assistants at the turning. And we men, of course, were merely following the women. While the women were being real men and striding on ahead. This is not a good beginning.

Our guide is in his forties, a short man with a belly. He has learnt the white-water instructor spiel in English. He can instruct: how to paddle, when to paddle, when to stop paddling, and he tells us never, never, ever to let go of our paddles. He instructs us in what to do if we fall in the water (lie on our backs); what to do if someone else falls in the water. And he shouts a good deal at the footballing German – I suspect because the German is the biggest member of our party and shouting at him reassures our small guide as to his own importance.

I help lift the raft into the river. People get in the side opposite me. This forces the raft my way. My paddle is under the raft – I have hold of the handle. Our guide yells at me to board. I yell back that my paddle is under the raft. He shouts at me to get in. I repeat that my paddle is under the raft. He screeches again. At which point I realise that he speaks the minimum necessary English. His understanding of the language is zero. So I shout at him in Spanish that he is a c— and that my paddle is under the raft.

The message reaches his brain. He pushes the raft out from the beach and my paddle is free. I board the raft. He gets in behind me. He says, in Spanish, that he's sorry for the misunderstanding. I say that that's fine, just so long as he doesn't drown me. He promises not to drown me. Good. We are making progress.

I am an old man. I have little fear of death. I fear being unable to cope. Paddling is easy. We hit the first rapid. Waves ram the blunt bow of the raft upward. Spray soaks us. I have a sudden memory of whizzing downriver in Kenya on truck tyres. A hydrologist, Basil Bell, was measuring the river's water flow. The local witchdoctor demanded that Basil buy a goat to sacrifice to the river. The goat belonged to the witchdoctor. I was twenty-one years old. This memory shoots us through the first rapid and I am having fun. More than fun – this is glorious.

We high-five our paddles and whack the blades in the water. We hit the next rapid. The waves are bigger. No problem. Alex and I are the rafting virgins. We grin and smack hands. I have found a sport that old men can enjoy. The river spits us out of the canyon, jungle on both sides. We swing close to the bank, orchids on the trees, a couple of optimistic vultures overhead. Yes, this is great.

More rapids, more high-fiving, shouts of exultation. Our guide orders us to paddle standing. Standing on a raft is not for old men. I have sufficient difficulty standing upright on dry land.

I return from the river to the hotel. Ming's Monster is parked beside the Honda. Ming is resting. I wake him and we recount our adventures. We eat at Marianne's with the two Germans and the two Canadians of my rafting trip. I order the Moroccan chicken. The other five order steak au poivre. Perfect.

Baños, Sunday 27 August

My Catholic and Spanish heritage pursues me. We ride today to a farm that Michel owned and sold to a Swiss. Michel is resting there a week. The farm is three miles down a dirt track. The track is new. Before the track, transport was by foot or mule or moke.

A foreign priest owned the farm and five foreign priests established a community there. A priestly cousin invited Michel to run a pharmacy at the entrance to the farm. The Versailles branch of the Knights of Malta donated the pharmaceuticals. Here is the heritage: my grandfather and my father were Knights, my brother is a Knight.

Insect bites did for the community – or a shaman.

Michel's cousin bought the farm and later sold it to Michel.

The present owner, the Swiss, has let the place go to ruin.

Ming and I climb with Michel up a steep hill and across a field of rushes to the community's church. The church is built of wood. It is narrow and has a steep roof and a small steeple. Steps lead up the back to what was the community's library and study room. The leader of the community lived in a house a further hundred metres or so beyond the church – until the bugs got him. Now the bugs devour his house and the church.

The field is edged by jungle. We walk in among the trees a little way and disturb a wild boar. Then we walk back down the hill to what was the dispensary and which Michel converted into a home. The terrace is ample. We sit at a wood table and eat too much and share two bottles of wine. The ex-dispensary has a good feel and Michel is a good kind man. The hill and the church and the gone community are different. Both Ming and I were disturbed up on the hill. We want to know more. Asking Michel seems impolite and dangerously intrusive.

On the ride back from the farm we see Tungurahua. The top of the volcano and the lower slopes are in cloud. The evening sun strikes the centre section. The effect is surprising, a giant sponge pudding streaked in icing sugar and chocolate. The river runs black with lava through the sluice gates at the hydroelectric station. Spray carries the stink of sulphur. Ming stops to photograph. I yell at him to keep going, not to inhale.

I am going to die, Monday 28 August

I wake at four and throw up. I throw up at half past four and at five and at half past five and at six. Mostly I control the direction and keep cleaning to a minimum.

Ming wakes me for breakfast at half past seven. I groan. He brings me a bottle of water and a glass of orange juice – my request. The juice is a disaster – although it completes the purging of my belly. The bug moves to my bowels. I become a rectal water pistol. Ming brings me antibiotics.

I don't want to die in Baños.

I want to go home.

Baños to Cuenca, Tuesday 29 August

I am recovered. Whatever was in my belly and bowels has been evacuated – totally. We leave Baños and ride across the Altiplano. The country is green and Scottish Borders. The hills to our right are streaked with snow. To our left, Tungurahua and its mates are blanketed in cloud. I brake and wait while a family crosses the road. The mother leads a black and white Friesian cow. Two small boys herd two black pigs with fawn snouts. A daughter and shaggy donkey bring up the rear. The mother wears a dark-green felt hat and a red jumper beneath a tweed coat. I raise a gloved hand in greeting and she gives me a big grin.

The land changes. The soil is grey and thin and over-farmed. Houses are small. Erosion scars the hillsides. Contour planting and contour ploughing would help – or building terraces. We ride through cloud. The women wear white festive bowler hats.

Later we are back into green uplands and dairy farms and large two-storey houses and felt hats. Is there a connection between white bowlers and poor land?

In Cuenca we find a hotel converted from a colonial house. We have rooms opening onto the rear patio. The water is hot. We have ridden across the Andes.

Cuenca, Wednesday 30 August

Ming has the bug. He threw up during the night. Now he lies curled up in bed, miserable and waif-like. I fetch him fresh yoghurt. I then attend early Mass in Cuenca's new cathedral. Completed in the 1890s, it is a great building. The architect was

German. I am amazed always by the courage and confidence of designers of great buildings. How can they be certain of the outcome? And the arrogance of architects of the massive mediocre – to so blight the cityscape.

The two young Canadians of my rafting are studying in Cuenca and live with host families. They fetch me from the hotel and take me to their favourite coffeehouse. The coffeehouse is warm. Bliss. Kay is a mixture of openness and enthusiasm and innocence. Tyler is both more watchful and thoughtful, and he has that quietness that is common to many Canadians and that differentiates them from their cross-border cousins.

As in Quito, the main museum in Cuenca is financed by the Central Bank. The bank has kept the best for Quito. There is an archaeological park that demonstrates the strata of building. I meet a German fund manager. We sit on a bench in the park in the sunshine and admire an elderly workman building a new ruin. Later I say to the workman, 'Working as in the old days.'

He grins and says, 'Much slower now.'

The fund manger was in Quito with his girlfriend. She wanted to go to the beach, he to Cuenca. They have separated for a few days. Later we meet a family from Virginia. The parents have taken their three children out of school for a year to journey round the world. The children are about seven, nine and thirteen. The two youngest are girls. The fund manger and his girlfriend are on a short break and disagreed on where to go. Imagine the arguments in this family. The parents are magnificent in their bravery – or crazy.

My stomach is acting up again. I take Ming a banana yoghurt, eat one myself and am in bed at seven thirty. I lie in bed much of the night wondering whether to throw up. Throwing up would eject my heart medication. Should I throw up and take more pills or not throw up and listen to my belly rumble and bubble?

I doze and a mosquito bites me. The bite is the size of a United States Treasury one-cent piece. I switch on the light and mount a major but unsuccessful mosquito hunt. I switch off the light and doze briefly.

The mosquito gets me. He is silent now. Perhaps he is merely sated. Or he may have caught the bug that has made Ming and me throw up – a cheering thought.

Do mosquitoes throw up?

Cuenca, Thursday 31 August

Ming and I were due out of Cuenca this morning. We both feel vomity and decide to give Cuenca a further day. I sit in the new cathedral a while. The side chapels are simply altars rather than walled enclosures. The space remains intact. The high altar is covered by a great golden canopy supported on four golden pillars. I am an addict of early Spanish colonial architecture. I praise a modern cathedral to prove my lack of bias. This cathedral is a space of prayer. I watch people enter, cross themselves, kneel a while, depart. An indigenous matron doffs her high-crowned Panama hat and lays it on the kneeler. She wears a knee-length pink skirt with blue edging. She rises and I glimpse her between the marble pillars, a ballet dancer waiting in the wings. Once recognised, the memory encompasses other women, their short skirts bulked out by petticoats, hair braided in a single pigtail – Degas, of course – and admiring God's creatures is a form of prayer.

I have my shoes polished. I am short of heart medication; Ming and I take a cab to a large pharmacy in the new city. The pharmacist diagnoses our suffering as a combination of food poisoning and altitude sickness. The altitude sickness should wear off in a few weeks. Gas is one of the symptoms. At altitude gas expands in your stomach and you continually break wind.

A few weeks of stomach gas? We are definitely out of here tomorrow. Aim to stop one night at Loja, a descent of 500 metres, followed the next day by the beach.

Meanwhile we sit in a café, belch, pass wind and watch the world pass. Ming sticks with soup. I risk a few mouthfuls of plain boiled white rice.

Writing of Degas and ballet dancers prompts a train of thought. Our hotel displays articles of indigenous art for sale. Two small paintings are appealing. My Canadian rafters know the painter. He is among the most prominent painters of indigenous art.

What is indigenous art?

I understand paintings painted by indigenous painters – although a genetic test might be necessary to prove the painter's bloodline; otherwise an art gallery might be accused of fraud. As for indigenous art – surely paintings are simply paintings and are judged on their merits rather than their heritage. Perhaps I am being dumb – or difficult. However, I have a nagging sense that indigenous art is a term of condescension: they are different from us, you know? The natives. Simple chaps. Isn't this painting cute?

Towards Peru, Friday 1 September

Today I discover bliss cruising the fells of southern Ecuador at eighty kilometres an hour on a 125 Honda pizza delivery bike. We are 11 000 feet above sea level on a broad ridge that stretches for forty kilometres. The sky is a patchwork of dark and white and brilliant blue. A stiff breeze chases shadow and sunlight across the road and through the tufted grass and scrub and down the valleys either side. The road dips and rises and curves and the view is forever in all directions. We meet a convoy of gravel trucks. The drivers see this old bearded foreign man on a small, heavily burdened bike and they wave out the window and honk and flash their lights. That friendship of the road does for me. I weep with happiness – real tears.

Down a couple of thousand metres. Catamayo is Cuenca's holiday resort. The people are jolly. I imagine that I am working for Catamayo's tourist bureau. What else can I write to persuade travellers to stay a night? A restaurant is recommended as the best in town. The restaurant is full of local citizenry. We eat a third-rate *churrasco*. We stay at a nine-dollar-a-night resort hotel up a dirt track. The rooms look onto a roofless corridor that shares odours with an over-watered mushroom tunnel. The pool is clean. I swim. The water becomes less cold once you have been in a while. Ming forgoes the joys of the pool. People raised in Indonesia don't do less cold. They do warm or they don't do. We are eaten by mosquitoes.

To the Peruvian Border, Saturday 2 September

The direct road south from Catamayo to the Peruvian border passes though Carlamanga, a small pleasant town where we breakfast for a dollar each at a small café on the central square. The altitude is a mere 6000 feet and I sit in the square after breakfast and enjoy the sun for the first time since leaving Cartagena. I am surrounded by a gang of miniature shoeshine terrorists. My choice is based on a flash assessment of which boy needs the money most. The boy polishes and I discuss life and the importance of education with his companions.

Ming takes photographs.

Beyond Catamayo, the road climbs steeply through mountains to a summit at 8600 feet. The mountains are near-desert; the soil is pale yellow and powdery. This powdery sand coats the road surface at the corners. A biker would be in trouble if he took a corner too fast and had to brake. On some corners, the outer lane has slipped down the mountain. At other corners, the mountain has slipped and blocked the inner lane. The drop is forever. Meeting a truck is for serious adrenalin addicts. The Honda is light and manoeuvrable. I would hate to do the climb on a big road cruiser.

We reach the frontier. Customs and immigration officials are friendly and fast with the paperwork. We shake hands and thank them. Ecuador has been a pleasure. It is the cleanest country I have ridden through yet; the people are open and friendly; much of the poverty is hidden and I never felt even remotely at danger or under threat. For caviar, add a superb museum (Central Bank) and the chapel of the Rosary, Santo Domingo – both in Quito. And, of course, there are hedges and fells and snow on the peaks and proper, cone-shaped volcanoes. Yes, I'd return.

Peru

To Chiclayo, Sunday 3 September

The Peruvian customs inspector sits at a table on a veranda outside the Customs House. The inspector is new to the job. This is his first shift. Ming and I are his first bikers. He says, 'Look, everything will be easy just so long as you don't hurry me.'

Guidebooks to South and Central America continually warn of corrupt officials. Perhaps I have been fortunate in my experiences – or possibly fulfilment follows expectation. I don't expect to be asked for a bribe. I presume the inspector is seeking compassion. He has come to the right man. I am panicked by paperwork.

A uniformed customs officer sits beside the inspector. The uniform is neat and carries a burnished pistol with burnished bullets in a polished leather holster on his polished leather belt. He has worked this beat for a while, sitting beside previous inspectors. Unfortunately, he hasn't paid attention and is less help than wet bread.

Completing the paperwork takes the best part of an hour. Success is accompanied by many sighs of relief and much shaking of hands and wishes of good luck. Ming and I leave the bikes and cross the road for a juice – freshly squeezed oranges – delicious.

The inspector calls us back. He is suffering doubts. He has a nagging fear that we are short of a document. We should wait. An experienced inspector is due on the next shift, a mere matter of thirty minutes.

The uniform considers our delay to be a great waste of everyone's time.

The inspector enquires when the uniform last experienced a foreign biker.

The uniform is unable to recall.

Ming and I sit and read our guidebooks while the inspector talks on the radio.

The radio advises him not to worry.

The inspector is a worrier (as am I). Why do people tell worriers not to worry? And the inspector is correct. Delving through back files, he discovers a foreign biker's papers. We require a customs permit to export our bikes from Peru. The inspector finds the permits, fills in our details, stamps and signs them and we are on our way – except for one final piece of advice: 'Be careful. Don't ride through Sullana. In Sullana you will get robbed. Lots of tourists are robbed.'

When officials in a country keen on tourism warn you to avoid a place, avoid it. Ming and I avoid Sullana – although not entirely. The highway south to Pirua forks left at the outskirts to Sullana. Hence my knowledge of the city ...

Not only is Sullana remarkable for its citizens' propensity for robbing tourists: Sullana has also discovered a method of counteracting global warming. Citizens spread plastic garbage across the country. The garbage helps retain the soil's humidity and reflects the heat back up at the sun. The city saves on garbage disposal and the world profits from the lack of pollution caused by garbage trucks. The sole disadvantage to this system is the stink. The surrounds of Sullana stink of wet putrid fish.

We ride in shirtsleeves across flat dry land. At Pirua we join the Pan-American Highway. Chiclayo is 264 kilometres south across the Sechura Desert. For the first fifty kilometres the desert is studded with flat-topped thorn trees. The trees are decorated with plastic bags and plastic sheeting blown by the wind off heaps of garbage dumped along the road edge. The road is straight bar a few gentle curves. White markers register the distance from Lima. A shrine at K931 is in memory of Riki. Was Riki driving? Did he lose control? Fall asleep? Did a tyre explode?

And what did for Tony Ramirez at K909?

The desert is full of mysteries.

Why did someone select the shade beneath a particular tree as home for his nine beehives? The tree is no different from its neighbours. Tracks cross from nowhere and lead to nowhere. An isolated hut stands sixty metres off the road. Why sixty? Why not one hundred – or fifty metres further south or north?

Everything strikes me as haphazard.

The greatest mystery is why people live here.

They live in low huts built of adobe brick. A fence of sticks offers minimal privacy and protects a yard against wind and sand. The sand, the poverty, the thorn trees are all familiar to me. This could be Somalia, Kenya's Northern Province or the Ogaden. Only the game is missing, and the camels.

I note small efforts at humanising existence: a sand football pitch, the net missing from the goals and the net supports broken, an adobe church, a basketball ring. Many huts are abandoned, stripped of their roofs. Other huts, exactly similar, are under construction.

Two women spur their donkeys across the road. The women are muffled against the wind. One carries a baby.

A family of three, mother, father, early teenager, plod across a clearing. Each is burdened with firewood. How far have they carried their loads? How far will they travel?

Ming and I zip by on our bikes. We come from a different planet. We possess untold riches – not of money but the riches of escape artists, immense freedom of choice. Our concern is which hotel we should stay at in Chiclayo.

The Royal Horse Artillery mount displays at London's Royal Tournament. Teams of horses dragging guns and ammunition weave between each other at full gallop. Chiclayo traffic is similar. No one halts at intersections, red lights are for chickens. Fortunately the vehicles are mostly slow and relatively harmless: a mix of yellow Daewoo Tiki taxis the size of fairground bumper cars and 100 cc motorbike rickshaws.

The Daewoo Tikis are manufactured in Korea. Import tax on used vehicles is lower than on new ones, and so all Tikis are pre-used or, as a cab driver tells me, almost new. I imagine an industry in Korea: drivers collect new Tikis from the factory and drive the necessary mileage to satisfy Peruvian customs. A great job for students.

Chiclayo, Monday 4 September

We have found an excellent small hotel. The hotel is a little out from the city centre – Hospedaje San Eduardo on the extension of 7 Jenero. Water is hot, the beds are new, we have tables in our respective windows at which to write. Good tourists, we eat an early breakfast and ride forty-five kilometres to inspect the pyramids at Tucume. The pyramids were built between 1000 and 1300 AD. They are vast and built of adobe bricks. Ming believes that kings wished to demonstrate their divinity by building mountains. I have a different theory. Adobe is made of clay bound with rice straw. Rice straw was the garbage of the period. The kings were attempting a clean-up programme.

Ming climbs a god-made hill to look down on the pyramids. I will look at his photographs. Meanwhile I sit with three students in the site museum's open-air caféteria. Food and maize beer are typical of the first millennium. I fast while the students chew on goat as old as and tougher than the pyramids. The students find the site magical (or have been told to find the site magical). Their professor tells them that without slaves there would be no monuments. I am delighted by this splendid excuse for slavery. Perhaps the kings, in their divinity, foresaw Peru's need for a tourist industry and way back in the first millennium set their slaves to work for Peru's future.

We have done the pyramids and the museum. The museum has the usual ceramics and crudely beaten gold ornaments. Ming descends from a culture that had discovered the wheel and bone china at a time when we Brits were running around in animal skins and painting ourselves blue. Ming is also accustomed to an accuracy in his work that is measured in fractions of millimetres. Peruvian arts and crafts don't do it for him. We head for the beach.

I lead down a dirt track beside an irrigation ditch. The track ends at a five-acre garbage dump. A small upmarket resort sits right up against the dump. We drive through the resort to a parking lot on the seafront. A dozen open-fronted seafood restaurants face the sea. Monday, and we are the only visitors. Waitresses compete in pleading for our custom.

First we stroll and inspect the fishermen's traditional boats of reeds bound to a chunk of balsa wood. A few fishermen paddle out through the surf; a few surfers ride the surf back in. The wind is chill. We eat shrimp *ceviche* – perfect – and crab cooked in a tomato, garlic and onion sauce. Ming drinks orange juice. I have a big bottle of beer. Our combined bill comes to fifteen dollars. The manageress at our hotel earns 150 dollars a month. She works a twelve-hour day. She lives with her mother and her grandmother. She longs to escape to a job in Spain. She can't. Her mother and grandmother need her. I take her to dinner at a pizza parlour.

Garbage to Cajamarca, Tuesday 5 September

The Pan-American Highway south from Chiclayo crosses what I think of as proper desert. Large road signs announce zones of dunes. The dunes are larger than the signs and announce themselves. Here, on the littoral, no one waves as we pass. Why would they? God created their environment on a bad-hair day. People have turned it into a vast rubbish dump. Not all garbage is dumped in the desert. Many a load is simply dumped on the highway's hard shoulder. Roadworthy garbage: broken bottles, cans ...

We pass an encampment of garbage pickers. Some have built small huts of adobe. Others have erected tents of discarded black plastic sheet – imagine the heat. Three men pick through a recently dumped truckload. Watchful vultures perch on a broken trailer. Cacti are nature's only representatives. The cacti stand on a ridge above the desert and hold their arms aloft in despair.

Ming wishes to discover whether Peru's uplands are as desecrated as the littoral. We turn inland through hills that resemble large heaps of builder's rubble – not a good beginning.

Cajamarca is situated 180 kilometres from the coast and at an altitude of 2750 metres. The road follows a river. The valley is narrow. The hills are naked rock. At their base grow lines of fruit trees. The trees shade water channels that irrigate every inch of flat land. Each small field is loved and cherished, each field a victory won through generations. The emerald of rice paddy gleams against grey rock face. Mango trees glitter with golden orbs.

We climb from valley to valley. Thirty kilometres to go and my rear tyre develops a slow puncture. Ming has a pump. We pump and I sprint. We overtake a convoy of tanker trucks heading for a recently opened gold mine. Cornering becomes difficult. We pump again. The tyre loses air more rapidly. Damn! Sprint and pump. Sprint and pump.

We reach the head of the pass. The terracotta roofs of Cajamarca spread below in a broad valley. Ming rides on ahead while I stop at the first puncture-repair shop. Dark and with tousled hair, the owner has the face of a fourteen-year-old. A baby crawls between his feet; two fighting cocks are tethered outside on a tiny patch of grass. He calls for his wife to care for the baby. The wife is heavily pregnant.

He fixes my tube while I admire his cocks. He is a cockfighting fanatic. His wife doesn't approve. She yells at him for wagering money they don't have. He finds two punctures in line with previous holes. He advises me to buy a new tyre. I pay him a dollar eighty for patching the punctures. I add two dollars and tell the kid the extra is to wager on the next cockfight. He giggles happily.

Ming is back. He has found rooms at a hotel where the cash goes to charity. We reach the hotel. In Ming's absence, the manageress has let all rooms for the night to a German tour group. So much for charity.

We find another hotel, big rooms, a rude manager. The handbasin in my bathroom leaks onto the floor. The towel might dry the nail on my little finger. Walls need painting. Floors require a clean. No undersheet and the mattress is stained. Yuk!

Built on the lower slopes of a mountain valley, Cajamarca is early Hispanic colonial. It is a town of small, mostly single-floor houses facing cobbled streets and should be charming. Cajamarca is dingy. Atahualpa, last of the Incas, was trapped and executed here by the Spaniards and their Inca allies. Now the inhabitants concentrate on tourists. Beggars beg, street traders pester, everything is overpriced.

And at high altitude the gas in one's belly expands and then escapes – often noisily. My advice? Give the town a miss.

We find one positive: a restaurant on the downhill side of the central plaza, Salas. Customers are local bourgeoisie. The food is excellent (main courses three to seven dollars), the waiters ancient, welcoming and professional.

Cajamarca, Wednesday 6 September

Cajamarca remains dingy. Stomach gas continues to expand and escape. Walking to breakfast, I fart as noisily as a flatulent cow. We ride six kilometres to the sulphur baths at the local spa. Ten dollars gets us the full treatment. First we are instructed to walk back and forth for ten minutes on a bed of loose cobbles. The exercise stretches our calf muscles and insteps. Better still, it demands no effort from the white-coated staff. Neither does the next twenty minutes in a single-seater plastic jacuzzi. A fifteen-minute massage completes the treatment. Fifteen minutes does little for biker's back. In the good old pre-Hispanic days, a visiting Inca would have had the staff's heads lopped.

This is my fourth month of travel. I have been cold each day that I have ridden across mountains. Ming asks how I expect to survive in the true Altiplano and for 2000 kilometres in early spring through Patagonia. I relent and buy myself a leather bomber jacket for fifty-five dollars.

To Huamachuco, Thursday 7 September

Early mornings are best. I am alert and physically fresh. Today we abandon Cajamarca at six-thirty and with no regrets. The road climbs. Ming freezes. I am enveloped in the warmth both of my new leather jacket and of sartorial superiority. I look splendid. Farmers wave.

The road crosses pale upland pastures where both air and soil are thin. Cows are lethargic. Dogs don't bother barking. Our destination is Huamachuco. The small town of San Marcos is our first halt. We breakfast at a restaurant on the square: eggs, rolls, coffee, fresh juice. Ming has thawed and the sun is up. We sit on the steps of a monument in the square. Small boys compete to polish my shoes. I ask why they aren't at school. It is a dumb question and they shrug and giggle among themselves.

We feel good. Ming is content at the lack of garbage. Then we hit dirt. The map doesn't say dirt. Short stretches of dirt are common in Latin America. Lack of road maintenance is the cause. The tar surface crumbles. Eventually it is scraped away by a mechanical grader. Further deterioration follows. I am confident that this will be a short stretch. The surface is loose stone, powder and deep ruts.

It continues and continues.

The Honda hates dirt. I achieve thirty kilometres an hour on the better straights, twenty on the climbs, down to ten on curves. The front wheel bucks in ruts and over rocks. The rear wheel kicks me in the butt. God knows what the countryside looks like. I dare not look. One moment's inattention and the bike will slide. The slide could be over a precipice and a thousand-foot drop.

Fifty kilometres of this purgatory brings us to Cajabamba, a neat, clean market town. I am exhausted. I am not having fun. We stop for fresh orange juice at a café. The owner tells us the dirt continues to Huamachuco, a minimum of three more hours. She suggests we put the bikes on the Horna Transport omnibus ('omnibus' is Peruvian for a standard coach). We try. Horna will take the Honda. The Suzuki is too large. At least the Suzuki is built for the rough stuff. The Honda is a city girl. I fear the road will destroy her. And I am holding Ming back.

I have three hours to wait before the bus departs. I watch *Seabiscuit* on TV in the café on the corner of the plaza. A gang of kindly helpers lays the Honda on its side in the rear luggage compartment. I pay a dollar sixty as a passenger and nine dollars for the bike. The omnibus takes three and a half hours to reach Huamachuco. The distance is sixty kilometres. The road surface is awful. Some corners are so tight that the bus has to back up a couple of times.

I sit next to a young lady with a plump face and a quiet voice. Her petticoats splay her skirt and she wears a broad-brimmed straw hat with a high crown. She grabs my knee on a couple of bad curves, curves where the edge is so close you look straight down the side of the bus into the abyss. A video of a jungle horror movie plays on TV. The dialogue is English drowned by Latino pop from the hi-fi speakers. I feel a fool having to ask my quiet-voiced companion to repeat herself as she comments on the passing scenery. She clearly believes that, in my old age, I am simple-minded – or that all foreigners are simple.

'That is a lake,' she says, spacing her words with care. 'There are many trout in the lake.'

'That is the river.'

'That is the irrigation ditch.'

'That is wheat.'

'Those are sheep.'

'That is rice.'

'Pardon me?' I say, and she repeats, with patience, 'Those are tiles for the roof.'

'There they are making adobe bricks.'

'That is a pig.'

My companion reports to fellow passengers the information she feeds me and on my lack of understanding. My fellow passengers listen and add further commentary. These layers of conversation become increasingly complicated. The bike ride has left me exhausted. Falling asleep would be extremely rude.

Ming reaches Huamachuco three hours ahead of the bus. He finds an excellent hotel. The Colonial is a converted colonial townhouse built around two patios. Ming checks the bathrooms: the water is piping hot. Ming books two rooms. He asks a cop outside the cop shop on the plaza for directions to the bus terminal. The cop drives Ming to the terminal in the police pickup.

We eat an excellent dinner at a small steakhouse on the square midway between the police station and the cathedral. The sky is clear. The moon is almost full. Ming is in the mood for wine. Dinner for two accompanied by a litre of surprisingly good Peruvian red sets us back ten dollars. We like Huamachuco. We don't feel cheated. Strange that two towns in the Andes, both Hispanic colonial and both sited at an altitude of over 3000 metres, should be so different in atmosphere.

On to Trujillo, Friday 8 September

Huamachuco boasts the largest Hispanic colonial plaza in Peru. Buildings are more charming than grand. The central gardens are imaginative and well maintained. The faithful and those without faith are united in their dislike of the cathedral. The original cathedral was built of adobe. It fell down. The new cathedral is a late twentieth-century industrial building in a seventeenth-century setting and resembles an aircraft hanger for small planes. The gates are locked. The janitor will open at eight.

I wait and talk with an elderly schoolteacher. She is an earnest lady, kindly. She cradles a large bunch of roses for the cathedral. A teacher's monthly salary of 260 dollars is insufficient to help buy medicine for her parents and small gifts for her grandchildren. She asks where I am going. I answer, 'To Trujillo.'

She tells me that the road should be paved. Funds were apportioned more than ten years ago. Officials embezzled the funds and decamped for Europe. Now the road is in a disastrous state. Huamachuco has become an island. She nods in agreement with herself as she relates the theft of the road funds. 'Corruption is the tremendous tragedy of our country, *señor*. Corruption is present at every level of government – even here in the municipality.'

The cathedral janitor is a poor timekeeper.

I go in search and discover a priest raised in Spain's Rioja. He has spent twenty-two years in Peru. As a young man, he travelled his first parish by mule. When he came to Huamachuco, the cathedral existed as concrete pillars and a curved roof. The parishioners made the bricks and built the walls. Their dream is to build a facade more in keeping with the plaza. A concrete crossbeam supporting the choir loft is the major obstacle.

'That beam would survive a nuclear war,' complains the priest.

We talk of the many Protestant sects proselytising in the province.

The priest doesn't view them as competition. His sole desire is that people come to God. What route they choose is immaterial: Hindu, Buddhist (looking at Ming), whatever ...

His might be an unpopular view with a conservative Vatican.

I suspect the priest is too busy struggling with the earthly and spiritual difficulties of his flock to give much care for such strictures. He struck both Ming and me as a remarkable man, kindly, gentle and deeply committed. A new facade for the cathedral would be a just reward for his years of service.

He asks whether I am aware of the first governor of the province under the Spanish. I admit my ignorance. He recites one of those splendid Spanish names that go on and on: Doña Isabella Francesca, Margarita Maria de ... de ... de ... etc., etc.

'Yes, a woman,' he says. 'A woman and an Inca. The names were those she took at baptism. Many of the early governors were Incas.'

The dirt road yesterday was a surprise. I hadn't prepared myself. I didn't know how long the dirt would continue or how much worse it might get. I felt that I was holding Ming back. Today I know. We face 160 kilometres of dirt and a wicked climb. I dress accordingly, two sets of long underwear, two pairs of pyjamas pants, two pairs of chinos – two undershirts, two shirts, two jerseys and my new leather bomber jacket. Mounting the Honda is a struggle.

I leave forty minutes ahead of Ming. The road is rutted at the corners. The ruts are filled with fine powder. I ease into the corners and use my feet to steady the bike. The straights are loose stone, ridges and craters. Some parts are only the width of a truck. The drop is terrifying. Traffic is minimal.

The road climbs and winds and climbs and finally frees itself to cross dry windswept fells. The grey crags ahead are lifted from the Scottish highlands. A reed-fringed tarn awakens childhood memories of casting for brown trout. The climb peaks at 13 700 feet. I have ridden forty kilometres in the first two hours. Rather than depressed, I feel elated.

This is tough. I am in my seventies. I am riding a small road bike. Surely I am achieving some kind of old man's record.

I pull off the road at a sod-roofed café. This is the first building I've seen in ten kilometres. I am greeted by a party of roadworkers about to leave in a pickup. A couple of holes in the wall are closed against the cold by wooden shutters. Light leaks between the shutters. Four men occupy one of a dozen crude tables. A woman serves the men and returns to the kitchen. The men ignore me. They wear wool ponchos and felt hats and sit hunched over their food. I sit and wait. I wait twenty minutes. No one acknowledges my existence. Finally I give up, go back outside and remount the bike.

I ride a further ten kilometres and stop at another café. Although equally isolated, this café has a tin roof and two windows with glass panes. I clamber off the Honda. A small dog barks and wags its tail. The dog follows me indoors. Six tables have bright plastic tablecloths.

A young woman peers briefly round the rear door and sees an immensely fat bearded European stroking a small dog. Her surprise is natural. She vanishes. I hear voices in the back. The woman reappears in company with an older woman. I explain my bulk by remarking that riding a bike across the fells demands much protection against the cold.

Both woman peek through the window. Sight of the Honda makes them less nervous.

'Yes,' the older woman says. 'Yes, it is cold.'

I ask whether it would be possible to eat.

'There is soup,' the older woman says. 'Soup, and there is meat.'

'Perfect,' I say. I sit at a table in the sunlight by a window and unzip my bomber jacket. The café sits on a slight rise with vast views of moors and crags and of distant mountain peaks. A dot appears way down the road. The dot grows. Ming has arrived. Being Chinese, he appears less foreign to the women. The potato soup is warming. The meat is old goat in a charcoal crust.

We ride together. The road rises to 4200 metres. We pass a silver mine owned by a Canadian mining company in which Ming holds shares. Air is thin and cold is permanent. The miners are small men.

They appear to crouch inside their coats as they shuffle along the road or ride in the back of a truck. We pass a village comprising mainly of tin huts. Compare the huts with a shipping container and the container would seem luxurious. Life has changed since the days of the Incas: miners have pneumatic drills.

Later, I ask Ming whether he is going to keep his shares in the mining company.

No, owning the shares makes him uncomfortable.

Thus are the perils for a capitalist who travels.

Finally we commence the descent. The road is tar and follows a river gorge, down, down, down. Ming stops to photograph. I stop to pee. I peek over the edge. Ming is photographing the skeletons of trucks that took a shortcut.

The gorge opens to a plain of vast sugar fields. Early evening and we stop at a gas station, drink good coffee and strip off a couple of layers of clothing. A further ten kilometres and we see the lights of Trujillo.

Trujillo has a good feel. It is a bright, open city. The buildings are painted in strong pastel colours. Much of the centre is Hispanic colonial. Our hotel is the Colonial on Independencia, two blocks from the main plaza. I am on the ground floor. Ming is on the first. I have two windows, one onto the rear patio. Our bikes are parked beside the fountain in the front patio. We stroll past tourist restaurants and up a pedestrian street to a small square with a fountain in the middle and four trees. We find a small bar-restaurant and eat shrimp *ceviche* at a table on the pavement. I follow with a steak. Ming orders calamari and rice. Ming drinks wine; I stick with beer. We have ridden one hell of a ride. We feel very proud of ourselves.

Trujillo, Sunday 10 September

A weekend in Trujillo and I have serviced my soul, the Honda, my belly and my writing obligations. The soul was easiest. Churches abound. El Carmen is a delight and full for Saturday evening Mass. The cathedral is splendid from the outside. I find the interior cold and Sunday service disappointing.

Honda HardCorp on Avenida Nicolás de Pierola services the bike. The mechanic wears slacks and polished shoes and a clean short-sleeved shirt – sufficient cause for suspicion. So I watch. I watch keenly. He completes every job by the book. He changes the oil, adjusts the valves, changes the plug, adjusts the points, greases this, oils that, on and on for three hours. He works while squatting on his polished heels and without getting a single drop of oil on his clothes or on the floor.

He dismounts the rear wheel, has a fresh tyre and tube fitted, remounts the wheel and remains clean. I mount the wheel and I have to sit in the dirt and balance the wheel between my feet. My hands get covered in oil and dirt. So do my trousers and my shirt. And I habitually wipe the sweat from my brow on the back of my hand.

HardCorp's general manager is a champion trials rider. The technical manager rides a 650 trial bike with the baffles removed from the exhaust. A full assault by a battalion of Special Forces would be quiet in comparison. He takes my little white Honda for a trial run. I tremble for the bike's innocence.

New rear tyre, tube and a spare tube, new plug, oil change and a full 3000-kilometre service sets me back fifty-six dollars. Back home I would pay fifty-six dollars to have a bike mechanic sneer.

Up in the Andes a Peruvian road rock tore loose one hinge on the Honda's rear rack box. I don't know which rock. Maybe it was a pot-hole. I ask where I can have the hinge fixed. The technical manager inspects the box. The fibreglass is weakened. A new hinge will tear loose. He heads for a biker's store. I follow. Ming brings up the rear. I am on a small bike and Trujillo traffic is scary. Being sandwiched between two maniacs on barking 650s is terrifying. The tech manager rides a race even when cruising round the block for a glass of milk. Other drivers are the enemy. One-way streets are a challenge. Red lights are for nursery maids. Across town takes twenty minutes. To hell with a bike shop. My nerves are shot. I need a pharmacy.

However, I buy a new box, bigger and stronger, for thirty dollars and, finally, a mirror to replace the mirror smashed when unloading from the hell ship.

Road to Lima, Monday 11 September

Ming the Adventurous scorns the Pan-American Highway as too easy a ride. He is convinced that a road marked as paved on his map is a paved road. I am a disbeliever. Now Ming is way up in the Andes scaring sheep while I take to the shifting sands of the littoral. The phrase sits easy on the tongue. Truth is seldom poetic. I am riding across real desert in a real sandstorm. Sand stings my cheeks. Visibility is fifty metres maximum. Cops nursemaid me.

The first two cops are surprised to see an old man with a sand-filled beard appear out of the mist of sand. They wave me down. Am I OK? Where am I going? Where have I come from? Mexico? On this little Honda? Never.

Except for the sea trip, I insist.

The cops think I'm nuts. A shortened version of the hell ship voyage convinces them.

They radio ahead a few kilometres to the next squad car. These cops disbelieve the first cops. In due course I appear out of the sandstorm. They wave me down. Is it true? That I rode from Mexico? That I am riding to Tierra del Fuego? That I am over seventy?

Absolutely.

They shake their heads and mutter the Peruvian cop equivalents of 'wow' and 'crazy'. They shake my hand and clap me on the back and tell me to be careful on the Pan-American Highway in a sandstorm. Bus and truck drivers have no respect for small bikes. Better keep to the hard shoulder.

I would be impolite in mentioning that truckers dump garbage on the hard shoulder.

So the ride continues all morning and through the first hours of the afternoon: squad car to squad car, worries as to my wellbeing, wonder at my adventure. The storm clears in mid-afternoon. Finally the desert is visible. Through millennia, the sea wind has scoured the hills bare and sculpted the sand into curls and peaks and steep ridges. Long lines of surf unfold across the beaches to my right. Despite the garbage, the landscape is extraordinarily beautiful. I am having a great time.

Peru is immense. Trujillo to Lima is 560 kilometres and this is a short leg. Lima to Cuzco comes next: 1100 kilometres. I stop at a small town that may have a name – if so, I missed it. A small single room with bathroom sets me back seven dollars. The shower is electrically heated. I check the wiring and choose to stay dirty. The internet café is safer. The guys and girls recommend a fish restaurant. They instruct a motor-rickshaw driver where to take me. The driver doesn't listen. He is in shock. Here is a real foreigner, an old man with a beard. The driver is already rehearsing the tale he will tell his kids back home. So he turns left at the end of the block. He should turn right. I tell him he should turn right. What's the point? He has no idea where the restaurant is. He can't recall its name. So I walk.

I find the restaurant and order *ceviche*, which is vast and mostly fish and octopus, with a few prawns, and a big bottle of Crystal lager.

I am halfway to Lima. I am warm. I am not breaking wind. I prepare to drift into well-earned sleep and dream of Ming freezing his butt as he bounces over a rock road. Ha!

Road to Lima, Tuesday 12 September

I ride the desert again. A young man stands beside the road. He wears freshly laundered red jogging pants, blue top, white baseball cap reversed, clean trainers with their laces loose. He is miles from anywhere; miles, even, from the nearest bush. He stands with his hands in his pockets. His dress and posture are familiar from a thousand bus stops, London, Paris, New York: the confident kid ready to bop.

A few miles separate the kid from a middle-aged couple tending a roadside shrine. To a son? A brother?

No car. Did they come by bus or by *collectivo* (shared taxi)?

How often do they make this pilgrimage?

Does loss dominate their lives?

I stop for breakfast at a restaurant in the middle of nowhere. The restaurant is an industrial building with windows on three sides. Continual wind has twisted the arched side doors and broken the glass panes. Two waitresses huddle from the wind at a table protected by a pillar on the extreme right of the big space. Fifty tables are laid with red tablecloths. I am the lone customer. Did the owner expect coach traffic?

The waitresses invite me to sit with them. I order American breakfast from the menu: fried eggs, fresh orange juice, rolls with butter and jam, coffee. I ask for the eggs to be fried English style (soft yolks) – such are the last small futile claims of English independence.

The waitresses are young and pretty and giggly. They earn seventy dollars a month plus room and board. Seventy dollars is slave money. Yes, they say, but needs must. They are unarmed by education yet TV informs them of alternative worlds – there is the cruelty. One had a *novio*. He left. What is their future? Marriage to a passing truck driver? Oh, for a magic wand with which to change their lives.

Two cops enter, nod to me and sit at the far side of the restaurant. They finish their meal while I am conversing with the waitresses. I ask for my bill. The cops have already paid. Has an old man's need for protection spread the entire length of the Pan-Americano?

The road passes vast chicken farms. Desert land is cheap. No need to clean up or reuse. Barns are full for a while, and then abandoned. Wind tears the sheeting. The barns become raggedy and spectral. Finally only the skeleton remains. The skeleton, too, buckles beneath the wind.

I take a late lunch at a four-table village restaurant: excellent tongue stew with rice, orange juice, coffee. Meals offer pot luck in whom I meet. Mada, six, and Rosita, twelve, join me. Mada shows me her schoolbook. Her handwriting is neat and her drawings are good and humorous. Rosita has left her schoolwork at home – or is shy of its quality (she has her backpack). They repeat for me my mantra: *education is the road to woman's liberty*. I give Mada eighty cents for chocolate. Mada spends twenty cents on two huge chocolate-coated Chupa Chups. She will give the change to her mother.

The Peruvian cops of the Pan-Americano are correct: truck drivers and coach drivers show neither respect nor mercy for the rider of a small bike. The freeway into Lima is terrifying. The spires and domes of the cathedral are visible above the rooftops. I turn right across the river and am in Lima's historic centre. The Hostal Roma is on Rica. I find it and am shown to a very basic room. Too basic. The *hostal* comes with the blessing of *Journey Latin America and the Footprint* guidebook. Sixteen dollars is way overpriced. I complain and am moved to a room with marginally more space and a bathtub of white tiles. The water is hot. The towel is adequate. Staff lift the Honda up the steps into the vestibule. Much is forgiven.

Onward through Peru

Lima, Tuesday 12 September

I sin in persecuting a young woman at the tourist information office close by the cathedral. She is three months into a job she enjoys. She is sweetly well meaning. She enquires of tourists their experiences of Peru and writes their polite replies in a large book. I speak of garbage and poverty: she doesn't write in the book. I ask, although certain of the answer, whether she was educated at a state or private school. Private, of course. The neat tweed suit is sufficient evidence.

Ashamed at my wickedness, I seek to shrive my soul – evening Mass at San Pedro. The church is Hispanic American baroque and a delight. The congregation fear for the celebrant, a doddery nonagenarian monsignor crowned with a pink cap. Has he died during the reading of the Epistle and Gospel or dozed off? Will he rise from his chair after the readings? Will he manage the steps to the altar? Whether he recalls the words of the service is immaterial. His voice is too weak and is buried within the coughs and shuffles of the congregation. This is Tuesday evening; I count over a hundred celebrants. Men are in the majority.

Lima, Wednesday 13 September

Francisco Pizzaro founded Lima in 1535. The university followed in 1551. I will recall the city for two beautiful patios and a grove of olive trees. Some of the trees are sufficiently holed and wizened to be survivors of the original planting by the Spanish founders of the city. The trees stand in a public park to the south of the city centre. The district is upmarket. The trees are surrounded by well-kept lawns. Private security guards are much in evidence. The poor are absent. A cab driver points to houses built by millionaires on privately expropriated corners of this public land – land reform for the super-rich. Their young speed on skateboards around a public fountain.

The sixteenth-century patios suffer a different arrogance. Imagine the temerity required to overshadow their beauty with the most mundane of late twentieth-century construction – such is the arrogance of architects and property developers.

I sat on my spectacles at the hotel on the road from Trujillo and Lima. Now I wear my spares. An optician makes me a new pair of bifocals in sprung frames. I order them in the morning. They are ready in the evening: thirty-seven dollars.

For dinner I eat *tomalis* (imagine a doughy sausage of cornflour stuffed with meat or whatever) and shellfish with rice. A six-year-old boy persecutes his mother at the next table: the usual games – unscrewing the salt and pepper pots and dumping the contents on the tablecloth; blowing the pepper at Mum; building towers of his food and then slapping the towers flat with his spoon so the food flies. A doting aunt finds the boy's antics cute. Doting Dad at most shakes his head in gentle reproof. Poor Mum. She does her utmost to control the brat. Aunt's and Dad's opposition is too strong. A hitching rail is the answer. Tie the brat up outside. Rain? The brat gets a free wash.

To Nazca, Thursday 14 September

Four hundred and forty kilometres to Nazca, city of mystical lines. Nazca is famous for its lines. The lines are kilometres long and drawn on the arid desert plateau. Some of the lines form patterns. Others represent animals. How were they drawn? By whom? How were artists at ground level able to envisage work that modern man can only appreciate from the seat of an aeroplane?

Beings from outer space are the suspects – or the children of visitors from outer space. The drawings don't impress me as sufficiently sophisticated to be the work of adults capable of crossing the universe.

I imagine a spacecraft breaking down. Dad is trying to fix the power supply. Mum is tut-tutting because the washing machine won't work. The kids are getting in the way.

Dad says to the kids, 'For Christ's sake, piss off and amuse yourselves.'

'There's nothing to do.' (No power – they can't play computer games.)

'Draw, for God's sake.'

'I've lost my pencil.'

'Use a stick. Draw in the damn desert.'

Yes, I am aware that the lines are kilometres long. Imagine the aliens as giant daddy-long-legs.

I leave Lima at seven and am in Nazca at half past four. The journey is across desert or near-desert. I stop for lunch at one of those crossroads in the middle of nowhere where passengers pee and change buses and eat food that has been a playground for flies for the past week.

Three cars and a couple of pickups are parked outside a diner on the corner. No buses. This may be a good sign. I risk a steak and onions, rice. A cop joins me.

I understand why I have contact with so many police. Police are accustomed to asking questions. They aren't shy. They see this old guy on a Mexican-registered bike. They say, hey, did you really ride from Mexico? Where are you from? Where are you going? How old are you? Are you married? How many kids do you have? What does your wife say, you being away so long? What job do you have? How much do you earn? What does this trip cost?

Non-cops are more fearful of being intrusive. They gather in the background, listen.

This cop is young. He earns 300 dollars a month. Enough to live on? Barely. He and I sit in the sun and drink orange juice and chat. The chat is interrupted by the cop rising to blow his whistle each time a bus passes. Why? Because blowing a whistle goes with the job.

Nazca, Friday 15 September

I have struck lucky in Nazca. I am staying at the Hostal Via Morburg. I have a small room with twin beds. The beds are comfortable and the wiring to the electric water heater on the shower appears vaguely safe. A small swimming pool with clean water occupies much of one patio. Better yet are the staff, one of whom has a daughter. The daughter is six. Last night she elected me her *novio*. Today I am Grandfather. Is this an upgrade or a downgrade? I am also a fearless explorer in partnership with the hotel administrator.

The Nazca lines attract tourists. Tourists tramp over the desert. Their footprints wreck the lines. Now the lines are protected territory. Fly over them in a small bumpy plane or watch them on video. Walking is forbidden.

Tour companies are in despair. What else can they show their prey? They search desperately for new lines, lines that are legally accessible.

The administrator of the Hostal Via Morburg is invited by a tour agency to sample their new tour. She invites me to join the freebie. First we visit a gold mine. The actual mine is three-quarters of the way up a shale precipice and inaccessible. The tour company has blasted a tunnel at the bottom of the precipice. This fake mine is our target. The tunnel is man-height and four metres long. The manageress is more practised at pretending interest. I prefer talking to one of the miners.

The miner earns 580 dollars a month. He lives in a shack on site and works five and a half days a week. He climbs the cliff to the mine. A tunnel 350 metres long leads to the workface. The miner has golden socks. The socks are the closest he'll get to personal wealth. The mine owner is North American. I am not being snide at the expense of the US. I am reporting fact.

Our guide stops on the return from the mine to show us his latest discovery. We are in a valley of boulders, shale and bare rock.

'Look,' he says, pointing at a chunk of mountainside. 'You can see a drawing of the sun and its rays.'

Our guide's partner in the tour agency points in a different direction, although with equal enthusiasm. 'There, look, see the drawing of a *cuy*? See? That's the tail.' *Cuy* is guinea-pig.

I am polite. I look. I see rock. The rock has the commonplace marks any rock face has.

The hotel administrator attempts loyalty to Nazca. Unfortunately she catches my eye. We get the giggles.

Nazca, Saturday 16 September

All the staff at the Hostal Via Morburg are female. They describe Juan Carlos as 'a Toby'. A Toby is a good-looking young man, amiable, lots of charm and perhaps a little too easy.

I will remember Juan Carlos with fondness as a merely moderately dangerous maniac. He speeds down desert tracks at a hundred kilometres an hour in an oversized blue dune buggy. He attacks dunes with the buggy. Most times he reaches the top. For serious sport, he rides a board down the dunes. These are not dunes as normal people imagine dunes. Juan Carlos' favourite is 1700 metres high. I need to put that in words lest readers believe they are reading a typo: one thousand, seven hundred metres. This is a dune taller than the highest mountain in Great Britain. Juan Carlos rides down this dune on a one-metre-twenty board. The sand is soft. My youngest son Jed rides down non-sand mountains on a board with wheels. He and Juan Carlos are soul brothers – or suffer from a similar mental illness.

I buggy-ride with Juan Carlos early this morning. He has an Italian couple as passengers, Barbara and Eduardo, honeymooners. Both speak good English. They are novices at sandboarding. They try out on a small dune, the equivalent of a blue run. They have a ball. So do I – although I don't board. The desert is spectacular and being driven by Juan Carlos has the adrenalin flowing.

We are back in town by midday. I have promised to watch my local grandchild dance at the Nazca primary school fête.

Nazca, Sunday 17 September

I ought to leave for Cuzco. My plans are frustrated by an electricity cut that will continue until late afternoon. The ATMs are down. I have no money.

I have been cooking for the past few days. I pretend that I am cooking for the staff at the Hostal Via Morburg. I am cooking for myself. Friday I bought live crab in the market and prepared a sauce: olive oil, onion, tomato, celery, garlic, red peppers, root ginger, chilli, fresh coriander. Yesterday I cooked prawns. Today I am using the remains of the prawns to flavour a pasta sauce. Two young sophisticates from the capital arrived late last night: Victor is first cousin to Juan Carlos. His *novia*, Carmen, is a dancer in a modern dance group. Sunday lunch of prawn pasta makes up for the lack of water (the pump is electric).

Replete, we commit ourselves to Juan Carlos and his buggy. We race down a dry river. Carmen is dismissive of the parched countryside. Then we hit the dunes. The dunes transform Carmen into a fanatic. Drop her three-quarters of the way up a dune with a 300-metre slide ahead – dissatisfied, she clambers the extra hundred metres to the summit. My youngest son, the mountain boarder, would do the same. I have watched him. Every metre of altitude counts, every extra degree of gradient.

While the kids play, I sit on a dune crest and watch the breeze obliterate our footsteps. The view is superb and extraordinary. The temperature is perfect. No flies, no mosquitoes. Nazca deserves more than the standard one-night stop on the tourist trail.

This evening we go to the cockfights. The small sand arena is ringed by banks of concrete benching. The fights are brief and unattractive. The birds wear long curved spurs on their legs. The handlers blow in the birds' faces (does garlic breath make the birds more combative?) and hold them aloft while punters shout bets at bookies. The birds are released. They eye each other with suspicion. Often they need further encouragement from their handlers – more garlic breath. Finally there is a flurry of wings as each bird attempts to gain height from which to strike down at its opponent's head. Cheers greet a few specks of blood. A bird collapses. The handler attempts resuscitation. The bell goes for the second round. A further brief flapping of feathers and the loser lies dead in the sand.

The audience is more interesting. The benches are full: grandads, mums and dads, teens, babes scarcely out of arms. The faces fascinate me. And the postures. They are so familiar: the bad-tempered minor official; the four men over-drinking beer from bottles; the teenage girl, a novice smoker, attempting to appear sophisticated as she puffs inexpertly on a cigarette.

An overweight mother makes a second dash to the caféteria. First she gives her five-year-old son a good shaking and plonks him on the tier behind us: 'Move from there and I'll murder you.'

The faces may be darker, but otherwise they are no different from any European crowd.

I recall the baseball game in Dallas. There I felt myself on unknown territory. I discovered no clues by which to assess what or who people were. Uniformity was the rule, faces equally groomed, equally bland, jeans or khaki drill obligatory. Here there is so much more individuality and character on display.

Escape from Nazca, Tuesday 19 September

None of the staff at the *hostal* has seen the Nazca lines (few locals can spare fifty dollars for the flight). I have seen innumerable photographs and read the theories and fictions and have wondered at the obsessiveness of archaeologists. I cooked for the staff and raced up and down dunes with Juan Carlos, Victor and Carmen. They treated me as a friend, made me feel at home. I had a ball – no need for lines. I thank them and I thank the people of Nazca – what joy to argue prices in the market, eat ghastly chemical-pink cake at the school fête, wander the streets at night without fear of assault. Now I head for Cuzco. My guidebook warns of frequent rapes and strangle muggings, and muggings by cab drivers, and pickpockets and con artists.

The road from Nazca twists up through dry mountains, a climb of over 3000 metres. I find a neat clean café at the top. Vases of brilliant wild flowers enliven the counter. The owner is in his sixties. He has lived here all his life. In his youth the hills were green. Farmers kept dairy cattle. Little rain has fallen over the past twenty years. The cattle have gone. Global warming.

The road crosses a dark bristly fell of tufted grass. I can see for miles. I wonder why vicuña graze beside the road. Do they enjoy traffic?

Puquio is 160 kilometres from Nazca. Mid-afternoon and I am

exhausted. Perhaps the altitude saps my will – or am I weakened by feeling alone and unprotected by friendships? I ride up a dirt street in search of a hotel. This is market day or all days are market days. Small dark people bundled in sweaters and wool jackets overflow the pavement. Men and women wear brown felt hats. Doorways overflow with used clothes.

The one hotel is on a street being laid with drains in a deep ditch alongside the pavement. The pavement is too narrow for the Honda and I park in the patio at the hotel owner's house. She directs me to the Estancia restaurant. If Peru has an arms industry, it could build tanks out of the beef. I chomp and read the newspaper. Pillaging of the military and police pension fund occupies the first four pages.

An electrical engineer sits at the next table. He has three sons. The eldest is also an engineer; the second is an architect; the third is studying computer science at university. My companion is a great reader and a student of current affairs. He asks my nationality and says, 'Your Tony Blair is a tremendous liar.'

'Yes,' I say.

'And now Bush makes torture legal. How do you feel?'

Few people I meet on this journey differentiate between the US and Britain. Blair has implicated us totally. How do I feel? I feel deeply sullied.

My daughter Anya complains that I accuse all Americans of torture. I accuse all Americans of complicity in torture. The US is a democracy: every citizen is responsible for the actions of the government. We Brits are accomplices. This is Blair's doing and the doing of our Parliament. We have been made accomplices to so much evil and to such stupidity. Yes, I feel sullied, but also enraged that one man should lead my nation down such a filth-strewn road.

Road to Cuzco, Wednesday 20 September

The road flows over high fells. I can see for miles. Way in the distance a lone truck creeps over a crest. A tarn to the left of the road reflects the deep blue of the sky. Small groups of vicuña graze the tufted grass. A couple of shaggy ponies watch from a rise. Snow covers a soft ridge between black rock peaks. A herdswoman chivvies a flock of alpaca. Riding here is easy. Free to muse, I dwell on yesterday's conversation with the engineer. I wrote yesterday in anger. Anger has been inescapable on much of this journey. I have been riding through the United States' backyard, a backyard that the US has been tilling for the past 200 years. Successive administrations have suborned governments, supported the vilest of dictators, trained military for whom murder and torture are the norm. Bush supports torture as necessary. Where does US society stand? Behind their president? Behind that great TV hero of *24*, an all-American hero to whom torturing prisoners is a noble act of self-sacrifice? This is the good guy. No wonder the US military is confused. No wonder Latin Americans are sickened by the US's claim to hold the moral high ground. I long to see Bush and Rumsfeld and Cheney strapped to boards and half-drowned in water tanks – the same treatment meted out to their prisoners. Blair I would dunk in a witch's chair.

The Altiplano ends. The road winds and backtracks down a steep mountain face. The drop is dizzying. I quake when forced by a truck to the outside of a curve. The road follows a river gorge. The gorge funnels a headwind and I crouch low over the gas tank. Tiny patches of tilled soil edge the water – 'fields' would be a misnomer. A woman shares the shade of a fruit tree with two sheep. She returns my wave. The gorge narrows to nothing and the road climbs. The Honda is valiant. Up we go, up and up. We hit the top and wow! The majestic sweep of the high Andes is spread across the horizon. The view of snow-capped peaks is magnificent. Surprise is total. The road drops again and follows another river. A hundred kilometres to Cuzco. Exhausted, I pull into a roadside inn.

I take a room with a bath. The hotel has flies. The flies bite. Each bite raises a purple bruise with a minute drop of blood dead in the centre. The bites itch. The beef at dinner is a further candidate for the Peruvian arms industry. I am out of cardiac medication. I can't sleep. I lie awake and itch and obsess over the state of my heart.

Cuzco, Thursday 21 September

A short ride takes me up to Cuzco – and a pharmacy where I fail to fill my prescriptions. The fault is mine. I take medication on trust. The pharmacist requires purpose: 'What are they for?'

'My heart.'

'Yes, but what do they do?'

'Keep me alive.'

I book into a Dutch-owned *hostal*, the Marani on Carmen Alto. Profits go to the Hope Foundation, a worthy cause. The Honda rests in an ample and pleasant patio. The street is narrow and cobbled. All streets are narrow and cobbled. Most are steep. Many have steps. Every doorway opens to a restaurant, a tour agency or an internet connection. Prices are high. I see foreigners everywhere. Down on the Plaza de Armas, the Cross Keys is a Brit-owned pub. I peek into a room packed with young foreigners competing in their mystical experiences of the Inca Trail and Machu Picchu. The Rat Hole is a bikers' bar with a visitors' book for passing bikers; the owner is a biker from Arizona.

Step outside and you require a fly whisk to dispatch the swarming hustlers. Antigua, Guatemala, has competition.

The cathedral is superb. A canvas is being relined in a side chapel. Restoration is undertaken by a department of the School of Belles Artes. Study is free – unlike in Ecuador. Peru has endless art in need of restoration and many trained restorers. Funds to pay the restorers are in short supply. I talk with the head of restoration. We talk of the artistic explosion that accompanied the Conquest. Indigenous artists were given the tools and were freed from constraint. They leapt from lugging boulders to creating the Rosario chapel. Their work will be marvelled at as long as this planet survives. In 1569 came the Inquisition. Thinking outside the box was again prohibited. Both Spain and Hispanic America atrophied.

Out of Cuzco, Friday 22 September

In Cuzco I am income, two-legged livestock. I will learn nothing of Peru. I am not enjoying myself. On arrival at the

Hostal Marani the Dutch manager asked me to tell her in the morning whether I wished to stay a further day. I tell her this morning. She tells me the hotel is fully booked. I have my excuse. Thirty minutes and I am packed and on the road to Puno.

Road and rail share a wide river valley. At first there are fields. The road climbs and I am back on the Altiplano. The clarity of light is extraordinary, the deep blue of the sky and feel of unlimited space. I stop at a plush roadhouse to use the lavatory. A Belgian coach party enjoys a buffet lunch. The tour group gathers round the Honda. We shake hands. They wish me happy travelling.

The road is straight, the surface excellent. The Honda cruises at eighty kilometres an hour. I inhale fresh chill air and revel in the intense beauty. The mountains are dark rock. A wedge of snow appears. The herds are mostly alpaca. I can differentiate them from llamas. I enquire of a herdswoman. The alpaca are shorter and have bulkier coats. The herdswoman's home is an adobe hovel. This is the truth of the Altiplano: poor soil, little food, nights of vicious cold, appalling accommodation. Many hovels stand empty. The people have fled. The squatter towns of Puno, Cuzco and Lima tempt with the possibility of a marginally better existence.

I have failed to get a handle on Peru. I am disturbed by the contrast between extreme poverty and dirt and the fact that Peru is a tourist Mecca. Inca worship is in fashion. I am out of fashion. I see 1000 years without change, without discovery. I look at Inca stonework and wonder how many slaves were killed and maimed on the construction site. Shifting a thirty-ton boulder up a mountain rather than using cut blocks is neither mystical nor meritorious. The drystone walls of Mediterranean olive terraces have stood for more than 2000 years. Inca terraces have already tumbled. I take on trust an expert's opinion as to the era of a ceramic or scrap of woven cloth; my interest is minimal.

I catch my first glimpse of the immense inland sea, Lake Titicaca. Sun sets as I ride the final kilometres into Puno. The drop in temperature is instant. I could weep icicles. A fiesta grips the city centre. The road to my chosen hotel is blocked. A cop suggests the Gran Puno Inn.

A young concierge runs to open the locked glass doors and laughs as he slides on the polished floor. Twenty-five dollars is beyond my budget. The manager settles for twenty dollars, to include a buffet breakfast. He and the concierge lift the Honda over the curb and into the lobby. My room is on the fourth floor, no elevator. The stairs are steep. I fear for my unmedicated heart. The concierge offers me coca leaves infused in hot water.

The room is spacious. So is the bathroom. The shower runs hot. The bath towels are thick and vast. The bath mat is a miraculous extra, as are an electric radiator and cable TV. I hope for the Ryder Cup. No luck.

Puno, Saturday 23 September

Puno is great for hats. Most common are chocolate soup plates bearing one of those round loaves that bulge above the baking tin. I admire a pink bowler with silk ribbon edging the underside of the brim. Another favourite is a mini-black bowler with a tassel worn at a jaunty angle by a plump lady in her fifties. She is dressed in black. White petticoats fluff up her skirt. A shy thin woman wears a yellow hat of plastic straw sprinkled with glitter. A teenage boy favours a red wool cloche. Then there is the man in the grey fedora who, hands in pockets, poses as an Italian Mafioso. An elderly grey Stetson talks to two junior baseball caps.

Backpackers favour a design on white wool, the top drawn to a point, a tuft on the crest and earflaps – apparently more indigenous than the hats worn by the indigenous.

Strangest is a wide-brim golden pentagon; blue lines mark the segments. Can it be a hat or is it a lampshade out for a walk? The owner is a severe schoolmistressy woman near retirement.

I walk down to the harbour. The first two steamships to sail the lake were imported from Britain. They were shipped as Ikea flat-packs and assembled on the lakeshore. The assemblers were competent. The first, the *Yavari*, was launched on Christmas Day 1870 and is still afloat. The *Ollanta* is more modern and sailed commercially from 1926 into the 1970s.

Puno, Sunday 24 September

Sunday is excellent for people-watching. I choose a table at a café on the harbour wharf. Cultural colonialism hits randomly. A young indigenous woman angles her head and flashes a smile at her father. She wants something. The flirtation is pure Hollywood. A tall, exceptionally dark-skinned young man is unique among his Puno contemporaries in wearing hip-hop.

I count eighteen restaurants on Puno's pedestrian street. All but Rica's Café are geared to tourists. Look in through any window – there we sit, we, the rich (by Peruvian standards). The restaurants employ hustlers. The altitude is above 3000 metres and the hustlers wrap up in ankle-length overcoats and matching mufflers in charcoal-grey wool. The colour is an unfortunate choice. One thinks of professional mourners at a funeral.

To Bolivia, Monday 25 September

The writer of my guidebook warns of corrupt practices at the Bolivian frontier with Peru. The writer mentions motorcyclists as victims. I am a motorcyclist. The road follows the lakeshore. I see thirty or more men seated on benches at the rear of an adobe house. The men are similarly dressed in black suits and black fedoras. They are silent and solemn. This must be a wake. They should take lessons from the Irish.

The road climbs behind a hill. Concrete steps mount the hill. Each step represents a Station of the Cross. Two tall radio masts dominate the hilltop. The shrine is insignificant.

I pause and look back across a bay. The water reflects the deep blue of the sky. A thousand mirrors gleam on the far shore – tin roofs catching the sunlight.

I note two rough-coated white donkeys on a pale beach.

And I worry. Ten kilometres to the frontier. Here comes the victim.

Peruvian immigration takes all of two minutes. Customs is a problem. Our friendly and helpful customs officer from the frontier with Ecuador completed the exit rather than the entry part of the Honda's transit permit.

'A tall man, talks a lot,' suggests the present officer as he scans the signature.

'Yes,' I say. 'A very amiable man.'

'Very amiable,' agrees his fellow official. 'Amiable is all he is. I've served with him.'

I wait while he writes an explanation of the error on pink paper. I add my signature. He affixes the report to the transit permit. We shake hands. I am out of Peru.

Bolivia

Copacabana, Monday 25 September

The vicious, corrupt Bolivian customs officer is a gardener. He is dressed in a wool jumper and is pushing a wheelbarrow. He directs me to immigration, where I fill in the standard tourist fiche (five minutes). I return to the customs office. The customs officer parks his wheelbarrow and we complete a transit permit for the Honda. Although patient, he is keen to get back to his barrow. He stamps and signs the permit and points me to the transit police for a countersignature. Total time at the Bolivian border? Barely fifteen minutes. For this I have worried.

I suspect that the writer of my guidebook is an irritating and arrogant young man – the type that officials hate on sight. Or perhaps I have been lucky. Perhaps my age helps. They imagine me dying on them and the paperwork and they think *Quick! Move the old fool on!*

Copacabana is built on the saddle between two hills. The town slopes steeply down to the shore and reminds me of a Mediterranean fishing village come tourist resort. The townsfolk seem friendlier, happier and more fun-loving than Peruvians. They may eat tourists, but they exercise charm. Peruvians prefer the bludgeon. A big white cathedral dominates the town. The tiled dome and the minarets at each corner of the vast courtyard belong to a mosque. The simplicity of the cathedral's interior is equally Islamic.

I book into the Colonial – big room with lake view and hot shower.

The bedside lamp doesn't work. I switch rooms. The shower doesn't work. However, the beds are comfortable and the room rate plus continental breakfast is five dollars.

A wet Brit on his gap year confronts me on the stairs. He has been swimming in the lake. He claims that the water is shallow and therefore warm. I am shivering from the bike ride. The swimmer, a second young Brit and two young North Americans make a foursome in the hotel garden. I would enjoy hearing their stories. Unfortunately, I carry a fatal disease, age, and they choose the table furthest from where I sit.

Lake Titicaca, Tuesday 26 September

Copacabana is on a peninsula. The peninsula is mountainous and projects from Peruvian territory, so it is a de facto island. You take a ferry to Bolivia proper. The ferry port is twenty-five kilometres from Cochabamaba. The road climbs to 4100 metres. Early morning is cold – especially for a biker. The road is under repair. Men lug stones. They don't wear gloves. Nor do the women who man the wheelbarrows. The hems of the women's petticoats and skirts show beneath yellow slickers. I consider myself a feminist. This isn't the equality I envisaged.

The road follows a high contour above Lake Titicaca. Thick rain clouds to the east dye the waters wine-dark. A lone white motor launch draws a white trail. West is sunshine and the water is brilliant blue. My guidebook reports that the lake is mystical, that the terraces on the peninsula are Inca and that La Paz has the best market for buying ingredients for witchcraft. Guidebooks also warned that the customs officers were crooks and warned that I would be raped, strangle mugged, abducted by guerrillas and shot by paramilitaries.

Forget the book and the mystic and the Incas. Stick with the facts: the fells are beautiful and the lake is beautiful. I am immensely privileged in riding these hills on such a glorious morning.

I eat a chicken roll and drink a large mug of hot black coffee in the caféteria by the ferry quay. The woman who serves me has lost an eye;

the socket has been sewn shut. She asks whether I am sometimes frightened riding alone. I say, no, I'm fine, just so long as I ignore guidebooks.

A dozen women sell fruit and whatever from stalls outside the cafeteria. One of them demonstrates the size of whatever she is discussing by holding her two forefingers a couple of inches apart.

'Me?' I say from the doorway, pointing a finger at myself. 'That's not very kind.'

A few seconds pass in which the women don't believe what they've heard. Then they break up. One has the laugh of an excited chicken. An old crone is doubled over: '*Mala, mala, mala!*' she shrieks. Bad, bad, bad!

Wooden barges ferry trucks and buses across the straits. The barges are outboard powered and the passage is some 400 metres. Ten or more of the barges wait in line. The crew won't cross for a lone biker.

A minibus drives onto the lead ferry and the coxswain waves me on board. He asks about my journey. He wants his photograph taken with the bike and me. One of his crewmen takes the picture. The crewman is a novice with a camera and cuts off part of my head. The coxswain is happy with the result.

La Paz is 120 kilometres from the ferry. The Spaniards founded the city in 1548. They longed for shelter from the viciously cold wind that blows across the Altiplano and sited the city at the bottom of a gorge. In those early days, rush hour was three horses and a mule. Imagine pouring the traffic of a major city into so constricted a space. On a bike I advance a hundred metres in twenty minutes.

I am staying two nights at the Hostal Republic two blocks off the cathedral square. The *hostal* was once the private house of an ex-president. An estate agent would describe it as a two-patio two-floor Spanish colonial. I have a single room on the upper floor overlooking the rear patio. The shower is reasonably hot and the towels are excellent. The building is romantic. Sixteen dollars is a reasonable room rate. The help found a plank so I could ride the Honda up the steps. The patios are cobbled and the Honda is happy.

I am a good tourist all afternoon: two museums, two churches and a cathedral. The cathedral is gloomy. One of the museums is under repair.

However, the coffee in the coffee shop at the Museum and Church of San Francisco is the best I have drunk in more than a month.

In the evening I chat with a German, a professor of philosophy. He has delivered a new book to his publishers and is taking a short break. Flying directly into La Paz often brings on altitude sickness. The professor is suffering – or I bore him to bed.

La Paz, Wednesday 27 September

Today I visited more museums and am overdosed. The streets are steep, and walking at over 4000 metres is tough on an old man. What did I see? More crude and unimaginative Inca gold, beautiful Tiwanachu ceramics. Fifteen hundred years of working with clay – why no potter's wheel?

Because of a culture in which no one dared think outside the box?

Or you can believe that the indigenous peoples are genetically uninventive.

Nonsense!

To Cochabamba, Thursday 28 September

La Paz is in a hole. A road leads in. A road leads out. Escape is simple. I ride one hundred kilometres across the Altiplano before pulling in at a roadhouse. I park beside an outsized Bolivian-registered 4×4 fitted with all the Chelsea extras: spotlights on the roof, spotlights on the bull bar, winch, cowcatcher, rocket launcher, smoke grenades, ejector seats. The passenger-side smoked window slides down. A neat Bolivian blonde asks where I've come from. 'Mexico? On that bike? Magnificent.'

I, of course, look humble.

'Where are you going? Argentina? Tierra del Fuego? Wow! Us too. That's really great.'

The man (ponytail) drums a finger on the padded leather steering wheel.

The blonde takes the message. The smoked window slides up.

I dismount and waddle into the roadhouse. I waddle because I have dressed for the altitude. First the lower half: underpants, long johns, two pairs of chinos, dull-blue waterproof trousers, red rugby socks, Church's shoes. The top: two undershirts, one cord shirt, one sleeveless jumper, two long-sleeved jumpers, scarf, leather jacket, bright-blue waterproof jacket, wool gloves, leather gauntlets. Why am I freezing?

Bolivia's Morales is the president of the urban poor, the subsistence farmers and the manual workers. A magic wand should go with the job. It doesn't. Morales is behind on his promises. His electorate is impatient. The miners have blockaded the road to Cochabamba.

This is the third day of the blockade. Cars can manage a U-turn. Trucks and buses are stuck. They are stuck in a double column tailing back for twenty-five kilometres. Local women are making a killing serving food. Bus passengers drag their gear in hope of a cab. I weave through the queue to the rock barrier.

A union meeting is in progress. I introduce myself to the picket as the father of an elected union official, a Trotskyite. *Un ingles, muy militante.*

A rock is dragged back to let me through. We embrace. The picket mounts a grass bank beside the road to be photographed. A miner takes the camera and photographs me in the centre of the picket. Sadly he doesn't push the button. I consider explaining his error. I also consider that a wise man would get the hell out of there fast.

The road climbs beyond the blockade. Snow sprinkles the fell. The snowline is well below the road. Cloud spits ice at my cheeks. My fingers freeze. I don't give a damn. Honda and I have set a new personal record: 4700 metres.

We have covered 420 kilometres from La Paz to Cochabamba. The Honda rests at a very smart Honda agency. I am in a hotel on the city's central square. The owners of the hotel are Serbian and friends of Jorge Stambuk whom I met in Girón, Colombia: he of the bio-diesel plant. The hotel bears that essential of a proper European family hotel: Madame sits behind the front desk and takes the money. I have a large room and large bathroom. The water is hot. The decor is 1930s. My relationship to Jorge Stambuk earns me a twenty percent discount. I am very comfortable.

Cochabamba, Friday 29 September

I sit in the sun and eat breakfast this morning at a pavement café. I am warm. Cochabamba is heaven. Rereading my writing of the past days, I realise that I have talked with few people since leaving Nazca. Opening conversations with strangers demands emotional energy. Cold is a sapper of energy. All those clothes form a barrier.

Now, in the sun, I am brave. I chat over breakfast at a café with an Argentinian architect, constructor of a cinema complex. Jewish. We talk of the conquest and the Jewish emigration from Spain to Latin America and of the Islamic influence on early Hispanic colonial architecture and of the friendships and business friendships and alliances between Jewish and Arab immigrants in Argentina.

The architect speaks of the Malvinas/Falklands war, of the young men whose lives were sacrificed to the demands of a drunk and to a woman's desire for re-election.

S.I.M. is the Honda agent. I watch the Honda being serviced. The mechanic is meticulous. I am about to start the bike. The mechanic orders me not to touch the throttle. I kick the starter. The engine burbles contentedly. The bill is twelve dollars.

Cochabamba, Saturday 30 September

The sun shines. I sit at a café with members of Cochabamba's Classic Bike Club. They insist I fetch my bike from the hotel garage. It is barely visible parked among its wealthy relatives, more a guinea-pig than a Hog. These men are wealthy. The custom seats on their Harleys and massive Hondas cost more than my entire 125. We exchange tales of accidents; politics are off the menu. Frustrating, as I long to learn their opinions.

The Bolivian chemical engineer in Girón, Colombia, has given me an introduction to a Bolivian icon, a footballer – goalkeeper for the national team. I am invited to lunch at his home. He is younger than me by a few years and yet he walks with a frame and is clumsy with his hands. 'Cortisone,' he explains. 'Playing when injured.'

We drink and talk while the TV displays extreme sports. I watch the crashes, kids bleeding, and I come near to vomiting with sudden fear for Jed, my youngest son: Jed, the mountain boarder, on first-name terms with ambulance crews.

The BBC's correspondent described last week's strike of the southern provinces of Bolivia as a strike of white Bolivians against the indigenous population of the north. Oddly, I find no mention on the BBC's site of the miners' blockade. Perhaps the correspondent is seeking to define the miners' colour.

I have been in Cochabamba for two and a half days. I have walked the streets, sat at cafés, eaten in restaurants. Where are these pure bloods of European descent? This white majority of the BBC correspondent's imagination?

My own perceptions are limited and probably equally erroneous. Cochabamba is a fun city. It is a city loved and cared for by its residents. Flowering trees line clean streets. After La Paz, you feel that you are in a different country. Here are a few quotations:

'There will be civil war.'

'What can you expect when the president is an Indian?'

'Morales is honourable but better an intelligent crook than an honourable incompetent.'

'The Americans should do something.'

'The Americans are to blame, always interfering.'

The poor of La Paz love Morales.

So do Europe's liberal intelligentsia.

I am ignorant. I have no facts. I have no opinion.

To Santa Cruz, Sunday 1 October

A TV crew will film my departure from Cochabamba. I pack, load the bike and wait in the central square. The cathedral is the far side, police headquarters on my left. A brass band is practising. Cops wander over to inspect the bike.

I tell them I intend riding the lowland road via Villa Turani to Santa Cruz. Villa Turani has been a centre for the US DEA and the War on Drugs, a campaign as corrupt and corrupting, ill-conceived and unsuccessful as the War on Terror.

The cops warn that I may be stopped by civilians posing as narcotics agents. There are no agents in civilian clothes. I must insist that the fake agents accompany me to the police station in the next town.

What if they are armed?

'Of course they will be armed. Everyone is armed. Insist,' insists a cop.

Sun shines. The TV journalist waves from the far side of the artificial lake. The lake water is clean. The flowerbeds are beautifully kept.

'Right,' I say. 'Yes, right, I'll insist.'

The band plays.

The cops shake my hand and wish me well.

The first 200 kilometres to Santa Cruz are biker heaven, easy climbs, swooping curves. I break at Villa Tunari. Midday and fish fresh from the river and grilled over charcoal is on the menu, with squeezed orange juice.

A further 470 kilometres to Santa Cruz.

Beyond the mountains the road runs straight across ranch land, dairy farms and huge fields of sugar cane. The heat is splendid: no need for a jumper or leather jacket. Dusk as I reach the city. Sunday and the boys on bikes are out and rowdy. I grin and pull in beside a clutch of Harleys revving at the pavement.

One of the riders (bearded) returns my grin and says, 'Yeah, I know.'

I find a nine-dollar hotel with hot water just a block away from the Plaza Central. I unload and leave my bags in the lobby while I park the bike in a parking lot. I return to the hotel and find that a young man has carried my gear up to my room. Such small unasked-for kindnesses give immense pleasure.

I lick great coffee ice-cream on the cathedral plaza. The population appears marginally paler-skinned than in Cochabamba. The cathedral is vast; the ceiling is inlaid with wood; standing room only for eight o'clock Mass.

South, Monday 2 October

My target is Yuquiba on the border with the Argentine. I fail to pick the left turn at kilometre thirteen and ride thirty kilometres on the hill road to Sucre. Dumb! I have a tail wind and cruising at a hundred kilometres an hour is easy on a great road across dry forest patched with rough fields. Hot as an oven and I stop wherever bottled water is available from an icebox.

The only service station midway is out of gas. The next gas station is a further hundred kilometres. I buy four litres from a drum at the next village.

I stop the night ninety kilometres short of the border at Villamontes. I try the Hotel Rancho first. It is recommended by the guidebooks. A surly receptionist gives a room rate of twenty-six dollars. The next two hotels are full. Finally I stop at the Hostal la Oyerencia on Avenida Heroes del Chaco: nine dollars for a large room with fan, hot water in a good bathroom, cable with CNN. I have ridden 1000 kilometres in two days.

Villamontes has a pleasant small-town feel. Although famous as a centre for sports fishing, the heat of its summers is infamous. The owner of the hotel sits in a rocking chair on the cool entrance porch and shares maté with young friends who stop by. I sit on the steps and join in the conversation. The owner is from La Paz. Her husband is an official. The hotel is a recent acquisition.

Yuquiba, Tuesday 3 October

Today I face a headwind and eighty kilometres is a maximum. Cold drizzle stings my cheeks. I stop at the roadside and pull on my jacket and rainwear. Miserable, I pull into Yuquiba and find a hotel on the square, with bathrooms and cable TV. A great restaurant on the square has an upstairs packed with Mennonites in fresh blue overalls and straw Stetsons. They don't drive cars, trucks or tractors. A Mennonite baby is sucking on a plastic pacifier.

Yuquiba is a border town and a bazaar. Shops overflow onto the pavement on my hotel's side of the street. A young woman walks ahead, mid-twenties. Her build is too square for fashionable taste. She wears short blue shorts, a sleeveless sports top, flip-flops. Add two teaspoons of creamy milk to a cup of good coffee and you have her skin tone. Her confidence and her independence strike me. Admiration is unimportant. She has dressed to please herself. I imagine her giving a nod to her reflection in the mirror: 'Yeah, girl, you look good.'

I sit at a pavement café in the evening and watch other women pass. This female confidence is new. The mid-thirties and younger have it. They are freed of servitude. They create their own roles. Meanwhile, Mennonite women cling to serfdom. They speak softly, avoid eye contact. Whether gift of God or genetics, beauty leads to sin. Cover it up. Hats and headscarves are obligatory. The route to hell lies in the glimpse of a pink earlobe.

The Mennonites share the headscarf with Islamic women. Little separates the scarf from the hijab. The hijab is a close relative to female circumcision.

Yuquiba is an odd place in which to meet a soulmate. Early evening and we sit together at the pavement café. He introduces himself: Luis Yudi.

Jewish?

Arab. Orthodox Christian.

Luis was seven when the family emigrated from Syria. Now he is in his early sixties. We are both early school leavers. Self-educated, we are suspicious of what we are told. University graduates are less enquiring: memorising the lecturer's notes is the route to success.

The exchange of opinions is serious stuff. Before speaking, Luis gathers himself and hunches his shoulders and dips his head the way a boxer does.

He is proudly Arab and full of odd scraps of Arab history. Did I know that Gibraltar is named after an Arab admiral?

He has contempt for George W. Bush and the US administration. Their ignorance offends him. The president's use of the term 'crusade' is typical. The Crusaders were liberal in whom they pillaged and butchered: Muslim, Orthodox Christian, Jew.

He has visited England and Scotland. He has warm memories of London. He judges as reprehensible Blair's failure to denounce Israel's recent destruction of Lebanon. Does Britain no longer have its own foreign policy?

He is, of course, a true Semite. Most Israelis are *mestizo*. Yet to be sympathetic to the Palestinian ordeal and to criticise Israel is to be anti-Semitic.

Although a businessman, he is also a writer. He has written a treatise on the Bolivian constitution. Eight copies of the book have been printed and bound. He fetches a copy from his house. He has dedicated the copy: *Para el amigo Gandolfi para que en tu tesis la midas con optimo calificaciones ...*

Luis, I thank you. Such meetings prove the value of travel.

Argentina

To Salta, Wednesday 4 October

I am in the Argentine. Or I am in Argentina? I prefer the former. Crossing the border was routine, although time-consuming. I have one more border to cross – that dividing Tierra del Fuego. Two young Frenchmen I met at the Bolivian frontier recounted their fears of the complications entailed in travelling by bike. There are no complications. A biker requires proof of ownership, a national driving licence, ample photocopies, patience and a good attitude. Attitude is essential. Officials scent arrogance or impatience or contempt faster than hounds scent a fox. Police are equally sensitive to attitude. I have been treated with courtesy throughout this journey. I have ridden 16 000 kilometres. Other than at a frontier, I have been asked for my papers only once: by a young cop on a bridge in Armenia, Colombia. A sergeant arrived and told the young cop not to be stupid.

I am in Salta. I have a room two blocks off the square at the Residencia Elena. The room opens off a patio full of flowers. Water is hot. The ceiling fan squeaks. The room rate is twenty dollars for a couple. I am alone and pay sixteen and a half dollars. I don't complain. I have ridden 400 kilometres today over country that is flat and boring. Agriculturally it is well organised in vast fields of sugar, a tall plant with a yellow flower, wheat and citrus. Mountains pretend to approach, only to retreat into the haze. Entering the city is easy. The centre is clearly signed.

Joy is to discover pavement cafés on the cathedral square that serve excellent coffee. I order a fruit salad, sip coffee and people-watch. I have been in a largely *mestizo* world for the past five months. Argentina is different. You see white people, white, white, white. A tall man selling fruit in the market is as white as an Irish nun in a closed order. Is he scared of the sun, frightened of skin cancer? What does he do at weekends? Watch football on TV?

Two pedestrian streets lead down from Salta's cathedral square. I stroll through a hippy craft market circa Ibiza 1970. The leather necklaces and pendants, wrist strings and bracelets arranged on carpets are indistinguishable from the wares in every other street craft market. The people are indistinguishable. Their conversation is indistinguishable, as is their certainty in their uniqueness. These people are different. They have dropped out. In 2006 – wow!

One man is Rasta-ing another's hair – symbol of that, to me, strange faith. Surely only ignorance can explain respect for Haile Selassie, king of kings (a throne he usurped)? Haile Selassie was a murderous autocrat. During the Italian conquest of Ethiopia, he fled to England while the great nobles of the country took to the mountains and fought and never surrendered. I lived in Ethiopia in my early twenties. My Ethiopian friends were desperate to modernise their country. Haile Selassie had many of them arrested, tortured and killed. And, of course, Haile Selassie was Amharic. The Amharas claim to be the only true white race (I am considered 'red'). They have two words for black people: 'slave' and 'outcast'. Typical Amhara proverb: *Should you come out of your house and see a black man, go back in for a black man brings bad luck.*

We all have our prejudices. I am in Salta. I am in a recognisably European city of pavement cafés, clean parks and smart shops. Normally I wear cargo pants. I carry my camera in one leg pocket, my wallet in the other. A thief would have to stoop and peel the Velcro flap. This evening I dress in smart corduroy trousers for a smart city (I bought the corduroys in La Paz for five dollars). I have escaped unscathed from the terrorist and bandit territory of indigenous America. I relax.

I have my pocket picked. Ha!

I report the loss of my wallet at the police station on the cathedral plaza. I am recompensed with two kisses. The police officer is young and pretty and kind. She says that I am in great shape for an oldie – that Bernadette must be a wonderful wife to have looked after me so well.

A second police officer groans under the weight of her pregnancy. I recall Bernadette visiting a dear friend on his deathbed. He had been a formidable rugby player in his youth and was a highly regarded gynaecologist. He was dismissive of women's aches and pains. Dying of cancer, he complained to Bernadette that every part of him hurt.

'At last you know what it feels like to be pregnant,' said Bernadette.

I report this tale to Salta's female police officers. Bernadette is their hero.

In England I belong to the Automobile Association. Here, in Salta, I join the Automobile Club of Argentina. Members gain a discount at ACA gas stations and at ACA motels and selected hotels. The discount on gas hardly benefits the rider of a Honda 125. As for the hotels, even with discounts they are beyond my budget. However, the ACA publishes an excellent guidebook with detailed road maps. The guidebook is well worth the subscription and the ACA logo will look good at home on our car.

Salta, Thursday 5 October

Midnight and I fetch a glass of water from the water cooler in the hotel lobby. Light is dim. The cooler has two taps. One tap appears a darker blue than the other. I put my four heart pills on my tongue, raise the glass, prepare to swallow. The water is boiling. I spit. The darker tap is water for tea or maté. My lower lip is scalded.

I lie in bed. It is half seven in the morning. The room is small and dark and dank. Plumbing gurgles. A man converses in German with his female companion and in Spanish with a member of the hotel staff. The German complains that his bedside light doesn't work, that the lavatory won't flush, that the ceiling fan screeches. He wants a discount on the room rate – or his wife or girlfriend demands that he demand a discount.

My bladder is demanding.

And my laptop is demanding. It waits on the table. I hate my laptop.

It is ancient and indestructible. It weighs a ton. It travels in the box on the bike's luggage rack. The box is black. Midday, the box becomes an oven. Heat murdered the batteries. I have to work indoors where I can connect to the power. The one chair sandwiched between the bed and the table has a cracked seat. The crack pinches my butt.

I feel inside my pyjama trousers for evidence of the pinch.

I find three spots.

Before riding, I need to put cream on the spots.

I don't want to ride.

I have been riding for months.

Tierra del Fuego is a further 5000 kilometres.

And Bernadette believes that I should ride north next year from Tierra del Fuego to New York.

My heart will give out.

I feel for my pulse.

Where the shit is my pulse?

Eight o'clock – I must get up.

The first movement and my years will stick knives in my spine and in my ankles. I will slip on the soap on the wet floor of the bathroom and crack my head open.

Where did I leave my teeth?

I need my spectacles.

Being old isn't fun.

I want to be home. I want to sprawl on the couch and watch TV and hug the kids (if they allow) and rest my head in Bernadette's lap and know that soon she and I will go upstairs to bed.

Salta is half the world away.

To Tafi, Friday 6 October

The Altiplano is beautiful to the traveller. He passes by. He doesn't stop. There is nowhere to stop. In Argentina, village after village tempts. I head south from Salta. Colonel Moldes comes first – surely an odd name for a town? Argentina is full of such names: Colonel This and General That.

Colonel Moldes is too charming to be military. Trees shade the main street. Pillared arcades shade the pavement. I stop for coffee at the Hospedaje Doña Lada. Birds enjoy the palm trees in the small park where a bust of the colonel holds sway. The coffee is excellent. The young woman who serves is delightful. Each passer-by greets me. This is bliss. I could stay a week. Townspeople would talk to me in the evenings. I would learn something of Argentina. Big cities don't work. People are too busy. I am invisible. I learn nothing.

The waitress brings me fresh coffee and I enquire as to the room rate: eight dollars for a room with private bath.

I paid double in Salta and had my pocket picked.

The gorge of El Rio de los Conchas should be on every traveller's list. Temperature is ideal. The curves and climbs and descents are set up to perfection for a biker. Take time out to admire the incredible scenery. The walls of the gorge are red rock. The rock has been crumpled and stretched and wrenched. Thorn trees and scrub along the river seem sprayed with emerald dust and lit with strobe lights. I share the gorge with a pushbike race. Cops clear the route. Three riders have a lead of a kilometre over the pack. A couple at the back catch a drag from attendants in a van. An ambulance brings up the rear.

Weird desire: to ride through such beauty with your head down, pedalling crazily and blinded with sweat. The riders may think me weird to be riding a pizza delivery bike the length of Hispanic America.

I intend sleeping in Santa Maria. Santa Maria is a small market town in the centre of nowhere. The road I take is surfaced with *ripli*. *Ripli* is Argentinian for corrugated dirt. Honda and I share an antipathy to dirt.

Should I have known that Santa Maria is holding a world conference on camel husbandry? South America is camel country: alpaca, llama and vicuña are members of the camel family. Morales, President of Bolivia, is due to attend the conference. Today he is officiating at a funeral of Bolivian miners killed in a fratricidal battle between miners from a cooperative and miners in the state sector. Miners from the co-op are militant. They detest the subsidies and state contracts that advantage miners in the public sector. Their weapons are sticks of dynamite. The dynamiters are those who welcomed me at their blockade.

President Morales or no President Morales, every hotel in Santa

Maria is full. The freeloaders of the international conference circuit have arrived. A pleasant elderly gentleman missing most of his teeth staffs the tourist office in the central square. He is a keen biker and owns an Alpina. He bought the Alpina as a rebuild job. It lies in bits in his garage. It has lain in bits for the past fifteen years. It requires spare parts. Parts require money. He doesn't have any. And he is getting older. Sixties?

Will my visit rekindle his dreams?

He advises Tafi as an alternative destination: ninety kilometres and two hours of daylight. Does he hate me? Is my liberty salt in the wounds of his disappointments? Why else would he fail to mention that the road to Tafi includes Altiplano and a mountain pass? The sky up there is overcast. The temperature falls faster than lead. My tears snap and tinkle on the rutted tar.

Tafi is a tiny tourist resort. Middle-class Argentinians escape to Tafi from the heat of the plains. I meet with a travelling couple. He is Scots New Zealand, Sara is Italian. We dine together at a restaurant where a gay magician acts as compère. The magician is brilliant. He leans over our table and makes coins and scarves appear and disappear. He works with his sleeves rolled up. Sara and I enjoy and admire. Our companion calculates how the tricks are done.

Meanwhile two men from the next table sing to us. The elder, a grey-haired sixties, sings soft Argentine ballads packed with sob and soul. For a pro, he would be good. As an amateur, he is amazing. The younger, a late-forties Dudley Moore, is equally talented. He plays and sings pop Latino rock. Call a title, he knows the song. I watch his wife. She has seen him perform 1000 times. She has admired him – probably why she fell for him. They are out to dinner, a party of six friends. They are up from San Juan. She hoped for a quiet weekend, a slow cuddle. Now she is faced with the same old need for confidence boosting every entertainer needs and craves.

I imagine the couple back in their hotel room. He asks, *How did I do? Did I get the notes right? Did people like me? Really like me? I didn't stay on too long? They didn't get bored?* Yeah, yeah, yeah ...

This is my first party night since eating out with Ming in Cartagena,

Colombia. Cartagena was full of holidaying Colombians. Tafi is full of holidaying Argentinians. We three are the only foreigners in the restaurant. We are guests. We want to stay, fine. We want to leave, that's also fine. We are unimportant. We are peripheral to the economy.

So often on the gringo route, all clientele are foreigners, essential income, prey to be targeted, territory to be occupied. There is no fun in being prey, territory or target. I prefer to be people. In Tafi I am returned to the human race.

To Chepes, Saturday 7 October

I leave Tafi del Valle at seven. One elderly man in a thick fawn coat and wool hat sweeps refuse back into a bin that dogs have rifled. No one else stirs. The city folk of Salta were equally late in rising. Eight in the morning had the feel of six o'clock in an English city. Argentinians siesta and shops stay open until ten or eleven at night. British shop assistants would strike.

The road dips past a lake, rises and then follows a stream down through a thickly forested gorge. The trees are peculiar. The leaves are sparse and small and curled. I have ridden a couple of kilometres before realisation strikes. 'Strikes' is an understatement for being smitten visually by a mass of yellow daffodils. The trees are deciduous; this is early spring; I am in a temperate microclimate. Sunrise tints the leaves with pink. One more gift of beauty from South America.

Twenty kilometres further and I reach a tropic floor of cane fields, citrus and wheat. The road crosses west into the next valley. Desert.

I ride 730 kilometres today to Chepes. I see no reason to stop. Present a Texan with a slice of this land and he would refer to it as his ranch. Normal people recognise desert. Vegetation is sparse and grey rather than green. Sand blows across the road and gets in your ears and in your eyes. The road runs straight to the horizon and all the way back to the horizon. A dot on the road finally materialises into a truck. A car driven fast overtakes and remains in view twenty minutes later.

A road sign welcomes me to Florida. A dust track leads off to the right and crosses a disused rail track. I pass a second sign the other side of the road – Florida is history.

The road crosses a dry lake. A fence runs across the lake parallel to the road. Two Aberdeen Angus bullocks walk beside the fence. They halt and look at me. I poop my klaxon. Perhaps they break wind.

Why didn't I take the scenic route? The scenic route is *ripli* – Honda and I don't ride *ripli*.

Chepes is a road junction. It used to be a rail junction. The railway died. What else can I write of Chepes? Dusty streets, a motorised procession of celebrating football fans. I find a *hostal* for seven dollars. A big beer and steak dinner sets me back three dollars. The steak is an escapee from a steel foundry. My bedroom has a low ceiling. I raise my arms to pull off my T-shirt, stick a hand in the ceiling fan and spray blood over my bed.

To Mendoza, Sunday 8 October

My wristwatch fell off some time yesterday. I bought the watch in Panama at a street stall for nine dollars. The one window in my room at the Chepes Hostal has venetian blinds that don't open. I need a morning call. I have parked in the garage behind the *hostal* owner's car. She warns me that she has to leave early.

What is early?

'By nine – half past at latest.'

Is late rising an Argentine religion?

Was Evita a late riser? She did much of her early work in bed.

The road from Chepes crosses desert to San Juan. I count three curves, each less than ten degrees. I stop at the first town. Town? A mini-Lourdes built around a hilltop shrine dedicated to the saint of travellers. Pilgrims arrive by bus. I am served the most disgusting cup of coffee of this entire trip, and the most revolting empanadas, and the toilet facilities are filthy. The saint is a fraud. Were she genuine, she would strike these exploiters dead.

Desert and more desert. Heat hazes the horizon. Out of the haze looms a faint darkening. The kilometres pass and the darkening gains shape and is recognisable as mountains. Further kilometres and a line of green appears in the far distance. The green is a boundary. The desert sprouts vineyards and citrus orchards and serial crops. Modern machinery and concrete have sown the desert with channels to carry the snow waters. This is Argentina: the scale is vast, the irrigated fields are flat. Close by soar the white-capped Andes.

A highway intersection heralds the approach to the town of San Juan. I ride into the town centre in fruitless search of a functioning ATM. I drink cold water, more water and a fresh juice. Then I search for a sign out of San Juan to Mendoza. Lost (or confused), I ask directions of a student in swimming trunks and a T-shirt. He has his dad's car for the day and leads me to the highway.

The wealth of Argentine agriculture is immense. I cross kilometre after kilometre of flat irrigated fields and vineyards. I don't recall a climb or dip of more than a few metres. To the right rise the Andes. Only a further 160 kilometres to Mendoza. I long for a visual foreplay of wooded foothills. Instead I get the visual foreplay common to the outskirts of a modern city: service stations, factories, warehouses, used car lots.

Mendoza, Tuesday 10 October

Mendoza is a clean safe modern city of shaded streets and watered parks and squares cooled by fountains. Plaza San Martín is the kernel. I check half a dozen hotels before taking a thirteen-dollar room on the third floor at the Imperial for two nights. The room has a full-size window and hot shower. The towels rate as adequate, the elevator functions, staff are helpful. I write eight hours straight at a table in the ground-floor restaurant (prices are reasonable for acceptable food). Three further hours on the internet and I am up to date.

In late evening, I meet with two young Canadians. They are riding big BMWs equipped with all the gear. The Canadians flew their bikes from Panama to Colombia and have made the trip from Nova Scotia in two months. I have ridden half the distance in five. The BMWs have comfortable seats. The Canadians are searching for a bar where they can drink beer with other North Americans. I prefer a pavement café and people-watching.

The temperature is ideal, no flies or mosquitoes. I think of Mendoza as a European city. I am wrong. In any European city I would see African and Asian faces. Here there remains a thin sprinkling of dark *mestizos* among older citizens. Among the young, Europe is triumphant, the indigenous visible only in the occasional slight natural tanning of skin and in a bright blackness of eye. Dress is casual. The young are confident in their sensuality. These are beautiful people and they are having fun.

To General Alvear, Wednesday 11 October

The road south from Mendoza traverses flat fields. The mountains are vertical stage flats, almost colourless in the fierce sun, and equally boring. I have been given an introduction to the regional president of the journalists' union in San Rafael. His cell phone is permanently busy. I wait an hour, give up and ride on.

Olive groves and terraces of ancient olive trees are familiars of European literature. Literature is passé and Argentina is agro-corporation. Kilometre upon kilometre of young olive trees march to the horizon either side of the road. I break for coffee at a service station. A young woman serves me. She is one of four daughters, no brothers. I have four sons and an adopted daughter. We compare ages, occupations.

Twenty or more shade-netted plant nurseries occupy the far corner of the intersection opposite the gas station: baby olive trees fresh from the genetic lab. The owners are Spanish. The town has become dependent on them. These same Spaniards have planted 3000 hectares of almonds. My informant is unsure as to how many thousand hectares of olives have been planted. The young woman tells me that a labourer earns 270 dollars a month and that many labourers are illegal immigrants from Bolivia. She asks what a farm labourer earns in England. I guess at 600–700 dollars a week.

I sip my coffee and wonder what the future holds for the European farmer, the Spaniard husbanding olives and almonds on a few cherished hectares of terrace high in the Sierra del Maestrazgo. Is the Spanish farmer aware of the intention of his compatriots here in Argentina? Perhaps a TV producer could bring them together in a debate. Imagine a judge as chair.

Is investing in the destruction of your compatriots' living an act of treason?

Or merely sensible business practice?

God bless the global economy, screw the loser.

General Alvear is a small modern town with a large tree-shaded plaza. What did General Alvear do? Why, in Argentina, this obsessive need to memorialise their military?

I find a hotel room, hot water, seven dollars. I check the internet and learn that England has lost to Croatia. For years the English sports journalists and fans have blamed a foreigner, Sven-Göran Eriksson, for any failure of the national team. Perhaps the Swede did well given the paucity of talent.

I eat steak and salad and return to the hotel. A small neat man in his sixties sits on the sofa in the lobby. He wears blue chinos, a blue jumper, blue socks and blue bedroom slippers. His moustache is parted in the middle and teased out into waxed daggers. The manager presents him as her friend (hence the slippers). Señor Hostility would be a better introduction. He settles himself on the sofa in the manner of a fighter pilot settling in the cockpit.

'You are English.'

'Yes,' I say.

'You English are arrogant. You don't wish to be part of Europe. You believe you are superior.'

I am pro-Europe – what should I say? I suggest that some Brits are nervous of being associated with nations where political corruption is the norm: that this fear is common to most members of the six nations comprising the original European community.

'Your Blair is more corrupt than anyone. More corrupt than Silvio Berlusconi. Blair and Berlusconi are friends. Look at Iraq – he is a liar, your Blair. There is proof that more than 650 000 civilians have been killed. What do you say to that?'

Señor Hostility is softening me up. Soon he will shift attack to the Falklands/Malvinas war.

'I agree,' I say. 'Absolutely. Now, please, if you'll excuse me, I have to be up and on the road by six-thirty.'

So sneaks away the cowardly Brit.

South, Thursday 12 October

Seven o'clock and the road leads dead straight across scrub desert. A cold fierce head wind plays smoky patterns of fine sand across the tar. I crouch over the fuel tank and edge the speedometer up to seventy kilometres an hour. The sand gets in my eyes and in my nostrils and in my ears. The road is endless. The country is featureless. Thousands of kilometres remain.

I check the speedometer. I have ridden six kilometres.

I check the speedometer. I have ridden eight kilometres.

I mark a post on the horizon. I won't check the speedometer again until I reach the post.

A pale spot becomes a truck. The truck becomes a monster. We pass and the bike shudders in the slipstream. Ten kilometres.

I need coffee.

Cochico, at ninety kilometres, is the first place name on the road map. Ninety kilometres at seventy kilometres an hour?

I have been crouching for an hour and my back aches. I sit upright and the speed drops to fifty-five.

Cochico is eight shacks and a police barrier. A kindly young cop advises me to pull off the road below a dead pickup. The shack behind the pickup serves coffee. I look for a sign – only a couple of thin dogs. The door is tacked together from old planks that have been used elsewhere. I tap. A balding head appears and is followed by a hand that scratches the scalp.

The door opens fully and the head extends into a man of my own decrepit generation. He is fresh from bed and hasn't completed his ablutions. Coffee? Of course I can have coffee.

He welcomes me into what passes for a restaurant: five tables, a bar, a TV, and a fireplace big enough to roast a whole sheep. Three layers of thick fish netting cover the unglazed windows. The netting keeps out some of the sand and most of the sunlight.

The owner seats me at a table and shuffles off to wherever the kitchen is. He returns after a while with two cups. He hasn't had time or the inclination or memory to wash or brush what is left of his hair. He asks whether I want a biscuit or a sandwich or a slice of cake.

'No,' I say. 'No, I don't think that I want a biscuit or a sandwich or a slice of cake.'

He sets the cups down on the table and sits opposite me. Where have I come from? Where am I going? How long have I been travelling? Do I have a wife? Children?

He has four children. All live and work near by – except for a daughter, aged twenty-seven, who is away studying at university in San Juan. The other daughter is married to the local ambulance driver. His wife is employed as cook somewhere close by (he expects me to know what or where the somewhere close is). He does the cooking in the restaurant. His kids dump the grandchildren on him. He is extraordinarily contented.

I imagine how good it would be for me and Bernadette to have my two elder sons close by and my daughter Anya running a local stud. Have Josh studying at a nearby university, and Jed at college. Have the door always open. Have my beloved daughter-out-of-law Sarah drop off my grandson Charlie Boo in the morning for me to babysit. Enjoy the entire family at table for Sunday lunch. It is the life I imagined for myself when I was young. I have made a real mess: divorced once, family scattered ... and riding a small motorbike.

Any biker riding through Cochico, please stop and pay the old man my respects and tell him of my gratitude. He pulled me out of a black depression. Perhaps all bikers suffer these dark moods one time or another, mostly when they are young and haven't dressed for the weather or are on the wrong bike for whatever it is they are trying to do. The old man's contentment did it – his contentment and my pleasure in human contact. I remounted with a changed vision. Instead of kilometres to be crossed, the desert had become something to look at and enjoy. I had been comparing it unfavourably with the game-filled

Ogaden that I had enjoyed in my youth. The Argentinian desert is no better or worse, neither prettier nor less attractive. It is different. That is all.

Either a light rain or a heavy dew must have fallen in the past weeks. The road is raised and the runoff has left green strips of fine grass each side of the tar. Three small coveys of a dun-coloured game bird, somewhat resembling guinea fowl, peck at the earth among the green grass. A small falcon with a white under-tail and white beneath the wings hunts the road edge. A small pink flower grows in patches. No names – and I am struck, as I ride, by how little I know of the world in which I have lived. I am old for a learner. I need to move along at a fair pace.

What began as a bad day becomes a great day. I stop for lunch at a shack in the middle of nowhere. The trucks and pickups parked outside are a good sign. A score of drivers occupy two long tables laid with tablecloths. A young pregnant woman serves platters of steamed trout and bottles of red and white wine.

I am pointed to a table without a tablecloth and am offered steak and salad or salad and steak. I choose the steak and salad. A driver, not of the party, joins me. He is familiar with the place. The pregnant woman's daughter, a six-year-old, kisses his cheek and fetches him a clean tumbler and a bottle of soda. The driver is anxious to be on the road ahead of the wine drinkers. Our food is served at the same time and we leave together. The rear tyre punctures right by the gas station in the next town. A neighbouring puncture specialist fixes the tube for a dollar sixty. I ride on through Nequeen and take Route 237 towards the mountains and San Carlos de Bariloche. Late evening and I am drenched by a couple of sharp rain squalls. The evening sun lights the underside of charcoal cloud above the lake at Villa El Chocón and transforms the water into a shimmering sheet of slate-coloured glass. The light on the water is intense and the far shore is hidden by the glare.

Villa El Chocón is a lakeshore tourist resort. The cops at the cop station warn me of the prices and recommend a *hostal* back on the highway.

Hostal El Alamo is a find. Any biker riding by should stop. The beds are perfect. Bathrooms have power showers. Tap water is potable. The lady of the house is welcoming and a great cook: ten dollars for the room plus four dollars for a dinner of delicious lasagne, fresh salad and a crème caramel.

I share a table with the only other guest, a man of interesting views. Self-educated, he is a building contractor. He finds modern society immoral. He places much of the blame on female liberation. Women, once educated, lose respect for their working husbands. They find their husbands limited and boring. They prefer the company of their educated female friends. Soon the women are out drinking together and smoking. Prostitution is the next step. The contractor tells me of a dance hall in Buenos Aires. A factory building, it holds 3000 couples. By two in the morning none of the women can dance – all are inebriated, all are for sale.

The contractor's father was killed in an earthquake when the contractor was a young child. He believes his father came from Syria or Iraq. Iraq is the birthplace of civilisation. Now look what the British are doing in Iraq and Afghanistan. They have killed 650 000 civilians – they and the Americans. The British in Australia were worse than the Spanish in America. Recently 300 Aboriginal bodies were discovered. Their British employer had murdered them rather than pay wages due – a common occurrence.

The contractor believes that the rich have instituted a great conspiracy. Consumerism is part of the conspiracy. Women are the chief targets (yes, we are back to women). Fifty-two percent of world income is spent on women. Cosmetics are the largest item. Women are weak and easily influenced. They have no resistance to temptation. Read the Bible. Remember Lot's wife.

So the contractor continues while I nod my understanding and marvel that his wife hasn't cut his throat.

To Bolsón, Friday 13 October

Another great day west on Route 327 from Villa El Chocón to the mountain resort of San Carlos del Bariloche. Bariloche? I wonder at the name. Was it born as Barry's loch?

Argentina excels in road signs. SINUADO is my favourite. Sad that they don't include SENSUADO. Any biker would know the meaning: sweeping curves, smooth dips, curving climbs, perfect camber, views to die for. Today's menu features rivers and lakes, dark, forbidding moors, pine forests and finally the snowfields. A familiar face observes me from the far side of a fence. He is a young chap, not fully grown, red coat, white nose.

I pull into the curb, dig out the camera and approach through coarse grass.

'Where are you from?' he asks.

'Colwall,' I reply.

'In Herefordshire? That's close to Ledbury.'

'Four miles,' I say.

'I believe that's where my great-great-grandfather came from,' he tells me.

'Very probably,' I say and take his photograph.

He is embarrassed at having spent so much time with an old fogey. Off he trots to join the rest of the herd.

Route 237 crosses the river only once before Bariloche. The gas station on the far side of the bridge has the appearance of a restaurant but isn't. Ride a few miles further and you find a restaurant down on your left beside the river. You can't miss it. It is the first building beyond the bridge. Don't stop. I was charged ten dollars for a half-full bowl of lentil soup, yesterday's salad and a small bottle of water.

The approach to Bariloche passes through a valley maybe half a mile in width. Black mountains rise on each flank, fierce crests of bare rock. Rain squalls scythe across the valley. The squalls pass and I catch glimpses of snow in the distance.

I am in want of the intimacy of a village. Bariloche is a town and too big for my tastes. The architecture is a jumble of concrete, cuckoo clock and the worst of Marbella Spanish. Pines edge the lakeshore. Above shine the ski slopes. Lift cables bisect the pistes. The road swings south towards Bolsón, a further 126 kilometres. I follow a second lake and a third. Pine forests end at the snow line. Rain closes in. The road climbs. Rain turns to sleet. My feet are soaked, toes and fingers numb. Sun finds a cleft in the clouds. The peaks glisten while I remain in semi-dark. My cheeks suffer a bombardment of ice crystals. I raise the speed by ten kilometres an hour to intensify the pain. I must be crazy. I even stop to photograph the peaks. I kneel beside the road and steady the camera on the crash rail. There, on my knees, illumination strikes. Bike size is of no account. Nor is speed. Age is immaterial. This is the test. The pass mark is having fun. Enjoy yourself under these conditions and you may wear the label proudly: BIKER.

Or lunatic.

Bolsón is a cute tourist town surrounded by mountains. Prices are high. So are the mountains. We are in early spring and the snows are retreating towards the summits. The tourist office finds me a hotel at fifteen dollars. I have a large pleasant room. The double bed has a comfortable mattress. The radiator is hot. The shower runs hot. Double windows open onto a neat garden. Add the luxury of a writing table. The brave resilient Honda sleeps undercover in the garage. The bike will rest tomorrow while I catch up with my blog and correspondence.

Patagonia, Sunday 15 October

Now for Patagonia. I leave Bolsón early and head south 193 kilometres to Esquel. The road climbs out of the valley to cross bleak treeless uplands. Flurries of rain turn to sleet near the crest, where two cops wait for something. The cops are wrapped in balaclavas and frost-retardant. I ask what happened to the central heating. One cop says, 'The government forgot to pay the gas bill.'

Esquel is the terminus for the antique narrow-gauge railway that once connected with the Buenos Aires–Bariloche main line. Paul Theroux named it 'The Patagonian Express'. In the seventies, Esquel was a hippie haven. Now it is a fashionable resort. Hippies on the make made good and now shop with platinum-grade credit cards. I top up with gas, coffee and mince empanadas before heading south to Tecka.

The road follows a wide flat river valley of vast sheep paddocks. Trees grow along the river. I startle a flight of green parrots. What are parrots doing up here on the Altiplano? And why haven't the farmers planted shelter strips to improve the grazing?

Tecka doesn't look much on the Auto Club map. So much for maps:

Tecka holds a treasure. I turn off the highway onto a dirt street. Tin-roof bungalows are sealed tight against the wind. The road becomes tar and I spot pickups parked outside a gas station. The gas station is out of use. The drivers are here for Sunday lunch.

A true restaurateur is a miracle to be discovered by grace of God and in the strangest places. Evidence starts with the greeting. In Tecka, the owner gives the impression that my arrival is the truffle on the toast of an already charmed existence. A good, solid man in his mid-fifties, he wears a white apron and a broad welcoming smile. Sunday is his day of rest: will the *plat du jour* suffice? A simple gnocchi?

Simple?

The gnocchi are al dente. The sauce is a combination of tomato, garlic, spring onion, herbs, wind-cured ham and Italian sausage. The quantity is as vast as Argentina. It is served in a dish cradled in a basket woven of willow wands. It is divine. So are the fresh-baked bread rolls.

Travellers, forget your schedules. Stop here and eat.

I ride out of Tecka into a full gale. A moment's inattention and the wind would slam me off the road. I consider turning back. A wonderful restaurant – maybe there is a great bed. However, Patagonia is famous for its winds. What I consider a gale is probably the standard Patagonian breeze.

Gobernador Costa is a further sixty kilometres south on Route 40. The streets are empty. Those out for a Sunday stroll have been blown away. I stop for gas and coffee. A pretty young woman operates both the gas pump and the espresso machine. She asks where I am going.

'Sarmiento,' I say.

'That's 260 kilometres,' she says.

I agree.

'There's a gale blowing,' she says.

I've noticed.

'You should stay the night here,' she says.

'Patagonia is famous for wind,' I say. 'Will there be less wind tomorrow?'

'Of course there will be less,' she says. 'This is a storm. We don't always have storms.'

She fails to convince me. A fresh storm tomorrow could bring a more intense wind. Weaken, and I could be stuck for weeks. I don't have weeks. I have a flight booked to Madrid out of Buenos Aires on the thirtieth.

This is sheep country. Cattle would be blown over and even the sheep face away from the gale and crouch for shelter among the sparse tufts of coarse grass. I bow as flat to the gas tank as is possible for an overweight blue balloon in a rain suit. The nearest pollution must be hundreds of kilometres away. I am struck by the clarity of light and the extraordinary depth of blue in the sky. The blue is reflected below in the lakes at the approach to Sarmiento. The lake at Villa El Chocón was the same amazing blue. So was Lake Titicaca. I have seen parrots today. I have seen flamingos graze in ponds alongside sheep and Hereford cattle. Awareness that flamingo breed in the Andes fails to make their presence any less surprising. Those long thin legs should freeze and snap.

Now, in the evening, the road descends from the bleakness of the uplands and I pass by the lakes. Waves break on the beach and the gale beats the water into foam. Seen in the distance, even the houses of Sarmiento seem to cower. Half a dozen cars are parked by a bridge on the outskirts of town and masochistic Sunday fisherman with fly rods struggle against the wind along a willow-sheltered riverbank.

I turn off the road at a sign offering B&B. Dogs greet me kindly. A woman shows me a bunkroom. She rents the room with its six beds and use of a kitchen for twenty dollars. I don't have use for six bunks. Nor can I use the kitchen. My logic confronts her prices. My logic fails. I take a room in town at the Hotel Ismir for fifteen dollars. The room is miserable. So am I. I am tired. I have ridden 600 kilometres. I have hayfever or a streaming head cold. I shower and walk a couple of blocks in search of a restaurant. Joy is foreign to Sarmiento in a gale. People huddle and watch TV. Bungalows shrink within themselves. The Hotel Colón is a rarity.

I spy, through the window, six men at the bar. I suspect that they missed morning church service and have been at the bar much of the day. How will they view an intruder? A Brit?

I pass by on the pavement half a dozen times before gaining sufficient courage to risk an entrance. A set of aluminium doors leads into a porch, from which more doors open to the bar. The doors are ill-fitting. They grate and squeak and clatter. An army tank would make less noise. Conversation ends. The six men at the bar turn on their stools and inspect me. So does the owner. So does his wife.

I hold my hands above my head in surrender. 'I am a Brit,' I say. 'Am I allowed?'

'They allow horses,' says a man in a flat leather gaucho hat.

The Hotel Colón in Sarmiento is the type of dump any respectable biker hankers after. The bar is the right length. Six people and it doesn't feel empty; twelve and it doesn't feel overcrowded. Sarmiento is a small town. I doubt there are more than twelve serious barstool occupiers. The six in possession are middle-aged. They have been on the same conversation for a while. Maybe it began yesterday or last week. It is one of those conversations that expand over time and develop threads that go nowhere and die a natural death. Mostly what is said now is in allusion to what has been said earlier and you would need to have been in on the conversation early to understand its direction – if it has a direction.

I sit at the far end of the bar, order a small beer and watch the last few minutes of a football match on TV. The conversationalists seem content with my presence. The pool table to the left of the bar hasn't been used in months; it is there because this type of bar requires a pool table. The girlie advertisements for beer exist for the same reason. They are expected, as are the three tables, each with four folding chairs, arranged along the wall. The barstool residents would be uncomfortable were they absent.

A young couple occupy the table closest to the door. I guess that they are students. She wears spectacles and is perhaps the more confident (or the more pressing) of their relationship. The obligatory guitar case protrudes from among the bags and backpacks heaped on the floor. I wonder whether the couple are waiting for a bus – or for a parent.

I imagine Josh or Jed calling home. 'Dad, can you pick us up?'

I wonder whether my sons are aware of the happiness I find in being asked. To be of use is a joy, no matter the time of day or night. I will bitch, of course. Bitching is expected. I don't ask how many 'us' is. I don't ask whether the girl is a friend or a girlfriend. Asking would be an infringement. Of course I want to know – not to judge, but because this is part of who they are. However, I do wish that they would sit a while in the kitchen once we get home, let me cook them something, talk to me, let me share a little of their lives. They tend to hurry straight upstairs to their rooms.

I guess it's my age. I'm sort of odd, an embarrassment. You know, having a dad in his seventies? And, yes, I am odd. I do odd things. Riding a pizza delivery bike 600 kilometres through Patagonia in a gale on a Sunday is more than odd. Perhaps I am a little crazy.

I ask Mrs Hotel Colón if there is a restaurant open nearby. She asks whether a steak and fries would satisfy. A steak and fries would be just dandy.

I drink a second beer and nod intelligently to asides from my barstool neighbour. The asides refer to the general conversation. A mystic would find them obtuse.

Mrs Hotel Colón summons me to a small dining room. She says, 'I put a couple of eggs on your steak.'

I thank her and ask for a third beer.

Three beers and dinner cost seven dollars.

Room rate for a single with bath is fifteen dollars. Should you ever pass through Sarmiento, you know where to stay. Take a right at the park, ride three blocks and turn left. The Colón is on your right. Don't bother with the conversation. It will be incomprehensible. You are a year or two late.

The coast, Monday 16 October

Wind buffets the Honda and I crouch low on the ride to Comodoro Rivadavia. Ahead lies the South Atlantic. I intended servicing the bike at the Honda agency. Comodoro Rivadavia appears deserted. Wind commands the streets. Dust devils snake across the tar. I stop for fuel. A lone truck pulls into the gas station. I have hit a national holiday: Mother's Day.

I turn south on the coastal road and halt on a cliff top. A fine sprinkling of minute wild flowers on the grass verge is the first sign of spring. The wind has brought clear skies. The sea is dark blue. Curling lines of surf, whiter than white, burst over the rocks. My camera is buried beneath layers of clothing. I pry through the layers. My fingers are numb and the wind whips the camera case over the cliff.

Caleta Olivia is an oil town. Here, too, the wind is in command. I stop at a small hotel near the plaza. The owners emigrated from Andalusia so let me call it the Hotel Andalusia. The wife appears from the kitchen, books me in and retreats back into the kitchen. I open my laptop on a table in the bar-lobby and work into late evening. The wind drops and the young come out to play. The women wear the standard uniform of the young, jeans or trousers supported by their backsides, two inches of bare belly, shoulder tattoos. The guys wear swagger and grease their hair against the wind. Piercings are in, mostly ears and eyebrows, a few noses, no lips that I notice.

The politics of Argentina have been tawdry in the extreme. Politicians are held in contempt and search for heroes with whom to associate themselves. Statues memorialise great men in even the smallest village. Caleta Olivia memorialises the oil field worker. An enormous statue dominates the central plaza. The statue is a direct descendant of Soviet art. Mother's Day and pizza parlours are doing great business.

I sit up late back at the hotel and talk with the owner. He is a short stocky man with square farmer's hands. He wears a tweed cap indoors and out and a dark suit. He is an only child of a farmer in Andalusia. Life on the land was hard when he was young. He sold his inheritance and has lived in Caleta Olivia for forty years. He was back in Spain for the first time last year. He sat in the village *bodega* and chatted with the friends of his youth. So much had changed. His friends own tractors and employ labour. They have a secure state pension and free health service.

Would he rather live in Spain?

He tilts his cap forward to scratch the back of his head. Then he shrugs and spreads his hands to indicate the hotel. To whom could he sell it? The middle classes lost all their capital in the recent crash.

To Puerto San Julián, Tuesday 17 October

The land between Caleta Olivia and Puerto San Julián began as a plateau. God got bored and chopped the plateau with the side of his hand every fifty kilometres or so. Rivers run through the valleys. Which direction the rivers drain depends on the angle at which God chopped: east into the South Atlantic or west to Lago Argentina. Geographers and geologists don't care for God and will give you a different explanation for the topography.

The road runs straight as a ruler across the plateaux. Have the wind in your face and you barely move. The clarity of light leads to confusion. You can see forever. You presume three bushes are a clump. The clump splits: the first bush is a mile closer than the second and the third is a further mile distant. A service station is the first stop at 150 kilometres; a new swanky *hostal* has been opened on the right a hundred kilometres short of San Julián. That's it. I may have seen a small tree. If so, it was a very small tree. Crossing the terrain on a small bike, you need to keep your mind occupied. God as a landscape artist served me well.

Most towns on the Patagonian plain seem built by the three little piggies. Along comes a wolf and he'll blow them away. Puerto San Julián is different. It possesses solidity and permanence. Being away from the highway and on a point, it is less of a transit stop than other towns. The citizenry are proud and make the best of where it is. A community of 18 000, it has three football clubs and a fives court. I tour in search of a hotel and find a monument out on the cliff front. The monument is a fighter plane from the Falklands/Malvinas war. The Hotel Municipal faces the monument. It is a good hotel. The room rate is higher than my want. Going elsewhere would be a retreat. I have been in Argentina for three weeks and have avoided the war. I am a Brit. The war is something I need to confront.

I do my internet work at a bar. The bar is the headquarters of the San Julián Athletic Club. The club's football team continuously exceeds expectations for a small-town club. Two walls are required to display the trophies. The trophies are massive. I chat at the bar with two young men. I had presumed that much of the town's wealth would come from the sea. They tell me that the fishing fleet is in the hands of a small clique and is of little benefit to the town. Mining supplies the major income: silver and gold

I am in a fishing port. I want to eat fresh fish. A tour group of elderly couples from Buenos Aires has booked the best restaurant. A table will be vacant at half past ten.

I wait in the hotel and talk with the manager. She is a reminder of the schoolteachers who told me of the US invasion of Panama. She has the same soft voice as she tells me of the young soldiers sent to the Malvinas. Poor boys, how they suffered. Most were from the north. They had never experienced cold and they had neither suitable clothes nor adequate food.

I reply that I recall reading of British officers' anger at discovering the condition of the Argentine soldiers and their contempt for Argentine officers, many of whom abandoned their men.

I walk back down the cliff road to the restaurant. Wind grabs at my jacket. I imagine the ancient Argentine battleship, the *Belgrano*, torpedoed. For how many minutes could a sailor survive in the freezing sea? The sinking was criminal. Both Brits and Argentinians were culpable. Surely a warning could have been given – through the US? Or was reasoning impossible with Galtieri and his officer clique? Galtieri was a graduate of the notorious School of the Americas – something to dwell on as I exchange the icy South Atlantic wind for the warmth of a restaurant famous for fresh fish.

The two bus drivers and the tour guide for the oldies invite me to their table. We chat of road conditions and distances and the countries we have visited. They insist on picking up my dinner tab and give me a ride back to the hotel in the double-decker coach. I lie in bed and think of the vile headlines in England's popular press. A good Argie was a dead Argie. And what of all those Brits who, over generations, have settled in Argentina?

To Santa Cruz, Wednesday 18 October

Morning and I am forced on foot to tack against the wind as I view Puerto San Julián's monument to the Argentine airmen killed in the war. The fighter plane seems so small, little more than a toy. I stagger under the wind. The South Atlantic rollers are white with foam. I imagine the sailors of the *Belgrano*, human flotsam. I circle and find the names of the dead inscribed on black plaques:

HEROES OF THE MALVINAS

Argentine or Brit, there were no heroes – only victims: victims of political ineptitude and politicians' vainglory.

I face another day of wind and cold and vast distances. I am accustomed now to the dress code for springtime in Patagonia. On the bottom half I wear underwear and long underwear, two pairs of pyjama bottoms, thick jeans and rain trousers. The top gets three undershirts, cord shirt, three jerseys, leather jacket, scarf, windproof rain jacket. I pad the front of the jerseys with newspaper.

Next I load the bike. One bag goes on the gas tank. I wedge a second bag into the gap between the seat and the cargo box. Maps, spare gloves and the Automobile Club guidebook go in rubber webbing on the box lid. I struggle into the backpack, settle the helmet and security glasses, pull on wool gloves and leather gauntlets. Ready.

Passers-by stop to watch this large blue balloon in a crash helmet prepare to mount. I know their thoughts.

Will the old weirdo get his leg over?

Will the bike fall?

Safely seated in the saddle, I kick the starter, no throttle: *Brrrmmmm* ...

I smile at the disbelievers, raise a disdainful paw, toe-tap the Honda into gear and ride off into the sun. And ride – and ride – and ride ...

I have seen a red lake and a green lake and blue lakes and dry lakes. I have shouted at fat married couples (birds) to get off the road. I have talked to Hereford cattle and road-repair gangs.

I whirl an arm to de-numb my fingers, stretch my legs, wriggle my toes. I bow to lessen wind buffeting by passing trucks, wave to gauchos, slalom the broken white line. I check my watch and the distance travelled against the distance remaining to the next gas stop. One hundred kilometres is the beginning of a countdown. One hundred kilometres is only sixty miles. Eighty kilometres is fifty miles. Twenty kilometres is nearly there.

My dismounting technique is ungainly – more a semi-fall sideways. I hobble to the lavatory and fumble deep within all the folds of clothing for something to pee with. I sip black coffee in the gas station caféteria, munch a sandwich, chat with whoever asks where I come from. These are the moments that make the trip worthwhile: so many different people, all content to share with me a little of themselves.

I fill the tank. Backpack, helmet, glasses, gloves: *Brrrrmmmm*.

Ahead lie a further 150 kilometres.

Is it fun?

In truth?

Fun is the wrong word.

Challenge comes closer. In my seventies, can I ride 22 000 kilometres on a small bike the length of Hispanic America? The start of each day is hardest. I wake and lie in bed and contemplate the distance ahead. One more night in a strange bed. Broken sleep. Every part of me aches – back, knees, ankles. I want to give up. I fumble for spectacles and the lamp switch. Check the ACA route guide. Tomorrow I will be on the final page. Get up, you old fool. Take a hot shower.

Santa Cruz is the provincial capital. It is packed with visiting officials and people needing to speak with officials. And it has the province's main hospital. I try six hotels before finding a bed. The shortage puts the room rate up to twenty dollars. I find a restaurant that professes to serve fresh fish. When will I learn? When in Argentina, stick with beef.

Tierra Del Fuego, Thursday 19 October

There are no gas stations between Santa Cruz and the border. Fill up in town. Wind as usual. The landscape has more shape; scrub has given way to vast grass paddocks. The grass is thin and tufty. Sheep graze alone rather than together. Despite the cold, this is springtime. Lambing has begun. The young butt their mothers' udders.

A road sign points left to Tierra del Fuego. An ostrich inspects me. He is one of eight. The other seven look the other way. I meet half a dozen trucks. The road dips. The channel lies ahead. A sailor is about to close the ferry ramp with a chain. He waves me on board. Drivers ask where I've come from. The driver of a new 4×4 pours me coffee from a flask. I go to the office to pay the ferry fare and am given free passage. I stand on the raised walkway and watch as we approach Tierra del Fuego. Rather than exhilaration, I feel relief. My journey is almost done.

I have four borders to cross: out of Argentina, into Chile; out of Chile, into Argentina. A young Argentine cop at the first border discusses the Malvinas war. He was a child, too young to remember much, and is uncertain as to the background of the conflict. He is certain that war was unnecessary. England and Argentina are friends. Many English have settled in Argentina.

'It was the politicians, the generals,' he says.

I share my thoughts of the monument in Porto San Julián: that there were no heroes, only sacrifices.

He agrees. 'Those poor boys from up north sent down there without proper clothes.'

Paperwork at the Chilean border takes half an hour. I have 180 kilometres to cross before reaching the next frontier. The first thirty kilometres is concrete; the rest is gravel. Gravel would have defeated me at the outset in Mexico. Now I am semi-expert and ride the dirt at sixty kilometres an hour. The knack is in staying relaxed and not tightening up when the wheels slither.

Expert or not, dirt is exhausting. Oncoming trucks drag clouds of dust and cut visibility to zero. When overtaken, I pull off the road and wait. I have reached serious sheep country. Not all are fenced and I beware of lambs bounding across the road. At last the Chilean border, a quick formality, and then eighteen kilometres to Argentina and a paved road.

I am half an hour at the Argentine border. I fly home at the end of the month and intend storing the Honda with the Honda agent in Ushuaia. The customs official tells me not to worry. The bike is on a temporary import permit for six months. I should show the permit to the customs at the quay in Ushuaia. I am very tired and consider stopping the night at the Automobile Club's *hostal* at the border. Doing so would leave me a long ride tomorrow into Ushuaia. I ride on.

What stopped me closing and fastening my bag properly? The bag that rests against my back and that holds all the bike's papers and the duplicates? The bag that I have unfastened and unzipped four times today at four frontiers?

Exhaustion?

Or did I relax with the journey almost finished?

I stop for a pee midway to Rio Grande and discover the document pocket gaping. I have lost the bike's registration papers, the temporary import permit and the Argentine Automobile Club guidebook.

I have been on the road the best part of six months and have been so careful.

Weeping won't help.

Maybe a sheep will find and eat them.

Shit!

Shit!

Shit!

There is a lot of water on the approach to Rio Grande. Early evening and mist smokes off the lakes and ponds and streams. Cold closes in. Visibility drops and my spectacles fog over. The fuel gauge is on reserve – this is a first in 22 000 kilometres. There must have been a gas pump at the Automobile Club *hostal*. Why didn't I stop? Had I stopped, I wouldn't have lost the bike's documents; I wouldn't be cold and tired and depressed. I wouldn't be scared of running out of gas and being stranded in the dark in the middle of nowhereland.

What has happened? Is it simply that I am near the end and want to get the journey over with? Or have the cold and distance finally reached into my brain and flicked the off switch?

I fill with gas, take a right at the Liverpool Pub, an immediate left and a second right on the main avenue. Hotel Argentina is the low, single-floor tin building on the right. I can't miss it. Graciela has worked it over with a bucket of yellow paint. Graciela is the owner. She has adult children and has kept young. I find her reading tarot cards at the kitchen table in company with three women friends. I ask whether they are a coven or the Rio Grande chapter of the Feminist Union.

'Both,' says Graciela.

Two student-age young men join us at the table. They are expert in that student skill of both being there and not being there while taking up considerable space.

Graciela tells one to take his cap off in the house so she can see his face and tells the other to shift his feet off the chair.

I love her.

I remark on a monument to Argentine ownership of the Malvinas coexisting with the Liverpool Pub. One of the coven tells me that the cost of maintaining the Malvinas will be too great for Britain. In a matter of years the islands will be absorbed by Argentina. She talks of the islands as if they are uninhabited. On TV the news shows a battle between two political factions. The factions are participating in the re-interment of Perón at San Vicente. Most are armed with staffs and base-ball bats. One man fires a pistol. Imagine a kelper, a Falkland Islander, watching on TV. Would he or she wish to be part of such political mayhem?

Rincón de Julio in Rio Grande is across the highway from the gas station. Julio is where the locals eat, those serious about food. Be there before half past nine of an evening or you won't get a table. I had intended dropping by the Liverpool Pub for a pre-dinner drink. The pub is closed. A cop is on guard at the door and a couple of officers are out back searching the grass. Disappointing – I wanted to ask the owner whether he had named his pub in honour of the city or the football club, whether he had visited England – and how he felt about Las Malvinas Son Argentinas at the next intersection.

Dinner at Julio's is excellent if you enjoy meat – although the cook apologises for the lamb chops. They will have to wait a few more weeks for this year's lambs.

I stroll back past the Liverpool Pub. The cops remain in occupation. The kitchen at the Hotel Argentina is welcoming. The coven and the students slope off to watch a couple of rented horror DVDs. Graciela and I sit and chat of this and that. Hotel Argentina is the best budget option in Rio Grande and Graciela gets the travellers. Most are good and easy. Some are weird; some have experimented with too many herbs and crystals; a few suffer from tangled wires in their heads.

A young Frenchman stayed two months. He believed that Graciela was the Virgin Mary reincarnated. He was John the Baptist. He tended to stare at Graciela; this put her off cooking. Imagine attempting a mayonnaise with someone gazing at you, someone with such expectations. Virginal is a tough demand when you have three grown kids and have suffered a recent divorce.

I sit there in the kitchen utterly content while Graciela tells me of her life. She is both extraordinarily youthful and very adult. She has humour and she reads books.

I have been biking five months and have enjoyed no proper (nor improper) female company apart from those few days in Nazca. I prefer a woman's company. Men don't do it for me. I miss Bernadette. I miss all four boys. I want to cuddle my grandson. And I want to visit with my daughter. Yeah, yeah, yeah ... get to bed, you old fool. It is half past one in the morning and you ride to Ushuaia in the morning. Thank you, Graciela.

Ushuaia, Friday 20 October

I ride out of Rio Grande with regret. The Hotel Argentina has been good for me. Losing the bike documents dumped me into a deep depression. Graciela dug me out. Wind is standard in Patagonia. So is the cold. I ride across sheep country, cross rivers, pass by ponds, see the occasional farmhouse tucked into a clump of trees, wave to a Hereford bull (he ignores me).

The tail end of the Andes squeezes in from the west. Snow-caps march across the horizon. A forest of strange conifers trails moss. A huge lake opens to the right. I enter a First World War battlefield. It is a scene of grim devastation in which shattered trees are tumbled one on another. The few trunks standing are stripped of branches; their peaks are sheared and ragged and resemble the rotting teeth of some huge prehistoric animal. What happened?

Honda and I are on the final climb of our journey. Snow closes in. Sunlit summits shimmer. I stop for lunch at a restaurant on the right of the road. The owner quizzes me. Where do I go next? Where will I leave my bike? At the Honda agency. I, in turn, ask what happened to the trees. Beavers did the killing. The beavers were imports from Canada.

I cross the final pass to Ushuaia. A few flecks of snow sting my cheeks. Snow turns to rain as I dip into town. Ahead lies the Beagle Channel. I stop at the Hostal Cruz del Sur. The owner, Luca, is Italian. He is a friend of Graciela's. Today is his birthday. He is thirty-three. Luca shows me to a bunkroom. Bunkrooms are unsuitable accommodation for an old man. How will I manage the climb to an upper bunk in the middle of the night?

I cross the street to a hotel with rooms that have private baths. I look back over my shoulder and see Luca watching me. Luca's Argentine friends are preparing the barbecue on the pavement. Luca has invited me. I feel a traitor. I circle to a grocery and buy three bottles of red wine.

I unload the bike and ride out of town to the Honda agency. The owner of the restaurant where I stopped for lunch has called to warn of my impending arrival. The manager expects me. The owner of the agency also owns a warehouse and cold store. The bike is to be garaged there. I ride back to town and park on the waterfront. A passing tourist takes my picture. I leave the bike in the warehouse and catch a cab back. I walk up two blocks to the Hostal Cruz del Sur. Steaks sizzle on the barbecue. Luca hands me a glass of red wine. My journey is done.

Except ... except that Bernadette believes that I should ride north next year. Although only as far as my daughter's home in Duchess County, New York. Bernadette swears that I'll enjoy myself – that I'll have fun.

Oh God, oh God, why hast thou forsaken me?